Cities of the World

Harper & Row Series in Geography
D. W. Meinig, Advisor

CITIES OF THE WORLD
World Regional Urban Development

STANLEY D. BRUNN
University of Kentucky

JACK F. WILLIAMS
Michigan State University

Contributing Authors:

Michael E. Bonine
University of Arizona

Ian M. Matley
Michigan State University

Joe T. Darden
Michigan State University

Assefa Mehretu
Michigan State University

Ashok K. Dutt
University of Akron

A. James Rose
Macquarie University, Australia

Larry Ford
San Diego State University

Lawrence M. Sommers
Michigan State University

Ernst Griffin
San Diego State University

Richard Ulack
University of Kentucky

Thomas R. Leinbach
University of Kentucky

Maurice Yeates
Queen's University, Kingston, Ontario

HarperCollins*Publishers*

Sponsoring Editor: Kathy Robinson
Project Editor: Rita Williams/Jon Dash
Production Manager: Willie Lane
Compositor: ComCom Division of Haddon Craftsmen, Inc.
Printer and Binder: R. R. Donnelley & Sons Company
Art Studio: Vantage Art, Inc.
Cartographer: Sherman Hollander

Cover photograph: Eastern North America, April 17, 1977. Produced from USAF DMSP (Defense Meteorological Satellite Program) film transparencies, archived for NOAA/EDIS at the Space Science and Engineering Center, University of Wisconsin-Madison.

CITIES OF THE WORLD: WORLD REGIONAL URBAN DEVELOPMENT

Copyright © 1983 by HarperCollins*Publishers*, Inc.

All rights reserved. Printed in the United States of America. No part of this book may be used or reproduced in any manner whatsoever without written permission, except in the case of brief quotations embodied in critical articles and reviews. For information address HarperCollins Publishers, Inc., 10 East 53d Street, New York, NY 10022.

Library of Congress Cataloging in Publication Data
Main entry under title:

Cities of the world.

  (Harper & Row series in geography)
  Includes bibliographies and index.
  1. Cities and towns. 2. City planning. 3. Urbanization. 4. Urban policy. I. Brunn, Stanley D.
II. Williams, Jack Francis. III. Bonine, Michael E., 1942– . IV. Series.
HT151.C569   1983   307′.14   82-11689
ISBN 0-06-381225-8

Contents

Foreword by Peter Haggett xv

Preface xvii

CHAPTER 1 *WORLD URBAN DEVELOPMENT* 3
    World Urbanism: Introduction 3
    World Urbanism: Concepts and Definitions 5
        Urbanism 5
        Urbanization 5
        Urbanized Area 5
        Metropolis and Metropolitan Area 6
        City 6
        Conurbation, Megalopolis, Superconurbation 6
        City System or Urban System 7
        Preindustrial City 7
        Postindustrial City 7
        Primate City 7
        Colonial City 8
        Socialist City 8
        New Towns 8
    The World Urban System 9
    World Urbanization: Past Trends 16
        The Middle Period (Fifth to Seventeenth Century A.D.) 18
        Industrial Urbanization (Eighteenth Century to Present) 21
    World Urbanization: Location and Growth of Cities 22
        Site and Situation 22
        Types of Cities 22
        Urban Growth and the Principle of Circular and Cumulative Causation 23
        Economic Base Concept 24
    World Urbanization: Theories on the Internal Spatial Structure of Cities 25
        Concentric Zone Theory 26
        Sector Theory 26
        Multiple Nuclei Theory 27
        Inverse Concentric Zone Theory 27
    An Overview of Urban Problems 30
        Excessive Size 30
        Overcrowding 30
        Shortage of Urban Services 31

Slums and Squatter Settlements 32
Traffic Congestion 32
Lack of Social Responsibility 34
Unemployment and Underemployment 34
Racial and Social Issues 35
Westernization versus Modernization 35
Environmental Degradation 36
Urban Expansion and Loss of Agricultural Land 36
Administrative Organization 37

CHAPTER 2   CITIES OF NORTH AMERICA 43
North America in the World Urban System 43
Development of the North American Urban System 44
   Sail/Wagon Epoch to 1830 45
   The Age of Steam and the Iron Rail, 1830–1870 48
   The Age of Steam and Steel, 1870–1920 49
   The Age of the Auto, the Truck, and Air Transport, 1920–1970 50
   Megalopolitan Developments 51
   The Deconcentration of Continental Urban Growth 52
   Suburbanization 53
   Counterurbanization, 1970–On 54
Internal Structure of North American Cities 56
   Manufacturing 56
   Commerce 58
   Retail Structure 58
   Business and Wholesaling 59
   People in Cities 60
Major Representative Cities 64
   New York City: A Global Metropolis 64
   Los Angeles: A Suburban Metropolis 67
   Houston: A Sun Belt City 70
   Toronto: A Cosmopolitan City 73
Urban Problems and Solutions 76
   Fragmentation 76
      The Inner City and the Outer City 77
      Governments in Metropolis in Competition 78
      The Fragmentation of Costs and Benefits 79
   Different Growth Within the Urban System 81

CHAPTER 3   CITIES OF WESTERN EUROPE 85
Western Europe in the World Urban System 85
Historical Evolution of Western European Cities 86

Early Beginnings 86
Industrial Revolution 87
Urban Regions 90
Nature of the Western European City 92
  Low Building Profile 92
  Compact Form 93
  Dominance of Multiple Family Residence 94
  Combination of Residence and Work 94
  Greater Use of Public Transportation 95
  Less Distinct Zonation of Land Use Types 95
  Lack of Slums but Appearance of Ghettos 95
  Frequency of Public Parks 97
  Brick, Cement, and Mortar as Dominant Building Materials 97
Major Urbanization Types in Western Europe 98
  The Large City 98
    London: A World City 98
    Paris: France's Primate City 101
  Other Large Cities 105
    East and West Berlin: A Divided City 105
    Copenhagen and Stockholm: Dominating Cities in Scandinavia 106
    Madrid: A Centralized Political City 106
    Rome and Vienna: Historical Cities of Previous Empires 107
    Other Major Nonprimate Large Cities 107
  Urban Agglomerations 107
    Randstadt 108
    Rhine-Ruhr Agglomeration 109
  The Medium-Sized City 111
  European Patterns of Life in Small Urban Places 112
Urban Problems Facing Western Europe 114
Some Solutions to Urban Problems 115
Future Western European Urban Trends 119

CHAPTER 4   **CITIES OF THE SOVIET UNION AND EASTERN EUROPE**   **123**
The Soviet Union/Eastern Europe in the World Urban System 123
Historical Development of Soviet Cities 124
  Early Urbanization 125
  Early Growth of Moscow 126
  Cities of the Commercial and Early Industrial Period, 1700–1917 128
    The Foundation of St. Petersburg 128
    Odessa 128
    Cities of the Urals 129
    The Donets Basin 129
  Cities of the Soviet Period: 1917 to the Second World War 129

   Accelerated Urbanization 129
   Moscow and Leningrad 130
   Kiev 134
   The Donets Basin 134
   Kharkov 134
   Gorki 134
   Cities of the Volga 135
  Major Representative Cities of the Soviet Union 135
   Moscow: The Skyscraper City 135
   Leningrad: An Old Industrial City 137
   Magnitogorsk and Volgograd: Ural and Volga Cities 139
   Omsk, Irkutsk, and Novosibirsk: Cities of Siberia 141
   Vladivostok and Bratsk: Cities of the Far East 141
   Norilsk and Murmansk: Arctic Cities 142
   Central Asian Cities: Dominance of Tashkent 142
   Cities of the Caucasus: Importance of Baku 143
   Baltic Cities: Riga and Kaliningrad 143
  Contemporary Soviet Urban Problems 144
   Housing 144
   Transportation 145
   Place of Work 145
   Shopping 145
   Entertainment 146
   Recreation 147
   Religious Institutions 147
  Solutions to Soviet Urban Problems 147
   Socialist Urban Planning 148
   The Socialist City 148
  Historical Development of Eastern European Cities 149
   German Influences 150
   Turkish Influences: Sarajevo 151
  Major Representative Cities of Eastern Europe 151
   Belgrade: Crossroads City 151
   Sofia: Bulgarian Capital 152
   Bucharest: Romanian Capital 153
   Warsaw: A Rebuilt City 154
   Budapest: Twin-City Origins 155
   Prague: Commercial and Administrative City 155
   New Socialist Cities: Heavy Industrial Base 158
  Major Urban Problems 159

CHAPTER 5 **CITIES OF OCEANIA** **163**
  Oceania in the World Urban System 163
  Nature and Evolution of the Urban System 164

Territorial Frameworks for Urban Evolution 165
  The Archipelagos 165
  New Zealand 165
  Papua New Guinea 166
  Australia and Its Sovereign States 166
Primacy and Subservience 168
  Colonial Seeds of Primate Dominance 170
  Technology and Urbanization Intensity 171
Major Representative Cities 172
  Sydney: Oceania's Primate City 173
    The Spreading City 175
    The Changing Physical Fabric 176
    Who Lives Where? 177
    Social Inversion in Progress 180
  Canberra: Planned Capital 180
  Melbourne: A Second Primate City 182
  Perth: Epitome of Regional Isolation 185
  Port Moresby: A City of Transformations 187
  Auckland: City of Polynesia 189
  Suva: An Archipelagic Capital 192
Problems and Solutions 193
  Tinkering with the Urban System 193
  Internal Metropolitan Changes 195
  The Island Cities 196

CHAPTER 6 CITIES OF LATIN AMERICA 199
Latin America in the World Urban System 199
Evolution of Cities in Latin America 200
  Pre-Columbian Urbanization 200
  European Urbanization of the New World 202
  Introduction of European Cities 203
  Traditional Internal Structure of Latin American Cities 206
  Transformation of Latin American City Structure 207
    Expansion of the Central Business District 207
    Industrialization 208
    Expansion of Urban Services and Suburbanization 210
    Architectural Change 211
    Filter-Down Housing and Squatter Settlements 211
  Internal Structure of Modern Latin American Cities 213
    Central Business District 213
    Spine and Elite Residential Sector 215
    Zones 216
      Zone of Maturity 216
      Zone of In Situ Accretion 217

Zone of Peripheral Squatter Settlements   218
Core Area Slums and Homelessness   218
Major Representative Cities   219
   Mexico City   219
   Tijuana   224
   Rio de Janeiro   226
   Brasilia   231
   Buenos Aires   234
Urban Problems and Solutions   237

CHAPTER 7   **CITIES OF SUBSAHARAN AFRICA**   **243**
Subsaharan Africa in the World Urban System   243
Evolution of Cities in Subsaharan Africa   244
   Historic Centers of Urbanization   244
   Medieval Trade Centers of Eastern Africa   247
   Prepartition European Influence on African Urbanization   248
   African Urbanization in the Postpartition Era   250
Major Representative Cities of Subsaharan Africa   252
   Nairobi   252
   Johannesburg   257
   Kinshasa   260
   Lagos   262
   Dakar   267
Problems of Urban Development in Subsaharan Africa   271
   Primate Cities   271
   Site and Situation   271
   Rural-to-Urban Migration   273
   Functional Concentration   274
   Internal Characteristics   275
Solutions to Urban Problems: Policy Implications of African Urban Growth   275

CHAPTER 8   **CITIES OF THE MIDDLE EAST AND NORTH AFRICA**   **281**
The Middle East and North Africa in the World Urban System   281
Evolution of Cities in the Middle East   282
   The Islamic City Model   284
   Processes of Urbanization: Traditional and Modern   287
Major Representative Cities   290
   Cairo: The Impoverished Metropolis   290
   Tehran: The Parvenu Capital   294
   Baghdad: Primate City on the Tigris   299
   Kuwait City: The Oil Urbanization   302

          Istanbul: Migrant Cosmopolis on the Bosporus   305
          Israeli New Towns: Central Places and Garden Cities   308
             Beersheba: Primate Town of the Negev   313
     Urban Problems and Prospects   314

CHAPTER 9   **CITIES OF SOUTH ASIA**   325
     South Asia in the World Urban System   325
     Evolution of Cities in South Asia   326
          The Indus Valley Era   326
          The Aryan Hindu Impact   327
          Dravidian Temple Cities   328
          The Moslem Imprint: Shahjahanabad (Delhi)   329
          The Colonial Period   330
          Presidency Towns   331
     Models of South Asian City Structure   336
          Colonial-Based-City Model   336
             Cantonment   339
             Railway Colony   340
             Hill Stations   340
          Bazaar-Based-City Model   340
          Mixture of Colonial and Bazaar Models   343
          Contemporary Urban and Urbanization Characteristics   344
     Major Representative Cities   346
          Calcutta   346
          Bombay   350
          Madras   352
          Delhi   353
          Karachi   355
          Dacca   356
     Urban Problems and Solutions   360
          Planning   363
          New Towns   365
             Islamabad   365
             Chandigarh   367
          Prospects   367

CHAPTER 10   **CITIES OF SOUTHEAST ASIA**   371
     Southeast Asia in the World Urban System   371
     Evolution of Cities in Southeast Asia   372
          Urban Southeast Asia in Precolonial Times   373
          Urban Southeast Asia in Colonial Times   375
     Major Representative Cities   382

The Largest Cities: Jakarta and Manila 383
A City-State: Singapore 385
A Modern Inland Capital: Kuala Lumpur 389
Examples of Regional Centers 391
Contemporary Major Urban Problems 392
　Urban Growth 392
　Causes of Urban Growth 393
　Migration to Urban Areas 393
　Migrants in Jakarta 394
　Other Problems in the Indonesian Capital 397
　Industry and Infrastructure 398
Solutions to Urban Problems 400
　Progress in Singapore 400
　Squatter Relocation 401
　Expanding Employment 401
　Solution Attempts in Indonesia 402
　Resettlement Programs 402
　Growth Diversion Strategies 403
　City Problems and Solutions in the Socialist Nations 404
　　Vietnam 404
　　Kampuchea 405

CHAPTER 11   CITIES OF EAST ASIA 409
East Asia in the World Urban System 409
Introduction 410
Evolution of Cities in East Asia 412
　The Traditional or Preindustrial City 412
　　Peking 413
　　Changan 414
　　The Chinese City as Model: Japan and Korea 417
　Colonial Cities 417
　　The First Footholds: The Portuguese and Dutch 417
　　Treaty Ports of China 418
　　Shanghai 420
　　Taiwan and Korea: The Japanese Impact 422
　　Hong Kong 423
　Japan: The Asian Exception 425
　　Osaka 425
　　Tokyo 425
Major Representative Cities of East Asia Today 426
　Superconurbations: Tokyo and the Tokaido Megalopolis 426
　Colonial Cities: The Anachronism of Hong Kong 430
　Primate Cities: Seoul 431

Regional Centers: Taipei   432
Socialist Cities: Shanghai   434
Major Urban Problems: The Experience of Nonsocialist East Asia   435
Solutions to Urban Problems   438
  The Nonsocialist Way   438
  The Socialist Way   440
    Urban Land Use   442
    Administration and Socialization   444
    Role of the City Center   445
    Housing   445
    Urban Services   446
    Urban Transportation   446
    Green Space   447
    Controlling Pollution   447
    Chinese Urban Planning: Portent of the Future?   447

CHAPTER 12 **CITIES OF THE FUTURE**   453
Global Urban Settlement in 2000   454
Urban Growth and Urban Primacy   457
  Stages and Rates of Growth   457
  Primacy Ratio   462
  Rank-Size Relationships   464
Major Agglomerations   466
Human Geography of Shrinking Urban Worlds   468
Emergence of City Systems and Systems of Cities   472
The Global Village and World Cities   476
Urban Forms and Functions   478
  Urban Forms   478
  Urban Functions   480
Future Urban Problems   483
  The Developing World   483
  The Developed World   484

APPENDIX I **MAJOR CITIES OF THE WORLD**   489

INDEX   500

Foreword
Peter Haggett

Cities of the World *catches the changing mood of geography in the 1980s in an exciting way. For the past two decades geographers concentrated on understanding the process of growth and change within the city by keeping a close-up camera focused on local detail and intimate transactions within individual cities. In this text, Stanley Brunn and Jack Williams use a wide-angle lens to sweep across the emerging world urban patterns, surveying from continent to continent. A complete global picture comes into view.*

The editors could hardly have chosen a better time in which to bring their team together. Most of the world's countries have completed their 1980 or 1981 population censuses and the results beginning to emerge show some startling turnabouts. Growth in some of the very large mega-cities, which seemed so inevitable and unstoppable only a decade ago, has faltered and—in a few cases—has started to move in reverse. The counterurbanization movement is expanding in many countries, and many smaller and middle-sized cities are the new leaders of growth.

To keep a team of 14 authors, all distinguished in their own fields, consistently pulling together along the trail is a feat in itself. Professors Brunn and Williams have managed a nice balance between the uniformity that gives cohesion and structure and the variety that allows each author to give his own stylistic imprint to the chapter. The result is a blend that students will find helpful and challenging.

As geography moves toward a more global form, texts like Cities of the World *will be needed. Combining a disciplined structure and immense variety (over 80 cities are given detailed consideration),* Cities of the World *is an invitation to consider the global picture in all its diversity.*

I hope many students will choose to join the authors on their exciting voyage of exploration: it will leave them with insights and enrichment long after their school days are over.

Preface

This volume is a study in comparative world urban development. The great interest today in global urban patterns, processes, and problems is a response to one of the most important phenomena in recent world history: the extraordinary growth of cities around the world, especially in the many newly independent nations that emerged from the crumbling colonial empires of the post-World War II era. More than half the world's population is expected to live in cities by the early twenty-first century. This urban explosion justifiably deserves the attention of geographers and other specialists; indeed, their attention is needed if there is to be any hope of bringing the enormous problems created by the relatively uncontrolled growth of cities—and the rural-to-urban migration that is a major component of their growth—under control.

There is a voluminous literature, both geographic and other, on the nature of cities and urbanism around the world. Nonetheless, we feel there is still a need for a single study to pull together and synthesize the existing literature on the urban history, patterns, processes, and problems of the major world regions. We believe there is a need for a volume that gives greater attention to urbanism in the non-Western and developing nations of the world. Thus, we have given roughly equal space in this study to each of the 10 major regions: North America, Western Europe, Eastern Europe and the Soviet Union, Oceania, Latin America, Subsaharan Africa, North Africa and the Middle East, South Asia, Southeast Asia, and East Asia.

Such a study can serve a number of functions. First, it can serve as a class text, either primary or supplemental, for undergraduate courses in urban geography, world urbanism, or urban studies in other disciplines. To be sure, relatively few courses in American universities and colleges treat world urbanism on a comparative regional basis, but this may be due as much to a lack of textbooks with this approach as to a reluctance to examine world urbanism in this way. Indeed, the lack of a real competitor to this volume may lie in the fact that no one person could hope to command the vast literature on world urbanism and have the intimate knowledge of each world region required to produce a truly sound study.

A second function of this text is service as a basic reference volume, a grand tour de force of the world urban landscape, designed to appeal to both student and teacher, layman and specialist. Again, this function is enhanced by the lack of any other volume with an equivalent approach and content. Nonetheless, this is basically not a text on urban geography per se, and certainly not one that deals with urban theory in any great depth. Rather, this study provides a primarily descriptive, humanistic, nontheoretical, and relatively nonquantitative analysis of the growth of world regional cities over time. It examines the processes involved in that growth, the urban patterns that result, the character of principal regional cities, the major problems besetting those cities, and the various efforts being made to attack or resolve those problems. In short, this is a study of world urbanism yesterday, today, and tomorrow. This relatively nontechnical, nontheoretical approach was deliberately chosen in order to produce a volume that would be intellectually sound yet at the same time have the broadest possible appeal. We believe that the message of this volume should be directed to the nonspecialist as well as the specialist: To prod laymen to think more deeply about the nature of cities and urban life outside of their own realms, and to prod specialists to broaden their perspectives beyond the quite commonly narrow focus on urbanism.

Because of the vastness of the topic, it was decided from the start to make this a multiauthored text. Indeed, the editors regard this approach as one of the great strengths of the study. Each of the regional chapter authors (three of the chapters are coauthored) is an area specialist first and foremost, but with a strong interest in urban geography. The editors felt that the basic objectives of this book could best be served by area specialists who have a thorough understanding of the totality of their respective region and extensive first-hand field experience in that region, including travel and residence in the cities about which they are writing. Only in this way, it was felt, could the true character of urbanism in that region be fully and accurately conveyed to the reader—the urban character that transcends mere quantitative data about numbers of people living here or there, which can be understood only after one has lived in a particular city and felt its tempo, known its people, and shared their problems. Each of the authors in this volume has done this.

In addition, there was the obvious recognition that geographers certainly are not alone in the study of cities and urbanism. Hence, there has been a conscious effort in the preparation of this book and the writing of the individual chapters to incorporate studies by geographers and nongeographers alike, with the aim of producing a volume that would go beyond the confines of a purely geographical examination of world urbanism and appeal to persons with other backgrounds and in other disciplines as well. The editors feel this objective has been achieved.

A problem, however, with multiauthored books is that continuity is often sacrificed because different authors have varying approaches and writing styles. To overcome these inherent limitations as much as possible, and to promote the objectives outlined above, the editors imposed on each regional author the following conditions. First, each regional chapter is built around four basic themes:

1. *Evolution of urban systems and settlements.* A presentation of the historical development of cities and urbanization patterns in the region, from earliest times to the present, but with emphasis on the post-World War II era. This theme covers not only the evolution of urban patterns but the forces and processes that produced urban growth and the development of specific cities.
2. *Major representative urban centers.* A discussion of the major urban centers in the region today, including such aspects as their site and situation characteristics, size and functions, economic base, internal morphology, and position within one or more urban systems peculiar to the region.
3. *Contemporary major urban problems.* This theme surveys the major urban problems facing the cities of the region in the contemporary period, including such thorny issues as rural-to-urban migration, squatter settlements, land-use conflicts, unemployment and underemployment, housing and social services, transportation problems, pollution and environmental degradation, socioeconomic inequalities, and urban administration. These problems are discussed for the most part in relation to the major representative cities introduced in the second point above. In addition, each author has tried to weave into the narrative some discussion of what it is actually like to live in the cities of the region from the perspective of the average citizen, as opposed to the very different view a foreign tourist typically has.
4. *Solutions to urban problems.* A thematic look at the various regional attempts or plans being made to attack and solve the major urban problems. These include the development of new towns, urban renewal, the closing of cities to rural migrants, socialist city planning, control of city growth through residence and work permits and internal passports, slum clearance and housing estates, and industrial parks and zoning ordinances. Again, attempts at solutions are discussed primarily in relation to the major representative cities of the region.

Besides the 10 regional chapters, there is also an introductory chapter providing an overview of world urbanism of the past, present, and future. This chapter discusses essentially the same four major themes that each regional chapter is built around, but does so on a world scale, in an effort to show the similarities as well as contrasts in urban patterns, processes, and problems between the 10 major world regions. The study concludes with a brief chapter tying together current ideas about possible future trends in world urbanism. These trends are introduced in several of the regional chapters.

Each of the chapters is illustrated with maps, graphics, and photographs to provide vital supplemental images. These illustrations are a critical part of fully comprehending the urban character of each region.

Obviously, the task assigned each author was formidable, considering the space limitations in relation to the amount of material and topics to be covered. However, there was never any intention to treat each region comprehensively, to discuss every city, or to exhaustively analyze every trend and problem. Rather, the objective was, as stated earlier, to provide the reader with a succinct overview of the urbanism of each region, and a framework for understanding that region and its urban character and problems. At the end of each regional chapter there is a short annotated list of suggested references that the reader can use to delve more deeply into the urbanism of the region. As much as possible, each regional author selected what he felt were among the best studies in current literature, particularly from the layperson's viewpoint.

The problem of standardization of measurements and spelling of place names always arises in a book of this kind. In the case of measurements, we have used English units followed by metric units in parentheses throughout the text as well as in the graphics (such as map scales). In the case of place names, we have followed the widely observed practice of using the common or popular English spelling, rather than the spelling used in individual countries, e.g., Moscow, rather than Moskva; Vienna, rather than Wien; Copenhagen, rather than Kobenhavn; Peking, rather than Beijing. In Chapter 11, however, we have included the new Chinese (pinyin) spelling system in parentheses after the first references to place names in the text, but not in the graphics.

The idea for this book evolved out of a class on world urbanism called "Cities of the World" that has been taught in the Department of Geography at Michigan State University for a number of years. Consistent student interest and enrollments in that course and the comparative regional approach employed, plus the lack of a single suitable book to use as a text—and hence the need to assign a variety of reserve readings—prompted us to develop this book.

Thanks are due to the contributing authors for their time, talents, and energy. Special thanks go to Sherm Hollander for the superb graphics that grace the volume. Bhagan Narine and Kathy Robinson, the geography editors, and the staff of Harper & Row, especially Rita Williams, deserve credit, too, for their support and patience in seeing the project through to completion after innumerable delays, due in no small way to the fact that the contributing authors are farflung all over North America and Australia. The editors and authors are also extremely grateful to the following people for reviewing various parts or all of the manuscript at some stage in its preparation: Melvin Albaum, John Brush, Sen-dou Chang, George

Hoffman, Laurence Ma, James McDonald, Peter Muller, Ray Northam, Clifton Pannell, Bruce Ryan, C. Sargent, Jean Vance, and Donald Zeigler. Lastly, we are most appreciative of those who helped type preliminary and final drafts of the manuscript. These include Harriet Ashbay, Cheryl Clark, Brenda Wallace, and Mona Kinkel at Michigan State University and Donna Vallance and Sylvia Henderson at the University of Kentucky.

STANLEY BRUNN
JACK WILLIAMS

CITIES OF THE WORLD

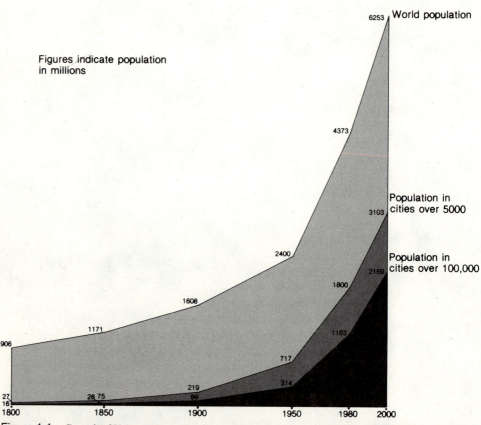

Figure 1.1 Growth of Urban Population and World Population, 1800–2000. (*Source:* Data derived from United Nations, Department of Economic and Social Affairs, *Global Review of Human Settlements, Statistical Annex,* published by Pergamon Press, New York, 1976.)

Chapter 1

World Urban Development

Jack F. Williams
Stanley D. Brunn
Joe T. Darden

World Urbanism: Introduction

If one compares a map of the world around the year 1900 with one of the world today, two changes are strikingly apparent: (1) the proliferation of nations, and (2) the mushrooming of the numbers and sizes of cities. The basically simple division of the world of 1900 between the independent, industrialized countries of Europe, North America, and Russia, and the vast colonial empires controlled by them in Latin America, Africa, and Asia, has been transformed into a far more complex mosaic of more than 160 independent nations of all sizes and levels of economic and political development. Likewise, the rather simple pattern of cities in 1900, with a relatively small number of major cities concentrated in the industrial countries, has also been transformed so that the greatest numbers of cities and the largest cities are increasingly found in the former colonial regions. With this growth of independent nations and cities, mankind is rapidly becoming urbanized, however poorly defined the concept of "urbanized" may be (see page 5). Around the year 1800 perhaps 3 percent of the world's population lived in urban places of 5000 people or more (Fig. 1.1). By 1900 the proportion had risen to over 13 percent. By 1980 the percentage had risen to over 40. According to statistical data provided for the United Nations Conference on Human Settlements, held in Vancouver in 1976, by the turn of the next century at least half of the world's population will live in urban places. Within the past century, the city has thus become the dominant center of modern civilization.

The present phenomenon of worldwide urbanization is as dramatic in its revolutionary implications for the history of civilization as were the earlier agricultural and industrial revolutions. In the industrial countries of Europe and North America, the *More Developed Countries* (MDCs) as the United Nations (UN) calls them, urbanization accompanied and was the consequence of industrialization and economic development. Thus, cities in those regions, although far from utopias, brought previously undreamed-of prosperity to the lives of millions. Industrial/economic growth combined with rapid urbanization produced a demographic transformation in those countries that brought declining population growth and, by and large, enabled the cities to expand apace with economic development. In the developing countries of Latin America, Africa, and Asia, the *Less Developed Countries* (LDCs) as the UN calls them, urbanization has occurred only partially as the result of industrial/economic growth and in many countries primarily as the result of rising and unfillable expectations of rural people who have flocked to the cities seeking escape from misery (and often not finding it). This "march to the cities," unaccompanied by significant declines in natural population growth, has resulted in the explosion of urban places in the LDCs.

Fundamental questions are raised by this extraordinary growth of cities, growth that is accelerating in the LDCs while showing signs of tapering off in the MDCs. For example, is urbanization a necessary concomitant of economic development? Or, to put it another way, is urbanization (a process associated with technological advance and the ability to multiply resources) the only way to outfit the earth for sustaining close to 6 billion people by the year 2000? Can rural development take some of the pressure off of cities in the LDCs? During the Maoist era, for instance, China appeared to be experimenting with this notion. New policies since the death of Mao in 1976 cast some doubt, though, on continuance of past development strategies regarding cities and urbanization (see Chapter 11).

There is also the question of the relationship between levels of urbanization and degree of political and economic power. It is a fact that the most powerful nations of the world today are highly urbanized, and that the highest standards of living, whether measured in per capita income figures or other standard indexes of economic well-being, are found in the countries with the highest percentages of urban population. Indeed, a strong correlation exists between per capita income and percent of urban population. Yet, does it automatically follow that the LDCs will see corresponding rises in per capita incomes as their percent of urban population grows? The answer to this question is probably no, until rates of urbanization are brought more closely in line with rates of economic growth. Otherwise, the problems of the cities multiply geometrically or logarithmically, while the financial resources of cities and governments to deal with the problems grow only arithmetically at best. Indeed, this is exactly what is happening throughout the LDCs today.

Even in the MDCs, however, where life for the vast majority of urban residents is incomparably better than for those living in the great cities of the LDCs, there are serious concerns about the future of the city. What, for example, is the optimum size of a city? Are cities in general getting too large for effective administration and to ensure an adequate, let alone ideal, urban environment to live in? Is the megalopolis or super-conurbation to be the norm for the twenty-first century? What will be the impact of these vast urban agglomerations on human society, on resource development, on environmental preservation?

Obviously, these are not easy questions to answer, and definitive answers will not

World Urbanism: Concepts and Definitions

be found in this book. But these and other questions are addressed in one way or another in the various regional chapters of this book, and in the concluding chapter, which looks at the future of cities of the world.

World Urbanism: Concepts and Definitions

A variety of terms or concepts associated with the theme of world urbanism are used throughout this book. The following discussion attempts to explain these terms in simple fashion and to clarify some of the ambiguities and similarities between various terms and concepts.

Urbanism

Urbanism is a broad concept which generally refers to all aspects—political, economic, social, etc.—of the urban way of life. Unlike urbanization, urbanism is not a process of urban growth, but rather the end result of urbanization. It is used in this book to convey the idea that all aspects of world urban patterns and problems are discussed.

Urbanization

Urbanization is a process involving two phases or aspects: (1) the movement of people from rural to urban places where they engage in primarily nonrural functions or occupations, and (2) the change in their life-style from rural to urban with its associated values, attitudes, and behaviors. The important variables in the former are population density and economic functions; the important variables in the latter depend on social, psychological, and behavorial factors. The two aspects are mutually supportive.

    The imprecision of the concept of urbanization is apparent in the wide variation from country to country as to exactly how many people must live in a concentrated area and engage in primarily nonrural activities to constitute an urban place. These minimum population concentration thresholds are derived by each country on the basis of varying mixes of population densities, land areas, and political/economic systems. In Albania and New Zealand, for example, places with a population of 400 and 1000, respectively, are considered urban; 1500 in Ireland; 2000 in France, Israel, and Argentina; 5000 in Belgium and Ghana and 10,000 in Greece and Senegal. In Denmark and Sweden, on the other hand, only 200 people are required for a place to be classified as urban. In the United States, places are defined as urban by the Bureau of the Census if they have at least 2500 people, the same minimum population used in Mexico and Venezuela.

Urbanized Area

As cities have spread spatially, the boundary between urban and rural has become increasingly blurred, especially in the industrialized countries such as the U.S., where modern transportation has particularly fostered urban sprawl. Thus, the *urbanized area* could be defined as the *built-up area,* where buildings, roads, and other essentially urban land uses predominate, even though these facilities spread beyond the political boundaries of cities and towns.

As cities have grown in size, both in population and spatially, a variety of terms have been coined to refer to these ever-larger cities and city regions.

Metropolis and Metropolitan Area

A *metropolis* is properly the chief city (but not necessarily the capital) of a country, state, or region, but is often loosely used to refer to any large city. The *metropolitan area* is generally regarded as a central city and peripheral jurisdictions plus all surrounding territory (urban or rural) integrated with the central city. In the U.S., however, the term has a much more precise meaning, embodied in the *Standard Metropolitan Statistical Area* (SMSA) or, as of 1982, now called simply the *Metropolitan Statistical Area* (MSA). Used by the Bureau of the Census since the 1950 census, the MSA refers to one or more central cities with at least 50,000 inhabitants in the urban core plus those contiguous counties that have more than 75 percent of their population engaged in nonagricultural activities, and using county boundaries as the statistical measuring units. The largest metropolitan census units are the Standard Consolidated Statistical Areas (SCSA), which are made up of several SMSAs. The largest SCSA is composed of New York, Newark, and Jersey City.

City

The term *city* is essentially a political designation, referring to a place governed by some kind of administrative body or organization. Thus, the term in itself has no size connotation, although normally a city is larger than a town or village. Two colloquial terms that do equate cities with size are *supercity* and *millionaire* (sometimes *million*) *city*. The former is sometimes used in general reference to any of the world's largest cities, those with a population over 5 million, say, although this term undoubtedly offends purists. Likewise, the latter term is sometimes used to refer to cities with a population of at least 1 million.

Conurbation, Megalopolis, Superconurbation

As cities have grown larger, they have begun to coalesce, or merge together, in the more congested regions of the world where many cities are located. *Conurbation* and *megalopolis* both mean essentially the same thing: the spatial merging (but not necessarily the political merging) of two or more cities along major transportation corridors. The term *conurbation* was originally coined in reference to British urban growth. *Megalopolis* was originally coined to refer to the merging of cities along the urban corridor in the eastern United States from Boston to Washington, but later became a generic term referring to urban coalescence. A *superconurbation* is simply a giant conurbation or megalopolis with a population of at least 12 million, based on a rather arbitrary population threshold. Another synonym for essentially the same concept that is also used in this text is *supermetropolitan region*. The ultimate expression of the merging of cities will be conurbations joining megalopolises to form a *world ecumenopolis*, as discussed in Chapter 12, in which city clusters in different regions will join with other agglomerations in a sort of vast interconnected continental-wide megalopolis. The beginning signs of this may already by evident.

City System or Urban System

As urbanization has grown and cities have multiplied throughout the world, every region or country has developed a *hierarchy* of cities, which can be ranked on the basis of population size and economic and other functions, and which are interlinked by increasingly sophisticated transportation and communication networks. Indeed, it is these integrating networks that provide the primary stimulus to the formation of conurbations.

Preindustrial City

The *preindustrial city,* sometimes referred to as the *traditional city,* sometimes inaccurately as the *non-Western city,* is, as the name suggests, a city that was founded and grew before the arrival of industrialization in the nineteenth and twentieth centuries and thus typically had quite different characteristics from the modern industrial cities of today. This type of city can still be seen in many of the LDCs today, although most major cities in even the LDCs now are in the process of industrializing to some degree and thus exhibit simultaneously elements of both preindustrial as well as commercial-industrial cities.

Postindustrial City

A relatively new type of city is emerging in the wealthy MDCs. The *postindustrial city* whose origin and economic raison d'être are not tied to an industrial base, but one where the employment in the services sector is high. Cities that are mainly the headquarters for corporations or a series of governmental and intergovernmental organizations are examples as are those specializing in research-and-development (R&D) institutes and tourism/recreation. With an increase in the number of people employed in tertiary and quaternary occupations, especially in such fields as finance, health, leisure, R&D, education, and telecommunications and in various levels of government, the cities with concentrations of these activities have an economic base in sharp contrast to those cities that originated in industrial economies.

Primate City

Another type of city, defined by size and function, is the *primate city.* The term derives from *urban primacy,* a concept first developed in the late 1930s to refer to the tendency for countries to have one city that is at least twice as large as the second largest city and has a dominance over the country's economic, political, and cultural life. This type of city is found throughout the world, but is especially prevalent in LDCs, in a few instances even occurring in the form of *dual primacy,* where two large cities share the dominant role, such as Rio de Janeiro and São Paulo in Brazil. Dual primacy is not to be confused with the concept of the *dual city,* which is also common in the LDCs and is the result primarily of colonialism in which a modern, relatively Western-style central city was built either independently or next to an existing traditional or indigenous city. The dual city is literally composed of two parts: one modern and Western, the other more traditional and indigenous in character.

One aspect of urban primacy is the *core-periphery concept,* introduced in Chapter 7, which is seen in the way African primate cities constitute a socioeconomic core that thrives on the parasitic relationship between them and the periphery. In fact, this concept is applicable to primate cities in other developing regions outside of Africa.

One concept that represents an alternative to primacy is the *rank-size rule,* explored more fully in Chapter 12, which evolved out of empirical research on the relationships between cities of different population size in a given region. Simply put, the rule states that the population of a particular city in an area is equal to the population of the largest city in the area divided by the rank of that particular city. In other words, in some countries there is a fairly well distributed growth in cities at many levels of size, and a natural mathematical relationship between their population sizes, whereas in other countries a single city (the primate city) utterly dominates the urban patterns. Some countries fall between those two models.

Colonial City

Another type of city, discussed extensively in several of the regional chapters (see particularly Chapters 6–11), is the *colonial city.* Although almost entirely gone from the face of the earth now, this type of city had the profoundest impact on urbanization and urban patterns throughout much of the world, starting around the year 1500 and culminating in the nineteenth and early twentieth centuries. The colonial city was a unique type, because of its special focus on commercial functions, its peculiar situation requirements, and the odd blend of European or Western urban forms with indigenous populations and cultures.

Socialist City

The *socialist city* is peculiar to the communist-socialist countries of the world, especially the Soviet Union and the People's Republic of China, in which a massive degree of government involvement, coupled with the absence of both private land ownership and free-market forces, have produced distinctly different cities in virtually all aspects of urbanism and internal spatial structure (see Chapters 4 and 11).

New Towns

The *new town,* narrowly interpreted, is a phenomenon of the twentieth century and refers to a comprehensively planned urban community built from scratch with the intent of becoming as self-contained as possible by encouraging the development of an economic base and full range of urban services and facilities. New towns have come into existence around the world to fulfill a number of functions, which include relieving overcrowding of the larger central cities (helping to redistribute urban population); providing an optimum living environment for the residents; helping to control urban sprawl and preserve open land; and in some countries serving as foci, or *growth poles,* for development of new industry and exploitation of natural resources. The modern new-town movement began in Britain in the early 1900s, and later diffused to other European countries, the United States, the Soviet Union, and in the post-World War II era to many other newly independent countries. The idealized form of the new town, in the West at least, tends to follow the Garden City concept of the British, with small population (generally under 100,000), heavy orientation toward the family, combinations of detached houses and apartments or condominium-style housing, carefully planned transportation to minimize the negative impact of automobiles, lots of green space and compactness to encourage walking and outdoor activities, and economic self-sufficiency so that the residents are within a very short distance of their jobs (thus cutting into the volume of suburban commuters to the large central cities). (See, for example, Chapters 3 and 8.)

This vision of the new town tends to have an aura of utopia to it, and like utopia is rarely achieved in entirety in actual new towns, although some new towns do come fairly close to fulfilling this vision. Nonetheless, the majority of new towns, whether in the West, in the Soviet Union, or in LDCs tend to fall quite short of these goals. Moreover, new towns have been even less successful in the West, at least in helping to solve broader urban problems of the congested and decaying central cities, in terms of shifting substantial segments of the urban population and solving problems of urban poverty. In the U.S., for instance, after several decades of effort, barely 100 new towns have been built, mostly under private developers. Few of these are new towns in the idealized British form. While people living in these new towns may indeed be quite happy with their situation, the existence of these new towns has done little to meet the urban problems of the U.S.

There are many reasons for this relative failure, including the cost of construction, difficulties in acquiring sufficient land, and the complex mix of social, economic, and political factors that govern where people and businesses opt to locate, not to mention relative lack of federal government interest since the brief spurt of interest and involvement in the mid-1960s. Without the nearly total control over land use, construction, and the lives of citizenry found in the communist states, governments and private groups in the West find it extremely difficult to use new towns as a major tool for urban development. In the LDCs also, though, new towns by and large have had no significant impact on the urban patterns and problems of those countries, even though some countries, such as Brazil with its dramatic new capital of Brasilia, have been quite bold in attempting to use new towns as instruments of change.

The World Urban System

The data on world urbanization, however imperfectly measured and subject to varying margins of error, vividly reveal the march to the cities that has been going on

TABLE 1.1 WORLD URBAN POPULATION, BY REGION, 1950 AND 1980

World Region	1950 Urban Population (Millions)	(%)	1980 (est.) Urban Population (Millions)	(%)
North America	105	64	196	79
Western Europe	177	60	260	74
Oceania	8	64	17	73
Latin America	67	41	237	64
Eastern Europe/Soviet Union	108	39	243	62
North Africa/Middle East	26	26	112	48
East Asia	112	17	358	33
Southeast Asia	23	13	90	24
South Asia	69	15	199	22
Subsaharan Africa	17	10	80	22
World	715	29	1792	41
More Developed Countries	457	53	842	72
Less Developed Countries	257	16	950	30

Source: Derived from Table 1 in *Global Review of Human Settlements, Statistical Annex,* United Nations: Department of Economic and Social Affairs, published by Pergamon Press, New York, 1976, pp. 22–49.

during the past 30 years. Table 1.1 and Fig. 1.2 compare the percentages of urban population in each of the 10 major regions, as delimited in this book, between 1950 and 1980 (estimated). The world population as a whole increased from 29 percent urban to about 41 percent urban in this period. The MDCs retained their lead in percent of urban population, rising from 53 to 72 percent, but the LDCs also showed substantial gains, from a mere 16 percent in 1950 to a nearly doubled 30 percent by 1980. Indeed, the percentage gains by the LDCs were much greater than for the rest of the world. Within the 10 regions, North America, Western Europe, and Oceania still are the most urbanized, while the vast region stretching from Subsaharan Africa through South and Southeast Asia still registers urban population percentages only in the 22 to 24 percent range, reflecting the fact that this realm contains the bulk of the LDCs, those with predominantly rural and poorly developed economies (Table 1.2 and Fig. 1.3).

The actual number of people involved in these percentage figures even better reveals the rising importance of the LDCs in world urbanism. In 1950 the MDCs had almost twice as many people in urban places as the LDCs; by 1980 the latter had overtaken the former by a margin of 100 million. In other words, a billion people now live in cities in the LDCs. Moreover, the number of cities in the LDCs has also overtaken the number in the MDCs (Table 1.3 and Fig. 1.4). In 1950 just over 900 cities in the world had a population of 100,000 or more. By 1980 that figure had risen to 2200. The number of those cities located in the MDCs increased from 557 to 1061, but at the same time the share found in the LDCs mushroomed from about 350 to 1140. In addition, the LDCs now have some 116 "million" cities, compared with 110 in the more developed countries. Particularly significant is the explosion in numbers

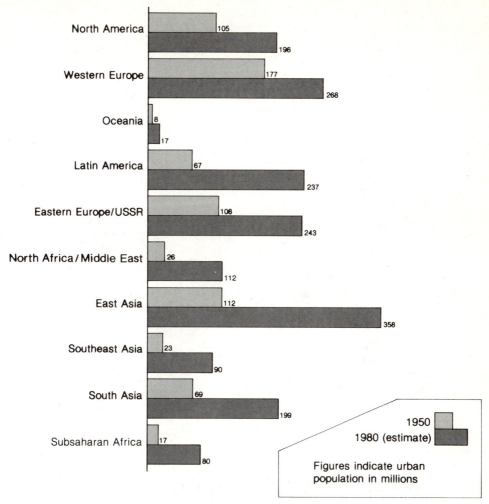

Figure 1.2 Urban Population of Major World Regions, 1950 and 1980. (*Source:* Data derived from United Nations, Department of Economic and Social Affairs, *Global Review of Human Settlements, Statistical Annex,* published by Pergamon Press, New York, 1976.)

of supercities, those with a population over 5 million. These giant agglomerations now total 15 in the LDCs and continue to grow at alarming rates, whereas the 11 such concentrations in the MDCs now have relatively low growth rates or are actually declining.

Irrespective of regional comparisons, these data show quite vividly the growing importance of the city as a focus of modern civilization, the number of cities with a population of at least 100,000 having more than doubled in the past 30 years. How long will it take for the number to double again? With no sign yet of a decline in the rate of urbanization in the LDCs (if anything, the rate may actually increase further),

TABLE 1.2 THE WORLD'S MOST URBANIZED NATIONS, 1980 (ESTIMATED)
(A population of at least 1 million, 50% or more urban)

Region and Nation	Urban Population (%)	Region and Nation	Urban Population (%)
Western Europe		Latin America (cont.)	
Sweden	86	Mexico	67
West Germany	85	Colombia	66
Denmark	84	Brazil	64
Netherlands	81	Cuba	64
United Kingdom	79	Peru	60
France	79	Panama	55
Belgium	74	Nicaragua	51
Spain	72	Jamaica	50
Greece	61	Subsaharan Africa	
Switzerland	60	South Africa	52
Finland	59	North Africa/Middle East	
Austria	55	Kuwait	92
Eastern Europe/Soviet Union		Israel	85
East Germany	76	Iraq	66
Soviet Union	64	Lebanon	65
Bulgaria	63	Algeria	55
Czechoslovakia	61	Egypt	51
Poland	60	Tunisia	51
North America		South Asia	
Canada	81	(None)	
United States	79		
Oceania		Southeast Asia	
Australia	87	Singapore	93
New Zealand	85	East Asia	
Latin America		Hong Kong	96
Chile	86	Japan	79
Venezuela	85	Taiwan	70
Uruguay	83	Mongolia	57
Argentina	82	South Korea	53

Source: Derived from Table 1 in *Global Review of Human Settlements, Statistical Annex,* United Nations: Department of Economic and Social Affairs, published by Pergamon Press, New York, 1976, pp. 22–49.

a number of predictions are warranted: (1) the percent of urban population will continue to increase in the LDCs, narrowing the gap further with the MDCs, whose percentage of urban population has more or less leveled off; (2) the total urban population in the LDCs will continue to grow beyond that found in the MDCs as the result of high natural population growth rates and continued rapid rural-to-urban migration; (3) the total numbers of cities and the number of "giant" cities in the LDCs will also continue to outdistance those in the MDCs.

Indeed, we seem to have entered the era of the superconurbation. The present pattern, particularly in the LDCs, is that the bigger the urban unit, the faster it grows.

The World Urban System 13

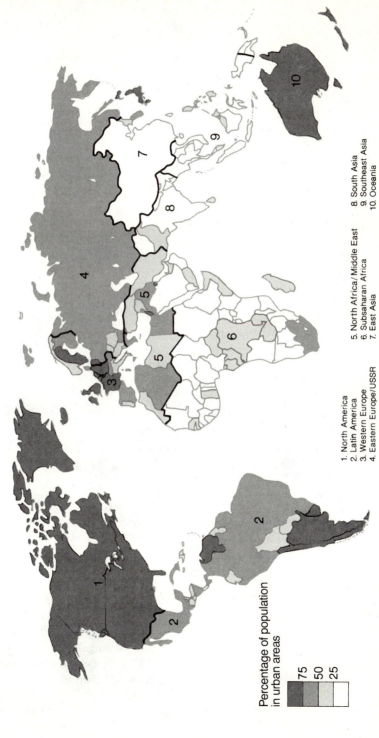

Figure 1.3 World Urbanization by Country. (*Source:* Data derived from United Nations, Department of Economic and Social Affairs, *Global Review of Human Settlements, Statistical Annex*, published by Pergamon Press, New York, 1976.)

TABLE 1.3 CITIES OF THE WORLD
Population 100,000 or More
1950 and 1980 (est.)

	1950	1980 (est.)
World Total		
Over 5 million	6	26
2–5 million	24	71
1–2 million	41	129
500,000–1 million	101	249
200,000–500,000	281	727
100,000–200,000	453	999
Total	906	2201
More Developed Countries		
Over 5 million	5	11
2–5 million	15	31
1–2 million	28	68
500,000–1 million	61	118
200,000–500,000	173	351
100,000–200,000	275	482
Total	557	1061
Less Developed Countries		
Over 5 million	1	15
2–5 million	9	40
1–2 million	13	61
500,000–1 million	40	131
200,000–500,000	108	376
100,000–200,000	178	517
Total	349	1140

Source: Derived from Table 5 in *Global Review of Human Settlements, Statistical Annex,* United Nations: Department of Economic and Social Affairs, published by Pergamon Press, New York, 1976, pp. 60–76.

Thus, towns are growing more rapidly than villages, cities faster than towns; cities with a population more than a million are growing faster than cities with less than a million, and multimillion cities with over 2.5 million are growing fastest of all. Assuming that the present growth rates of 2 percent for the MDCs and 4.2 percent for the LDCs continue, the result is that by the year 2000 the following cities will become superconurbations: Mexico City, Mexico; São Paulo and Rio de Janeiro, Brazil; Shanghai and Peking, China; Bombay, New Delhi, Calcutta, India; Seoul, Korea; Buenos Aires, Argentina; Cairo, Egypt; Tehran, Iran; Bangkok, Thailand; Manila, the Philippines; Lima, Peru; Bogotá, Colombia; and Los Angeles-Long Beach, U.S. Thus, most of the superconurbations will be in the LDCs, areas least able to provide the necessary resources for dealing with the problems of urban life. This era of the superconurbation has reordered social relations and has brought forth new patterns of political, familial, and religious institutions. Power relationships between the LDCs and MDCs are

The World Urban System 15

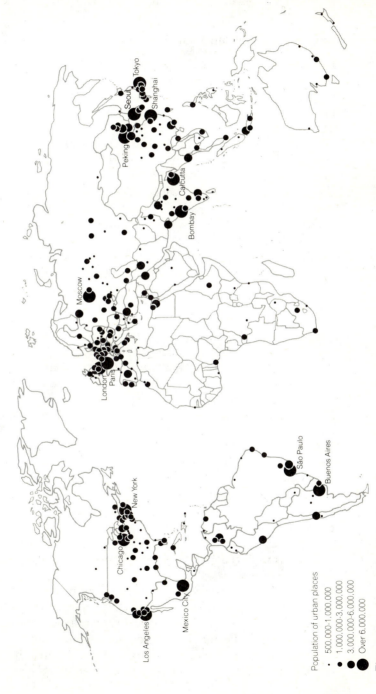

Figure 1.4 Major Cities of the World. (*Source:* Data derived from United Nations, Department of Economic and Social Affairs, *Global Review of Human Settlements, Statistical Annex*, published by Pergamon Press, New York, 1976.)

changing as countries in the less developed world begin experiencing some of the benefits and problems of modern urbanization and industrialization.

World Urbanization: Past Trends

It is remarkable that the present urban pattern, although largely the creation of the last century, had its origins thousands of years ago in several of the very regions currently experiencing explosive urban growth. From these early centers of human civilization, the concept of the city diffused to Europe and then tens of centuries later returned in the form of the colonial city, which was to have such a radical impact and forever alter the urban character of these ancient regions.

Four main regions in the Old World and one region in the New World were the earliest centers of preindustrial or traditional cities, the first cities in human history (Fig. 1.5). The first cities were located in Mesopotamia, probably about 4000 B.C. Cities were found in the Nile Valley about 3000 B.C., in the Indus Valley (present Pakistan) by 2500 B.C., in the Yellow River Valley of China by 2000 B.C., and in Mexico and Peru in A.D. 500. Estimates as to the size of these early cities indicate that they were relatively small. The city of Ur may have had a population of 200,000. Thebes, as the capital of Egypt, could have had around 225,000 inhabitants in 1600 B.C. However, ancient cities on the average did not increase significantly in number, and in general their populations remained in the range of 2,000 to 20,000 until well into the first thousand years of their existence. The largest ancient city was Rome. In the second century A.D., Rome may have had 1 million inhabitants, making it the first "million" city in history. But after the second century, Rome's population began to decrease, declining below 200,000 by the ninth century. No other city in the Western world reached Rome's maximum population until London attained 1 million people early in the 1800s.

These ancient cities appeared at a time and at places where the state of technology and the social and natural conditions of the environment enabled cultivators to produce more than they needed to subsist. From that time onward, a system of division of labor and distribution of surplus products developed. Cities were the residential form adopted by those members of society whose direct presence at the places of agricultural production was not necessary. They were religious, administrative, and political centers. These ancient cities represented a new social system, but one that was not separate from the rural one because they were both closely linked to the same process of production and distribution of the surplus.

In these ancient cities were specialists working full time such as priests and service workers as well as a population that appreciated the arts and the use of writing and arithmetic. There was also a system of taxation, there was external trade, and there were social classes. Each city was surrounded by a countryside of farms, villages, and even towns. Ancient cities demonstrated the emergence of specialization. Rural life limited the exchange of goods, ideas, and people, as well as the complexity of technology and the division of labor. Thus, trade was a basic function of ancient cities, which were linked to the surrounding rural areas and to other cities by a relatively complex system of production and distribution, as well as religious, military, and economic institutions.

World Urbanization: Past Trends 17

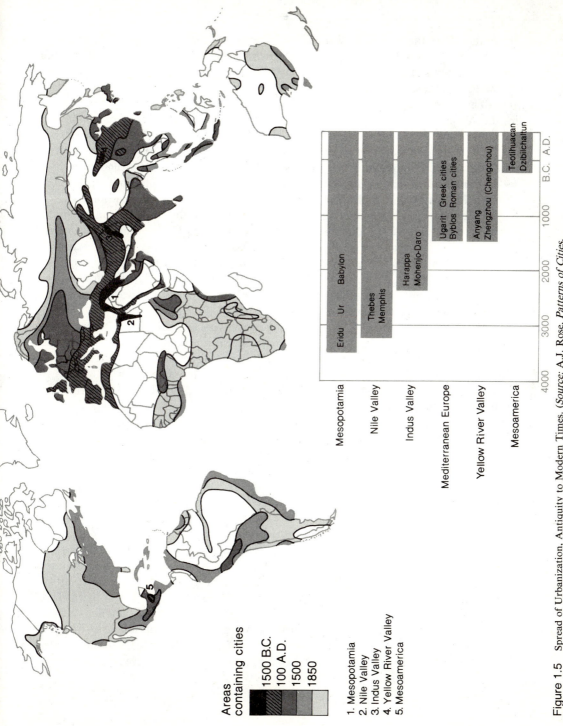

Figure 1.5 Spread of Urbanization, Antiquity to Modern Times. (*Source*: A.J. Rose, *Patterns of Cities*, Sydney, Australia: Thomas Nelson, 1967, p. 21. Reprinted with permission, which is based on "The Origin and Evolution of Cities" by Gideon Sjoberg. Copyright © 1965 by Scientific American, Inc. All rights reserved.)

The Middle Period (Fifth to Seventeenth Century A.D.)

From the fall of the Roman Empire to the seventeenth century, cities in Europe grew only slowly or not at all. The few large cities declined in size and function. Thus, the Roman Empire's fall in the fifth century A.D. marked the effective end of urbanization in Western Europe for over 600 years.

The important question is why urbanization ceased there for so long or why cities did not grow. The major reason was a decrease in spatial interaction. After the collapse of the Roman Empire, urban localities became isolated from one other and had to become self-sufficient in order to survive. From their very beginnings, cities had survived and increased in size because of spatial interaction with their rural hinterland and with other cities, forming a system of production, distribution, and exchange. The disruption of the Roman transportation system, the spread of Islam in the seventh and eighth centuries, and the pillaging raids of the Norsemen in the ninth century almost completely eliminated trade between cities. These events, plus the periodic attacks by barbarians on the rural areas, resulted in an almost complete disruption of urban and rural interaction. Both the rural and urban populations declined. With the loss of trade, entire regions became isolated, with the result that urban ideas had little diffusion, agricultural productivity declined, and people became preoccupied with defense and survival.

Related to the decline in agricultural productivity and diffusion of urban ideas was an ineffective governmental administration. Services, especially transportation and communication networks, were not maintained, resulting in internal interaction only. The lack of innovation and technical change reinforced the no-growth pattern.

Although urban revival did occur 600 years after the fall of the Roman Empire via fortified settlements and ecclesiastical centers, growth in population and production remained quite small. The reason is quite simply that exchange was limited, and was conducted largely with people of the immediate surrounding region. Most urban residents spent their lives within the walls of their city. Thus, urban communities developed very close-knit social structures. Power was shared between feudal lords and religious leaders. The urban population was organized into guilds, with each craftsman, artisan, and merchant belonging to a particular guild. Within the social organization, each person had a clearly defined place. One's social status was determined by one's position in guild, family, church, and feudal administration. Merchants and craftsmen in guilds saw the innovative possibilities of free cities, where a person could reach his or her full potential within a community setting. Over time, however, commerce expanded the function of the city and linked it to the expanding power of the state, resulting in a system called *mercantilism*. The purpose of the economic policy of mercantilism was the use of the power of the state to help the nation develop its economic potential and population. The policy of mercantilism included protection of merchant interests through the control of trade subsidies, the creation of trade monopolies, and the maintenance of a strong armed force to defend commercial aims. Cities were its growth centers, and specialization and trade kept it alive.

Mercantilism, though based on new economic ideas and practices, had one important element in common with beliefs of the previous period. It restrained and controlled individual merchants in favor of the needs of society. However, the rising new middle class of merchants and industrial capitalists were against any restrictions on their profits. They opposed economic regulaton and used their growing power to demand freedom from state control. They desired an end to mercantilism. As the power of the capitalists increased, the goal of the economy became expansion, with economic profit the function of city growth. While the new market economy provided means to social recognition, the social costs were high. The greatest hardship fell on those receiving the fewest benefits—poor farmers and members of the rising industrial working class. This new force, *capitalism,* pushed aside the last vestiges of feudal life and created a new central function for the city—industrialization. It was capitalism that ushered in the Industrial Revolution and led to the emergence of the *industrial city* (Fig. 1.6).

While Europe was going through this process of decline and then rebirth in its cities, areas of the non-Western world experienced quite different patterns. In East Asia, for example, the city did not suffer the decline that it went through in medieval Europe. In China, numerous cities founded before the Christian era remained continuously occupied and economically viable down through the centuries. Moreover, long before any city in Europe grew to a size to rival ancient Rome, "million" cities were

Figure 1.6 Hamburg, the largest city of West Germany, with a population over 2.2 million, is a good example of an older major industrial city in Western Europe's urban-industrial core. Rebuilt from the ruins of World War II, Hamburg exhibits a mixture of structures typical of such cities, ranging from cathedrals of the medieval past to industrial plants of the nineteenth century to ultramodern office buildings of the postwar period. (Courtesy German Information Service)

thriving in East Asia. Changan (present-day Sian or Xi'an), for example, reputedly had more than 1 million people when it was the capital of Tang China in the seventh century. Kyoto, the capital of Japan for over a thousand years and modeled after ancient Changan, had a population exceeding 1 million by the 1700s. Likewise, Tokyo, a relatively young city by Asian standards, had grown to 1 million by the middle of the eighteenth century. Although most of the ancient non-Western cities of Asia had a population of less than 1 million, for the most part they were still far larger than cities in Europe until the commercial/industrial revolutions there. The principal explanation for this historical pattern of urban growth lies, of course, in the very different political/cultural systems and geographical environments of the great Asian civilizations. Although empires waxed and waned in Asia, just as in Europe, the city in premodern Asia continued to serve a vital function, as the center of political administration, as the cultural and religious center, and as the commercial center for the highly developed traditional agrarian societies of Asia.

It was not until the arrival of Western colonialism that the traditional societies, and the cities of those societies, began to be threatened. The several centuries of Western colonialism in Asia added a new kind of city to the region, a Western commercial city sometimes grafted onto a traditional city, sometimes created anew from virgin land. In either case, these new cities came eventually to dominate the urban landscape of most of Asia until the end of colonialism in the middle of the twentieth century. Indeed, that dominance has continued right into the contemporary period.

In the Middle East and North Africa, in the Islamic world, the traditional city had also existed and thrived down through the centuries long before Europeans began to claim pieces of the region as their colonial territories. But once colonialism was fully asserted in the region, the same process of grafting and creating of new Western commercial cities occurred, with similar consequences to those experienced in Asia.

In Subsaharan Africa and Latin America, the urban experience varied somewhat from that of much of Asia and the Middle East. In the case of Latin America, the traditional city—and the societies that created that city, such as the Mayan, Inca, and Aztec—were completely obliterated by Spanish conquest and colonization. The Spanish, as well as the Portuguese and other Europeans, thus created new cities in the vast realm of Latin America, cities that reflected the cultures of Europe. In Subsaharan Africa, the indigenous cities of various black African kingdoms and tribal groups that had existed for a number of centuries also felt the impact of European colonialism, especially by the nineteenth century, and were largely obliterated as viable urban centers, with few exceptions. Thus, in that vast subcontinent the Europeans also carved out their colonial territories and created innumerable European commercial cities that quickly grew to dominate the region and have continued to dominate in the postindependence period.

Hence, throughout most of the world outside of Europe, the principal historical pattern in urban development has been the profound impact of the European-created city transported to other parts of the world, sometimes to largely virgin territories where indigenous societies were exterminated or shoved aside (as in North and South America and in Oceania), sometimes to regions with large populations and long histories of indigenous cultures and urban life where Europeans had to conquer and rule (as in most of Asia, the Middle East, and Africa).

Industrial Urbanization (Eighteenth Century to Present)

Only after the Industrial Revolution did significant urbanization occur, in that for the first time a sizable proportion of the population came to live in urban areas. As places of human residence and employment, urban areas did not absorb a large proportion of the population until the nineteenth century, and even then only in selected areas of the world. Thus, the division of the world's population into categories of urban and rural residence did not acquire demographic significance until modern times. Not more than three percent of the world's population could have been considered urban in 1800. The emergence of cities as important places of population concentration can be regarded as a major event of the nineteenth century.

The emergence of urbanized nations in which a majority of the population resides in urban places occurred during the twentieth century. At the beginning of this century, only one nation, Great Britain, could be regarded as an urbanized society in the sense that more than one-half of its inhabitants resided in urban places. The United States had become an urban nation by 1920. By 1955, there were at least 18 such nations, and by 1965 there were at least 30. By 1980 an estimated 47 nations (those of at least 1 million population) were urbanized (Table 1.2). Nonetheless, the majority of nations are still predominantly rural.

In most of the world's large cities (at least those outside the socialist bloc), the residents live in urban areas produced by basically unregulated market and social forces. For the most part, the pricing mechanism is operating to produce an economic city with countless simultaneous and successive decisions affecting a market-oriented allocation of resources. In reading the section on the problems of urbanization, keep in mind that the market system has channeled investment to produce a great variety of cities, specialized and diversified, large and small, growing and declining. The important point to remember, however, is that the problems of the average citizen will reflect the general prosperity of his or her city. The position and importance of a city (i.e., its rank in the international and national systems of cities) is a vital measure in an assessment of the problems of the residents.

It is also important to note that the city is not a static entity, but a system in flux. Within the city, some sectors may decline and die as investment is withdrawn or withheld while others grow and prosper as investments increase. Every change in urban function has its effect. Adjustment to the changed situation may occur slowly. If the change is a reduction in functions, poverty levels will usually rise as unemployment spreads through the city in a cumulative manner but produces greater effects in some neighborhoods and among some groups than others. Whether the city is growing or declining, spatial change within it will occur as a result of the decline of older neighborhoods, an influx of poor rural families, or immigrants from foreign areas, labor-shedding as a result of automation, development of new suburbs or satellite towns, and the migration of businesses and industries to the suburbs. In a city that is changing its functions, those without access to opportunities, skills, or transportation will be left out by the market system operating. Whenever the market system operates, it is designed to serve the affluent rather than the poor. Thus, the problems of urbanization are in a sense the problems of the poor.

World Urbanization: Location and Growth of Cities

Site and Situation

Why are cities located where they are? How and why do they grow? Why do some cities expand in certain directions and grow economically while others do not? Two concepts used by urban geographers to answer these and related questions are *site* and *situation*. Site refers to the physical environment on which the city originated and evolved. The city's geologic structure, surface landforms, elevation, water table, and other features are included in its site characteristics. Situation, on the other hand, refers to the relative location of a city with respect to other places with which it interacts. The term also connotes a city's relations with other cities, for example, whether it is centrally located, at the mouth of a major river, or at a point of low transport costs. Site and situation are both important in examining the origins of a city, as well as its relations with others in an urban system.

Site characteristics were probably more important in the location of ancient or preindustrial cities than in modern industrial cities. Having defensible positions, available drinking water supplies, and food-producing areas nearby were influential in the viability of early cities. In measuring a city's growth over time what is usually more important is its proximity to neighboring cities, the distances raw materials are sent for processing, and the specific functions performed. The functions, which may be of an economic, social, or administrative nature, are provided for city residents and those in the city's hinterlands.

Types of Cities

Geographers have traditionally explained the location of cities by classifying them into three categories based on their major types of functions. These categories include cities performing *marketing functions,* called market centers, cities performing *transportation functions,* called transportation centers, and cities performing *specialized functions,* which may be political, recreational, or religious centers. Cities performing a variety of retail functions for themselves and their surrounding area are identified as central places. A large body of literature within urban geography is concerned with explaining the numbers, hierarchies, spacings, distributions, functions, and trade areas of central places. *Central place theory* is concerned with examining these features of urban settlements. Central places offer a variety of goods and services, including retail, wholesale, administrative, social, and financial. Even though such services are urban centered, the location of cities does not depend on the characteristics of a particular site. Instead, the most important reason for the location of such cities is "centrality" with respect to service establishments and their hinterland. Central places thus are located at points most accessible to the inhabitants of the surrounding trade area. Their number, size, and spacing follow a regular pattern, according to the theory. Small central places or market centers tend to locate within the hinterlands of larger cities; they depend on these larger centers for more specialized functions which require a larger threshold population. There is thus a spatial order to the settlements and their functional composition. Cities of a particular size or level in the urban hierarchy tend to be evenly distributed throughout a service area, at least according to theory. The largest cities, or highest-order centers, are surrounded by medium-sized cities that are in turn surrounded by still smaller cities, all forming an integrated part of a spatially organized nested hierarchy. The spatial patterns of central places or market centers are quite different from the locations of transport and specialized function cities.

Transport cities perform *break-of-bulk or break-in-transport functions* along transportation routes. Where raw materials or semifinished products are transferred from one mode of transport to another, for example, from water to rail, or rail to highway, cities emerge either as processing (manufacturing) centers or as transshipment centers. Unlike central places, whose regularity in location is accounted for by marketing principles that operate over a large area, transport cities are located in linear patterns along rail lines, coastlines, or major rivers. Frequently, major transport cities are the focus of two or more modes of transportation, for example, the coastal city which is the hub of a number of railways and major highways.

Cities that perform a single function, such as recreation, mining, administration, or manufacturing, are labeled *specialized function cities.* A very high percentage of the population in one or two related activities is evidence of specialization. Within most countries it is not difficult to distinguish university, medical, military, government, and tourist cities whose economy is highly specialized. Specialization is evident not only in those cities offering services, recreation, or government, but in those where the extraction or processing of a resource is the major activity. Cities labeled as mining and manufacturing cities have much more specialization than those with a diversified economic base.

Urban Growth and the Principle of Circular and Cumulative Causation

As mentioned above, cities perform a variety of functions, and their population size directly reflects the number and variety performed. To understand why some cities grow and others do not, we can use the *principle of circular and cumulative causation.* This principle has broad application to society, particularly as it applies to urban growth. Very simply, the principle states that a change in urban economic functions causes changes in population. Increases in urban functions bring about increases in urban population. Growth is a cumulative process. Conversely, any decline in the number and variety of urban economic functions brings about a concomitant decline in the urban population. When seen in this light, decline is also a cumulative process.

To illustrate the principle, we can use the adoption of manufacturing establishments in a city, a process that has been one of the major ways cities grew in the past. The decision to locate a factory in an urban area stimulates general economic development and also accounts for population growth. The reasons for development and population growth are obvious. Opportunities for employment and increased incomes are provided; business output increases due to a greater demand for products. Rising profits increase savings, which also causes investments to rise, in turn pushing up the demand for and level of profits. Increased productivity results in an increased demand for labor. The growing population then reaches a new level or threshold, again resulting in a new round of demands. As cities move to a new population level, whether 250,000 or 1 million, they are able to offer a greater number and variety of services than they could with fewer inhabitants. In sum, the growth of cities is cumulative and is strongly influenced by changes in the economic functions provided. To explain why some cities fail to grow or even decline, we can merely reverse the cycle or process. Cities stagnate or die because they lose industries and population, conditions which create a negative circular and cumulative causation.

Economic Base Concept

Economic functions thus are keys to the growth of cities. An approach geographers use to study urban functions follows the *economic base concept,* which states that two types of activities or functions exist, viz., those that are necessary for urban growth and those that exist primarily to supplement those necessary functions. The former functions are called *basic functions* or city-forming activities. They consist of functions which involve the manufacturing, processing, or trading of goods or the providing of services for populations or businesses located outside the city's boundaries. Economic functions primarily of a city-serving nature are called *nonbasic functions.* Activities that include grocery stores, restaurants, furniture stores, beauty salons, etc., are economic functions that cater to residents within the city itself.

Of the two functions, the basic functions are the key to the levels of growth in urban population, employment, and income. A city with a high percentage of its labor force in, and its income generated by, the production of such things as automobiles, furniture, and electronic equipment, depends on sales beyond the city's boundaries for its growth and prosperity. Of course, some goods are destined also for markets within the city where they are produced. Income generated by the sales of those industrial goods is channeled back into the city, where employees for those industries then spend money on groceries, gasoline, hardware, entertainment, etc. While the city depends on basic activities for its economic base, the nature of the nonbasic activities is also critical in measuring the city's total economic health.

One of the most commonly used indexes to measure the economic base of a city is the size and proportion of the labor force in the industrial sector. Of the several measures devised to determine the industrial economic base, two of the more frequently used are the ratio of an industry's share in the local employment to its share of national employment, and the ratio of a city's share of national employment in a particular industry to the city's share of total national employment. If the ratios reveal a higher concentration at the city level than at the national level, the city is considered to have a strong industrial economic base. Defining the economic base in this light suggests that an industrial base is necessary for the existence of cities, which is not the case if we consider cities whose economy is based on income generated by services. Cities with large percentages of their labor force in tourism, recreation, government, education, and health-related activities depend on income brought in by individuals and businesses outside the city itself. Postindustrial cities have as one of their salient characteristics an economy dependent on generating income by performing services, often of a specialized nature, to regional and national service areas. In summary, the location and growth of cities is depending less on site characteristics, but more on the number and variety of functions and services performed.

World Urbanization: Theories on the Internal Spatial Structure of Cities

In addition to interest in the origin and growth of cities, geographers and others have long been intrigued by the great variation in the internal spatial structure of cities around the world. The locations of industry, commercial districts, transportation routes, residential patterns (especially between high- and low-income groups), the number and nature of parks and amount of "green space," and the areas or directions in which a city is growing the fastest are included in the geography of a particular city. Even today, with the increasing homogenization of urban life and many physical features of the modern large city around the world, such as skyscrapers, Western clothing styles and food habits, and the automobile society, distinctive differences remain in the internal arrangement of cities in different regions of the world as well as within individual countries. Many reasons account for those variations.

A variety of theories have been developed to describe and explain the pattern of land uses and the distribution of population groups within cities. The four most widely accepted theories that are useful in analyzing the internal spatial structure of cities in the 10 world regions identified in this book are the concentric zone theory, the sector theory, the multiple nuclei theory, and the inverse concentric zone theory (Fig. 1.7).

Figure 1.7 Generalized Patterns of Internal Urban Structure. [*Source:* Adapted from C. Harris and E. Ullman, "The Nature of Cities," *Annals of the American Academy of Political and Social Science,* 242 (1945), 7–17, as shown in Dean S. Rugg, *Spatial Foundations of Urbanism,* 2nd ed., New York: Wm. C. Brown, 1979, p. 216.]

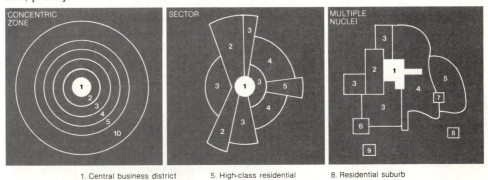

1. Central business district
2. Wholesale light manufacturing
3. Low-class residential
4. Medium-class residential
5. High-class residential
6. Heavy manufacturing
7. Outlying business district
8. Residential suburb
9. Industrial suburb
10. Commuter zone

Concentric Zone Theory

The *concentric zone theory* was first conceptualized by Friedrich Engels in the mid-nineteenth century. Engels noted that the population of Manchester, England, in 1844 was residentially segregated on the basis of class. He noted that the commercial district, consisting almost totally of offices and warehouses, was located in the center of Manchester. The commercial district extended about half a mile in all four directions. With the exception of this commercial district, Manchester, in Engels's time, consisted of unmixed working people's quarters, which extended a mile and a half around the commercial district. Next to the working people's quarters, extending outward, were the homes of the middle bourgeoisie, or capitalist class. Outward from the middle bourgeoisie were the homes of the upper bourgeoisie who lived in remote villas with gardens or in free, wholesome country air in fine, comfortable homes. Engels implied that commercial growth followed a sector or strip pattern. Engels believed this general plan or pattern to be more or less common to all great cities.

Although Engels was the first author to describe the spatial pattern of the city in class stratification terms, most geographers and other social scientists consider E. W. Burgess, a University of Chicago sociologist, responsible for the concentric zone model and theory in 1925. According to the Burgess theory, the growth of any town or city occurs through a radial expansion from the center so as to form a series of concentric zones or circles. These circles may be numbered to designate both the successive zones of urban extension and the types of areas differentiated in the process of expansion. The five zones Burgess observed and described in Chicago were: (1) the central business district (CBD), (2) the zone of transition and social deterioration invaded by business and light manufacture, (3) the homes of factory workers, (4) the residential zone of high-class apartment buildings or single-family dwellings, and (5) the commuter's zone which extended beyond the city limits and consisted of suburban areas or satellite cities. The process Burgess used to explain these successive rings was called *invasion and succession.* Each type of land use and each socioeconomic group in the inner zone tends to extend its zone by the invasion of the next outer zone. The spatial structure of a city is reflected in its social structure. As the city grows or expands, there is a spatial redistribution of population groups by residence and occupation. Burgess further demonstrated that many social phenomena are spatially distributed in a series of gradients away from the central business district. Such phenomena include the percentage of foreign-born groups, poverty, and delinquency rates. Each tends to decrease outwards from the center of the city.

Sector Theory

The *sector theory* was developed in 1939 by Homer Hoyt, an economist. Hoyt examined spatial variations in household rent in 142 American cities. He concluded, among other things, that a general pattern of rent applies to all cities and that rent patterns are not in the form of successive concentric circles but tend rather to appear as sectors. Hoyt was primarily concerned in his study with residential land use. His major contribution to urban structure was the identification of a directional element in city growth. He considered the movement of the high-rent residential sector to be the most important group in explaining city growth because it tends to pull the growth of the entire city in the same direction. That growth usually extends outward along transportation axes and does not encircle the city at its outer limits. The sectorial pattern of city growth can be explained in part by a filtering process. When new housing is constructed, it is located primarily on the outer edges of the high-rent sector. The homes of community leaders, new offices, and stores are attracted to the same areas. As inner middle class areas are abandoned, lower-class rental groups filter into them. In this process the city grows over time in the direction of the high-rent residential sector, which is nourished with new housing and marked as well by declines in the low-rent residential sectors.

Multiple Nuclei Theory

In 1945, two geographers, Chauncy Harris and Edward Ullman, developed a third model to explain urban growth, the *multiple nuclei theory.* According to this theory, cities tend to grow around not one but several distinct nuclei, thus forming a multiple nuclei pattern. The process that explains this multiple nuclei pattern is a historical one which results because of the following factors:

1. Certain activities are limited to particular sites because they have highly specialized needs. For example, the retail district needs accessibility, which can best be found in a central location, while the manufacturing district needs transportation facilities.
2. Certain related activities or economic functions tend to cluster in the same district because they can carry on their activities more efficiently as a cohesive unit. New- and used-automobile dealers, auto repair shops, tire, and auto glass shops are examples.
3. Certain unrelated activities, by their very nature, repel each other. A high class residential district will normally locate in a separate area from the heavy manufacturing district.
4. Certain activities, unable to generate enough income to pay the high rents of certain sites, may be relegated to more inaccessible locations. Examples may include some specialty shops.

The number of distinct nuclei occurring within a city is likely to be a function of city size and recency of development. Auto-oriented cities, which often have a distinct horizontal as opposed to vertical appearance, display industrial parks, regional shopping centers, and layered (by ages of residents, incomes, and housing values) suburbs. Rampant urban sprawl is likely to be reflected in a mixed pattern of industrial, commercial, and residential areas in peripheral locations.

Inverse Concentric Zone Theory

The preceding three theories of urban spatial structure apply primarily to cities of the MDCs and to American cities in particular. Many cities in the LDCs follow somewhat different patterns. A frequent one is the *inverse concentric zone pattern.* Cities where this pattern exist have been called preindustrial; that is, they are primarily administrative and/or religious centers or were at the time of their initial founding and growth. In such cities, the central area is the place of residence of the elite or upper class. The poor live on the periphery. Unlike most cities in the MDCs, social class is inversely related to distance from the center of the city.

The reasons for this pattern are twofold: (1) lack of an adequate and dependable transportation system, which thus restricts the elite or upper class to the center of the city in order to be close to their place of work; and (2) the functions of the city, which are primarily administrative and religious/cultural, functions dominated by the elite and concentrated in the center of the city (government buildings, cultural institutions, places of worship, etc.).

Three examples of internal spatial structure can be seen in the cities of Belfast (Northern Ireland), Popayán (Colombia), and Baghdad (Iraq) (Fig. 1.8). The social regions of Belfast are fairly compact and easy to distinguish. The high-status areas appear as distinct sectors north, east, and south of the city center. Low-status regions are readily identifiable west and east of the downtown. Distinct segregated areas of Catholics and Protestants are mainly concentrated in the city's low-status regions. Popayán, a major city in southern Colombia, is a good example of the inverse concentric zone model described above. The upper class lives near the center, where the religious, cultural, and administrative activities are clustered, while the lower classes live on the periphery. The city follows the classic preindustrial-city pattern of social regions. Baghdad, another preindustrial city, depicts patterns sharply distinct from those of European and North American cities. The concentrations of industries, middle class, and workers in several areas gives the appearance of a random process. However, there is some regularity to the location of workers near the major industrial sites, the middle class near the downtown areas, and ethnic/religious quarters near the older part of the city. Baghdad is not unique among old Middle Eastern cities in having the upper class, middle class, and working class living in close proximity.

As many of the LDCs have begun to industrialize, especially in the last 30 years, that industry has been primarily urban oriented, in much the same way that industry was established in the MDCs many decades ago. However, the newer and larger industrial establishments tend to locate not in the city centers but in the periphery or suburban areas of the cities, often in industrial parks established by the governments for the purpose of attracting both domestic and foreign investors. The city centers tend to be far too congested and with little land or few other advantages for industrial plants of any considerable size. Moreover, the elites in the city centers often do not want large industrial plants near their places of work and residence. (There is some parallel with the problems currently being experienced by cities of the MDCs, especially those in the United States, which are having difficulties in maintaining sound economic bases and healthy CBDs in the face of industry fleeing to the suburbs, or worse yet, to the Sun Belt cities.) Hence, what is emerging gradually in many of the larger cities of the LDCs is the pattern of the multiple nuclei theory, with the new industrial plants or parks serving as the nuclei. In other words, the inverse concentric zone pattern, while still valid in many LDCs, is merging with the evolving multiple nuclei pattern.

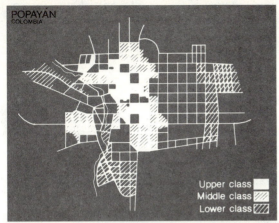
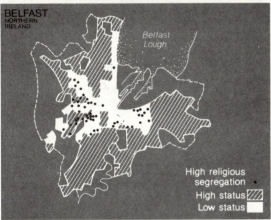
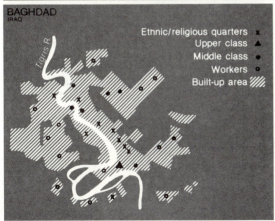

Figure 1.8 Internal Structure of Three Cities: Belfast, Popoyán, and Baghdad. [*Sources:* Belfast: after *A Social Geography of Belfast* by E. Jones © Oxford University Press 1960; Popoyán: after A.H. Whiteford, *Two Cities of Latin America*, Beloit, WI: Logan Museum of Anthropology, 1960; Baghdad: after J. Gulick, "Baghdad: Portrait of a City in Physical and Cultural Change," *Journal, American Institute of Planners,* 33 (1967), 247.]

Interesting and useful as these four theories of the internal spatial structure of cities are, they must be viewed with caution as generalizations of the extremely complex mix of factors that influence and determine the use of land within cities in any region or country. Even in the United States or Western Europe, where empirical research on the applicability of the patterns has been extensive and sophisticated, one can commonly find elements of more than one theory present in a given city. Moreover, each of the models and the land uses associated with them must be viewed as dynamic. There are changes going on all the time in economic functions, social and administrative services, transportation, and population groups that will alter the size and shape of specific sectors or zones. Furthermore, the complexities of applying these theories multiply severalfold when working with non-Western cultures and economic systems.

Nowhere is this more apparent than in the communist nations, particularly the Soviet Union and China, where various forms of the so-called socialist city are being created (see Chapters 4 and 11), which have internal spatial structures quite unlike those described by any of the four theories mentioned. But even outside the communist nations, it is quite possible that cities of some LDCs also do not fit any of the four theories of internal structure, and that newer models or theories to fit these cities are needed. But at the least, the four existing models provide forms with which to compare cities of the LDCs, and if the fit is not good, one is then led to question why. In those cases where the fit is, in fact, not good, part of the explanation may lie in the very different urban problems confronting those cities of the LDCs as compared with the major problems that cities of the MDCs are contending with.

An Overview of Urban Problems

Each of the regional chapters deals extensively with the urban problems peculiar to the region and with solutions or attempts at solution being made. Hence, not a great deal needs to be said about this matter at this point in the text. Nonetheless, some broad generalizations can be made about the nature of some key urban problems that are worldwide in their character and severity, to set the stage for the succeeding chapters.

Excessive Size

Excessive size, both in population and in geographical area occupied by cities, might more properly be described as a cause of problems than a problem in itself. But, as has already been made clear, excessive size exists worldwide as a problem or condition, with the greatest severity now in the LDCs, where the economic base of the cities is inadequate to cope with the problems created by excessive size.

Overcrowding

A logical outgrowth or consequence of excessive size is overcrowding, meaning too many people occupying too little space and competing for too few services and jobs. Again, this is particularly acute in the LDCs (Fig. 1.9). It is sometimes difficult for Americans or Europeans, who have not traveled outside of their country or region,

Figure 1.9 Shanghai. Nanking Road, the main thoroughfare of Shanghai's central business district, is thronged with people and traffic at midday. The problems of urban overcrowding in LDCs are nowhere more apparent than in teeming Shanghai, although in China more effort may be going toward solving these problems than in many other LDCs. (J. Williams)

to fully comprehend the magnitude and effect of really severe urban overcrowding. Seeing or being caught up in the tidal wave of humanity that one can find in the larger cities of the LDCs is a vivid lesson on the consequences of excessive urbanization that one never forgets.

Shortage of Urban Services

With too many people in the cities, city governments are hard pressed to provide all the human services that the residents would like or expect. This is often true even in the affluent MDCs. It is virtually a truism in the LDCs. *Housing shortages,* for example, occur worldwide. Typically, it is the poorest people who suffer the most, since in at least the free-market (noncommunist) countries, land rents in the cities get pushed up to sometimes astronomical heights, to the point where the majority of the populace cannot afford decent housing. Even in the communist states, however, because the governments usually give highest priority to investment in industry and armaments, the amount of capital sunk into public housing (and all housing is built by the government) is far from adequate to meet demand. The result is also substandard and inadequate housing space for the majority of the population. In addition to housing, though, other basic urban services are often deficient in relation to demand. *Basic human needs* such as *piped sewage systems,* hot and cold *running water,* decent *telephone service,* reliable *electricity supply,* adequate *garbage disposal systems,* which residents of many cities in the more affluent MDCs take more or less for granted, are anything but certain, reliable, or of high quality in the cities of the LDCs. *Educational, health care,* and *recreational systems and facilities,* other basic human needs, are commonly inadequate in the larger cities of the world, especially in the LDCs.

Slums and Squatter Settlements

Most cities of the world have slums and/or squatter settlements. While both concepts may represent the depressed areas or sections of the population of cities which are not fully integrated, socially or economically, into the development process, there are differences in national attitudes, standards, and definitions toward what constitutes a slum or squatter settlement. *Slums* are areas of authorized, usually older housing which are deteriorating or decaying in the sense that they are underserviced, overcrowded, and dilapidated. Slums are usually located on valuable land adjacent to the central business district (i.e., near the center of cities), although in some LDCs slums can be found throughout the urban areas. *Squatter settlements,* on the other hand, contain makeshift dwellings erected without official permission (i.e., unauthorized on land which the squatters do not own) (Fig. 1.10). They are usually located on the periphery instead of near the center of cities. In a sense, they are new areas created by their own inhabitants to protect themselves and mobilize minimal resources. The dwellings are constructed of any available materials such as cardboard, tin, straw mats, or sacks. There are no minimum sanitation standards, the construction is primarily uncontrolled, and the areas tend to lack the essential services of an urban environment such as sewage, water, and lighting. As a result, squatter settlements commonly are areas of health problems, not to mention socioeconomic problems. Squatter settlements go by various names in different countries. For example, they are *barriadas* in Peru, *gecekondu* in Turkey, *favelas* in Brazil, *bustees* in India, and *bidonvilles* in former French colonies such as Algeria and Morocco. Although squatter settlements are most prevalent in LDCs, they also exist in MDCs, albeit rarely of the same magnitude.

Traffic Congestion

Another obvious effect of overcrowding, produced in part by the appearance of the automobile society in most large cities of the world today, is *traffic congestion.* Superficially, this might be viewed as merely a nuisance of urban life, an aggravation of much less consequence than survival-level problems of employment, housing, social services, etc. Nonetheless, traffic congestion is a serious dilemma that is choking many cities to a standstill in terms of the movement of people and goods within the cities, with extremely serious consequences of waste of resources (time and energy of people, gasoline, etc.) and deleterious effects on the productivity of the city's economic base, which in turn affects growth of jobs and employment levels.

An Overview of Urban Problems

Figure 1.10 Squatters are a common sight in cities around the world. In Hong Kong, squatter settlements such as this, thrown together from scrap material, cling precariously to the steep, scraggly hillsides. Although the Hong Kong government has one of the best public housing programs in the world, thousands of people in Hong Kong still make do with wretched conditions such as these. (J. Williams)

Lack of Social Responsibility

Perhaps one of the most insidious effects of the overcrowding of cities throughout the world, but especially in the LDCs, is to reduce people's *sense of social responsibility.* As more and more people compete for space and services, the competition tends to breed an everyman-for-himself attitude. Hence, people resist queuing for services, think nothing of littering or despoiling public property (not to mention stealing private property), disregard traffic regulations (and all rules in general, for that matter, if they can get away with it, and they usually can because of grossly overburdened police forces), and show a callous disregard for the rights of fellow citizens. While many cultures in the world have always been characterized by the showing of great courtesy and respect to people one knows, while displaying indifference to everyone else, the rapid urbanization of the past 30 years definitely seems to have exacerbated this cultural failing and made urban life that much more miserable for many.

Unemployment and Underemployment

The matter of employment would probably top most people's lists of serious urban problems, since virtually everything else connected with the city and its people is related in one way or another to the economic health of the city. This is certainly a worldwide problem, but again the magnitude varies. In the MDCs, the problem is primarily *unemployment,* with the greatest burden felt by the poor and unskilled. In the United States, for example, unemployment continues to be borne disproportionately by marginal labor force groups such as teenagers, older workers, women, racial minorities, and unskilled workers in general. In addition, large numbers of persons working earn so little that they remain essentially in poverty. But the situation is not all that different in the cities of Western Europe, nor for that matter in the cities of the LDCs.

However, because the cities of the LDCs are far more overcrowded as a rule than those of the MDCs, and because high natural population growth rates continue in most of the LDCs, a huge proportion of the population is young, in the early employment period of 15 to 30 years of age. In many LDC cities, as much as half the population may be under the age of 30. This creates tremendous strains on the job markets. Unemployment rates of 30 to 40 percent or more are not uncommon. Hundreds, even thousands, of young people may apply for a handful of job openings in a particular company. The lucky ones may, in fact, end up with a job that is below their capabilities—in effect, *underemployment.* This is particularly true for college graduates whose numbers each year in most of the LDCs is far greater than the creation of jobs equivalent to their skills. The unlucky ones may resort to self-employment, such as hawking, opening up small food stands, or turn to begging or street crime, especially petty theft. The streets of the major cities in the LDCs are cluttered with tens of thousands of such members of the *informal working sector,* eking out a marginal existence with long hours and no fringe benefits. Families manage to barely make ends meet by having every able-bodied member participating in some kind of such employment. The really unlucky ones starve. While malnutrition can be found even among urban residents of affluent countries such as the United States, outright starvation is rare in such places. Starvation is not so rare in many LDC cities, and malnutrition is readily apparent in large numbers of people.

One aftereffect of employment problems in the LDCs especially is the large proportion of people employed in the service sector, both by the government civil service and also in private establishments that deal with the public, including such places as government offices, banks, post offices, department stores, and restaurants. One commonly sees unusually large numbers of service personnel in these establishments. They neither seem to work hard nor to be expected to work hard, since their wages are usually very low. But the hiring of more personnel than really needed is one way of absorbing some of the excess labor force.

Racial and Social Issues

Unemployment and underemployment, along with other factors, breed a variety of subsidiary problems related to *racial and social issues.* These vary from region to region, of course. For example, in the United States relative economic prosperity has produced a tidal wave of illegal immigration, primarily from Mexicans and other Latin Americans seeking employment and a better life. These people commonly settle in the cities, as do, for that matter, the large numbers of refugees as well as legal immigrants allowed into the country in the last few decades. For example, Cuban refugees dramatically transformed the population composition and economic base of Miami, Florida. The influx of these peoples becomes a problem when it breeds resentment and outright conflict with other groups in the U.S., such as blacks and other low income groups who normally are the major competitors for the jobs sought by the legal and illegal immigrants (see Chapter 2). In Europe, a similar situation has developed, particulary in West Germany, where large numbers of so-called guest workers from southern and eastern Europe were allowed in to help meet the labor shortage in Germany's booming industrial economy. These "temporary" immigrants have also spawned resentment and tensions, often simply from cultural differences rather than economic competition (see Chapter 3). In South Africa, the unique situation of *apartheid,* or nationally legalized segregation of races, is also the result of mixing of different racial groups in the cities and the inability (or unwillingness of the whites, more properly) to live with that situation (see Chapter 7). In Southeast Asia, the importation of millions of Chinese and Indians during the colonial era left those countries, after independence, with very distorted socioeconomic patterns, concentrated in the former colonial cities, that tend to divide the races and work against efforts at development of national unity (see Chapter 10). In short, throughout the world, many cities face severe internal tensions that create centrifugal forces to work against efforts at solving many of the urban problems facing those cities.

Westernization versus Modernization

One phenomenon that is sweeping the world's cities, especially the larger ones, and which might properly be termed a problem is the dilemma of *Westernization* versus *modernization.* This theme, addressed in several of the regional chapters, refers to the problem facing the LDCs in trying to modernize their economies and cities, to industrialize and raise standards of living, without at the same time completely abandoning traditional cultural values and ways of life. Some might argue that tradition and modernization are incompatible, that modernization automatically entails change, and that change is likely to take the form of Westernization, since it is the West, the MDCs, that developed the lead in creating the modern industrial city and the life-style that goes with it. To be sure, there are ample signs of this Westernization (some might wish to call it "homogenization" or "internationalization") of the world's major cities, in the form of skyscrapers and modern architecture, the automobile society, Western high technology, advertising, etc. Nonetheless, as anyone who has lived in cities of the LDCs for any length of time can attest, traditional cultural values and life-styles do somehow manage to persist even in the middle of the most modern metropolis.

Environmental Degradation

Environmental degradation—pollution of the air and water, excessive noise levels, the uglification of the landscape through lack of planning and urban poverty—is another serious worldwide problem concentrated in the cities. The chief difference between the MDCs and the LDCs is that in the MDCs people and governments are doing something about it. The LDCs, by and large, regard such concerns as frivolous in the face of more immediate life-and-death issues of employment, housing, control of infectious diseases, etc. Thus, in general, the degree of urban degradation is most severe today in the cities of the LDCs, not in the more industrialized cities of the MDCs, which may have had the dubious distinction some decades ago. The cities with the greatest air pollution, for example, are no longer those such as Los Angeles (not that that city has solved its air pollution problem!), but rather those such as Seoul, Mexico City, and São Paulo of the giant agglomerations or conurbations group. Levels of noise, dirt, ugliness, health hazards, congestion, and confusion in countless cities of the LDCs easily surpass the levels in the worst cities in the MDCs.

Urban Expansion and Loss of Agricultural Land

Part of the process of environmental degradation is the tremendous amounts of land being gobbled up by sprawl of cities, especially the giant conurbations. In some countries, such as the United States with its relative wealth of land resources, the problem is seen by some as unfortunate but not life-threatening. In many other countries, however, where land resources in relation to population are less favorable, the *loss of agricultural land to urban/industrial sprawl* is of grave concern. Many countries in Asia particularly face this problem, perhaps none worse than Japan. On the one hand, these countries use land for industrial growth and economic advancement, while at the same time losing part of their ability to feed themselves. Food self-sufficiency ratios for Japan, Taiwan, South Korea, and a number of other rapidly urbanizing, industrializing states of Asia have been declining in real terms for several decades. Unfortunately, too, the best agricultural land is commonly found close to the major cities, since this was one of the site factors that accounted for the initial founding of many of those cities in the preindustrial era. Once lost, this prime land cannot be replaced, and marginal land being reclaimed for agriculture does not begin to compensate in productivity for the land lost.

Administrative Organization

Cities in the LDCs that are growing rapidly in numbers and in area face problems of how to extend health care, water, sanitation, transportation, fire, police, and other services to inhabitants of fragmented suburbs and even to inhabitants of cities who have traditionally been excluded from governmental services. Problems arise over *how to organize spatially new administrative structures,* how to prevent rampant and uncontrolled expansion, how to finance public services and to allocate funds on a priority basis, and how to develop and implement a comprehensive urban plan. Conflicts occur over spending priorities, the location of new facilities (schools, hospitals, public housing projects, etc.). The task of governing or administering services to a mushrooming city whose population, areal extent, and quality of services are unknown is mind boggling. It is little wonder that portions of large cities in the LDCs may lack vital services, representation, and much hope. Government leaders faced with diminished revenues and higher costs to provide human services may eventually have to select which cities or portions of cities can be saved with remedial and emergency care. Such a selection process may mean some urban areas and urban residents will experience little relief from the many economic, social, and environmental ills they face.

Problems of political organization are not unique to the LDCs. In many MDCs, declining central city tax bases, central city population decline, independent balkanized suburbs, and population growth in fringe areas are current problems. Reorganization of school, park, health, fire, police, sanitation, and other districts is needed to provide an effective and efficient delivery of services. Competing and conflicting jurisdictions, be they townships, counties, individual cities, or states, often jealously guard their political turf. The preservation of the status quo among the dozens or hundreds of administrative units within a metropolitan area stands in the way of effective comprehensive planning schemes. The United States has a mixed record of metropolitan governments, city-county consolidations, and regional government structures. Reorganization seems to be much more popular and acceptable in the Sun Belt than Frost Belt states. In Canada, metropolitan reorganization efforts have been more successful than within the U.S. It seems likely that with declining populations, diminished tax bases, and higher costs for transportation, welfare, education, health, and police a greater amount of administrative reorganization and region-wide planning are needed. Metropolitan planning schemes for future housing, energy, sanitation, water, health, and other needs should be easier to accomplish in many MDCs than LDCs in part because their populations will remain fairly stable.

Governmental organization is significant when measuring the priorities for specific programs. Are governments promoting policies to increase industrialization in major cities, to intensify transport networks in already overdeveloped urban areas, and to support industrial development over basic human needs? Critical choices are made

38 Chapter 1, World Urban Development

that impact how urban nodes and systems are developed and what levels of goods and services the residents will receive. In the interest of obtaining economic progress, governments may tolerate unhealthy heavy industrial pollution, traffic congestion, and unhealthy overcrowding rather than improve antiquated water systems, ineffective health delivery, and outdated educational programs. MDCs as well as LDCs may decide that the social costs of improving the quality of life of urban (and rural) residents are not commensurate with the economic benefits of short-term economic development. Physical quality of life measures appear to be gaining ground in importance within the MDCs, at the same time that economic and industrial growth have slowed. Many European and North American cities have spawned programs to clean up the air and clean water and eradicate social blight. Similar efforts have not yet been successfully introduced within most LDCs.

The picture painted is a bleak one, but it is not without hope. At least some countries among the LDCs and a great many among the MDCs, including Japan, which was often cited in the past as a notorious example of these problems in the MDCs, are attacking the problems of urban life and urban growth. The solutions tried or planned are far too numerous and complex to even attempt a summary or generalizations here (Fig. 1.11). The reader is advised to see each regional chapter for an appreciation of the panoply of approaches taken. There are pessimists who undoubtedly contend it is too late to solve the urban ills of mankind. Optimists hope this is not so.

Figure 1.11 One of the many solutions being attempted to solve world urban problems is the construction of new towns, totally planned new communities that theoretically are supposed to avoid the problems of older, unplanned urban places. This scene is of a multilevel apartment complex in Eury, a new town just south of Paris, France. (L. Sommers)

RECOMMENDED READINGS

Abu-Lughod, Janet and Richard Hay, Jr., eds. *Third World Urbanization.* Chicago: Maaroufa Press, 1977.
 A multidisciplinary book, in 30 brief chapters, by 28 authors, of many facets of urbanization in the Third World. Some of the chapters deal only tangentially with urban matters, but the volume is nonetheless useful.

Berry, Brian J. L. *The Human Consequences of Urbanization.* London: Macmillan, 1973.
 Examines salient causes and consequences of urbanization paths in North America, the Third World, and Europe in the twentieth century. A succinct primer on global urbanization.

Berry, Brian J. L., ed. *Urbanization and Counterurbanization.* Beverly Hills, CA: Sage Publications, 1976.
 Statement by number of leading social scientists on economic, social, and political impacts of urbanization in developed and developing countries and regions. Good mix of studies on theories and policies related to contrasting paths of urban development.

Bourne, L. S. *Urban Systems: Strategies for Regulation.* New York: 1975.
 Introduces the spatial processes operating to produce urban systems and compares urban system development and policy in the United Kingdom, Sweden, Australia, and Canada.

Bourne, L. S. and J. W. Simmons, eds. *Systems of Cities: Readings on Structure, Growth, and Policy.* New York: Oxford University Press, 1978.
 The 39 articles examine the concept of urban systems, their evolution, types of linkages, and role in national urban policies. An excellent set of statements by geographers, regional scientists, economists, and sociologists.

Brunn, Stanley D. *Urbanization in Developing Countries: An International Bibliography.* East Lansing, MI: Latin American Studies Center and the Center for Urban Affairs, Michigan State University, 1971.
 An unannotated list of over 7000 publications on all facets of urbanization in Latin America, Africa, and Asia.

Burgess, Ernest W. "The Growth of the City." In *The City,* edited by Robert E. Park, E. W. Burgess, and Roderick McKenzie. Chicago: University of Chicago Press, 1925, pp. 47–62.
 This article, which describes the pattern and process of invasion and succession of population groups in the city of Chicago, is the classic work explaining the concentric zone theory of urban growth.

Castells, Manuel. *The Urban Question: A Marxist Approach.* Cambridge, MA: The MIT Press, 1977.
 A fundamental aim of this book is to develop new tools of research while criticizing the traditional categories with which the social sciences and mass media have usually conceived urban problems. The book examines the urban sociological literature of several countries in relation to different themes and constructs the mechanisms by which these categories displace questions and distort our vision of reality.

Cities: Their Growth, Origin, and Human Impact. San Francisco: W. H. Freeman, 1973.
 These 27 articles from previous issues of *Scientific American* focus on early urban development in various regions, the quality of life in urban environments, and contemporary social and economic problems. Specific articles deal with Stockholm and Calcutta; general ones examine cities in MDCs and LDCs.

Coates, B. E., R. J. Johnston, and P. L. Knox. *Geography and Inequality.* New York: Oxford University Press, 1977.
> This book provides an understanding of some of the spatial aspects of the development, maintenance, and possible solutions to one of the world's major problems, i.e., inequality. It describes the spatial patterns of inequalities and tries to explain why they occur.

Davis, Kingsley. "The Urbanization of Human Population." *Scientific American,* 213 (1965), 41–54.
> Davis presents an excellent illustrated discussion and explanation of world and regional variation in urbanization trends. He uses one index of urbanization—the proportion of the population living in cities of 100,000 or larger—to predict that more than half the world's people will probably be living in cities of 100,000 or more by 1990.

Eldridge, H. Wentworth. *World Capitals: Toward Guided Urbanization.* Garden City, NY: Anchor Press/Doubleday, 1975.
> Between an introductory chapter on world urbanization and three chapters on global urbanism are detailed descriptions of the historical and architectural plans of 11 major cities (Stockholm, Paris, London, Moscow, Washington, Toronto, Tokyo, Brasilia, Caracas, Dakar, and Chandigar). The volume includes a number of useful maps and photos.

Fava, Sylvia Fleis, ed. *Urbanism in World Perspective: A Reader.* New York: Crowell, 1968.
> Urban sociology reader that includes 51 articles on urban housing, social psychology, ecology, social mobility, and policy. A rich set of readings that consider urbanism at a global level as well as within individual societies and cities.

Geruson, Richard T. and Dennis McGrath. *Cities and Urbanization.* New York: Praeger, 1977.
> This work focuses on the city in the history of civilization. It attempts to develop a general perspective on cities and urbanization and to examine in detail the American urban experience.

Hall, Peter. *The World Cities.* New York: McGraw-Hill, 1977.
> A brief volume that focuses on just seven major world urban centers and analyzes their growth, characteristics, and problems. Only one of the cities (Tokyo) is outside of the Western world.

Harris, Chauncy and Ullman, Edward. "The Nature of Cities." *Annals of the American Academy of Political and Social Science,* 242 (1945), 7–17.
> This is the classic work that introduced the multiple nuclei theory of urban growth. In addition, the authors discuss cities within the contexts of three categories—cities as central places, cities as transport and break-of-bulk points, and cities as concentration points for specialized services.

Hoyt, Homer. *The Structure and Growth of Residential Neighborhoods in American Cities.* Washington, DC: Federal Housing Administration, 1939.
> The sector theory of urban growth was introduced by this work. This volume provides an excellent background on the establishment and growth of rental housing in urban America.

Lampard, Eric E. "Historical Aspects of Urbanization." In *The Study of Urbanization,* edited by Philip M. Hauser and Leo F. Schnore. New York: Wiley, 1965, pp. 519–554.
> This article discusses urbanization within the ecological framework. The author's primary concern is with the historical incidence and the organization of urbanization. In addition, the author presents a critique of the behavioral, structural, and demographic approaches to the study of urbanization.

Mountjoy, Alan B. "Urbanization, the Squatter and Development in the Third World." *Tijdschrift Voor Economic Sociale Geografie,* 67 (1976), 130–137.
    The author explains the concept of squatter settlements in this work and presents the severe problems faced by the inhabitants of these settlements in cities in the less developed countries. The author also emphasizes the growth and spread of squatter settlements.

Mumford, Lewis. *The City in History: Its Origins, Its Transformations, and Its Prospects.* New York: Harcourt Brace Jovanovich, 1961.
    This major work on the forms and functions of Western cities answers such basic questions as: What is a city? How did it come into existence? What processes does it further and what purposes does it fulfill?

Rose, A. J. *Patterns of Cities.* Sydney, Australia: Thomas Nelson, 1967.
    A well-illustrated overview of urbanism and the spatial location of cities as well as internal structures and hierarchies, with primary focus on Australian cities.

Rugg, Dean S. *Spatial Foundations of Urbanism.* 2nd ed. Dubuque, IA: Wm. C. Brown, 1979.
    An interesting book that relates the external and internal relations of cities to current theoretical research as well as to actual urban patterns in the world today. The book gives heavy emphasis to Western cities. In many ways, the first edition of this book (1972) was more useful.

Sjoberg, Gideon. *The Preindustrial City.* Glencoe, IL: The Free Press, 1960.
    This book analyzes the urban structure of preindustrial societies and introduces the inverse concentric zone theory of urban growth.

Thomlinson, Ralph. *Urban Structure: The Social and Spatial Character of Cities.* New York: Random House, 1969.
    This book takes an urban ecological approach to an understanding of cities, their nature, their spread, how they are arranged, and how they might be changed in the future through urban planning policies.

Vance, James E. *This Scene of Man: Role and Structure of the City in the Geography of Western Civilization.* New York: Harper & Row, 1977.
    Detailed treatment of urban morphogenesis, that is, the role and purposes of cities in Western societies and the various institutional processes those societies have used to create and transform the physical structure of cities.

Weber, Adna F. *The Growth of Cities in the Nineteenth Century.* New York: Columbia University Press, 1899.
    This book demonstrates the tremendous impact industrialization had on the growth of cities.

Figure 2.1 Major Cities of North America. (*Source:* Data derived from United Nations, Department of Economic and Social Affairs, *Global Review of Human Settlements, Statistical Annex,* published by Pergamon Press, New York, 1976.)

Chapter 2

Cities of North America

Maurice H. Yeates
Stanley D. Brunn

North America in the World Urban System

The region of North America (which consists of just the U.S. and Canada as the region is delimited in this book) is one of the most highly urbanized parts of the world. Canada slightly leads the U.S. in percentage of urban population, 81 to 79 percent, respectively. Because of its large population, the U.S. has the distinction of having the largest total urban population of any country in the world, approximately 180 million (out of North America's 227 million urban residents). In addition, the U.S. has the largest number of major cities (78 SMSAs in 1980 with a population of half a million or larger, 38 of which have a population of 1 million or more) of any country in the world (second place in numbers of major cities goes to, interestingly, China) (Fig. 2.1). Canada, because of its much smaller population, naturally has far fewer urban residents and cities and is on a par with a number of Western European countries.

Because of its large urban population and numbers of cities, plus its high level of economic development, the United States plays a pivotal role in world urbanism. The American city as developed in the U.S. has become a distinctive type of modern city. On the one hand, the American city (with its peculiar racial composition and morphology, skyscraper profile, suburbanization, and glorification of the automobile and high technology) is still quite different from that found in almost every other part of the world. On the other hand, various aspects of American urban society are rapidly diffusing around the world, to both developed and developing countries, particularly in the form of the automobile society, high-rise construction, and mass consumerism. If any one thing could be singled out as contributing the most to the increasing homogenization of the world's major cities, it would have to be the pervasive influence of the American urban model. Critics may decry this influence, but it cannot be ignored.

Within the U.S. itself, however, the American city is by no means static. The largest cities of the past, such as New York, Chicago, Philadelphia, and Detroit, remain the largest, and the greatest number of major cities remains concentrated in the old industrial Northeast. Nonetheless, the decade of the 1970s, which brought along such events as the energy crisis, hastened along a trend that had already been emerging, that of counterurbanization, or movement out of cities to smaller towns and even rural areas, and movement to the Sunbelt states of the southern tier of the country. As a result, cities in the Sun Belt, best typified by Houston, Phoenix, Miami, Atlanta, and a few others, have emerged as million-plus centers of modern America, stimulated economically and culturally by the sizable migrations of Americans South and West, as well as by influxes of new immigrants, such as the Cubans to Miami. These new-growth cities have joined the ranks of earlier growth cities of the Sun Belt, such as Los Angeles and Tampa, which have moderated in their growth rates.

Canada's urban pattern is also changing, but far less dramatically than that of the U.S., since Canada's population and urban centers have always been located in a narrow strip along the southern border with the United States. Nonetheless, the last 30 years have seen the emergence of a number of major cities, some of which, such as handsome, cosmopolitan Toronto, or Vancouver with its spectacular natural setting, have become symbols of desirable urban environments for modern man.

Development of the North American Urban System

The urban development in North America has occurred primarily over the last 100 years as a response to the geography of the changing economic system in which we live. In general, the North American urban system has developed from east to west along with the settlement of the continent as a result of European immigration. Thus, the changes that have occurred, and that are taking place, must be expressed within the context of the technologies that fostered this east-west settlement. Four major stages in urban evolution can be identified, and to these could be added a fifth epoch into which our present urban system is probably entering. These five epochs and the general dates during which they occurred can be defined as:

1. the period up to about 1830, in which the location and spread of cities was primarily influenced by wagon/sail technology;
2. 1830–1870, in which the innovation of the iron rail, canals, and steamboat greatly influenced the spread of cities;
3. 1870–1920, which were tumultuous years in North American urban growth, in which the steel rail, steam-driven oceangoing vessels, industrialization, and massive immigration combined to produce the basic urban system that we know today;
4. 1920–1970, in which the automobile reshaped North American cities, and the innovation of air travel reinforced the interrelationships of the urban system that had developed earlier; and

5. the period from 1970 onward, which involves a process of counterurbanization occurring in part as a result of the innovation of a continental, limited-access, high-speed highway system.

Four maps illustrate the population size of the major cities in the urban system of each epoch (Figs. 2.2 and 2.3). The map for 1830–1831 indicates the size distribution of 38 cities in North America with a population of about 4000 or more. The benchmark population figure for inclusion of cities in the maps for 1870–1871, 1920–1921, and 1970–1971 increases fivefold for each era, reflecting the growth in urban population that has occurred. Thus, the map for 1870–1871 contains all cities in North America with a population of about 20,000 or more, that for 1920–1921 contains all cities with a population of about 100,000 or more, and the map for 1970–1971 contains all metropolitan statistical areas with a population of about 500,000 or more.

Sail/Wagon Epoch to 1830

The economy of North America throughout the eighteenth and early nineteenth centuries was based almost entirely on agriculture and the export of staple products. Even by 1830, the proportion of the population residing in urban places of 5000 or more in the U.S. was only 8 percent; in the area that became Canada the proportion was undoubtedly somewhat less. The major function of the few cities that existed was mercantile, involving the import of manufactured products from Britain and Europe, the export of fish, furs, timber, and farm products.

Consequently, the largest cities were to be found along the Atlantic coast, with New York (202,600), Philadelphia (161,400), Baltimore (80,600), and Boston (61,400) dominating the trade of the original thirteen colonies. Each of these cities was competing for the new hinterland opening up west of the Appalachians. The next three largest cities were located along the routes that traditionally led into the heart of North America. New Orleans (46,300), at the delta of the Mississippi, received the produce from the hinterland, but the difficulty of up-river passage impeded the flow of two-way traffic. Quebec City (27,700) and Montreal (27,000), located along the St. Lawrence river, controlled the northern route into the continent, but the relative growth of these two cities was already suffering from the loss of hinterland resulting from the separation of the United States from British colonial rule.

Most of the cities located in the hinterland, which stretched as far as the Mississippi River, were very small, and served as centers of commerce for the surrounding agricultural settlements. In 1830, Cincinnati was the largest of these interior towns (24,800). It acted as a service town for the rich Ohio Valley, with its merchants importing manufactured products and agricultural supplies directly across the Appalachians from the East Coast ports and arranging for the export of products from the region down the Ohio and Mississippi rivers via New Orleans to Europe.

Although there were a few industrial towns such as Lowell, New Bedford, and Springfield, the economic base of most cities was commerce, and so the cities that grew and dominated were those which could control the largest and richest hinterlands. New

46 Chapter 2, Cities of North America

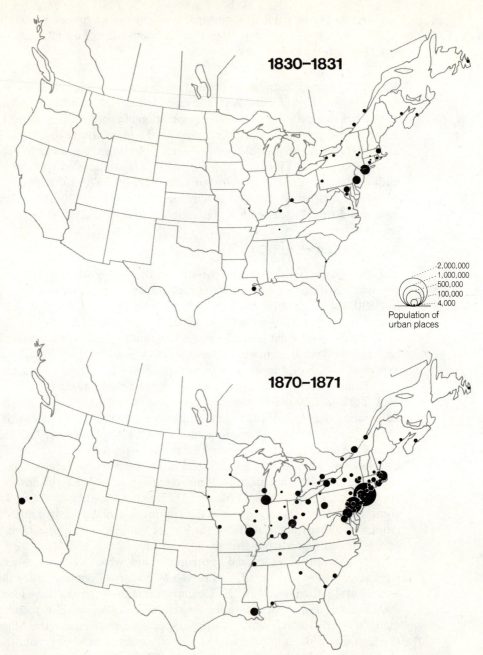

Figure 2.2 Urban Places of North America, 1830–1831 and 1870–1871. (*Source:* Compiled by M. Yeates.)

Development of the North American Urban System 47

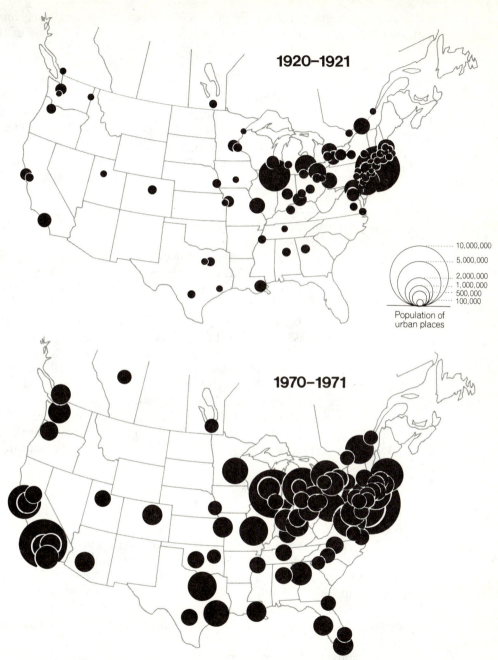

Figure 2.3 Urban Places of North America, 1920–1921 and 1970–1971. (*Source:* Data compiled by M. Yeates.)

York engineered a major coup in this regard when its entrepreneurs constructed the Erie Canal, which linked the Hudson River to Lake Erie at Buffalo in 1825.

The Age of Steam and the Iron Rail, 1830–1870

Between 1830 and 1870 the proportion of the population residing in urban areas in the United States almost tripled, rising from 8 percent in 1830 to 23 percent in 1870. In Canada, the first census of the new Dominion records 12 percent of the population residing in cities of more than 5000 in 1871. The map for 1870–1871 indicates that by the end of the era urban growth, particularly along the East Coast between Boston and Washington DC, had continued at a rapid pace. By 1870 New York City had become the dominant urban place in North America, and combined with Brooklyn had a population in excess of 1.2 million. The cities of the U.S. East Coast had enlarged their role as commercial centers for the developing continent, had grown as financial centers linking European capital with high-yielding but often speculative investment opportunities, and had become centers of manufacturing as a result of protective tariffs and the influx of many thousands of poor immigrants. By comparison, urban growth in Canada had languished, as its economy was still tied to that of Britain.

Apart from the tremendous growth of urban areas between Boston and Washington, DC, the most dramatic outcome of the era was the spread of urban areas through the Middle West and lower Great Lakes areas. This development was associated with the rapid increase in transportation as a result of the construction of canals and railways. The railroad mileage alone tells much of the story. In 1850 there were 9,000 mi. (14,490 km.) of track in the U.S.; by 1860, 31,000 mi. (49,910 km.); and by 1870, 53,000 mi. (85,330 km.). The network linked all the cities of the East Coast, spread inland most extensively through the Middle West and lower Great Lakes, and by 1869 had reached Oakland in San Francisco Bay. The spread of canals and canalized rivers was vital for the transport of heavy goods because the iron rail could not support weighty loads.

Thus, inland cities in opportune locations for both rail and water transportation grew phenomenally. St. Louis, on the Mississippi, connected to New Orleans by steamboat and barge, which plied upstream as well as down, increased in population from 6,000 in 1830 to 311,000 in 1870. Chicago, on Lake Michigan, with an all-water transport route via the lakes and Erie Canal, had become the self-proclaimed "Greatest Primary Grain Port in the World," competed directly with New York as a wholesaling center, and had, on the strength of trade, established itself as a city of almost 300,000 by 1870. Cincinnati, the other big inland city of the Middle West, had grown less dramatically, reaching a population of 216,000 by 1870, with a more diversified economy based on manufacturing (particularly pork meat packing), commerce, and transportation.

The only two large cities beyond the East Coast and Middle West were New Orleans (191,000) and San Francisco (150,000). New Orleans, by far the largest city in the South, was now in its heyday, with the steamboat and barge linking it to a rich hinterland of cotton, grain, and salted meat products. The east-west development of the

North American railroad system, built and controlled by East Coast big-city capital, was, however, soon to syphon off most of this trade. On the West Coast, the growth of San Francisco had occurred as a result of the force-feeding of new capital derived from the gold rush of '49, and the control by San Franciscans of the Comstock Lode, which was discovered in 1859.

Thus, by 1870, the cities of North America had increased in population and number along the East Coast of the U.S. and had also developed inland in the area of the Middle West and lower Great Lakes. Manufacturing, as well as trade and transportation, had become a dominant economic activity, particularly in East Coast cities. The urban system of the continent was shaped by the developing network of railroads, canals, and rivers, and the control that the capitalist-owners of these transport systems exerted in the direction and extent of their construction. The Civil War, which occurred toward the end of this period (1861–1865), boosted the development of manufacturing in the East Coast cities, and it was from this base that city development continued into the twentieth century.

The Age of Steam and Steel, 1870–1920

Between 1870 and 1920 the proportion of the population residing in urban areas in the U.S. more than doubled, and the actual number of people residing in cities of more than 5000 people experienced a fivefold increase to 41 million. A similar increase occurred in Canada, where the urban population rose to 2.7 million, or nearly six times its number in 1870.

The urban areas on the East Coast of the U.S. continued to grow rapidly in population, with the New York metropolitan area quadrupling in population to 5.3 million by 1920, Philadelphia nearly tripling to 1.8 million, and Boston and Baltimore maintaining similar rates of growth. In total, 28 cities extending in a 500-mi. (800 km.) arc from Lynn, Massachusetts, to Norfolk, Virginia, had populations exceeding 100,000 in 1920. There was also great growth in cities in the Middle West and lower Great Lakes, with Chicago moving from a position of fifth largest city in North America in 1870 to second largest in 1920, and experiencing a ninefold increase in urban population to 2.7 million. Also noteworthy is the increase in number of cities along the West Coast with populations in excess of 100,000, led, particularly, by Los Angeles. Finally, there was some development of larger urban areas in the South and Texas, though this was only in an incipient stage by 1920.

A large number of forces, some with historical antecedents, and others that were new innovations of the period, exerted a joint impact to yield this continent-wide urbanization. These forces included: (1) the increasing integration of the North American transport system; (2) the influx of vast numbers of poor immigrants, which provided a continuous supply of low-cost labor; (3) the innovation of the assembly-line factory system, most dramatically exemplified in Detroit, which spread rapidly through all types of manufacturing; (4) the large surpluses being produced by a mechanized agricultural system which demanded less labor; and (5) the entrepreneurial activity of the family-owned corporation. All of these forces focused on the accelerated importance of manufacturing as a major cause of urban growth in the cities of the East Coast, Middle West, and lower Great Lakes. Trade, of course, continued to stimulate the growth of some cities, particularly that related to the export of staple products from the regions served by the newer cities of the West Coast and Texas.

No doubt the urban growth that occurred was in large part the result of the creation of a continent-wide market due to the increased level of integration of the North American transport system. This was brought about by the standardization of rail gauges in the 1870s, the increase in railroad mileage and transcontinental lines (the Canadian Pacific Railroad reached Vancouver in 1886), and the general decrease in transport costs that occurred as a result of the innovation of the steel rail, which could support longer trains and heavier loads.

Some of the cities that grew most in this period exemplify these forces in action. Detroit, Cleveland, Montreal, and Pittsburgh moved to positions of fourth, fifth, ninth, and tenth largest cities in North America, respectively, by 1920. Detroit, chosen by Ford and Durant as the home of the automobile industry, grew along with the adoption of the automobile. Whereas there were 8000 automobile registrations in the United States in 1900, there were 8 million registrations in 1920. Cleveland and Pittsburgh, always manufacturing centers, grew particularly rapidly as producers of iron and steel. Cleveland, well served by rail and Great Lakes transportation, developed an iron and steel industry as part of its iron ore transport function and later became the center of the burgeoning petroleum and petrochemical industry. Pittsburgh, located on the coal fields, became the home of the Carnegie corporation, which in 1901 merged with other producers to become U.S. Steel. Montreal experienced rapid growth from 1870 to 1920 as a result of the tremendous outflow of energy to create a united country following confederation in 1867. The city had always been the center of trade and finance, and now it became the headquarters of the Canadian Pacific Railroad connecting the Canadian hinterland with water transport to Europe.

By 1920 the basic features of the North American urban system had been established. It was a system that had developed as a result of decisions concerning the location of transport facilities, and various innovations that made this transport system more efficient. The urban system had also developed and grown in response to changing investment decisions and the need for resources. One must not, however, forget that the base of this urban growth was the people who flooded into the cities from the farms and smaller towns, and from Europe. In particular, between 1860 and 1920 over 30 million people entered the U.S. from Europe, and between 1901 and 1921 over 1 million people entered Canada from Europe. This continuous supply of cheap labor was the foundation of the urban and economic growth that occurred.

The Age of the Auto, the Truck, and Air Transport, 1920–1970

Between 1920 and 1970 the proportion of the population residing in urban places of 5000 or more people in the U.S. increased from 47 percent to almost 70 percent, while the urban proportion in Canada nearly doubled from 37 percent in 1921 to 70 percent in 1971. The period was one of considerable changes in the scale and size of urban developments as well as quite massive changes in the organization of business and governmental structures. The First World War acted as a stimulus to the growth of manufacturing in the U.S. and Canada, and also greatly weakened the financial strength of Europe while enhancing that of North America. Urban growth was therefore quite rapid during the 1920s, but in the 1930s overspeculation led to one of the recurring downswings in the economic cycle that turned into the deepest economic depression in the history of the continent and there was little increase in the general level of urbanization. The years of the Second World War were associated with renewed growth of the larger urban areas, particularly the port cities on the West Coast and the manufacturing centers of the East Coast, Middle West, and lower Great Lakes. Finally, the postwar years were a period of rapid urban growth as a result of high rates of natural population increase and accelerating personal consumption associated with rising real income.

The relative size and distribution of the 80 largest metropolitan areas in 1970–1971 varies widely with the smallest now with a population of about half a million. The changes in the distribution of urban population that occurred between 1920 and 1970 can perhaps be characterized as relating to:

1. an increase in scale of urbanization which led to the emergence of supermetropolitan and megalopolitan urban formations;
2. the deconcentration of continental urban growth, resulting in metropolitan urban developments across much of the continent; and
3. the spectacular growth of urban areas beyond the old central cities that contained most of the urban population in 1920.

The general deconcentration and metropolitanization of the population between 1920 and 1970 is related directly to the way in which the automobile, truck, and air transport shaped urban development. In particular, the widespread adoption of the automobile facilitated the decentralization of population in metropolitan areas. The construction of federally financed highways in the 1930s, the Pennsylvania, Ohio, and Indiana turnpikes in the 1950s, and the high-capacity, limited-access Interstate Highway System in the 1960s and 1970s resulted in a new network of surface transportation which allowed the truck to replace the railroad in the carrying of nonbulk traffic and created a continental market that could be well served from a number of different locations. As a consequence, metropolitan areas spread out and metropolitan growth was widespread across North America.

Megalopolitan Developments

A distinctive development of the post-World War II era has been the emergence of megalopolises. Many of the SMSAs in Fig. 2.4 are merging together into regional agglomerations of central cities and suburban sprawl, growing primarily along key transportation arteries, especially the interstate highway system. Best known is the Bowash Megalopolis, a 500-mi. (800-km.) stretch of urban population between Boston and

Figure 2.4 SMSAs and CMAs in North America Containing 250,000 People or More. (*Source:* Data compiled by M. Yeates)

Washington along the East Coast of the United States. By 1970, this whole area contained 43 million people, and was the first example in the world of supermetropolitan development on a massive scale.

Other supermetropolitan regions also have emerged. For example, the "Great Lakes Megalopolis," with more than 40 million people, stretches from Milwaukee and Chicago through to Detroit, Cleveland, Pittsburgh, Buffalo, Toronto, and Montreal, a total distance of about 1100 mi. (1760 km.). This megalopolis actually consists of two main parts. On the U.S. side of the Great Lakes, the major urban areas from Milwaukee through to Syracuse contain about 28 million people, and are the location of a wide variety of manufacturing activities, of which the best known relate to iron and steel, automobiles and general transport equipment, and the many industries based on petrochemicals. On the Canadian side of the Great Lakes, the Windsor-Quebec City axis embraces 12 million people, or 55 percent of the population of Canada, and within the area is concentrated 70 percent of the manufacturing of the entire country.

The Deconcentration of Continental Urban Growth

Probably the most publicized changes in the North American urban system between 1920 and 1970 occurred in the South, in Texas, and along the West Coast. Much of this area has been referred to as the Sun Belt, and no doubt warmth has a certain amenity attraction. Nowhere is this more apparent than in Florida, where four urban areas grew in response to recreation amenity/retirement stimuli. There has also been a noticeable growth in manufacturing in the South, particularly associated with the shift from the Northeast textile and furniture industries and the emergence of Atlanta as a major financial and business center for the region. Urban areas along the Gulf Coast, and in Texas and Oklahoma, increased in population because of the initial development of oil fields and petrochemicals, and more recently with electronics and aerospace industries. Dallas, in particular, has emerged as a center of finance for the region based on the capital accumulated from oil.

Likewise, and even more spectacular, has been the oil-triggered growth of Los Angeles to be the second largest metropolis on the continent. Capital accumulated from oil, land speculation, food processing, recreation, the film and television industry, petrochemicals, electronics, and aerospace activities, has resulted in a supermetropolitan area containing 12 million people extending some 250 miles (403 km.) from Santa Barbara to San Diego. Small supermetropolitan areas have developed around San Francisco Bay (4.5 million) based on a variety of manufacturing, food-processing, electronics, and port-related activities; and in the Puget Sound area between Seattle and Vancouver, which contains 3.5 million people. The economy of Seattle is very much influenced by the health of the aircraft industry, and Vancouver is still predominantly a resource-based city and port connecting the Canadian West with the trade routes of the Pacific Ocean and Japan.

Suburbanization

Although the expansion of suburbs around North American inner cities has been most apparent during the past 30 years, suburbanization is not a new phenomenon. The suburbanization process has been a part of the North American urban scene since the middle nineteenth century, and it is the spatial expression of the class divisions in society that emerged with the growth of employment in manufacturing, commerce, business, and financial activities. Suburbs have always existed in response to a desire by the more wealthy for differentiation, a wish for separation from the city's problems, and an affectation for a more "rural" landscape. The process has reached a peak at certain periods, however, especially those in which increases in wealth as a result of upswings in the economy have been associated with innovations in urban transportation. One of the most dramatic of these was the development of "streetcar" suburbs between 1890 and 1910 following the innovation of the electric streetcar in 1888.

The period between 1920 and 1970 was, however, one in which the automobile shaped the city from the fringe. The automobile provided the middle classes with a personal means of transportation, freeing the population from reliance on public transport and permitting expansion of residential areas into lower-density and even more "rural" environments. As a consequence, the suburbs developed an automobile-oriented work, social, and commercial structure which dominated the development of the metropolis. The greatest volume of suburbanization occurred following the Second World War, when the supply of new housing was low due to limited wartime construction, and the demand for housing was high as the population turned to peacetime activities. One consequence was the "baby boom," which reached a peak in the United States in 1955, in Canada in 1959, and which added an unusual urgency to the need for housing. This need was met by the expansion of federal housing programs to provide low-interest, low-downpayment, federally insured mortgages for new housing. As new housing invariably requires new urban land, the government did in effect help to promote the rapid suburbanization as well as to subsidize home ownership.

The consequences of this suburbanization can be detailed in terms of the total distribution of the population, the location of employment, and racial differences. By 1970, the majority of the urban population of North America resided in the suburbs. Though, taken as a whole, there was growth in the populations of the central cities of the metropolitan areas of the continent, the growth of the suburbs between 1950 and 1970 was four times greater. Whereas in 1950 about 56 percent of the population of the metropolitan United States lived in central cities, in 1970 only 32 percent resided in these areas, and by 1977 the figure was only 28 percent. Along with this relative decentralization of the population to the suburbs has been a decentralization of employment. It is estimated that 65 percent of all metropolitan area employment was located in central cities in 1960 as compared with 56 percent in 1970. Although both blue-collar and white-collar jobs increased greatly in number in the suburbs, there was a decline in blue-collar jobs in the central city and a small increase in those of the white-collar variety.

The implication of the change in distribution of white- and blue-collar jobs becomes apparent when one looks at the differential suburbanization of the white and nonwhite populations. The period from 1920 to 1970 witnessed a tremendous migration of the black population from the large and small towns of the South to the growing metropolitan areas of the U.S. Like the waves of immigrants before them, most blacks and immigrants from Puerto Rico and Mexico moved in to the older rental accommodations of the inner city, but as a result of discrimination they have been concentrated into distinct neighborhoods that have ghettos. Almost every urban area in North America, whatever the size, that has a considerable proportion of nonwhite inhabitants has a nonwhite ghetto. As the nonwhite population increased in numbers, and the area of the ghettos spread, the white population has moved to the suburbs. By 1980, the central cities of the U.S. had become the home of the nonwhite population, and the suburbs had become the home of the majority of the white urbanized population. Furthermore, as families residing in the suburbs tend to be wealthier than those in the central city, it is evident that by 1980, the suburban process had resulted in the formation, in the U.S., of two urban worlds, one poor and containing a large proportion of the black urban population, the other richer and containing a slight majority of the white urban population.

Counterurbanization, 1970–On

Trends existing during the latter part of the 1920–1970 period but accentuated during the 1970s lead one to conclude that the U.S. urban system is now firmly in a period of counterurbanization. This is defined as a decreasing size of the larger metropolitan areas, a decreasing density of the urban population, and an increasing uniformity of groupings of people in communities according to class, race, age, or language. Given this definition, it could also be argued that the urban system in Canada is developing similarly.

Evidence for this counterurbanization hypothesis is fairly widespread, and some specific examples can be cited as follows:

1. The larger metropolitan areas are now growing at a rate somewhat less than that of the population of North America as a whole.
2. Some of the larger metropolitan areas are actually decreasing in population for the first time. The obvious examples are in the older urbanized parts of the continent, such as New York, Pittsburgh, Cleveland, and Philadelphia; but others are in the newer urbanized regions, such as Los Angeles and Tacoma.
3. Nearly all central cities decreased in population after 1970, and most of this decrease is accounted for by an outmigration of the white population. Hence the central city has become even more the home of the nonwhite population, the poor, and the aged.
4. Rapid population growth has taken place in smaller cities and metropolitan areas, particularly those of the South, Florida, and the West. Examples include Atlanta, Miami, Albuquerque, Edmonton, and Victoria.

Furthermore, the nonmetropolitan urban areas of both the U.S. and Canada have, since 1970, grown at a faster rate than the metropolitan areas.

The forces leading to counterurbanization, or migration from the big metropolitan areas, are many and varied. Some of the more important are industrial decentralization, metropolitan insecurity and discomfort, the search for amenities and retirement, and improved transportation and communications, which have extended the urban way of life far beyond the immediate boundaries of metropolitan areas. Of these, transportation and communication improvements are especially interesting because industries and people are now beginning to feel that they can have reasonably good access to markets, resources, and new ideas without necessarily having to be physically located all the time in the big metropolitan areas.

This counterurbanization trend has presented a new and complicating wrinkle to the array of issues faced by urban North America. This new complication relates to the combined impact of the trend toward much lower birth rates (zero population growth) and marked changes in migration flows that is resulting in population decline in some areas and population increases in others. By 1970, the post-World War II baby boom was over, and the trend in North America is now clearly toward levels of natural increase at, or only slightly above, the replacement level. Thus, internal migration now plays a most important role in determining which places grow, and which decline. In 1960–1965 internal migration accounted for only about 11 percent of the relative change in population in North America, but in 1970–1975, internal migration accounted for about 27 percent of the relative change in population.

Internal Structure of North American Cities

The internal spatial structure of North American cities is the product of numerous locational decisions made over many years in response to situations occurring, or forecast to occur, at the time the decision was made. The results of these decisions are overlaying patterns of manufacturing, commerce, population, and connecting transport networks, each of which influences the location of others in a cumulative fashion.

Manufacturing

Suppose that you are an entrepreneur with a certain amount of capital (or credit) who wishes to establish a plant manufacturing footwear in a city. Where would you locate the plant in 1850, 1900, 1935, and 1980? As an entrepreneur you are concerned with access to raw materials, markets, equipment, energy, and efficient labor and the lowest cost site at which it is feasible to operate. In 1850 the locational decision is fairly simple, for the chief means of transportation is water, whether by ocean or river, and so most manufacturing activities are clustered around the harbor and its associated commercial area. The labor force also clusters tightly around the employment opportunities in the port area and the developing Central Business District because most people have to walk to work.

    By 1900, rail transportation, and innovations in urban transportation such as the streetcar, have extended the area of possible plant location. Access to raw materials, markets, and energy (coal) is now possible via rail as well as waterfront. Furthermore, the streetcar has made it possible for people to live farther from work, though the streetcar lines focusing on the CBD still make locations around the commercial district served by rail and water the most likely to be selected. Furthermore, the existence of an industrial labor force, greatly increased in volume by the influx of hard-working, poverty-stricken immigrants who flood into the older housing and tenements in the central part of the city, increases the attractiveness of central locations. The railroad companies do, however, offer attractive alternative locations along their tracks because much of the railroad land is offered at low prices to attract occupancy.

    In 1935, the entrepreneur has many more possible sites to choose between because the widespread use of automobiles and trucks, with the associated construction of arterial roads and ring roads within cities, has greatly increased the general level of accessibility in all parts of the city. Furthermore, the widespread use of electricity has eliminated the low cost transportation requirements for bulk fuel. The population (in the U.S.) is now recovering from the Depression, and the demand for housing and other aspects of personal consumption are increasing greatly in total volume. Suburbanization is accelerating, and the entrepreneur can now consider locations in the industrial land zoned alongside some of the arterial highways, as well as the more traditional fringe of the CBD locations.

    By 1980, the entrepreneur has to consider locating in a metropolis in which many political and tax considerations influence his decision. Interstate highways and limited-access belt lines have succeeded in opening many suburban areas to industrialization.

But, the metropolis is fragmented in political structure, with the old and new suburban communities competing with the older central city for the types of jobs and people they want. Some communities simply do not provide land for manufacturing, while others provide inducements for light-manufacturing such as footwear. Federal inducements may, however, offset the perceived disadvantages of inner city locations by providing sufficient tax incentives to overcome the costs of theft or chronic absenteeism. Thus, by 1980 the location decision is extremely complex, and the accessibility considerations are much less important than in early years.

The result is a pattern of location of manufacturing that is dispersed throughout much of the metropolis. But, certain features of this pattern are still quite marked. For example, in the map showing the location of manufacturing in Minneapolis-St. Paul it is evident that industrial activity of this type is concentrated in (1) the areas surrounding central business districts of the Twin Cities, (2) land adjacent to the railroad lines serving the metropolis, and (3) blocks of land along the major road arterials and interstate highways either circling or passing through the metropolis (Fig. 2.5). This type

Figure 2.5 Land Devoted to Manufacturing in Minneapolis-St. Paul, 1971. (*Source: Focus,* New York: American Geographical Society, February, 1970, after map #1.)

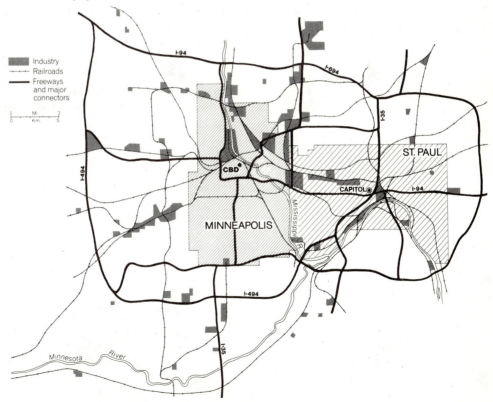

of pattern is repeated over and over in North American cities, with variations from the Minneapolis-St. Paul pattern occurring as a result of differences in the availability of transport facilities.

Commerce

Although commercial activities are not great users of land in cities, they are prominent because they intrude into most every part of the metropolis. For the sake of convenience, we can divide commercial activities into three kinds: business and finance, wholesale, and retail. Probably the greatest single change in the structure and behavior of people living in cities since 1950 has occurred as a result of changes in retailing. If there is any single feature that distinguishes North American cities from cities in the rest of the world it is the planned regional shopping center.

Retail Structure

The retail structure of cities is the product of a composite of two main forces. The first, which resulted in strips of stores and shops along the main urban arterials, with concentrations of larger department-type stores and banks at major intersections, is the product of relatively urban population densities and a society in which public transportation was more important than transportation by automobile. Thus, the older inner city (or central city) contains strips of retailing activities along arterials that are, or used to be, major routes for public transportation, and the largest and greatest number of stores are found around intersections that were or still are the foci of heavy traffic from four different directions. The central part of the city around which the urban area grew often remained the focus of traffic because public transportation fed into the center of the city, and highways also converged on the downtown area. Thus, the CBD served the entire city for infrequent or special purchases (often found in big department stores), while the strips and shops found at intersections serve a local neighborhood or community for more frequent needs such as groceries.

The second force influencing the retail structure of North American cities is the product of lower population densities, found initially in the suburbs, and a society in which automobile transportation has replaced public transportation. The result is the planned shopping center, or mall, around which there is abundant "free" parking. The parking is not, of course, "free" because the user is in effect paying for the privilege as a portion of the price of the purchase. Shopping centers are found primarily in suburban areas, and the largest of these can serve a considerable population and achieve a sales volume similar to that of the CBD (Fig. 2.6).

The trend during the 1970s was for the central city, in its process of readjustment to population change and environment-controlled shopping centers, to try to establish the same type of facility within the city. These have been in the form of either new shopping malls, such as the Zion Mercantile Center in Salt Lake City, or interlinked shopping facilities built in conjunction with new hotels and office buildings, such as Ville Place Marie and Place Bonaventure in Montreal, or Eaton Place in Toronto.

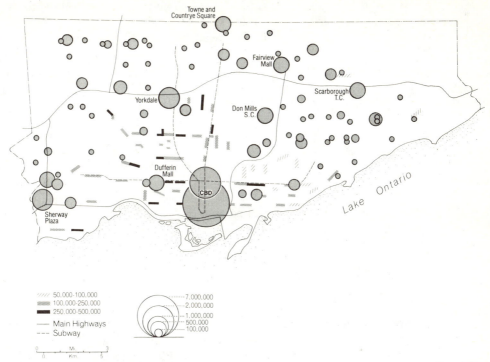

Figure 2.6 Strip Retailing and Shopping Centers in Metropolitan Toronto, 1976. (*Source:* City of Toronto Planning Department.)

Business and Wholesaling

One of the most noticeable features of urbanization is the clustering of offices, financial activities, and wholesale firms within or adjacent to the central business areas of major cities. This clustering arises as a result of a complex array of forces among which the need to serve the urban market, or draw on the labor force of the entire urban area, and face-to-face contact, are probably the most important. The focusing of railroads, transit, and highways on the downtown area gives that location a unique accessibility to the whole metropolis. Furthermore, many activities undertaken in the area depend upon quick response, competitive decision making, whether this be in the form of price quotations, bank loans and interest rates, or "old boy" network-obtained contracts. The central commercial area is thus the location of a high level of information concerning any matter that might influence a business decision.

The consequence of these forces is a concentration of employment in business activities in high rise office buildings, which dominate the skyline of the central city. During the 1960s and early 1970s, most larger urban areas increased employment in these types of activities, and the result has been a construction of a number of new high rise office buildings in downtown areas. This, coupled with the tremendous growth of employment in governmental activities, has helped boost building in many CBDs.

But, there has also been a decentralization of offices out to the vicinity of the newer regional shopping centers in the suburbs. In particular, the "office park" concept has been widely applied within the megalopolis and the supermetropolitan centers, with the financing often coming from the large multinational corporations that wish to decentralize their own operations.

People in Cities

In most cities of the world, one basic characteristic of the distribution of the population is quite repetitive. Population densities are generally highest close to the CBD of the city, and decrease fairly regularly with distance from the center to the periphery. The reason for this is that the central area, though not the location of all jobs in the city, is the location of the greatest number, and as a consequence access to these employment opportunities is the most important consideration. Furthermore, accessibility costs money, and in poorer societies, where a larger portion of income is spent on food and habitation than in a North American society, travel costs have to be kept to a minimum. People therefore tend to try to minimize their transport costs, and this can be achieved by renting or purchasing small amounts of space, that is, living at high densities, close to the center of the city.

The pattern of urban population densities in North American cities used to be similar to this, but since 1950 the situation has changed substantially. The great increase in level of real incomes since 1950, the shorter working week, the public provision of expressways and arterials within cities, and the concomitant decentralization of manufacturing employment and office employment to locations beyond the old core area has resulted in a population density that is now fairly even over the entire metropolitan area. Certainly higher densities are still perceived in the core area of the older cities, but the urban region now contains many foci of economic activity, and the urban dweller is hardly constrained at all by a need to locate close to any particular zone.

In fact, the locational criterion that has become more important is to find a situation that is perceived to be safe and allows people to live in a neighborhood that contains other people of similar background and common interests. The result is a spatial separation of cities into neighborhoods of similar economic status, stage in the life cycle, and race. Some of these are also neighborhoods of exclusion and prejudice.

The way in which the characteristics of economic status, stage in the life cycle, and race interact to produce spatial separation of groups and classes within cities is indicated in a general model which can be applied to most any North American city. Economic status appears to vary sectorally. Parts of the city have always contained the more wealthy, and as the city has grown that part has continued to maintain its status (Fig. 2.7). Conversely, other parts of the city have always contained the less wealthy, and as the city has grown outward that sector too has been perpetuated (Fig. 2.8).

Stage in the life cycle, or family status, tends to be distributed concentrically. This is partially the product of housing policies in North America, for low down payment, federally insured, low interest mortgages have, for the most part, only been avail-

Internal Structure of North American Cities 61

Figure 2.7 Parts of the North American city have always contained the more wealthy, and as the city has grown, that part has continued to maintain its status, as illustrated by this scene of Grosse Pointe Farms outside Detroit. (Courtesy John Jakle)

Figure 2.8 Parts of the North American city have always contained the less wealthy, as illustrated in this scene of a low-income multiracial and multilingual neighborhood in Brooklyn, New York. (Courtesy John Jakle)

able for new homes. As new homes are usually only available at the periphery of cities, families with young children tend to have little choice other than locations at the periphery (Fig. 2.9). Conversely, young singles, unmarrieds, or marrieds find apartments more congruent with their life-style, and they tend to occupy locations that give them greater access to a good social life. The elderly, who are often poor, also tend to live in central locations, for here are available low rent rooms in older, rundown buildings.

Minority groups, be they black, Puerto Rican, Mexican American (Chicano), oriental, or recent immigrants from Italy or Portugal, usually locate in distinct parts of the city that are clearly separated from the majority population. These communities are subdivided internally with different groups in a manner similar to the rest of the city, a situation which can also be represented diagramatically (Fig. 2.10). In fact, minority communities can be regarded as a distinct city, or cities, within the metropolis as a whole that occurs as a result of voluntary or involuntary segregation. Voluntary segregation occurs when the members of a particular minority group concentrate in a section of the city in order to maintain certain linguistic, cultural, or religious values. They group together because they themselves wish to reside in a separated neighborhood. Involuntary segregation occurs when the majority perceives a minority to be of an undesirable status and, through a variety of institutional procedures (such as "redlining"), manages to contain that minority in a certain part of the metropolis.

Nonwhite ghettos are, perhaps, the single most obvious illustration of cleavage

Figure 2.9 Since new homes are generally only available on the periphery of cities, families with young children tend to have little choice other than locations on the periphery, such as this suburban tract development outside Chicago. (Courtesy John Jakle)

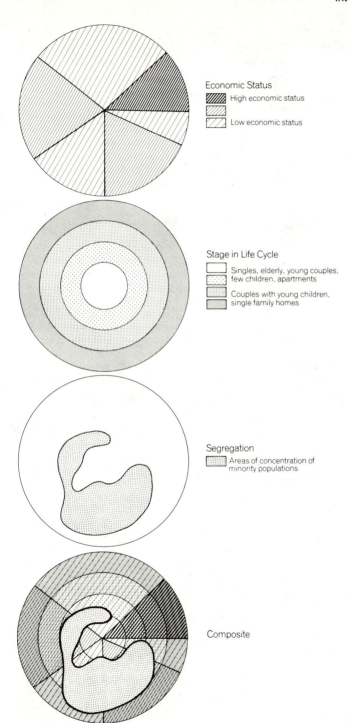

Figure 2.10 Typical Distribution of People in North American Metropolitan Areas by Various Classifications. (*Source:* Compiled by M. Yeates.)

in American society. The extent of residential segregation has been declining over the past few decades, but it is still very high. Information in Table 2.1 crystallizes the situation. The numbers in the table are simply an index of segregation calculated for 109 U.S. cities over four decades. A number of 100 would indicate complete separation of whites and nonwhites, and 0 would indicate complete integration of the two groups. One interpretation of the index numbers is that in 1970 the level of segregation was still such as to require the redistribution of 88 percent of the nonwhite population in the southern sample cities, and 77 percent of the nonwhite population in the sample cities in the rest of the country, to achieve complete desegregation.

Major Representative Cities

In what is probably the most important region of the world from an urban viewpoint, with such a large number of important world cities to choose from, it is no easy task to select a few major representative cities. Nonetheless, four major cities—New York, Los Angeles, Houston, and Toronto—have been chosen because they are not only among the largest in North America but also four of the most important in terms of urban functions and the characteristics of different types of cities that they illustrate.

New York City: A Global Metropolis

The premier city in the United States measured in terms of population, economic assets, corporation offices, and cultural attractions is New York City (Fig. 2.11). The 7.1 million people in the city and nearly 11 million in the surrounding areas overshadow both the Chicago and Los Angeles-Long Beach metropolitan areas. More people live in the metropolis than in all but five states. To many Americans, New York is the "pulse" of the nation and the world, as much of what occurs here affects the rest of the world directly and indirectly. New York is more than a collection of major streets, high-rise office buildings, and world culture; it is the home of millions of people of all walks

TABLE 2.1 AN INDEX OF RESIDENTIAL SEGREGATION BETWEEN WHITE AND NONWHITE HOUSEHOLDS FOR 109 SELECTED CITIES 1940–1970

Date	All Cities	South	Non-South
1970	82	88	77
1960	86	91	83
1950	87	89	86
1940	85	85	85
Number of cities	109	45	64

Source: H. Winsborough et al., "Models of Change in Residential Segregation," Madison: University of Wisconsin, Center for Demography and Ecology, 1975, WP 75–76, p. 2.

Figure 2.11 Manhattan, looking north from the top of the Empire State Building, a scene familiar to millions around the world, and symbolizing the distinctive character as well as world importance of New York City. The high-rise building, rapidly becoming a common feature of the world's major cities, had its origin in New York. (Courtesy John Jakle)

of life and occupations. For nearly two centuries the city has been a destination for destitute European immigrants seeking a home in a new land, for poor blacks and Puerto Ricans seeking better jobs, for corporate executives seeking to expand their global networks, and for artists, musicians, and writers seeking the creative atmosphere of a city in constant touch with the rest of the world. The "mecca" image that the city has enjoyed in the past continues to be one of its chief attractions.

Greater New York comprises five boroughs. Each has a rather distinct character of ethnic communities, commercial and industrial land uses, and problems. The borough of Manhattan (1 million) is the island with the greatest wealth and the greatest concentration of vertical development in the country. On the streets of Manhattan are the super-rich, aristocrats, middle-class suburbanites, as well as peddlers, prostitutes, down-and-outers, new immigrants, and prophets of fads and doom. The dress reveals a host of cultures and tastes, and the languages readily attest to New York being a world city. The remaining four boroughs have a different character and convey different impressions. Brooklyn (2.5 million), southeast of Manhattan, is noted for its beaches, parks, historic residential areas, cemeteries, and shipyards. The Bronx (1.5 million), north of Manhattan, is mainly a residential borough of extremes; the rich live along the Hudson River in Riverdale and the poor in an area south of Bronx Park. Queens (2 million), east of Brooklyn, is a residential suburb that developed after World War

II. Staten Island (under 300,000) remained virtually undeveloped as a residential and industrial area until the 1960s, when a bridge connected it to Brooklyn.

The city may also be thought of as a group of islands (Manhattan, Staten Island, Liberty Island, and Long Island among others) at the southern tip of New York State. The city is at the junction of two rivers, the Hudson and East (more a strait); it is flat to very gently rolling. The situation of the city was as important historically to its growth in a North American context as was its bedrock. The basement rocks on Manhattan are hard metamorphic that permit the construction of skyscrapers. The extreme height of the skyscrapers (seven over 60 floors) reflects the high cost of land on the island; the filling in around the peripheries for warehouses and dock facilities also shows the intense competition for land.

The earliest residents of what is presently New York City were the Algonquian Indians who lived along the shores of the Hudson and East rivers. The first European to enter New York harbor was the Italian explorer, Verrazano, in 1524. Other explorers followed, but none reported seeing the island the local Indians called Man-a-hat-ta, which meant "island of hills." Henry Hudson is credited with reaching Manhattan in 1609 and sailing up the river that bears his name. The Dutch West Indies Company, interested in establishing a trading base on the continent, sent a group of settlers in 1624. Two years later the settlement was laid out and was called Fort Amsterdam. It was that same year (1626) that the governor of the settlement, Peter Minuit, bought Manhattan Island for goods worth about $24 from local Indians, an economic transaction that is heralded as one of the most prudent purchases of all times, from the settlers' viewpoint. The new settlement grew slowly; by 1650 there were only about one thousand residents, mainly in the southern half of the island. A wall was built for protection at the northern edge of the settlement; it was torn down later and became a major road, Wall Street.

The English, Danes, and Dutch were among the early settlers on Manhattan and on the new settlements of the Bronx, Brooklyn, and Queens. The English and Dutch fought several major naval battles from 1652–1674 which eventually led to the English obtaining possession of Fort Amsterdam, which they renamed New York. In the hands of the English the population and economy of the colony grew rapidly; there were an estimated 7000 inhabitants by 1700. During the Revolutionary War and following, the city was important as both an economic and political center. In 1785 New York City was the temporary national capital. Congress met here in 1789, and George Washington was inaugurated as president in the city in the same year.

Since its beginning, New York was destined to become a major regional, national, and international city. During the earliest decades of settlement along the Atlantic coast, the city vied with Philadelphia and Boston for commercial leadership. However, by 1790, the year of the first U.S. census, New York City had nearly 50,000 inhabitants; it was then, and has continued to be, the largest city in the nation. The major advantage the city enjoyed was its excellent natural harbor. That harbor, when coupled with its access to the interior of an expanding continent, enhanced with the construction of the Erie Canal in 1825, and its situation with respect to the Atlantic Coast and Europe, meant the city was certain to see prolonged growth and prosperity.

The city's rich history and economy are enhanced by the dozens of nationalities that make up its present fabric. Three major waves of new migrants can be distinguished. Before 1890 the largest number were from Germany, Ireland, and northwest Europe. After 1900 they were mainly from southern and eastern Europe: Italians, Portuguese, Greeks, Syrians, and others. During the mid-twentieth century, blacks, especially from the rural South, and Puerto Ricans sought better jobs and living conditions in the nation's largest city. Today, however, five major ethnic groups dominate—blacks, Irish, Italians, Jews, and Puerto Ricans.

The economic preeminence of New York City is one of its major trademarks. Without doubt it is the nation's leading financial, shipping, transportation, communications, and convention center. With its 20,000 manufacturing establishments, New York ranks third after Chicago and Los Angeles-Long Beach in manufacturing. Altogether more than 7 million employees in the metropolitan area work in business, government, industry, and entertainment.

It should come as no surprise that New York City is not immune from problems, some of which are serious and have been for several decades. A partial listing would include the large number (more than 1 million) dependent upon public welfare, the persistence of segregated housing and job discrimination by white ethnics against the newly arrived Puerto Ricans and blacks, and the problems of crime, environmental pollution, and clogged sidewalks and streets. Housing is an acute problem, since about 70 percent of the housing was built before 1940. Sixty percent of New Yorkers live in apartments, and almost three-quarters rent the places in which they live. Very little new housing is under construction; many of the old tenements and brownstone houses built in the late 1800s or early 1900s are in varying states of deterioration. The city, in spite of its wealth, experiences not infrequent problems of its public workers, including the police, fire, sanitation, and transportation workers, and teachers who strike for higher pay and improved benefits. New York City attracted nationwide attention during 1975 when financial support from Congress was needed to save the "Big Apple" from its financial crisis. In spite of the breakdowns in human services, the depersonalization residents and out-of-towners feel toward institutions and themselves, poverty and racism, and a deteriorating quality of life for many residents, New York remains one of the major world cities, a position it will always hold.

Los Angeles: A Suburban Metropolis

Los Angeles is a city that contrasts sharply from New York. It not only is a younger city, but it developed as a major metropolis differently from East Coast and Middle West cities. The form of its growth (horizontal and sprawling) indicated a different mode of transportation (automobile) from the railroad and water commerce that were instrumental in those cities that developed in the early and late 1800s (Fig. 2.12). The sprawl of Greater Los Angeles extends 70 mi. (113 km.) east to west and covers 464 sq. mi. (1166 sq. km.) That gargantuan sprawl is also apparent in the massive use of concrete for almost every structure.

Images of Los Angeles that readily come to mind include (1) the worship of the

Figure 2.12　Los Angeles is commonly regarded as the epitome of the sprawling modern American metropolis, with its overwhelming emphasis on the automobile. Los Angeles was also one of the first major world cities to introduce the ills of motor-vehicle-produced air pollution or smog. (Courtesy John Jakle)

automobile, evident in the 650 mi. (1050 km.) of freeway serving the city, the ubiquitous parking ramps and lots, drive-in establishments of every kind, wide streets, and numerous sprawling shopping centers; (2) the neatly arranged subdivisions that almost all look alike with single family ranch houses equipped with outdoor patios, barbecue grills, and swimming pools; (3) the prevalence and seeming acceptance of widely held differences in political philosphy (extremes on the right are more acceptable here than in San Francisco), life-styles, and religious practices; (4) the apparent disregard for many potentially serious environmental hazards, including earthquakes (treated on evening news in the same manner as baseball scores), brush fires, and mud slides; (5) the affinity for glamor and glitter that is attributed to movie and television stars and recreational amenities of Southern California; and (6) the slightly more relaxed and open atmosphere than is evident in either New York City or Chicago. Los Angeles is a cosmopolitan center of a different cast than New York City. The major difference is that Los Angeles has a rich mixture of people from other states rather than from numerous foreign countries. Mexican Americans represent the largest minority, but there are also Chinese, Japanese, Filipinos, Vietnamese, Germans, Canadians, and British. The creativity of Los Angeles is the result of individuals and groups who only came to the city this century and many since World War II. That frontier spirit and footloose character of its highly mobile residents is a sharp departure from the longer established traditions held by many New Yorkers.

　　The city of Los Angeles (with a population of almost 3 million in 1980) is the nation's second largest. The metropolitan area, often referred to as the Los Angeles-Long Beach SMSA, includes parts of five counties and has a population of over 11 million. Los Angeles County, the nation's largest county in population (7 million), has more people than all but five states (excluding California). Los Angeles is only one of 81 independent cities within the county; many are physically indistinguishable from one another. The look-alike character of Southern California communities stems from their rapid development on land that was often vacant or used to grow vegetables or fruit.

The site that is presently Los Angeles was originally occupied by a small branch of the Shoshone Indians. They lived in the area in the 1500s and were there when the Portuguese explorer Cabrillo discovered the village of Yang-na in 1542; Cabrillo was supported by the Spanish government, which was interested in what is today the California coast. The next contact the Spanish had with this area was in 1769 when a captain and Franciscan priest led an expedition north of San Diego. They likewise visited the Indian village, liked the site, and called it El Pueblo Nuestra Señora la Reina de Los Angeles de Porciuncula (The Town of Our Lady the Queen of the Angels of Porciuncula) after an Italian chapel associated with St. Francis of Assisi. The Spanish began to settle the area in earnest in the late 1700s; they established a mission in 1771 and founded the town (pueblo) of Los Angeles in 1781. The pueblo of Los Angeles comprised a mixture of Indians, Mexicans, blacks, and Spanish, and the city became a center for farming and ranching. The first white settlers to arrive by land came in 1841; Mexicans and Spanish remained the dominant populations. When Mexico lost the Mexican War in 1848, the United States obtained control of both the city and the territory. In 1850 the village had only 1610 inhabitants. Growth continued at a slow pace until railroads came in 1876 and 1885 that linked the city to the rest of the country. Once rail routes were open to northern California, to San Francisco, and to the Middle West, the population leaped to 50,000 by 1890 and to 100,000 by 1900. Thus at the beginning of the century this West Coast city was insignificant in importance compared to large industrial centers in the Northeast and the Middle West.

The city's growth started in earnest this century with the completion of the artificial harbor in 1914. Tourism and the entertainment business brought in additional jobs and investment dollars as did the oil industry, which had begun somewhat earlier. Thousands of unemployed workers moved into Los Angeles and Southern California during the Great Depression of the 1930s. While the city was not as hard hit as others, it did benefit by having a large talent pool for manufacturing a variety of industrial and military goods needed for World War II. Petroleum, chemicals, aircraft, tires, and motor vehicles were all in great demand. The new companies and industries attracted new migrants from all over the U.S., but particularly from the South and the Middle West. By 1945 the city had mushroomed and was still growing because of the area's situation vis-à-vis expanding West Coast markets, the physical amenities which attracted tourists and retirees, and the huge outlays of federal monies supporting military and aerospace industries.

Los Angeles ranks after New York City and Chicago in the volume of retail sales (more than $5 billion annually). It is second to Chicago in manufacturing establishments (about 16,000) and is the West Coast's leading wholesale distribution center, financial center, and port. The city's port handles more trade with Japan, Southeast Asia, Oceania, and Latin America than any other U.S. port. International Los Angeles airport is the third busiest nationwide (after O'Hare in Chicago and Hartsfield in Atlanta). The presence of many financial institutions is an indication of the amount of monies invested in helping to develop the city's and region's economy. In terms of industry the city is the leader in the production of aircraft and space equipment and the motion picture and television industry. Other major industries include women's clothing, petroleum products, electronics, chemicals, furniture, toys, pottery, rubber, printing and publishing, autos, and auto parts. The city's diverse commercial and industrial base and its location as the center of rail, highway, and airline routes in the Southwest and West have helped it become the major center of economic activity in the western half of the country. Three additional components of the city's economy that are very important in dollars they bring in are tourism and conventions, agriculture, and federal contracts.

The dependence of the city and the county of Los Angeles on the federal government is only one of several problems the city is faced with. Four additional ones are critical. A major one is the extremely high cost of living in the city. Small, single-family dwellings not more than thirty years old may cost $150,000 to $200,000; apartments for a middle income couple may range from $500 to $800 a month. Transportation costs are also high, as one must depend on private automobiles to go almost anywhere in this sprawling metropolis. Another major problem is the extremes of wealth and poverty that remain in spite of riots by blacks in Watts during 1965 and by Mexican Americans in 1970 and 1971. Large numbers of both groups feel the brunt of discrimination in housing, employment, and education; they are not part of the packaged and publicized Southern California life-style and glamor. The reluctance of the city to assume a more progressive policy in resolving social ills may be due to its antecedents (many of rural Deep South heritage) or the footloose frontier philosophy that "anyone can make it." The third problem the city and county face is the lack of a good effective public mass transit system. The system that exists is unsatisfactory given the preponderance of private cars used (driven by single drivers), clogged freeways most daytime hours, and the unhealthy smog that permeates the basin much of the time. It is unfortunate the residents themselves fail to support mass transit as well as energy conservation measures. Automobile- and industrial-based smog is only one of the several environmental problems the city faces. Smog alerts warn residents of unhealthy atmospheric conditions; when they occur, one is advised to remain indoors. Until very recently, the city was without a downtown skyline of significance because most tall buildings were thought not to be earthquake proof. With the San Andreas fault in the vicinity, the city is awaiting some future catastrophe.

Houston: A Sun Belt City

Houston is rightly identified as a product of the last half of the twentieth century; in fact, to some observers it is a city of the twenty-first century (Fig. 2.13). Houston is currently ranked fifth in size (compared to thirteenth in 1960) and has had one of the most rapid population increases of any large metropolitan area in the country. The 1980 census revealed that the city had a population of 1.7 million and the SMSA 2.9 million. The meteoric rise in population is mostly a post-World War II phenomenon attributed to expanding space and petrochemical industries, low energy costs, a leisure-cosmopolitan image, little governmental regulation, and an economic climate favorable to the energetic, enterprising, and swashbuckling tactics of new Texan millionaires. By its economic output, population, areal extent (541 sq. mi. or 1401 sq. km. for the city and 6,931 sq. mi. or 17,951 sq. km. for the metropolitan area), downtown skyscrapers, and massive traffic jams on its expressways, Houston would seem to qualify as a major urban center on the continent. To some Houston may be defined in several ways: unregulated sprawl, susceptibility to major natural disasters (hurricanes), the best of middle class America, relegation of large masses of Mexican Americans and blacks to a perpetual life of poverty and discrimination. Some of these views contrast sharply with those promoting the city as a living symbol of continued American economic growth (amidst decline elsewhere); the last vestige of free enterprise; a city with little regard for energy conservation; the prototype of postindustrial urbanization, a citadel of aspiring, free-swinging, jet-setting, pleasure-seeking Americans.

Like Los Angeles, Houston is a relatively recent city in a North American context: a century ago only about 10,000 people were in the settlement. Prior to the arrival

Figure 2.13 Houston has emerged in the post-World War II era as one of the most dynamic American cities, an urban frontier experiencing explosive growth as perhaps the most famous of the Sun Belt cities. (Courtesy Charles Tatum)

of the first white settlers in 1822, the site of present-day Houston was occupied by the Karakawa Indians. Not until four years later (1826) did John Richardson Harris settle and survey a site at the junction of the Buffalo and White Oak bayous. This site was later sold in 1836 for $9428 to two New York land speculators who foresaw the site of eventual commercial importance to the expanding nation and entire continent. The site, originally called Harrisburg, was renamed Houston, in honor of General Sam Houston, commander of the Texas army in its struggle for independence from Mexico in 1836. Houston, with a population of 1500, served briefly as the temporary capital.

As long as Houston served as the state capital, it stimulated growth. The population grew to 2396 by 1850, primarily because the city served as a center for the east Texas cotton economy and because of its location on the navigable Buffalo Bayou. Sustained growth was not recorded until the railroad connections were expanded within the state and to major eastern and western cities, in particular New Orleans and San Francisco, and until the ship channel between Galveston and Houston was widened and deepened. Federal assistance helped with the channel development, not only to develop a major inland port that would be safe from hurricane damage (6000 were killed by a hurricane that struck Galveston Bay in 1900), but to be near the huge Spindletop oil fields, northeast of Houston, that were discovered in 1901.

From a population of less than 10,000 in 1870, Houston grew to 44,000 in 1900 and to 78,000 in 1910. World War I (1914–1918) also enhanced Houston's economy in a major way. The city already was receiving ocean-going vessels, and it became a center for petroleum-based products, of which there was a growing demand. As an industrial and transportation (rail and water) center serving expanding national and international markets, the city grew to 138,000 by 1920 and 292,000 in 1930. World War II also was a boom to the city's economy; Houston's population reached 384,000 by 1940.

While the city's economy and population were steadily increasing during the two world wars, the real boom did not materialize until the end of World War II. This period marked the beginning of suburbanization, national economies, and heavy petroleum usage. In population rank the city jumped from twenty-first in 1940 to thirteenth in 1960 to fifth place in 1980. The Houston-Southeast Gulf Coast area is the largest concentration of oil refinery operations in the country. The "Golden Strip" of the Houston Ship Channel (25 mi. or 40 km.) has 30 oil refineries, which command one-third of the nation's petroleum refining capacity. The channel has, as well, numerous shipyards, grain elevators, and cement factories, making it a very industrialized and heavily polluted part of the city. The city is the nation's leader in the production of oil field equipment, fertilizers, insecticides, and synthetic rubber. The huge maze of pipelines connecting the numerous petrochemical, natural gas, and petroleum refining companies has given the industrial area the label "Spaghetti Bowl." Efforts during the past two decades to diversify the city (away from dependence on energy industries) have been successful; Houston is now a major producer of food products, scientific equipment, paper products, sheet metal products, electrical machinery, and motor vehicles. There are currently more than 3000 manufacturing firms in the city, which produce more than $4 billion in goods annually.

A major component of Houston's growth during the 1960s and 1970s can be traced to the nation's space programs. The political decision to locate the headquarters of NASA's Manned Spacecraft Center (renamed Johnson Spacecraft Center in 1973) in the Houston area has been responsible for attracting some 1200 space-oriented firms and thousands of scientists and engineers into the area.

A city and metropolitan area that has experienced the growth of Houston's proportions during the past two decades is not without its problems. In fact, the glitter of affluence and newness often overshadows serious problems facing the city and its inhabitants. One of the major problems is the virtual absence of zoning and government regulations. It is not unusual to find large vacant land (formerly rich lands for rice, vegetables, or livestock) now totally abandoned, and awaiting development, or the sight of acres of concrete freeways, shopping centers with huge parking lots, or tracts for homes or condominiums. Houston, like Los Angeles, is a city developed by and for the automobile. There are more than 300 mi. (480 km.) of freeway in the city. In what is termed the "energy capital" of the country, there is little evidence of voluntary or enforced lower speed limits for conservation and safety. Crime and violence are also recognized within the city as major problems that may reflect the footloose cosmopolitan nature of new residents and vast socioeconomic differences. In a city considered affluent (third largest in per-capita income of the 10 most populous urban areas in 1979 with $10,638), there remain vast differences within the city. Elite subdivisions for millionares, clean, modern single family suburbs, and substandard housing for poor Mexican Americans and blacks (some that are within the shadows of the CBD's glittering energy company offices and hotels) all make up the city's residential character. Houston has the largest population of blacks of any city in the Sun Belt except Los Angeles. Minorities, comprising blacks (20 percent) and Mexican Americans (10 percent), feel they continue to be discriminated against in employment, housing, education, and the judicial process by the dominant white population comprised of people of German, British, Canadian, Italian, and Polish descent. The migrants—rich, middle class, and poor—that have arrived from the Northeast, Middle West, South, and West with a mixture of skills and ages (average age 26) give the city its cosmopolitan character; the large influx is seen as a mixed blessing. They represent a tremendous pool of talent that enhances the city's image of being creative and innovative, but they also put pressure on public services (water and transit especially) and the development process itself.

Toronto: A Cosmopolitan City

This largest Canadian metropolis, with a population of 2,864,700 (1979 estimate), is composed of the city of Toronto (640,000) and five surrounding boroughs: North York, York, East York, Scarborough, and Etobicoke. As the capital of the Province of Ontario and one of the leading industrial, commercial, and financial centers in Canada, it has many striking parallels to New York City (Fig. 2.14). Toronto also resembles New York City visually, with its waterfront skyline, skyscrapers, and sprawling suburbs. Nearly one-third of all Ontario's residents live within the metropolitan area. It

Figure 2.14 Toronto graces the north shore of Lake Ontario with its dynamic central business district as seen from the spectacular Canadian National Tower. Toronto is commonly regarded as one of the most successful North American cities to adapt to the challenges of the postwar era. (Courtesy John Jakle)

has as well about one-tenth of all Canadians and 13 percent of all wealth generated within the country. Without doubt the major reasons why Toronto is one of the fastest growing large metropolitan areas on the continent are its cosmopolitan character, its active program of downtown development, the positive image the city evokes with the public, and the benefits accrued from successful metrogovernment federation.

Toronto was once composed primarily of single family homes. However, that has changed during the past two decades with the construction of numerous multiple unit complexes. Today almost one-quarter of all residents live in apartments. The sprawl of Toronto is extensive: the municipality covers 241 sq. mi. (624 sq. km.) and the Census Metropolitan Area 1041 sq. mi. (2629 sq. km.).

The city's past and present have been shaped by its favored situation in the province and country. Prior to the arrival of Europeans in the early 1600s, the Iroquois and Hurons used the site as a portage between Lake Ontario and Huron. Toronto is a Huron word meaning "meeting place." The French explorer Étienne Brulé was the first European to visit the site of present-day Toronto in 1615. Much later, the French recognized the strategic position of the site for trading and missionary purposes. They built Fort Rouillé, also called Fort Toronto, in 1720, only to destroy it in 1759; later the site was ceded to the British, as was the rest of French Canada, with the Treaty of Paris in 1763. The British, recognizing the value of the site, bought land on the Toronto peninsula from the Mississauga Indians in 1787 on which to build a capital for

Upper Canada (later Ontario). Settlement did not occur until 1793; the town was called York, after the Duke of York, a name which remained until 1834 when it reverted again to Toronto.

Two decisions in the early 1800s helped insure Toronto's importance as a commercial and government center. One was the decision to make it a major administrative and military center. The second was to invest government monies to build a fort, government buildings, and roads, and to develop agricultural lands. These investments helped the settlement to become a political, military, manufacturing, and transportation center. Toronto ceased to become a provincial capital when Upper and Lower Canada (Quebec) were united in 1841; however, when the two colonies separated at the time of the Confederation of 1867, Toronto became the capital of the new Province of Ontario.

During the last half of the nineteenth century, two further factors were instrumental in the city's growth. One was the construction of transcontinental railroads, which made the city a hub of the province's and much of the nation's emerging railway systems. The second, indirectly related to the first, were a series of decisions made by the Canadian government to adopt policies that would protect new Canadian industries from American companies and to open frontier lands to the west for agricultural (especially grain and livestock) and mineral development. Businesses within Toronto, in particular the financial institutions, used these policies to help to attract new and larger industries into the city and to expand the city's markets to the Prairie Provinces and Western Canada.

Toronto's economy expanded substantially during the two world wars, in part because of the greater demand for wartime industrial goods. Growth has continued since the end of World War II, in large part because of the city's strategic location vis-à-vis markets in Canada and North America, the various transportation routes that converge on the city, and the diversity and balance of its economy. Toronto, in a prosperous part of Canada's agricultural heartland, has a good blend of commercial, industrial, financial, governmental, and tourist-related activities. Almost one-third of the country's manufacturing industries are located within 100 mi. (160 km.) of the city. The highest concentration of industry is in the Toronto area; the city is part of one arm of the Golden Horseshoe that stretches from Toronto to Hamilton to southern Lake Ontario.

Prior to World War II Toronto was predominantly a city of white Anglo-Saxon Protestants (WASPS). Since then, due to the influx of European immigrants and the in-migration of rural French- and English-speaking Canadians from Quebec, the Maritimes, Ontario, and the Prairie Provinces, the city has become more cosmopolitan. This feature, along with a high standard of living (per capita disposable income approaching $9800), is one of the major reasons why Toronto is considered a highly desirable place to live. Almost one-third of Toronto's residents were born outside of Canada. The European groups that have arrived since 1945 reside in fairly distinct sections: the Italians in the west and north, the Germans in the east and south, the Jews in the Forest Hills section, and the Ukrainians, Poles, and other East Europeans in Etobicoke. A goodly number of English, Scots, and Irish have also arrived since 1950, as have lesser numbers of Chinese, Greeks, Portuguese, Indians, and West Indians. The cosmopolitan character is evident in neighborhood groceries, restaurants, and churches, especially in some of the older sections near downtown Toronto. It is not unusual to travel the streetcars, subways, or buses and hear a half-dozen different languages. The suburbs house not only recently arrived French Canadians but many English-speaking families who have sought the havens of single-family dwellings and high rise apartments closer to their jobs. Numerous industrial parks and regional shopping centers dot the suburban landscapes.

Toronto is not without many problems facing other cities. A partial list would include blight and decay (in some older areas near downtown), traffic congestion on expressways and on old, narrow streets, environmental pollution, and assorted land use conflicts. A major decision to resolve these at the metropolitan level was made by provincial legislation in 1954 that created the Municipality of Metropolitan Toronto. The province felt some comprehensive approach was needed as the individual suburbs were often not making decisions in concert. Toronto's growth during the early 1900s was one of basically separated communities which eventually grew together. Several suburban municipalities were annexed to Toronto between 1893 and 1912, but no further boundary changes occurred until the formation of the federation in 1954. The Municipality of Metropolitan Toronto consisted originally of 12 suburbs and the city of Toronto. In 1967 the 13 political units merged to form five boroughs and the city of Toronto. The council that governs the city is composed of 12 elected members from the city of Toronto and 20 from the five boroughs; the 32 appoint a chair. The tax assessments are set by individual municipalities. By pooling the tax resources of the six member municipalities, funding is provided for the construction of public highways, sewers, and other projects. The police forces are coordinated as are libraries, planning boards, public housing, welfare, transit, parks, water supply, and emergency services. Fire fighting services are handled by the municipalities themselves. Pollution control is a provincial responsibility. In spite of a number of administrative and logistical problems that surfaced during the early years of this metrogovernment, this first system of urban federated government in North America is generally viewed as a success.

Urban Problems and Solutions

Two very general groups of issues arising out of the discussion of the evolution of North American cities, the internal structure of cities, and the profiles of four major cities can be presented. These issues concern (1) the fragmentation of the metropolitan region and (2) the management of differential growth, stagnation, and decline of metropolises within the North American system of cities.

Fragmentation

Spatial differentiation, enshrined in political fragmentation, is an important issue not simply because it occurs, but because it results in inequalities of access to employment, education, amenities, housing, safety, shopping, and so forth. For the sake of brevity, three aspects of this fragmentation issue are examined. The first relates to the inner city-outer city question, the second relates to the number and competition between governmental units, and the third relates to one way in which inequities are created in an urban context.

The Inner City and the Outer City Conceptually, the inner city contains the original central business area, and the economic activities and houses built prior to the massive suburbanization which followed the widespread use of the automobile. Practically, the inner city is defined as the central city in the census. Given the practical definition of the inner city, it is evident that the degree to which the central city represents an era prior to heavy dependence on the automobile is directly related to the political extent of the central city. The outer city consists conceptually of the more recent automobile-oriented suburbs, especially those that have developed since 1945. Practically, the outer city is defined in the census as the remaining area of the SMSA beyond the central city.

The inner city is the consequence of a number of different processes, some measures of which are presented for a few selected SMSAs in Table 2.2. The most obvious process is one of aging, relating to the housing, social services, infrastructure, industrial base, and population itself. The result of this aging is much housing in need of renovation or replacement, social services housed in understaffed facilities and often poorly funded, a transportation system that may be decrepit and streets in need of repair, old factories that are ill suited to modern technology, and the loss of many family households. But, it must be recognized that this process of aging faces all parts of the metropolis sooner or later, and what is important is the way in which the resultant issues are

TABLE 2.2 SOME INDICES OF DISPARITY BETWEEN SELECTED U.S. CENTRAL CITIES AND SUBURBS

Central City and SMSA	% of SMSA Population in City, 1973	% City Population Black, 1970	% Increase in Black Population, 1960–1970	Index of Income Disparity	% Change in Jobs, 1960–1970	% Change in Population Aged 18–64	Number of Local Government Units
Newark	19	54.2	20.1	0.56	−12.5	−12	207
Cleveland	33	38.3	9.7	0.66	−12.9	−16	210
St. Louis	23	40.9	12.3	0.78	−14.2	−21	483
Baltimore	41	46.4	11.7	0.79	−4.6	−5	29
Boston	22	16.4	7.3	0.79	−4.0	−8	147
Chicago	45	32.7	9.8	0.80	−12.1	−8	1172
Detroit	33	43.7	14.8	0.80	−18.8	−12	241
Milwaukee	48	14.7	6.3	0.82	−10.2	−5	149
Philadelphia	38	33.6	7.2	0.83	−4.1	−5	852
New York	67	21.2	7.2	0.84	−1.9	−1	538
Birmingham	39	42.9	2.4	0.84	5.7	−11	92
Washington	24	71.1	17.2	0.84	8.2	−2	90
Atlanta	30	51.3	13.0	0.84	19.5	+1	86

Source: Advisory Commission on Intergovernmental Relations, *Trends in Metropolitan America,* Washington, D.C., 1977.

tackled. Some of the older suburbs of the outer city are also experiencing aging, so it is narrow minded to regard this particular process as relating to the inner city alone.

A second process, somewhat complementary to that of aging, relates to changing land uses, which in the case of the inner city can result in quite dramatic transformations in the fabric of local neighborhoods. These changes may result from new construction related to the activities of the central business area, new highways, the building of hospitals, and so forth. Positive effects can result from well planned renovations, and the careful replacement of older housing with better new housing at reasonable prices. Negative effects, which have usually been the case, result from carving up neighborhoods with expressways, the construction of discordant buildings, and simply allowing property to depreciate while land is being assembled for future development. The process of changing land uses is not, however, restricted to the inner city, though some of the effects have been more obvious in this section of the metropolis.

A third process relates to the changing social structure of the population of the inner city. This has resulted in minority groups, such as blacks or new immigrants, concentrating in parts of the area and occasionally becoming the dominant group. One result of this is that when the nature of the infrastructure is changed to cater to the special needs of minorities or new immigrants, the changes are not accepted or are regarded as unnecessary by the majority. Probably one of the best examples in this regard is education, where the established majority sees no need for an educational system that tries to support the values and heritage of a minority.

The essential point is, therefore, that the inner city-outer city dichotomy is a false dichotomy. Even if the metropolis can be divided into these two parts, sections of the metropolis will always have to change under the impact of the processes described above, and if these impacts are dominant in the inner city today they will be dominant in parts of the outer city tomorrow.

Governments in Metropolis in Competition Two of the main reasons why the results of the processes described above are not tackled more resolutely are that metropolises have neither the financial resources nor the political organization to deal with the issues in a comprehensive manner. These two aspects of the urban dilemma are particularly endemic to the North American situation, for in other parts of the world (such as Europe) they are issues that have been faced through political and fiscal reorganization. The Canadian situation in this regard is a great deal better than that found in the United States, which may be one reason why Canadian inner cities are in a healthier condition than those south of the border.

The number of municipal councils found in many metropolitan areas is overwhelming, and results in a political fragmentation within a metropolis that makes coordination difficult. In fact, when different municipalities do see a need for coordination, they often establish a special purpose body to deal with that particular issue. There is therefore little wonder that the possibilities for partisan behavior, and corruption, in local government are quite high. The move toward a resolution of this type of fragmentation has been slow. Some of the best examples of one-tier federation and two-tier federation are found in Winnipeg and Toronto in Canada. Miami took advantage of the county level of government to form Metro in the early fifties, and a move has been made toward greater coordination in a number of metropolises such as Boston and San Francisco in recent years. It is difficult, however, to conclude that anything other than wholesale local government reform is now required for most large urban areas in the United States.

The financial problems of large metropolises such as New York City have hit the headlines in recent years. Apart from any bad management, which is likely to be the norm in a fragmented government situation, the fiscal squeeze stems in large part from the changed role of local government and the inadequate taxation system on which it is based. Traditionally, local governments are in the business of providing for the needs and upkeep of the physical structure of the city. They have been responsible for roads, sewers, policing, fire protection, sanitation, snowplowing, and so forth. Since the 1930s, however, this role has been gradually changing, and now urban areas have become involved in social issues relating to the population. This involvement has of course been with the assistance of state and federal governments, and it includes welfare, rental housing, homes for the elderly, alcohol and drug clinics, and many services related to school children through local boards of education.

There are three problems with this switch to a social orientation. First, local governments were established to provide for physical needs, not social needs. Hence they are slow to develop social services. Second, the demands for social services fall disproportionately in those parts of the metropolis that have the greatest number of poor people, single-parent families, unemployed, and so forth. Unfortunately, the parts of the metropolis with the greatest need are usually within the central city, hence it is that area that experiences the greatest burden. Third, the financial basis of metropolitan governments is inadequate to provide many of the services required, and so large transfers of federal and state funds are necessary to support the services. The federal and state funds are earmarked, however, for specific purposes. They may be tied to certain short-run party objectives or they may be provided in response to perceived national rather than local needs. The money that local governments themselves raise is derived from property taxes, sales and other indirect taxes, and in some cases, payroll levies.

The result is competition between local governments within metropolitan areas to maximize their property tax base, and minimize expenditures. Thus, local governments compete with each other to attract clean light industry and attractive shopping centers and zone for large lots and high income families. They try to keep out unsightly-looking manufacturing activities and people who may impose a burden on local services and restrict the construction of amusements that might attract undesirable inhabitants. It is therefore the entire metropolitan area that is the arena in which control must be enforced on the basis of equity.

The Fragmentation of Costs and Benefits The last issue to be discussed in this section is the fragmentation, or separation, made in society between costs and benefits. This is an important issue to understand in North American urbanism because it underlies nearly every problem that may be raised, and certainly provides a foundation for discussion of the concerns outlined in this chapter. North American society seems to

80 Chapter 2, Cities of North America

have an amazing ability to share the costs of urban infrastructure among a large number of people, but to allow the benefits to be enjoyed or appropriated by very few. This sharing of costs but privatizing the benefits occurs both spatially and in time. Two examples may explain.

The spatial example is drawn from the West Coast, where all innovations are controversial, and none more so than the Bay Area Rapid Transit system (BART)

Figure 2.15 Region Served by the Bay Area Rapid Transit System. [*Source:* M. M. Webber, "The BART Experience—What Have We Learned?" University of California, Berkeley, Institute of Urban and Regional Research, Monograph 26, 1976, p. 3.]

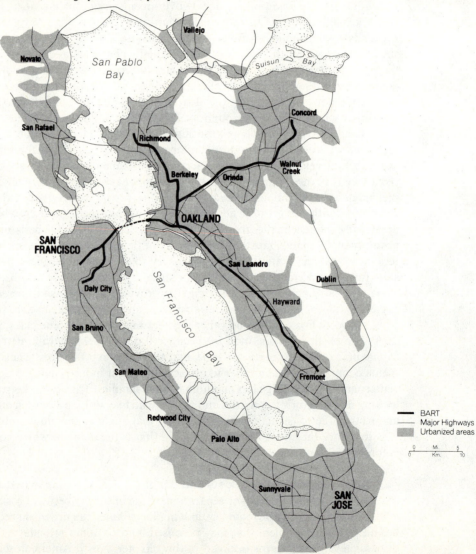

(Fig. 2.15). BART is a regional rail system extending for 71 mi. (114 km.) over three counties connecting the communities around San Francisco as far apart as Fremont, Concord, and Richmond with the central city of San Francisco. Planning for the system commenced in the 1950s. Funds were authorized in 1962, and the first section of the system opened in 1972. Over 60 percent of the capital costs of the project ($1.5 billion and still counting), and 55 percent of the annual operating costs ($64 million in 1975–1976), are being paid by all residents of the three-county area primarily through property taxes and secondarily retail sales taxes. Both property taxes and sales taxes in the BART area are regressive, falling disproportionately heavier on low income households than on those of higher income. The benefits of the system are accrued, however, by the people owning property within easy reach of the stations, and the riders who are drawn disproportionately from the higher-income groups. Thus, the costs are borne by all, and fall heaviest on the poor, while the benefits are reaped by a few property owners and higher-income commuters to the San Francisco business district.

The second example, the one of sharing the costs but privatizing the benefits in a temporal context, is rather more conceptual and relates to the inner city-outer city discussion. The reader should by now recognize that a metropolitan area is a functional economic and social system, and that this system has developed over time in an interrelated manner. But, some suburban communities try to appropriate the benefits of this accumulated investment by discriminatory zoning and discouraging all but the most attractive business and commercial investments. These communities are therefore privatizing the benefits of an urban accumulation that has occurred over a long period of time, while avoiding the accumulated costs that have also occurred. These costs are in the form of an aging physical plant, social services for the disadvantaged, and so forth, that have to be born in other parts of the urban area such as the inner city. Furthermore, in the process of privatizing the benefits of the urban accumulation today, they are helping to accentuate the natural and inevitable costs of urbanization that will occur tomorrow.

Thus, the fragmentation, or separation, between those individuals or groups who receive the benefits, and the more general sharing of the costs among society as a whole, is at the core of many of the urban issues facing North America. It may be argued that the solution to this particular facet of the issues lies in the development of a package of reforms. This package involves local government reform, continued change in the source of finance for cities, and a taxation system which permits governments to recoup the localized benefits received from public investment.

Different Growth Within the Urban System

Looking ahead over the next 25 years it is now clear that a major issue of continental importance derives from the decline in overall population growth and the increased importance of migration as a determinant of growth or decline. This issue has been examined with respect to the inner city-outer city question, and some of the same principles apply at the more national level. In an era of counterurbanization, migration determines which areas of North America will grow and which will not. This issue is important because it is now becoming quite apparent that a decrease in population and a contraction of services cannot be accomplished by simply reversing the organizational and political mechanisms that have in the past catered for growth.

As an illustration of this latter comment consider the school closing issue now faced in many areas across the continent. In an era of growth and high birth rates, the needs of an increased population of actual and projected children of school age was met by building new schools and training more teachers. It is, however, extraordinarily difficult, to throw this procedure into reverse; that is, close schools and fire teachers, though this is being done. The question of contraction involves considerations of the relationship between a school and the community in which it is located, and the values that a community wishes to retain in the educational system. Thus the decisions concerning which schools to close, and which values to pay for and which to delete, are complex issues requiring close consultation with the people involved in the area.

The result of the increased importance of migration in growth and decline can perhaps be examined in the context of three questions. These are: (1) how do we cater to contraction; (2) how do we prevent too much growth; and (3) how do we deal with the political consequences of population shifts? These questions will be dealt with only briefly, but it is hoped that some of the points raised will assist a discussion of alternatives.

Although a great deal is known about the pressures created in periods of growth, little is known about the socioeconomic characteristics of metropolises in decline. What is known, however, is that the potential migrant group in any city is limited in number, and once the bulk of the migration has occurred metropolitan areas become resistant to decline in population size. Rather than leave their community, many people accept lower paying jobs or withdraw from the labor force. Thus nongrowth cities have a per-capita income level significantly less than growing cities, and this results in a declining level of local demand. The declining level of local demand leads to obsolescence of some service facilities, and institutions funded out of the local tax base receive the greatest cutbacks. Education is therefore particularly vulnerable, and a decline in the quality of education leads to a lowering in the level of skills in the labor force and a consequent decrease in productivity.

It is therefore clear that contraction has to be managed in such a way that the quality of both public and private services must not be allowed to decline. Obsolescent service functions must be replaced by facilities that can be supported by the lower level of demand. The inherent stability of nongrowth areas is a positive inducement to careful and sensitive planning of this type. Furthermore, it should be recognized that a period of nongrowth may well be followed by a short period of growth as some economic activities enter the area to take advantage of lower wage levels.

Most public decision making is predicated upon the notion of growth. New ideas can be tried out when new physical plant is created or new institutions developed. It is clear, however, that rapid growth creates problems associated with too much demand, which can force up prices and provide an environment conducive to exploitation by speculators. This has happened especially with respect to house and land prices in growing North American cities. Also, residents of some of the more favored areas perceive environmental damage and overcrowding occurring with continued growth. Hence the movements toward discouraging immigration by some West Coast communities. In an era in which migration determines growth, quite possibly some of the more attractive areas may begin to develop discriminatory practices on a regional scale in much the same manner as some of the rich suburban communities. In fact, some regions already use the cloak of environmental protection to limit growth and preserve the area for those favored by prior residence.

The sectional bias in areas of growth (the Sun Belt) and areas of decline (some of the lower Great Lakes and East Coast cities) could well lead to political schisms of some consequence. Political power is based on economic strength and number of votes, and the areas in which decline is occurring are beginning to witness some disappearance of this power, hence the formation of the Coalition of Northeast Governors, the Northeast-Midwest Economic Advancement Coalition, the Southern Growth Policies Board, and, perhaps, even separatism in Quebec. In fact, the myopic recent cries from the Sun Belt of "to hell with New York City" resemble the disregard of narrow-minded suburbanites for the issues facing the inner city.

RECOMMENDED READINGS

Adams, J. S., ed. *Contemporary Metropolitan America: Cities of the Nation's Historic Metropolitan Core.* Cambridge, MA: Ballinger, 1976.

Advisory Commission on Intergovernmental Relations. *Trends in Metropolitan America.* Washington, DC, 1977.

Berry, B. J. L. and D. C. Dahmann. "Population Redistribution in the United States in the 1970s." *Population and Development Review,* Vol. 3 (1977), 443–471.

Borchert, J. R., "America's Changing Metropolitan Regions." *Annals of the Association of American Geographers,* 62 (1972), 352–373.

Bourne, L. *Perspectives on the Inner City: Its Changing Character, Reasons for Decline and Revival.* Toronto: CUCS, Res. Paper No. 94, 1978.

Cutler, I. *Chicago: Metropolis of the Mid-Continent.* Dubuque, IA: Kendall, Hunt, 1976.

Gottman, J. *Megalopolis.* New York: Twentieth Century Fund, 1961.

Muller, P. O. *The Outer City.* Washington, DC: Association of American Geographers, 1976.

Nader, G. *Cities of Canada: Profiles of Fifteen Metropolitan Centres.* Toronto: Macmillan of Canada, 1976.

Nader, G. *Cities of Canada: Theoretical, Historical, and Planning Perspectives.* Toronto: Macmillan of Canada, 1975.

Rose, H. M. *The Black Ghetto: A Spatial Behavioral Perspective.* New York: McGraw-Hill, 1971.

Rose, H. M. *Black Suburbanization: Access to Improved Quality of Life or Maintenance of the Status Quo?* Cambridge, MA: Ballinger, 1976.

Rust, E. *No Growth: Impacts on Metropolitan Areas.* Lexington, MA: Heath, 1975.

Yeates, M. *Main Street: Windsor to Quebec City.* Toronto: Macmillan of Canada, 1975.

Yeates, M. and B. Garner. *The North American City.* New York: Harper & Row, 1980.

Figure 3.1 Major Cities of Western Europe (*Source:* Data derived from United Nations, Department of Economic and Social Affairs. *Global Review of Human Settlements, Statistical Annex,* published by Pergamon Press, New York, 1976.)

Chapter 3

Cities of Western Europe

Lawrence M. Sommers

Western Europe in the World Urban System

Western Europe is one of the most highly urbanized regions (74 percent) in the world, although the percentage of people classified as urban varies greatly within the region as it does within individual countries. The heaviest concentrations of urban dwellers are in West Central Europe, including the United Kingdom, where the Industrial Revolution has had the greatest influence. Sweden is the most urbanized country in Western Europe, with 86 percent of the population classified as urban. West Germany is 80 percent urban, France and the United Kingdom are both 79 percent, and Belgium is 74 percent. Outside of this core area the proportion of the population that is urban drops off to under 50 percent in some of the peripheral areas of the Mediterranean and Scandinavia.

Because of the large population in Western Europe, the high percentages of urban population represent a large urban population as well, about 260 million (out of a total population of 350 million) in 1980. Because of this, Western Europe contained 15 percent of the world's total urban population.

From the perspective of numbers and sizes of cities, Western Europe stands out even more clearly as one of the most important urban regions of the world. Many of the world's largest and most important cities are located here. Indeed, in several of the countries of the urban core, vast urban agglomerations dominate each of the countries (Fig. 3.1). In the Netherlands, for example, the Randstadt, a series of large, more or less contiguous cities, contains 46 percent of the population of the country. In West Germany, a similar belt of cities in the Rhine-Ruhr contains 41 percent of the population of that country. In several other countries, the primate city is a common phenomenon, for example, Copenhagen (26 percent of the population), Greater London (13 percent), Greater Paris (19 percent), Stockholm (17 percent), Brussels (11 percent), and Oslo (16 percent). As of 1980, Western Europe had two cities each with a population of more than 5 million (London and Paris), six with 2 to 5 million, and 18 with 1 to 2 million. The dominance of the urban core in West Central Europe is even more apparent from knowing that in 1980 West Germany had six of the 34 cities with populations exceeding 1 million, the United Kingdom had seven (one of them, London, at more than 10 million, one of the 5 largest cities in the world and the largest in all of Europe), France had three, with 10 others scattered among the remaining countries of the core region.

The cities of Western Europe are among the world's oldest, with many, including such present-day major centers as London, Paris, and Rome, dating back to Greek and Roman times. Nonetheless, the large numbers of cities, the great sizes of many of them, and the large urban population are primarily the result of the Industrial Revolution of the nineteenth and twentieth centuries. Hence, from a historical perspective, Western Europe today contains predominantly modern industrial/commercial cities, often grafted onto or grown out of older urban areas dating back to the Renaissance/Baroque period, the Medieval period, and in some cases even back to Greco-Roman times. It is this long historical continuity that gives Western European cities their distinctive character and clearly sets them apart from the newer industrial/commercial cities of North America and Oceania. Western Europe's cities also distinctly differ from the cities of Eastern Europe, even though the latter went through similar historical periods and processes of growth. But the imposition of socialist systems on the cities of Eastern Europe in the post-World War II era has changed those cities, some more than others, and diverted that part of Europe onto an alternative path of development that has had an important impact on the urban landscape.

Historical Evolution of Western European Cities

Early Beginnings

Concentrations of people in urban settlements, which began in Europe with the early civilizations in the Western Mediterranean, are important features in the economic, social, and political histories of most countries and are also dominating phenomena on the landscape. The earliest towns, probably established in the Tigris-Euphrates River Valley, were market centers developed to exchange the surplus production of irrigated agriculture. Somewhat later, between 5000 and 700 B.C., Phoenicians and Greeks dominated the lands of the Mediterranean Basin and added fishing, commerce, and incipient primitive industry to agriculture as bases of their livelihood. They developed small ports on the Mediterranean such as Carthage, Cartagena, Syracuse on Sicily, Marseilles, and Korinthos (Corinth). The Greek town, usually small and rather nondescript in appearance, was built within walls and usually contained a dominating fortress. Streets were narrow and winding, houses were low and poorly built, and a few public buildings were found along with structures housing craft industries. The population rarely exceeded a few thousand, although Athinai (Athens) reached an estimated 300,000 at the height of Greek civilization.

The development of towns and cities was accentuated during the Roman period (500 B.C. to A.D. 250). Roman settlements also became the primary basis for the resurgence of towns in the Middle Ages. Ports, road centers, defense points, agricultural and mineral processing centers, industry, and trade centers were the bases for the rapid increase of urban settlements during the Roman period. At the height of the Roman Empire, Rome reached an estimated population of 1 million crowded into less than 25 sq. km. The existence of Rome was a truly phenomenal accomplishment for that period, as food and raw materials had to be transported long distances to supply the large urban population. The Romans created over 400 cities in Italy alone, and towns were developed throughout the Empire from Spain to England as well as in France and Germany.

With the fall of the Holy Roman Empire and the subsequent control of many areas by barbarian tribes, urban life declined as did the need for cities. Towns again became important during the Middle Ages under the pressure of larger numbers of people, strong religious movements and leaders, and the material desires of feudal lords. By the end of the medieval period (roughly A.D. 1500), the area once controlled by the Holy Roman Empire contained about 3,000 towns. A small number of these were major metropolitan agglomerations for that period, usually serving as seaports and regional and political capitals with 1,000 to more than 10,000 inhabitants. About 2,800 were market towns with a population of 100 to 1,000 that served limited hinterlands of 40 sq. mi. (104 sq. km.) in the more densely populated regions and up to 200 sq. mi. (518 sq. km.) in sparsely populated areas. The spacing and frequency of market towns was based on the distance the peasants could go and return in one day on foot or using animals to market their produce and obtain essential goods. This spacing concept was later studied in detail in Southern Germany by Walter Cristaller and became the basis for central place theory (see Chapter 1).

Industrial Revolution

The next surge of urban development in Europe came with the Industrial Revolution after 1800. Prior to this, towns in West Central Europe had developed largely as marketplaces for agricultural produce, as centers for merchants to exchange goods, and for artisans to create and trade handicraft articles of various kinds. They were small preindustrial urban places with agriculture and limited market activity dominating the totality of human development. The predominantly rural character of the population is indicated by the 90 percent so classified in France and nearly 80 percent in England and Wales in the early 1800s. With the Industrial Revolution, manufacturing powered by coal became the major activity in most cities, and retail and service industries grew rapidly to supply the needs of a burgeoning urban population.

Manufacturing establishments required a reliable source of power as well as labor and raw materials, some of which were available locally, others which had to be imported. Industrialization created a need for warehousing raw and finished materials and led to the development of retail and service industries to supply the needs of factory workers. The new jobs also created a flow of people from rural areas to towns, thus increasing the rate of rural depopulation. One or more cities grew up in areas which had advantages for the development of certain kinds of industry. As the landscape became increasingly urbanized, regions changed from subsistence to exchange economies. Towns became central places or marketing centers which served their urban population as well as the tributary rural areas which surrounded them. The functions of retail and wholesale commerce, transportation, trade, finance, services, construction, and government became significant in addition to the production of goods.

As processing centers grew in size and number, the arrangement of cities as well as the specializations of each became more complex. Access to natural resources including productive soils, domestic and industrial water, biotic resources, coal, and water power became important. Clusters of urban settlements were created, and sharper distinctions in function and specialization began to grow among cities and within sections of individual cities. The development of transportation facilities such as waterways and railways to facilitate the movement of raw materials, finished goods, and people accelerated the growth and size of urban centers.

The growth of industry and urban centers during the past two centuries has been far from even throughout Western Europe. Norway and Sweden, for instance, remained predominantly rural much longer than did England or West Germany. Partially this reflected a difference in the availability of resources. Partly it was a matter of location, and partly the nature of the stage of development and technology (the slower arrival of the Industrial Revolution) and the degree of availability of capital to invest in industry. The colonial empires of England, France, Belgium, and the Netherlands fed a great deal of raw materials into the home country and provided markets for finished goods. Overseas interests also fostered the large scale development of merchant marines and the development of ports and transportation facilities within the home countries to move goods to inland areas for further processing, use, or reexport. As the process of urbanization continued, certain large centers began to predominate and became primate cities, metropolitan centers, or the focus of a cluster of smaller cities, as for example in the Ruhr area of West Germany.

Growth and expansion during the Industrial Revolution became characteristic for the individual city as well as groups of centers. In some cases, a single invention or available resource tended to be the major reason for the concentration of urban population. An example is Cartwright's power loom, essential in the development of the textile industry, which was largely responsible for the concentration of development in a series of cities in England, notably Manchester, Liverpool, and Leeds. Coal was the available energy source that powered textile development; thus most of the textile towns are located on or near coal fields. More recently, a set of inventions related to the modern office building has had a great deal to do with the focus of development in the central business districts of urban areas. These include commercial shorthand, the electric telegraph, cheap universal postage, the freight and human elevator, the typewriter, skyscraper building techniques, the telephone, the adding machine, electric light, reinforced steel and concrete buildings, mimeograph and dictating machines, carbon paper as applied to typing, and a whole series of printing and photo reproduction processes. This set of inventions led to concentrations of types of services or functions in the downtowns of European cities. Certain cities or parts of cities specialized and became corporate headquarters of industries, finance centers, or centers for specialized services and government activity. White-collar occupations increased, and urban development was given additional impetus by scientific research centered in universities and research sections of large corporations. In turn, research results fostered new urban activities.

As a result of this increased concentration of people in urban centers, the mode of life and the cultural and physical landscape of Western Europe changed. Large metropolitan centers became predominant and contained a significant portion of a nation's people, for example, 26 percent in Copenhagen, Denmark. Such dominating centers tend to have a significant influence on the spatial organization of the country in which they are found. In the city itself, specializations of functions developed, giving rise to sectors or successive rings outward from the central business district. As Cristaller noted, around a major marketing center other centers will emerge at given distances and will be connected to it by various means of transportation.

In the late nineteenth and early twentieth centuries, industrial cities or central places grew in size and complexity and became more numerous in the core region of Western Europe. The following facilitated the diffusion of industrial economies: coal was abundant as a source of power; excellent seaports were available to carry on ocean trade; the climate was reliable; good soil facilitated intense agriculture; water power was available; rail, water and road transportation facilities were well developed; and a variety of local raw materials were available as a basis for manufacturing. The impact of the Industrial Revolution, which began in England, spread quickly to nearby areas of the continent. The rapid growth of industrial cities on the continent was largely a post-1870 phenomenon, as indicated by the growth of such German urban centers as Essen, Chemnitz, Düsseldorf, and Duisburg (Table 3.1). The old established capital, seaport, or medieval city grew during the industrial period, but the rate of growth was not as spectacular as in the new manufacturing city that was changing the economic face of the continent. The growth of representative established cities from 1800 to 1975 is shown in Table 3.2.

Rapid change has been a major characteristic of urban Western Europe since the advent of the Industrial Revolution. First people moved from rural areas to villages, towns, and cities to find employment in the factories and accompanying growing ser-

TABLE 3.1 GROWTH OF GERMAN CITIES 1800–1920

City	1800	1850	1880	1920
Munich	30,000	110,000	230,000	631,000
Cologne	50,000	97,000	145,000	634,000
Essen	4,000	9,000	57,000	439,000
Chemnitz	14,000	32,000	95,000	304,000
Düsseldorf	10,000	27,000	95,000	407,000
Duisburg	—	—	41,000	244,000

Source: W. Gordon East, *An Historical Geography of Europe,* London: Meuthen, 1966, p. 415.

TABLE 3.2 POPULATION IN URBAN AGGLOMERATIONS (IN THOUSANDS)

City	1800	1850	1880	1900	1950	1975
London	1117	2363	3830	6586	8348	7281
Paris	547	1053	2269	2714	5441	9863
Berlin	172	419	1122	1889	3337	3142
Rome	163	175	300	463	1701	2868

Source: Compiled by the author.

vice, retail, and government activities. Then movement took place to the suburbs and nearby urban places as towns and cities became crowded and large scale industry could only find room in satellite communities for new urban development. As these growth trends developed, the concentration of urban population increased rapidly in the core region of Western Europe, particularly in larger cities (population over 10,000). Industrial growth triggered a number of major movements: rural to urban, south and north Europe to core, and expanding city to previously rural areas. Along with the rapidity of urban growth came numerous problems, such as congestion, noise and ecological pollution, inadequate transportation and housing, high crime rates, administrative and jurisdictional governmental difficulties, and lack of green or recreational space. The implications of these problems are covered in more detail later in this chapter.

Urban Regions

The frequency and size of cities and the proportion of population classified as urban decreases to the north, south, and east from the highly industrialized urban core of West Central Europe. The patterns of distribution and density of urban population in Western Europe are largely correlated with the degree of industrialization. Three distinct regions can be identified as: (1) the densely populated urban-industrialized core, (2) the sparsely populated primary-industry-dependent periphery, and (3) the transition region between the two extremes with moderate urban development (Fig. 3.2). The degree of urbanization in the three regions reflects the type and concentrations of industry and related economic activities. Manufacturing, retail and service industries, intensive agriculture, and urban population dominate the core region. Limited extensive agriculture, the processing of products of the primary sectors of the economy (agriculture, forestry, fishing, and minerals), and sparse urban population characterize the periphery. The transition region has moderate levels of agriculture, manufacturing, and commerce and a moderate proportion of the population living in cities. Cities, larger and more frequent in the core, become smaller and more widely scattered urban settlements toward the periphery.

The dominant recent movement of people in Western Europe has been into the cities, particularly those in the core region. Cities in the core region attract or "pull" those "pushed" from the peripheral areas because of less economic opportunity. The European Economic Community (Common Market) has facilitated the movement by allowing labor to move freely within member countries. Also, large numbers of people

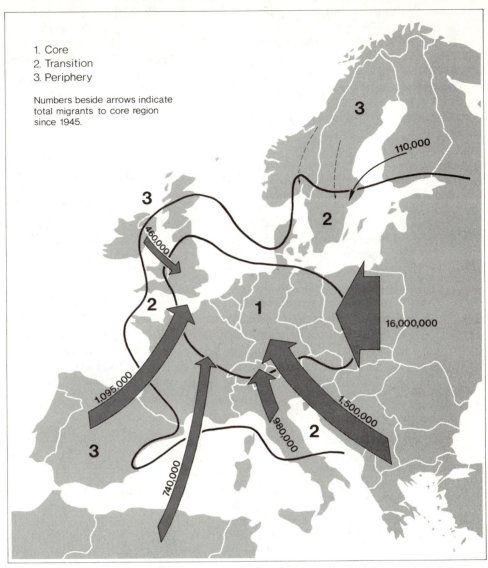

Figure 3.2 Urban Regions of Western Europe. (*Source:* Reprinted from *U.S. News and World Report*, October 29, 1979, p. 74, © 1979 by U.S. News and World Report, Inc.)

were added to urban places in Germany as a result of forced movement of 16 to 18 million ethnic Germans from Eastern Europe after World War II. The ethnic French and some Algerians moved from Algeria to France as a result of the war in Algeria. The breakup of other overseas empires has led to migration to the appropriate European country, for example, West Indians, Indians, and Pakistanis to England, Moluccans and others from Indonesia to the Netherlands, and Africans from the Belgian

Congo (Zaire) to Belgium. More recently people from Southern Europe have moved to cities throughout Western Europe to take jobs largely as service personnel in hotels, restaurants, and large buildings but also other low status jobs such as in construction.

These recent migrations have led to a change in the ethnic makeup of many European cities. West Indians are now a major minority in London, Birmingham, and several other English industrial cities. Pakistanis form a minority group in Oslo, Syrians in several Swedish cities. Italians form major minority groups in several German and Swiss cities. These populations have had an impact on the culture and spatial character of the urban places in which they settled and are changing the urban character of a number of cities in Western Europe.

Nature of the Western European City

The Western European city differs from cities in other parts of the world settled by European immigrants, primarily because the settlements are hundreds of years older. For instance, the average European city predates most American cities by several centuries. Many cities still reflect influences of previous peoples or civilizations, including the Romans; most had their origin in preindustrial periods. Thus, the present shape of the town, the size of the buildings, and the street pattern reflect the needs, technology, and culture of people when agriculture, handicrafts, local markets, and limited trade were the major economic functions. Streets were narrow and winding footpaths or roads were made for humans or animal drawn vehicles. The major characteristics of the Western European city can be summarized as follows, with the North American (United States and Canada) city serving as the basis of comparison.

Low Building Profile

Most European cities have buildings averaging three to five stories in height. They were constructed before technology permitted the skyscraper, a building type possible only when the elevator was available to carry people and freight up many stories, and when reinforced steel and concrete building techniques permitted the support of much more weight and, subsequently, higher buildings (Fig. 3.3). A number of cities, including Paris, had legal restrictions on building height and other structural characteristics; often buildings had to be lower than the dome of the cathedral. As mentioned above, inventions, including the elevator (1857), telephone (1876), and the steel-frame skyscraper (1875), facilitated centralization of company headquarters in modern office buildings in the CBDs of major cities. Since 1850, and particularly since World War II, taller buildings have gradually penetrated most large West European cities to house various service functions and to serve as apartment buildings. This vertical development was accelerated by the rebuilding of many cities destroyed during World War II, notably Hamburg, Essen, Rotterdam, and London. Today the low profile is broken by buildings of 10 to 50 or more stories in most large cities, both downtown and in the suburbs. Such buildings are not universally welcomed by the population, as indi-

Nature of the Western European City   93

Figure 3.1 Major Cities of Western Europe (*Source:* Data derived from United Nations, Department of Economic and Social Affairs. *Global Review of Human Settlements, Statistical Annex,* published by Pergamon Press, New York, 1976.)

cated by the controversy surrounding the building of the Post Office Tower Building in London and the tall building which interferes with the traditional view of the Arc de Triomphe in Paris (Fig. 3.4).

Compact Form

The Western European city usually occupies much less total area than a comparable American city with the same population. Historically, workers lived in close proximity to shops and businesses. Foot and carriage traffic permitted residents to be near those places they frequented. The compactness is most evident in the high densities of housing; most people live in apartments rather than single family homes. Streets are narrow, and open "green spaces" around residences are few or nonexistent. A departure from the compactness is a recent trend of large factories to utilize extensive amounts of land in suburbs and satellite towns rather than in the city proper. The sprawl associated with the less intensely developed rural-urban fringe of the American city is often lacking or very poorly represented in Western Europe. Planning practices traditionally have resulted in a well defined urban-rural land use boundary. There are exceptions to the compact city characteristic, especially in residential parts of a city such as Stockholm, which is spread out more like an American city.

94 Chapter 3, Cities of Western Europe

Figure 3.4 Paris from the roof of the Galeris Lafeyette department store, illustrating the low building profiles and the Eiffel Tower in the background. (L. Sommers)

Dominance of Multiple Family Residence

The multiple family residence dominates the Western European city. Families live in the third to fifth floors in downtown buildings as well as in apartment buildings in various parts of the city. This feature is a sharp difference between European and American cities. As income permits, the Western European increasingly aspires to the single family home, but high costs and insufficient supplies both of available homes and of the space planned for such by governments are currently available to meet demand.

Combination of Residence and Work

The most common pattern of land use in the CBD of the Western European city is for the first, second, and often the third floors to be occupied by retail, wholesale, handicraft, or service functions, with the operators of a business living on the same floor as their business or the floor above (Fig. 3.5). This pattern exists to some extent in other parts of the city but is less characteristic in areas dominated by newer apartment buildings. The European psyche seems to be more attuned to high density living than the American psyche.

Figure 3.5 Street scene in Newcastle, England. Note the row houses with business establishments on the first floor and apartments on the second and third floors. The chimney pots are typical. (L. Sommers)

Greater Use of Public Transportation

The compact city, high population densities, apartment buildings, and low income levels have facilitated widespread development and use of public transportation in Western Europe. Surface transportation has often been supplemented by underground facilities, especially in such large cities as London, Paris, Hamburg, Munich, Stockholm, and Oslo. The narrow streets do not lend themselves to large scale automobile use; parking space is often limited both on and off the streets.

Less Distinct Zonation of Land Use Types

The concentric zone or sector theories (see Chapter 1) only partially fit the land use patterns of most Western European cities. Land uses are usually quite mixed as a result of the preindustrial age of many cities and towns. The CBDs of the largest cities have readily identifiable retail, financial, entertainment, office building, and government and public building districts, but the recent large industrial and wholesale sectors are generally located outside the city where more space is available (Fig. 3.6).

Lack of Slums but Appearance of Ghettos

Though some portions of Western European cities are poorer than sections of other cities in terms of housing quality, the zones of deterioration or slums usually associated

Figure 3.6 The central portion of Düsseldorf, West Germany, depicting the Autostrasse, modernistic theater, park, high rise office buildings, and apartments. (Courtesy German Information Center)

with the U.S. city are generally lacking. One of the major reasons for this phenomenon is the more homogeneous character of the population. However, in recent years ghettos have developed in selected areas, which are attributed in part to the large scale influx of black West Indians to British cities; Algerians to France, especially Paris; and Italians to cities in Switzerland and Germany. The equivalent of New York's Harlem can now be found in London, Birmingham, and several other English industrial cities, and Italian enclaves are quite evident in such cities as Zurich and Wolfsburg.

Frequency of Public Parks

Public parks have been placed frequently throughout the Western European city even in and near the CBD. Often they are adjacent to city walls and properties of royal families, both past and present, and attest to an appreciation for nature and preservation of the physical environment. In earlier periods, most parks could only be reached on foot or by public transportation. The main government buildings, historical buildings, churches and cathedrals, and monuments often have park areas attached to them. A central square containing some park land is a feature found in most cities. Larger parks, zoos, and various types of recreational areas are usually found in the outer parts of the city.

Brick, Cement, and Mortar as Dominant Building Materials

The lack of wood for building purposes and the ravages of fire over the centuries have meant that most Western European cities are constructed of brick, cement, and mortar. The major exceptions are the single family homes in forested areas such as Scandinavia and in the small cities and villages in mountainous areas like the Alps and Pyrenees.

In summary, the Western European city has quite a different face from its North American counterpart. Age is a principal factor, but ethnic and environmental differences also play major roles in the appearance of the European city. Politics, war, fire, religion, culture, and economics also have played a role. Land is expensive due to its scarcity, and capital for private enterprise development has been insufficient, so government-built housing is quite common. Land ownership has been fragmented over the years due to inheritance systems that often split land among sons. Prices for real estate and rent have been government controlled in many countries. Planning and zoning codes as well as the development of utilities are determined by government policies. These are charactristics of a region with a long history, dense population, scarce land, and strong government control of urban land development.

The most salient post-World War II trend has been to "Americanize" the Western European city. This process was made possible first by the rebuilding of war-ravaged cities and second by the greater affluence of the average postwar European, which meant more money was available for housing, for motor vehicles, and for recreation. Greater mobility has brought more American-type characteristics to the European city, such as wider streets, more parking space, and more commuting from outskirts, nearby cities, and scattered urban developments. The urban fringe and string developments along major highways out from the cities have grown rapidly during the last 20 years. The tall building of cement, steel, and glass, that is, the skyscraper, continues to penetrate at an increasing rate in all parts of major cities in the region (Fig. 3.7).

Major Urbanization Types in Western Europe

The Large City

The Industrial Revolution and subsequent population growth ushered in the large city to Western Europe in a major way. Today almost every country has one or more cities with a population over 1 million; the metropolitan type of urban settlement has become a dominant force in the daily lives of an increasing number of inhabitants. London and Paris are selected to examine the characteristics of many large cities in Europe.

London: A World City The city, located in the London Basin at the head of the Thames River estuary, was an important city in Roman times but was probably settled even much earlier. The city's site and situation offer many advantages which have helped London become the major city of England and indeed one of the leading cities in the world. It was the first bridging point on the Thames; high ground just to the

Figure 3.7   Two-level main thoroughfare in Brussels, Belgium, showing low- and high-rise building profiles. (L. Sommers)

north of the river made it quite defensible. Nearby alluvial gravel and sand deposits provided building materials and a good water supply; the area was lightly wooded and could be cultivated easily for agriculture. The lower Thames is navigable for oceangoing ships and facilitated the city's easy access to the North Sea, the Atlantic Ocean, and the world. London has long been a leader in entrepôt trade, as raw materials imported from all over the world were classified, processed, and then reexported as finished goods to other parts of Europe, the colonial empire, and elsewhere on all continents.

London had reached a population of 225,000 by 1600, 500,000 by 1700, and 1,117,000 by 1800. At the beginning of the nineteenth century the city began to grow very rapidly with the stimulation provided by the Industrial Revolution and the beginnings of global commercial ties. The city was becoming a major land transport and trade center for England. By 1850, Greater London (conurbation) had reached a population of 2,365,000; by 1900 it had grown to 6,590,000 and by 1950 to 8,350,000. The 1974 population of Greater London was only 7,167,000, however, a result of the recent major growth areas outside the conurbation and the migration of a number of Londoners to cities out of the city proper. The total urban region of London contained nearly 11 million inhabitants by 1980.

Greater London covers 610 sq. mi. (1580 sq. km.) and has an average population density of 11,751 people per square mile (4536 per square kilometer). The city can be divided into zones, each with certain distinguishing characteristics. The Central Area or CBD is bounded by the main railway stations which were built during the railway age of the late 1800s (Fig. 3.8). The heart of London covers only about one-hundredth of the total built-up area of the city. Only about 25,000 people live in the CBD, but 1.25 million find employment here during the day, largely in retail stores, as office workers in finance, government, publishing, and advertising, and as service personnel in hotels and restaurants. There is some small scale manufacturing in the central city as well as a large part of England's cultural life in the form of museums, concert halls, public buildings, and theaters. Most workers commute by train, bus, underground, and automobile to the city center from the outer metropolitan area, which adds to the congestion, itself one of London's major problems.

Surrounding the Central Area is Inner London, or the inner ring, an irregular area 3 to 4 mi. (4.8 to 6.4 km.) wide. Houses and buildings in this area are more than 100 years old, most being built during the nineteenth century. Most inhabitants of Inner London, both rich and poor, live in apartments; here the population density is the highest, more than 23,575 per square mile (9,100 per square kilometer). Poorer residents live largely in the south and east, while the more affluent professional and managerial categories are in the north and west. Although Inner London is mainly a residential area, there are many small industrial workshops throughout the region. Industries are also found along the Thames, particularly on the south bank.

The Outer Zone has developed during the twentieth century, primarily between the two world wars. Population densities are lower as there are more single family houses and more open spaces. Many commute to the Central Area for work. There are frequent shops and factories in the Outer Zone. Industrial concentrations appear along the Thames, near Heathrow Airport, and scattered throughout the area, as in

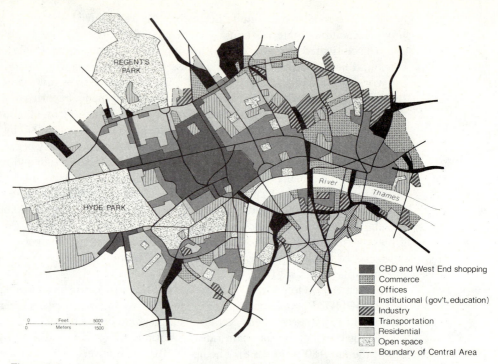

Figure 3.8 London: Land Use in the CBD. (*Source:* Adapted from Peter Hall, "General Introduction to the Excursions in Central London," 30th International Geographical Congress, London, 1964.)

the Lea Valley. The important dock area extends 10 mi. (16 km.) downstream from London Bridge, as the docks were built largely on the tidelands and marshy regions of the Thames. The dredged Thames channel can handle oceangoing freighters, and locks have been built to cope with the tidal range of 8 ft. (2.4 m.) or more. The docks handle a wide variety of goods and have resulted in a complex association of warehousing and industries in the east end of London. Most docks near the central city have been abandoned.

Surrounding Outer London is the Green Belt, an area of parkland and green open space that was proposed as such as early as 1890 but not implemented until 1935. The object was to assure that a belt of land approximately 10 mi. (16 km.) wide surrounding the city would be open to the public for recreation and zoned against the anticipated urban expansion. This belt has since been encroached upon from both within and without, but it remains a definite break in concentrated urban development between London and those suburban villages, towns, and industries beyond the Green Belt. The fast-growing region beyond the Green Belt, called the Outer Metropolitan Area, extends as much as 50 mi. (80 km.) from the center of London and contains the new towns and expanded towns which were planned to take some of the pressure and congestion from Central London (Fig. 3.9).

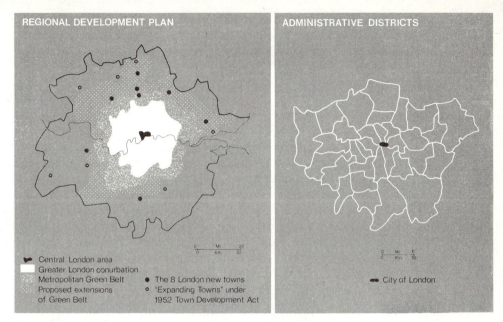

Figure 3.9 London: Regional Development Plan. (*Source:* Left: Adapted from *The South East: A Framework for Planning,* London, 1968; Right: adapted from Arthur E. Smailes, "The Site, Growth, and Changing Face of London," in R. Clayton, ed., *The Geography of London,* London: George Philip & Son, 1964, p. 4.) Reprinted with permission.

The major problems of the London region are centered around the large demand for labor of all types in Central London, the decay in Inner London, congestion of the major traffic arteries, and the unseemly growth of Outer London. As Peter Hall indicates in his *London 2000,* the major question is, "Shall London grow?" The pressure on London comes from within and without. Limitations on office space development as well as the out-migration to new towns has permitted the development of a "hotel boom." The skyscraper is also a distinct feature in the city's profile. The number of tourists visiting London now exceeds 7 million annually and overtaxes the hotels and other facilities at peak periods. The surplus of jobs in central London, inadequate housing, and pressures on transportation cause major congestion problems on the streets, buses, underground, railways, and taxis. If the growth of central city employment opportunities is not controlled in some way, the development of new and expanded towns is seen as only a partial solution to London's problems.

Paris: France's Primate City The French capital is a good example of a primate city concept, as Paris completely dominates the political, economic, cultural, and social life of France. Greater Paris contains 9.9 million people or 19 percent of the total population of France and is the eleventh largest agglomeration in the world. The central city is excessively crowded, and the outer districts have developed with little planning or organization. The average resident density in Inner Paris is 91,000 people per square mile (35,160 people per square kilometer), over three times the density of Inner London. About 87 percent of the area of Paris is covered with buildings, contrasted to 73 percent in London and 70 percent in New York. The daytime population density of central Paris exceeds 200,000 people per square mile (77,220 per square kilometer).

Paris was first developed on an island in the center of the Seine River called Île de la Cité. The island provided a bridging point on the Seine and was a defendable settlement for early occupants. By the Middle Ages the city had grown and extended to both banks of the river, and about 1200 King Philip Augustus built the first circular wall. Additional walls were built successively farther out in the seventeenth century, in 1789, and in 1840; these have influenced the street pattern and overall shape of the city. Only in the twentieth century have suburban expansion and tentacles of growth along major radiating highways taken place. Paris grew to be the major city of France despite not being a major ocean port, nor having a significant natural resource such as coal on which to base growth. It was first made the capital of France temporarily in the tenth century and then permanently by the twelfth century. This provided a continual impetus for growth and hampered development of regional capitals in France, leading to the popular phrase "Paris and the French Desert"—indicating a comparative lack of urban and cultural development outside of Paris (Fig. 3.10).

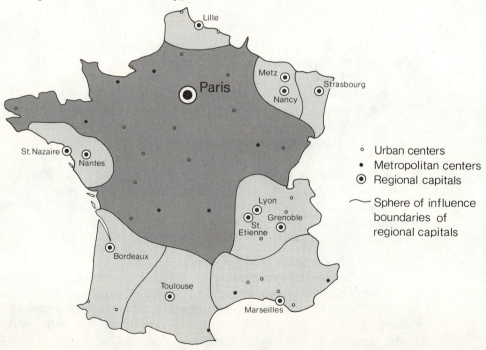

Figure 3.10   Paris: Regional Influence. (*Source:* Adapted from *France, Town and Country Environment Planning,* New York: French Embassy.)

The population of Paris grew from 200,000 in 1300 to 500,000 by 1700, to 1 million in 1850 and about 2,714,000 in 1900. The metropolitan region now has nearly 10 million in the conurbation (Fig. 3.11). Rapid growth took place after the Industrial Revolution, since much of the industry of France was concentrated in the Paris Basin. Paris occupies a central site in this rich agricultural region and is the focus of most of the roads, railways, and waterways of France. Through the impetus of the political strength derived from being the capital city, industrial, intellectual, cultural, recreational, and government activities have also concentrated in Greater Paris.

The early walls of Paris have given the city a roughly circular form. About two-thirds of the city is on the north or right bank of the Seine. The central core is very compact and crowded with narrow streets except for the major boulevards and traffic circles, which were superimposed by the Haussmann plan in the nineteenth century. Baron Haussmann was responsible for planning the system of boulevards and places or traffic circles in the mid-1800s. These boulevards add to the attractiveness of Paris but have not facilitated traffic flow; in many ways they are impediments. As in London,

Figure 3.11 Paris: Historical Urban Growth. (*Source:* Compiled by the author.)

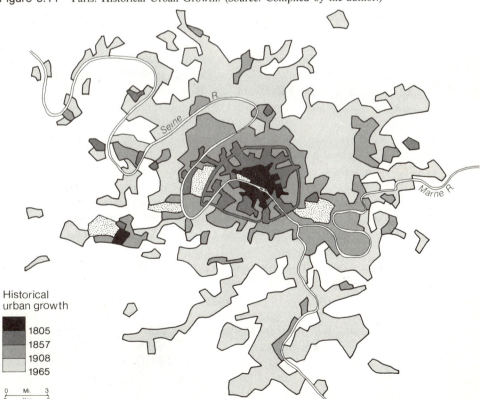

the main railway stations, outlining the limits of the CBD, were built during the railway-building age of the 1800s and were built on the edge of Central Paris in that period. On the right bank are found the shops, banks, government buildings, historical buildings and monuments, office buildings, hotels, restaurants, foreign embassies and consuls, small-scale handicraft industries, and apartments. On the left bank is the Latin Quarter with the famous Sorbonne University, student quarters, bookshops, theaters, government buildings, publishing firms, shops, restaurants, hotels, and much poorer-quality housing. The only large open space in the entire core area is the Tuileries Gardens.

Outside the central core is the inner ring of suburbs, which is a continuous built-up area largely completed during the nineteenth century. This ring has concentrations of industry along the Seine, railways, and canals with much heavy industry including engineering, automobiles, and chemicals. The area also has a residential emphasis but is less crowded than the central core. The Inner Suburbs lack adequate planned development of transportation and other public services; there are also no strongly organized suburban core areas, as the population must depend on railways, the subway and automobiles to move them to the central city for shopping or to the many nearby industrial regions for work.

The next zone, the Outer Suburban Ring, is a series of noncontinuous suburbs and housing developments. After World War II, large apartment complexes called "grands ensembles" were built with access to major highways and railways and located near existing towns or in undeveloped open space. The three major airports are in this zone: Orly, Le Bourget, and the newest, Charles de Gaulle. Industry, a considerable part of which has moved out from Paris in decentralization efforts, is scattered throughout the area. The Outer Suburban Ring still contains a considerable amount of green open space, largely agricultural land and forest, which provides recreation potential for the millions in the Paris region. The outer suburbs have mushroomed rapidly, and with the predominantly young age structure of residents, growth will likely continue. The dispersed population and settlements depend heavily upon mobility via roads and railways for travel to jobs, shops, and the amenities of the central city.

Among the serious problems of the Paris agglomeration are congestion, renewal needs of old sections, overloading of commuting transport facilities, inadequate public services, insufficient housing, insufficient decentralization of industry from Paris, and overconcentration of power and influence within one urban agglomeration in France. A "Schema Directeur," or master plan, was proposed in 1965 and subsequently revised to deal with these problems (Fig. 3.12). It is a comprehensive, innovative plan which incorporates developments and changes in the entire Seine River Valley and proposes to meet the needs of the area by the year 2000. The plan includes transport improvements, industrial parks, new-town proposals, and recreational land use designations which would help put some order in the future urban developments of Greater Paris. Unfortunately the master plan does not include the central city, where improvements are more difficult to implement and coordinate. The main problems of Central Paris are the exorbitant costs of land, the lack of consistent control over skyscraper-type developments, and the difficulties and costs of controlling increased traffic, noise, and pol-

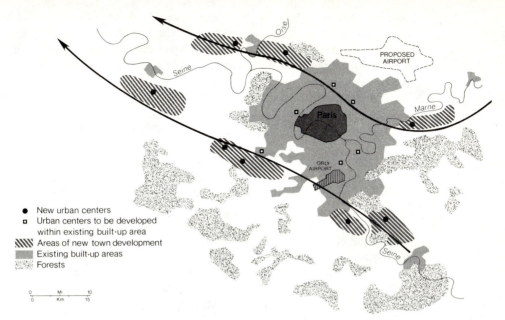

Figure 3.12 Paris: Master Plan. (*Source: France,* New York: French Embassy, Press and Information Division.)

lution. Whether current efforts can overcome the problems caused by lack of planning in the past remains to be seen.

Other Large Cities

London and Paris are dominant urban centers in Western Europe, but there are a number of other large and important ones. Their character and significance differ from region to region depending on age, history, natural setting, previous natural and human disasters, economic function, culture, and the goals of the people and their governments. Cities of Northern Europe, including Stockholm and Copenhagen, are modern appearing, with much water space and wide major thoroughfares. Buildings were originally constructed of wood, but major fires have meant several rebuildings of the central city over historical time. Most cities of West Central Europe suffered war destruction, especially during the two world wars, and recently have been rebuilt with much use of steel and glass skyscrapers in the central city. This trend is exemplified by Hamburg, West Berlin, Essen, Rotterdam, and Amsterdam. The larger cities of Mediterranean Europe, including Rome, Milan, Athens, Lisbon, and Madrid, with walls, gateways, and the dominating cathedrals reflect the influence of the Greeks, Romans, and Moors. Some major characteristics of the remaining cities of Western Europe whose population exceeds 1 million are examined below.

East and West Berlin: A Divided City   Berlin was the major governmental, industrial, commercial, intellectual, and cultural center of prewar Germany. The Potsdam agreement divided the city into unequal sections based on prewar functions. For instance, the major part of the former CBD was placed in East Berlin (population 1 million); West Berlin (2 million) has had to develop a new CBD. West Berlin is physically isolated from the rest of West Germany and has had many economic problems in the postwar period as a result. A wall erected in 1961 now separates East and West Berlin; it is a major barrier to movement between the two cities. Both cities remain major cities in their respective parts of divided Germany. Their character reflects the impact of a political decision on changing the nature and function of a major city.

Copenhagen and Stockholm: Dominating Cities in Scandinavia Copenhagen (1.4 million), a strategic and charming capital city situated on the Straits of Oresund and guarding the entrance to the Baltic Sea, completely dominates the political, economic, social, and cultural life of Denmark. The city was built around its port facilities, which include an international free port. Industry has added concentric rings of growth around the old city, and Copenhagen is now expanding out along major highways in a star-shaped pattern. The growth of the city in narrow bands along highways and railways is called the "finger principle" of planning. Copenhagen is a major tourist center with a number of attractions such as the delightful downtown park called Tivoli and Hans Christian Anderson's Little Mermaid statue on the waterfront. Copenhagen is a prime example of a primate city.

Stockholm (1.3 million) has an attractive location on the entrance to Lake Malar and is built on a series of islands and the rocky mainland facing the Baltic Sea. The city thus has a port function on the Baltic and is the capital and the major industrial, financial, and cultural center for the nation. The surrounding water and channels have been instrumental in its being labeled the "Venice of the North." The city has been planned since 1640 and often serves as a world model of desirable urban planning. In recent years the inner city has been redeveloped and new towns have been built as well to help solve some severe transportation and housing problems the city faced. The central city today connects other business, industrial, and residential nuclei by underground and surface mass transportation. Each citizen is within five minutes' walking distance of efficient public transportation. Stockholm retains many styles of old and new architecture in its palaces, 42 bridges, Town Hall, and other government, apartment, and business buildings. A regional planning agency exerts some influence in the development of Stockholm and 45 surrounding municipalities.

Madrid: A Centralized Political City The city (4 million) has no natural site advantages but has become Spain's major city through the centralization of political power, which in turn led to it becoming the major transportation, industrial, commercial, and cultural center of Spain. King Philip II selected Madrid for his capital in 1561, and this centrally located city has been the dominant city in Spain since that time. Its relative recent development compared with that of other European cities gives it a more modern appearance. Madrid's basin location contributes to air pollution problems during stagnant air periods, pollution due to heavy automobile traffic and industrial emissions.

Rome and Vienna: Historical Cities of Previous Empires Rome (3.5 million) has capitalized on its early start in the Roman period to maintain its importance in Italy. Besides being the capital of Italy, it contains the Vatican City, the world focus of Catholicism. Early Rome was built on hills but has since expanded over the swampy terrain which dominates much of the surrounding area. The city ranks as one of the world's most attractive cities, with its ancient palaces and monuments, churches, fountains, shops, cafes, parks, and tree-lined boulevards. The Vatican City attracts thousands of tourists annually to Rome.

For almost 1000 years Vienna (1.9 million) was a capital of the outer regions of the Holy Roman Empire and later the Hapsburg Empire. It was built to serve the needs of a much larger population during the historical past and has had serious problems adjusting to being the capital of present-day Austria (population 7.5 million). The city occupies an excellent site on the Danube River and is situated between the Alps and the plains of the Danube Valley. Vienna is the largest city, except for West Berlin, near the communist borders of Europe, and because of its location has served as the site for several East-West political meetings. Since World War II the city has assumed an international role because of its location and because it functions as the headquarters of the International Atomic Energy Agency, OPEC, and other organizations. The inner city is bounded by the Danube and the famous boulevard called the Ring. Vienna contains many famous historical buildings, palaces, gardens, and theaters and opera houses. It also is the country's major industrial center and has a diversified manufacturing base.

Other Major Nonprimate Large Cities Barcelona (population 2 million), Amsterdam (1 million), Milan (6.5 million), Turin (2 million), Naples (4 million), Birmingham (2.9 million), Hamburg (2.2 million), and Munich (1.9 million) are eight additional major European industrial cities with a population of more than 1 million. All have developed rapidly in the postwar period by catering to the many industrial and commercial needs of modern, urban technological societies. Their CBDs are heavily dominated by the glass and steel buildings of corporation headquarters which affect industry throughout the respective countries. As with most large cities, these cities are also plagued by the related problems of traffic congestion and air pollution.

Urban Agglomerations

With the high degree of urbanization that characterizes much of Western Europe, one would expect clusters or concentrations of cities. The most important clusters that exist are found in the Southern Pennines, in the Scottish Lowlands, in Belgium-Northern France, in Randstadt-Holland, in the Rhine-Ruhr, on the Swiss Plateau, and in the Po Valley. These areas enjoy the advantages of available coal or water power, locations on favorable land and water transportation networks, and proximity to large national and regional markets. Each city in the cluster began initially as a small market center but expanded in size, functions, and influence during the industrial period. In all the above countries, the clusters of cities are coalescing into a megalopolitan region where the boundaries of political units and hinterlands are sometimes hard to delimit. Rand-

108　Chapter 3, Cities of Western Europe

stadt and the Rhine-Ruhr are discussed in some detail, as they illustrate the character and some of the problems of the Western Europe urban agglomerations.

Randstadt　A high degree of urbanization exists in the western Netherlands between the Ijsselmeer and the estuaries of the Rhine. A more or less continuous string of cities arranged in a rough "c" shape extends from Dordrecht through Rotterdam, The Hague, Leiden, Haarlem, Amsterdam, Hilversum, and Utrecht (Fig. 3.13). Collectively these cities are called the Randstadt ("rim city") by the Dutch since their loca-

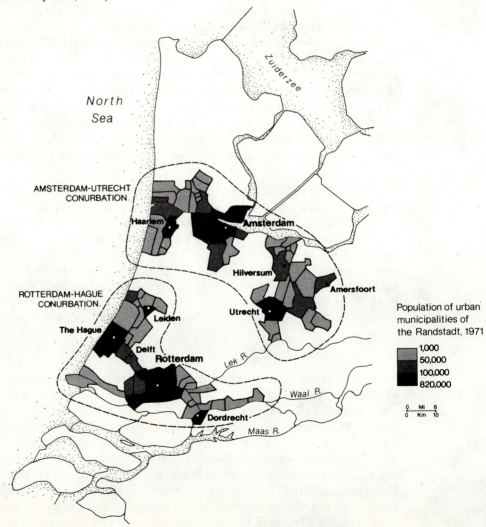

Figure 3.13　Randstadt Conurbation. (*Source:* From *Randstad Holland* by G.R.P. Lawrence, © Oxford University Press, 1973.)

tions resemble the rim of a saucer. The cities are surrounded by green areas which are largely agricultural polders, often referred to as the "greenheart." The provinces containing these cities comprise about 46 percent of the population of the Netherlands but only about 20 percent of the urban area. The cities have favorable water transportation locations with access to both the Rhine River and the North Sea as well as easy highway and railroad connections with all of Western Europe. Despite government attempts to decentralize industrial development into eastern and northern regions of the country, population and urban growth continues more rapidly within and between cities of the Randstadt than elsewhere.

A number of problems face the Randstadt; some are serious, including potential flood danger when unusual North Sea storm and high-tide conditions overflow the protecting dikes and seawalls and sea water penetrates into coastal domestic, industrial, and agricultural water supplies. Additional problems faced are building site difficulties because of a lack of bedrock for construction or foundation materials to provide stability for large buildings, the universal need for drainage of excess water, and the encroachment of urban development on the greenheart area, a problem because a limited amount of open space is available to the urban populations for recreation. Utilizing more land for urban expansion decreases the amount of available agricultural land, which is one of the principal bases of the economy of the Netherlands. Further problems facing Randstadt are increasing traffic congestion, increased air and water pollution, shortages of available labor for burgeoning industry and commercial, retail, and wholesale activities, and higher land costs for new buildings as well as construction, maintenance, and service costs.

The major challenge facing planners and politicians is how to control the future development of the Randstadt while still meeting the national needs of industry, agriculture, transport, housing, services, and recreation. Further encroachment upon the greenheart is deemed undesirable, yet the pressure continues. New towns have been developed, including Zotemeer, which has removed some pressure from The Hague, but the sites of these new settlements eliminate agricultural land and green open space in the process. Adjusting the plans of individual communities for the good of the region and the country will require tolerance and ingenuity.

Rhine-Ruhr Agglomeration This agglomeration is one of the most important urbanized industrial districts in Western Europe and the world (Fig. 3.14). The region contains about 10 million inhabitants (one-sixth of West Germany's total) and 13 cities of more than 200,000, including four of the top seven cities in West Germany: Cologne (832,000), Essen (674,000), Düsseldorf (632,000), and Dortmund (628,000). The excellent Ruhr coal resource was the original impetus for urban growth and still provides much of the energy for industry in the area. Besides coal mining, engineering, chemicals, and textiles are major industries. The region occupies a prime location in West Germany and Western Europe. Since the development of intense industrialization in Europe, the Ruhr has been the key to a successful economy in West Germany, the European Economic Community, and all of Western Europe.

The urban problems faced by the Rhine-Ruhr region are similar to those of the

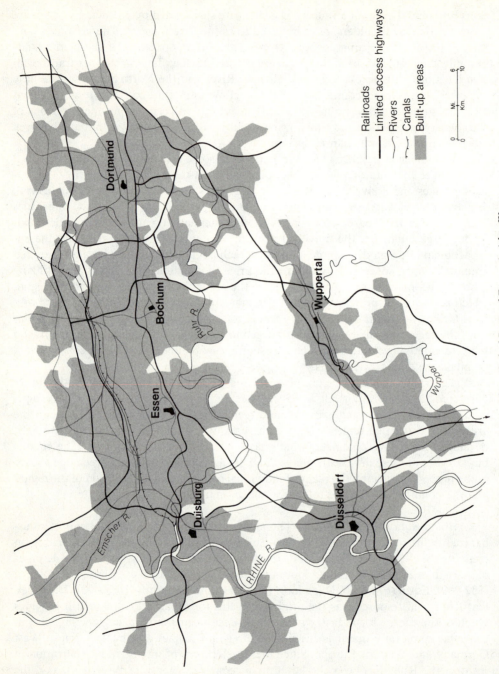

Figure 3.14 Rhine-Ruhr Conurbation. (*Source:* Adapted from *Oxford Regional Economic Atlas, Western Europe*, London: Oxford University Press, 1971.)

Randstadt. The major difference is a much greater emphasis upon coal and heavy industry with the accompanying problems of large space requirements for factories, the reclamation of surface coal mining areas, the huge water needs for coal mining and for chemical, engineering, and textile-type industries, and the tremendous potential for land, air, water, and noise pollution associated with heavy industrial activities. Within the region additional problems are the declining quality of coal, increasing costs, and a transportation system in need of modernization.

The region's projected population is expected to exceed 12 million by the year 2000. As the Rhine-Ruhr region grows, along with cities in France, Belgium, the Netherlands, and West Germany, there is the increasing potential of one huge megalopolis in West Central Europe. Growth will create increasing congestion and associated transportation, housing, recreation, industrial, agricultural, and public services problems throughout the area. Plans for individual cities in the Rhine-Ruhr will have to be reconciled with the needs and problems of individual countries, the region, the European Economic Community, and the continent. Rhine-Ruhr development brings into focus the problems of coordinating policies and plans among political units within a region and country as well as between countries and within international bodies representing groups of countries. For instance, pollution of the Rhine River has major consequences on practices and policies in the several nations through which it flows. Millions in France, West Germany, and the Netherlands depend upon the Rhine for transport, as a source of domestic and industrial water, and as a medium to carry away wastes. An international body has been created to deal with economic and environmental problems of the Rhine, but to date it lacks the power to be effective. Among the more pressing problems are finding ways to resolve conflicting and competing uses of land as the Rhine-Ruhr agglomeration continues to expand in population and area.

The Medium-Sized City

A number of important cities in Western Europe have fewer than 500,000 inhabitants. They are often regional capitals, industrial centers, exchange centers, or ports that have developed as a result of specific situational or resource advantages. As mentioned above, more than 320 cities in Western Europe have between 100,000 and 500,000 inhabitants and a still larger number have less than 100,000.

An example of a medium-sized city is Newcastle-upon-Tyne, England. The city has a population exceeding 300,000 in the city proper (1.1 million in the conurbation) and is the regional capital and principal port of northeast England. Newcastle is an old city which owes its growth to being a major port and industrial center after the discovery of nearby coal, a major source of power during the Industrial Revolution. Newcastle provided London with coal as early as the fourteenth century and during the nineteenth-century heyday of the steamship shipped coal to coaling stations and ports throughout the world. Local coal production has declined in importance, but the industry, port, and regional function of Newcastle remains significant. Offshore oil and natural gas developments in the North Sea during the 1970s have accentuated growth in Newcastle and surrounding cities. Oil is coming ashore just to the south of Teesside, and materials for drilling and production are funneling in and out of the port facilities along the mouth of the Tyne River.

The location of Newcastle is doubly advantageous as it is situated on the navigable mouth of the Tyne as well as being near the coalfields of northeast England. A variety of industries have developed, including shipbuilding and repair, machinery and metals, and chemicals. Newcastle and the surrounding industrial region were hard hit by the Depression of the 1920s and 1930s, especially by declines in the nearby coal industry. The area received government assistance as a "development area" after 1945, and Newcastle benefited considerably. Lighter industries have been established in designated "industrial estates" or parks, poor housing areas have been renovated, the street and highway system within and surrounding the city has been vastly improved, a new university has been established, and an impressive civic center was developed. The city still has high unemployment and severe urban renewal problems, but the government assistance program, the innovative urban renewal plan, and the economic resurgence sparked by the offshore oil and natural gas give the hope of coping with its many problems. Within Western Europe there are numerous other medium sized cities with histories similar to Newcastle and whose problems of adjusting to new and different economic conditions are challenges to urban and regional planners.

European Patterns of Life in Small Urban Places

In every country of Western Europe, large numbers of people live in small cities with populations between 5,000 and 20,000. In France, for instance, 533 such urban centers play a significant role in the country's economic, political, and social life. One out of ten French citizens lives in these small places. The populations of French small cities are increasing while the populations of large and medium-sized cities are remaining stable or decreasing. Those migrating from rural to urban areas will most often make the small city their first stop. The creation of new jobs through the establishment of a new factory is an example of what will draw laborers to a town. Many newcomers are young and mobile; the shopkeepers and property owners are usually older and more likely to be residents with longer histories in the city.

One of the principal features of life in a French small town is the proximity of residential neighborhoods to places of work. Most people prefer to live in single family homes, so the apartment building is a much less important type of residence than in the larger French or European city. The small urban center usually consists of several distinct sections, including upper, middle, and lower class residential areas; a CBD with shops, restaurants, theaters, the town square with government buildings, and the church or cathedral; and an industrial sector often with only one major factory and several small scale enterprises.

The French small towns can be classified by the nature and importance of their major economic activity. Most towns in eastern, northeastern, and northern France may be classified as industrial. The major economic advantages these towns enjoy over the large city are lower labor costs and a more stable, often nonunionized, labor force. The government is encouraging Paris companies, including textile firms, to relocate in small towns in the Paris Basin. Most of the French small cities are based on a single industry such as textiles, leather processing, and cutlery. Of the 533 small towns with a population between 5,000 and 20,000, only 41 have more than one industry. This overdependence on one industry or company may cause a problem if the company fails or does not provide satisfactory working conditions or pay.

The remaining small towns, mostly located in the South and West, can be classified as nonindustrial and agricultural. They serve as government and marketing centers for predominantly rural districts. Others are supported by spas, resorts, fishing, and military bases, which are the focal point for the social, cultural, and political life of the community.

The survival of the small towns of France in a society that emphasizes bigness remains rather precarious. To counter possibly uncertain futures, the French Industrial Development Agency has implemented a system of cash grants to create better jobs, improve the economic activity, and provide better community services for small towns. By 1977, about 10 percent of the small towns had signed government contracts to improve their community life. The small town plays an important role in a country and in this light it is the goal of both national and local governments to preserve their existence and make them better places to live and work.

The definition of a village varies from country to country but usually is an urban agglomeration of less than 2000 to 2500. Sometimes lower populations are used, as in Norway, where 200 or more persons defines a village. The specific limits depend on the density of the population and the historical or traditional settlement characteristics of a region. The small village is more common in central and southern Europe, since farmers live in villages rather than on isolated farmsteads as in the case in Scandinavia and most of the British Isles. In additon to small populations, villages usually do not have their own government but are part of a larger commune (township) or minor civil division. The village normally has a few stores, perhaps a small industry, and selected services, but is an important ingredient in the total settlement fabric of a country.

Vollen, an example of a village in Norway, is located on Oslo Fjord about 30 mi. (48 km.) south of Oslo, the capital city. It has a small harbor and a marina, and its origin is due largely to its formerly being a stopping point of a passenger boat service on Oslo Fjord. The village is now a residential community of several hundred people, many of whom work in Oslo, the cement factory in nearby Slemmestad, or the commune (township) government and trade center of Asker. There are a small boat-building and boat repair industry, a small furniture factory, a post office, school, library, limited-service-type hotel, grocery store, and a small commercial gardening enterprise based largely on greenhouses. Two fjord fishing boats have their home base in Vollen.

Vollen expanded in the postwar period; most housing sites have now been developed. Further expansion is limited by lack of sufficient utility services. The village has increasingly come under the economic, shopping, and amenity dominance of both Oslo and Asker in recent years, a trend likely to continue. Buses connect Vollen with Oslo and other nearby communities hourly, while the family automobile provides additional mobility. This mobility has decreased the number of grocery stores in the village from three to one; other services are disappearing as the residents go to larger shopping centers. This small village remains a desirable residential community with the recreation and aesthetic advantages of the fjord location. The economic descriptions of Vollen are duplicated in thousands of other villages throughout the region. While not as significant in population or in economic productivity as the larger cities, such villages are integral elements in a total settlement geography.

Urban Problems Facing Western Europe

Major urban problems, some cited above, have accompanied the rapid industrialization and urbanization of Western Europe. Large scale modern industry has brought about the increasing concentration of people in central places to supply the labor for the factories, as well as the retail, wholesale, and service enterprises that emerge to serve a growing population. Along with the growth of cities, which has slowed considerably in the past two decades, there are problems in maintaining a satisfactory quality of life for all inhabitants in the face of congestion and frequently unsatisfactory working, transportation, and housing conditions and inadequate recreational facilities. Concentrations of industries near the downtowns of old commercial cores along with heavy densities of vehicle traffic often result in high levels of land, water, air, and noise pollution. Sewage disposal is often a problem, as is maintaining a reliable water supply. Rising crime rates are a problem in some cities as are the difficulties of providing adequate educational, amenity, and governmental services of all kinds.

The cities and streets of Western Europe were not built for heavy modern automobile traffic. The origin of many Western, Southern, and Central European cities goes back to Greek and Roman times and these cities have grown since that time largely without benefit of consistent planning. The result is intense traffic and housing congestion, especially in the old central parts of the city. Urban renewal is difficult because of cost, lack of space for change, popular resistance to change, and overlapping government jurisdictions, all of which make for conflicting opinions and slow or insignificant progress. The pressure for more housing and office and commercial space in downtown areas has resulted in cities growing vertically with increasing numbers of high rise buildings. Such vertical development increases the density of population and pedestrian and vehicular traffic, and it places greater stress on streets and in other downtown services and facilities.

Large scale manufacturing, retail, and wholesale activity in European cities has developed in the outskirts or in suburbs in order to find sufficient space. Decentralization creates commuting problems, since many laborers continue to live in city centers and must travel outward to work, while others living in outlying regions or suburbs find they need to travel to the central city for work as well as the amenities of entertainment and shopping. The large concentrations of heavy industry found in the Rhine-Ruhr and Midlands cause local as well as regional pollution problems. Sewage disposal and an inadequate water supply are additional local problems. Polluted air is often carried by prevailing winds over nearby countries; for instance, the sulfur which comes from burning coal and oil is so concentrated in the water of certain lakes in Scandinavia that most aquatic forms of life have been eliminated. The major source of this acid rain, a byproduct of burning fossil fuels, is from iron and steel plants and chemical and petroleum refineries in West Germany, England, and the Benelux countries.

The urban dweller faces other economic problems than those of a corporate or institutional nature, including being able to afford a satisfactory place to live, to purchase and maintain a car, especially with high gasoline costs, and to be able to meet the higher costs of food, home heating oil, repairs, recreation, and rent. Many young couples are finding it extremely difficult to rent apartments and purchase single family residences. Economic hardships are also acute for the elderly, of which there are growing numbers in many of the old, large cities.

A number of social problems are created by tensions between religious groups (Catholics and Protestants in Northern Ireland), linguistic and nationalistic differences (Belgium), and long established residents and recently arrived foreign immigrant groups. Indonesians (Moluccans) in Dutch cities; Pakistanis, Saudis, and West Indians in London; Italians and Turks in Munich and West German cities; and Algerians in Paris, Marseilles, and other French cities have been the victims of social alienation and the focus of conflicts. Discrimination in housing and employment, racism, and bloody, violent protests and clashes are not unknown. Terrorist groups in Spain, Italy, West Germany, and France have often targeted major industries, airlines, banks, and government offices in large Western European cities. While terrorists' damage to an entire city is small considering the size of the urban area, the impact on the daily urban life of residents and on seasonal tourist traffic is perceived to be much greater. Changes in the urban social geography of another sort is evidenced in cities which have experienced recent economic booms, such as that stemming from North Sea oil and gas discovery and exploration. Aberdeen, Scotland, and Stavanger, Norway, are but two ports that have experienced economic growth and an influx of petroleum company workers and firms from Texas, Oklahoma, and California. The new businesses built for and by outsiders have created some conflict with long-established residents who are less than totally satisfied with changes in the urban landscape and population.

Some Solutions to Urban Problems

Improvement in the quality of urban life in Western Europe is often difficult, costly, and slow. Nevertheless, major efforts have been made to implement change. New towns have been established to try and decrease the pressure and population density in the large city. Urban renewal efforts have been initiated, decentralization of government offices and industry to less congested areas has taken place, and efficient mass transit facilities and new highways have been implemented to move large numbers of people more effectively. Western Europe had an advantage in planning and rebuilding many cities that were destroyed in World War II.

A massive experiment in new-town development is taking place in heavily urbanized areas throughout Western Europe. The world's first comprehensive plan was developed for Greater Stockholm, which includes the new towns of Vallingby and Farsta (Fig. 3.15). King Kristian built perhaps the earliest new town at Kristiansand in southern Norway in 1641; he had to bribe people to settle there. Most of the more than 100 planned communities in Western Europe have been developed since World War II. Eight new towns were located around London beginning in 1946; by 1976 these contained 412,000 inhabitants (Fig. 3.16). Forty-four other new towns that now exist throughout the United Kingdom contain 1.7 million inhabitants. Similar new-town developments can be found around Paris and in the Netherlands, West Germany, Italy, Spain, and Switzerland.

Figure 3.15 European New Towns: CBD and apartment buildings in Vallingby, Sweden, above, and a modernistic apartment complex in Wulfen, West Germany, below. (L. Sommers)

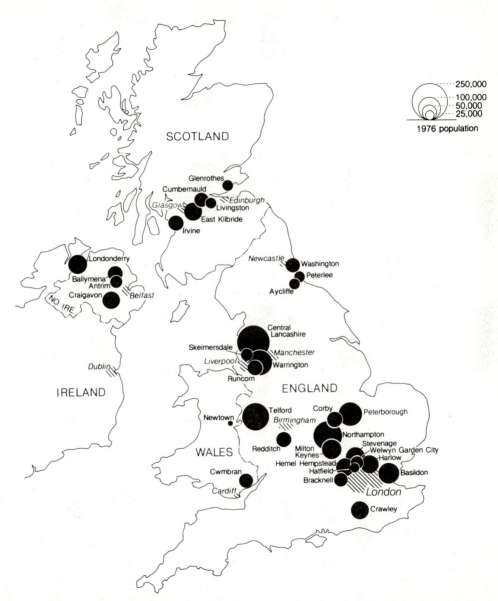

Figure 3.16 United Kingdom New Towns. [*Source:* Based on data from Pat Blake, "Britain's New Towns: Facts and Figures," *Town and Country Planning,* 45 (February 1977) 89–110.]

The success of the new towns is dependent upon the extent to which they mesh with the greater-city region or conurbation. In some cases a regional authority plans all aspects of a region from mass transportation to recreational space to all other kinds of land use. Stockholm has served as a world model of such successful planning; the oldest part of the central city, Gamla Stan, has been preserved and restored to retain its charm and contains numerous attractive restaurants, antique shops, and old residences. The design for the rest of the city is a radial mass transit system which connects new central subcenters of the city with the still newer suburban satellites. The subway, heart of the mass transportation system, has five spokes currently radiating out from the center and three others in planning stages. The subcenters of Stockholm and the satellite towns are connected by surface bus lines. This "finger principle" of urban development has subcenters along the fingers and satellite cities at the tips, a planning technique used today in many European cities. The design is such that no resident will be more than a 10-minute walk, 0.6 mi. (about 1 km.), from a subway station and that no one will live more than 45 minutes from any other point in the city by a combination of walking and public transport. Certain downtown major avenues have express lanes for buses and taxis to facilitate movement and entice people to switch from private auto to public transportation. Farsta and Vallingby are new towns created at the "tips" of the "fingers" in Stockholm (Fig. 3.17). They are completely planned cities with various kinds of apartment sizes and architecture, a pedestrian mall-type central business district, planned park and recreational space, churches, schools, and a major employer, such as the power and light works in Farsta. Stockholm's new towns are planned to be attractive, convenient, and functional. Helsinki's new-town garden city, Tapiola, is aesthetically more pleasing. The goal of new towns in general is that they have adequate local employment and can be functionally independent of the nearby major city. In most instances this goal has been only partially achieved in Europe.

Decentralization efforts are illustrated by efforts to move major office functions from London to the nearby new town of Crawley. Moving industry from Paris and its outskirts to suburbs and satellite towns in the Paris region and farther out into regional capitals is decentralization policy in France. Urban renewal efforts are common throughout Europe, but there are attempts as well to preserve the old, medieval appearance of the cities. The steel and glass skyscraper, which Americanizes the appearance of the European city, is becoming increasingly common.

More emphasis on planning the "city region" as opposed to the individual city is a key to solving many of the urban problems. The *city region* concept considers urban conurbations as a total system, that is, their physical, social, political, and economic character. Obtaining the cooperation of overlapping political jurisdictions and advancing solutions which are best for the entire city region is crucial to solving urgent urban problems. The city region consists of a complex set of communities that have distinctive spatial characteristics and problems; these attributes and how they are created must be understood. An example of the difficulties facing regionwide planning is Greater London, which contains 130 political units that must be included in planning proposals. The city region approach, if adopted throughout Western Europe, would aid in dealing with problems in London and other major Western European large and medium sized agglomerations.

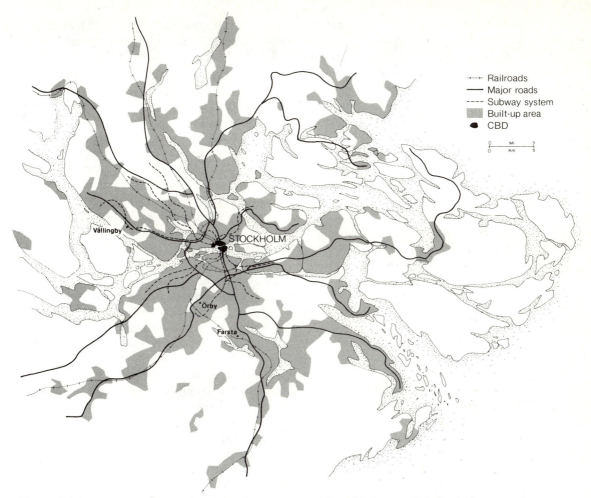

Figure 3.17 Stockholm Metropolitan Region. (*Source:* Adapted from Bilatlas over Hela Sverige.)

Future Western European Urban Trends

The nature and evolution of the Western European city varies from country to country, from one region to another within a given country, and often from city to city within the same region. Cities reflect the social mores and objectives of their residents, merchants, politicians, and rulers over a period of time. Four types of cities that remain in the landscape today are the medieval burgher city of the feudal state, the nobility city created by the absolutist state, the manufacturing city of the liberal laissez-faire era, and the planned new towns developed under the social welfare political system. Recent emphasis has been upon the large apartment complexes such as those in the Randstadt, under the Schema Directeur in France, and in the new towns near Stockholm and other large cities. Planners have designed these complexes to take care of anticipated housing needs, but many people throughout Western Europe now aspire to more private space and separate housing types. Whether this will be possible on a large scale will depend upon continuing favorable economic conditions, the space to permit such development, and assuring necessary future energy at a price that will permit more dispersed development.

Urban growth continues in Europe and change in the nature of its cities is inevitable. Suburbs, string developments along major highways out from cities, and satellite and new-town development near large cities will continue. Many new ideas about urban form and function are continually being advanced by planners and urban specialists in all countries, but it is up to politicians and policy boards to implement plans that will satisfy the desires of people. According to Brian Berry in his *The Human Consequences of Urbanization,* the five major goals and objectives of urban growth are related to: (1) achieving a more balanced distribution of income and social well-being among regions and social classes of a country; (2) whether a government (local, regional, or national) wishes to centralize or decentralize future growth; (3) the environmental protection problems of a given area; (4) the use of new transportation systems, land use controls, new towns, housing construction, tax incentives and disincentives, and land use controls such as zoning in future metropolitan development; and (5) the stimulation of growth in little or lesser developed parts of a country by means of growth poles, new transportation links between growth centers and established areas, the relocation of government activities, and the use of other incentives and disincentives. The implementation of the above goals and objectives will vary considerably from place to place and government to government among countries of Western Europe.

Within the region the following four trends are taking place and will continue into the near future. First, the metropolitan regions will continue to grow at the expense of the central city and rural areas. Second, new towns will become larger in size and will be used as growth points rather than primarily as places for surplus population of the large city. Third, the role of the CBD will change as ideas and technology related to communications and electronics permit change in the space required and kind and amount of labor needed to perform various kinds of tasks. And fourth, planners and politicians will have greater influence in the placing of new towns, open and recreational space, development of more efficient mass transportation, and more consistent layout of new or renewed cities and the design of buildings.

RECOMMENDED READINGS

Clout, Hugh D., ed. *Regional Development in Western Europe.* London: John Wiley, 1975.
    Recent economic, urban, and social trends are developed in the regional context of all Western Europe. The regional planning and economic policy developments are analyzed in a chapter for each country.

Coppock, J. T. and Hugh C. Prince, eds. *Greater London.* London: Faber and Faber, 1964.
    A multiauthored book covering such topics as the climate, communications, housing, industry, the green belt, new towns, parks, and the future of London. The objective is to indicate the problems of London and to suggest potential solutions.

Cotter, John V. "New Towns as an International Phenomenon: A Bibliography." Monticello, IL: Council of Planning Librarians, 1977. Exchange Bibliography 1315.
   A recent bibliography of the new-town literature with emphasis upon Western Europe. Most items are English-language sources, but some material written in other European languages is included.

Dickinson, Robert E. *The West European City.* 2nd ed. London: Routledge and Kegan Paul, 1964.
   A classic work on the nature of the Western European city with emphasis upon the historical factor. Specifics on most major cities in this area are included.

Gottmann, Jean. *A Geography of Europe.* New York: Holt, Rinehart and Winston, 1969.
   A regional coverage of the countries of Europe with emphasis upon social, political, and cultural factors. The cities of each country are analyzed in their regional context.

Hall, John M. *London: Metropolis and Region.* Oxford: Oxford University Press, 1976.
   As one of a series on the "problem regions" in Europe, this short volume covers the inherited past, current problems of the city and region, and future of London. Covent Garden and Docklands are used as two case studies of change.

Hall, Peter. *London 2000.* 2nd ed. London: Faber and Faber, 1971.
   A comprehensive look at the nature of London and the projected problems by the year 2000. The author poses one central problem—shall London grow?—and discusses the vastly different consequences and decisions as to whether or not London expands in size, function, and population.

Hellen, J. A. *North Rhine-Westphalia.* London: Oxford University Press, 1974.
   North Rhine-Westphalia, the major industrial-urban concentration in West Germany, is covered in terms of past character and contemporary problems. The volume closes with an analysis of future plans.

Jones, Emrys. *Towns and Cities,* London: Oxford University Press, 1966.
   The book introduces the reader to urban geography covering such topics as the process of urbanization, preindustrial cities, city classification, and the city in its region. Of particular importance is a chapter on the western city.

Lawrence, G. R. P. *Randstadt, Holland.* London: Oxford University Press, 1973.
   A good, brief treatise of the urban concentrations in the Netherlands and their problems. The role of Randstadt is characterized and potential future outlined.

Thompson, Dan B. *The Paris Basin.* London: Oxford University Press, 1973.
   A short analysis of Paris in the larger context of the Paris Basin. Emphasis is on the problems of Greater Paris and the strategies for solutions including the new towns and the future role of the Lower Seine Valley.

Wild, Trevor. *West Germany: A Geography of Its People.* Totowa, NJ: Barnes & Noble, 1979.
   A recent analysis of population changes in post-World War II West Germany. One chapter deals directly with the urban dimension, but others cover the character of the cities in West Germany.

Wise, Michael. "The City Region." *Advancement of Science,* 27 (February 1966), 571–588.
   The city region concept is evaluated as to its importance in planning the future of urban areas. The emphasis is on the city as a system portraying interrelationships of numerous factors. Several European cities are used as examples.

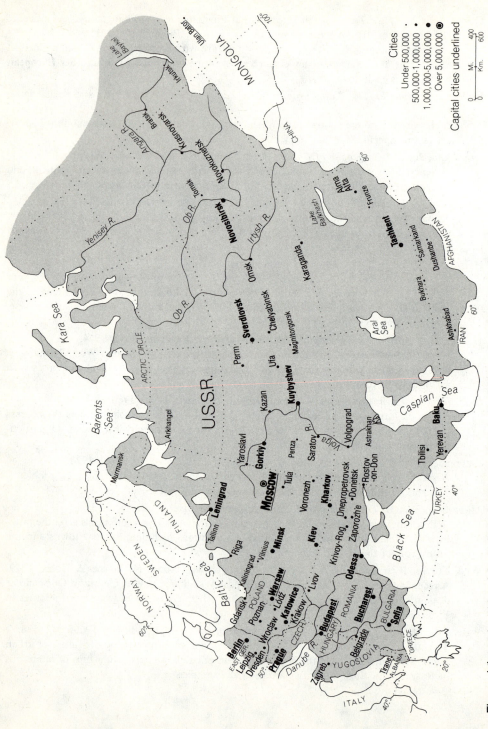

Figure 4.1 Major Cities of the Soviet Union/Eastern Europe. (*Source:* Data derived from United Nations, Department of Economic and Social Affairs, *Global Review of Human Settlements, Statistical Annex*, published by Pergamon Press, New York, 1976.)

Chapter 4

Cities of the Soviet Union and Eastern Europe

Ian M. Matley

The Soviet Union/Eastern Europe in the World Urban System

Although the Soviet Union and Eastern Europe are not among the most urbanized regions of the world, certainly they rank above most of the countries of Africa and Asia. With approximately 62 percent of their populations living in cities in 1980 (compared with only 39 percent in 1950), Eastern Europe and the Soviet Union together account for nearly 250 million urban residents. This region as a whole is about where North America and Western Europe stood in degree of urbanization back in the early 1950s.

  As with all the world regions, there is great variation in levels of urbanization within the Soviet Union and Eastern Europe. East Germany, for example, is the most urbanized at 76 percent, reflecting its historical association with a unified and highly urbanized/industrialized Germany of the past. The Soviet Union, at 64 percent urban, is second in the region, followed by Bulgaria, Czechoslovakia, and Poland, at 63, 61, and 60 percent, respectively. Parts of Eastern Europe are still largely rural, however, particularly the Balkan states, with Albania only 41 percent urbanized, Romania 49 percent, and Yugoslavia 42 percent.

  In all there are some 225 cities with a population of at least 100,000 people in the Soviet Union, but relatively few really large cities. Only 23 cities have a population of more than 1 million, and only two contain 2 to 5 million (Leningrad and Kiev) (Fig. 4.1). The urban pattern of the Soviet Union is overwhelmingly dominated by the giant city of Moscow, at more than 8 million people a primate city in many respects, and one of the largest cities in the world. The dominance of Moscow as the supreme Central Place in the Soviet Union and the hold it has had over the lives and culture of the Russians down through the centuries is matched by few other cities in the world. The continued importance of Moscow and the preponderance of relatively smaller cities is a reflection of the urban/industrial development policies pursued by the government since Stalin began industrialization in the 1930s and of the character of the Soviet system, with its monolithic centralization of power in the national capital of Moscow.

As a region Eastern Europe also has remarkably few large cities, certainly far fewer than Western Europe, whether compared on the basis of region or individual country. There are no giant cities (population greater than 5 million), only two with a population of 2 to 5 million, and just five more with 1 to 2 million. Budapest and Warsaw, each with just over 2 million, are the largest cities in Eastern Europe. As with the Soviet Union, the socialist development of Eastern Europe in the past 30 years explains in large part the relatively small numbers of cities and smaller urban population vis-à-vis Western Europe.

Indeed, the vast realm of the Soviet Union and Eastern Europe is treated as a single entity in this book because of the dominance of Eastern Europe by the Soviet Union since the late 1940s and also because of long historical linkages between the two regions. From an urban perspective, certainly, there are strong similarities between the two regions in the contemporary period, because of the efforts to create the so-called socialist city in both the Soviet Union and the various countries of Eastern Europe, even though the character and degree of success in creation of the socialist city vary widely between countries in the Soviet bloc.

Historical Development of Soviet Cities

The vast area of the country, the diversity of natural regions, and the variety of peoples of different ethnic origins and historical backgrounds have all influenced the development and distribution of Soviet urban settlements. The area of the country most suitable for human settlement is relatively small. The northern and eastern regions are covered with large areas of coniferous forest and have cold winter temperatures, a short growing season, and relatively infertile soils. Most of the area lying to the east of the Ural Mountains, known as Siberia, has these characteristics. Much of the southern part of the country contains deserts, semideserts, or dry grasslands, where agriculture is possible only with the use of irrigation. Much of this arid land lies within the borders of the region known as Central Asia. Between these two regions is an area of deciduous and mixed forest with a belt of grassland (steppe) to the south. In the steppes sufficient moisture for agriculture is generally available, the growing season is long enough to permit a variety of crops to mature, and soils vary from brown and gray soils of moderate fertility in the forested areas to *chernozem* (black earth) soils of great fertility in the steppes. It is this area, totaling only some 8.5 percent of the total land area of the country, which offers the best conditions for human settlement. It includes most of the central and southern part of the European area of the Soviet Union and a narrow zone to the east of the Ural Mountains. The northern border of this "agricultural triangle" lies approximately along a line drawn from the city of Leningrad in the northwest to the southern tip of Lake Baikal in eastern Siberia, while its southern border extends from Odessa on the Black Sea to the southern tip of Lake Baikal. Most of the population of the country lives within this triangle and most of the agriculture and industry is located there. Consequently, most of the urban settlement has taken place within the agricultural triangle or in the few other areas of favorable climate, including the Caucasus Mountains, the southern part of the Pacific Coast region (Ussuri-Amur Valley), the irrigated areas of Central Asia, and the area of exceptionally mild winters along the north coast of the Kola Peninsula, warmed by the North Atlantic current.

Within the bounds of the settled areas of the Soviet Union there lives a variety of peoples of different ethnic origins, many of whom have widely divergent historical roots. This diversity is reflected in the architecture and street plans as well as in the periods of development of Soviet cities, from the ancient Moslem cities of Central Asia with their mosques and minarets, to the old cities of Russia with their kremlins and orthodox churches, to the German-built cities of the Baltic region, with their Lutheran churches and round towers. There are, in fact, several regional groups of urban settlements, each with their own characteristics and periods of historical development.

Early Urbanization

The earliest urban settlements in the territory of the present-day Soviet Union took place in Central Asia. Samarkand, the oldest city in the country, dates from the fourth or third millenium B.C. The urban settlements of the Slavs started at a much later date. The first Slav settlement of importance was the city of Kiev, which was first mentioned in the ninth century. Although an important trade center at an early period, it suffered from the attacks of the Pechenegs, Mongols, and Tatars and was destroyed in the thirteenth and fifteenth centuries. The annexation by Russia of the southern steppes in the eighteenth century removed the Tatar menace, and Kiev was left in peace to develop as a provincial capital.

During the period of the decline of Kiev the second of the early Slav urban settlements was established. Sheltered by the forests of the north, the city of Novgorod became an important trading center located on the river routes of the north and protected by a *kremlin* or fort. From the thirteenth to the fifteenth century Novgorod became part of the network of Hanseatic trade centers established by the Germans in the Baltic region. However, the rise of Moscow resulted in the subjugation of Novgorod in the late fifteenth century and its eclipse as a trade and political center. In the seventeenth century it suffered in the wars with the Swedes, from which it never recovered its former importance. It has remained a relatively unimportant provincial town.

Several minor towns such as Vladimir, Suzdal, Tver (now called Kalinin), and Pskov experienced periods of early importance as the centers of principalities, but were eclipsed by the rise of Moscow. The existence of Moscow was first recorded in the twelfth century, although a settlement had existed on the site since prehistoric times. A wooden fortress, later to become the famed Kremlin, was built on the high northern bank of the Moscow River. Not only was the site of the settlement good for defense, but so was its location in the forests with the swamps of the Oka River to the east. The local princes were also very successful in their dealings with the Tatars and saved the city from further attacks through a combination of cunning and bribery. In spite of attacks by Tatars, Poles, and Lithuanians, Moscow managed to survive the critical years of its early growth.

Early Growth of Moscow

The rise of Moscow cannot be explained only in terms of security from attack. The early settlement was located at the center of a river system which permitted movement by water in several directions. Access to the Volga and Oka Rivers gave a route to the east, although in early days this was blocked by the Tatar khanate of Kazan, which controlled the central and lower Volga. The Western Dvina led to the Baltic and the Don and Dnepr Rivers to the Black Sea. The headwaters of all these river systems were within easy reach of Moscow. During the early period of the development of the Russian state the role of rivers as a means of trade and communication was very important and the favorable location of Moscow with relation to the major river routes was an important factor in explaining its growth.

In the fourteenth century Moscow began to take on the appearance of a major city. The Kremlin was surrounded by stone walls and extended to its present size. In the fifteenth century new brick walls with towers were built. To the east of the Kremlin merchants and artisans lived in the Kitay Gorod (probably from Pecheneg *katay:* "fortress" and Russian *gorod:* "city"), which was also protected by brick walls in the sixteenth century. The Kitay Gorod consisted of one-story wooden buildings until it was destroyed in a fire in 1596, after which stone buildings appeared. The center of the Kitay Gorod was the large square first mentioned in the fifteenth century as the *torg* (marketplace), which became known in the seventeenth century as Red Square (Krasnaya Ploshchad). Its first function was as a marketplace and site of a fair where merchants from all Russia and surrounding territories displayed their wares, but later it became the main square of the city, where executions, demonstrations, parades, and other gatherings took place and where the decrees of the czar were announced. In the middle of the sixteenth century Ivan the Terrible erected the great cathedral of St. Basil at the southern end of the square to commemorate his great victory over the Tatars at Kazan; this victory effectively opened up the Volga and Ural regions for Russian settlement.

Encircling the Kremlin and the Kitay Gorod on the north bank of the river was the Bely Gorod ("white city"), which was enclosed by stone walls at the end of the sixteenth century (Fig. 4.2). It contained the houses of merchants and nobles as well as churches and shops. Beyond the Bely Gorod and extending south as well as north of the river was the Zemlyanoy Gorod ("earthen city"), so named because of its earthern walls, erected at the end of the sixteenth century. (These walls were pulled down in the nineteenth century and replaced by ring boulevards.) Apart from shops and houses the Zemlyanoy Gorod contained military barracks, located south of the river, and several fortified monasteries, such as the Novodevichi and Donskoy, which protected the approaches to the city from the south. Other kremlins and fortified monasteries were built in smaller towns surrounding Moscow, including Kolomna, Zaraysk, and Serpukhov, which added to the security of the city from attack from the east and the south.

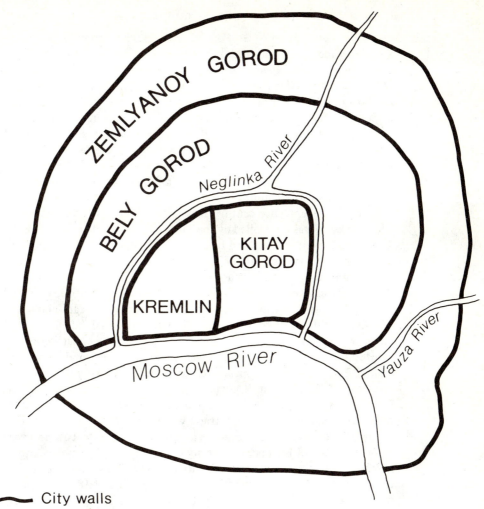

Figure 4.2   Old Moscow. (*Source:* Adapted from W. H. Parker, *An Historical Geography of Russia,* Chicago: Aldine, 1969, p. 96.)

    In the sixteenth century the population of Moscow was probably more than 100,000. By the beginning of the eighteenth century the city had between 150,000 and 200,000 inhabitants. Although the general outlines of the city around 1700 were not much different from those of a hundred years earlier, there had been some changes within the major divisions of the city. A number of new ecclesiastical and other buildings were erected. Workshops and factories began to appear as Moscow became the major trade and manufacturing center of Russia. Several of the villages surrounding the city also began to develop handicraft industries, leading to the growth of a number of industrial suburbs. The industries included textile, clothing, glass, leather, and weapons. To the south, the city of Tula became an important producer of iron, using local iron ore and charcoal from the forests.

Cities of the Commerical and Early Industrial Period, 1700–1917

The Foundation of St. Petersburg The development of Moscow as the capital and major industrial and trade center of Russia was temporarily eclipsed by the founding of the city of St. Petersburg in 1703. The birth of St. Petersburg marked the beginning of a period of commercial and industrial expansion which placed Russia within the ranks of other European military and economic powers. The one individual most responsible for this expansion was Czar Peter the Great, who came to the throne in 1682. With a series of reforms which shook Russian society to its roots and which earned him many enemies, Peter tried singlehandedly to turn Russia from a barbaric, Oriental country into a modern Western society. His changes profoundly affected Russian religious, economic, social, and political life and had a great effect upon the future development of the country.

In the seventeenth century Russia had problems of access to the outside world. The Black Sea was controlled by the Turks and their allies and the Baltic by the Swedes. The Poles prevented overland trade with the West. The only available trade route was by the northern rivers to the White Sea through the port of Archangel (Arkhangelsk). This route was very unsatisfactory, due to distance and the winter ice on the White Sea. Peter the Great's decision to clear the Swedes out of the eastern Baltic was based on his vision of a new major port for Russia and a new capital city closer to the West. The first buildings of this new city, located on the islands at the mouth of the Neva River, were a fortress and a shipbuilding yard for the construction of a Russian navy. The foundation of the city in 1703 was followed by the rapid construction of a Western-style city designed by European architects but built by conscripted labor and prisoners-of-war. In 1712 the seat of government was moved to the new city of St. Petersburg from Moscow and the nobles and merchants were forced by decree to establish homes in the new capital. All foreign trade was routed through the port. By the nineteenth century St. Petersburg had become as large a city as Moscow and was one of the most attractive cities of Europe, with many beautiful churches, palaces and public buildings. Moscow never recovered from the loss of its role as capital city until after the 1917 revolution; the French occupation and the great fire of 1812 further hindered its development. By 1914 St. Petersburg had a population of 2.1 million, compared with Moscow's 1.8 million. The two cities contained just under one-third of the total urban population of the country.

During the nineteenth century both cities experienced rapid industrial growth. St. Petersburg became a center for engineering and metalworking, while Moscow's industrial development was helped by the growth of the railroad network which centered on the city. Moscow had a better location from the point of view of transportation and the assembly of raw materials. St. Petersburg began to find itself on the fringe of the major areas of economic development.

Odessa During the period of development of commerce and industry in Russia after 1700, several other important cities arose. After the conquest of the Black Sea coastal region by Catherine the Great, the city and port of Odessa was built as an outlet to the south. Founded in 1792, the city was populated largely by foreigners. In 1866 the railroad reached Odessa, which then became the second port in the country after St. Petersburg. It was the third largest city in Russia at that time, with about 120,000 inhabitants. Odessa's commercial importance was chiefly due to the large exports of grain from the southern steppes that passed through the port on the way to Western Europe. By 1914 the population of the city reached 500,000, but competition from North American grain led to decreasing Russian exports and Odessa never regained its earlier prosperity.

Cities of the Urals The rise of the Russian metallurgical industry was hampered by the lack of good supplies of iron ore and fuel in the Moscow and St. Petersburg areas. This situation led to the development of the iron ore deposits in the southern Urals, about 1000 mi. (1600 km.) to the east. Foundries were set up on the banks of the Ural rivers, and the metal was brought by inland waterway routes to Moscow and St. Petersburg. By 1800 the Urals were producing 80 percent of Russia's iron, much of which was exported. In 1721 Peter the Great founded the city of Yekaterinburg (now Sverdlovsk) in the Urals. It soon became the largest city of the region and its administrative center; it was also located on a major route to Siberia. By 1917 it had some 70,000 inhabitants. Other Ural cities that later became important were Ufa, Chelyabinsk, and Perm.

The Donets Basin The Ural region maintained its supremacy as a supplier of iron until the 1890s, when the development of the Donets Basin coalfield and the iron ore deposits of Krivoy Rog in the Ukraine led to a major shift in the location of the main centers of iron and steel production. By 1913 almost 70 percent of Russia's iron came from the Ukraine and only 20 percent from the Urals. A number of new industrial cities arose in the Ukraine. The most important of these was Yuzovka (now Donetsk), which was founded in 1869 and named after John Hughes, a Welshman who had built the first foundry. By 1917 the city had 49,000 inhabitants. Another metallurgical center was Lugansk, which by 1917 had 60,000 inhabitants. The late nineteenth century saw the growth of several other mining and metallurgical centers in the region. After the Russian Revolution (1917) the Donets Basin cities became one of the largest concentrations of industrial cities in the country.

Cities of the Soviet Period: 1917 to the Second World War

Accelerated Urbanization Some Soviet writers on the subject of urbanization in their country give the impression that little of significance took place until after the 1917 revolution. As already noted, however, many of the major urban centers are of ancient origin and a knowledge of their history is essential to the understanding of their present form and function. Nevertheless, the advent of Soviet rule had a great effect on the growth and direction of urbanization. During this period three basic trends can be seen. First, many of the cities which had shown a healthy rate of growth during the czarist period continued to expand after the revolution. Such were Moscow, St.

Petersburg, Kiev, and the cities of the Urals and the Ukraine. Second, several cities which had been important at an earlier period saw little or no development under Soviet rule. Among these were Novgorod, the capitals of the old principalities around Moscow, including Suzdal, Ryazan and Pskov, and, to a certain extent, Odessa. Third, a number of new cities were founded or relatively unimportant cities were developed into major industrial or administrative centers. Such were Kharkov in the Ukraine, Gorki, Kuibyshev, and Volgograd (formerly called Stalingrad) on the Volga, and several industrial cities in the Donets Basin. (The cities of Siberia, Central Asia, and the Caucasus will be discussed separately later.) Because of the effects of World War II on the growth of Soviet cities, the period 1917 to 1941 is examined first.

The 1926 census listed only two cities with a population of over 1 million: Moscow (2 million) and Leningrad (formerly called St. Petersburg, 1.7 million). Kiev was the only other city with over 500,000 inhabitants (514,000). At that time the population of the Soviet Union was still predominantly rural, with only 18 percent of the people living in urban settlements. It should be noted that there are two official categories of Soviet urban settlements; cities proper and settlements of the urban type. Their definition depends mainly on size, although function also plays a role. In general, cities are settlements with more than 10,000 inhabitants, and settlements of urban type those with less than 10,000. Most of the large cities are in western Russia, that is, west of the Urals (Fig. 4.3). In 1926 there were 1,925 urban settlements of both types, of which only 31 had more than 100,000 inhabitants. By the time of the 1939 census, 33 percent of the total population was living in urban settlements (Fig. 4.4) and the number of such settlements had risen to 2,373, with 89 cities with over 100,000 inhabitants. The basic reason for this rapid growth in the number and size of urban settlements was the industrialization program of Stalin, carried out in a number of five-year plans, starting in 1928 (Fig. 4.5). Industrialization resulted in the large-scale migration of peasants to the cities, the transformation of many farm villages into urban settlements, the incorporation of many villages into the larger cities, and the construction of new industrial centers.

Moscow and Leningrad From 1926 until 1939 the population of Moscow more than doubled, reaching just over 4 million in the latter year. Lenin had moved the government back to Moscow in 1918, and as the capital of the country as well as its major industrial and transportation center, the city thrived. The former St. Petersburg, however, entered a period of increasing problems. Renamed Petrograd during World War I, its name was changed again to Leningrad in 1924 because of its German-sounding name. During the civil war that followed the revolution, Leningrad was threatened by the White armies, which failed in attempts to take the city. Its industry ground to a halt and many people died of starvation during this period. By 1920 the population of the city had dropped to around 720,000, compared with 2.5 million in 1917. The rapid industrialization of the Stalin period contributed to the revival of the city and led to a population of 3.1 million in 1939. At that time about 11 percent of total Soviet industrial production came from Leningrad. The city gradually found itself located more and more on the fringe of Soviet industrial development, with few local raw mate-

Historical Development of Soviet Cities 131

Figure 4.3 Major Cities of European Soviet Union. (*Source:* Data derived from United Nations, Department of Economic and Social Affairs, *Global Review of Human Settlements, Statistical Annex,* published by Pergamon Press, New York, 1976.)

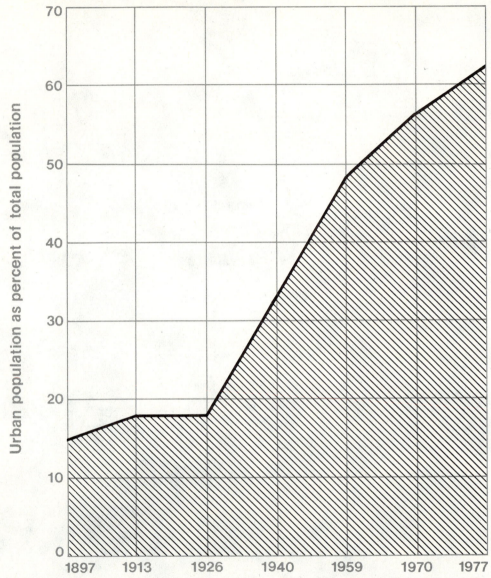

Figure 4.4 Growth of Urban Population in the Soviet Union, 1897–1977. (*Source:* Narodnoe Khozyaystvo S.S.S.R. za 60 let, Statistika, Moscow, 1977, p. 44.)

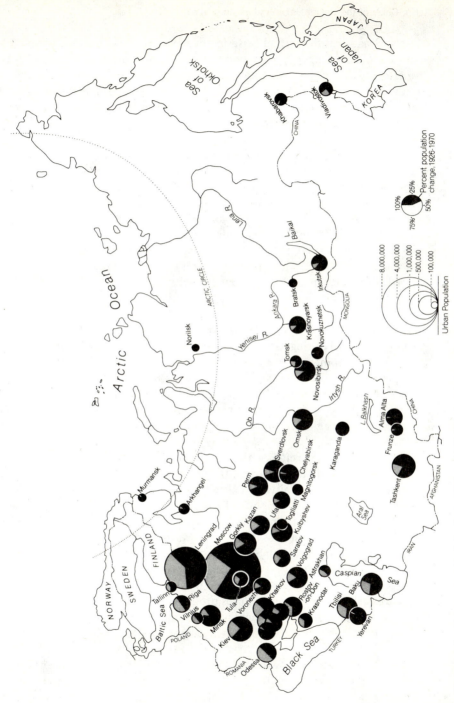

Figure 4.5 Urban Growth of the Soviet Union, 1926–1970. (*Source:* Adapted from S. V. Kalesnk and V. F. Pavlenko, *Soviet Union: A Geographical Survey, Progress,* Moscow, 1976, p. 146.)

rials. Because of the virtual cessation of Soviet trade with the outside world, its industries could no longer rely on imported coal and iron ore; Leningrad was faced with increasing difficulties to maintain its economic growth. Although Moscow also suffered from a lack of local industrial resources during this period, its location was more favorable for economic development and its renewed role as the administrative and cultural center of the country ensured its future growth.

Kiev The city of Kiev remained a small town in the early nineteenth century, but with the removal of the Tatar threat and the settlement of the Ukrainian steppes it expanded rapidly and by 1897 had 248,000 inhabitants. Further development of the industrial and agricultural riches of the Ukraine around the turn of the century led to its even more rapid growth as an administrative and cultural center, and by 1914 Kiev had 521,000 inhabitants. During the early years of Soviet rule the government of the Ukrainian Soviet Socialist Republic was established at Kharkov, but in 1934 it was moved to Kiev. At the same time a number of important industries were developed in the city, including various branches of engineering, light industry, and food processing. The population rose rapidly and by 1939 reached 847,000.

The Donets Basin The industrial cities of the Donets Basin experienced a period of rapid growth during the Stalin period due to the priorities given in the five-year plans for the development of heavy industry. Yuzovka, now rechristened Stalino, increased in population from 174,000 in 1926 to 462,000 in 1939. Several other cities, including Lugansk and Makayevka, had passed the 200,000 mark. Many other smaller coal-mining and iron and steel towns were in this region, which together formed one of the largest urban agglomerations in the Soviet Union.

Kharkov Two cities which have experienced a remarkable growth during the period of Soviet rule are Kharkov in the Ukraine and Gorki on the Volga to the east of Moscow. Kharkov already existed in the seventeenth century as a fortress on the steppe frontier and by the time of the Revolution had a population of some 350,000. Its proximity to the Donets Basin and its heavy industry led to the development of several important branches of the engineering industry. From 1919 until 1934 it was the capital of the Ukrainian S. S. R. and during the Stalin period investment in its industries increased. Its location at the center of the railroad network of the Ukraine helped its economic development. By 1939 Kharkov was the largest industrial city of the Ukraine, with engineering factories producing railroad equipment, machine tools, tractors and other agricultural machinery, mining equipment, and other products. Its population on the eve of the Second World War was 833,000.

Gorki Gorki, known until 1932 as Nizhni Novgorod ("lower Novgorod"), is located on the upper Volga. It is an ancient city and was known in the nineteenth century for its huge annual fair, which attracted merchants from all over Russia and also from abroad. The city saw some industrial development during the same period, but its period of greatest growth began in 1932 with the establishment of a huge automobile factory, built with the help of the American Ford company. This development earned the city the title of the "Detroit of Russia," but it should be emphasized that the total production of trucks and cars from this and other Soviet automobile factories is considerably less than from their American counterparts. The population of the city rose from 222,000 in 1926 to 644,000 in 1939, and Gorki was well on its way to becoming one of the most important industrial centers in the country. Its location on the Volga, near its confluence with the Oka River, helped it to become not only an important trade center in the past but also the largest river port in the Soviet Union at present.

Cities of the Volga The cities of the lower Volga also saw a period of rapid growth in the 1930s. The city of Volgograd (called Tsaritsyn until 1925 and Stalingrad until 1961) started as a fortress on the river in the sixteenth century and was relatively unimportant until the Revolution. In 1917 it had 133,000 inhabitants, but by 1939 this number had risen to 445,000, an increase due primarily to the establishment of a large tractor factory in the 1930s and other industries. The city of Kuybyshev (named Samara until 1935) was also an early Volga fortress, becoming a provincial center in the nineteenth century. During the 1930s rapid industrial development took place, and by 1939 the population was 390,000. Although other Volga cities, such as Saratov and Kazan, had similar populations at this time, Kuybyshev was destined to become the largest city of the Volga region.

Major Representative Cities of the Soviet Period

The Second World War had a great impact on the rate and direction of urbanization in the Soviet Union. An estimated 1700 cities and towns were destroyed or badly damaged and 6 million buildings were demolished, while over 20 million persons perished. Other cities were scarcely affected by the war and even flourished in secure locations far from the front lines, where their industries could be expanded to serve the war effort.

Moscow: The Skyscraper City

Moscow was fortunate to have suffered little damage during the war. Although the German armies were stopped only a few miles from the city, destruction to buildings and losses of population were not so great as in many other cities. After the war Stalin decided to make the city a showplace of Soviet urban planning and architecture. A grandiose plan had already been drawn up for the future city in 1935, most of which was never accomplished. Among the more successful ventures was the Moscow subway, known as the Metro. Begun in 1933, it was expanded to become an efficient urban transportation system; it is also universally admired for the cleanliness and artistic quality of its stations. The Metro served as a model for subways in other Soviet cities such as Leningrad, Kiev, Tashkent, Baku, and Tbilisi. Less successful, at least from the aesthetic point of view, were Stalin's attempts to introduce the skyscraper to the Moscow scene. A number of these huge buildings in an elaborate "wedding cake" style of architecture were built in the early 1950s, mainly in the center of the city (Fig. 4.6). They

Figure 4.6 Downtown Moscow: Kalinin Prospekt with new office and apartment buildings and stores. In the background is the Ukraina Hotel. (I. Matley)

have various functions, and include a hotel, an apartment building, and government offices. The most spectacular is the 32-story building housing the science departments of Moscow University, located in the southwest part of the city. A number of other high rise buildings, mainly apartments, were started in various districts of the city; this trend has continued to the present. Not only is large-scale construction of whole complexes of apartments and other buildings taking place on the outskirts of the city, but the downtown area, especially along Kalinin Prospekt, has been transformed with glass-and-concrete buildings in a style which is now international. A large Palace of Congresses was opened in 1961 inside the Kremlin for sessions of the Supreme Soviet and Party congresses (Fig. 4.7). Near the Kremlin a vast hotel, the Rossiya, was built in 1967 to house the increasing flow of visitors to the city. To the north of the city a huge television tower was built in 1968 with a revolving restaurant near the top.

Much of this recent construction has taken place since 1960, when a new general plan for the city was inaugurated (Fig. 4.8). Along with new buildings, seven bridges have been built, the Metro expanded, and a 68-mi.-long (110 km.) circular highway laid around the city. In spite of occasional attempts to limit the population of the city, it has expanded rapidly from 6 million in 1959 to 8 million in 1979, making it not only

Figure 4.7 Moscow: View from the Kremlin Walls. To the right is Red Square with Lenin's Tomb and the usual line of visitors. In the background is the Historical Museum. The high-rise building is the Intourist Hotel. (I. Matley)

the largest city in the Soviet Union by far, but also a world metropolis on the scale of New York, London, or Tokyo.

Leningrad: An Old Industrial City

Leningrad suffered a different fate from that of Moscow during World War II. Besieged by the German armies for 900 days and supplied by only a limited route in winter over the frozen surface of neighboring Lake Ladoga, the city lost thousands of inhabitants and saw most of its buildings destroyed or damaged. At the first postwar census in 1959 the population of the city was only 3,003,000, compared with 3,119,000 in 1939. Although the buildings of this beautiful city were restored at great expense and the population had increased to 4.1 million by 1979, Leningrad never regained its previous dominant role in Russian affairs. Leningrad is still the second most important city in terms of national industrial production, even though it does not have the dynamism of Moscow. Its port, the largest in the Soviet Union, has only a small turnover compared with other similar ports abroad, and in general the city finds itself on the fringe of the core region of Soviet economic development. In contrast to Moscow, which has a large number of smaller industrial cities and towns around it, Leningrad is virtually the only city of any size in its region. In spite of its industrial importance it is to a certain extent a *museum city* (Figs. 4.9 and 4.10).

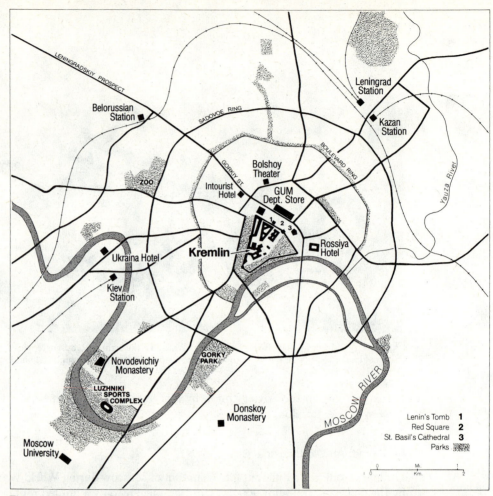

Figure 4.8 Greater Moscow. (*Source:* adapted from *Moscow,* Lausanne: Verlitz, 1976, pp. 32–33.)

Many smaller Soviet cities suffered heavy damage during the war. In particular, the cities of western Russia, the Ukraine, and Belorussia, which lay in the zones of heaviest fighting, were in many cases almost totally destroyed. Kiev and Kharkov were largely ruined; the latter changing hands several times during the war. Volgograd (Stalingrad) was totally destroyed, while such cities as Smolensk, Minsk, and Voronezh were severely damaged. Many of them were rebuilt with new city centers containing large buildings in the florid architectural style typical of the Stalin period. In most cases the cities lost their prewar appearance, but gained new, broad tree-lined streets and green parks. The reconstruction of these destroyed cities and their industries cost the Soviet government and people a great deal of capital and effort in the postwar years and put a considerable strain on the economy already weakened by the war.

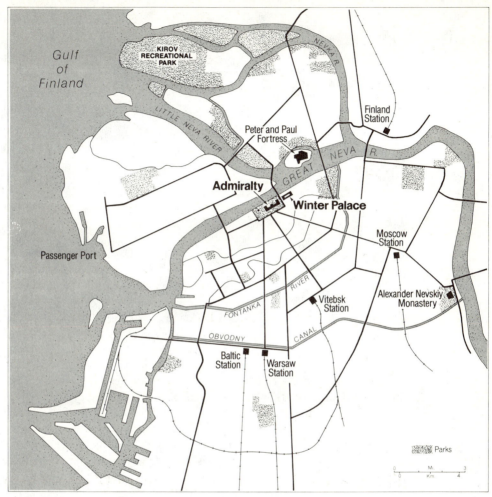

Figure 4.9 Leningrad. (*Source:* Adapted from L. G. Chertov, *Leningrad, Prosveshchenie,* Moscow, 1972, pp. 104–105.)

Magnitogorsk and Volgograd: Ural and Volga Cities

Other cities thrived during the war. In particular the cities of the Urals experienced a period of rapid growth which had begun in the 1930s and which was accelerated by the evacuation of industries and population to this secure area far behind the front lines. A large iron and steel plant was built at Magnitogorsk in the 1930s and became the largest in the Soviet Union. At present the city of Magnitogorsk has over 400,000 inhabitants. The supply of coal for this plant came from the Kuznetsk Basin in Western Siberia, where another large iron and steel plant was built at Stalinsk (now Novokuznetsk). Iron ore was brought by rail from the Urals. In 1979 Novokuznetsk had 541,000 inhabitants. During the war the Urals and the Kuznetsk Basin became the main heavy-

Figure 4.10 Leningrad: the Nevsky Prospekt, the Main Street of the City. The buildings, in prerevolutionary architectural style, are the Comedy Theater and a gift store. (I. Matley)

industrial bases of the country, as most of the cities of the Donets Basin had fallen into enemy hands or lay in the front line of the fighting. Other Ural cities grew rapidly during the war. In particular, the evacuation of industries from Moscow and other western cities to the region around Sverdlovsk gave that city a great impetus to further growth. Its population rose from 423,000 in 1939 to its present figure of 1.2 million, making it the largest city in the Urals. Both Chelyabinsk and Perm have also reached the million-inhabitant mark. The Ural region became established as one of the most important industrial regions of the country.

The cities along the lower Volga also saw some growth during World War II. Although Volgograd (Stalingrad) was totally destroyed, Kuybyshev became the temporary capital of the country while Moscow was directly threatened by the German armies. Other cities like Saratov and Kazan also experienced some development. However, the period of most rapid growth for the Volga cities began in the 1950s with the completion of the Volga-Don Canal, which linked the river directly with the Black Sea, and with the construction of the large hydroelectric dams and power stations at Kuybyshev and Volgograd. The exploitation of the large oil field in the Volga region also gave local industry a boost. The Volga cities developed the aluminum industry, based on plentiful electric power, the oil-refining industry, and a variety of others. The new city of Togliatti was built near Kuybyshev to house the workers of a large automobile plant designed by Fiat of Italy. The city, named after the Italian Communist leader, is the largest producer of cars in the country and has a population of over 500,000.

Volgograd was rebuilt and is now an important industrial city and oil-refining center of 930,000 inhabitants. Kuybyshev remains the largest city of the Volga region with a population of 1.2 million.

Omsk, Irkutsk, and Novosibirsk: Cities of Siberia

Perhaps the most dramatic urban growth in the Soviet Union has taken place in its eastern and northern regions, in other words, in Siberia, the Far East, and the Arctic. Although settlement of Siberia began in the seventeenth century, the size of the towns remained small until the construction of the trans-Siberian railroad in the 1891–1901 period. Omsk, located where the railroad crosses the Irtysh River, became the largest city in Siberia, with 135,000 inhabitants by 1914. It was the major commerical and administrative center of the region. Irkutsk, on the Angara River near Lake Baikal in Eastern Siberia, started as a fort in the seventeenth century and developed into a town with a population composed largely of persons banished from western Russia, especially after the 1825 uprising and the Polish revolts of 1831. By 1917 it had 90,000 inhabitants. After the 1917 revolution both Omsk and Irkutsk flourished as the major urban centers of Western and Eastern Siberia, respectively. Irkutsk became industrialized in the 1930s and grew especially rapidly. By 1979 its population had reached 550,000. Omsk has recently become the major center of the oil-refining and petrochemical industries in Western Siberia and has passed the million-inhabitant figure.

    Both cities have been surpassed in both size and importance by Novosibirsk ("New Siberia"), located where the Trans-Siberian railroad crosses the Ob River, a relatively new city, having been founded only at the beginning of the century. Industrialization only began in the 1930s, but by 1939 the population had surpassed 400,000. Novosibirsk's present population is 1.3 million, making it the largest city in all Siberia and the eighth largest in the Soviet Union. Its importance is due not only to its location as a transportation and commerical center, but also to its proximity to the industries of the Kuznetsk Basin. Novosibirsk has important engineering and metallurgical factories. Nearby a town known as Akademgorodok ("academic town") houses several scientific institutes, their staffs and families. It is one of the most important research facilities in the entire country. Another city which has grown rapidly in recent years is Krasnoyarsk, at the junction of the railroad and the Yenisei River. It has surpassed Irkutsk in size and is now the largest city of Eastern Siberia, with 796,000 inhabitants. Its growth is due to its function as a transport center and to the construction of a large hydroelectric plant on the Yenisei in the 1960s, which stimulated development of the aluminum, lumber, and pulp industries among others.

Vladivostok and Bratsk: Cities of the Far East

The city of Vladivostok on the Pacific Ocean is relatively new. The Far East territories of the Soviet Union were annexed from China between 1858 and 1860, and Vladivostok was founded in the latter year as Russia's major port and naval base on the Pacific. In 1979 its population was 550,000. Because of problems of icing of the narrow bay on which the port is situated, two new ports, Nakhodka and Vostochnii, have been built further to the east.

Since the 1917 Revolution a number of new cities have been built in Siberia with the aim of exploiting the resources of the region. The most publicized of these has been the city of Bratsk, built on the Angara River in 1955 to house the workers on the huge dam and electric power station under construction there. The population of the city reached 214,000 in 1979. Many are employed in the large aluminum and timber-processing factories which have recently been built. Bratsk has been the subject of several poems and novels by prominent Soviet writers, and at the time of its construction the city and its dam were hailed as a major achievement of the Soviet regime.

Norilsk and Murmansk: Arctic Cities

An even more remarkable urban settlement is the city of Norilsk, near the mouth of the Yenisei River, north of the Arctic Circle. It was founded in the 1930s as a mining town to exploit the nickel and other nonferrous metals of the region. Built in an area of permafrost (permanently frozen ground) and with no links to the outside world except by air or water along the Yenisei River or via the Arctic Ocean, the city has nevertheless seen rapid development and now has broad streets and multistory buildings. Its population in 1979 was 180,000. The inhabitants must withstand not only extremely low winter temperatures, but also arctic night for almost six months of the year. Norilsk is unique in being by far the largest settlement of its type north of the Arctic Circle.

The port of Murmansk, situated on the Kola Peninsula north of the Arctic Circle, is in fact larger than Norilsk but lies in an area of exceptionally mild climate for its latitude. The northern coasts of the Kola Peninsula are washed by the warm waters of the North Atlantic current, which vanishes in the cold Arctic Ocean to the east. The waters in the area are virtually ice free, and it is not surprising that the Tsarist authorities decided to build a railroad to the Arctic coast during World War I and establish a port there to facilitate contact with the outside world. Murmansk was founded in 1915 and serves as the northern port of the Soviet Union during the winter period when Leningrad and Archangel are closed by ice. Murmansk is also an important naval base and home port for part of the Soviet fishing fleet. During World War II it was the end point for Allied convoys bringing aid to Russia and was severely damaged by German air attacks. The city has 381,000 inhabitants.

Central Asian Cities: Dominance of Tashkent

The historical development of Central Asian cities has followed a different pattern from those of the European regions of the Soviet Union. Central Asia consists of the regions of Uzbekistan, Tadzhikistan, Turkmenistan, and Kirghizistan, with the vast region of Kazakhstan, often regarded as separate from Central Asia proper, to the north. Most of these regions were only incorporated into the Russian Empire in the mid-nineteenth century and had experienced a long period of urbanization before this period, as mentioned above. Many of these ancient Moslem cities, such as Samarkand, Bukhara, and Tashkent, retained their old form with the mosques, palaces and bazaars typical of the

Middle Eastern city, but received the addition of a new European-style city built by the Russians. In particular, Tashkent saw a period of rapid development, especially after the 1917 revolution, when it was declared the capital of the Uzbek S.S.R. and became the main administrative and political center for the whole of Central Asia. By 1939 its population had reached 550,000, double that of 1914. During World War II the evacuation of large numbers of persons from the war zone to Central Asia resulted in an even greater rate of growth of the city. At present its population exceeds 1.8 million, about half being Russians and Ukrainians, making it the fourth largest city of the Soviet Union. Throughout its history, Tashkent has suffered from several serious earthquakes, the most recent being in 1966. Consequently, much of the city has been rebuilt in recent years with earthquake-proof buildings. An attempt has been made to modify modern architectural styles to include Central Asian motifs. The modern city is now considered the show place of Soviet Central Asia. Most other Central Asian cities are much smaller. Several, including Alma Ata and Frunze (both capitals of republics), were founded by the Russians around fortresses and have few features typical of a Central Asian city.

Cities of the Caucasus: Importance of Baku

The Caucasus region was also incorporated into the Russian Empire only in the nineteenth century. The most important city of the region is Baku on the Caspian Sea, once the oil capital of Russia. In 1914 it already had a population of 232,000, mostly Azerbaijanis, Russians, and Armenians. Further development of the Caucasus oil industry led to the rapid growth of the city, and by 1939 the population had reached 773,000 (including surrounding settlements). Even after the shift of the major center of Soviet oil production to the Volga region, Baku continued to grow and by 1979 had a population of 1 million. The city's importance is enhanced by its being the largest Soviet port on the Caspian Sea and the capital of the Azerbaijan S.S.R. Other Caucasian cities are Tbilisi, capital of the Georgian republic (1979 population: 1.1 million), and Yerevan, capital of the Armenian S.S.R. (1979 population: 1 million).

Baltic Cities: Riga and Kaliningrad

Another region with a history of urbanization which differs considerably from the rest of the Soviet Union is the Baltic region. During the Middle Ages the Baltic Sea was largely dominated by the Germans, who established several commercial ports, including Konigsberg, which was also an important military and administrative center, as well as Riga and Tallin. Along with Novgorod, these cities played an important role in the activities of the Hanseatic League until their seizure by the Swedes in the seventeenth century. After the defeat of the Swedes by Peter the Great, Riga and Tallin were incorporated into the Russian Empire and remained so until the 1917 Revolution. Riga grew extremely rapidly between the 1860s and 1917. Konigsberg remained all this time under German control during this period.

In 1918 Latvia and Estonia became independent states with their capitals at Riga and Tallin, respectively. In 1940, however, the two republics again found themselves under Russian control. The city of Konigsberg was also annexed by the Soviet Union in 1945 and renamed Kaliningrad; it is the most westerly port in the Soviet Union and is virtually ice free. The city is used both for naval and fishing purposes. In spite of its strategic and economic importance, at present Kaliningrad has only about two-thirds of its prewar population, due to the expulsion of the original German population and their replacement by Russians brought from various parts of the Soviet Union. Riga is the largest of these Baltic cities, with a population of 835,000 as of 1979. The Baltic cities have old medieval centers with typical German architecture of the period, although most of the newer residential districts consist of standard Soviet-style apartment blocks found as well in most other cities from Central Asia to the Arctic. Vilnius, the capital of the Lithuanian S.S.R., differs from these other Baltic cities in that it was not a Protestant German city, but a Polish Catholic city with a large Jewish population. It was annexed by the Soviet Union from Poland in 1940.

Contemporary Soviet Urban Problems

The problems of urban life in the Soviet Union are best understood by looking at the daily life of a citizen of Moscow or of another large Soviet city. Following an examination of a number of problems, how they are solved is discussed.

Housing

The average Soviet family lives in an apartment in a large block. This block may either be an older one near the center of the city or a newer one on the outskirts. Residential areas in Soviet cities are often located much closer to the center of the city than is generally the case in the United States. In recent years, however, large new housing areas have arisen on the outskirts of most cities. Many of the new apartment blocks are of a standard architectural style which is ubiquitous in all regions of the country. Concrete panels, internal walls, and bathroom and kitchen units are prefabricated and put into place by cranes or by lifting jacks. In some cases mobile plants are erected near building sites for the prefabrication of parts and then dismantled later. Although these new blocks may look impressive from a distance, construction standards are low and both the exterior and interior finishing is shoddy. The apartments themselves are often very small and poorly equipped with amenities. Although a small kitchen, bath, and toilet are included in most modern flats, there is usually no dining room and the living room may have to double as a bedroom. A large number of people living in older apartment blocks or converted houses may have to share a kitchen and toilet with other residents. In many cases a couple may be living with parents and couples with a child may often have a grandmother living with them in an apartment meant originally for two. In spite of the inconvenience, grandmother may in fact play an important role as baby sitter when mother is at work, a common situation in the Soviet Union. In spite of the large number of new blocks built in recent years, a good apartment remains difficult to find. Tight housing conditions largely account for the small size of families in Soviet cities and the high rate of divorce. It must be remembered, however, that housing is subsidized heavily and rents are low. Thus, housing costs form only a small part of a family's total living expenses.

Transportation

The citizen who cannot walk to his or her place of work usually travels by some form of public transportation. Travel to work by private car is virtually unknown, unless one is an important government official, in which case a car from a government car pool may be made available. The average person travels by bus, trolley bus (which takes power from overhead electric lines), streetcar, or subway, which are often very crowded during rush hours. People will often walk considerable distances to work to avoid waiting for crowded buses. The subway system (Metro) provides the best and quickest way of getting to work in a number of cities, although it can often be crowded. In some cities, including Leningrad, the size of the network is inadequate. The low fares encourage the use of mass transportation in general. Taxis, also available, sometimes follow regular routes at rush hours and thus can take several passengers having the same destination.

Place of Work

Most Soviet citizens work in a state-run enterprise, which may be anything from an iron and steel plant to a local dairy store. Many work in ministries or other government offices. It must be remembered that the role of large industrial corporations and other business enterprises of Western type is filled in the Soviet Union by a large number of ministries and other state organizations. These offices are often housed in buildings in the central districts of the city, especially in Moscow and the capitals of the republics. The office work force tends to be more concentrated and centrally located than in some Western cities.

Shopping

Shopping presents some problems for the Soviet citizen. Department stores are found in most cities but are sometimes contained in antiquated buildings, such as the huge G.U.M. (state department store) on the Red Square in Moscow, built in Tsarist times as a merchants' arcade. Because of the lack of competition, generally only one or two major department stores are in each city. Since stores of all types are state owned, their number and location are not decided by market forces but by government planners. In general, an attempt is made to locate stores which sell everyday items in residential areas, so that consumers will not have far to walk for their daily shopping. Soviet housewives usually shop every day for food and often have to stop at separate stores for dairy products, meat, and bread. Supermarkets exist, but are often in the downtown area and have to be visited by bus or streetcar. Shopping takes a long time, as one often has to stand in line for scarce goods. Within the store there are separate lines to choose your purchase, to pay for it, and to pick it up. There are usually a number of kiosks on the streets of Soviet cities, where not only newspapers are sold, but also bus and streetcar tickets, postage stamps, and other items. Some kiosks supply information on local addresses and transportation. There are also stands on the sidewalks selling beer and kvass (a drink made from fermented grain bread).

Each city has a "collective farm" market, which corresponds to the farmers' market found in many Western cities. Here the farmers bring produce grown on their private plots on the collective farms and sell it at a price decided by supply and demand. Many Soviet housewives shop for vegetables and other foodstuff at these markets. Although prices are generally higher than in state-owned stores, the quality of the produce is usually better and there is greater variety. In order to get the largest selection the housewife has to be at the market at an early hour. In general, shopping is a major operation for the Soviet citizen, and the purchase of food and clothing consumes a large part of his or her time as well as a major portion of the monthly budget.

Entertainment

Restaurants, theaters, cinemas, and other forms of entertainment exist in Soviet cities. The theater, opera, and ballet are very popular, and tickets are often difficult to get, especially when favorite performers are appearing. The cinema is also popular, and the Soviet film industry is very productive. Only a few selected Western films are shown. The circus is also a popular form of entertainment, for children and adults, and many cities have a large permanent building for the circus. Night clubs exist, but are not as numerous as in many Western cities. On the whole, Soviet urban entertainment is conservative by Western standards. As in other countries, a large number of Soviet families have a television set (the price of which is relatively cheap), and many stay at home after work to watch the programs. Again, Soviet television programs are in general conservative and have a strong educational and ideological character.

Restaurants are popular places to visit for a special night out. Several large restaurants in Moscow, for example, specialize in regional dishes from the Caucasus, Central Asia, and other parts of the Soviet Union, while the major hotels have restaurants catering to local citizens as well as to tourists. There is usually an orchestra and singers. Most people, however, do not use restaurants as a place to eat everyday meals to the extent that the average American does. Most meals are eaten at home or at the place of work, where a canteen may be available. There are few snack bars or fast-food restaurants in Soviet cities.

The "palace of culture" is a unique feature of cities in the communist world. It is a large building, often in the center of the city, where there may be a theater, cinema, or restaurant, as well as lecture rooms for cultural or political meetings or talks, a gymnasium, practice rooms for choirs and orchestras, and rooms where various hobbies can be carried out. The palace of culture may be run by the city itself or may belong to a major factory or enterprise. For example, the big electrical engineering plant in Riga has a palace of culture which can accommodate 3000 persons in 44 different activity groups. Salaried instructors teach such divergent hobbies as ballet, sculpture, and stamp collecting.

Recreation

Parks, sports arenas, and other forms of outdoor recreation are also provided in most Soviet cities. Parks are popular with the citizens during the summer and are generally well kept, with trees and ornamental flower beds. Many of the cities destroyed during the war were rebuilt with new parks in the city center. In general, the level of crime in Soviet cities is low and parks are safe places for the whole family. Even on cold winter days a surprisingly large number of women with their warmly clothed children can be seen sitting on park benches. Sports arenas and swimming pools are provided in all cities. In Moscow there is a large stadium along with a whole complex of sports buildings along the banks of the Moscow River to the southwest of the city. These facilities and others were used for the 1980 Olympic Games.

Religious Institutions

Although churches or mosques are a prominent feature of the skyline in the older districts of Soviet cities, few are used for religious purposes and many are now museums or are empty. Their place as the location of weddings or baptisms has been replaced by two new Soviet institutions, the "palace of weddings" and the "palace of infants." The palace of weddings, a special building where the ceremony takes place, has a large hall where guests can attend and also toast the happy couple. The wedding party is later held in a restaurant or at home. The palace of infants is used for baptisms. In Leningrad, for example, it is a two-storied building, with rooms for the mother and child, a doctor in attendance, a banquet hall, and a room for ceremonies. These institutions have obviously been developed to replace the religious ceremonies which were popular with Russians in the old days.

Solutions to Soviet Urban Problems

The growth of urbanization has clearly been exceptionally rapid in the Soviet Union since the 1917 revolution, especially during the period of the Stalin five-year plans (1928–1941) and since World War II. In 1926 only 18 percent of the total population was classified as urban, while in 1940 it was 33 percent. In 1977 over 62 percent of the population lived in urban settlements (Fig. 4.4). Much of this growth has taken place in the large cities. The number of cities with a population over 100,000 rose from 31 in 1926 to 236 in 1973, while cities with a population of over 500,000 rose from 3 in 1926 (Moscow, Leningrad, and Kiev) to 35 in 1973. (Fig. 4.5). In the latter year about 28 percent of the urban population of the country lived in cities with 500,000 or more inhabitants, while about 29 percent lived in cities with a population between 100,000 and 500,000. In other words, the Soviet Union has become a country of large cities with a rapid rate of urban population growth. Between 1959 and 1973 the urban population of the country increased from 100 million to 146 million, a rate of about 3.3 percent per annum. Although this may be slower than the 6.5 percent rate of the prewar period, the rate of urbanization is nevertheless quite high.

Socialist Urban Planning

Faced with this situation of rapid growth, it is not surprising that in a country devoted to the concept of socialist planning much attention has been given to the question of the optimum size of cities and methods of control. In particular, Soviet planners have stressed the necessity of limiting the size of the largest cities and of developing small and middle-sized cities, either from expanding existing ones or creating new towns of various types. At present, many new industrial plants are being built in smaller cities.

The Soviet authorities have a means of controlling the population movement and place of residence which enables them to limit or restrict population more effectively than in many other countries. Every worker must receive a permit to live and work in a particular city, and no housing will be made available to him or her without this permit. Even then the worker may be put on a waiting list for an apartment, control of which lies in the hands of either the enterprise for which he or she works or the city government. Each citizen must carry a domestic passport in which basic information on the owner is recorded, including permission granted to reside in a particular city. A residential permit is difficult to obtain in any city where the authorities are attempting to restrict population growth. There are about 20 of these cities, including Moscow, Leningrad and Kiev, where residence permits are hard to obtain. In spite of this control, people who have connections or whose talents are particularly attractive to a factory or enterprise may be able to arrange for permission to live in a restricted city. It is also possible for authorities to deny peasants permission to leave a collective or state farm to move to the city, a policy which partially controls migration from rural to urban areas.

The Socialist City

Apart from attempts to control city size, Soviet planners have also been active in designing cities which they consider more suitable for a country with avowed socialist principles. This concept of the *socialist city* has been applied not only in planning of new towns but also in reconstructing older cities and developing new districts and suburbs.

The socialist city is seen as a classless city. This means that in theory no residential areas are designed for housing low-income workers or upper-middle-class executives. Everybody lives in the same districts in the same type of apartment block. This concept leads to standardized housing: rows of uniform, generally uninteresting-looking blocks of poor design and construction. In spite of claims to having developed a classless society, the higher officials, economic managers, top Communist party officials and other important people generally have better quality housing, often segregated in a form of residential ghetto of modern style buildings with big windows and nicely tended lawns. They use special stores for their shopping and have a country villa for summer use.

The central area of a socialist city is also conceived along rather different lines than the downtown area of a Western city. In place of the commercial establishments and offices typical of the Western central business district, the socialist city has more buildings housing political, cultural, and educational activities, often located around or near to a large central square. In some cases this central square already existed from an earlier period of urban development, but in many cities in both the Soviet Union and Eastern Europe these squares are a feature of socialist planning. The square is often used for military parades, for mass demonstrations in support of the regime, or as standing space for crowds attending a speech by one of the leaders. Besides palaces of culture, Party headquarters, museums, theaters, and opera houses, the central area of the city also has department stores and tourist hotels. Many buildings in the city center carry communist slogans and are sometimes surmounted with red stars and other symbols. It should also be remembered that in some Soviet cities residential areas are found much closer to the downtown area than in the case of American cities.

In the ideal socialist city the concept of self-contained neighborhoods is stressed. People should be able to conduct most of their everyday affairs without leaving a small area around their apartment building. Ideally, one's home should be close to the place of work, either office or factory. In the immediate neighborhood there should be shops, a school, a post office, a small park, and other recreational facilities. These residential units, known as *mikrorayons* ("microneighborhoods"), form the basis of present residential planning. In a large city the mikrorayon is the basic unit, containing about 15,000 people. A school is within walking distance, and other facilities should not be further than between a quarter and a third of a mile from home. Next in size is the residential district, containing up to 50,000 people. Shopping, cultural, and recreational facilities of a higher order are available (such as theaters, clubs, libraries, and medical centers) and may be up to a mile from home. Each district contains several mikrorayons. In practice many communities lack the services which in theory they should have, and many people have to commute considerable distances to work. In many cases workers may have to live in suburban villages or smaller towns and travel to work every day by train. It should also be noted that the neighborhood complex of shops and services is found in many Western cities and is thus not a peculiarly Soviet development.

On the whole, the socialist city concept has not worked out too well in practice in the communist countries. It has often been difficult to convert older cities to this model, and often distinct socialist features can only be found in the newer residential districts of the city. Poor standards of construction, lack of investment, and delays in implementing or completing plans have led to poor results.

Historical Development of Eastern European Cities

It is more difficult to generalize about urbanization in Eastern Europe than in the case of the Soviet Union. A group of countries is involved which have had varied historical experiences and which at different periods have come under the control or influence of other European continental powers. For example, Poland has been partitioned on several occasions in its history between Germany, Russia, and Austria, and its cities and towns reflect these foreign influences. In Southeastern Europe the long period of control by the Turks is reflected in the architecture of many cities in southern Yugoslavia, Bulgaria, and Albania.

In general, the highest levels of urbanization are found in East Germany, western Czechoslovakia, and southern and central Poland, while the lowest levels are in southern and eastern Yugoslavia, Bulgaria, and Albania (Fig. 4.11). Hungary and western Romania occupy an intermediate position. This situation is largely due to the economic and political policies of the major powers which controlled these countries and regions in the past.

German Influences

German and Austrian influences were most influential in encouraging the growth of urbanization. Many of the old cities of Central Europe owe their origin to the activities

Figure 4.11 Major Cities of Eastern Europe. (*Source:* Adapted from Roy E. H. Mellor, *Eastern Europe: A Geography of the Comecon Countries,* New York: Columbia University Press, 1975 p. 140.)

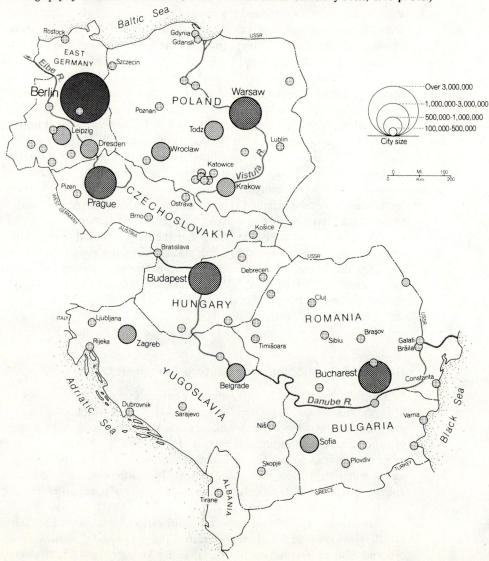

of German or Austrian architects and town planners. Prague, Plzen, Brno, and many other cities and towns in Czechoslovakia; Kracow, Gdansk (Danzig), Poznan, and Wroclaw (Breslau) in Poland; Budapest in Hungary; Zagreb and Ljubljana in northern Yugoslavia; and, of course, the cities of East Germany—these are basically German or Austrian in style and appearance, although their inhabitants may have been neither, in either language or culture. At one time all these cities were within either the German or the Austro-Hungarian empires.

Even beyond the area of their political control, the Germans had a great influence on the growth of urbanization in Eastern Europe. Numbers of German miners, merchants and soldiers, many invited by local rulers, settled in regions including Transylvania in western Romania and in Slovakia. They established towns such as Cluj (Kausenburgh), Sighisoara (Schassburg), Brasov (Kronstadt), and Sibiu (Hermannstadt) in Transylvania and several small mining towns in Slovakia.

Turkish Influences: Sarajevo

Turkish influence was limited basically to the area of the southern part of present-day Yugoslavia, as well as to Bulgaria and Albania. Although Hungary was occupied by the Turks for some time, the only remaining signs are a few old mosques left standing in the center of cities such as Pecs. Romania was also part of the Ottoman Empire, but again little Turkish influence can be seen in Romanian cities. The Turks did nothing to encourage the economy of their conquered territories, and with a lack of industrial activity, it is not surprising that few large cities developed. The Turks developed several military and commerical centers, however, which bear the mark of their origin in the shape of mosques, *hamams* (Turkish baths), religious schools, bazaars, and other features typical of Islamic cities.

One of the cities established by the Turks as the residence for a governor was Sarajevo in the province of Bosnia in central Yugoslavia. Founded in 1462, it still retains a typical Turkish appearance, with mosques, houses with courtyards, a *hamam,* and the remains of an old caravansary. By the middle of the sixteenth century Sarajevo had a population of around 50,000. Sarajevo was also important because it lay on a major trade route between Istanbul and Turkish possessions to the north. In 1878 Austria occupied Bosnia and later annexed it, with the result that Sarajevo became an Austrian city with the addition of some large, Western-style administrative buildings. After World War II Sarajevo became the capital of the Yugoslav republic of Bosnia and Hercegovina; since then, both the city center and residential areas have experienced considerable development. Its population was 244,000 in 1975.

Major Representative Cities of Eastern Europe

Belgrade: Crossroads City

The site of the city of Belgrade was occupied by a settlement long before the period of Turkish control. A fort already existed in prehistoric times at the confluence of the Sava and Danube rivers, and during the period of Roman control it became an important frontier fortress known as Singidunum. The site was later occupied by the Slavs and became part of the Bulgarian and, later, the Byzantine empires. Although the population consisted of Serbs, the town fell into the hands of the Hungarians in the fifteenth century and later was captured by the Turks in 1521. After a short period of Austrian control and subsequent reoccupation by the Turks, Belgrade finally came under Serbian control in 1815. The Turkish garrison did not leave until 1867, however. Belgrade was damaged by artillery bombardment in the First World War and by German and Allied air attacks in the Second World War. The result was the destruction of much of the old Turkish city. Most of the city center today is modern. Belgrade has suffered through the centuries because of its strategic location in a region disputed by the major powers of Austria, Hungary, and Turkey. It lies on important land and water routes and is the major river port of Yugoslavia. The banks of the Sava are lined with quays, and there is an important railroad terminal. Most of the city's industry lies to the east, although the suburbs of Zemun to the west and Rakovica and Zeleznki to the south contain some modern engineering plants. To the west of the city the new district of Novi Beograd (New Belgrade) contains high rise apartment blocks and government buildings. The population of Belgrade expanded from 250,000 in 1939 to 746,000 at the census of 1971, and is currently around 1 million.

Sofia: Bulgarian Capital

The capital of Bulgaria dates back to the time of the Romans, who named it Serdica after a local tribe, the Serdi, It lay on an important east-west route and during the reign of Constantine the Great in the fourth century became one of the major cities of the Balkans. In the following century Serdica was destroyed by the Huns. The city was later rebuilt and in the time of Justinian regained much of its former glory. With the arrival of the Slavs in the region the name of the city was changed to Sredets ("the center"), reflecting its location at a focal point of routes. A number of churches existed in the city, the largest of which, the church of St. Sophia, gave the city its present name. This sixth-century church is still standing.

In 1386 the city was captured by the Turks and a long period of Turkish control began. Although at this time the capital of the Bulgarian state was Velikovo Turnovo, the Turks made Sofia the capital of the province of Rumelia. The city lost much of its former importance, however, and in 1879 when it became the capital of liberated Bulgaria, it was a small Turkish town of only 12,000 inhabitants. As the administrative center of the country it began to grow and soon attracted several industries. Much of the city was rebuilt, and the large Alexander Nevsky cathedral, the National Assembly, the university, and the National Theater were built at the end of the nineteenth and the beginning of the twentieth century. By 1912 about 18 percent of the country's industrial enterprises were concentrated in Sofia. Although the planning of the city center left much to be desired, the existence of a number of parks gives the city a pleasant appearance. Much of the center was destroyed by Allied air raids during the Second World War, requiring considerable reconstruction. Since the period of communist control, a large party headquarters and a mausoleum to house the body of former leader

Georgi Dimitrov have been added to the monumental buildings of the city center. Several large hotels and a central department store have also been built in recent years. At present, Sofia is the most important industrial city of Bulgaria and accounts for about one-quarter of total industrial production.

Sofia is fortunate in having a large park on its southern outskirts in the shape of Mount Vitosha, which provides the inhabitants of Sofia with opportunities for outdoor exercise, including winter sports. The basin in which Sofia lies permits the expansion of the city and its industries, and several new districts and suburbs have been developed in recent years (Fig. 4.12). The city's current population is over 1 million, compared with 516,000 in 1946.

Bucharest: Romanian Capital

Although many of the cities of Eastern Europe were founded during the Roman period or at another early time, several of the major cities of the region saw their period of greatest development during the years after they became the capitals of new nation states. Bucharest, the capital of Romania, had attained some importance as a provincial capital before the independence of the country in 1861. At that time it had about 121,000 inhabitants and was a major trade center between Turkey and Central Europe. Industrial development led to the rapid growth of the city between World War I and the present. By 1941 the population had almost reached the million mark and by 1980 totalled 1.9 million (Fig. 4.13). The center of the city, partly damaged by bombing,

Figure 4.12 Sofia: the Supermarket of a New Housing Development. (I. Matley)

Figure 4.13 Bucharest: the Headquarters of the Romanian Communist Party. This building is typical of the monumental government buildings erected in socialist cities in Eastern Europe. (I. Matley)

was to a great extent rebuilt after World War II in a mixture of architectural styles. Large new residential areas were also developed. However, the disastrous earthquake of 1976 destroyed many of the new, cheaply built buildings, including many apartment blocks in the central areas of the city, with great loss of life. A major rebuilding program is now underway.

Warsaw: A Rebuilt City

Warsaw, the capital of Poland, was first mentioned as a town in the fourteenth century, when it functioned as a river port on the Vistula. In the sixteenth century it became the capital, but during the next century the city suffered greatly from the Swedish invasions. In the eighteenth century the Saxon kings of Poland were instrumental in developing and beautifying the city, which had about 100,000 inhabitants by the end of the century. Between 1815 and 1830 Warsaw was the capital of an autonomous kingdom, but after that Warsaw found itself in the part of Poland under Russian control. It lost its role as a capital city, but nevertheless grew into an important industrial and commercial center on the railroad from Vienna to St. Petersburg. Warsaw was badly planned, however, and by 1914 its 800,000 inhabitants were living in a congested and crowded city. When Poland became an independent country again after World War I, development was more carefully planned. But in 1939 the German invasion and the subsequent bombardment of the city resulted in the destruction of much of the city. What remained was further destroyed during the uprisings against the German occupiers in 1943 and

1944. In 1945 only 162,000 persons were left in the city, compared with 1.3 million in 1939. After the war the old part of the city was restored at great cost (Fig. 4.14A and B). A new center was developed with a large square dominated by a large Palace of Science and Culture donated by the Soviet Union. It is built in the typical Stalinist "wedding cake" skyscraper style of the early 1950s. Apart from the old town and some surrounding streets, much of the city has been replanned, including access routes. The city has seen a great deal of industrial development; its population had reached 2 million by 1980.

Budapest: Twin-City Origins

Budapest has had a rather different pattern of development compared with Warsaw. Originally a Roman fortress on the Danube, it was developed as a trading town by the Hungarians after their settlement in the Mid-Danube region. Buda, on the west bank of the river, became the capital of Hungary in the early Middle Ages, but it was destroyed by the Tatars, along with the settlement of Pest on the opposite bank. After the Tatars left, a new site was chosen for Buda, a limestone hill facing Pest across the river. Here a castle was built, which was expanded at later periods until its virtual destruction during World War II. The Turks held Buda and Pest between 1541 and 1686, and the cities took on a Turkish appearance. When the Turks withdrew, the two cities were badly damaged; reconstruction did not take place until the eighteenth century, when an Austrian-style city arose. In 1849 a permanent bridge was built over the river, joining the two cities, which in 1873 were united as Budapest. This bridge has been followed by seven others. In the nineteenth-century, Pest, on the flat east bank of the river, developed particularly rapidly and several major boulevards and numerous government and commercial buildings were constructed (Fig. 4.15). The first subway on the European continent was built here in 1896. Pest became the administrative center of the whole city, while Buda remained essentially an area of historic buildings and villas. In 1900 Budapest had 863,000 inhabitants. During the period between the two World Wars it industrialized rapidly and at present is by far the largest city of Hungary, containing as many people as all of Hungary together. Budapest also contains much of the country's industry, including engineering and metallurgy. The current population exceeds 2 million.

Prague: Commercial and Administrative City

The capital of Czechoslovakia began as a settlement on the hill known as the Vyšehrad. At the beginning of the Middle Ages the Hradčany castle was built to the north on the high west bank of the Vltava River. It contained the cathedral of the bishop of Prague. Beside it, the district known as Mala Strana arose for persons of the court. In the fourteenth century Charles IV expanded the city from the area on the bank opposite the Hradčany toward the east and south. The old core of the city, known as the Staré Město ("old town"), contained a commercial and a Jewish quarter, while the construction of the Nové Město ("new town") added a further commercial district. The city was surrounded by a wall. Charles also built one of the first universities in

Figure 4.14A   Warsaw: the City Center in 1963. (I. Matley)

Figure 4.14B   Warsaw: the same view at present. The multistoried building in the center is the Hotel Forum. The streets at this busy intersection are linked by pedestrian tunnels. (I. Matley)

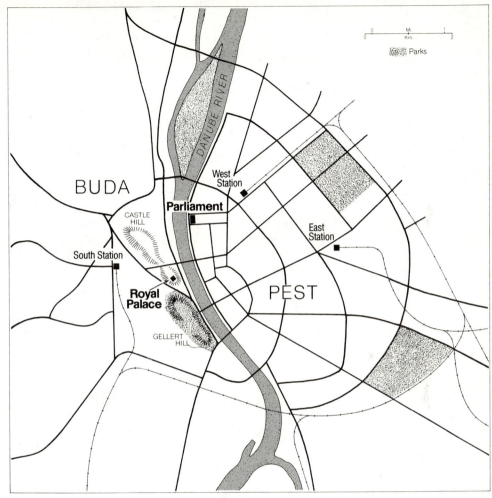

Figure 4.15 Budapest. (*Source:* Adapted from R. H. Osborne, *East-Central Europe,* New York: Praeger, 1967, p. 179.)

Europe, which, when added to the political functions of the city as the capital of the Holy Roman Empire, made Prague one of the most important cities of the time.

The city saw little growth until the nineteenth century. Part of the city walls were removed, and new residential and industrial districts were developed. As a city of the Austro-Hungarian Empire, Prague was a focus of Austrian and German investment and became an important industrial and transportation center, with engineering and chemical factories and manufacturers of a variety of consumer goods. A river port was also established. By 1938 the city had about 900,000 inhabitants. In spite of new construction, the older parts of the city were relatively little touched, while damage in World War II was minimal. Prague remains one of the most beautiful cities of Europe, with a remarkable collection of Gothic and Baroque buildings (Fig. 4.16). The population in 1980 was over 1.1 million.

Czechoslovakia also contains a large number of smaller cities and towns of great historical interest. Such cities as Plzeň, České Budějovice, Hradec Králové, and Bratislava have old centers, where buildings of historical and architectural importance have been carefully preserved. Many Czechoslovak cities have also been built with new suburbs according to the principles of socialist planning.

New Socialist Cities: Heavy Industrial Base

As in the Soviet Union, the period of communist control, which began in the Eastern European countries only after World War II, has seen the development not only of existing cities, but of new socialist cities, mainly connected with the rapid development of heavy industry. Most of the Eastern European countries, with the exception of the western parts of Czechoslovakia and of East Germany, had seen little industrial development before World War II. According to Soviet planning theory, an iron and steel industry was essential to the future growth of national industry, and in several countries large new plants were built, which formed the core of new cities. In Hungary the city of Dunaújváros ("Danube new town") was founded on the Danube River south of Budapest, where local and Polish coal and iron ore from the Ukraine could be assembled. In Poland a similar development took place at Nowa Huta (New Foundry), on the outskirts of the old Polish city of Kracow. This large plant uses iron ore from the

Figure 4.16   Prague: the Hradcany with the Cathedral of St. Vitus. In the right background is the Vltava River. (I. Matley)

Ukraine and local coal and employs people from the predominantly rural areas to the east of Kracow. In 1970 the population of Nowa Huta had reached 161,000. In Czechoslovakia, as in East Germany, much of the recent development of heavy industry has been based on existing iron and steel manufacturing centers, which have been expanded in many cases with new plants and residential districts. However, large new metallurgical works have been built at Košice in Eastern Slovakia in order to bring industry to a basically rural area. A new town has arisen around the plant.

In Yugoslavia several socialist cities have arisen, not all of them associated with heavy industry. For example, Titograd was built next to the old Turkish town of Podgorica to serve as the new capital of the republic of Montenegro. Although it has some industry, its function is mainly administrative and cultural. It is also the site of a new university. Romania also has several new cities, of which the most important is Gheorghe Gheorghiu-Dej, named after a communist leader. It is a major center of the Romanian petrochemical industry and rose in a few years from a village to a city; its 1971 population was 56,000. Several other cities have had new districts added to them. An example is the old mining town of Baia Mare, which has a new city center and residential area.

In general, most of these new cities in Eastern Europe are laid out according to the basic principles developed by Soviet planners and architects. As in the case of the Soviet Union, the results have been mixed, with a great deal of monotonous standardization of buildings and poor construction.

Major Urban Problems

Many of the problems found in Soviet cities also exist in those of Eastern Europe. A major difference is that the cities of Eastern Europe have experienced a more recent period of urban development under capitalism than did those of the Soviet Union. Cities such as Budapest and Prague contain many buildings and residential areas which were built during the capitalist period between the two world wars. In particular much more former middle class housing is still left in these cities than in Moscow or other Soviet cities. Although many of these houses, villas, and apartments have since been subdivided or shared by families, some families still occupy the same house they owned before World War II. In most cities, however, housing is in short supply and the remarks made earlier about Soviet housing problems also apply to the countries of Eastern Europe.

Urban mass transportation is organized in much the same fashion as in Soviet cities. Private ownership of cars is more common in some Eastern European countries, however, and traffic jams develop regularly in such cities as Belgrade and Budapest. The recreation and entertainment picture is somewhat brighter. Not only do many of the Eastern European cities have large and beautiful parks, dating in most cases from an earlier period of city planning, but there are many more restaurants and cafes than in Soviet cities. These differences are mainly due to a different urban tradition from that of the Russians. In Warsaw or Budapest, for example, many people meet in their favorite cafes in the evening or sit on terraces where they can drink their coffee and watch the world go by. Urban entertainments have more the flavor of Vienna than of Moscow. In the southern countries such as Yugoslavia and Romania life is lived more on the street, in the sidewalk cafe, and during the evening promenade, where people can meet their friends. In some Yugoslav cities certain streets are closed to traffic for a period in the evening so that an evening promenade can take place uninterrupted. As a whole there are more compensations for inadequate housing and lack of consumer goods in the cities of Eastern Europe than in those of the Soviet Union. In fact, to many Soviet tourists, Prague, Warsaw, and Budapest represent the West rather than an extension of their own society.

RECOMMENDED READINGS

Bater, James H. *St. Petersburg: Industrialization and Change.* Montreal: McGill-Queen's University Press, 1976.
    An excellent and detailed study of the economic and social development of the city.
Fedor, Thomas S. *Patterns of Urban Growth in the Russian Empire During the Nineteenth Century.* Chicago: University of Chicago, Department of Geography, Research Paper No. 163, 1975.
    A good historical account of an important period in the growth of Russian cities.
Fisher, Jack C. "Urban Planning in the Soviet Union and Eastern Europe." In *Taming Megalopolis,* edited by H. W. Eldredge. Vol. 2. Garden City, NY: Doubleday, 1967, pp. 1068–1099.
    Covers the basic principles of socialist urban planning.
French, R. A. and F. E. Ian Hamilton, eds. *The Socialist City.* Chichester, John Wiley, 1979.
Frolic, B. Michael. "Moscow: The Socialist Alternative." In *World Capitals,* edited by H. Wentworth Eldredge. Garden City, NY: Anchor/Doubleday, 1975, pp. 295–337.
    Good general description, including discussion of city organization and major problems.
Gutkind, Erwin A., ed. *Urban Development in East-Central Europe: Poland, Czechoslovakia, and Hungary.* International History of City Development, Vol. 7. New York: The Free Press, 1972.
    Covers the growth of cities up to the early modern period.
Gutkind, Erwin A., ed. *Urban Development in Eastern Europe: Bulgaria, Romania, and the U.S.S.R.* International History of City Development, Vol. 8. New York: The Free Press, 1972.
Hall, Peter. "Moscow." In *The World's Cities,* edited by Peter Hall. New York: McGraw-Hill, 1977, pp. 150–177.
    A good general description with maps.
Hamilton, F. E. Ian. *The Moscow City Region.* Oxford: Oxford University Press, 1976.
Hamm, Michael F., ed. *The City in Russian History.* Lexington, KY: University Press of Kentucky, 1976.
    An account of the role of cities in Russian history.
Harris, Chauncy D. *Cities of the Soviet Union.* Monograph Series of the Association of American Geographers. Chicago: Rand McNally, 1970.
    A detailed analysis of the growth and functions of cities during the Soviet period.
Lappo, G. et al. *Moscow: Capital of the Soviet Union.* Moscow: Progress Publishers, 1976.
    A good general description of the city by Soviet geographers.

Posokhin, M. V. *Cities to Live In.* Moscow: Novosti Press, Agency Publishing House, 1974.
  A Soviet scholar looks at modern urban development with special attention to Moscow.

Pounds, Norman J. G. "The Urbanization of East-Central and Southeast Europe: An Historical Perspective," with comments by Ian M. Matley. In *Eastern Europe: Essays in Geographical Problems,* edited by George W. Hoffman. London: Methuen 1971, pp. 45–81.
  A general historical review of East European urban development.

Underhill, Jack A. *Soviet New Towns: Housing and National Urban Policy Growth.* Washington DC: U.S. Department of Housing and Urban Development, July 1976.
  An American assessment of new socialist cities and their planning.

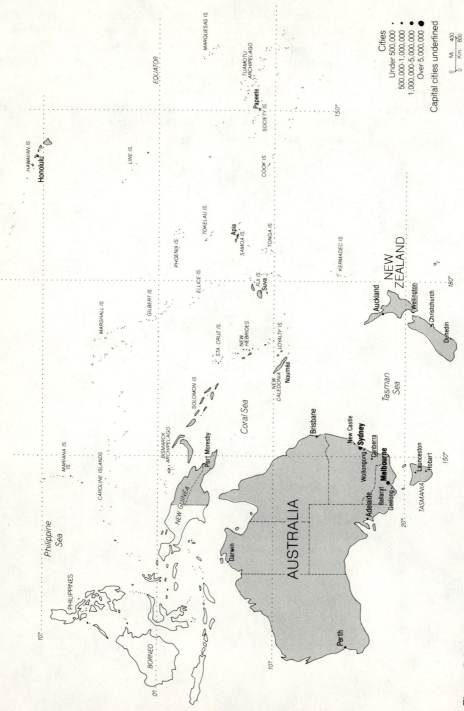

Figure 5.1 Major Cities of Oceania. (*Source:* Data derived from United Nations, Department of Economic and Social Affairs, *Global Review of Human Settlements, Statistical Annex*, published by Pergamon Press, New York, 1976.)

Chapter 5

Cities of Oceania

A. James Rose

Oceania in the World Urban System

Oceania is the least neatly defined of the 10 world regions examined in this book. From the perspective of urbanization and urban systems, the most important geographical areas included in Oceania are Australia, first and foremost, and New Zealand secondarily, with urban places far smaller and less important in the many islands that make up the remainder of Oceania. A unique feature of Oceania is that this is one of the most urbanized regions of the world, at 73 percent, yet the total urban population is the smallest of the 10 world regions, a trifling 17 million in 1980. This curious standing is due, of course, to the small total population throughout Oceania, and to the fact that most of that population is located in Australia, an arid continent that encouraged peripheral settlement and whose historical pattern of growth stimulated concentration of population in urban places. Actually, Australia and New Zealand are among the most highly urbanized countries of the world, at 87 and 85 percent, respectively. Together, they contain 18 of Oceania's more than 24 million inhabitants.

In terms of numbers and specific cities, Oceania has few major cities (Fig. 5.1). Only four cities have a population greater than 1 million, all of them in Australia: Sydney and Melbourne dominate with more than 3 million each, followed in size by Adelaide and Brisbane. The largest city in New Zealand, Auckland, has fewer than 1 million inhabitants, and none of the cities ("towns" would be more appropriate titles) in the rest of Oceania amount to much, although a few, such as Suva (Fiji) and Port Moresby (New Guinea), have populations around 100,000. That is not to say these towns do not serve important, albeit limited, roles as regional centers in the various island groupings. But when comparing Oceania with the rest of the world from an urban perspective, the big cities of Australia provide the primary basis of comparison.

One of the dominant themes throughout Oceania, best expressed in Australia, but also evident even in the rest of the region, is the dominance of urban primacy, with a single city serving as the focal point for a large geographical area. Although the primate city is found throughout the world, this phenomenon is unusually well developed in Oceania, as the result of the peculiar geography, vast distances, and limited population of the region, as well as the historical processes of settlement and development, especially in Australia.

Oceania has no generally accepted boundary. As used in this chapter the region comprises the lands and waters lying south of the equator and southward and eastward from Indonesia. Its major landmasses include Australia, the eastern half of New Guinea, and New Zealand; in addition a number of significant island groups cluster around the main islands of the Solomons, New Caledonia, Fiji, and Samoa. Eastward from Fiji the island groups are more thinly spread, their units smaller and their isolation greater; from Tonga eastward through the Cook Islands, the Societies, and the Tuamotus the only unity is supplied by the common tongue of Polynesia and the shared experience of European cultural and political domination. The outstanding geographical characteristic of Oceania is distance, distance between its settled points and distance from the major population concentrations of the world.

The total land area of Oceania is about 3.4 million sq. mi. (8.8 million sq. km.), 90 percent of which lies in Australia. This total is a little less than the area of the United States, including Alaska, or of Canada. The area supports a population of some 24 million spread thinly through 50 degrees of latitude from the equator to southernmost New Zealand, and through 110 degrees of longitude, from the offshore islands of Western Australia eastward to the Society Islands. An equivalent global span in the northern hemisphere would incorporate a sector stretching northward from the Amazon to the Canada-U.S. border, and westward across the breadth of South America and far into the central Pacific to the longitude of Hawaii. Sydney, the major city of Oceania, lies in its central southern zone. Distances from Sydney to selected cities within and beyond the region illustrate the daunting character of the isolation that must be overcome in linking Oceania with the outside world and in developing internal regional networks. San Francisco lies 7400 mi. (11,910 km.) across the Pacific to the northeast; Singapore, the nearest city on mainland Asia, is 3900 mi. (6280 km.) to the northwest. Within the region, Perth is 2000 mi. (3220 km) away; Rarotonga in the Cook Islands, is 3100 mi. (4990 km.); and relatively nearby Wellington, capital of New Zealand, lies 1400 mi. (2250 km.) southeast, across empty ocean. Port Moresby, capital of Papua New Guinea, is 1800 mi. (2900 km.) north of Sydney.

Given these factors—of distance and isolation—the role of transport and communication facilities provides a prominent common theme in the fabric of all the major centers of the region. The imperative need to conquer distance provides a common link between the navigators of ancient Polynesia and the jet pilots of today.

Nature and Evolution of the Urban System

Two hundred years ago neither cities nor towns existed in Oceania. Today no part of the world is so completely dominated by its major metropolitan concentrations. Two centuries ago the entire Australian continent, Tasmania, and most of southern New Zealand were devoid of permanent settlements; in the remaining 10 percent of the total land area, in northern New Zealand and the remainder of Polynesia together with the island clusters of Melanesia, permanent settlements were limited in size to the villages housing the gardening populations in each self-contained and isolated patch of cultivable land. Today, each major territory is knit together by the flows of political organization and commerce emanating from its metropolitan capital, which also serves as the link point of that territory with the outside world. In the modern era the basic parameter for each of the urban systems that has evolved is provided by the political-territorial framework established in the early phase of European penetration and colonization.

Territorial Frameworks for Urban Evolution

In some major world regions the relationship of political boundaries to urban systems is not always apparent. In Oceania (as in much of Latin America) the coincidence of political territory with the polarized concentration of the entire settlement array contained therein is invariably striking and in some instances spectacular in its intensity. Primacy is the common denominator of the Oceanian urban system, primacy with respect to the political territory within which the particular system evolved. Thus an understanding of the urban systems of the Oceania region requires an understanding of the geographical character of the territories themselves, as well as of the political-economic basis of their territorial organization.

The Archipelagos There is a logic to the political organization of Oceania that is based in the geographical disposition of its land areas. There are many small islands, but these generally cluster in archipelagos. In pre-European days seldom did any measure of political integration exist even between neighboring island units within the archipelagos; generally the largest political units did not exceed in scale the integration of a limited number of villages within a single tribal area on any one island. When the Europeans came they imposed common political rule over the whole archipelago, and these new colonial entities became the womb for the embryonic urban systems and the modern national states that have now emerged, such as Fiji and the Solomons, Western Samoa, and Cook Islands; isolated islands such as Nauru and Tuvalu have taken on separate political identities with independence.

New Zealand This island country is much larger in scale than the other island groups. Since the firm establishment of the European population, and the conclusive subjugation of the Maoris by 1874, the country has been governed as a unitary state. In 1865 the capital was shifted from the relatively peripheral northern town of Auckland to the comparatively central location of Wellington, at the southern extremity of the North Island. Wellington thus gained political ascendancy over the string of settlements and towns that has been springing up along the coasts of the thousand-mile (1600 km.) length of the two main islands since 1840. This ascendancy, combined with the general disposition of the colonial settlements and with the firm establishment of two major centers, Dunedin and Christchurch on the South Island, appeared to ensure the perpetuation of a geographically and statistically balanced hierarchy of urban settlements in New Zealand. However, access to the most productive hinterland within the small national economy led to the emergence of Auckland as the undisputed primate city before the mid-twentieth century. This city is unique among the primates of Oceania in that it is not the seat of territorial government but merely the preeminent center of commerce and industry.

Papua New Guinea This country occupies the eastern half of the large island of New Guinea (largest of the Bismarck Archipelago) and numerous smaller island groups, as well as Bougainville and nearby islands at the northern end of the Solomons archipelago. Prior to European penetration there was some measure of integration by way of commerce among various regional clusters of coastal settlements, but political integration beyond the village scale was virtually absent when the European empires began to take a positive interest in the area during the closing decades of the nineteenth century. Imperial Germany established a claim to northern portions of mainland New Guinea and the islands lying to the east, while Britain claimed the southern part of the mainland, Papua, together with the Solomons to the south of German-held Bougainville. Australia took over administration of Papua from Britain in 1906 and was given the mandate to administer German New Guinea in 1919. Urban development throughout present Papua New Guinea languished until after World War II; none of the three largest towns in the area had more than 10,000 inhabitants when Japanese bombs began to fall in early 1942. Following the war the Australians amalgamated the administrations of Papua and the Territory of New Guinea into a central government at Port Moresby, the original Western capital of Papua. This administrative union provided the stimulus for the subsequent rapid urban development. Despite its eccentric position relative to the major areas of population and economic production in the northeast and in the highlands, Port Moresby had the advantages of comparatively easy access to Australia, reasonable port facilities, and regular air service south to the Australian cities. Under the Australian thrust, the city rapidly emerged as the primate city to create the fabric of an integrated nation-state in response to pressures from the United Nations. By the time Papua New Guinea became self-governing in 1975, Port Moresby's population exceeded 80,000, making it twice the size of Lae, its north-coast competitor, and more than three times the size of distant Rabaul, the former German capital at the eastern end of the island of New Britain.

Australia and Its Sovereign States The world's largest island and smallest continent is marginally smaller than the contiguous United States of America. Together with the neighboring island of Tasmania it has been constituted as a political federation, the Commonwealth of Australia, since 1901. The country's settlement pattern took shape as a series of coastal colonies, each functioning as a separate entity within the British Empire. The present capitals of three of these colonies (now states) formed the primary foci of British settlement in the continent: Sydney in New South Wales, Adelaide in South Australia, and Perth in Western Australia. The original territory of New South Wales incorporated all the eastern third of the continent plus Tasmania—an area comparable in size to all the United States lying east of the Mississippi. Distance and slow transport combined to stimulate secessionist movements in the areas distant from Sydney, and in due course Tasmania, Victoria, and Queensland were accorded equivalent colonial status to their mother colony of New South Wales by the Imperial government in London. Thereafter the settlement pattern in each of the six colonies evolved internally within its own political territory, each in fierce economic competition with its neighbors. The intensity of this competition was mitigated only by the sense of common origin among the inhabitants and by a common allegiance to the British Crown.

Sharing as they did the occupation of a continental area, each of the five mainland colonies also had the shared experience of trying to effectively settle immense territories where farming proved possible only in the quite limited coastward reaches. The interior remained forbidden to the farmer by its aridity. In competition with its neighbors, each colonial government bent its efforts to stimulate settlement by sponsoring immigration from Britain and to hasten the exploitation of its natural resources by the construction (and operation) of rail nets spreading inland to the maximum feasible reach within the colonial territory.

As the railways tapped interior wealth and funneled it to the seaboard, so prospered the merchants in the capital cities who then were able to turn their wealth to the development of manufactures. The Australian colonies partitioned the continent into a functional "economic archipelago," each unit as effectively separated from its neighbors by competitive trade practices and tariffs as were the economies developing simultaneously among the natural archipelagos of the great ocean to the northeast. As the commerce of each Australian "archipelago" unit increased, so too did the wealth and drawing power of its capital city.

Federation in 1901 has not yet succeeded in modifying to any noticeable degree the basic pattern of intense primacy of each colonial capital within its territory, a pattern that was firmly cemented during the half-century of rail-net development after 1850. Indeed, the emergence of Australia as a unified industrialized nation this century has tended to accentuate rather than to diminish the metropolitan dominance of earlier date. Industries flourish best where raw materials converge from scattered sources, where labor is most plentiful, and where markets are most insistent in demand. In Australia, with its large population nodes beaded around 3000 mi. (4800 km.) of coast and its thin veneer of rural population spreading not more than from a few score to about 200 mi. (320 km.) inland, the growth of a national economy has benefited mainly the primary population concentrations of the colonial era.

The most obvious manifestation within the Australian settlement pattern of the direct effects of the political and economic federation of 1901 is the existence of another capital city. Canberra is the seat of federal authority, deliberately sited at a respectable distance inland from the sea and itself a major beneficiary of the taxation powers of the Commonwealth government. Canberra, formerly open grazing country, was formally inaugurated as the seat of national government in 1927; in 1957 it still contained fewer than 40,000 inhabitants, but by 1980 it was approaching 240,000, a sixfold increase in less than 25 years.

The Australian urban system is geared to and governed by a string of colonial-era primate cities. The power of these cities, of their taxpayers and political leaders, remains of such magnitude even into the ninth decade of federal union that their interests are still strong enough to dictate that national government shall not seek to substantially modify the existing structure of the urban system. Australia remains firmly wedded to a blissful state of metropolitan dominance and provincial subservience.

Primacy and Subservience

The nature and dimensions of urban systems are fundamentally conditioned by the scale of operations in terms of both sheer space and of absolute population size. Thus a continent of Australia's dimensions represents a basically different framework for urban evolution from that of a scattered handful of islands spread, like the Cook Islands, across a million square miles of ocean but containing only a few square miles of land and fewer than 25,000 inhabitants. Again, while Australia's territory is comparable in size to that of the United States, the Commonwealth has a population only one-sixteenth that of the Union, smaller indeed than that of California. Because of that population difference the opportunity for certain forms of development is simply not available. Making due allowance for the parameters of territorial size and configuration and of population scale, it is clear that the outstanding features of the urban systems of Oceania are the universal incidence of "primacy" and, wherever the magnitude of urban populations permits it to occur within a particular system, the existence of extremely large metropolitan units.

An additional element may set Oceania apart from other world regions. Whereas some observers identify a movement toward "normal rank-size" patterns in the array of different-sized urban centers through time, no such trend is yet evident in Oceania. The reverse is the case, and with every elaboration of the region's urban hierarchies during the present century every one of its territorial units has witnessed the enhancement of the primacy status of its major metropolis. Given the size and configuration of the various territorial units, such a situation is not unnatural. But the circumstance of intensifying primacy throughout the region raises the question of the relative meaning of primacy itself and emphasizes the point made at the outset of this present discussion, viz., that the nature of any given urban system is fundamentally conditioned by the characteristics of the particular political territory the system is designed to serve. If political boundaries are altered, so are the statistical relationships of the territorial urban array as well.

This dependency of the perception of primacy status upon political boundaries is nowhere better illustrated than by the Australian example. In 1900 there was no such political entity as "Australia," but rather six independently functioning countries, each with a high primacy level. In the following year there was a new political entity, a unification of the previous colonies. In this new unit, primacy was low, with the second city, Melbourne, only slightly smaller than the leader, Sydney. In the formal statistical sense the primacy index for Australia remains relatively low, but within each of Australia's constituent states the index of concentration is far higher now than it was in 1900. The reality of the Australian settlement pattern remains unimpaired as being outstandingly primate dominated, whatever the boundary-dependent statistics may suggest to the contrary.

A condition of metropolitan primacy is the normal state throughout Oceania. Substantial cities have everywhere emerged to outrank by far their nearest rivals in each territory. Although primacy everywhere prevails, it reaches its extreme manifestation in several of the Australian states, where urban inhabitants must choose to live in either the "city or the bush," as there are simply no urban centers of intermediate size. Where cities of intermediate size do exist, as in Newcastle and Wollongong in New South Wales, Geelong in Victoria, or Gold Coast in Queensland, they in fact function as outliers of the central metropolitan mass itself. The situation for selected territories of Oceania is illustrated in Table 5.1.

The concomitant of the intense levels of primacy illustrated in Table 5.1 is the extremely weak position, the very limited opportunity for further growth, of the urban units operating at the provincial level in each of the administrative units. The various territories of Oceania display in acute form the problems of *center and periphery,* that at the global level bedevil relations between the MDCs and LDCs. At the level of the nation-states the contrast is much in evidence between relatively prosperous and economically expansive "core" areas and economically stagnating and relatively poor zones. In Oceania prosperity goes with economic growth and such growth is strongly focused toward the established metropolitan centers of activity. Where the "primate mass," that is, the share of total urban population of the country concentrated in the leading metropolis exceeds about 35 percent, there must inevitably be a marked falling

TABLE 5.1 METROPOLITAN PRIMACY IN OCEANIA
1976 Censuses—Populations (in thousands)

Territory	Total Population	Primate City	Population	Second City	Population	Primate Mass*
		Mainland Australia				
New South Wales	4777	Sydney	2924	Newcastle	339	69
Victoria	3647	Melbourne	2529	Geelong	127	79
Queensland	2037	Brisbane	905	Gold Coast	95	55
South Australia	1245	Adelaide	873	Whyalla	33	83
Western Australia	1145	Perth	765	Bunbury	20	80
		Island States				
Papua New Guinea	†2490	Pt. Moresby	77	Lae	39	36
New Zealand	3129	Auckland	744	Wellington	328	35
Tasmania	403	Hobart	151	Launceston	73	50
		Archipelagic States				
Fiji	588	Suva	118	Lautoka	29	61
New Caledonia	133	Noumea	71	—	—	87
Western Samoa	152	Apia	32	—	—	100
The Solomons	197	Honiara	15	—	—	82

Primate Mass is the percentage of the total *urban* population of the particular territory that is massed in the metropolis.
†1971 figures.

off in the attractiveness of alternative centers for the location of new economically vibrant enterprises or investments.

Given the relative attractiveness of the metropolis in each territory to private and governmental investor alike, under the prevailing Oceanian conditions of high primacy mass, the opportunities for competing provincial centers to attract growth capital are dim indeed. This situation prevails throughout the region. It is the common experience of the outlying islands of the Fiji archipelago, competing with developments clustering around the capital of Suva and the towns of southern New Zealand seeking to divert a modicum from the streams of investment flowing into that country's beautiful, self-styled Queen City of Auckland. The weakness of provincial location is just as apparent on the Australian continent, where the profits from even the most remote mining towns, and with these profits also the growth of population, flows into such capitals as Perth, Sydney, or Melbourne.

Provincial subservience is as much a part of the currency of the urban systems of Oceania as is the more apparent fact of metropolitan primacy; it is indeed the other side of the coin.

Colonial Seeds of Primate Dominance

The entire postcontact development of Oceania has been carried through within the era of global commerce, technological revolution, and industrialization. Because the region lacked even the levels of urbanization commonly found among the agrarian civilizations of the preindustrial world, it follows logically that the present-day urban systems are absolutely the creations of the expansive colonial mechanisms of mercantile and industrial Europe. This commercial basis for the entire urban pattern is true just as much in the areas of substantial pre-contact gardening populations in Oceania as it is where the Europeans themselves totally replaced the thinly scattered pretribal nomads.

It has become fashionable in certain intellectual circles to decry the patterns of urban systems generated under colonial systems and to ascribe to them some measure of inherent malignancy. Such interpretations suggest an absence of contact with real-life conditions among these critics, a lamentable lack of insight into the spatial requirements of technological needs and the necessity to distribute terribly limited resources in the most economical way feasible into hitherto unorganized territory being brought into contact with the wider world. In any case, to bemoan such outcomes in the case of Oceania is to cry over spilt milk. The hierarchical patterns necessary for all forms of human social organization, be they political or social, spiritual, or commercial, have already set the urban frame for all future modifications of urban systems in Oceania. Furthermore, the forces tending toward the polarization of settlement in primate patterns seem to be of such universal potency, even in countries of long-standing political independence, that to claim "colonial dependency" as their exclusive basis is an extremely simplistic view.

When the European contact in Oceania started, with the unloading of the first fleet at Sydney Cove on January 26, 1788, it was not only the phenomenon of a new population being transplanted from a far corner of the globe that was significant to the region. After all, such immigrations of seaborne people had been the necessary preliminary to the establishment of human beings from time immemorial in every part of Oceania. From the first landing of humans coming from Southeast Asia to the Australian landmass some 50,000 years before the first fleet of the Europeans, through the hazardous peopling of the far-strewn archipelagos, islands, and atolls of Melanesia and Polynesia and until the last major Oceanian migration thrust, which as recently as only 900 years before the European arrival had seen the Maoris from the central Pacific first colonize New Zealand, humans have stepped to the shore from frail craft to survive and implant their promise of future generations in new lands.

The difference between the peopling of Oceania in 1788 and those previous occurrences was that this newest penetration began with an unprecedented set of aims and intentions, and the material equipment necessary for their achievement, viz., equipment like large ships, navigational aids, hierarchy of command. Prime among the revolutionary intentions of these newcomers was the notion of maintaining continuous contact and interaction with the home base, an intention which may have been a wish in the minds but never a real possibility for the early navigators. Next among the intentions of the newcomers was the notion that extensive territory should, and could, be brought under the organized control of the central intruding government. Third was the single and unwritten notion in the minds of the expedition commanders that the proper and orderly mode of settlement for new lands is the town. The town must provide the center necessary for the organization of space, the linkage of frontiers of settlement with the areas already established; government and town are synonymous, so that trade, agriculture, and commerce will all follow the town.

Technology and Urbanization Intensity

The degree of urbanization of a population is measured in terms of the proportion of town dwellers against those living under rural conditions. In preindustrial times, with low levels of agrarian productivity, few economies could sustain any significant degree of urbanization. In Oceania there were no towns whatever and the populations were totally rural. Before the Europeans had established themselves in significant numbers in Oceania, say, by 1860, the wider society of which they were merely a part was already well advanced toward the level of technological enrichment which would make the necessity for dense agricultural populations anachronistic. The railroad, the application of horsepower to agriculture, and machinery to mining operations, all rapidly transmitted the message that primary production could be achieved with the employment of very little manpower. The European exploitation of the soil resources of Oceania began in this era of limited, and progressively lessening, needs for rural labor. With every new invention, production from land resources increased while the call for labor to achieve this production diminished as machines progressively increased the number of acres and the number of animals that could be managed by one pair of human hands.

The tapping of land resources has never required dense populations of rural workers in the parts of Oceania settled by Europeans, and thus from its inception the pattern of occupance has involved predominantly urban populations. A high level of urbanization historically has been the norm in Australia and New Zealand, and in these countries today there are few significant areas where rural populations make up as much as one-quarter of the total. For Australia as a whole the proportion of nonurban population stood at only 14 percent in 1976 and was still declining; the comparable figure for New Zealand was 17 percent. These figures do not mean that in these two countries there has been a cessation of the flow of people from rural to urban areas, but in the future the scale of this flow must be a quite modest contributor to urban expansion, simply because its source now constitutes such a small share of the total. Future urban growth in Australia and New Zealand will have to depend more on transfers of population from other towns, and from overseas immigration, than on any contribution that the local rural sources can provide. In New Zealand further movement of the indigenous Maori population from their small rural holdings into the towns is now much diminished.

The level of urbanization in Papua New Guinea and the other tropical archipelagos is understandably lower than in Australia and New Zealand. Local densities of the gardening populations in these areas were quite high, to as many as 200 persons to the square mile (77 per square kilometer) in some of the richer areas of highland New Guinea. The prevalent systems of communal land tenure also have hindered the conversion of rural production to the commercial mode. The mechanical transformation that has revolutionized agrarian production in the temperate lands has been relatively late arriving in tropical areas, so that benefits still derive from a plentiful labor supply. These facts combine with the relatively late date of full European penetration into the Islands to give a situation in which the process of urbanization of the populations is patchy in its incidence and early in its stage of impact. The slowness of penetration is best illustrated in Papua New Guinea, where significant highland village populations were being brought into first "contact" as late as 1960. In such areas, a major aim of the national government today is establishing the very first markets in the remoter areas. Accompanying this development is the prospect of rapid urbanization in New Guinea, even though at present the urban component in the total population of some 3 million is under 300,000, or less than 10 percent. Elsewhere in the archipelagos total populations are much smaller and the opportunity for the emergence of really large cities is absent.

Major Representative Cities

Not only do the major cities of Oceania have positions of power within their various primate-dominated settlement systems, but with the single exception of Canberra, all the cities discussed below were founded in the brief historical span between 1788 (Sydney) and 1886 (Port Moresby). With the exception of Auckland, all are the political capitals of their respective territories; and except for Canberra, all attest to the significance of their colonial origins and commercial integration with the outside world by their seaboard locations and their roles as the dominant general ports for handling international and local coastwise traffic. Canberra was not a colonial foundation, and those responsible for its creation deliberately sought a location for the new federated Commonwealth capital which could symbolize independence from outside influence. So Canberra was located at an inland point.

While the elements of function-linked siting and their role in territorial government impart a common theme to the character of the major Oceanian centers, other facets further blur the distinctions which might be expectable over such a broad space. The Australian and New Zealand cities were founded by people of a common tradition, during a single era in which much attention was being given to the formal elements of town design, and were during their formative years administered by a cadre of governors all subject to the direction and expectations of a single directing authority, the British Colonial Office. Not only did British town design notions prevail in these areas, but they were also transmitted to the islands that came under British or Australian control. Only in the French territories of New Caledonia and Polynesia, and in Rabaul (Papua New Guinea) and Apia (West Samoa), which were foundations of the brief German presence in Oceania, were other patterns available. An additional characteristic for at least the six largest cities of the region is their functional diversity; no major city of Oceania is dominated by a prime activity in the manner of, say, Pittsburgh or Birmingham. Functional specialization is a feature only of the units lower in the hierarchy, such as Newcastle or Wollongong (coal and steel), or, surprisingly for a capital, the nickel smelters in Nouméa, New Caledonia.

Sydney: Oceania's Primate City

Sydney was the first town established in Oceania. Its maritime merchants who early probed the resources of the adjoining ocean were responsible for integrating the islands of Oceania into the web of world commerce. Sydney was the base for the explorers and pastoralists who first penetrated the (to European eyes) hitherto trackless and unused wastes of empty Inland Australia. The city remained unchallenged throughout Oceania until the discovery of gold in Victoria to the south in 1851 led to the meteoric rise of the stripling town of Melbourne to eminence. For a few decades it was the largest city of Oceania, before Sydney again reasserted its leadership. Despite commercial inroads into its territory of New South Wales, directed from Brisbane to the north, Adelaide to the west, and Melbourne to the south, Sydney still exerts trading leadership over the most productive and diversified hinterland of any of Australia's primate cities. It is wealthy in the staples of wool, wheat, and meat, its coalfields are the sinews of the not inconsiderable Australian iron and steel industry and major providers of energy to Japan. These same coalfields will meet future energy demands which are to make Australia one of the world's leading aluminum producers before 1990. Sydney has the further advantage of having firmly imbedded within its commercial hinterland the Australian Capital Territory, with the national capital only 20 minutes away by jet.

Sydney exercises intense primacy over most of its attendant political territory and also exercises another variety of primacy of the spiritual sort, over a much more extensive zone, much in the manner of New York. To the villagers of Polynesia, the traders along the coasts of Melanesia, the younger sons of New Zealand dairymen, and the iron miners of Western Australia, Sydney is the bright lights, the "big pineapple" of Oceania. Sydney exercises a degree of primacy over a hinterland more extensive than all France, and with an intensity even greater than does Paris over its tributary territory.

The site of Sydney matches its ramifying oceanic and continental linkages. In this vicinity the alternating headlands and sandy beaches of the coast are broken by three major openings to the sea, Broken Bay in the north, Port Jackson (Sydney Harbour) in the center, and Botany Bay to the south; tidal influence spreads up these intricate waterways for 20 or more mi. (32 km.) inland (Fig. 5.2). Sydney Cove was site of the first European settlement in Oceania. This point is now the shop window of the city's central business district, flanked by the skyscrapers of the financial district, the Opera House, and the Harbour Bridge (Fig. 5.3). Five miles (8 km.) to the south, the runway of the international airport projects into Botany Bay. Sydney's ocean frontage and its inland waterways impart a maritime quality rivaled by few major cities on earth; three-quarters of its people live within 5 mi. (8 km.) of tidewater. Within 70 mi. (112

Figure 5.2 Sydney Metropolitan Area. (*Source:* Compiled by the author.)

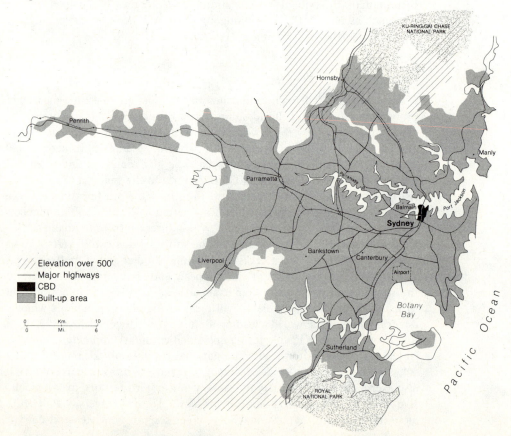

Figure 5.3 Sydney Harbor, 192 years after Captain Arthur Phillip landed. He raised the British flag in Sydney Cove, the small bay just to the left of the Opera House. The latter has become a symbol of modern Sydney. (Courtesy Australian Information Service)

km.) of Sydney Cove live one-quarter of Australia's population and one-sixth the entire population of Oceania.

From its cramped original site in the valley of the Tank Stream draining into Sydney Cove, the encampment of 1788 has been transformed into a sprawling metropolis whose outer suburbs creep steadily up the slopes of the Blue Mountains 40 mi. (64 km.) west of the original urban focus. The ocean frontages provide space for parks and suburbs through a 30-mi. (48 km.) stretch, and to the south and north the city sprawls to its limits on the margins of rugged sandstone country which is protected from further urban encroachment by virtue of being a national park.

The Spreading City In Sydney the point of first settlement is still the functional heart of the metropolitan mass (Fig. 5.4). As the settlement grew it spread up the valley of the Tank Stream and onto the low ridge to the west; subsequent expansion then followed along the roads that fanned out from the original focus to the west, southwest, and east. By 1850 the rail net was already growing rapidly and dominated the settlement pattern until automobile numbers grew to a respectable total during the 1930s. Continuous growth from immigration and rapid natural increase transformed the modest town of 1840 into a city comparatively large in world terms by the beginning of

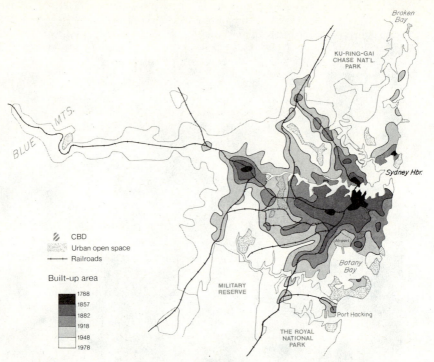

Figure 5.4 Sydney: Historical Growth. (Reprinted by permission of The Department of Environment and Planning, Sydney, Australia, from Denis Winston, *Sydney's Great Experiment: The Progress of The Cumberland County Plan,* 1957.)

the present century; by 1911 the population of the sprawling urban area had reached 652,000.

Between 1911 and 1947 expansion continued, based in part on continuing immigration from Britain and supplemented after 1935 by the initial arrivals fleeing from the Hitlerian persecutions in Europe. In 1947 the Australians began a sustained drive to obtain immigrants from Europe, initially as a relief measure for war refugees and subsequently as a general policy to enhance the national numbers. The major contribution, however, came from a healthy natural population growth and substantial rural-to-urban migration. In 1947 the metropolitan population stood at 1,475,000. With an average increase of about 500,000 each decade since 1947, Sydney sprawled out through its former limits to assume its present form and a 1980 population of 3.3 million.

The Changing Physical Fabric As the population expanded, the physical fabric kept pace and molded its form to meet new needs, new tastes, and new technologies. Before 1880 Sydney built tight with most of its housing in terraces (rows); water supply and sewage disposal were constant problems, so that summer intestinal disorders were rife and infant mortality levels high. During the city's first century only the rich could afford separate solid houses. But row houses gave lower general densities than were the rule in many contemporary cities of comparable size. The main roads radiating from the early-imposed rectangular grid of the original town were notable for following ridge lines in the direction of the open country, rather than adhering to the compass points as in the new American urban foundations. Sydney today has a heritage of major highways whose directions tend to wander in accordance with the needs of nineteenth-century bullock teams to minimize steep grades. As suburbia expanded it filled the interstices between these roads, frequently alining the local streets at right angles to the particular courses of the early major arteries. One Sydney view has it that San Francisco is a good site for a city that has been ruined by fanatic devotion to the worship of the grid and the right angle; in Sydney, terrain has always evoked a response from developers.

The rail net that began developing in 1850 soon supplanted the roads as the major determinant of the direction of expansion; trains were always challenged as a provider of public transport by the trams (streetcars) and harbor ferries. Well into the present century most development occurred south of the harbor, mainly in single cottage houses on individual plots of land after 1890. The inner area remained the focus, providing employment in commerce, transport, manufacturing, and government. In 1932 the first Harbour Bridge was built, directly joining the CBD to the north shore; since that day the metropolis has spread both north and south of the harbor.

The rapid expansion in car ownership from about 1930, plus the huge increase in population after 1947, has grafted the patterns of the automobile urban format onto the previously rail-condition fabric of Sydney. Suburbs have sprawled, and shipping centers have grown to serve them. Industry has expanded and moved out from central locations into spaces reserved and provided by the metropolitan County of Cumberland Plan of 1951. The office buildings of the CBD have erupted skywards, and high rise apartment buildings have appeared at choice harborside sites in inner redevelopment areas and at favored points of high-transport access. Established preferences die hard: two-thirds of the housing units built in Sydney between 1965 and 1980 were still of the single-house type. The individualism of the city is further demonstrated by the paucity of freeway development; within the built-up parts of the metropolis there was less than 5 mi. (8 km.) of freeway in 1980, a remarkably low figure for a place almost as addicted to the private car as is Los Angeles. Air pollution levels, however, have achieved major-city status.

Who Lives Where? Functional patterns and terrain divide Sydney into two general areas. Along the harborside and across its northern reaches the land tends to be hilly and the scenery pleasant; to the south and west the surface is relatively monotonous, the scenery is boring, and summer temperatures are high. The north, free of noxious industry, is primarily residential. The south and west, heavily industrial, carry the most heavy transport; housing tracts never seem far away from the generators of noise and atmospheric pollution. There are some pockets of industrial land in the north, and areas of residential greenery in the south, but this broad and somewhat generalized division of the urban area holds true. This division is parallelled in significant measure by many of the patterns of its social geography.

Until the beginnings of large-scale continental European immigration shortly before World War II, social division in Sydney had been essentially based on socioeconomic class. In 1940 the localities of choice for those in the favored strata of society were on the harborside, especially east from the Center to the ocean, along the upper reaches of the north-shore railway, and in Strathfield (Fig. 5.5). These salubrious suburbs were very much WASP territory, with Presbyterians disproportionately represented. The more crowded inner industrial suburbs were blue collar in the main, with a heavy admixture of White Anglo-Celtic Catholics. The silvertail (wealthier white collar) suburbs regularly voted conservative in politics, and their opposite numbers just as avidly supported Labor, the party of the left; mixed suburbs provided venues for changes in the affiliations of parliamentary members. The social map of Sydney easily could be read by any student of the writings of Burgess or Hoyt.

By 1980 the urban population had more than doubled and the physical expanse of the metropolis more than tripled. More than a quarter of the population are foreign born, and probably more than 40 percent of the total are either postwar immigrants or the children of immigrants. Although the single largest immigrant group is still the British, there are substantial numbers of Italians, Greeks, and Lebanese, with smaller but still significant numbers from Eastern Europe, Germany and Holland, Malta and Turkey, and dozens of other countries, including those elite Japanese and American businessmen whose companies prefer to locate in Sydney. The two most recent immigrant streams of significance have come from Vietnam and New Zealand.

Figure 5.5 Sydney: Ethnic Concentrations. (*Source:* Compiled by the author.)

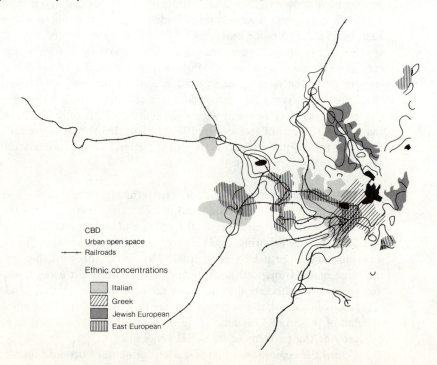

The new immigrants have tended to be added to the lower echelons of the social pyramid; the long-standing Anglo-Celtic Catholic element has been correspondingly elevated, with the mixture of Catholic, Orthodox, and Moslem Mediterraneans now forming an acceptable but socially "less equal" stratum. These new immigrants are most strongly represented in the laboring occupations, especially in the building industry and in industrial process work, such as automobile assembly lines. Some, including the Jewish people from Hungary and elsewhere in Central Europe, have achieved marked economic and social acceptance in the worlds of finance and management. The Dutch have been successful in achieving occupational and residential patterns similar to those of the WASP population. A feature in the rather ready acceptance of the newcomers has been the great strength of the trade unions; their power has been sufficient to insure that immigrants are unable to undercut established pay levels.

The residential pattern adopted by immigrant groups is strongly conditioned by general forces which have been transforming the social map with gathering momentum since about 1960 (Fig. 5.6). Prior to that date most immigrants found the inner suburbs, the traditional working-class area of low environmental quality and low rents, to be the most attractive. The aging populations in these areas meant that for two decades after the war many houses were becoming vacant which readily could be purchased by immigrant families. Gradually significant concentrations of particular immigrant

Figure 5.6   Sydney: Socioeconomic Status. (*Source:* Adapted from Michael Poulsen and Peter Spearritt, *Sydney, A Social and Political Atlas,* North Sydney, N.S.W., George Allen and Unwin, 1981. Reprinted with permission.)

groups developed in these and adjacent, somewhat newer suburbs. The tight concentrations and packed clusters of ethnic groups common in many other countries in periods of heavy immigration, failed to develop, as within a very few years of initial establishment most immigrant groups have tended to appear into the growing outer fringe areas, where clustering has been less tight. Whole groups, such as the Maltese, have shifted their primary focus from the inner city to the outer suburbs.

Social Inversion in Progress Today the working-class suburbs of 1940 are being invaded by white-collar "trendies" who are largely WASP in origin and were mainly reared in the more affluent outer suburbs. The movement began in near-city Paddington before 1960 and has completely transformed that formerly decrepit suburb. The process of upgrading decaying buildings and replacing their former inhabitants has now spread to other areas including Balmain and Glebe, with pockets of "trendification" (few of these new residents are "gentry") spreading like a rash through all the inner areas. The Burgess sectoral zonal model of metropolitan structure (see Chapter 1) is now the opposite of the truth in Sydney, and the only "transition" occurring is a change from blue-collar and immigrant occupancy to a predominance of white collars and the native born. The rising cost of inner city rentals and increased property values makes such areas much less attractive to immigrant groups than previously.

The reasons for this inversion are linked to shifts in employment patterns that have been gaining momentum throughout the last two decades. Industrial and heavy-transport functions have been drifting away from the inner areas, while the CBD has increasingly specialized its structure in the direction of white-collar professional and office employment. New accretions to the housing stock have occurred at the fringes of urban settlement, and tradeoff situations have developed in which many younger people have found it preferable to buy and refurbish an old inner-area house rather than engage in the long trek from outer green suburb to Center and return each day. Many of the older parts of Sydney inherently have charm, the sea is always near, and most recently, energy price rises have markedly raised the costs of long-distance commuting. The less successful in Sydney society are being silently transferred to outer suburbia.

Canberra: Planned Capital

Canberra is one of a handful of the world's cities built specifically to undertake the role of government. Like its counterparts, Washington, Ottawa, Brasilia, and Islamabad, Canberra was developed to fulfill a symbolic function, to be a "national" city in a federal union rising above the specific rivalries and interests of preexisting centers. Thus it was necessary that the new city not be located on the coast. As a sop to the feelings of the Foundation Colony it was agreed that the new capital should be located within the territory of New South Wales, but more than 100 mi. (160 km.) from Sydney. The site for Canberra was chosen in 1913, and the legislature began functioning there in 1928 (Fig. 5.7).

Canberra was initially planned to occupy a shallow basin in the southern uplands

Figure 5.7 Canberra, Australia's national capital, as seen from Mt. Ainslie overlooking the city. Canberra is Australia's largest inland city. Rising out of the central basin of Lake Burley Griffin, the manmade lake around which Canberra is built can be seen the Water Jet, a memorial to commemorate the bicentennial in 1970 of Captain James Cook's discovery of the eastern Australian coast. (Courtesy Australian Information Service)

of New South Wales. It was conveniently close to the already-established township of Queanbeyan on land held in a few large pastoral properties that readily could be purchased by the new government without disrupting too many private interests. Placing the new center 190 mi. (306 km.) from Sydney assured that it would be untainted by the sins of Sydney and that the New Jerusalem could grow in purity as well as tranquillity. Among the first acts of the founders was the establishment of a brickworks, under government ownership; this was closely followed by the establishment of a tree nursery. When the population had reached 16,000 in 1947, a million shrubs and trees were already in the ground.

The city was not sufficiently established to cater to the great expansion of government activity that occurred during the war years 1939–1945; however, after 1947 growth accelerated with the gradual transfer of government departments from Melbourne. In 1954 the population was 28,000; in 1966 the population was 94,000; and at the 1976 census the population of the Canberra Statistical District was 215,000. Despite this rapid growth, expansion has proceeded in a smooth and orderly manner. No shanty towns mar the sylvan scene, and industry finds little favor among the planners.

Canberra contrasts with its opposite numbers overseas: capitals converted into industrial towns with annexations of capital city functions.

Unlike its counterparts in other lands, Canberra has hesitated to grasp the monumental and the grandiose. Here, avenues tend to be avenues, and you cannot see the buildings for the trees. Both the House of Representatives and the Senate still sit in a simple squat building with no hint of dome or tower. Apartment buildings rise only to three stories, and at the National University the fountains outnumber the libraries and the magpies terrorize the pedestrians. Naturally, there are good suburbs and poorer suburbs, but being "ethnic" in Canberra may indicate high status through affiliation with a foreign embassy.

The center of Canberra is occupied by a lake around whose shores stretch golf and yacht clubs, lawns, and the major government buildings. Suburbia spreads across all the lower surrounding levels, with the hilltops left unencumbered by buildings other than communications facilities. The urban area is preposterously extensive for such a small population. In its extreme suburbanization Canberra takes the domestic dream of the average Australian beyond any reasonable limit. Nevertheless the planners, a numerous and influential element in the bureaucracy, have taken pains to relieve the shortcomings of hypersprawl and have successfully decreed that office employment, the mainstay of the city, shall be located at various suburban points away from the original center. Canberra is thus a company town locked into dependency on the automobile. The city is fast becoming Australia's major retirement center away from the warmer eastern coastal zone. It is an exceedingly civil city built by and for civil servants, an example of how Washington might have been if Californians had built it.

Canberra's original design came not from California but from Chicago, the brainchild of the architect Walter Burley Griffin. No greater physical contrast could be found between his design and that of Adelaide, most formally laid out of all the older Australasian cities with a rigid and regular plan. The mould for Canberra was set by the early-twentieth-century English "garden cities," strongly laced by a central governmental zone of avenues and vistas. Its chief defect as a design is the excessive provision of open space. It is a sobering reflection on Burley Griffin's vision that he provided sufficient space in inner urban Canberra for offices to house up to twenty times the present number of civil servants without undue crowding. These minor blemishes fail to distract from what is probably the world's most comfortable and humane capital city structure.

Melbourne: A Second Primate City

Spawned as a settlement at the outset of the age of pastoral expansion in eastern Australia, Melbourne shot to eminence as port and metropolis for the gold fields opening during the 1850s and 1860s. The city cemented its commercial supremacy over the southern bulge of the Australian continent by ensuring that the rail system tapping the inland areas focused unequivocally on its commercial center and port facilities. The first white settlers arrived on the banks of the Yarra River, a little upstream from its mouth in Port Phillip Bay in 1835, as spearheads of the pastoral invasion of the mainland from Tasmania. The settlement gained official recognition as a town in 1842 and was the natural choice to be the center of government when separation (from New South Wales) was achieved by the new Colony of Victoria in 1851, the year in which the first large gold discoveries were made.

By 1860 Melbourne was Oceania's largest city, its annual Melbourne Cup horse race already the outstanding sporting event in the recreational calendar of Britain's antipodean colonies. Its financial houses and mining companies had also begun to assert their control over all future mineral developments in Australia, a hallmark that it retains today. Melbourne achieved primacy in the Victorian settlement network almost from the outset; by 1891 with a population approaching 480,000, it contained more than two in every five inhabitants within the colony. The urban system of Victoria has revolved around the sun of Melbourne virtually from the inception of settlement.

Melbourne spreads broadly across the undulating land that rises gently from the northeastern shores of Port Phillip Bay (Fig. 5.8). The central business core is set inland from the bay around the first settlement site. The regular grid of the original "city" is arranged with broad streets alternating with relatively narrow "little" streets to give a rather distinctive pattern; the grid orientation is northeast-southwest and northwest-southeast. Outside the original city area grid regularity prevails in a north-south orientation that is unlike the orientation in Sydney but is familiar to most North Americans. Melbourne has felt little need to unduly confine the width of its streets; the broad major avenues present a further contrast to the older city of Sydney. From its inception Mel-

Figure 5.8 Melbourne Metropolitan Area. (*Source:* Compiled by the author.)

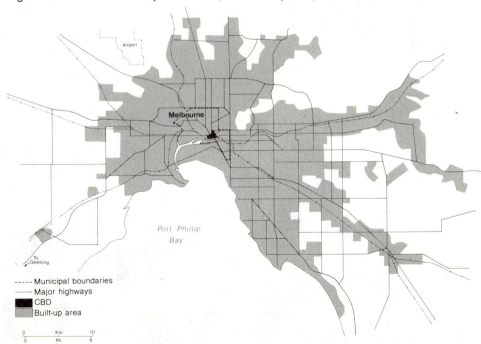

bourne has strived to create itself as a gracious and spacious example of all that was best in the urban tradition of Queen Victoria's British Empire. This aim was aided by the relatively level terrain; the vistas and architectural balance of the major avenues and parklands of inner Melbourne possess a certain grandiosity that is more commonly the hallmark of Iberian than Anglo-Saxon urban foundations.

Twentieth-century expansion in Melbourne has been much greater east than west of the downtown (Fig. 5.9). To the west there have been two general and significant hindrances to residential urban development: the lower reaches of the Yarra, with their concentrated industrial and port functions, which have not attracted residences; and further north and west, the margins of the extensive basaltic lava plains, which stretch away to the South Australian border. These plains yield soils and drainage problems little to the liking of industrialists and suburban gardeners. Most expansion in Melbourne has been to the higher ground to the northeast, in the direction of the attractive Dandenong Range, along the bayside leading south from the Center, and in the direction of the rich farmlands and brown-coal-mining region of Gippsland to the southeast.

Primate cities everywhere tend to be highly diversified, and Melbourne is no exception. Much of the urban growth of the late nineteenth century was deliberately designed to stimulate industrial production. As the Victorian gold fields declined during this period, their workers streamed to the towns, mainly to Melbourne, where many found employment in the factories established under the shelter of the import tariffs. Thus Melbourne expanded, not only as Australia's leading center of mining-generated capital, but as an industrial producer, with special emphasis on textiles and other apparel. When the Australian colonies finally federated in 1901, they adopted the policy of

Figure 5.9 Princes Bridge, Melbourne, one of the main arteries across the Yarra River into the CBD of the City. Modern office buildings, symbolic of Melbourne's growth and importance, stand near older, more ornate buildings of the past, including St. Paul's Anglican Cathedral and the Flinders Street Station (the domed building on the left). (Courtesy Australian Information Service)

free and unrestricted trade among themselves and the Victorian preference for high import tariffs.

The result of these actions was that Melbourne companies have dominated the national markets for apparel items and, by virtue of their financial strength, have also skimmed off much of the profit from the heavy industries, which for reasons of raw-material location, are located in other states; the latter is true for the largest Australian company, BHP (originally Broken Hill Proprietary Limited). BHP has its headquarters in Melbourne, but its major plants are in Newcastle and Wollongong (New South Wales) and Whyalla (South Australia). The combination of corporate capital and the skills built up in its numerous industries make Melbourne most commonly the first choice for plants to produce new items for the national market.

The continuing industrial and commercial strength of Melbourne has made the city the prime attraction for overseas immigration in recent decades. Together with the neighboring town of Geelong, also on Port Phillip Bay, Melbourne, in addition to its apparel and light-engineering strengths, has become the center of Australian automobile production and the location of the limited airplane manufacturing industry. Generally, Melbourne caters to the solid and established industries and enterprises; its tone is much more sober, so it is claimed, than that of comparatively flighty Sydney. The conservative governments which have dominated Australian national politics since 1949 have drawn much of their strength and the bulk of their moral fiber from Melbourne and its affiliated rural region, whereas the leadership of the brief period of non-conservative Labor Party rule from 1972 to 1975 was drawn from Sydney.

In a nation where two cities, both intensely primate within their own territories, vie for primacy within an imposed frame of territorial reference, there is bound to be intense rivalry. Together Melbourne and Sydney constitute over 40 percent of the national market, and given the relatively limited size of this market, it is not always possible to support more than one plant to serve its entire demand. So state governments compete with each other for new industrial enterprises, and the source of the capital being used in their establishment is of little relevance. The issue is that if the plant goes to one state, it cannot go to another. In reality, given the distribution of Australian productive resources, the competition between states for new enterprises ends up being competition between cities. States as well compete for control over energy sources which may serve as lures for enterprises. The major cities, as the sources of the wealth and labor needed for the operation of such a national system, become not simply cities but combinations of industrial and commercial entities sprawling across areas of provincial dimensions. Such are Melbourne and Sydney.

Perth: Epitome of Regional Isolation

The capital of Western Australia is separated from the other Australian cities by ocean and by desert. No other major city on earth is so isolated; its rail connection with eastern Australia was completed only during the First World War. Perth controls the western third of the continent, an area of 1 million sq. mi. (2.6 million sq. km.), almost twice the size of Alaska or four times that of Texas. In this area live 1.5 million people, two-thirds of them in Perth; the city is more than 20 times larger than the next city in its territory. Perth is, in extreme measure, completely primate throughout its hinterland, in every measure of urban function—industrial, commercial, social and political. Like its eastern fellows, Perth commands the rail net that spreads inland and along the coast north and south to tap the small portion of the state that has sufficient rain to permit agriculture and forestry. More than three-quarters of the state lies more than 100 mi. (160 km.) from the nearest railroad. Perth also commands the richest iron ore field on earth, in the Pilbara district 800 mi. (1290 km.) to the north. The city remains resentful of its incorporation within the Australian federation, and many residents support secession.

In its site and general position Perth is in some ways the mirror image of Sydney, facing the ocean to the west rather than to the east, a city built along sandy ocean beaches and embracing a broad estuary, the Swan River, from whose shores the inner-city skyscrapers rise at a distance of some miles from the sea (Fig. 5.10). A difference of detail arises from the fact that the general cargo port in Sydney is immediately adjacent to the CBD, whereas in Perth it is at Fremantle, at the mouth of the estuary and several miles from the Center. Perth and Sydney stand at the two ends of the Transcontinental Railway, linked by regular services of the Indian-Pacific Express. As in Sydney

Figure 5.10 Perth, the capital of Western Australia, basks in the warm sun of a Mediterranean-type climate, flanking the pleasant wide waters of the Swan River. The city has the insular charm of the world's most isolated capital, but also mirrors the progress of Australia's biggest and fastest-growing state. (Courtesy Australian Information Service)

there is social preference for waterside scenery; the more prestigious suburbs front the estuary waters.

Perth is hampered within the Australian economy both by its isolation and by the small size of the local population; both together tremendously handicap its full integration with the rest of the nation. Manufactured goods have only a small local market and must be capable of absorbing the high freight costs involved in being transported more than 2000 mi. (3220 km.) before they can hope to tap into the larger markets of the east. For these reasons Perth remains basically a major service center rather than part of the national manufacturing economy; it meets the needs of the farmers and pastoralists, miners and foresters, of its vast territory. Since 1960 the gold mines, notably at Kalgoorlie to the east, have been supplemented by the iron ore developments to the north, by the exploitation of nickel deposits, and by the intensification of wheat farming. Prospects for development of major gas deposits exist offshore on the continental shelf to the north, and if these hopes are realized, Perth could draw revenue from large energy exports, just as Brisbane and Sydney do from their coal deposits.

The city has grown markedly in recent decades, especially with the expansion of the various facets of the mining industry. With every surge in mining activity, there is a corresponding surge in the activity of Perth's real estate industry, enough to stimulate continued low density sprawl across the sandy coastal plain on which it is built as well as southward to incorporate the new heavy industrial suburbs and northward to embrace virgin surf-front territory.

With Perth's pleasant houses with red tile roofs, its emphasis on water-oriented recreation, the flavors of its excellent wines grown on the foothills of the escarpment to the east, and its clean air constantly refreshed by ocean breezes, the city presents an image for outsiders of freshly scrubbed beauty, a place to be cherished for its dearth of industry and for the way geography has set it so apart from all other cities.

Port Moresby: A City of Transformations

Like Canberra, the capital of Papua New Guinea was created specifically by and for government, and like its southern counterpart it achieves eminence less from its size as from its role in integrating a hitherto fragmented land. Port Moresby was created as the seat of British government on the Papuan coast in 1886 on a site selected because of its relatively good potential for development as a harbor. Despite the change from British to Australian administration in 1906, the little town languished through the closing decades of the colonial era. The administrative amalgamation of Papua with the richer Territory of New Guinea in 1949, and the choice of Port Moresby as capital by an Australian administration determined to assure the country to full independence, ensured the city's future growth. By 1961, just 12 years after amalgamation, the population had soared to a heady total of 29,000; by 1966 it was 42,000. The city had 76,500 inhabitants in 1971 and now probably has over 90,000. Port Moresby is twice the size of Lae, the second largest town, and three times the size of Rabaul, the former capital of German New Guinea on the island of New Britain.

The commercial center of the early town, at the wharves of the original port,

188 Chapter 5, Cities of Oceania

is now remote from the geographical center of the urban area, which has spread eastward toward Jacksons Airport and northward in the direction of the campus of the University of Papua New Guinea (Fig. 5.11). The old town is largely separated from the "new" Port Moresby by steep hills and a sharp escarpment. The layout of the new areas on the upland surface is strongly reminiscent of Canberra, with tidy, intricately platted suburban tracts separated from each other by much empty space. But it differs

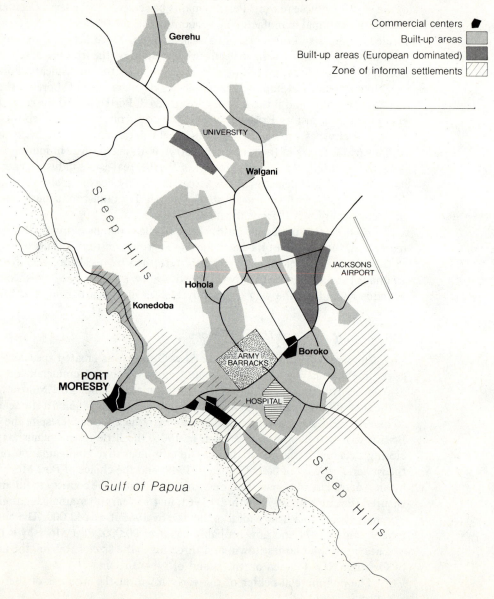

Figure 5.11 Port Moresby. (*Source:* Compiled by the author.)

from its Australian prototype in that scattered through the open areas are clusters of unofficial settlements of villagers come to town. These villagers are the source of unskilled labor for the capital; their hutments are something of an embarrassment for officials trained to gauge housing standards through Canberra-tinted spectacles. These settlements are also the focal points of simmering resentments among the rival tribal groups. Melanesians are entering a new experience, the enforced toleration of different groups brought together in an environment that is new and puzzling, but extremely attractive, when compared with the state of deprivation in their home villages. Most visible among the diverse groups are the fair-skinned foreigners.

Papua New Guinea is engaged in the task of transforming its society literally from Stone Age conditions to integration in the modern world within two generations. The Australians had barely laid the necessary infrastructure of communications and transport links and the rule of law and development of local government and education systems when independence overtook the country. The new leaders have recognized the need for outside assistance to achieve the aims of national integration. Assisting them are the revenues from the major copper and gold deposit on Bougainville together with substantial grants from the Australian government. Skilled managerial and commercial personnel remain the new country's critical shortage. For Port Moresby this situation implants a distinctive foreign element in the social geography of the urban fabric. The lineal descendants of the former colonial governors, indeed sometimes the very same individuals, continue to occupy many of the choicer residential areas.

Port Moresby is enacting in microcosm the difficult task of welding into a single entity mutually unintelligible language groups culturally attuned to warfare, village against village, coastal man against highlander, Papuan against New Guinean. The nation has more ethnic diversity and less physical unity than all Europe, and the risks of disaster are exceeded only by the spirit of determination among the educated leading groups that the experiment must not fail. Some of the difficulty is apparent in the magnitude of the physical communication problems in the country. Port Moresby has road contact only with its neighboring coastal strip. The major population concentrations lie beyond the mountains, around the coasts and islands of New Guinea and in the highland valleys to the north; contact with these areas is possible now only by radio, by sea transport, or by air. Jacksons Airport is the key point in the slender line of air connections that holds together this exceedingly difficult land.

Auckland: City of Polynesia

Auckland is the only primate city in Oceania that grew to primacy in an urban system despite the fact that the national capital lay elsewhere. The rise of this New Zealand city to national eminence is fundamentally due to the relative wealth and diversity of the provincial hinterland that has looked to it for general port and commercial services ever since the foundation of the European settlement in 1840. In 1976 Auckland's leadership was so marked that it held a quarter of the total population and a third of the urban population of the whole country; in 1980 the metropolitan population approached 800,000, making Auckland comparable in size with Adelaide (Fig. 5.12), Brisbane, and Perth.

The city is even more maritime than Sydney. It spreads across an isthmus separating two intricate harbors, and focuses on the deeper northern one of these, Waitemata Harbour, which opens toward the Pacific on the east. The original township of 1840 was planted on the south shore of the Waitemata. A century later the urban area had spread clear across the isthmus, and to points along the shores north of the Waitemata; by 1964 the metropolitan suburban outliers had developed along the main south road and rail to a distance of 30 miles (48 km.) from the center. "Corridor growth" is virtually a necessity for Auckland, given the disposition of land and sea, and the major new industrial suburbs in recent decades have developed along or close to the southern corridor.

The Auckland isthmus is a low, undulating plateau, its surface punctuated by numerous small scoria cones and the sunken craters of volcanic eruptions. Some of these date back to 60,000 years ago, and others more recently, for example, the island of Rangitoto near the Waitemata Harbour entrance; Auckland has been described as the "city of volcanoes." Their low eminences provide excellent viewing points for the tourists of today; prior to the advent of the Europeans some of the larger cones formed redoubts for the local Maoris against the attacks of tribal rivals. This isthmus site was of much strategic importance during the Polynesian era in New Zealand, as it is today.

Unlike Australia, New Zealand has not resorted to large-scale immigration from continental Europe and the eastern Mediterranean in recent decades to fuel the growth of its economy and national strength. Apart from the customary significant accretions from Britain, with some admixture of Dutch, the population growth from 1.5 million in 1940 to 3 million in 1980 has been accomplished largely by natural growth. Auckland has shared disproportionately in this growth, and in particular has benefited from a direct flow of surplus farm population from its commercial hinterland, the northern half of the North Island, and from a steady northward drift of people from the southern parts of the country. While Auckland was already the largest city before the end of the last century, its national preeminence was not conclusive until about 1920; today it is more than twice as large as its nearest rival.

Metropolitan Auckland contains some 60,000 Maoris and another 40,000 settlers originating from elsewhere in Polynesia, especially from Samoa and the Cook Islands. The Polynesians form rather disparate groups, characterized by fairly distinctive locational patterns and affiliation networks, while the indigenous Maoris, with their advantage of familiarity with the local scene and their relatively full degree of integration into the social patterns of the dominant European ancestry, fare somewhat better in the urban milieu. As a group the Polynesians rank relatively low in the social scale, find employment mainly in the less prestigious occupations, and locate themselves notably in part of the inner city and in several newer outer industrial suburbs. In some restricted quarters of the inner zone, Polynesians may make up almost half of their population, but it would be an exaggeration to suggest that Auckland contains any area of ghetto character.

In its physical setting and lineaments of its street plan, Auckland is strongly remi-

Major Representative Cities 191

Figure 5.12 Adelaide, the capital of South Australia, is Australia's third biggest city. This aerial shot looks south toward the CBD and the Torrens River in the foreground. (Courtesy Australian Information Service)

niscent of Sydney. The intricacies of the shorelines, and the sharp declivities of the drainage lines in combination with the volcanic features, give a terrain better suited to the development of road patterns than to the rigid imposition of a regular rectangular grid. The similarity is enhanced by the preference for subtropical species in street tree plantings. Auckland lays claim to being the "Queen City" not only of New Zealand but of all Polynesia. In large measure this claim is justified in terms of its commercial and industrial preeminence at home and its commercial and social integration with the island world of tropical Polynesia.

Suva: An Archipelagic Capital

Suva is the capital of the complex Fiji archipelago, and with a 1976 population of 118,000 it contains one-fifth of the national population and three-fifths of the urban population. Initial white settlement began at Suva in 1868, against spirited opposition from the local people, and the site was soon chosen as the administrative capital for the British colonial government. Early developments were located close to the landing wharf on a peninsula jutting southward from the eastern flank of Viti Levu island into the reef-rimmed Koro Sea at a point where a break in the coral gave deep water close inshore. The normal pattern of penetration and urban establishment in Oceania was followed. Security generated by the governmental presence and the early presence of Australian and other companies favored Suva from the outset. In the closing decades of the last century the economy and sugar cane estates were developed to fit into world demand patterns. The Sydney-based Colonial Sugar Refineries Limited (now CSR) and gold mining in the interior were dominated by Australian companies; foreign capital as well was important in harnessing copra from the coastal areas and small islands into world commerce.

The postcontact development of Fijian resources met with little support from the indigenous population as indentured laborers from the Indian subcontinent were brought in to supply the labor needs of the plantations. Native Fijians and the descendants of the Indians have maintained a rather high degree of social and locational distance ever since. The indigenous Fijians express a preference for rural environments and are protected by law in that they alone have rights of land ownership. The Indo-Fijians may lease and cultivate land, but are most active in commerce and small industrial activities; the indigenous people have something of a stranglehold on employment in the (now independent) government service and the military forces.

The ethnic divisions carry over into the urban situation. Major companies and banks and their staffs remain under outside (generally Australian or New Zealand) control; in Suva they reside on the southern part of the peninsula, in and near the original government area. Europeans form only about 10 percent of the Suva City population. The Indo-Fijians are the most numerous group, totaling more than half; indigenous Fijians compose some 40 percent of the Suva City total and are clustered about the port and the industrial area immediately to the north. Overt rivalry between the two major groups is absent, but restraint and undercurrents remain.

As in the other port towns of Oceania, Suva presents a substantial but geographically concentrated distillation of the problems of its society at large. In Fiji the rural population is still almost twice as large as the urban, a fact which in combination with continuing high rates of natural increase indicates an ample reservoir of immigrants to ensure the future growth of Suva.

Problems and Solutions

For the balance of the present century the problems facing the cities of Oceania will seem but pale reflections of those facing cities elsewhere in the world. No vast reservoirs of rural folk are seeking the liberation that an urban location supposedly confers, unlike the situation throughout Asia, Africa, and Latin America. But relative to their limited populations, and available resources, the integration of further influxes of rural people will undoubtedly tax the authorities of Port Moresby and Suva through the coming decades. In both Australia and New Zealand there is at present a marked lull in the upsurge in numbers, and this has come at a time when already there is little demand for the further reduction of labor in rural occupations. In the future, internal migration, the prime engine of urban growth in most countries, will be essentially interurban migration rather than rural-urban movement.

Tinkering with the Urban System

Changes in the general structure of the urban system now loom as the matter of most direct concern in Australia and New Zealand, rather than the matter of urbanization itself. For the past half-century and more there has been continuing debate about the proper balance of the urban systems in both countries, with attention focused on the presumed evils and disadvantages stemming from primacy. On one plane these worries express themselves as concern with economic issues; on another, appropriate life-styles and the maintenance of suitable human environments. These concerns imply considerable attention to the internal functions and structures of the cities themselves. In both countries these issues received considerable ventilation during the early 1970s, under Labor administrations, but have since muted during a period of economic downturn and conservative governments.

The economic arguments about primacy center on the issue of the advantages of concentration over dispersion. Certainly in New Zealand, where primacy is steadily emerging into sheer dominance, as in the case of Auckland, there is much to the argument that such a pattern is tending to leave human investments, in the urban and settlement fabrics already extant elsewhere in the country, in a state of relative underemployment. Few countries can readily afford to allow much underemployment of their basic capital resources, so the New Zealand government is continually faced with pressures both to maintain old industries and to ensure that new enterprises are established in the wide range of significant settlements and cities outside the orbit of the metropolis. Such arguments in New Zealand can be buttressed by the fact that the population is still widely dispersed, and sites more centrally located along the length of the two islands can just as economically serve the national market as can Auckland with little adverse effect on infrastructures already well developed.

The arguments for positive policies to redirect the settlement trends away from primacy in the Australian states are less clear. The pendulum swing toward primacy has already gone so far that it now seems permanently weighted in that direction. In the Australian states, extreme primacy must be regarded as "the normal state." That is, in economic terms, where the viability of an industrial or a commercial enterprise must depend basically on minimum-cost access to major markets and the availability of large supplies of skilled and unskilled labor, there are no realistic alternatives to locating within or on the margins of an established metropolitan area. This situation does not apply where bulky local raw materials form critical inputs in the product mix of the enterprise, as is the case in iron and steel production.

The above views do not go unchallenged. Large cities, it is argued, generate diseconomies of scale. These appear as unnecessarily high internal transport costs and as overloading of the capacity of the local environmental systems. Thus they can no longer absorb and disperse the wastes and pollution stemming from the seething activities of the major cities. Much waste is indeed caused simply by overcoming the disabilities generated by congestion itself.

Under the Labor administrations of the 1970s in both Australia and New Zealand, steps were put in train to modify the existing settlement array by stimulating the growth of a number of new or already existing centers. It has been said of the existing Australian urban system that its distinctive pattern of primate dominance was achieved "by proclamation," meaning that once a town was proclaimed as the political capital, it was inevitably slated to assume primate status. The drive in the 1970s was to achieve dispersion by proclamation, and to underwrite the proclamations by pouring large volumes of governmental money into new urban foundations situated well outside the existing centers; the overall aim is to create a significant number of medium-sized cities with populations on the order of 400,000 to 500,000. Underlying this development toward an integrated national approach to the shaping of a more balanced urban hierarchy was the anticipation that the population would increase from its existing 13 million in about 1970 to some 24 million by the year 2000. Without such positive measures, this prospective increase would inevitably cluster within and around the five major existing cities, for no "natural" forces exist that might bring about a more widespread distribution.

The primary new component in the policies of the Australian settlement planners was to modify and give federal government support to long-established but hitherto ineffectual policies of the state governments to aid "decentralization" of economic activities to small country towns. The new wave of planners sought to create substantial cities in country areas by concentrating the traditional effort into a selected and limited number of expanded settlements. A major early component in this drive would be to transfer government employment, to the greatest extent compatible with efficiency, out from the capitals to the new growth centers. Additionally, local governmental administration would as far as possible be concentrated in these towns instead of being dispersed throughout many smaller centers at random. The guarantee of continued public funding over several decades implicit in these policies would, it was hoped, provide attractive opportunities for the investment of private capital and the establishment of new enterprises in the chosen centers.

A few such centers were nominated for forced-draft development when the economy took a sharp downturn in 1975 and the Labor government in Canberra was prematurely dismissed at the end of the same year. Today only one city is still receiving any significant input of federal funding. This is Albury-Wodonga, straddling the Victoria-New South Wales border on the main route linking Melbourne and Sydney. However, despite assistance and a favorable location this center is not being unduly successful in attracting private investment; indeed its growth is little if any faster than that of the neighboring town of Wagga Wagga some distance to the north and firmly within New South Wales territory. Elsewhere the grandiose plans for regional growth centers have been quietly shelved. Underlying these negative policies has been the reality of diminished population growth rates occasioned by declining births and reduced immigration. The 1970 expectation of a total population of 24 million by the year 2000 has more recently been lowered to only 18 million.

Internal Metropolitan Changes

Part of the intellectual underpinning for the drive toward regional growth centers was the conviction that the major cities were overcrowded and that their entire inner fabric was decaying to a positively unhealthy extent, that is, scarcely fit environments for civilized people. Only part of the solution was deemed to lie in the development of new centers. A primary solution was believed to lie in the extension of the metropolitan areas themselves through properly planned and serviced "system cities" located a modest distance beyond the existing metropolitan boundaries. Similar entities are known elsewhere as *corridor cities*. Such places were, and are, being designed to cater to the overflow from the inner areas and for anticipated accretions from natural growth and immigration. It is somewhat difficult to distinguish such areas as being anything other than officially sanctioned prolongations of traditional suburban sprawl. But a determined attempt is being made at Campbelltown 32 mi. (52 km.) southwest from the Sydney CBD to develop a reasonably self-contained city of about 400,000 containing a balanced range of industrial activities and its own significant commercial center. The city is sufficiently close to the existing metropolis to benefit from its diversified employment opportunities and not so far away from the major source of industrial labor as to appear disheartening to industrialists attracted by the low-priced serviced land available by the Development Corporation.

In the metropolis itself the signs point to a reversal of previous conceptions of declining environmental quality of the inner areas. Not only in Sydney but also in Melbourne, Adelaide, and Perth, there is a noticeable revival of interest in home purchase in the inner areas, despite the relatively old age of many houses. In Sydney through 1979 and 1980 a resurgent real estate market saw price rises in excess of 50 percent through the inner areas and 15 to 25 percent in the outer suburbs. In part this difference stems from Sydney's lack of any effective metropolitan freeway network and with the attendant problems of slow travel times and enhanced pollution levels. The coming age of high-transport fuel costs and the increases in density implied by the new thrust back toward the central areas may not be desirable.

The Island Cities

The problems of the major towns in the archipelagos of Oceania are not so much those stemming from sheer large scale, for Suva, Apia, Nouméa, and Papeete have limits to the size they can attain over the coming decades arising quite simply from the small size of their territorial populations. Rather, their problems are those of societies in which village people from the outer islands find themselves in situations where costs must be met in cash payments and where the home village is far away. These are the traditional problems attending the urbanization of rural folk. They are already being met by modified forms of village and kinship structure applied within the new urban milieu of the cities.

The situation facing Port Moresby is potentially different from these in that this city has the potential to become a large metropolis in view of the present size and continuing rapid growth. While the quasi-tribal solution to the transition from village to city is certainly operating in Port Moresby, the town has prospects of becoming sufficiently large to generate other problems. These include the maintenance of a reasonably hygenic urban fabric, the heavy capital outlays needed for the provision of basic water and energy supplies well above the levels of the immediate environment and the ever-present concern for intertribal strife should the fiercely competing immigrant groups attain major proportions. The social problem within Port Moresby is increasingly likely to be seen as a microcosm of the national problem of generating unity in a land where, even after 7000 years of settled agriculture, loyalties have never for long extended beyond the immediate village group.

RECOMMENDED READINGS

Bourne, Larry S. *Urban Systems: Strategies for Regulation.* Oxford: Clarendon Press, 1975.
    Comparative study of attempts to modify urban systems in Australia, Britain, Canada, and Sweden.

Brookfield, Harold C. and Doreen Hart. *Melanesia: A Geographical Interpretation of an Island World.* London: Methuen, 1971.
    Excellent discussions cover development of urban centers and systems through New Guinea and eastward as far as Fiji.

Jackson, Richard, ed. *Urban Geography of Papua New Guinea: An Introduction.* New Guinea: University of Papua, 1976.
    General discussion of urban development and specific descriptions of all towns.

Johnston, Ronald J. *Urbanisation in New Zealand,* Wellington, England: Reed, 1973.
    Concentrates on the development of the urban system and says little about individual centers.

Mamak, Alexander. *Colour Culture and Conflict: A Study of Pluralism in Fiji.* Sydney: Pergamon, 1978.
    Excellent examination of the developing plural society, with particular attention to the situation in Suva.

Moran, Warren and Michael J. Taylor, eds. *Auckland and the Central North Island.* Auckland: Longman Paul, 1979.
    More than 100 pages deal compactly and professionally with physical environment, peripheral agriculture, manufacturing, population, and historical development of the city.

Neutze, G. Max. *Australian Urban Policy.* Sydney: Allen and Unwin, 1978.
    Best general discussion of past and prospective policies, and their philosophical underpinnings, for the Australian urban systems.

Neutze, G. Max. *Urban Development in Australia.* Sydney: Allen and Unwin, 1977.
    Best general discussion of structural development of Australian cities.

Oram, Nigel D. *Colonial Town of Melanesian City, Port Moresby 1874–1974.* Canberra: Australian National University Press, 1976.
    Detailed historical-social discussion of the development of the largest Melanesian city.

Powell, Joseph M. ed. *Urban and Industrial Australia.* Melbourne: Sorrett, 1974.
    Readings on the growth of the urban system and analyses of internal urban growth forces.

Rapoport, Amos. *Australia as Human Setting.* Sydney: Angus and Robertson, 1972.
    The Australian cultural landscape in the context of its physical, historical, and societal settings; a carefully structured work of 16 chapters from various authors.

Rose, A. James. *Patterns of Cities.* Melbourne: Nelson, 1968.
    Australian urban patterns set in context of world urban development; detailed discussions of Sydney and Canberra.

Sandercock, Leonie. *Cities for Sale: Property Politics and Urban Planning in Australia.* Melbourne: Melbourne University Press, 1977.
    Analyzes the role of property ownership in the expansion of Adelaide, Melbourne, and Sydney.

Seddon, George. *Sense of Place.* Perth: University of Western Australia Press, 1972.
    Deals in detail with the physical environment and in summary with past and prospective development of Perth.

Spoehr, Alexander, ed. *Pacific Port Towns and Cities.* Honolulu: Bishop Museum, 1963.
    Deals with general problems of urbanization for island rural communities and deals, in Oceania, with Nouméa, Suva, and Papeete.

Figure 6.1 Major Cities of Latin America. (*Source:* Data derived from United Nations, Department of Economic and Social Affairs, *Global Review of Human Settlements, Statistical Annex,* published by Pergamon Press, New York, 1976.)

Chapter 6

Cities of Latin America

Ernst Griffin
Larry Ford

Latin America in the World Urban System

Latin America, which consists of those countries from Mexico southward through Central America including the Caribbean Islands and encompassing all of South America, is commonly regarded as part of the world of the LDCs. As a whole, Latin America is the most urbanized region in the developing world, with 64 percent of its population urban, exceeding even the Soviet Union/Eastern Europe (at 62 percent). This is a marked change from 1950, when the population in Latin America was only 41 percent urban. The increase in total urban population is an even more vivid indication, however, of the extraordinary march to the cities that has been going on in Latin America over the past 30 years, with some of the fastest-growing cities in the world. Whereas only 67 million people lived in cities there in 1950, by 1980 the total had increased more than 250 percent to 237 million, more people than the total rural and urban population combined in 1960. Latin America is thus the first region of the LDCs examined in this book to exhibit the peculiar combination of rapid rural-to-urban migration and high natural population growth. The consequence is the population explosion of cities.

While primate cities have been a longtime characteristic of the region, the growth of these cities has accelerated unbelievably in the past 30 years (Fig. 6.1). In 1950 only 66 Latin American cities had a population of at least 100,000; none had more than 5 million. In 1980, 245 had a population of at least 100,000, of which 25 had a population of 1 million or more; and five cities had at least 5 million inhabitants. The giant, of course, is Mexico City, its estimated population of 14 million making it one of the largest urban agglomerations in the world. Others, such as Buenos Aires, Argentina, and Rio de Janeiro and São Paulo, Brazil, with populations in excess of 5 million, also merit the status of "world cities." Altogether, the 25 cities of 1 million or more hold in excess of 93 million people, or 38 percent of Latin America's urban population. Few other regions of the world have experienced such a rapid and dramatic transformation in the post–World War II era (Fig. 6.2).

Naturally, there is considerable variation throughout Latin America, both in the percentage of urban population and in the size and dominance of the cities. Not surprisingly, the most urbanized countries are Chile, Venezuela, Uruguay, and Argentina, all with more than 80 percent urban populations, all of them the most European, most industrialized, and wealthiest, and all having the smallest proportions of indigenous (Amerind) populations. Many other countries in the region, especially in the Caribbean and Central America, are substantially less than 50 percent urbanized. Little effort has been made in Latin America to disperse growth to smaller urban centers. As a result, primate cities within the region frequently have one-fourth to one-third of a country's total population. Montevideo, among the most primate cities in the world, contains about 52 percent of Uruguay's total population. By contrast, Mexico City, although the largest city in the region, contains "only" about 20 percent of Mexico's total population, because of the huge and still rapidly growing rural population in that country.

Although the great cities of Latin America are beset with urban problems of incredible magnitude, the region nonetheless is reknowned for having some of the world's most beautiful and lively urban places, the result of a combination of exquisite natural settings for some cities (most notably, Rio de Janeiro), and the unique character stamped on Latin American cities by the Spanish and Portuguese. The distinctive and attractive character of the classic Latin American city has somehow managed to persist down to the present time, even while the processes of industrialization/economic growth and rapid urbanization have been putting severe stresses on that classic city type.

Evolution of Cities in Latin America

Pre-Columbian Urbanization

While the urbanization process has accelerated at an unprecedented rate during this century, cities have played a major role in Latin American civilization for more than 1500 years. Many pre-Columbian cultures had developed elaborate urban systems as the focal points of societal interaction. A number of Mayan cities, such as Chichén Itzá, Uzmal, Palenque, Cobal, Cobán, and Tolum had flowered and been abandoned prior to European contact. Indeed, some of these had been abandoned several centuries prior to European arrival. Others, such as the Aztec center of Tenochtitlán and the Incan capital of Cuzco, were magnificent urban centers surpassing in grandeur and size most of their Old World counterparts. Early Spanish chroniclers described with awe the wealth and opulence of these and other major Amerind cities. While reports of urban population varied widely, it is reasonable to assume that with at least 100,000 inhabitants (and possibly two or three times that) Tenochtitlán was the largest city in the New World and one of the larger cities in the world at that time.

Pre-Columbian cities were major administrative and marketing centers as well

Evolution of Cities in Latin America 201

Figure 6.2 Population Concentrations in Latin America. (*Source:* Compiled by the authors.)

as religious sites whose symbolic importance acted as a catalyst to culturally unite the various tribal groups within a political empire. These cities were frequently designed to recreate the cosmos as envisioned by the culture involved. Huge, monumental buildings, including pyramids and astronomical observatories of religious significance, were often linked by massive avenues tens of yards wide. Some urban sites are believed to have been purely ceremonial in nature, but most served a variety of urban functions. As was the case in the Old World, these cities were supported by densely populated rural hinterlands where sophisticated intensive irrigation agriculture was practiced.

European Urbanization of the New World

This legacy of pre-Columbian urbanization was largely destroyed by the Spanish, who viewed the pyramids and other religious monuments of Amerind cities as an affront to Christianity. Major edifices in these cities were dismantled, often stone by stone, to symbolically demonstrate the power of European institutions and the frailty of indigenous ones. Interestingly, many of the oldest buildings in Latin America are constructed from stones taken from razed Aztec, Mayan, or Incan structures. The Spanish frequently constructed their Christian cathedrals and main governmental buildings on sites previously occupied by Amerind religious or administrative structures. By using this principle of "transference of sanctity," the holiness of the indigenous places was transferred to their Christian successors and the power of the old order was subsumed by the new. Thus, the newly conquered were impressed with the might and right of the Europeans and their God. The penchant of Spaniards to locate on top of earlier Amerind cities meant that those urban centers which were functioning upon the arrival of Europeans have been obliterated, the details of their form and function having been largely lost to time. Remote, abandoned sites, on the other hand, have become tourist attractions during this century.

While indigenous urban structure and organization have long since been eradicated, pre-Columbian urbanization patterns have had an enduring impact upon Latin American urban location. If Europeans left only sparse vestiges of the pre-Columbian cities, they almost universally adopted the active sites selected by Amerinds for their urban centers, especially in the highland areas. From Mexico to Chile major Amerind towns were located in relatively mild upland or highland valleys in the most productive agricultural areas available. Many of these early cities had site and situational advantages not found elsewhere. In terms of interior, noncoastal locations, these urban centers were especially well located. The mainland pre-Columbian civilizations of present-day Latin America were internally oriented. At the time of European arrival, coastal areas were on the periphery of settlement of the higher civilizations. Port cities were unneeded within such a land-bound context and were never developed. Urban hierarchies did develop, however, and in some instances were quite pronounced, Incan towns and cities offering a good example. Well-organized and well-maintained road and bridge networks connected towns and cities, permitting the relatively easy flow of goods and people within the empires. Many historians have argued that the pre-Columbian inland transportation network was far superior to that of their European successors.

Introduction of European Cities

Although urbanization was an important part of many Amerind cultures, the spread of cities throughout Latin America began in earnest with the advent of European settlement. The early voyages of Columbus led to colonization of several of the Caribbean Islands, the most important among these Hispaniola. The town of Santo Domingo was founded in 1496 and became the first European city in the Americas. By the middle of the next century, however, the Spanish and Portuguese conquerors had established permanent town sites from St. Augustine, Florida, and Taos, New Mexico, on the north to Santiago, Chile, and Buenos Aires on the south.

To understand the rapid diffusion of towns in Latin America, and to appreciate the magnitude of such an accomplishment under the circumstances, a number of considerations must be kept in mind. First, Europeans came into the New World in extremely small numbers, especially at the onset. By most estimates, fewer than 200,000 Europeans were in the Americas by 1570. In the early 1500s tiny groups of Spanish and Portuguese residents were superimposing themselves on a native population conservatively estimated to number somewhere between 13 and 25 million. This limited presence in a sea of indigenous people meant that to have a reasonable chance of organizing the newly discovered areas Europeans would have to congregate in central nodes. Furthermore, few early settlers came with the idea of staying permanently. Most hoped to earn a fortune and then return to Iberia to live a comfortable life. As a result, their attitude toward the colonies was logically exploitive and their desire to remit to the Old World the wealth generated in the New World is understandable within that historical context.

Second, both Spanish and Portuguese society, while largely rural in nature, had highly structured urban hierarchies where administrative control was centralized. It is reasonable to assume the transference of urban administrative centers would be a part of their settlement strategy. The characteristic of highly centralized administrative control was exaggerated by the legal intricacies of colonization policies enacted by the Spanish and to a lesser degree by the Portuguese. Under the reigning economic theory of the day, mercantilism, colonies existed for the aggrandizement of the motherland. Most goods produced in the New World were to be remitted to the homeland so that the wealth could be accumulated and utilized there. Conversely, imports to the colonies could come only from the parent nation. Close attention had to be paid to inventorying goods and collecting royal taxes as well as administering directives from king or queen if such a system were to function effectively. Therefore, centralization was mandatory to accomplish such tasks.

Further, mercantilism demanded a need for port facilities to send and receive goods. As literally no ports existed prior to European colonization and trade was internally oriented, the Spanish and Portuguese were quick to establish coastal settlements. The Spanish severely restricted trade between homeland and colonies. A very few cities were allowed to participate in such commercial interaction, often only a single city within each viceroyalty in the New World. Goods entering or leaving the colonies had to move through these designated ports, thus strongly enhancing the importance of

Vera Cruz, Mexico, or Lima, Peru. This high degree of administratively mandated commercial centralization insured the dominance of designated ports over all other coastal settlements.

It is often said that the conquest of the New World was motivated by the three g's: God, gold, and greed (but not necessarily in that order). On this basis, four types of urban settlements emerged. Theoretically, at least, New World conquest was primarily an effort to convert heathen souls to Christianity. As mentioned previously, most early European cities were located on active pre-Columbian urban sites with large indigenous populations. Such cities were invariably located in relatively productive agricultural areas. The reservoir of convertible souls also represented a labor source for agriculture and other economic activities. Most capitals of viceroyalties and captaincy generals were located in these areas, insuring the long-term importance of the sites selected. Some of these pre-Columbian urban sites, such as Mexico City and Bogotá, Colombia, have remained the primate centers in their settlement areas through several centuries and a variety of cultural contexts. Furthermore, Spanish towns were established in virtually every major Amerind concentration in Latin America and formed the basis of urbanization in the region.

Valuable mineral resources, particularly gold and silver, had a magnetic attraction for the European conquerors. Mining towns were established wherever substantial deposits of exploitable minerals were found, regardless of the disamenities presented by climatic conditions, altitude, lack of native population, or other limitations. Cities such as Potosi, Bolivia; Taxco or Zacatecas, Mexico; and Tegucigalpa, Honduras, were originally established because they were adjacent to sources of precious minerals. Mining centers were to provide the most visible and coveted type of wealth generated in the Americas. In true boom-town fashion, many gold and silver towns grew to major proportions. Potosi, Bolivia, for example, was probably the single wealthiest site in the New World from the late 1500s to the mid-1600s and as such attracted a large population. Despite the fact that many mining communities experienced a depletion of their mineral resources, only the most intolerable sites were abandoned. Therefore, even most early mining towns were to form a lasting part of the urban pattern of Latin America.

One of the most significant geographic imprints of Europeans on the New World was the drastic reorientation of movements from continental interiors to coastal exteriors. The products from mines and fields, in large part, were destined for Europe. Ports were to play a major role in the urban hierarchy, but were extremely limited in number (Fig. 6.3). A combination of few good natural harbors and the restriction of trade through officially designated posts emphasized the importance of a handful of coastal sites. Santo Domingo, Dominican Republic; Havana, Cuba; Acapulco and Vera Cruz, Mexico; Balboa and Colón (the transshipment points across the Isthmus of Panama); Cartagena, Colombia; Guayaquil, Ecuador; Lima, Peru; Salvador and Bahia, Brazil; and Rio de Janeiro were the only ports to become major colonial towns. Santa Marta, Colombia; Buenos Aires, Argentina; Asunción, Paraguay; and Valparaiso, Chile, along with a number of smaller contraband ports, were less significant until after 1800. Natural site advantages, such as sheltered anchorage and easy access to the productive por-

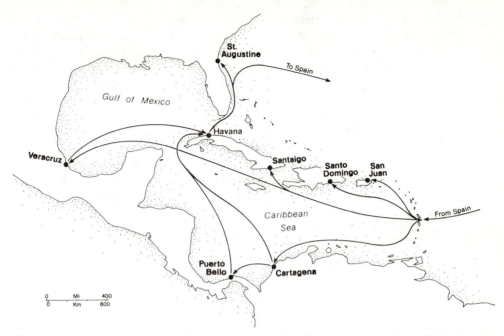

Figure 6.3 Spanish Colonial Ports in Central America and The Caribbean and Route of The Spanish Convoy System. (*Source:* Robert C. West and John P. Augelli, *Middle America: Its Lands and Peoples,* 2d ed., Englewood Cliffs, NJ: Prentice-Hall, © 1976, p. 64. Reprinted by permission of Prentice-Hall, Inc.)

tions of the hinterland, particularly mining centers, were key locational factors in the successful port cities. Lima, the queen of Latin American colonial cities, was also named the capital of the viceroyalty of Peru, enormously enhancing the power and prestige of the city. Lima was unique among Spanish cities in possessing the dual functions of administrative and port center. Only Rio de Janeiro filled a similar role in Latin America.

Functionally, the fourth type of Hispanic urban places were defensive sites designed to protect the limits of European settlement. At the onset of conquest all Spanish and Portuguese enclaves had essentially defensive functions. The earlier towns usually were surrounded by walls to repel attacks by hostile natives. Soon after initial colonization, however, aside from coastal cities subject to attack by privateers, such problems became inconsequential except in frontier towns, which became the major defensive sites after the mid-1500s. Places like Santiago were established to ward off attack by warlike indigenous groups such as the Arucanians. Such towns often marked the limit of effective settlement within their settlement regions.

Taken together, these several types of towns within a specific political unit formed the basis for the urban network that would last through the colonial period and that in many cases remains largely intact today. With political independence from Spain in the early 1800s, only minor changes occurred in the significance of individual urban places and for all intents and purposes, the relative importance of cities within newly independent countries was unaffected. Since the late 1800s new mining centers were founded with the rise in importance of industrial minerals, the most notable among these the oil-producing city of Maracaibo, Venezuela. The introduction of new agricultural technologies and industrialization has had a striking impact upon the development of some cities, with the emergence of São Paulo as Latin America's industrial giant providing, perhaps, the most striking example. New ports like Buenaventura, Colombia, or Antofagasta, Chile, have arisen to serve economically advancing hinterlands. And even planned special-function cities, such as the political center of Brasilia or the industrial city of Ciudad Guyana, have been developed. Nonetheless, the great mass of Latin American cities trace their origins to the colonial and pre-twentieth-century republican periods. This colonial legacy influenced much more than just the location of urban sites. More than any culture region, Latin American cities have shared a common urban structure which derived from their colonial roots and has persisted into this century.

Traditional Internal Structure of Latin American Cities

During the colonial period, the Spanish-American city was thoroughly controlled by the Laws of the Indies, which mandated everything from the treatment of Indians to the width of streets in towns and cities. Portuguese-American cities, while not subject to these laws, were designed according to the Roman planning tradition that inspired them and so were remarkably similar. The Laws called for a grid pattern of geometrically regular east-west and north-south streets radiating outward from a central plaza. The city's development outward from the plaza, including land uses around the plaza and social gradient away from it, block sizes, orientation toward the sun, and location of important urban activities, such as the slaughterhouse, were determined by the Laws.

Urban life centered on the main plaza. All major governmental offices, the great majority of commercial activities, and essentially all of the social amenities from theaters to the best restaurants were located within a relatively short distance from the plaza. As a result, employment opportunities also were concentrated in the city center. Living in proximity to the ebb and flow of city life was a symbol of status which is still an important consideration in location decisions in Latin American cities. The hustle and bustle of city life, *movimiento* as it is termed in Spanish, is viewed as a positive quality by Latins. As public transportation was introduced, access lines focused on the downtown, reinforcing the long-standing importance of the urban core.

Much of the traditional structure still remains. Because most Latin American cities were administrative centers and market towns experiencing neither rapid immigration nor industrialization during the nineteenth century, urban growth and the type of structural change associated with North American cities was quite limited. With the exception of southern South America, where cities such as Buenos Aires and Montevideo early adopted many of the traits of Paris and Chicago, Latin American cities remained traditional, specialized, and relatively small. Even Mexico City had only about 300,000 inhabitants in the year 1900. Because of slow growth and a lack of industrialization in many smaller Latin American cities, many studies have concluded that traditional patterns largely remain. Studies conducted since the 1940s of such cities as Popoyán, Colombia; Oaxaca, Mexico; and Guatemala City have concluded that the socioeconomic organization of Latin American cities is little changed from colonial times.

The stability of urban internal structure was enhanced by other factors. The dualistic nature of Latin American societies severely limited social and economic mobility. With few exceptions, the urban middle class was small and grew slowly until the mid-1900s, when the rate of its expansion increased markedly. Traditional urban social structure buttressed traditional distributions of housing, thus reducing the need to modify urban residential land use patterns. Because of the location of the small number of elites in the city's central core and of the majority (low income groups) on the urban periphery, the provision of urban services to outlying areas was slow at best. This limited expansion of public services led to a compacting of urbanization as the spread of a city was often accompanied by increasing disamenity levels for those living farthest out on the urban fringe. From the colonial era through the 1930s, urban areas in most countries experienced only minor changes in architectural preferences, particularly in terms of residential structures. Some cities, most notably Buenos Aires, Montevideo, São Paulo, Rio de Janeiro, and Mexico City, did undergo a dramatic transformation in architectural stock during the late 1800s and early 1900s as a result of modernization processes spurred by economic development, but they were exceptions to the general trend. Where traditional housing styles remained unchallenged by innovations from abroad, little incentive or impulse existed to change either type of house or residential locations. An important mechanism for bringing about standard change in other cultural contexts was absent in Latin America.

Transformation of Latin American City Structure

As long as slow growth, minimal industrialization, limited provision and expansion of urban services, and restricted transportation and mobility prevailed, so too did the traditional grid plan. The plan was set and there was simply little reason to change it. Many cities took centuries to fill up the original grid laid out with the founding of the city, and so morphological change was difficult if not impossible even long after colonial regulations had ended. In the preindustrial, administrative, artisan city, there was no threat from incompatible land uses, and in cultures characterized by architectural stability and tradition the appeal of a new house was little different from the appeal of an old one.

While grid pattern organization and associated social status still prevail in a number of small, stable Latin American cities, they are obviously of little use toward understanding most large, dynamic urban centers in the region today. A large number of factors have caused a transformation of the traditional urban forms and a breakdown of traditional social organization. Some of these factors merit closer attention.

Expansion of the Central Business District Discussions of North American downtowns or CBDs are replete with such terms as *zone of assimilation, zone of discard,* *transition zone, sequent occupance,* and *segregation and extension.* The basic idea is that as cities grow and change, so, too, do their CBDs in both area and intensity of use. In addition, it is usually assumed that the areal expansion of intensive downtown land uses will be viewed as a threat to residential neighborhoods nearby. Massive, rapid, and disruptive change has been the major force in creating the much maligned transition zone around most North American CBDs. In Latin American cities the CBD was the economic and administrative core of the city, but its expansion was rarely evident prior to the 1930s. Such expansion is certainly the norm, at least in larger cities today. In a number of Latin American urban centers in recent decades, streets have been widened, old mansions demolished, parking garages and lots carved out, skyscraper office towers built, shopping malls created, bus terminals constructed, and a variety of hotels, restaurants, and arenas put up in and around the downtown. In short, the sleepy, stable central plaza has become the node around which a very North American-style CBD has evolved. While many of the old, multistoried courtyard mansions proved amenable to conversion to commercial uses, this strategy, as in North America and Europe, was viewed as temporary at best. Soon, the demand for space and increasing land values mandated abrupt changes in the type and scale of the architectural stock. Perhaps the clearest example of the arrival of this process in Latin America is provided by Mexico City, which has seen its CBD expand over the years from the traditional core at the Zócalo, past the Alameda, and for more than a mile down the Paseo de la Reforma. In the best Wilshire Boulevard (in Los Angeles) tradition, mansions have been replaced by skyscraper offices, chic nightspots, and theaters all along the "Mexican Miracle Mile" (Fig. 6.4).

Meanwhile, much of the space north of the Zócalo has reverted to zone-of-discard markets and tenements. The upper classes traditionally occupying residences in the path of this downtown expansion were largely pushed outward, partly because of their inability or unwillingness to pay commercial prices for a central city location and partly by the congestion and disruption of the new, dynamic cityscape. Those finding themselves "on the other side of the plaza" moved outward along the same path so as to avoid increasing deterioration and to be close to the relocating "action." In many ways, the processes shaping North American and Latin American CBDs are similar, but the resulting downtowns are hardly carbon copies.

Industrialization Few Latin American cities can rival Cleveland, Detroit, or Chicago as industrial cities, but many are becoming important centers for everything from food processing to automobile assembly. While little of this industrialization has occurred in the heart of the downtown as it did in Cleveland, it does, nevertheless, require a fairly central location, accessible to major highways and railroad links. Industrialization also requires a number of urban services, such as water and electricity, many of which have not been ubiquitously expanded in Latin American cities to the point that industry can be built just about anywhere as is nearly the case in North America. Cities from Lima to Monterrey (Mexico) have large areas near their cores that could, to one degree or another, be called industrial. Often these areas are less specialized than comparable districts in Anglo America, although they bear a distinct

Figure 6.4 Paseo de la Reforma, Mexico City's spine. This "Mexican Miracle Mile," which forms part of the CBD, is an area of skyscrapers, chic nightspots, and theaters. (E. Griffin and L. Ford)

resemblance to some types of older, prezoning neighborhoods found along the tracks in older eastern North American cities, usually encompassing a variety of heavy industries, artisan shops, storefronts, and residences. Large-scale industry helps to further disorganize the traditional social structure and landscape and to bid up the cost of central-city space. In addition, the noise and pollution created by industry and the numbers of vehicles servicing industry looms large in creating the image of the central city as a disamenity zone.

Still, "high class" land uses are found much closer to industrial areas in Latin America than in Europe or North America since access to paved highways and modern services is essential for industry and such things tend to be most well developed in the "wealthy sector." To some extent, the attraction is mutual since an increasing number of elites are corporate executives who work in industry, and access to work in an inadequately paved, truck- and cart-filled urban milieu is undesirable. Once again, North American trends are evident, but so are the constraints. The options are limited.

Expansion of Urban Services and Suburbanization Even though Mexico City was the first city in the Western Hemisphere to have gas-lit streets, North American and European cities have generally been far ahead of those in Latin America in developing and expanding a full range of urban services. Not only were North American cities among the first in the world to provide such things as water, sewage, police and fire protection, street paving and cleaning, street lighting, public schools and parks, mass transportation systems, and even tree planting, but perhaps more importantly, affluence and rapid economic growth made it possible to extend those services great distances rapidly. For nearly 60 years, someone moving to the periphery of a North American city could expect to be serviced with everything from running water to telephones. While Latin American cities are still nowhere near so universally serviced, in most cases the basic conveniences of urban living have been developed and extended into at least some areas beyond the urban core. While relatively limited service extension still constrains exurban living of the kind found 20 to 30 mi. (32 to 48 km.) outside many North American cities, suburban living is possible. In recent years, a number of large-scale suburban developments have arisen in Latin America, complete with minimum lot sizes and architectural controls, thus alleviating the fear of random encroachment by squatters, which may well have limited individual suburban moves in the past. Since urban services are difficult and expensive to extend, it follows that wealthy areas will be the first and in some cases the only areas to get them. Most cities have only one wealthy sector because extending services rapidly in several directions normally is fiscally impossible. Indeed, wealthy suburban developments expand in the same direction as the business district, since that area is the best serviced and mutual access exists. Important natural and man-made amenities, such as parks, golf courses, and race tracks, further lock-in the direction of suburban expansion.

Upward socioeconomic mobility is relatively limited in much of Latin America, and only a small, though in some cases increasing, percentage of the population can afford professionally built housing. Usually, only a few residential suburbs are located in juxtaposition so as if to reinforce a new idea. Recently, modern automobile-oriented shopping centers and office parks have grown up around these high-status communities just as they do in North American cities. This new social and economic centrality, or sense of being "someplace" (an important cultural requisite in the Latin American milieu), may be especially important in attracting further suburbanization. Increasingly, the large suburban developments are providing some type of financing, an attractive inducement in high-interest, money-tight economies.

Architectural Change   Another factor affecting the transformation of Latin America cities in this century is the increasing rate of architectural change. Until the 1920s much of Latin America was characterized by architectural stability. The single or multistoried courtyard house remained the accepted ideal. During the 1920s and especially with the advent of the 1930s, however, foreign-trained architects began to introduce variety into the Latin cityscape, running the gamut from English Tudor to art deco. Many of these new designs featured freestanding houses with front yards, and upper class residents seeking to emulate a "modern" life-style moved into them. A filter-down process had begun.

Filter-Down Housing and Squatter Settlements   The prerequisites for the filter-down process are less often met in Latin American cities than in North American cities. Because of drastic differences in income distribution, a much smaller percentage of the population is able to participate in the housing market either as purchasers or renters. Also, since loan money is scarce and interest rates are high, fewer developers are operating in marginal lower-middle-class housing markets in Latin America than in North America, especially away from the proven upper class neighborhoods. Since new, freestanding housing tends to be built largely for the upper class, emerging middle class renters and buyers are more likely to improve existing dwellings than to seek housing in filtered-down upper class areas.

The biggest and most obvious difference between cities in the two Americas, however, is the Latin American phenomenon of squatter settlements and self-built housing (Fig. 6.5). Recent in-migration from the countryside has brought large numbers of people who cannot be readily absorbed into the urban economy, not only because of their low incomes and social positions, but because of the rate and scale of population increase. Large numbers of people earn so little and earn it so irregularly that paying rent or making mortgage payments with interest rates of 20 to 25 percent on 10-year loans is out of the question. If housing were available, which is rarely the case, it would be unaffordable to the mass of recent in-migrants at any price. Even the low rents charged in government-subsidized housing projects creates an impossible financial burden for the great majority of urban residents. These people must simply take over unoccupied land, or in some cases undeveloped lots, and build their own dwellings.

Self-built housing can be, and is, made from just about anything, including cardboard, plastic, tin, scrap wood, branches, cloth, concrete, bricks, highway signs, and roofing material. Since such housing need not be finished before it is inhabited, it enables people to get a start in the city and even to save money. Most of the houses simply

Figure 6.5 A new government-built school rises in the background of a typical squatter settlement in Mexico City, an indication of the gradual modernization of these poverty zones that takes place over time, although seldom fast enough to keep pace with new in-migrants from the rural areas. (E. Griffin and L. Ford)

"accrete" over time, with better materials being substituted for makeshift ones as money is obtained. Urban services are often provided to these settlements in time, but for a long while people must simply do without or improvise through the use of water trucks, sewer trenches, stone pathways, and the like. In some cases, government authorities or private landowners have sought to evict squatters, but their sheer numbers and the political realities of the situation (there is no place for them to go) make expulsions rare indeed. In some cases, centrally located areas which are extremely inhospitable to development and servicing, such as steep slopes, canyons, areas subject to flooding, or garbage dumps, are utilized for squatter settlements, although here the pressures for removal may be more intense. Normally, therefore, the newest squatter settlements tend to be in the most peripheral locations.

Given time and the provision of at least minimal government services such as schools, water, and sewage disposal, squatter settlements can become stable and substantial neighborhoods. Since filtered-down middle class housing is seldom available, especially in cities experiencing rapid growth, people simply improve their homes and neighborhoods *in situ*. In general, the older the settlement, the better and more substantial it is. It is not uncommon to find entire neighborhoods of two-story concrete houses that have evolved over a decade or two from one-room cardboard shacks. With the gradual addition of paved roads, street lights, and vegetation, many early squatter settlements are now indistinguishable from neighborhoods with less checkered histories.

Meanwhile, new squatter settlements grow up even farther out, and so the poorest people continue to live on the edge of town.

Internal Structure of Modern Latin American Cities

It is apparent that the processes of modernization have had a significant impact upon all major Latin American cities. Indeed, many researchers have argued that urban areas in the region are evolving in much the same way as cities have in North America. Accordingly, Mexico City, Bogotá, and Lima, say, should become structurally akin to New York, Denver, and Los Angeles. But this line of logic ignores the significant cultural, technological and socioeconomic differences between North America and Latin America. Therefore, it is more reasonable to assume that both the process of city growth and the form cities take is to a large degree culturally specific regardless of the rates of growth and modernization. While the forces of urban change may result in considerable worldwide similarity in city structure, attitudes toward such things as density, mixed land uses, open spaces, architectural ideals and aesthetics, and the value of "city life" are bound to vary. In addition, institutional factors such as zoning laws, building codes, financial arrangements, construction technology and available materials, the role of government in providing housing, and the establishment or expansion of urban services vary with both culture and level of technology.

As a result, Latin American cities have developed a distinctive structural pattern in which traditional elements of Latin American culture have been merged with the modernizing processes altering them (Fig. 6.6). In general terms Latin American cities are dominated by several components: a viable CBD, a commercial Spine and an associated Elite Residential Sector, and a series of concentric zones in which residential quality decreases outward from the center of the city. Using this as a model for understanding Latin American urban morphology provides insights into the dynamics of Latin American urbanization. A discussion of each of these structural elements will help to clarify how urban space is utilized in this cultural context.

Central Business District

Latin American cities are characterized by vibrant, highly dynamic, and increasingly specialized CBDs. In contrast to most North American cities they have remained the prime employment, commercial, and entertainment nodes for the city. Skyscraper office and condominium towers, department stores, movie theaters, and speciality shops have long been a part of the Latin American downtown, but these cities have either resisted or have not yet experienced many of the segregating and sterilizing trends evident in the downtown of U.S. cities. The relative dominance of the CBD can be explained in part by a reliance upon public transit, which has continued to center on the CBD and in part by the existence of a large and relatively affluent population in the inner rings of the city.

As in North America this dynamism, with its rapid rate of change in scale and function, is threatening smaller and older buildings within the downtown core. But

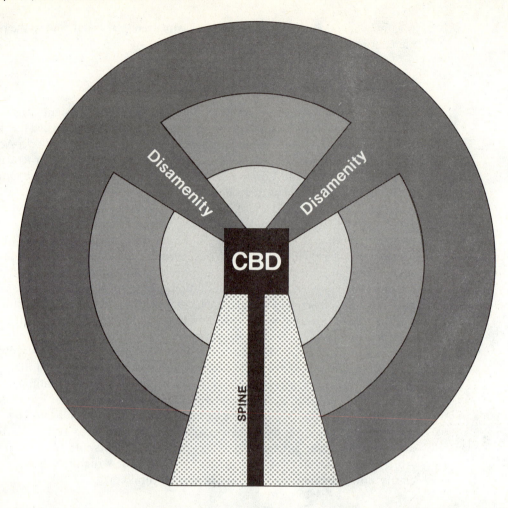

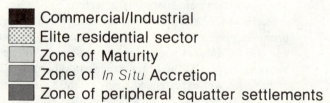

Figure 6.6 A Model of Latin American City Structure. (*Source:* Reprinted from E. Griffin and L. Ford, *Geographical Review,* vol. 70, 1980, with the permission of The American Geographical Society.)

space in Latin American cities is simply too much in demand to be thrown away or underutilized as it is in many overbuilt North American cities. Thus, while Latin American cities do have areas similar in many ways to North American zones of discard, these have a much greater economic viability and serve as market districts and low-income shopping zones as well as temporary homes for new in-migrants or transients. While there is a zone in transition in most large Latin American cities, it is much less important and visible than in North America.

The fact that Bogotá veritably bristles with high rise corporate headquarters, hotels and apartments, while Lima features a large number of relatively compact central-city buildings highlighted by restored two- and three-storied colonial structures has little bearing on the shape and structure of the two cities. Therefore, while the CBD is the literal heart of the city, other structural elements distinguish the morphology of Latin American urban areas from those in other major culture regions.

Spine and Elite Residential Sector

Outside of the area of the CBD, the dominant element of Latin American city structure is a commercial Spine surrounded by an Elite Residential Sector (which shall be referred to as the Spine/Sector from time to time). The Spine/Sector is present in all Latin American cities, and the process of its formation differs substantially from the processes shaping the rest of the city. The Spine/Sector is essentially an extension of the CBD lined with the city's most important amenities, including nearly all of the professionally built upper-class and upper-middle-class housing stock. The Spine/Sector encompasses virtually all of the important people and activities not located downtown: the major tree-lined boulevards, golf courses, and the major parks with museums and zoos; the best theaters, restaurants, and office buildings; and the wealthiest suburbs. Thus, the Spine/Sector provides a "good address" from the downtown to the edge of the city. All urban services are provided and are the best available in the city. Zoning and other land controls are strict.

Socioeconomic elites occupy an inordinate amount of space in relation to their numbers in nearly all urban contexts, and in Latin America this relationship is further exaggerated. An extremely limited percentage of a city's total population, normally less than 5 percent, dominates a disproportionately large area, sometimes as much as a quarter or third of total urban space. The Elite Residential Sector forms a wedge in the Hoytian sense. Within the Spine/Sector, the market for residential and commercial space operates much as it does in North American cities. For example, as the wealthy move outward toward newer, larger, modern homes with more open space, the upper middle class accepts filter-down housing in once fashionable neighborhoods closer to the center of the city. Increasingly, upper-middle-class apartments and houses are being built on the fringes of the Elite Residential Sector, partly because of increasing demand in this market and partly as a buffer against ever-present squatter settlements not far away.

The width, and thus the areal extent, of the Elite Residential Sector, typically varies with the percentage of the population that can afford to participate in the "North

American-style" housing market. The Spine/Sector provides a type of North American-style suburban amenities without sacrificing the Latin American requirements of centrality and access. Because the life of the city ebbs and flows along the Spine and because travel through the sector is easy, "the action" is never far away.

The Spine and Elite Residential Sector constitutes a morphological response to the limited ability to extend urban services, limited mortgage money coupled with conservative lending policies and high interest rates, the relatively recent acquisition of suburban values by the elites, and the inability of Latin American cities to plan, build for, and otherwise cope with massive growth. Within the Spine/Sector, the forces molding and shaping the Latin American metropolis are largely similar to those operating in North American cities, while elsewhere within the urban milieu the Latin American city reflects more traditional characteristics.

Zones

While the Spine/Sector represents an important and in some cases dominant aspect of the morphology of the Latin American city, it houses only a small percentage of the total metropolitan population. As an example, according to 1974 income data 86 percent of Bogotá's households had a total monthly income of less than $250, while 52 percent reported a monthly income of less than $100, dramatizing the inability of the vast majority of the city's residents of ever having a serious chance of participating in the professional housing market. Away from the Spine/Sector, the Latin American city's structure consists of a series of more or less concentric zones with socioeconomic characteristics roughly opposite to those postulated by Burgess for North American cities. In general, socioeconomic levels and housing quality decrease with increasing distance from the central core.

The Latin American city is typified by three distinctive zones or rings: (1) a Zone of Maturity, (2) a Zone of *in Situ* Accretion, and (3) a Zone of Peripheral Squatter Settlements. The relative size of the three zones is a function of the rate of in-migration compared with the pace of individual *in situ* improvement of housing and the city's ability to expand urban services. For example, cities which experience relatively slow population growth will appear to have a larger Zone of Maturity and therefore a less chaotic, more organized cityscape than cities with extremely rapid in-migration, which are apt to have large Zones of Peripheral Squatter Settlements, thus lending an air of disorganization and chaos to the landscape (Fig. 6.7). The Zone of *in Situ* Accretion represents the area in which the process of assimilation between the inner and outer zones is most dramatically occurring. Although these zones exist in a generalized form, areas of high disamenity such as flood-prone river channels or steep slopes or canyons often remain unimproved settlement areas even when centrally located. While all three zones are characterized by mixed land uses, aside from small-scale "corner stores" and services, there is little important commercial activity outside of the CBD and the Spine.

Zone of Maturity In the Latin American context, an inner city location carries a positive connotation. Outside of the Spine/Sector, the Zone of Maturity is the area

Figure 6.7 Street vendors, a traditional part of Latin American cities, are often young children who help supplement family income. (E. Griffin and L. Ford)

of "better residences" within a city. While in most older cities the zone includes many filtered-down traditional colonial homes, it is more typically an area of gradually improved, significantly upgraded self-built housing. This zone may or may not include professionally built dwellings financed through bank mortgages, but it almost always contains solid, sometimes quite large brick or concrete homes. These homes have been improved and enlarged gradually *in situ* by residents unable to participate in the housing market of the Elite Residential Sector. This upward transformation is a morphological response to the extremely limited geographic mobility possible within urban space despite the increased socioeconomic mobility achieved by the zone's residents. Because such neighborhood improvements have occurred over time *in situ,* dwelling unit density is about the same as in more peripheral zones. But because the population is somewhat older, there are fewer children and population density may be lower. The zone is fully serviced with paved streets, lighting, good public transportation, schools, and sewerage. While sometimes showing signs of age, the zone is gradually improving and the population is relatively stable.

Zone of *in Situ* Accretion In most Latin American cities, the Zone of *in Situ* Accretion is one of modest residential quality moving toward a state of maturity. This zone is characterized by a great variety of housing types, sizes, and quality. Some of it is "completed" and is similar to that found in the Zone of Maturity, while on the same block might be located a hovel. The zone is in a constant state of ongoing construction. Piles of bricks and concrete blocks seem to be everywhere. Many of the houses have unfinished rooms or second stories, and a wild variety of fences abound. Often only the main thoroughfares are paved, but small shops and schools are present. Not all of the neighborhoods have electricity, although some households have television sets eagerly awaiting its arrival. In many instances deliveries by water and butane trucks are still vital. The generally disheveled appearance of the zone, along with the bright colors often used to brighten up houses as soon as money for paint is available, creates an extremely chaotic landscape by North American or European standards. Nonetheless, things are definitely on the upswing as public services are expanded and the overall level of housing quality and landscaping improve with time. Because it is at least partially serviced and some buildable sites are still available, this is the zone where large government-sponsored building projects are likely to be located. The density of the landscape reflects to a degree the uneven assimilation of the zone's residents into the economic and social structure of the city. The rate of the Zone of *in Situ* Accretion's improvement is based on the city's ability to provide services and the continued economic mobility of its residents.

Zone of Peripheral Squatter Settlements Life on the Latin American urban fringe does not conjure up the same idyllic images that it does in North America. This zone houses the impoverished, recent in-migrants to the city and in terms of housing quality and services is the worst part of the city. Since in-migration exceeds home construction by a wide margin, many people must simply scavenge materials and make do. The landscape has been denuded of all vegetation for building materials or fuel and often gives the appearance of a refugee camp. The houses are small and extremely fragile. The zone is almost totally unserviced. Open trenches carry waste down the rutted, unpaved streets, and people carry buckets of water long distances from communal taps. Sometimes electricity is "pirated" by attaching as many as several hundred wires to a utility pole in or close to the neighborhoods, but most often there is no power at all. The journey to work, if there is work, is long and difficult since it often involves walking to the nearest bus line through eroding, unlit streets. Often "urban villages" emerge made up largely of in-migrants from a particular rural area. All in all, the zone's quality of life is marginal. Despite what appears to the outsider to be wretched conditions, the residents perceive that neighborhood improvement is possible and will, with time, transform their communities. After all, even parts of the Zone of Maturity and more recently the Zone of *in Situ* Accretion had the same characteristics that now exist here. The vast literature on squatter settlements confirms the process of gradual upgrading of neighborhoods which has occurred in cities throughout Latin America.

Core Area Slums and Homelessness As was alluded to earlier, certain parts of Latin American cities remain disamenity areas for long periods of time and do not evolve through *in situ* accretion processes as just described. Areas such as the *favelas* of Rio de Janeiro have become infamous for the substandard living conditions and teeming poverty endured by its residents. Fortunately, such slums represent the exception rather than the rule in terms of long-term residential conditions for most of the region's marginal urban population. However, such slum areas can be truly repulsive examples of inadequate housing, lack of services, social stagnation, criminality, and hopelessness.

In many cities within Latin America significant numbers of people, normally those with the most limited economic means and the least ability to adapt to urban life-styles, have no housing whatsoever. They simply live in the streets, often in doorways or in cardboard boxes they carry with them. Gangs of abandoned children, called *gamines* in Colombia and elsewhere, form a growing percentage of the homeless population.

Major Representative Cities

Of any number of cities that could be selected as major representative cities of Latin America, a handful of the most important have been chosen: Mexico City, Tijuana (Mexico), Rio de Janeiro, Brasilia, and Buenos Aires. These five illustrate especially well the urbanization trends, internal spatial structure, and urban problems of Latin American cities.

Mexico City

Mexico City is both the largest and the oldest city in all of Latin America. When the Spanish arrived in Tenochtitlán, the Aztec name for what is now Mexico City, they found a bustling metropolis of perhaps 100,000 inhabitants situated upon a series of islands in a shallow lake in the central plateau of Mexico. Nestled among picturesque volcanic peaks at an altitude of over 7000 feet (2100 m.), the city provided a classic example of a defensible site as well as one with an awe-inspiring and perhaps religiously significant setting. The Aztec city consisted of a series of compact rectangular islands separated by navigational canals and dominated by ceremonial centers which replicated the Aztec conception of the cosmos, replete with monumental pyramids and temples to a plethora of gods. The Spanish razed the Aztec city, but built their Roman-inspired planned rectangular city in many ways conforming to the design of the preexisting Aztec city. While the city officially changed hands in 1519 with the European takeover, in reality the focal point of Mexico remained unchanged and has remained so down to the present time (Fig. 6.8).

The city superimposed by the Spanish focused upon the Zócalo, a large central plaza "parade ground" surrounded by the cathedral, national palace, and important government and commercial structures (Fig. 6.9). Today, 450 years later, the Zócalo remains the symbolic center of the city and the focal point for all of Mexico. Indeed, the area around the Zócalo has remained perhaps more stable in function and appearance than the core of any other major Latin American metropolis. The colonial Zócalo area continues to exist because the city has continually moved to the west toward higher, better-drained ground rather than redeveloping older areas. Mexico City was by far the largest, most sophisticated, perhaps best designed and serviced city in the Western Hemisphere in the year 1800, before immigration and industrialization trans-

220   Chapter 6, Cities of Latin America

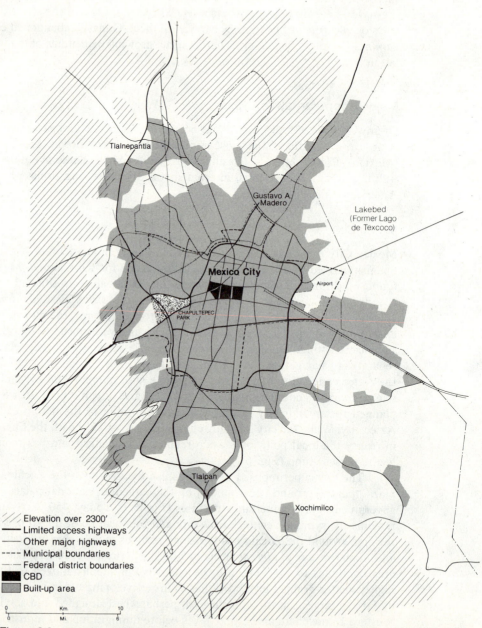

Figure 6.8   Mexico City. (*Source:* Compiled by the authors.)

Figure 6.9 The Zócalo, in downtown Mexico City, is the cultural and financial center of the nation. It shows a mix of nineteenth-century colonial-style architecture and modern skyscrapers. (E. Griffin and L. Ford)

formed the cities of both North and South America at a more rapid rate. Nevertheless, virtually the entire city at that time occupied only the original colonial grid surrounding the Zócalo. During the nineteenth century, however, the form of the city changed significantly. By the end of the century, the downtown core had reached the tree-filled Alameda and wealthy residential areas were springing up well beyond toward the hills of Chapultepec. Today the Alameda area provides a continuing focal point for the "downtown," with its 500-foot (167 m.) Latin American Tower skyscraper and Belles Artes Theater. High rise hotels and office buildings dating from the 1930s through the 1950s enclose the Alameda, giving it a "Central Park" ambience.

Perhaps the seminal event in the transformation of Mexico City from a colonial capital to a world city occurred in the 1860s during the French interlude of Emperor Maximillian. At this time, the Paseo de la Reforma, a 2-mi.-long, eight-lane wide, tree-lined boulevard in the tradition of the Champs Élysées connected the city with Chapultepec Castle and Park to the west. The Reforma was quickly lined with the elegant homes, shops, embassies, and cafes which to this day remain where the elite congregate. The Reforma now forms a commercial spine lined with luxury hotels, condominiums, chic restaurants, and posh office buildings. The Zona Rosa, a European-style zone of cafes and shops, is perhaps best characterized as the Beverly Hills of Mexico City. Indeed, the area is worldly in the sense that there are few clues to national indentity here—it could be Paris, Rome, or New York by the looks of the people and activities. Over the last three or four decades, the Reforma's high class residences have been replaced by higher-value commercial land uses, causing the elites to move progressively westward into new, sprawling, suburban developments such as Lomas de Chapultepec. These new areas, further out along the extended Reforma, are characterized by continuing easy access to the Zona Rosa hub.

The core area described above constituted nearly the entire city up until the early 1900s and is generally the only part of the city that tourists, elites, and diplomats see. Nearly everything that happens of any importance happens in this CBD core and Spine. Since the early 1900s, however, the population of the city has exploded from about 350,000 to nearly 14 million today. Much of this growth has come since 1950. Mexico City could be called a "late blooming" metropolis in that it largely sat out the industrial revolution of the late 1800s and early 1900s that so greatly transformed North American and European cities, as well as Buenos Aires and to a lesser degree São Paulo. Since World War II, though, the population explosion in Mexico, coupled with the continuing dominance of Mexico City in the country's urban hierarchy, has led to unparalleled population growth. Mexico City has always been located in the heart of the most densely populated region of the country, and now that the perception of opportunity in the rural landscape has diminished, all roads lead to Mexico City. From a population of about 2 million people in 1950 to some 7 million in the mid-1960s, Mexico City is becoming the largest single-centered metropolis in the entire world.

The end is nowhere in sight. The city's housing infrastructure, transportation system, and social services have simply been overwhelmed. The city, long hemmed in by low, swampy soils on the east and limited transportation, has sprawled spectacularly across the lake bed and into the hills beyond during the past decade. In spite of the construction of an extensive freeway and subway system in the last 20 years, the city lives with the constant possibility of total strangulation due to massive and uncontrolled in-migration. Experts project that if growth rates continue at their present level until 2000, Mexico City's population will reach 32 million, roughly the population of the entire nation in 1950. Traffic moves at a snail's pace during rush hours in the morning, at noon, and in the evening. Finding an empty taxi, a seat on the bus, or standing room on the subway presents a real challenge for all but the most aggressive. In addition, the sheer number of people walking, standing, and milling about on downtown streets can make almost any movement difficult. All of this movement also creates a tremendous pollution problem in the Valle de México, since vehicular exhaust from literally thousands of untuned buses and trucks is trapped by the mountains which surround the 7000-foot-high (2100m.) valley, making breathing an exhausting experience. The smog problem is among the worst in the world.

In spite of its problems, Mexico City remains one of the major attractions of the world and by far the leading magnet of internal migration within Mexico. It is rapidly becoming the undisputed cultural center of the Spanish-speaking world, as well. It is the major center of book publishing in Latin America, vying only with Buenos Aires for the honor. Mexico City's film industry is now so successful that exports are being sent to Spain as well as throughout the Americas. Mexico City's artists, recording stars, and television personalities are renowned in Latin America, making the city a cultural mecca in the tradition of London, Paris, and New York. This is also true in architecture.

Because of its unstable soil and heritage of destructive earthquakes, Mexico City remains primarily a low-profile metropolis. Compared with most other world cities such as New York, São Paulo, or Hong Kong, Mexico City appears to be a city of low- and mid-rise houses and apartments. Much of the central city is characterized by boxy, two- to four-story apartments made of brick or reinforced concrete covered with bright or pastel-colored stucco. The vast majority of these structures cover the entire lot; yards and other open spaces are rare. In spite of the low profile, the density of the city is quite high. Since this Zone of Maturity accreted over time, some architectural diversity exists, but even so, much of the residential landscape appears bland and monotonous. Occasional stores, churches, factories, and markets enliven the scene. Since about one-half of all the automobiles registered in Mexico are in Mexico City, traffic is both incredible and constant.

Because of the tremendous in-migration of people into Mexico City, the housing market of the metropolitan area has been engulfed. Massive numbers of people are unable to find suitable accommodations. As a result, huge expanses of peripheral squatter settlements have developed to the north, east, and south of the city. These squatter settlements mushroomed despite the concerted efforts of the government to provide subsidized housing. Massive tracts of government-sponsored housing dot the eastern lake plain of Mexico City and serve as home for thousands of families. The scale of the housing problem is so immense, however, that government housing is available for only a small percentage of those who desire it. Meanwhile the city continues to grow.

Tijuana

Although far from being one of the largest cities in Latin America, Tijuana is one of the world's most rapidly growing urban places, and is a dynamic cultural hybrid city. With a current population approaching 1 million and an annual growth rate of more than 8 percent, Tijuana could become the second largest city in Mexico before the end of the 1980s. Though not a typical Latin American city, Tijuana may be a prototype of the future (Fig. 6.10). Its landscape and morphology have resulted from a volatile mixture of central Mexican tradition and Southern California pizzazz. Because of its small core and recent rapid growth, Tijuana provides an easily observable laboratory in which to study the processes currently shaping Latin American cities. Additionally, as a border city, Tijuana along with Mexicali, Juarez, and Laredo, provides an example of an increasingly important aspect of urban growth in Mexico. The city has become a significant industrial center and a destination for massive migration within the country. In many ways it epitomizes the ideas of a classic frontier city.

Tijuana is almost entirely a product of the twentieth century. During the 1890s Tijuana was said to have more saloons than buildings, and the city's population reached 1000 only around 1900. As a result, little in Tijuana's landscape can be described as traditionally Latin American in appearance. During the first decade of the 1900s, Tijuana grew slowly because it was difficult and expensive for people to get there from

Figure 6.10 Tijuana, as seen in this aerial photo, fronts abruptly on the U.S. border (the road in the center that neatly divides rural and urban landscapes). This unique Mexican city has prospered as well as suffered from its proximity to the U.S. (E. Griffin and L. Ford)

central Mexico and because the economy was based on bullfights, boxing, gambling, and, during Prohibition, liquor. By 1930 the population of Tijuana had reached 11,000. During this period the prevailing image of the city as a strip of bars across the international border from Southern California was formed. This tainted image persisted during the boisterous days of World War II and still lingers on.

In the 1930s Tijuana was designated a free-trade zone by the Mexican government and the pace of growth began to quicken in spite of the repeal of Prohibition in the United States and a ban on gambling in Mexico. "Sin City," as Tijuana was known, slowly began to diversify economically and during the decade grew at approximately 5 percent annually, more than twice the Mexican national average. Primarily through migration from interior Mexico and the repatriation of Mexican citizens from the United States during the Great Depression, the city's population grew to nearly 22,000 by 1940. The 1940s witnessed a tripling of Tijuana's population. New employment opportunities were created by tremendous increases in tourism (especially sailors and marines) from burgeoning Southern California and by the presence of large numbers of jobs in California for legal and illegal Mexican agricultural laborers after the *bracero* program began in 1942. By 1950 Tijuana had more than 65,000 inhabitants and ranked fifth among the Mexican border cities. Since then, Tijuana has been the fastest growing of all Mexican frontier cities. By the mid-1970s it had well over 500,000 people and has added perhaps as many as 500,000 more since then.

The recent growth of Tijuana is due to a number of factors. First in importance is the fact that Tijuana has the highest federally established minimum wages in Mexico. Second, Tijuana remains a free-trade zone, which means that many consumer and luxury goods are available in the city at low cost, while they are out of reach for low-income Mexicans elsewhere in the country. Third, the federal government has encouraged industrial growth in the border zone through its Programa Nacional Fronteriza. A number of industrial parks have been developed in the city to accommodate new plants which provide jobs for several thousand employees.

Most of Tijuana's growth has occurred without the benefit of land use planning, building codes, or zoning ordinances in a city with limited financial capabilities to cope with extremely rapid growth. Like other Mexican cities, Tijuana has little taxing or spending power, for most revenue collecting and most planning is done at the federal and state levels. The Mexican government long considered the city a remote, semi-American outpost and has only recently allocated substantial funds for paving, flood control, and subsidized housing programs. Since much of Tijuana's landscape is makeshift, to the uninitiated it seems to be a giant, amorphous hodgepodge that defies rational description. But on closer examination it is apparent that Tijuana has a strong sectoral appearance due in part to the fact that the city is located astride a major river channel. The relatively compact CBD is functionally bifurcated into a tourist section and a Mexican business zone. Numerous tourist-oriented curio shops and bars dominate the Avenida Revolución, while government offices, professional services, and commercial activities intended for residents of the city are located on thoroughfares paralleling the Avenida. The "downtown" has extended southward with the residential growth of the city and away from the cantina-filled zone of discard along the immediate border.

The southward expansion of the commercial core of Tijuana led in recent years to the development of a classic spine. The spine extends southeastward for approximately five miles, although it is seldom more than a block wide on either side of Agua Caliente-Diaz Ordaz Boulevard, the main arterial. Almost everything of major importance to the city of Tijuana is located there. During the last decade, the spine has grown dramatically as major elite residential developments have paralleled the spine's extension, on the west side of Ordaz Boulevard. In the early days of Tijuana the elite occupied houses adjacent to the CBD, but by the late 1930s had begun the gradual drift along the emerging spine south of the CBD, a trend firmly established with the development of the luxury neighborhood of Chapultepec starting in the early 1950s. Although the high class residential section is quintessentially suburban in character, it is equivalent to living "downtown" in the preindustrial city.

Tijuana's zonal structure conforms fairly well to the model presented earlier, although the relative newness of the city has created a seemingly chaotic cityscape. Thousands of people have migrated to Tijuana, chiefly from such traditional areas as the states of Jalisco and Michoacán, usually with little money and only the possibility of a job. Many if not most of the new migrants who have flooded into Tijuana since 1950 might best be described as squatters. Few have been able to afford the high prices charged for existing housing in the city or the high interest rates on mortgage loans, so they headed for the hills and put together a "house" as best they could.

To the uninitiated observer, most housing in Tijuana appears to be marginal. Chaos abounds. This impression reflects the disproportionately large size of the Zone of *in Situ* Accretion compared with the sizes of the other zones in the city. Unlike the traditional Latin American city, there is no perceptible organization with regard to features such as age and style of houses, changing preferences for building materials and landscaping, or status of maintenance.

Rio de Janeiro

Probably no other city of Latin America conjures up an image of a beautiful and vibrant urban environment, however erroneous some of that image may be, than Rio. No major city in Latin America has been more strongly influenced by its physical setting than Rio de Janeiro. Nestled snugly between a precipitous coastal mountain range and the island-studded expanses of Guanabara Bay, Rio has perhaps the most magnificent site of any world city (Fig. 6.11). Yet, this physical environment has been a mixed blessing. While the protected harbor provided the reason for initial settlement and the scenic mountains and broad beaches provide a continuing attraction for tourists and migrants alike, the limited buildable lands available have been a severe constraint on the city's expansion over the last century. There is little land for development, and attempts to build on marginal sites have led to destructive mud slides and disruption of public services. Additionally, the mountainous terrain surrounding Rio has greatly limited access to the interior and the effective integration of its natural hinterland. Nonetheless, by the eighteenth century, Rio de Janeiro had become Brazil's most important city and by the twentieth century had become an international playground.

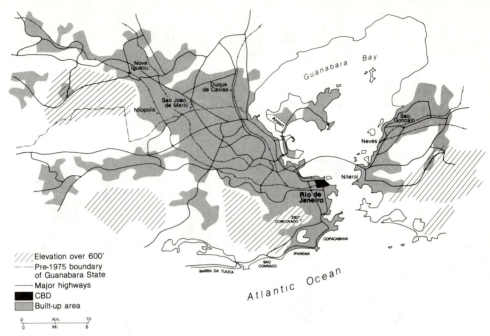

Figure 6.11 Rio de Janeiro. (*Source:* Compiled by the authors.)

Rio was established in the sixteenth century. Its initial importance derived from its role as the coastal entrepôt for the rich gold-mining centers which flourished in the interior. In 1763 Rio became the capital of colonial Brazil and grew in stature with the arrival of the exiled Portuguese royal court in 1808. This new function saved the city from the possible stagnation which likely would have occurred when the mineral wealth of the interior was depleted in the late 1700s. Rio reached a population of 100,000 in the 1820s, and with the advent of the Kingdom of Brazil in the 1830s it was made the capital of the nation, a role it retained until the inauguration of Brasilia in 1960. Brasilia's rise as the country's political capital, and São Paulo's emergence as the undisputed economic and population focal point, has caused Rio to lose its former dominance (Fig. 6.12). Yet the city has retained its image as the epitome of the Brazilian way of life. If Buenos Aires is the city of sidewalk cafes and sophisticated theater, then Rio is the city of beaches and "carnival." The atmosphere of the place is uniquely hedonistic among world cities.

Rio, with a population of over 600,000 in 1900, was at that time Latin America's second largest city. It grew to over 1 million by 1920 and reached 2 million in the 1940s. By the early 1960s Rio had again doubled its population, but had been surpassed in size by its national sibling São Paulo as well as by Mexico City, thus falling to fourth place in the hierarchy of Latin American urban centers. With a metropolitan area totaling over 8 million inhabitants, Rio today remains Brazil's second largest city.

Figure 6.12 São Paulo, the giant industrial/commercial city of Brazil, projects its economic muscle in this photo of towering modern skyscrapers. Not visible in this scene, however, are the appalling urban problems that afflict this overgrown metropolis. (Courtesy Brazilian Embassy)

Because of its site characteristics, Rio's urban structure is unlike that of almost any other Latin American city. Although Portuguese colonial cities had no prescribed geometric plan, sixteenth-century Rio was characterized by a more or less regular grid pattern. The core of the city developed amid four hills, and from this beginning its expansion was limited by topographic considerations. In the 1870s Rio embarked on a plan to efface its lingering colonial architectural stock and replace it with newer buildings worthy of an empire. From a preservationist's point of view, one of the most lamentable aspects of this project occurred in 1920 when the remaining portion of the original settlement of Rio (built in 1567), a complex of over 470 of the oldest structures in the city which lined a picturesque maze of narrow lanes, was totally obliterated in order to create fill land for an exhibition site commemorating Brazilian independence. On a more positive note, a series of major arterials, such as Biera-Mar, a landscaped boulevard which extends to the beach of Botafogo, and Avenida Central, connecting the emerging North and South zones of Rio, facilitated circulation and emerged as some of the most beautiful, scenic boulevards in the world. A number of monumental civic complexes were also developed at this time. Avenida Central (since 1912 renamed Avenida Rio Branco) remains the main street of the downtown.

The rapid areal expansion of the nineteenth-century city was encouraged by the growth of railroads and tram lines. By the late 1800s Rio spilled out of its original grid zone as commuter railways led to the creation of a string of industrial and working class residential areas in the North Zone. An Elite Residential Sector grew in the South Zone along the extension of magnificent tree-lined boulevards which reached the beaches. Access to the beaches in the South has been greatly enhanced by a series of tunnels through the mountains which permitted a large population to squeeze into this area. Gradually, the narrow strips of beachfront land in Botafogo, Copacabana, and Ipanema became some of the most highly prized and valuable residential properties on earth. Today these areas are characterized almost exclusively by modernistic high rise apartments and hotels inserted among the rounded peaks, such as Sugar Loaf and Corcovado, which give Rio its sense of place (Fig. 6.13). This elite sector has extremely high population densities, reaching 80,000 people per square mile, (32,000 per square kilometer), while the lower- and middle-class neighborhoods to the north and west are more commonly characterized by one- and two-story dwellings and much lower densities.

Because of the extreme scarcity of buildable land due to the position of the original core between ocean, bay, and mountains, commercial and industrial activities have grown to the north and west of the city along highways and rail lines. Even here the limited quantity of flat land has caused the city's expansion to be channeled primarily in a single direction. Virtually all the urban area's economic activities take place in one sector northwest of the historical downtown. To alleviate this lack of building sites, fill land has been created all around the traditional core and has been used intensively for activities ranging from port facilities to the city's airport. With the construction in the 1970s of the bridge across Guanabara Bay to Niterói, much additional growth has occurred there.

The residential structure of Rio provides one of the great anomalies of the modern urban world in that the poorest squatters live on hillsides with panoramic views of the luxurious beach communities that lie within a stone's throw of truly squalid living conditions. Rio has had squatter settlements since at least the 1880s when freed slaves occupied the hillsides above the city. *Favela* was the name of one of the hills occupied in the 1890s and has become the generic name for slums within Brazil. Because Rio was one of the first Latin American cities to develop large-scale squatter settlements and because those settlements occupied scenic slopes close to the wealthy and prestigious core of the city, the contrast generated caused the favelas to gain worldwide notoriety.

Figure 6.13 The magnificence of Rio de Janeiro's site is evident in this scene of one of the many famous beaches that front on the Atlantic Ocean outside Guanabara Bay (in the background). Luxury apartment buildings crowd the avenue facing this famous Latin American playground. (Courtesy Brazilian Embassy)

Population of the favelas is difficult to determine, but it is estimated that between 500,000 and 1 million people occupy shanties immediately adjacent to the downtown. Although the squatter settlements are in juxtaposition to the core of the city, they were unserviceable and inaccessible without enormous government expenditure. There have been several piecemeal attempts to clear the favelas from the most highly visible or desirable locations, but given the huge numbers of people involved, eradication of these slums has been politically impractical.

The favelas have been a main destination for poverty-stricken migrants from the

Brazilian northeast. This former sugar-producing area was occupied largely by blacks and mulattos, who form the bulk of the favelas residents. It is estimated that more than 70 percent of favelados are black or mulatto, while in the rest of Rio less than a third of the population consists of people of color. It has been argued that the favelas represent stepping stones for new migrants to be assimilated into urban life. It is undoubtedly true that many former favelados have been able to escape the substandard conditions of their squatter settlements, but many become permanently entrapped in the hopelessness and desperation of the favelas.

Brasilia

Brasilia is unique among Latin American cities because it is a totally planned urban center. For nearly two centuries Brazilians talked of placing the country's capital in the interior to signify the nation's determination to effectively occupy its national territory. The idea was institutionalized in the constitution of 1889 but was not brought to fruition until 1960. Throughout Brazilian history more than 90 percent of the country's population has lived within 50 miles of the coast. The huge expanse of the interior remained a virgin wilderness filled with unexploited potential. From time to time political leaders advocated moving the capital from Rio de Janeiro, but money was never available to do so. In the late 1940s and early 1950s serious efforts were undertaken to find a site for the proposed capital. With the election of Julicino Kubischek de Oliveira as president in 1956, a crash program to develop the city was begun. An international competition was held to select a plan for Brasilia. The winning design, submitted by Lucio Costa, consisted of a crossaxial scheme roughly conforming to the cosmic ideal of a city and the topography of the selected site. Brasilia was meant to be a highly symbolic place (Fig. 6.14).

In almost every way, Brasilia offers a contrast to Rio. Rio represents a city which evolved almost without plan or design in an extremely complex and difficult setting, while Brasilia was planned for a site chosen because it offered no obstacles to urban development. The overall ambience of the two places could not be more different. Brasilia's stark plainness and austere landscape reflect perhaps the last gasp of the modernist movement in architecture and the desire to create an urban utopia. From its beginning Brasilia was not designed for human interaction, but as a highly visible monument to national pride. This lack of human scale remains the city's major drawback.

Based loosely on the ideas of the architect Le Corbusier, the city consists of a series of glass boxes, wide superhighways, and open spaces set in the middle of a barren tropical plateau. Perhaps more than any urban center in the world, Brasilia epitomizes the ideal of the city as a perfectly efficient machine. From end to end, Brasilia consists of a series of "superblocks" separated by vast, underutilized open zones. It is a city characterized by highly segregated land uses and designed for single-purpose interaction, conforming to the 1950s notion that mixed land use and multipurpose space somehow represented an imperfect and messy urban landscape. Ironically, Brasilia was officially inaugurated in 1960 just as the modernist movement began its death throes.

232 Chapter 6, Cities of Latin America

1. Plaza of the Three Powers
2. Esplanade of the Ministries
3. Embassies and legations
4. Residential Palace
5. High density residential
6. Medium density residential
7. Single family residential
8. Suburban residences
9. Commercial
10. Industrial
11. Offices
12. Hotels
13. Tourist's hotel
14. Entertainment
15. Cultural
16. University
17. Cemetery
18. Airport
19. Railroad station

Figure 6.14 Brasilia. (*Source:* Compiled by the authors.)

Although the construction of Brasilia provided a focal point for Brazilian pride and enhanced the country's unity during the late 1950s and early 1960s, the final product was definitely flawed. The design of the city suffered from two major imperfections; the cold, sterile, segregated spaces are devoid of almost any kind of interaction; and the city, designed as a final perfect form, resists all efforts to alter or modify its character. In spite of the fact that Brasilia is only twenty years old, it has not aged gracefully. As its buildings have stained and its concrete plazas have cracked, the city has been likened to a "ceremonial slum."

Throughout the 1960s the Brazilian government moved its official functions to the new capital, but enormous resistance was met from several sources. Foreign embassies refused to relocate from the excitement of Rio to the total blandness of Brasilia. In fact, in 1970 the Brazilian government issued an ultimatum to all foreign governments threatening to withdraw diplomatic accreditation to those embassies not located in Brasilia. The capital became known as "the three-day city" because businessmen, politicians, and diplomats commuted by air to and from Rio, choosing to spend only Tuesday through Thursday in Brasilia. Such underwhelming acceptance reflected as much the lack of appeal of Brasilia as the attraction of Rio.

Structurally, Brasilia's east-west axis is divided between the Plaza of the Three Powers, site of governmental offices and ministries, and Municipal Square. The "downtown" is located near the intersection of the east-west and north-south axis. This core of mid-rise hotels, banks, and commercial buildings sits astride the arcuate north-south axis, which is dominated by superblocks of apartment complexes. (Fig. 6.15). Single-family housing for the elite has been built on an artificial peninsula which juts into man-made Lake Paranoa. Some low income housing has been constructed to the west of the city, but the poor who built Brasilia and service its more affluent population live in a series of satellite communities, such as Sobradinho, Planaltina, Taguatinga, Ipe, Gama, and Nucleo Bandierante. A population roughly equivalent to Brasilia's is housed in these surrounding towns. The contrast between the spontaneous peripheral communities and the Orwellian imperfection of the capital proper is stunning.

Brasilia was developed around a series of broad super highways and monumental interchanges symbolizing the futuristic image of automobiles constantly in motion. In such an environment, walking is unrewarding if not impossible and most people must rely on private autos or public conveyance, which makes the city seem inert and lifeless. However, one of the goals reached in creating the capital was the highway connection of the northeast and the south with the interior of the nation. When initially selected, the site of Brasilia was not linked by road or rail with existing population centers. Thus Brasilia served as major justification for construction of all-purpose roads linking the coastal margins and opening up potentially productive regions for exploitation.

In a locational sense Brasilia has been a moderate success. It has led to increased utilization of the interior and, to an extent, has redefined the historic Brazilian desire to look inward for national growth. But in a design sense the capital has failed to develop into the kind of urban magnet that could compete with the traditional centers of Rio de Janeiro or São Paulo. While Brasilia has few of the urban problems plaguing other Latin American cities, such as air pollution, massive tracts of substandard hous-

Figure 6.15 Part of Brasilia's unique morphology is shown in this photo of the north-south arcuate axis of the city, dominated by superblocks of apartment complexes. Brasilia epitomizes the ideal of the city as a perfectly efficient machine. (E. Griffin and L. Ford)

ing, traffic congestion, or inadequate services, it is not without serious shortcomings. Perhaps the cultural sterility of Brasilia creates a greater handicap to its long-term potential success than the more basic problems present elsewhere. The totally planned environment, with its lack of human scale, provides an insight into this totally unexplored dimension of urban malaise.

Buenos Aires

When one thinks of a large, cosmopolitan Latin American city, Buenos Aires historically comes to mind. Indeed, until the 1960s, Buenos Aires was by far the largest and culturally most significant urban center in the region (Fig. 6.16). In many ways the city has more in common with Paris or Chicago than it does with Mexico City or Bogotá. Although it was founded in the 1530s, Buenos Aires languished as a forgotten backwater of the Spanish colonial empire until the late 1700s. In 1776 it was made the capital of the viceroyalty of La Plata and began a steady rise to primacy in Argentina and Latin America. Unlike most of the hemisphere's cities, Buenos Aires was an eager participant in, and a major beneficiary of, the commercial activities resulting from the industrial and agricultural innovations arising during the late nineteenth and early twentieth centuries. Like Chicago, Buenos Aires grew as a result of massive European immigration in the 1800s and through the processing and exportation of products de-

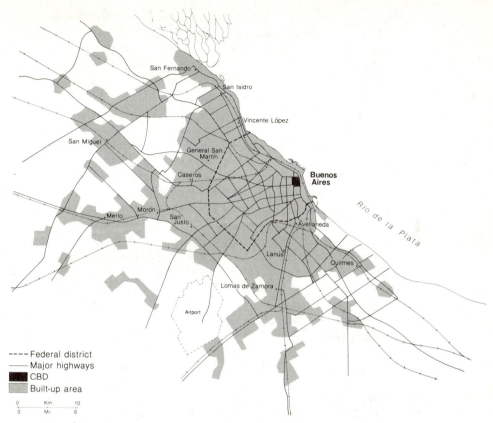

Figure 6.16   Buenos Aires. (*Source:* Compiled by the authors.)

rived from an extensive agricultural hinterland. As a result, Buenos Aires has grown progressively for nearly 150 years rather than exploding onto the urban scene as has been typical of other major cities in the region. Because of its relative importance during the nineteenth century and its "European" population, Buenos Aires, with its sidewalk cafes, industrial base, and Parisian architecture, exudes a sophisticated ambience atypical of other Latin American cities.

As late as 1850 Buenos Aires was a traditional preindustrial city with a population of around 100,000. Functionally it was a large village centered around a primitive roadstead port. Even today residents of the city are known as *portenos*. Buenos Aires' growth was initially retarded both by the early economic insignificance of the pampas and by its remoteness from the traditional northwestern core of the country. Because of its relative unimportance, the city lacked an impressive colonial architectural stock comparable to cities such as Lima or Bogotá. The role of the city changed radically as the result of a number of factors beginning in the early 1800s. The pampas were to become a primary food-producing area for Europe's increasingly urbanized industrial population, and Buenos Aires served as the commercial entrepôt for the dynamic interchange of Argentine food products and European manufactured goods. By the turn of the century, Buenos Aires had achieved the status of world city with a population approaching 1 million. At this time Buenos Aires seemed to belong not to Latin America but rather to the progressive world of Europe and North America.

As if to separate itself from Latin America and perhaps to overcome its meager traditional architectural tradition, Buenos Aires adopted mansard roofs, impressive obelisks, monumental statuary, wide boulevards, canopied sidewalk cafes, and European-styled governmental buildings to highlight its newfound importance in the world. Equally important, by the 1880s the city had developed a transportation network consisting of a variety of commuter railroads, trolley lines, and a subway system which gave it a spider-web morphology of "street car suburbs" more typically found in North America. In the late 1800s and early 1900s Buenos Aires, in terms of living standards and urban amenities, rivaled the wealthiest cities in the world.

By the 1920s the city was experiencing significant land use segregation, with wealthy suburban chalets and summer home communities springing up to the north along the Rio de la Plata while breweries, assembly plants, meat packing, oil refineries, and tightly knit ethnic neighborhoods emerged in the south. Meanwhile, a nonresidential CBD consisting of banks, government offices, theaters and major retailing outlets evolved in the traditional core. Because of its role as a major food producer, Argentina, especially Buenos Aires, was provided an enormous economic bonanza by World War I. By the 1930s Buenos Aires bristled with art deco *rascacielos* (skyscrapers), including the tallest building in Latin America, inserted randomly into the Parisian Second Empire cityscape. In addition, a large number of 8- to 12-story apartment buildings were constructed along the city's extensive system of transport arterials, giving Buenos Aires a massive appearance uncommon in Latin American cities. Further, a well-developed system of tree-filled parks and plazas added an element of maturity and completeness to the landscape not found elsewhere in the region's urban areas. By 1930 the population of greater Buenos Aires exceeded three million, making it about three times as large as the next largest cities in Latin America (Mexico City and Rio de Janeiro) and 10 times as large as many important capitals (Lima and Bogotá). In terms of population, economic importance, and cultural activities, Buenos Aires became the archtypical primate city not only for Argentina but also for Spanish-speaking Latin America. Today, with a population of approximately 10 million, Greater Buenos Aires is only the third largest metropolitan area in Latin America. However, the urban area's population represents nearly 40 percent of Argentina's total population.

Because of its nineteenth-century growth, reliance upon fixed-rail public transportation, a relatively affluent "European" population, and its relatively slow recent growth, Buenos Aires has an enormously large Zone of Maturity. This zone consists of a wide variety of housing types, from mid- to high-rise apartments, traditional one- and two-story freestanding houses, row houses, and converted mansions. Unlike many rapidly growing cities, Buenos Aires has almost no Zone of *in Situ* Accretion, as the housing was developed mainly through professional builders. The Zone of Peripheral Squatter Settlements is relatively small compared with that of other Latin American cities but is increasingly significant. Rather than surrounding the city, the zone is highly concentrated in swampy areas and the low-lying flood plains to the southwest of the city.

The Elite Residential Sector extends northwestward along the Rio de la Plata from Barrio Norte outward. Much of the area is experiencing densification as high rise apartments replace the freestanding chalets and mansions built during earlier periods. As in North America, suburbs are becoming an important component of urban life, since well over two-thirds of the metropolitan population lives outside of the official city boundaries of Buenos Aires.

The CBD is still the undisputed heart of Buenos Aires. Despite a significant suburbanization of entertainment and retailing functions along major thoroughfares leading out of the city, no dominant spine has emerged to challenge the supremacy of downtown. With a large number of live theaters, museums, libraries, universities, fine hotels, good restaurants, department stores, and exotic pedestrian malls, downtown Buenos Aires is truly vibrant and dynamic, comparable in many ways to Manhattan, London, and Paris.

Urban Problems and Solutions

The urban problems of Latin American cities have already been discussed in various forms in the preceding sections. Thus, it is sufficient here to provide merely a wrapup look at the most serious issues. Latin American cities share a number of problems, among them rapid population growth, extensive areas of substandard housing, inadequate public services, increasing marginality due to high rates of under- and unemployment, serious traffic congestion, and in many cases severe air pollution. Many of the urban problems experienced in the region are common to Third World nations in Africa and Asia as well and are not unique to Latin America. The dynamics of urbanization have resulted in similar consequences in most developing nations.

Within Latin America major urban areas have grown rapidly over the last three decades. For the region as a whole, cities of over 100,000 have expanded at about 6 percent annually. Massive flows of migrants from small towns and rural communities have been enticed to the larger cities by the relative modernity and perceived greater economic opportunity which exists there. Ironically, many of the fastest-growing cities are the largest urban centers. Metropolitan areas such as São Paulo and Mexico City have had extended periods of growth at rates of 8 to 12 percent annually, which results in a doubling of population in as little as six to nine years. Such hyperurbanization leads to projected city sizes which stagger the imagination.

No city, whether in the developed or developing world, can hope to accommodate such rapid increases in numbers, but the problem is exaggerated in Latin American countries because of their relatively limited financial ability to cope with such growth. The bulk of urbanward migrants are low income individuals, most of whom are unable to afford the limited existing housing that is available. As a result, many migrants initially settle in squatter settlements or core area slums where living conditions are marginal at best. In peripheral squatter settlements shacks are created willy-nilly in an effort to provide basic shelter. Amazingly, an interesting metamorphosis takes place in these areas as *in situ* improvements occur over time, converting "slums" into respectable low income neighborhoods. Core area slums and squatter sites in areas of extreme disamenity often remain permanently beyond reasonable hope of remedy, but time and individual industriousness have brought about significant changes to most original peripheral squatter settlements. In nearly all major cities low cost government housing is being built in an attempt to alleviate some of the backlogged housing needs, but given the magnitude of the problem such efforts are totally inadequate.

Only the most draconian steps to limit individual mobility can stem the tide of migrants to the cities, and in all of Latin America only the Cuban government has had it within its power to effectively limit such movements. Migration to Havana was essentially curtailed by not permitting migrants into the urban area unless they could prove that they had housing available. As housing permits were issued only to existing residents of the city, migrants were all but excluded. Other countries in the region have found it politically impractical to impose such controls and are highly unlikely to do so. After all, migration to the city acts as a release valve in alleviating rural problems.

While the provision of adequate housing is a major problem, the unavailability of public services exacerbates the difficulty of upgrading living standards. The virtual flood of in-migrants has created rapid areal expansion in many cities. The building of water lines, sewerage, electrical hookups, and roads to service these new urbanites constantly lags behind existing need. Part of the difficulty is financial. Metropolitan areas simply do not have enough money to build new facilities fast enough to satisfy demand. Even if the money existed, it is doubtful that such quantities of public services could be extended as rapidly as new needs emerge. Additionally, new schools and hospitals, as well as the staffs to operate them, are required if the basic demands of newer residents are to be met. In reality, the increasing number of urban inhabitants outpaces creation of new social infrastructure. A complicating element in this equation is the fact that many of Latin America's biggest cities are also old with infrastructures badly in need of upgrading or replacement, which is on top of the new demands resulting from hyperurbanization. Only a leveling-off of growth and a period of massive capital infusion will allow the region's urban centers to catch up with the dimensions of the current problems.

The real key to solving Latin America's urban problems is the successful assimilation of migrants into the urban economy. Unfortunately, this is easier said than done. By all indications marginality among urban populations is increasing rather than decreasing for most major cities. Unemployment rates of 25 to 33 percent or more are common. When underemployment figures are included, the total often reaches 40 to 50 percent of the urban work force. Hyperurbanization has often been false urbanization in Latin America in that much of the new urban population is unassimilated economically and culturally. Creation of jobs—massive numbers of jobs—is fundamental to the transformation of the current economic dilemma.

Increased population numbers have also led to greater congestion in the region's cities. The strongly dynamic character of CBDs in major Latin American urban centers heightens this problem. Most employment opportunities and commercial interaction focus on the downtown or its attendant spine, funneling more and more people into the same amount of space. Various innovative experiments have been tried to reduce traffic into the urban core, such as building subways (Mexico City in 1968, Rio in 1972); creating "walking cities" by banning automobiles from sections of the downtown (Buenos Aires, Bogotá); and modernizing traffic flow patterns, widening streets, and building urban expressways (Tijuana, Caracas). In some instances positive results have accrued, but in the central cores of most big Latin American cities traffic moves at a snail's pace, if it moves at all. A concomitant to the increased number of vehicles is increased air pollution resulting from auto emissions. Latin American cities share a common trait: during rush hour they reek of diesel fumes and have serious ground-level air pollution. Indeed, places like Mexico City, Caracas, Santiago, and São Paulo are now infamous for their air pollution. As North American cities have shown, such problems can be ameliorated but are difficult to solve on a permanent basis.

Such a litany of problems, as serious as they are, creates a highly negative image of Latin American cities. Contrary to what might be thought, however, Latin Americans perceive cities positively. Despite substandard housing, limited public services, congestion and pollution, real progress is being made in the region's urban centers. In a sense, migrants vote with their feet. They come to the cities and remain in the cities. Large numbers of them progress socially and economically. From generation to generation substantial gains are being made by the masses. It can be argued, and with ample justification, that the rate of such progress is slower than it should be and that if income distributions were altered or if the political process provided the poor with more power, progress would be more rapid. But one need look no further than the former "peripheral" squatter settlements which have evolved to become habitable, well-serviced communities to realize that positive change is taking place in Latin America's cities.

RECOMMENDED READINGS

Evenson, Norma. *Two Brazilian Capitals*. New Haven, Conn.: Yale University Press, 1973.
  A comparison of the architecture and urban design, focusing on the physical design and art, of Brasilia and Rio de Janeiro.

Griffin, Ernst and Larry Ford. "Tijuana: Landscape of a Culture Hybrid." *Geographical Review*, 66 (1976), 435–447.
  A detailed statement of the dynamic landscape changes that have occurred since the 1950s. Traditional Mexican cultural images and preferences remain, but they are constantly bombarded by the impress of Southern Californians. Tijuana fence types illustrate this hybridization process.

Griffin, Ernst and Larry Ford. "A Model of Latin American City Structure." *Geographical Review*, 70 (1980), 397–422.
  North American models of urban morphology fail to satisfactorily explain the patterns of land use in Latin American cities. A descriptive and graphic model is presented that reflects the dramatic internal changes. An Elite Residential Sector and commercial Spine exist with concentric zones of decreasing residential quality toward the city periphery.

Hardoy, Jorge E., ed. *Urbanization in Latin America: Approaches and Issues*. Garden City, NY: Anchor/Doubleday, 1975.

An anthology of 12 essays which emphasizes the economic and sociopolitical background of urbanization in Latin America. Most of the selected contributions were originally published in Spanish. The individual readings about the Latin American city are organized in three broad themes: (1) the historical antecedents, (2) the contemporary city in transition, and (3) the future.

Levine, D. H. "Urbanization in Latin America: Changing Perspectives." *Latin American Research Review,* 14 (1979), 170–183.

A review of nine books, including the collected works of John Friedmann *(Urbanization, Planning, and National Development)* and the first five annual volumes of *Latin American Urban Research;* it identifies the shift in analyses of the urbanization process from the external manifestations of "positivism" toward the more internalized and experiential phenomenological approach evident in the research literature of the 1970s.

Lloyd, Peter C. *Slums of No Hope? Shanty Towns of the Third World.* New York: St. Martin's Press, 1979.

Based upon his research among the Yoruba in Nigeria and more recently the urban migrants of Lima, the author presents a more positive and universal picture of the Third World shanty, countering the earlier and more conventional images of slums of despair.

Margolies, L. "Rural-Urban Migration and Urbanization in Latin America." *Cultural Anthropology,* 19 (1978), 130.

The author is critical of the tendency to treat "migration" and "urbanization" as separate processes, which fails to incorporate the changing sociopolitical context within which the migration process develops. The migration process must be evaluated within the broader rubric of the urbanization process, not just as the major component of urban growth.

Walton, John. "From Cities to Systems: Recent Research on Latin American Urbanization." *Latin American Research Review,* 14 (1979), 159–169.

Ward, Peter M. "Self-Help Housing in Mexico City." *Town Planning Review,* 49 (1978), 38–50.

An analysis based on stepwise regression on the "consolidation" or residential improvement of three squatter settlements which originated by organized invasion in Mexico City. The author found that residential improvements at the household level are most importantly a product of investment surplus, which is closely related to the level of income generated by the head-of-household and the combined household income.

White, P. and Robert Woods, eds. *The Geographic Impact of Migration.* London: Longman, 1980.

A geographical inquiry examining how changes in population redistribution through migration affect the organization of human society. The first part of the book deals with the socioeconomic and demographic impacts of migration on origin and destination areas; the second part deals with specific case studies from the Third World (East Africa and Bolivia) and from England and France.

Figure 7.1 Major Cities of Subsaharan Africa. (*Source:* Data derived from United Nations, Department of Economic and Social Affairs, *Global Review of Human Settlements, Statistical Annex,* published by Pergamon Press, New York, 1976.)

Chapter 7

Cities of Subsaharan Africa

Assefa Mehretu

Subsaharan Africa in the World Urban System

Subsaharan Africa remains the least urbanized region in the world, despite substantial increases in urbanization in the past 30 years. At about 22 percent urban population for the region as a whole, Subsaharan Africa sits at the bottom of the ladder with South Asia. This is not really surprising, given the low levels of economic development from which most of the states of the region started as independence from colonialism was achieved in the past decades. There is a fairly direct correlation worldwide between level of economic development and degree of urbanization, and Subsaharan Africa (along with South Asia) remains at the bottom on both counts. Here again, though, there is inevitably substantial regional variation between countries and within countries. Only one major nation, South Africa, is more than 50 percent urbanized (52 percent), but that country's urban system is hardly typical of the region. Among the remaining 35 nations of Subsaharan Africa, all but two are less than 50 percent urbanized and run in the spectrum from barely 4 to 5 percent urban as in Burundi and Rwanda, to figures in the 30 and 40 percent range, such as in the Central African Republic, the Congo, Ghana, Gabon, Senegal, and Somalia. Two political units, Equatorial Guinea and Djibouti, are more than 50 percent urban, but these tiny states, with miniscule populations under 300,000 each, are statistical quirks that do not alter the basic pattern for Subsaharan Africa as a whole.

The relatively small number of major cities in the region reflects the still fledgling development of urban places (Fig. 7.1). Only 12 cities on the entire subcontinent have a population greater than 1 million, and four of these are in South Africa. Only two of these cities have a population of more than 2 million: Kinshasa, Zaire, is the largest, at about 3 million; Lagos, Nigeria, has just under 3 million. The remainder have a population ranging from 1 to 2 million.

In spite of the relatively low levels of urbanization and few numbers of large cities, it would be a mistake to dismiss Subsaharan Africa as unimportant from an urban perspective. For one thing, some 80 million of the subcontinent's more than 360 million inhabitants now live in urban places, a more than fourfold increase since 1950. This area has among the world's highest rates of urbanization, meaning that the march to the cities is proceeding at a rate far above that of natural population growth. Hence, cities such as Kinshasa (Zaire), Lagos (Nigeria), Dakar (Senegal), Nairobi (Kenya), and Accra (Ghana), are growing much too fast for the abilities of the governments concerned to deal effectively with the problems created. In addition, this region is also afflicted with the primate city problem, a legacy of the colonial period. Hence, the few big cities that do exist tend to grow much more rapidly than smaller cities, contributing further to regional imbalances that have long plagued Subsaharan Africa.

Although the history and nature of urban development in Subsaharan Africa is still far from perfectly understood, several other major patterns are discernible (Fig. 7.2). First, earlier views that tropical Africa did not have a history of urbanization and urban morphology before the coming of the white man, as tested by rigid definitional requirements of Western analytical models, have lost validity, primarily because they were couched in European ethnocentric approaches to the history of Africa. Second, one of the more significant effects of the colonial period, nonetheless, was its creation of coastal settlements to the detriment of historical centers of trade and civilization. Third, the distribution of urban places is extremely uneven over the continent. Fourth, most African towns are characterized today by varied forms of internal morphology that for the most part do not fit the existing Western-derived models of internal spatial structure (see Chapter 1). Fifth, African primate cities and major urban agglomerations constitute socioeconomic cores or central regions that depend for their existence on the parasitic relationship between them and the periphery or hinterland.

Evolution of Cities in Subsaharan Africa

Historic Centers of Urbanization

The fact that the history of cities in Africa runs for millennia is beyond doubt, although it is true that a great number of the cities either are extinct or no longer assume a great deal of significance partly because of the advent of colonialism, and partly because of the continuous internal shifts of centers of influence (Fig. 7.3). But the imprint of great civilizations around Meroe, Axum, and Adulis in Eastern Africa, which flourished for centuries before Christ, is a vivid reminder of ancient glory. Lying westward along the Sudan belt were the kingdoms of Darfur, Wadai, Kanem Bornu, Hausaland, Songhai, Mali, and Ghana, whose urban centers such as Kumbi-Saleh of Ghana; Ngazargamo of Bornu; Katsina, Kano, and Zaria of Hausaland States; and Gao and Timbuktu of Songhai were the termini of a network of caravan routes that crisscrossed the Sahara supplying goods to Tripoli, the oases of Ghadames, Algiers, Marrakech, and Fez in the Maghreb. West African commodities reached Western Europe through the ports of the Maghreb, particularly Tunis and Algiers.

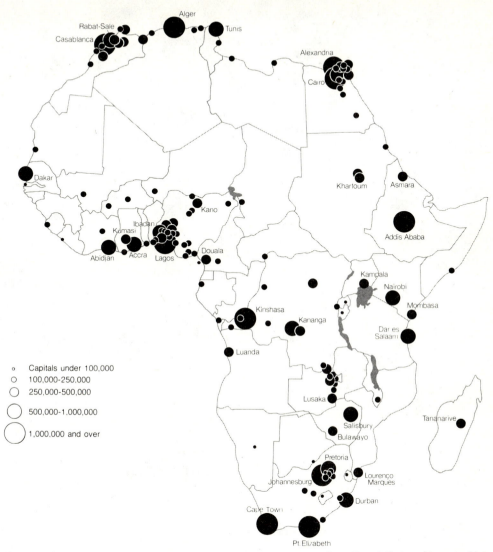

Figure 7.2 Principal African Urban Centers. (*Source:* Data derived from *United Nations, Demographic Yearbook, 1978,* New York: United Nations, Department of International Economic and Social Affairs, 1979.)

Some of the Sudanic centers had achieved such repute in the medieval world that they became centers of centralized empires; Ghana, Mali, and Songhai retained prominence and considerable influence until the period between the thirteenth and seventeenth centuries. In the Zaire Basin, it was witnessed that well before the advent of Portuguese sailors, the Kongo, Bateke, and Luango kingdoms contained major populated centers like Mbanza and Kintambo (present site of Kinshasa). Although they were not placed to benefit from the intercontinental and intra-African trade such as

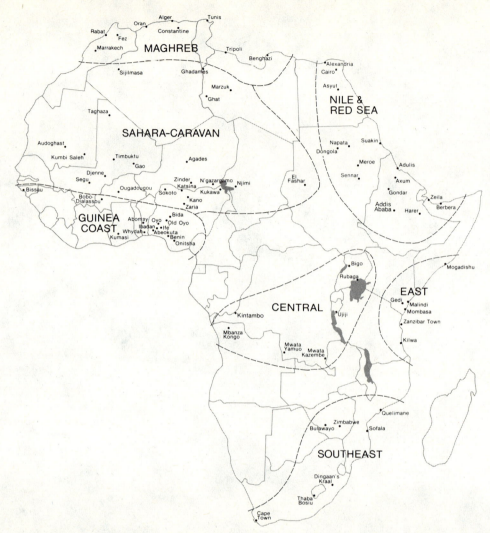

Figure 7.3   Historical Centers of Urbanization in Africa. (*Source:* Compiled by the author.)

those of Sudanic and northeastern states, they were characterized by highly centralized systems of government, each headed by a supreme leader who drew allegiance from smaller constituencies in the estuarine civilization. Around the same period, within the Zaire Basin and along the southern reaches of the river, the kingdoms of Luba and Lunda had developed in what is now the southern province of Zaire. Although major cities did not materialize before the colonial period, the prosperity of the area and more hospitable climate conditions had supported centralized kingdoms and extensive interregional trade beginning in the early fifteenth century. To the east of the Zaire Basin, a number of "interlacustrine kingdoms" came into existence perhaps beginning in the sixteenth century, but in this part of Africa large towns did not appear until after this period.

In southern Africa lay two important centers, one perhaps the oldest empire and intensive settlement center in Africa. The ruins of Great Zimbabwe, the capital of the Rozvi Mutapa Empire, which flourished between the fourth and nineteenth centuries, demonstrate one of the most remarkable organizational and architectural features of African civilizations. Although Zimbabwe itself may not have reached great urban status in number of inhabitants, it served as the most influential locus of political control for numerous towns that developed around the gold and ivory hinterlands found between the Zambesi and Limpopo rivers. West of Great Zimbabwe, Bulawayo sprang up as the capital of one of the Bantu empires and continued to dominate the area until the colonial scramble. The Zulu kingdoms, probably of more recent origin, also had influential centers around which they formed perhaps one of the most powerful political organizations and military powers on the continent. From these centers, Zulu chiefs launched periodic raids on neighboring peoples, and their success and growth in power enabled them to organize one of the only major challenges against the mass movements of the Dutch settlers from around the Cape to the interior plateau of southern Africa which the Zulu controlled. Although the ensuing conflict between the Dutch *trekers* (Boers) and the Zulu did not turn in favor of the latter, the tough resistance of the Zulu, with their superior numbers, proved the sophistication of precolonial central leadership, organization, and settlement in southern Africa.

As mentioned before, many of the ancient African cities lost their influence to newer indigenous towns or colonial capitals, but it must be remembered that many of these ancient cities have since been transformed into some of the major metropolises on the continent. Omdurman (Sudan), Addis Ababa (Ethiopia), Kumasi (Ghana), Kano and Ibadan (Nigeria), Kinshasa (Zaire), and Bulawayo (Zimbabwe) are just a few of the old urban centers in Subsaharan Africa that predate foreign intervention.

Medieval Trade Centers of Eastern Africa

Of particular significance to the development of urbanization in Eastern Africa are the ancient coastal trade centers on the Red Sea and Indian Ocean around which flourished extensive trade with the Arab and Persian nations in Asia. Some of these centers acted as coastal city-states; beginning in the ninth century, they became important beachheads for Arab maritime traffic, which included the exportation of gold, ivory, and slaves from Africa in exchange for textiles and jewelry. These East African coastal centers also derived their growth, character, and political organization from the increasing number of Asian settlers who used the trade contacts as a vehicle to escape political problems and ostracism in their countries and made permanent homes in Africa. Major urban centers grew out of this contact, among them Adulis, Mogadishu, Malindi, Gidi, Mombasa, Pemba, Zanzibar Town, Kilwa, and Sofala (see Fig. 7.3 for precise locations). The urban structures of these cities, some of which are still important, incorporated African as well as Arabic and Persian building styles.

Precolonial external influence on African urbanization was of course not limited to the Arabic and Persian beachheads on the Red Sea and the Indian Ocean. Although this region has received by far the higher degree of influence, a number of centers in the interior have also been affected, especially with the expansion of Islam south from the Maghreb and west from the Red Sea and the Gulf of Aden.

Prepartition European Influence on African Urbanization

European contribution to the growth of African urbanization took place in two major phases, the first of which was the precolonial intermittent and coastal contact dominated particularly by the Portuguese starting from the first half of the fifteenth century. For about two and a half centuries, most contact between European traders and Africans was carried out in coastal settlements whose size and infrastructure grew as European traders gradually developed their appetite for tropical commodities, such as rubber, ivory, gold, hardwoods, and hides and skins. The slave trade of course contributed to the development of coastal trade centers where warehouses and permanent installations were needed to accommodate commodities and men drawn from the interior.

One of the first Portuguese centers in West Africa was established at the northern margin of Subsaharan Africa at a place called Saint Louis at the mouth of the Senegal River. The Portuguese made their first contact here in 1445, and for the following centuries they conducted trade with the region and also used it as a revictualing point for their subsequent explorations further down the coast of Africa and eventually all the way around the Cape to East Africa. Dominating the sixteenth-century scene in trade and prepartition urban development, the Portuguese were responsible for founding a number of centers, among which were Bissau in Guinea; Luanda, Benguela, and São Salvador do Congo in Angola; and Lourenço Marques, Seña, and Mozambique in present-day Mozambique. They also managed to wrench control from the Arabs of existing centers like Zanzibar City in Zanzibar and Mombasa in Kenya. At the invitation of Ethiopian emperors of the time, partly to get involved in the internal strife between Christian and Islamic peoples of the country, the Portuguese made their only significant penetration into the African interior and helped build Gondar, the former Ethiopian capital.

After the end of the sixteenth century, the Portuguese role in African exploration and trade declined and Portugal could hardly maintain control of centers it established or took control of. Its Arab rivals pushed out the new settlers of Mombasa, and most of the centers in eastern Africa were also lost to the original founders. As the Dutch, British, and French strengthened their hold on African coastal commerce in both West and southern Africa, and as the Arabs retrieved their supremacy in the East, the Portuguese role in Africa declined remarkably.

The Dutch founded Cape Town in 1652 (Fig. 7.4), and the French and British got busy establishing forts along the West African coasts at times with severe competition leading to clashes among the European powers. From this period emerged towns such as Conakry in Guinea; Accra, Sekondi, and Cape Coast in Ghana; and Calabar in Nigeria. Most of these towns were of course merely forts, for example, Accra, origi-

Figure 7.4 A statue of Jan van Riebeeck, the Dutch navigator who established the first settlement at Table Bay in 1652, stands in Heerengracht in modern Cape Town in front of the dramatic backdrop of Table Mountain, symbolizing the profound role that European settlement played in the founding and growth not only of Cape Town but also of other cities throughout much of Subsaharan Africa. (Courtesy South African Consulate General)

nally the site of Fort Usher, was established in 1650 by the Dutch and Fort James was founded in 1673 by the British. During the seventeenth century a few centers also emerged as a result of European initiative, but major urban developments in eastern Africa as a result of post-Portuguese European intervention had to wait until after the colonial partitioning in the nineteenth century.

The first half of the nineteenth century witnessed the mushrooming of a number of new urban centers in western as well as eastern Africa. By far the most significant development occurred in Nigeria with the development of the Yoruba towns. Although a number of the Yoruba towns, such as Ife, which perhaps served as the parent settlement since the Yoruba migrations in the latter part of the first millennium, were of pre-nineteenth-century origin, most of the larger Yoruba towns such as Oshogbo, Ibadan, Abeokuta, and Oyo were established in the early nineteenth century. Elsewhere in West Africa, Monrovia in Liberia, Banjul in Gambia, and Libreville in Gabon were also founded in the same period.

In eastern Africa, Khartoum and El Obeid in the Sudan were established in this period. In southern Africa a number of South Africa's major cities like Port Elizabeth,

Durban, Pietermaritzburg, Bloemfontein, East London, and Pretoria were established during the same period.

The period of European contact before the colonial partition of Africa is characterized by three distinct factors. The first is that most of the European contribution in settlement development was coastal and no significant penetration of the continent occurred during this period. The second characteristic is that many of the coastal settlements were intended as transshipment points for trade and hence little happened in terms of planned urban infrastructure except those structures used for defense, commodity storage, and temporary accommodations for laborers to be exported. A third characteristic is the lack of diffusion of European technology and culture to the interior indigenous urban centers. The interior towns, while they served as important agents for prepartition trade and may have even grown in size as a result of it, obtained little in terms of European technology.

African Urbanization in the Postpartition Era

The European role in the development of African urbanization underwent a major shift after the colonial partition. With the abolition of slavery but a growing interest in African raw materials, the supply of raw materials had to be insured. Beginning with the pioneering effort (albeit an infamous act of exploitation) by King Leopold of Belgium to consolidate his interests in the Congo (now Zaire), the European powers saw that they had to make an aggressive thrust into the interior to support the flow of commodities to Europe. The required infrastructure and colonial settlements to ensure the smooth flow of commodities were built. By the end of the nineteenth century the colonial powers made massive efforts in building penetration routes composed primarily of railways linking the port cities with major hinterland centers in the interior. By the beginning of the present century the railway pattern in Africa resembled that of a system of coastal rivers draining the continent to the sea. Virtually all of the coastal termini from Dakar to Luanda became the capital and primate cities in their respective countries, with external trade as their major function. In eastern Africa, although the physical resource situation forced the colonial settlers to focus attention on the major towns in the interior such as Khartoum, Addis Ababa, Kampala, Nairobi, and Salisbury, these towns were soon linked to one major port in each country with railway penetration lines such as Port Sudan in Sudan, Djibouti in Ethiopia, Mombasa in Kenya, and Beira serving Rhodesia (now Zimbabwe). Some eastern African centers such as Dar es Salaam and Maputo experienced the West African pattern (Fig. 7.5). In some cases some of the major towns sprang up as a result of the railway construction process to penetrate the hinterland; one such town is Nairobi.

In South Africa, the pattern is quite different. Major European penetration predated colonial partition, with the Dutch launching massive migrations into the interior plateau region of southern Africa starting in 1836 from coastal holdings they had had since the mid-seventeenth century. Because of the tenacious expatriate settlements that resulted, urban development, commodity flows, and infrastructure are distinctly different from elsewhere in Africa. In South Africa, as a result, numerous urban centers in

Figure 7.5 A section of the downtown district of Dar es Salaam reveals a city characterized by building styles from various cultures. In response to the Ujamaa development policy of Tanzania, Dar es Salaam does not exercise as much primacy in that country as is true in most other Subsaharan capital cities. (Courtesy Tanzania Information Services)

the interior are presently served by over seven major ports all around the southern tip of the continent. The railway pattern is much more intensive, with a high degree of connectivity between urban centers in the plateau hinterland as well as between the interior settlements and the port cities.

Although the dynamics of the growth of urban inhabitants in most African principal centers did not start until after the Second World War, most if not all of the primate cities had been established in the majority of the cases by the colonial powers and in the case of the Horn from existing indigenous centers. As indicated above, transportation development along with commerce were by far the most important factors for the growth in urban centers. Since the colonial policy did not encourage real industrialization except to facilitate efficient transfer of minerals and commodities to the metropolitan centers, fixed capital in secondary activities had not been a major factor in urban development. However, primary processing for export has been responsible for growth of urban population in mineral-rich regions. Good examples are the mining towns of the Zambian copper belt and Shaba Province of Zaire, in which present-day Lubumbashi, Likasi, and Kolwezi in Zaire, and Ndola, Kitwe, Chingola, Luanshya, and Mufulira in Zambia have become major urban centers; their populations surpass the 100,000 mark, and some have half a million inhabitants.

The colonial period also introduced other factors which have played an important role in urban growth. In order to support the scale of trade that flowed between Africa and Europe, a commensurate administrative function, and appropriate accommodations for the colonial functionaries of indigenous as well as foreign origin, had to be established. Modern social infrastructure and amenities required by the bureaucratic and business elite led to the introduction of European urban nodalities which were later to be inherited as the most important problem facing primate cities in Africa.

The nineteenth century and early twentieth century witnessed a number of additions to the cities of Africa. Sahelian towns established in this period included Bamako in Mali and N'Djamena in Chad. The Guinea coastal region produced Abidjan and Bouake in Ivory Coast; Port Harcourt, Maiduguri, Enugu, and Kaduna in Nigeria; and Yaoundé in Cameroon. Within the central African region rose Bangui in the Central African Republic; Brazzaville in Congo; and Matadi, Kisangani, Lubumbashi, and Likasi in Zaire. In the southern African region Kimberley and Johannesburg emerged in South Africa; Maseru and Mbabane were established in Lesotho and Swaziland, respectively. The southeastern region produced Salisbury and Bulawayo in Zimbabwe, Kabwe in Zambia, and Blantyre in Malawi. In East Africa Nairobi was established in Kenya, Kampala in Uganda, and Dar es Salaam in Tanzania. During the same period in the Horn, Addis Ababa and Asmara were established in Ethiopia, and Omdurman and Port Sudan in the Sudan.

Of the 146 African centers which had 100,000 or more inhabitants in 1980, only about 28, or hardly 20 percent of the total, are attributed to the colonial period. Contrary to what may be thought, a great many of the present urban centers claim their origin from historical centers of indigenous civilizations. A good number also emerged, particularly in the coastal regions of Africa, during the precolonial period of African exploration and trade between Asiatic states and Europe. A few have also been established in the post independence era. The task is not easy to separate those cities that were indigenously initiated and those that were contributed by precolonial and colonial European intervention, partly because at various times the colonial powers took over some indigenous centers and altered them to the point where the original characteristics have disappeared. It is no wonder that according to one writer Kinshasa of Zaire is said to have originated as one of the largest centers of the Kongo kingdom, after being founded before 1530, while another writer claims that Kinshasa was established by colonial powers in 1881 as Leopoldville.

Major Representative Cities of Subsaharan Africa

Nairobi

The history of Nairobi is one of the most unusual of African cities (Fig. 7.6). The site was known as Enkare Nairobi, or "cold water," by the pastoral Masai, who also re-

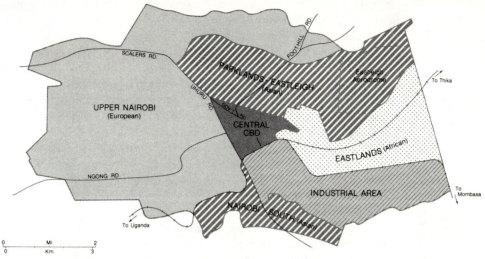

Figure 7.6 Nairobi's Major Inner-City Land Use Zones. (*Source:* Adapted from W. T. W. Morgan, *Nairobi City and Region,* Nairobi: Oxford University Press, 1967, p 105.)

garded this area, uninhabited and fully covered by virgin forest and swamp, as a natural buffer between them and their traditional enemies the Kikuyu to the north on the plateau. The Nairobi River, however, was a strategic resting and camping spot for the traveler from the coast (Mombasa) into the hinterland in Uganda. In 1896 the first rail was laid in Mombasa to link the coast with Uganda. The railway reached the site of Nairobi in 1899. Because of the natural site advantages, Nairobi was chosen as the headquarters of the railway, taking that function away from Mombasa. In addition, the government administrative center of the province to which Nairobi belonged, which was located at Machakos, about 40 mi. (64 km.) to the southeast, was also moved to Nairobi in 1899. Thus, from a nucleus of a railway camp, the town expanded its function to include government. Although drainage and health problems plagued the early settlement of Nairobi, in 1906 the colonial government endorsed the location, fixing Nairobi where it was for good.

By 1906 the new city contained over 13,000 inhabitants within its municipal boundary limited to a circular area of 1.5 mi. (2.4 km.), a radius arbitrarily fixed in 1900 by the Nairobi Municipal Regulation. Nairobi soon became the most important colonial capital in East Africa. This importance was greatly strengthened during the two world wars, when the city was an important base of operations by British military forces in Africa. By 1948 the city's population exceeded 100,000. After that, Nairobi shared with other African primate cities the postwar boom in growth which continued until the independence movements of the 1950s.

The factors that stimulated the establishment and growth of Nairobi were to produce some of the important problems the city faces as a burgeoning African metropolis. At the outset, its site, considered ideal for railway sidings, proved disastrous when it came to sanitation, a problem which still features as an important constraint in the city's development. Second, Nairobi has never been considered a suitable place to live by the Africans. For reasons based on absence of any indigenous base or rationale for its creation and an initial monopoly of the site by foreigners of European or Indian origin, Africans always considered the city a place of work and not a permanent residence. This was of course exacerbated by colonial policies of marginalization of the local population. There have always been more men in the city and a relative scarcity of women and children. The average length of residence in the city by Africans is considered to be below 10 years. Although Nairobi is a city in Kenya, few characteristic features made it a viable city for Kenyans.

Third, Nairobi's three major ethnics—Africans, Asians, and Europeans—were stratified by occupation and also separated residentially. The Europeans have been responsible for all administration, resource ownership, and financial institutions. The Asians, who were initially introduced into the area to work on the railway construction, occupied themselves as artisans, merchants, and shopkeepers. From the outset, the Africans were relegated to whatever menial jobs the city was able to create. Residentially, once again the three peoples essentially were separated into three zones within the city.

Fourth, responses to growth, especially of the African population, are similar now to what they were during the colonial days. Unlike the European and Asian property owners in their carefully demarcated zones, most Africans lived in rented housing built by the city or by their employers. The African residential zone of Eastlands was also characterized by the unstable situation, not only in frequent turnovers of inhabitants but also in the continuous turmoil of wrecking and building that continued throughout the colonial period. Another major development is the recent growth of squatter settlements in Nairobi as a result of population pressure in the city proper and the growing labor force, which has marginal or no employment in the formal sector.

Nairobi has now achieved a status of a major African metropolis with diverse local as well as international functions. Its population soared to over 1 million by 1980. As a primate city with exclusive advantages in attracting important secondary, tertiary, and quaternary functions, Nairobi plays the dominant role in a core/periphery relation in a highly dualistic economy. As the major core in Kenya, Nairobi displays an internal morphology in which a modern enclave continues to operate with almost the same colonial mode of operation, abated only by the emerging indigenous elite, which has started to make inroads in the traditionally European and Asian niche.

Nairobi continues to suffer from the inertia of history. Its most important problem emerges from the way the African regards the city as an alien introduction; as far as the African is concerned, its sole purpose is to offer nonagricultural employment just as an industrial enclave would in a rural environment. In fact the city has hardly been regarded as a permanent dwelling by any of the major ethnics in the city. The Europeans, who still consider Europe their home, use it as a means of economic enterprise. The Asians maintain their primary connections with India and Pakistan. The Africans have neither been fully integrated in the "core" function of the city nor have they been attracted by it as a permanent residence. For the African, the rural homestead has always been more important; it is there that he or she goes every year for rest and recreation and eventually for retirement.

Postindependence development of an urban elite of indigenous origin has of course initiated a change in the ethnic character of employment strata, residential separation, and residential stability of the city. Many Africans are moving into traditionally European- and Asian-dominated occupations. Among the elite, a good number were born and/or raised and educated in the city and consider it their home. Some of these who are prosperous enough to afford the price have moved into traditionally European and Asian ghettos. Although such trends are quite significant, for the time being, they are only of cosmetic value.

By and large the economy is in the hands of expatriates. Upper Nairobi and the "Hill" residential areas continue to be dominated by European single-unit and fashionable homes complete with servant quarters. Most of the Asians of the city live in Parklands Eastleigh, where they have tried to maintain their cultural uniqueness by the styles of their architecture and community and religious functions. The quality of their dwellings, however, is not uniform. The well-to-do Asians inhabit Parklands, adjacent to the European sector, and have higher-quality surroundings. The poorer Asians live in Eastleigh, which borders Eastlands—the African sector. Some of the Asian population has moved to a second Asian quarter recently constructed in Nairobi South.

The preponderant majority of Africans live in Eastlands. This sector contains the working class estates often built by the city or employers. The western section of Eastlands contains older units. More recently, newer and better-quality units have been built to the east. But overall, the quality of residence here cannot be compared to the other two discussed above. The Eastlands residential area is flat, monotonous, short on amenities, with a residentially unstable population. The three major ethnic residential areas are therefore still separated. The new Africans that inhabit other sectors are either servants or members of the post independence elite who have the means to acquire property in these areas.

Three other functions complete the picture of Nairobi's land use, and all three are found in the central and southern areas, which are the oldest localities to be developed. The industrial area was highly influenced by the location of the railway yard in the south of the city. The environs of the railway station contain a number of industries. In order to facilitate transportation, an industrial estate has been laid out to the east of the railway station, complete with railway sidings and access roads.

The CBD is located in the heart of the city, enclosed by natural as well as man-made boundaries (Fig. 7.7). The CBD is bounded by the Nairobi River to the north and east; the former Uganda railway line, now the Uhuru Highway, to the west; and the railway station and the rail line to Uganda to the south. This central area of Nairobi represents one of the busiest spots on the continent. The CBD's most prominent functions are commerce, retailing, tourism, banking, government, international functions, and education. It is also very modern, with multistory buildings, wide, double-lane painted streets with street lights, buses, traffic congestion, gigantic billboards, neon lights, and automobiles from all over the world. This is the heartbeat of Kenya. As in all African countries, the primate city monopolizes major economic, political, and cultural activities. It is here where virtually every modern intervention is decided upon and also where all new major urban functions gravitate. The ultramodern city that Nai-

Figure 7.7 Downtown Nairobi with Parliament Building and the Kenyata Conference Center on the right. The Intercontinental Hotel and the CBD are on the left; Uhuru Park is in the foreground. (Courtesy David Campbell)

robi has become is a mosaic of the three subcultures it represents. The average African sets out from his Eastlands home to work in the CBD's menial jobs and the industrial estates. There is little for him in Nairobi in terms of recreation except perhaps the bars in his residential zone. The average European and Asian drives his car from his comfortable home in Upper Nairobi and Parklands and works in the CBD or a similar enclave, often in extremely modern, clean, and comfortable surroundings, with occasional interruptions to visit the plush hotels, bars, and supermodern shops in the CBD. Before dusk he would probably go for a game of golf or tennis at the golf club or the railway sports grounds located conveniently between the CBD and The "Hill," a section of the fashionable bedroom district of the Europeans.

Nairobi's future challenges are immense. An important task that still waits to be done is to transform the city into a place where the bulk of its activities would be relevant for the rural as well as the urban majority of the Africans. It has to shed its excessive primary position, which has made it the busiest tourist center in East Africa and the location of more than half of the country's industrial establishments. It has to ameliorate more vigorously the status of the African Kenyans by opening more employment in the more prestigious and high-paying jobs. Advances made on behalf of the Africans in the job and residential sectors of the city would go a long way to alleviate existing resentment and forestall potential conflicts between the relatively small number of expatriates and indigenous elite who control the means and enjoy the comforts, and the citizens who are still struggling in the margin.

Johannesburg

Johannesburg, once a mine digger's camp, is now the largest city in South Africa, boasting a population of close to 2 million (Fig. 7.8). The city owes its establishment and phenomenal growth to the discovery of gold, presumably by an Australian miner named George Harrison, in 1886. The rush of settler communities from the south to share in the riches of the land caused the town's population to increase to 10,000 within a year of the birth of the settlement. Things changed fast for the mining town. By 1890 not only did it have its first electric light but it also had horse trams for public transportation. By 1895, hardly 10 years after its establishment, the city had a population of about 100,000, half of European origin. Johannesburg was the creation of the mining companies, which to this day have perhaps more to do in determining the spatial organization of the city, particularly as it relates to the Africans, than any force in Johannesburg.

From its early beginnings, Johannesburg was a microcosm of what South Africa has become as a social challenge to the peoples of southern Africa. It started by the

Figure 7.8 The Witwatersrand and African Townships around Johannesburg. (*Source:* Compiled by the author.)

assertion that in 1886 no native tribes lived within 70 mi. (113 km.) of the site of the new town. According to the Europeans, the history of the settlement goes like this. The Africans were attracted to the site of their own free will in search of employment, to earn cash with the objective of returning to their Kraal, where they invested in cattle. When the "native" problem arose as far back as 1903, and then later in 1932, with the creation of the Native Economic Commission, the white settlers argued that Johannesburg was built by the white man, for the white man, and belonged to him and him alone. They maintained that the "natives" were needed for unskilled labor; they came to the city to work but not to live in it, mainly because of their inability to handle white civilization. In this manner, the largest of the "white" cities in southern Africa came into being. Consistent with the ideological position that the African cannot be detribalized and will always continue to have his links with his tribal village, the African was denied permanence of dwelling and a life with family while he worked for the city. By the same token, he was absolutely barred from the life of the city and even the city itself and was restricted to guarded compounds during the tenure of his employment. The "pass law" inaugurated in 1890 and the "compounding system" became the parameters of the movement of the African who chose to work in Johannesburg.

Johannesburg became South Africa's largest manufacturing center, and the "city of gold" was also a principal center of culture and education. The prosperity of the city, which was derived from the labors of all the races, was co-opted by a European minority that has one of the highest living standards in the world. The city is clean, with well-planned streets, skyscrapers, and extremely plush residential quarters (Fig. 7.9). The downtown area is similar to that of any industrial city in Europe and North America, with vertical development to house the offices of the numerous companies, trading firms, and offices. In the suburbs of Johannesburg, such as Houghton and Hyde Park, the residential homes for the well-to-do whites may, in architecture and amenities, more than match their counterparts in Europe and the United States.

The policy of separate development called *apartheid* is enforced by the minority whites as a tool to maintain the privileged status of the white population, so that their fewer number can take advantage of the vast amount of wealth generated in the country. The impact of this policy is felt more in the urban areas like Johannesburg, which have attracted a great number of Africans to work in the city's mines and factories, than anywhere in the country. The dilemma faced by the whites is that their policy of separate development is clashing head on with their need for black labor to maintain their high standard of living. They have done everything they can do to achieve these two inherently contradictory objectives in the long run.

The problem is centered in one major phenomenon. The urban black population is now by and large a resident population. Most of the black urban residents do not necessarily maintain their tribal linkages, and a good number are fourth- and fifth-generation urbanized residents. The advantages derived by the government from the destabilization of urban residents by constant turnovers and movement is declining. More Africans are being added to those already in and around the city, and the rate of increase of the black population can not be matched by provision of facilities. This has produced, especially around Johannesburg, some of the worst slum conditions in Africa.

Figure 7.9 The modernity and economic power of Johannesburg (and South Africa in a broader sense) are conveyed in this scene of the city's CBD, its high-rise buildings and layout strikingly similar to those of any industrial city in Europe or North America. (Courtesy South African Consulate General)

The South Africans are trying to meet this challenge in a number of ways. They still maintain racial segregation under the Group Areas Act by which they are trying to partition sprawling Johannesburg into a white urban zone and scattered townships for the black, colored, and Asian populations in the outskirts of the city. In the name of slum clearance, the various black populations are now quartered in new townships whose monotony and oppressive situation are exemplified by Soweto, the largest of the black townships in South Africa. In the mid-1970s, responding to increasing international pressure and increased dissent and civil disorder, the government began a series of largely cosmetic changes, especially in the so-called petty apartheid, which separates the races in such aspects as use of public facilities. But the fundamental basis of apartheid remained unchanged. As a result, in June 1976 Johannesburg was rocked by the most violent show of dissent in the Soweto township, marking a watershed in the history of interracial conflict in South Africa. The dissent spread to other townships in the country, and troubles continued for about two years, with considerable loss of life and great disorder in the economy and urban life, for all the races.

The future of Johannesburg lies in how the root cause of urban instability is eradicated in order to maintain the city's ability to continue as South Africa's most important industrial and business center. It is in the throes of becoming a megalopolis with a series of mining towns and industrial areas merging together. Added to this are such black townships as Soweto and Alexandra, scattered around the city within 6 to 19 mi. (10 to 30 km.) and containing over 1 million inhabitants. Most of these black townships were deliberately located adjacent to or in mining areas separated from the city proper by all sorts of buffer zones to control the movement of blacks. As the country is divided into white areas and Bantustans (homelands), it is expected by the official apartheid position that the blacks now working in and around white urban areas like Johannesburg, considered only "temporary sojourners," would eventually be repatriated to their homelands. This situation has virtually eliminated any political rights of the blacks in the urban areas.

Kinshasa

Kinshasa is one of the most rapidly growing cities of Subsaharan Africa (Fig. 7.10). Its modern history dates back to 1881 when Henry M. Stanley, an explorer of Africa, returned to what was then called the Congo to survey the region on behalf of King Leopold II of Belgium, who had designs on the prosperous central African region. After

Figure 7.10   Kinshasa, Zaire. (*Source:* Adapted from Paul Raymaekers, *L'Organization Des Zones de Squatting,* Paris: Editions Universitaires, 1964, pp. 182–183.)

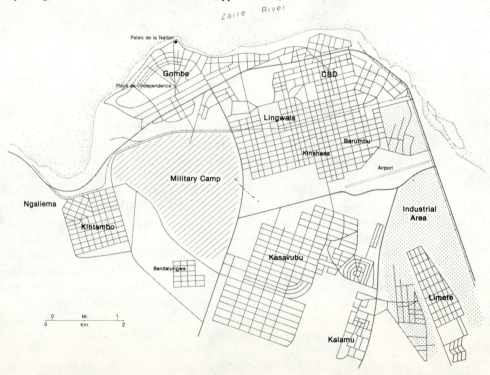

two years of preparation and expedition, Stanley reached the present site of Kinshasa in 1881 and set up his first camp on a small hill called Ngaliema, after the chief with whom Stanley negotiated for the acquisition of the area. The original site, which Stanley chose because of its beautiful panoramic view of the Zaire River, was located just west of the ancient village of Kintambo and was to become perhaps the most prestigious quarter of Kinshasa (Leopoldville, as it was called until the country's independence in the 1960s). Kinshasa's favorable location between the regions of upper and lower Zaire made it a strategic point to conduct trade. Commercial relationships expanded and accelerated between the various tribes in the interior and those nearer the coast. By 1883, Kinshasa had become the most important post in upper Zaire and according to Stanley the most prosperous, presumably on account of the good relationship between the new settler community and the indigenous population.

In 1885, Zaire became a virtual private property of Leopold II under the banner of the Congo Free State, at which time perhaps the most ruthless overseas exploitation in Africa started. When Zaire became a colony of Belgium in 1908, ending Leopold's private tenure of the region, Kinshasa had accumulated so much capital in the form of plantations, boat yards, and transportation and commercial facilities that it had become an important point of supply for primary commodities. Soon Kinshasa was connected by rail to the port at Matadi downstream on the Zaire River. This boosted its importance as a break-of-bulk and transshipment point, and before too long it became a major city in central Africa.

In 1910 Kinshasa had a population of 10,000; by 1930 this number had grown to 30,000, most of whom were African. Kinshasa became a center of influence for Belgian control of central Africa, and in 1929, Kinshasa housed the governor general of the Belgian Congo and Ruanda-Urundi. World War II brought increased importance to the Zaire capital, with increased activities in the primary-product sectors as well as in manufacturing, which attracted more people to the city. In 1946 Kinshasa had grown to 110,000, and in the next 10 years it more than tripled its population to 367,000, which included 16,000 expatriates. At independence in 1960, Kinshasa had over 400,000 inhabitants when the Belgians left. Kinshasa was a big city but had fewer than 50 university graduates to take over the administration of the country from the Belgians. By 1980, the population had exploded to nearly 3 million, almost the same as that of Lagos.

With the busiest port in central Africa, bungalows and high rise buildings adorning its European quarter, and wide, grid-patterned streets with trees and flowers giving beauty to its downtown area, Kinshasa was considered by the Europeans to be the choice town to live in in central Africa. This of course was not the case for the African, who looks at the city from his old, crowded commune of Kasavubu and Barumbu or one of the half-dozen bidonvilles (squatter settlements) in the southern sections of the city where life for the Africans can be extremely poor, unsanitary, and disorderly.

Kinshasa has five major sections. The structure of the city has been greatly influenced by the bend of the Zaire River. Along the coast, which used to be called *quartier éuropean,* the city is in three sections. In the west is the fashionable and modernistic area composed of the Ngaliema and Gombe quarters, used mostly for high class residence and government offices. The presidential palace and the glamorous OAU village are also found in this section. Other impressive landmarks such as the Palais de la Nation and Place de l'Independence are also located here. To the east of Gombe is the CBD of Kinshasa. This is also a modern sector, with high rise buildings, shops, centers of entertainment, hotels, and other commercial establishments. This is the busiest sector of Kinshasa, where prices are reportedly the most exorbitant. Following the bend of the river to the east of the CBD is the industrial zone of Kinshasa. The location of the railway complex here and port facilities have attracted a number of industries to this area. It is also located adjacent to the source of labor in the poor residential quarters to the west of the zone.

The fourth section of the city is composed of the old Kinshasa and Barumba, which are poor residential areas intermingled with retail establishments. The principal market is also located here. The quality of this area has been on the decline and is mostly used by Africans. To the south of this section are found more recent African communes whose quality ranges from poor housing to shanty squatter dwellings. This section has recently grown to cover a vast area to the south of the city. The expansion of the squatter dwellings is considered one of the major urban problems of Kinshasa, and the causes are both internal to the city as well as external. A good number of the squatter dwellers are people leaving the old sections of the city, which are becoming inhospitable because of increased densities and inadequate amenities. New migrants, who are flowing to Kinshasa at an alarming rate, are also a major cause for the expansion of the squatter areas. Kinshasa's rate of growth has been one of the highest in Subsaharan Africa.

Kinshasa's problems clearly derive from its rapid growth and follow from the socioeconomic structure, which, as in the case of many African primate cities, reflects the colonial duality of modern and traditional enclaves trying to forge harmony within the context of a modern town. Herein lies the major contradiction. The systems that operate within Kinshasa are two: those that govern the activities and life-styles of the indigenous elite and the European community, and those that are followed by the masses of urban dwellers in the pseudo-urban or traditional subsystem. The former has the means to carve out its own domain from the urban area and give it the physical and cultural attributes of a modern town. The latter does not. In many cases, it simply extends its rural mode of living with crude forms of adaptation to the urban milieu. The result is, on the one hand, a well-planned and well-administered modern section and, on the other hand, a mass of disorganized, high-density, and unsanitary slum or squatter settlements. The gaps are immense. A major challenge for Kinshasa lies in reducing rural-urban migrations as a top priority, instituting more vigorous programs to increase urban employment, and attempting to reduce the large disparity within the city. Like Dakar, Abidjan, and Nairobi, Kinshasa is a long way from becoming a truly viable and relevant city for the ordinary citizen.

Lagos

It is often said that Lagos owes its growth and dynamism to European influence. But Lagos is also one of the few major metropolises in Subsaharan Africa in whose cre-

Figure 7.11 Ibadan, Nigeria, is unusual in Subsaharan Africa. Although one of the largest cities in Nigeria (and on the subcontinent as well), Ibadan shows very little modern physical development because of the relative primacy of Lagos on the coast. (A. Mehretu)

ation and development Africans participated (Fig. 7.11). Lagos was probably established in the seventeenth century, when a group of Awari decided to cross over the lagoons and settle on the more secure island of Iddo. Later they crossed over to Lagos Island in search of more farm land (Fig. 7.12). In this manner the three important parts of the city of Lagos started out as fishing and farming villages by the indigenous population well before major external influences became important in the eighteenth century.

Another important historical note in the development of Lagos was its importance in the slave trade between 1786 and 1851, in which the Africans, especially the Yoruba, were willing participants in the marketing of slaves brought mainly from Hausaland. Lagos Island became an important center where slaves were barricaded awaiting their export along with primary commodities, particularly foodstuffs and Yoruba cloth, which reached markets as far as Brazil. Although in 1807 the British passed an act to abolish slavery, Lagos, because of its locational advantage, continued the trade until 1851. The slave trade finally was halted in 1851 by the British bombardment of the city, which also caused a temporary decline in the city's population. With the cession of Lagos to Britain as a colony in 1861, the colonial era for Lagos was formally begun and growth resumed.

From the interior, people still flowed to the "free colony," leaving slavery, war, and instability behind in the interior. Freed slaves also returned from Brazil as well as from Sierra Leone and made their home in Lagos. Toward the end of the eighteenth

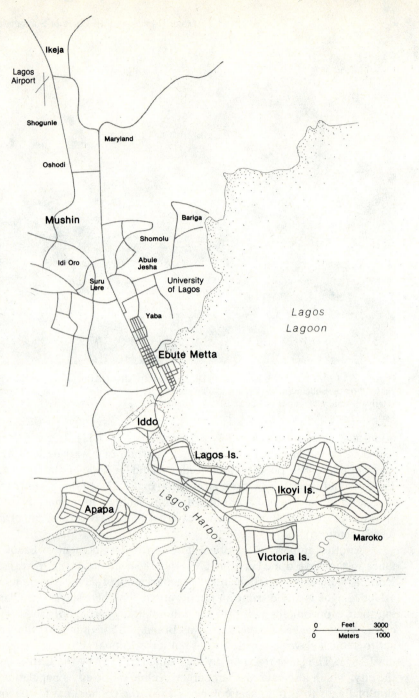

Figure 7.12 Lagos Metropolitan Area. (*Source:* Adapted from A. B. Aderibigbe, ed., *Lagos: The Development of an African City,* Lagos: Longmans Nigeria, 1975, p. 105.)

century, Britain established a protectorate over the whole of Nigeria. A railway from Lagos was begun in 1895, reaching Kano in 1912.

Its effective hinterland now expanded to the interior of Nigeria, Lagos became even more important in its function as a trade and administrative center of the colony as well as the Protectorate of Nigeria. The British consulate was built on Lagos Island, and quarters for public servants of the colonial administration also sprang up in what became known as the Marina and on Ikoye Island. By 1901 Lagos had a population of more than 40,000, and by this time the future prominence of the "modern metropolis" was pretty much established.

Lagos now has just under 3 million inhabitants, after Kinshasa the largest urban agglomeration in Subsaharan Africa. Lagos is also a city with many problems rooted in its rapid growth. The city has been called the biggest disaster area that ever passed for a city. That may be overstating it, but Lagos has acute, sometimes incomprehensible problems of traffic, sanitation, housing, urban decay, and social services. With the discovery of oil and sudden wealth reaching the population, the problems have been aggravated on all fronts.

The city is spread out over a large area on the mainland and four small islands to the south. The internal structure consists of eight zones of development. On the mainland is the sector of Ebute Metta, a major industrial area that contains the Nigerian Railway Corporation and other firms. Some high- to medium-class residential areas also adjoin the industrial zone. West of Ebute Metta is the new development area of Suru Lere, which also contains medium-grade residential housing.

The second principal sector on the mainland is the Apapa area, which has not only an industrial estate and a transport center but also a high class residential area adjoining the industrial estate. The third and fourth sectors are Mushin and Ikeja, respectively, which are further to the north. Both have developed mostly as industrial estates, but they also contain a considerable amount of peripheral low-grade residential dwellings; Ikeja also has Lagos's international airport.

Iddo Island is the fifth unit, and its most important function is transport. Since Iddo is located between the mainland and the other islands as a stepping stone, the principal roads and bridges all pass through it. Lagos Island, the most important and most densely used of the islands, contains the CBD along the Marina, government offices, embassies, very old slum dwellings, and some tracts of middle- and high-class residential areas (Fig. 7.13). Lagos Island is the heartbeat of Lagos not only for the elite but also for the poor and transitional class who inhabit the slums and gravitate around the more traditional centers of exchange. Southeast of Lagos Island are the two "dormitory" sectors of the well-to-do Nigerians—the islands of Ikoyi and Victoria.

Lagos is a primate city. That means it exhibits all the problems that cities of this character portray in Africa. The disparity in socioeconomic status between the elite and the mass of urbanites is wide. That means the city reflects two contradictory modes of living—one is an extension of European style brought about by those who can afford the luxuries of high-level technology; the other is an extension of the traditional mode distorted to fit an urban milieu. As it reflects itself in an African urban milieu the curi-

Figure 7.13 Downtown Lagos with older colonial buildings in the foreground and more modern structures in the background. Lagos is undergoing rapid changes as older structures and empty areas give way to new buildings in this bustling West African metropolis. (Courtesy Shell-BP and the Nigerian Oil Corporation)

ous amalgam loses the beauty, charm, and convenience of either and becomes a nuisance exemplified by the traffic congestion and slum dwellings in Lagos.

As a primate city Lagos has the typical problem of rapid population growth that lacks sufficient employment opportunities. The net effect of this is vast. It depresses urban wages to almost marginal subsistence levels and adds to the pressure of urban amenities and housing. In addition, numerous social problems ensue as a result of unemployment and underemployment, especially in the slums of Lagos and peripheral communities. Lagos is a good example of African primate cities whose growth rates and attendant problems in distorted consumption patterns have created a stultifying problem that a weak and often disorganized city government is incapable of handling. Lagos seems to follow its own momentum, and one only hopes that some day the city authorities and planners will catch up with it.

Some positive developments are on the way. The capital of the country is to be moved to a more central location in the vicinity of the confluence between the Niger and Benue rivers at a place called Abuja. This will definitely mean a major step in decentralization to reduce the concentration of functions in Lagos. The building of a second bridge connecting Lagos Island with Iddo Island should reduce the traffic problem, but the long-term solution of Lagos lies in the systematic and holistic planning of the entire metropolitan region, including Mushin and Ikeja. Unlike Dakar and Abidjan, Lagos is a long way from ever receiving compliments, but then Lagos, like Ibadan and

Addis Ababa, is closer to the expression of the more realistic African response to social transformation under the influence of urban modernity. It should be remembered that Lagos, even in the colonial period, had fewer than 5000 expatriates. Hence, the character of the city and its spatial organization were considerably less a function of the impact of the Europeans than was clearly the case for Dakar, Abidjan, Nairobi, and Kinshasa. The process that Lagos is experiencing, if there is any recognizable process at all, may throw light on the problems of African primate cities that have been, and in most cases still are, enclaves of European economic systems often as alien to their people as are cities in Europe. Lagos is a bona fide African city and, as disorganized as it is, may be one of the few cities in Africa to offer a lesson on the transition from colonial to indigenous urban environment.

Dakar

Dakar is known for its beauty, modernity, charm, and style. Because of its agreeable climate, excellent location, and urban morphology, Dakar is often described as the Marseilles or Nice of West Africa. But of course this image depends on which part of Dakar one wishes to describe. Dakar is a city of phenomenal contradictions (Fig. 7.14).

The city was founded in 1444, when Portuguese sailors made a small settlement on the tiny island Gorée, located about 1.9 mi. (3 km.) off the Dakar peninsula. In 1588 the Dutch also made the island of Gorée a resting point; the French followed in 1675. None of the settlers, however, ventured onto the mainland until 1857. The Dakar peninsula was settled by indigenous people, and access to it was not easy.

Inevitably, the French forced themselves onto the mainland in 1857 and used Dakar as a refueling and coal-bunkering point, but a number of developments expanded its functions until in a relatively short time Dakar became the most important colonial point on the west coast of Africa. Dakar was preceded by St. Louis at the mouth of the Senegal River as an important trade center after St. Louis was established by the Portuguese in the fifteenth century. In 1885 Dakar was linked to St. Louis by rail, which gave it an added importance as a trading center. Its situation and site advantages as well as its Mediterranean-type climate soon led Dakar to be a focus for a number of colonial functions which France wanted to introduce in the region. In 1898 Dakar was chosen as a naval base, and in 1904 it became the capital of the Federation of French West Africa.

Dakar is situated on the westernmost part of the continent. This gave it an important function as the most strategic point for ships moving between Europe and southern Africa and from Africa to the New World. As a capital of the Federation of French West Africa until 1956, Dakar served the hinterland stretching from the west coast to Mali, Upper Volta, and Niger. Site was also one of the important factors that made Dakar the most colonized city in West Africa. The aforementioned qualities and attributes, combined with Dakar's site on a peninsula at the end of Cape Verde blessed with a moderate climate—unlike that of any of the localities in West Africa—and its protected harbor made Dakar an ideal colony.

The evolution of Dakar's internal structure and spatial organization has an inter-

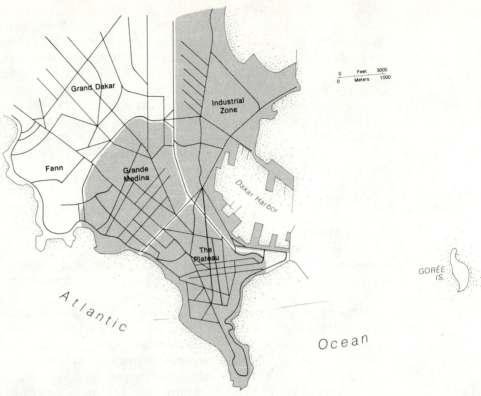

Figure 7.14 Dakar: Principal Land Use Zones. (*Source:* Adapted from IFAN, *Dakar: Metropole Ouest-Africaine,* Dakar: Institut Fondamental D'Afrique Noire, 1970, p. 149.)

esting background. When the French moved from the island of Gorée to the peninsula in 1857, there was some uneasiness about living in quarters surrounded by African villages. Although a policy of racial segregation was not officially pursued, as it was in southern Africa, the settlers had always wanted to separate the two communities. However, the settlers had to await a natural calamity that befell the Africans before they could accelerate the extent of their exclusive holdings. Although progressive displacement of African dwellings was underway before the outbreak of a yellow fever epidemic in 1900, the Europeans, invoking sanitation requirements, used the epidemic as a pretext to displace the Africans by pushing them northward. Between 1900 and 1902 numerous African homesteads were burnt down as a "sanitary measure" and the occupants relocated further to the north after being compensated for the holdings they lost. Another epidemic hit in 1914, and this once again brought about destruction of African homesteads in the south and more relocation of Africans again to the north. The 1914 epidemic and World War I coincided, and both phenomena intensified the disinheritance of the Africans.

On the eve of World War II the French succeeded in almost completely dominating downtown Dakar, often called Le Plateau or Dakar Ville, concentrating the Africans in what became known as the African Medina in the north-central part of the peninsula. The problem of "cohabitation," as the French called it, was at the root of the whole displacement campaign, but the colonial authorities would never admit a policy of official segregation, although many recommendations were made to openly enforce a system based on race. A commission charged with the study of Dakar in 1889 recommended separate residential quarters for European and African populations. In 1901 another report proposed relocating the African outside the confines of the city. A new plan, implemented in 1950–1951, gave the colonial administrators further excuse to displace more Africans, especially those who had formed squatter dwellings in open spaces in the north of the Plateau.

The present internal morphology of Dakar reflects this historical background. Le Plateau contains one of the most Westernized sectors in Africa, which easily can compare with any decent-looking urban sector of a European city. On the other hand the African Medina reflects its background as a concentration of Africans into a high-density mass of housing projects and bidonvilles.

Modern Dakar has four main divisions. Le Plateau, the most modern sector of the city, contains high class residential quarters, commercial and retail functions, government offices, and institutions (Fig. 7.15). To the east is the port of Dakar, where port administration and numerous port functions are handled. This part of the city

Figure 7.15 The CBD of Dakar exhibits a high density of modern structures. The first floors are invariably used for shops, travel agencies, bars, and the like, while the higher floors are devoted to offices and residential use. (A. Mehretu)

still has an atmosphere reminiscent of its European background, with high rise buildings, expensive shops, exclusive restaurants, business offices, and many Europeans. The Grande Medina, located north of Le Plateau, contains the old African Medina: this is the African Dakar. Its functions are primarily residential, but there are also shops, markets, and cultural features. The Medina contains the industrial laborers and those employed in the informal sector both outside and inside the Medina. The population of the Medina and the adjacent bidonvilles of Ouakem and Grand Yof is uniformly poor, living in high-density, sometimes inadequately serviced quarters of the city.

East and northeast of the Grande Medina is the industrial sector of Dakar. Conveniently located with its southern flanks resting on the port section of Dakar, this sector contains the bulk of Dakar's industrial activity. North of the Medina recent expansions of the city have resulted in a sector called Grand Dakar, which contains a mixture of some modern residential quarters, some industries, and bidonvilles. Southwest of Grand Dakar is Fann, comprising modern and plush residential quarters and the university.

As with many African primate cities, Dakar faces the problems that accompany rapid population growth. In 1914 the city had a total population of 18,000. By 1945 the population had increased to 132,000, and 10 years later that figure had more than doubled, to 300,000. By 1968, the population had once again doubled, to 600,000; in 1975 it stood at 808,000; and in 1980, 1.05 million. Clearly most of the growth is attributable to rural-urban migration. The rate of natural increase of the city's population has also been much higher than the national average on account of better sanitation and medical services.

The rapid population growth makes planning a crucial problem. Since 1956, when the city ceased to be the capital of the Federation of French West Africa, Dakar has lost a considerable amount of its significance as a seat of government, commercial, and industrial activity. The French had one of the most elaborate colonial administrative machineries in Dakar, supported by a budgetary allocation from France. It had the largest contingent of French expatriates in government, education, commerce, and industry. The question after 1956 was, could Dakar survive as a Senegalese capital stripped of much of its initial reason for existence?

No doubt Dakar is still an important center whose functions reach far beyond its national boundaries. Its ideal location still makes it a center of maritime and air traffic. Many international organizations are located in Dakar on account of its situation and agreeable urban environment. Many international conferences and meetings are also held here. Above all, Dakar is one of the most favored vacation spots in West Africa for European tourists, especially those from the Mediterranean who find a similar climatic comfort in exotic and at times intriguing surroundings. Nevertheless, the future of Dakar depends largely on the solution of two major problems—stemming the tide of rural-to-urban migration by a sound policy of regional and rural development, including development of satellite cities and subsequent decentralization; and reducing the disparity and severe duality within its urban boundary between its ultramodern sectors and the bidonvilles. One major challenge should be to make Dakar a de facto African city.

Problems of Urban Development in Subsaharan Africa

Primate Cities

Observed from the preceding discussion of representative city profiles, the phenomenon of urban primacy continues to dominate the African urban scene. In fact, the study of urbanization in Africa has often been the study of the primate cities whose background, character, and dynamics are usually quite different from indigenous urban phenomena. In most instances the primate cities of African countries contain a good proportion of the total urban population. What makes them primate is of course restricted not only to the criterion of size but also to the unique character of such centers in relation to the socioeconomic environment in which they are found.

One of the more significant factors in urban transformation in Africa in the post-World War II and postindependence period has been the dramatic population growth of the primate cities, a growth that shows no sign of slackening (Fig. 7.16). In fact, recent years have been characterized by even higher rates of growth. As measured by the proportion of urban population contained in each primate city in 1980, the degree of primacy in Africa ranged between 14 percent in South Africa to 100 percent in countries like Lesotho, Seychelles, and Djibouti. As observed earlier, countries where urbanization has a relatively long history generally have lower proportions. Nigeria shows the lowest proportion in its region; although Lagos has grown to a staggering size in recent years, its proportion is lower than expected. Considering the relatively low rate of growth of urban population in traditionally urbanized areas like South Africa, and at the same time observing the acceleration of their primate cities, the degree of primacy can be concluded to be a significant pattern in Africa's urban development for quite a long time if processes continue to operate in the current fashion.

The overall pattern seems to indicate that the primate cities contain a good portion of the urban population. On the average, a third of the urban population lives in these cities. Study of the growth trends of many of the primate cities, especially those found in mineral-rich nations, indicates that over the last decade and a half, higher and higher portions of the urban population are flocking into them. In 1960 Lagos and Kinshasa accounted for only 9 and 11 percent of the total urban population in their respective countries. By 1980 Lagos had increased its portion to 20 percent, while Kinshasa had raised its share to 34 percent. Other centers, such as Accra, Nairobi, Addis Ababa, Luanda, Dakar, and even Cairo, increased their share of the total urban population in their respective countries from between 5 and 10 percent in 1960 to between 30 and 65 percent in 1980.

Site and Situation

The growth of African cities has generated problems tied in with site and situation. As with many other aspects of African development, the growth of the majority of African cities has not resulted from careful planning. With perhaps a few exceptions, neither has it resulted from spontaneous growth reflected by genuine indigenous requirements of spatial organization. Situation has been by far more important than site

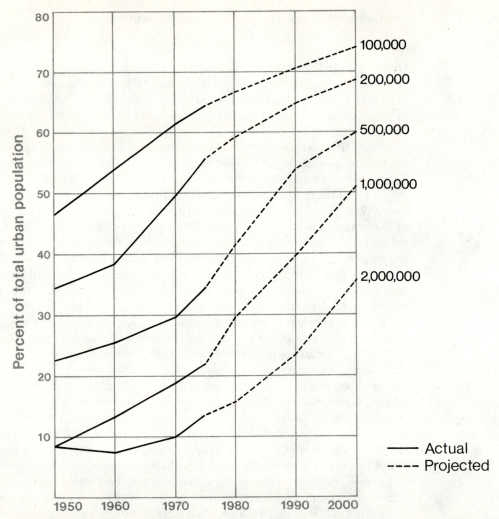

Figure 7.16 Growth of Cities, Actual and Projected, 1950–2000. (*Source:* Data derived from UN *Demographic Yearbooks,* 1970, 1976, 1978.)

in the founding of a good number of cities in Africa. Furthermore, since cities were founded by the colonial powers to function as transshipment centers for efficient handling of raw-material exports and, since it was not in the interest of colonial administrators to build functional towns to serve indigenous interests, site and situation of towns in terms of internal space organization requirements were unimportant considerations so long as the outward flow of commodities was insured.

Consequently the sites of some of the largest cities in Africa suffer from limited area for expansion and development. Cities such as Lagos, Dakar, Conakry, Monrovia, and Durban are restricted to island or peninsular sites. Cape Town, Freetown, Addis Ababa, and Nairobi are among African towns handicapped by mountain barriers, hilly

Figure 7.17   Tananarive (Anatananarivo) in the Malagasy Republic (island of Madagascar), shows a mix of old and new buildings typical of African cities. The city is located in the highlands of the interior and thus is characterized by narrow, one-way streets and many hills and curves. (Courtesy David Campbell)

sites, or historical background (Fig. 7.17). Others, like Khartoum and Banjul, which are sited on flat areas and flood plains, have drainage problems.

Most large cities, particularly those in the Guinea coastal region, continue to be located at the margins of the terrestrial hinterland of the respective nations, reflecting maritime orientation.

As interior cities such as Bouaké in Ivory Coast, Kumasi in Ghana, Kano in Nigeria, and Yaoundé in Cameroon increase in importance, the present maritime bias may be altered. In some countries, Tanzania and Nigeria, for example, plans are definite to develop new capitals that will have a more central location. Although a shift of this magnitude is unlikely elsewhere in Africa, functional specialization, such as Kano's possible emergence as a major transport center, may be a way to change the existing concentration and external orientation of cities especially in the Guinea coastal region.

Rural-to-Urban Migration

As we have seen, African primate cities exhibit some of the highest population growth rates in the world: most major cities are growing more than 5 percent per annum, with some like Lagos and Kinshasa growing at about 10 percent. Migration experts point out that almost 60 percent of LDC urban growth is due to rural-to-urban migration. It is therefore not surprising that one of the most crucial problems afflicting African cities is the current wave of rural-to-urban migration.

Rural-urban migration represents an unprecedented massive flow of people into the few urban centers that became the locus of power and investment, particularly in the period following decolonization of the continent. Concern about the rate of African urbanization would hardly seem justifiable considering the magnitude of the rural population. However, the urban growth pattern often dominated by the primate city and the high growth rate of such centers tax the ability of the urban socioeconomic system to generate the required employment opportunities, housing, and social services. As a consequence, the primate city has become, in most instances, a liability to the overall development process because of the disproportionately large amount of resources needed to insure its stability.

It has now been established beyond doubt that rates of rural-to-urban migration continue to exceed rates of urban job creation and seriously jeopardize traditional views that rural-to-urban migration was a healthy developmental process.

The paradoxical fact that rural-to-urban migration continues to grow in spite of rising unemployment in urban centers of LDCs has given rise to a migration theory based on rural-urban income differentials. This theory assumes that migration is "primarily an economic phenomenon" and that the potential migrant makes a move in order to maximize his "expected" earnings.

Whether in fact the current massive rural-to-urban migration is caused primarily by economic phenomena related to rural-urban income differences might be open to debate. Clearly, however, the African city constitutes a major factor in the contradictions between urban and rural life; because of its monopoly of "economic wealth and political power" it has created a false perception on the part of rural-to-urban migrants of certain and immediate opportunities for socioeconomic improvement which the African urban reality cannot support.

Functional Concentration

The primate city in Africa is disproportionately larger than the other cities. The rank-size rule, which to a great extent characterizes the structure of urban development in industrialized nations, does not apply to urban-center relationships in Africa.

The African primate city also enjoys a monopoly of urban functions. A bulk of the major secondary, tertiary, and quaternary services are located in the primate city. The city embraces virtually all of the important urban functions, including government, international affairs, educational and cultural institutions, transport, and industry. In most African countries the primate city is so much an important nerve center that its effective control is tantamount to control of the nation as a whole. Its dominance of the rest of the country is often absolute, and although its prosperity and growth derive from the rest of the country, this transfer of resources is not reciprocated by a reverse flow in terms of development services and significant diffusion of relevant technology.

The African primate city contains the most important dynamics in the *center-periphery* dichotomy, where the city, being the core of economic activity, derives a disproportionate share of the development benefits. The rapid growth of the cities' economic prosperity relative to their rural peripheries has produced a socioeconomic disparity in which a spatially differentiated process of development has made it possible for primate cities or economic "core areas" to monopolize the benefits of development.

On the other hand, the outlying areas are made to suffer from sacrificing their manpower and resources to maintain the centralized prosperity of the primate cities.

Internal Characteristics

As demonstrated by the profiles of selected African cities, a form of development disparity also exists within African primate cities. The inhabitants of an African city are differentiated on the basis of ethnic background and rural domicile, culture, occupational characteristics, residential stability, and overall levels of living standards. African cities somewhat resemble cities of the industrialized countries, but the resemblance is limited to the physical structure of the domain of the African and expatriate elite who have surrounded themselves with the trappings of a modern environment for work, residence, social services, recreation, and communication. The difference between them lies in the existence, within the same municipal boundary, of a population which is poor and finds itself in a condition of subservience to the more privileged social classes in the modern system. As a result of this condition, the African city exhibits in microcosm the disparity that exists between city and countryside as a whole. The system seems to portray two enclaves operating within the African city, one composed of the urban elite and having strong functional linkages with the international system, the other composed of poorer masses who maintain stronger economic, political, and social affinity with the rural population of the country. From the viewpoint of the urban masses, the crucial problem that militates against an integrated development is the fact that the African urban elite has been unable to disengage its political, economic, and cultural dependence and turn its face toward its own environment.

Corresponding to this disparity in modernization processes within the urban milieu, the physical attributes of the urban structure have also been made to reflect sharp social and spatial contrasts (Fig. 7.18). The elite spatial domain represents a highly modernized work, social-service, and residential environment complete with macadamed roads, telephones, financial institutions, indoor running water, computers, television, and similar luxuries. On the other hand, the poorer segment of the urban inhabitants, whose daily affairs are hardly affected by such modernizing phenomena, live in shanty areas and slum conditions. Although the existence of extreme disparities in internal urban structure is not limited to African cities, an important distinction of the African modernizing process is its discontinuous and dichotomous character in terms affecting the two segments of the urban population. Whereas modern technology is within relatively easy access to the people within the modern system, it is virtually unattainable to the inhabitants within the more traditional system.

Solutions to Urban Problems: Policy Implications of African Urban Growth

The solutions to the current problems associated with rapid urbanization under the existing socioeconomic structures imply policies whose impact should go beyond the confines of the African city.

One of the chief factors inhibiting growth and integration of the African economy is the balkanization of the continent into economically and potentially weak entities

Figure 7.18 A major intersection in downtown Ougadougou, Upper Volta. Since there is no public transport system, people depend on bicycles and motorcycles to get around, creating traffic congestion. (A. Mehretu)

which in most instances can hardly hope to develop into viable economies in the foreseeable future. To make matters worse, a majority of African nations also operate under conditions in which political boundaries act as socioeconomic sheds across which virtually no trade, migration, or diffusion of ideas takes place. Instead, most significant flows in this insular spatial economy gravitate toward the primate city. In order to solve the deleterious effects of small and balkanized economies in which primate cities dominate, a system of subregional integration and common-market arrangements should be seriously considered in the long run. Although most African nations seem to be a bit too rigid about yielding any form of authority, a lasting solution to the problems of economic insularity can only be effectively solved by encouraging direct links between the economic core areas of the African nations at least on a subregional basis. This would not only bring about all of the advantages of coalesced markets but also would help to restructure the spatial orientation of the economy by integrating "peripheral" areas into the economy, which would be enhanced by the expanding trade and resource transfers between neighboring states.

The problem of primate city dominance can also be abated by a sound internal regional development policy which would introduce measures for improving the flow of development investment and infrastructural development. Development poles, satellite towns, and rural service centers can be identified from the existing system of central places and made to receive a higher share of the development investment than has been the case before. The selection of a hierarchy of central places and the assignment of services to each center in the hierarchy should be done in accordance with the rural economy and technology and with a view to increasing the efficiency in the delivery of central place services to the rural population. The new system of investment and settlement planning should aim at making the primate city shed those services and activities that can be effectively handled by smaller and more accessible centers.

Transport and social infrastructure are perhaps the most important factors for spatial organization of settlement. Surface transport policy is particularly crucial in restructuring existing orientations, which exhibit a tendency of unimodal dominance. Improving road connectivity between selected lower-order central places and supplying the rural population with alternative accessible centers for urban functions would significantly reduce the centripetal force of the primate city. The supply of a range of social services, including government, education, health, and recreation, would also enhance decentralization efforts.

A focus on rural development has taken hold in many African countries. Although results are not dramatic, experience indicates that increased commitment in this area could have a significant impact on the transformation of urban-rural relations. If planned and executed in a more integrated fashion, rural development based on the productive potentials of agriculture and natural resources can help redress existing rural-urban disparities and also alter the present trade and resource transfer relations whose terms of exchange favor the primate cities and other major urban centers in each country. A rural development strategy not only would bring about improvement in rural productivity and hence opportunities for better levels of living, but also would enable the development of a system for a more equitable distribution of development benefits.

A major problem posed by primate cities in Africa is their relative advantage to attract and hold on to the bulk of the human capital of the nation. Most trained people prefer to live in the primate cities, and although governments and developers deplore this trend, few intelligent and positive measures have been made to make smaller urban centers and rural areas more attractive to work and live in. Instead of developing incentives to reverse such trends, governments, perhaps inadvertently, have shown to be the prime offenders in perpetuating the unattractiveness of outlying areas by using them for punitive deposition of rival functionaries and for alienating those who insist on changes in the status quo.

The space structure of socioeconomic indicators shows a high concentration in the primate cities and an abrupt decline with distance away from them. Levels of adjusted income and development benefits accordingly exhibit rapid distance decay from the primate cities. The willingness to live and work away from the primate city is also a mirror image of the incentive function of the space economy governed by the primate cities, which of course behaves in a similar manner as adjusted income and development infrastructure. The quantitative and qualitative differences in "quality of life" that result from this condition make the primate city the most attractive center in the national space. Consequently, the ultimate goal of most rural elite and their offspring, and of those functionaries assigned rural jobs, is to eventually make a permanent home in the primate city. Few people with an educational achievement higher than elementary school or equivalent would consider small towns and rural areas as a permanent domicile.

The solution for this state of affairs does not seem to lie in the frequent self-righteous pronouncements that come from the leadership in Africa for selflessness and sacrifice on the part of a segment of the population. To use coercion to either dispatch people to serve in outlying areas or to try to stem the tide of rural-to-urban migration by force would only lead to counterproductive consequences. The only viable option must be based in making outlying areas more attractive to live and work in. Smaller towns and rural centers must be made to acquire competitive conditions of adjusted income and amenities so that they can attract people on their own merit. The willingness to work outside the primate city must be dealt with spatially by effecting adjustments in income and provision of social services so that the centripetal force toward the primate city is significantly reduced. Few African countries can afford a large-scale decentralization policy involving many towns. However, a concerted effort to restructure the spatial organization of the socioeconomic system, which is now dominated by the primate city, should be a major goal for development planning for many years to come.

RECOMMENDED READINGS

Aderibigbe, A. B. et al. *Lagos: The Development of an African City.* London: Longman, 1975.
Assembled on the occasion of the Second World Black and African Festival of Arts, this book represents a detailed historical as well as contemporary study of Lagos as a developing metropolis in West Africa.

Barbour, K. M. and R. M. Prothero, eds. *Essays on African Population.* London: Routledge and Kegan Paul, 1961.
In this collection of essays on the general topic of the African population, a few chapters deal with growth, migration, and wage-labor phenomena connected with the African urbanization process.

Bugnicourt, J. "Which Urban Alternative for Africa?" *African Environment,* 2, No. 3 (1976).
This paper deals with the most important components of a typical African city. After dividing the urban unit into modern subsystem and transitional subsystem, the author tries to characterize direction, magnitude, and nature of linkages between the two subsystems.

El-Shakhs, Salah and Robert Obudho, eds. *Urbanization, National Development, and Regional Planning in Africa.* New York: Praeger, 1974.
The book deals with a number of issues on the problems of urbanization and development in Africa. The process of urbanization is examined from various angles, including growth, problems of internal structure, polarization, and function.

Hake, Andrew. *African Metropolis, Nairobi's Self-Help City.* London: Sussex University Press, 1977.
This study of problems faced by most developing primate cities in Africa deals with the problem of the dual structure of Nairobi, its formal and modern sector on the one hand, its slums on the other.

Hamdan, G. "Capitals of the New Africa." *Economic Geography,* 40, No. 3 (1964), 239–253.

This paper deals with the African primate cities and describes the major developmental phenomena along the lines of centrality, nodality, and size. It focuses on how the primate city in Africa dominates the urban scene.

Hance, William A. *Population, Migration, and Urbanization in Africa.* New York: Columbia University Press, 1970.
One of the best readings available on the general character of African urban systems, their problems and possible solutions, this book also has a section on profiles of some African cities.

Hanna, William J. and Judith L. Hanna. *Urban Dynamics in Black Africa.* Washington, DC: Center for Research in School Systems, 1969.
This book offers a detailed treatment of some of the major urban dynamics in Africa, including migration, employment, ethnicity, political conflict and accommodation, and patterns of change in urban life.

Hull, Richard W. *African Cities and Towns Before the European Conquest.* New York: W. W. Norton, 1976.
An excellent summary of the background of major urban regions that have been investigated so far.

Hutton, John. *Urban Challenge in East Africa.* Nairobi: East African Publishing House, 1972.
This survey of problems of urban development in East Africa deals mostly with housing problems.

Mabogunje, A. L. *Urbanization in Nigeria.* London: University of London Press, 1968.

Mabogunje, A. L. "Urban-Rural Relationships in a Developing Economy: The Parable of the Old Wineskins." Paper presented at the 20th Annual Meeting of the African Studies Association, Houston, Texas, 1977.
The development of Nigerian towns is examined: historical background as well as contemporary problems of urbanization.

Miner, Horance. ed., *The City in Modern Africa.* New York: Praeger, 1967.
A number of problems of African urbanization are discussed. The chapters on processes of modernization and size classification are particularly interesting.

Riddell, J. Barry. "The Migration to the Cities of West Africa: Some Policy Considerations." *Modern African Studies,* 16, No. 2 (1978), 241–260.
There is an attempt to explain some of the factors of migration, but even more interesting is the discussion of policy issues to solve the problem of excessive migration into cities.

Skinner, Elliot. *African Urban Life: The Transformation of Ouagadougou.* Princeton, NJ: Princeton University Press, 1974.
This work, which reflects an anthropologist's view of a changing urban structure, deals with the background of Ouagadougou and the factors that influenced its present developmental structure.

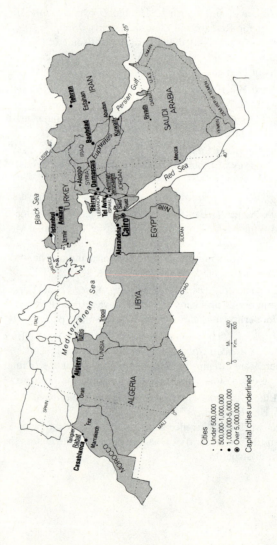

Figure 8.1 Major Cities of the Middle East and North Africa. (*Source:* Data derived from United Nations, Department of Economic and Social Affairs, *Global Review of Human Settlements, Statistical Annex,* published by Pergamon Press, New York, 1976.)

Chapter 8

Cities of the Middle East and North Africa

Michael E. Bonine

The Middle East and North Africa in the World Urban System

The Middle East and North Africa form another of the 10 world regions that is somewhat difficult to define and whose boundaries are relatively amorphous. The chief distinguishing characteristics that bind this region together are the religion of Islam and the impact of that religion on virtually all aspects of the region's cultural environment. That impact has been great, as well, on the urban pattern and urbanism, with the historic role of the Islamic city, or more properly, the Middle Eastern city. As the chapter notes, this unique type of city, which has survived into the contemporary period in many parts of the region, is actually the amalgam of many cultures and religions and contains elements that existed long before Islam emerged in the region. The Middle Eastern city thus is one type of preindustrial city that has shown remarkable resiliency.

As a region, the Middle East and North Africa are close to being more than 50 percent urbanized, having nearly doubled their percentage of urban population since 1950 while the total urban population increased about sixfold, to over 110 million in 1980 (out of a regional population total of some 230 million). Historically, however, this region has contained some of the oldest cities in the world. Indeed, parts of the area, in Mesopotamia and the Nile Valley, contained two of the earliest centers of the city in human civilization. Thus, it is not surprising that this region has always been more urbanized and has had larger and more important cities than Subsaharan Africa. Indeed, within the region, seven nations are already urbanized, in the sense of having more than 50 percent of their population in cities. Kuwait is at the top, at 92 percent urban probably the single most urbanized state in the entire world; but the peculiar geography and nature of the economy in Kuwait must be kept in mind in noting that high figure. Israel is second in the region, at 85 percent urban, again extremely high but also the result of the peculiar geography and character of the Israeli state. Among the more "traditional" states of the region, Iraq and Lebanon are fairly highly urbanized, at 66 and 65 percent, respectively, followed by Algeria, Egypt, and Tunisia, which have just passed the 50 percent mark in recent years. The remainder of the region is less than 50 percent urban.

The relatively high degree of urbanization is reflected, not surprisingly, in the fairly large number of cities and the sizes of those cities. There are 14 cities with a population of a million or more, with virtually every country in the region having at least one such city. The urban hierarchy is dominated at the top, of course, by Cairo, with more than 8 million people the largest city by far in the region and one of the largest in the world. But at least three other major cities in the region also rank high in the hierarchy: Tehran, the primate city of Iran, has a population of nearly 6 million; Baghdad, also a primate city of Iraq, has 4.5 million; and ancient Istanbul, the historic steppingstone between Europe and Asia, has 4 million (Fig. 8.1). All the cities of the region have witnessed explosive growth in the past 30 years, but perhaps few cities in the region or the rest of the world can match Kuwait City, which began as an insignificant desert center of a mere 85,000 people back in 1950 and by 1980 emerged, as the result of oil revenues, as a modern metropolis of 1.3 million (a 14-fold increase) and still rapidly growing. Indeed, this is one of the dominant themes, and problems, in the region today: the impact of inflated oil revenues on the total level of economic development, and hence urban development, throughout much of the Middle East and North Africa. From an urban perspective, this is thus one of the most fascinating regions of the world today, because of the strength of the preindustrial city, the legacy of the colonial city, and the powerful forces for change that are sweeping the region as the result of the world energy situation and resulting geopolitical tensions.

Evolution of Cities in the Middle East

Cities originated many millennia ago in the Middle East. The first urban settlements appeared as early as the fourth millennium B.C. in Mesopotamia (Iraq), and since that time towns have been important nodes of population and culture in the Middle East. As the fortunes of individual cities waxed and waned, so the importance and impact of urbanism varied both spatially and temporally over the many centuries.

Compared with the metropolises of today, the ancient cities of this region were small. Many had only several thousand inhabitants, and few had more than 5,000 or 10,000. One exception was Uruk, a Sumerian city in southern Mesopotamia that in one period occupied over a thousand acres, was surrounded by a double city wall 5.9 mi. (9.5 km.) in circumference, and had a population of 40,000 to 50,000. Despite the small size, these ancient settlements functionally were cities. They served as a focus for a nearby surrounding agricultural (and village) population. Temples, a literary and religious elite, palaces and rulers, specialized trades and crafts, storage facilities for grains, and many other features characterized these cities and distinguished them from agricultural villages.

The ancient Middle Eastern city had a rather distinct morphology; the basic pattern was a round city with a large wall to protect the inhabitants. In the center was a concentration of temples and public buildings, while wide streets radiated outward from this complex. By the end of the third millennium this temple complex had developed into a great stepped ziggurat. Palaces also became more prominent as the secular rulers grew in power compared with the high priests. The housing was rectangular and built around an open courtyard, the rooms being arranged around this open space. The morphology of the residences is strikingly similar to the traditional housing of the later periods, until the modern era—a continuity of form for over five millennia!

Some changes in the organization of the Middle Eastern city occurred as a result of the introduction of the Greek city and its ideals into the region. Although Greek settlements had long existed in western Anatolia, Alexander the Great's conquest in the fourth century B.C. furnished the main impetus for the spread of Hellenistic urban ideals. Many new cities were founded, and Greek colonists also were settled in many of the native cities, the aliens living in separate neighborhoods. The grid street pattern as well as important morphological structures such as the agora, basilica, and public baths were introduced with the Greeks. Hellenization of the indigenous urban elite occurred as they adopted Greek names, dress, and even the language. Although the successors of Alexander, such as the Seleucids, continued to found cities with Greek colonists, the subsequent centuries began the absorption of the Greeks and the gradual loss of the influence of Hellenization.

In the seventh century A.D. the religion of Islam began in the Arabian peninsula and was spread swiftly by Arab armies across North Africa and Southwest Asia. The Arabs founded a number of cities, although many of the Arabs and their allies settled in existing cities or villages or even set up nomadic camps in the frontier areas. Many of the new "cities" established were tent or makeshift encampments, including Basra, Kufa, and Fustat.

By the eighth century Islam stretched from Spain and northwest Africa on the west and to India on the east. In terms of urban development entirely new cities were not as significant as the more common pattern of establishing a separate Arab neighborhood outside of existing ancient cities. Inhabited by different ethnic, social, and religious groups, the Arab sections and the traditional city soon were divided. This division remained for several centuries until an Islamic urban society emerged as the result of the transformation of the Arab tribal and kinship organization into a complex, differentiated society. It was Islamic because religious communities evolved based upon schools of Islamic law, creating a new context for organizing Moslem social and religious life.

By the Middle Ages some Middle Eastern cities, such as Cairo, became dominated by an alien slave-military dynasty, the Mamelukes. They were interested only in collecting taxes, and ignored the welfare of the inhabitants. Also at this time a new urban elite, the *ulema* (Moslem clergy), emerged as an influential force by marrying into the important merchant, landowning, and administrative families. It was, in fact, only by the eleventh or twelfth centuries that most of the inhabitants of Middle Eastern cities had converted to Islam and that we can speak of a truly Islamic urban society.

The traditional city in the Islamic Middle East did not change considerably after the Middle Ages, although there were certainly differences between Ottoman, Safavid, and other cities, especially in the administrative structure of municipalities. Regional variations in morphology also could be found, but these differences were due largely to environmental factors and the heritage of structure and form from antiquity. It was the modern period, the nineteenth and especially twentieth centuries, in which major changes began to take place in the Middle Eastern city.

The Islamic City Model

The religion of Islam and its influence on the society and culture of the Middle East for over 13 centuries is one of the underlying characteristics of this region. Islam pervades all aspects of the life of a traditional, religious Moslem. By extension the Middle Eastern city in the Islamic period has been viewed as an Islamic or "Moslem" city. This idea was largely formulated in the first half of the twentieth century by Orientalists, individuals knowledgeable in the languages, religions, and cultures of the Middle East. They consider Islam one of the overriding factors in the lives of Middle Eastern inhabitants, and this viewpoint includes the urban environment. Cities are seen as manifestations of religious ideals, and so the structure and morphology of the Islamic city reflects the religion of Islam.

The model's basic premise is that Islam is an urban religion because only in a city can faithful Moslems adhere to all requirements of the Koran and the *Shari'a* or religious law. Therefore, Islam fosters the development of cities. With the spread of Islam went the spread of urban settlements. According to the model, the Moslem city is formless, irregular, a mass of confusion. This is because Islamic law does not recognize separate or special status for cities or urbanites, all individuals being equal before the law. Winding alleyways and cul-de-sacs develop because no civil authority exists to prevent the encroachment of houses onto the public lanes.

The Islamic city is a compact mass of residences, open courtyard houses which create a cellular urban texture (Fig. 8.2). The house is very private, and elaborate precautions are taken to shelter Moslem women. Entrances are L shaped and not across from one another to prevent seeing into a house, walls on the alleyways are windowless, and separate guest rooms or courtyards for the men are present. The residences are arranged and organized into quarters or neighborhoods, which often can be based on ethnic groups, religious sects or minorities, and occupations. Many activities are organized by quarters, and each has a representative or headman.

Structures and institutions in the Islamic city include a permanent central market (bazaar or *suq*), mosques, shrines, public baths, a city wall, a citadel, inns, and small markets in the individual quarters. Each city has one major mosque called the Friday Mosque, which is the most important symbolic place of worship (except that a major shrine or even another mosque may overshadow the Friday Mosque in some cities).

The bazaar is one of the most important distinguishing characteristics of the Moslem city. This marketplace comprises small, contiguous stalls located in numerous passageways or branches which usually are covered by a series of vaults or domes (Fig. 8.3). The individual branches may be occupied principally by coppersmiths, blacksmiths, cloth sellers, or other individual retailers and craftsmen. Complementary trades

Figure 8.2 Compact open-courtyard houses in the city of Yazd, Iran, are typical of the traditional Middle Eastern city's residential areas. (M. Bonine)

often are next to one another, such as the leather sellers next to the shoemakers, so the latter will have ready access to their principal raw material. The individual trades were organized into guilds, and these associations not only assured the quality of products and served the interests of the members, but were also vehicles by which governments collected taxes.

There are problems with the Islamic city model. Most of the characteristics described and attributed to this city actually can be found in many preindustrial cities. Similarly, most morphologic characteristics of the Islamic city can be found in the pre-Islamic urban forms of the region. The windowless house with an L-shaped entrance can be found in pre-Islamic houses, so it is rather fallacious to say this form derived from Islamic social customs. Public baths, citadels, city walls, narrow alleyways, and quarters based on ethnic or religious affiliations can be found in cities outside the region as well as among pre-Islamic settlements. Of course, mosques, shrines, and religious schools are specifically Moslem, but their location and significance in urban society differs little from religious institutions in other traditional cultures.

The Islamic city is less disorganized or confusing than postulated by the model. The "formlessness" and "disorder" reflect the perceptions of Western observers and scholars who consciously or unconsciously compare them with Western, industrialized cities. For its inhabitants and a preindustrial technology the Islamic city is rationally, logically organized. For instance, the narrow alleyways provide shade for the inhabi-

Figure 8.3 The covered bazaar, or market area, is another distinctive feature of the traditional Middle Eastern city, as in this photo of the bazaar at Yazd, Iran. (M. Bonine)

tants, who still have to walk in hot weather. Such lanes also reduce the impact of frequently blowing wind and dust, and do not waste space which can be used for housing and other buildings.

The alleyways are not so irregular either. In Iran, for example, the traditional cities have major lanes in an orthogonal network. The direction of one axis of this grid is downslope and for good reason: the water channels for irrigation systems are laid out in a grid system, and the streets follow the channels to reach various rectangular plots of cultivated land. Cities grew by expanding along the existing streets and water channels, filling in the rectangular plots. Instead of a maze of twisting alleyways, a rather orthogonal network of lanes results, including cul-de-sacs at right angles to the main grid.

The concentric zones of residential quarters based upon social status are seldom present in the Islamic city. Quarters often are a mixture of rich and poor, although some neighborhoods are more prestigious. In Iranian cities the traditional elite quarters tend to be in the upslope direction.

Other aspects of the model could be countered, but the refutation needs no belaboring. It should be pointed out, however, that Islam is not necessarily an urban religion, nor did it necessarily foster urbanism throughout the Middle East. Moslem society is built upon a heritage of millennia, and cities reflect that foundation. Rather than the Islamic city we must refer to the traditional urban settlement of this cultural region as the Middle Eastern city.

Processes of Urbanization: Traditional and Modern

Traditional cities in the Middle East developed for different and multiple causes. Cities always were a focus for a surrounding agricultural hinterland, but such settlements remained small unless other factors were operative. Similarly, numerous garrisons or outposts established by many dynasties in frontier areas evolved into cities only due to other stimuli.

Cities could exist only with a reliable water supply, often a difficult requirement in the arid Middle East. Generally, except for settlements on the largest rivers, such as the Nile, Tigris, and Euphrates, cities are located in a lowland area near highlands or mountains. It is these highlands which receive relatively greater precipitation and furnish the source of water for the lowland cities—either by rivers, by springs, or as ground water. There are even cases in which the source of a city's water supply may be hundreds of miles away; for instance, the spring water for many of the settlements in the eastern Arabian peninsula originates far to the west. Only a few cities, such as Jerusalem, are located in the main highlands of a region.

Trade also has been one of the more important factors for the location of cities. Long-distance trade networks connected parts of the Middle East with each other and with outside regions at least since the beginning of cities. Early Mesopotamian settlements imported goods from Anatolia, Oman, India, and other areas. Sea routes were important, although overland trade connectons also were significant, especially after the increased use of camel caravans about 2000 years ago. Although coastal cities such as Carthage/Tunis and Alexandria were located on major sea trade routes, the great number of cities on major inland trading routes generally characterized the Middle East. Even Mecca, the birthplace of Islam and still its most important sacred city, is an inland city, despite being near the Red Sea. The settlement evolved several centuries before Islam because of its location on the caravan route for frankincense and myrrh from southern Arabia to the developed cities to the north (and because it was a pagan religious center for surrounding tribes).

The largest cities of the premodern Middle East developed not only because of trade, but also from political circumstances. The myriad dynasties and empires which form the long, complicated history of this region resulted in countless capitals and provincial centers. Considering only the Islamic period, such cities as Damascus, Baghdad, Cairo, Istanbul, Isfahan, and Tehran owe their great expansion before modern times to their role as capitals of major empires.

The settling of nomadic groups and rural migrants into cities influenced the growth of traditional settlements. Villagers tended to have ties to specific quarters of a city, which aided the migration process. Nomads had similar relations and often settled as a group, constituting a separate quarter. Nomads sometimes were forcibly settled by a ruler, while in other circumstances droughts, intertribal warfare, or other economic conditions caused the sedentarization.

One further important impetus for the location and growth of some cities in the Middle East is the importance of shrines and other religious buildings. This is an example where Islam has played a role in the development of urbanism, although religious shrines also were important in pre-Islamic cities. Mecca continued to be viable after it lost its pivotal role in the trade from southern Arabia because the pilgrimage to Mecca (the *hajj*) is required for all Moslems who can physically and financially survive the journey. Not only was money brought into the Holy City, supporting the town's businesses, but pilgrims from Morocco to Afghanistan (and farther east) settled permanently. With modern transportation the hajj has increased in scope considerably, although settling for non-Saudi Arabians is now very difficult.

Other cities that also are important pilgrimage centers are Jerusalem, which is sacred to Moslems, Jews, and Christians; and the important Shiite Moslem cities of Nagaf and Karbala in Iraq and Qum and Mashhad in Iran. Such Shiite cities (Moslems divide into two main sects: Shiites and Sunnites) are usually the location of the burial and shrine of one or more of the Shiite Twelve Imans, and most of these settlements owe their founding and initial growth to the shrines. Local saints are particularly prevalent in Sudan, Morocco, and other areas of North Africa and have contributed to the growth or even foundation of numerous cities in this region.

Within the last several centuries urbanization in the Middle East has been affected by many of the same factors which have influenced the growth of cities throughout the developing world. Except for most of North Africa, however, the European colonial impact was less in the Middle East than in many other parts of the world. The Ottoman Empire controlled most of Southwest Asia until World War I, while Iran remained independent under the Qajar and Pahlavi dynasties.

Although in North Africa the European economy began to dominate the area as early as the seventeenth century, not until the nineteenth and early twentieth centuries did the French conquer Algeria, Tunisia, and Morocco and did the British or Italians control Egypt, Sudan, and Libya. A new urban hierarchy developed under the colonial economy, one in which the port cities dominated. Europeans came in great numbers and soon constituted—and controlled—a substantial proportion of the population of these cities. Indigenous migrants flocked to these ports as interior towns declined and peasants were displaced by a changing economy (or by Europeans in the case of Algeria). Nomads added to the influx, especially since many had been pushed to marginal areas where their herds could not survive. Older cities such as Alexandria, Algiers, and Tunis and newer ones such as Casablanca and Suez grew considerably.

European colonial policies also affected the cities of Southwest Asia in the same period, although not nearly to the same degree. Indigenous handicrafts declined drastically as European goods undermined the local economies, and so the traditional structure of the cities was also somewhat altered. In some areas rural-to-urban migration increased because cash crops became more prevalent and left the peasantry more vulnerable to external, international market fluctuations. Some major changes in cities began after World War I, as concerted modernization programs began in Turkey and Iran and the British and French controlled many of the remnants of the Ottoman Empire. But it is the period after World War II in which the most dramatic changes occurred in the cities of the Middle East.

Within the last several decades rapid urbanization has taken place in the Middle East, and in many countries a great percentage, if not the majority, of the urban population reside in a few of the largest cities. A primate city dominates most of these countries. Many of the largest cities are national capitals, and the role of administration and centralization is most important in their development. A cumbersome, unwieldy bureaucracy has evolved, and the thousands of government officials produce a multiplier effect, providing jobs in the tertiary sector. Industrialization has concentrated in the same cities, with a similar effect.

Urbanization has greatly accelerated in many countries of the Middle East more recently for one principal reason—oil. The development of the petroleum industry itself has provided some employment, largely in terms of labor for construction and services. However, it is the vast sums of revenue from this resource which have provided the main impetus for what only can be called the fantastic city growth and development characteristic of Libya, Saudi Arabia, Iran, Iraq, Kuwait, the United Arab Emirates, Qatar, and Bahrain.

The vast oil revenues have provided the means to finance gigantic industrial schemes and even the construction of entire cities. For instance, in Saudi Arabia the new city of Jabail is being constructed to house 175,000 persons as part of a new industrial node on the Persian Gulf, while a $1 billion city with major military facilities and a planned population of 70,000 is being built in the northern part of the country near Kuwait. The revenues also are responsible for many of the large housing projects constructed in existing cities. The spectacular overnight growth of Kuwait City, Dubai, and Abu Dhabi are directly related to petroleum.

The rapid expansion of the economies of the petroleum-producing nations have caused acute labor shortages, and millions of foreign workers have migrated to fill the need, many from the capital-poor Arab states of Egypt, Yemen (North and South), and Jordan, but also from Pakistan, India, Korea, and other Asian countries. Although most of these aliens are considered temporary, in reality they are part of the urbanization of the Middle East and the problems of these cities. Indigenous inhabitants, including villagers and nomads, also have responded to the employment opportunities.

Of course, migrants contribute to the growth of all the major cities of the Middle East. Migration from the countryside continues due to population pressure in the rural areas, the mechanization of agriculture, and land-reform schemes. The establishment and expansion of Israel have added millions of displaced Arabs to the migrant pool. But it also should be remembered that with the improved medical and health conditions there have been a greater number of live births and better chances of survival for infants. With a longer life span the natural increase of the urban population in many instances has become as important as or even more significant for city growth than the increase by migration.

Major Representative Cities

Cairo: The Impoverished Metropolis

The metropolis of Greater Cairo reached a population of about 9 million by 1980. The city has been one of the most important centers of power and culture throughout much of the Islamic period, and even today the Egyptian capital serves as a symbolic focus of the Arab world, although tarnished by the Egyptian-Israeli accords.

Cairo began as the military encampment of Fustat, established on the Nile in A.D. 640 by an Arab army near the preexisting Christian town of Babylon-in-Egypt. Fustat grew into an important city, but in A.D. 969 a dissident branch of Moslems, the Shiite Fatimids, conquered Egypt and established a walled palace and city northeast of Fustat. It was named Al-Qahirah ("the victorious"), which in English has become known as Cairo. After the unwalled Fustat was destroyed in the twelfth century, Cairo became the principal settlement. By the fourteenth century Cairo was the capital of the Mamelukes and was a city of half a million.

Cairo was occupied by the Ottoman Turks in 1516, and even though the city served as a provincial capital for the Turks, it declined over the next several centuries to a population of only a quarter million. The city was then abruptly introduced to the modern era by Napoleon's occupation of Egypt in 1798. Although the occupation lasted only three years, the French destroyed or damaged large sections of Cairo. They straightened and enlarged a number of major streets and reorganized the city's administrative districts into eight large *arrondissements*. These administrative divisions have, with some boundary changes, remained for this part of the city until today, and the streets rebuilt by the French continue to be major thoroughfares.

After the French exodus, contacts with Europe were numerous, and the rule of Mohammed Ali in the first half of the nineteenth century encouraged the introduction of European goods and ideas into Egypt. Yet not until the last half of that century did major changes begin to occur in the morphology of Cairo. In 1867 the head of the Egyptian throne, Ismail, attended the Exposition Universelle in Paris. He was so impressed by the redeveloped Paris that he decided to duplicate the feat in Cairo within two years to celebrate the opening of the Suez Canal. He brought in French consultants and by 1869 new, extensive grid pattern streets and parks were built north and west of the old city, although the latter suburb, Ismailia, actually was occupied only slowly over the succeeding years.

Ismail's grand schemes helped drive Egypt into bankruptcy, and even though the country nominally was still a Turkish province, Great Britain controlled Egypt after 1882. With this protection the Europeans built a self-contained, modern city in Ismailia and expanded it westward to the Nile itself. A luxurious waterfront development soon followed, made possible by the control of floods by a dam at Aswan. The development expanded to one of the islands within the Nile (the Gezira) and, with the completion of several bridges, onto the west side of the great river. The new colonial appendage had wide, tree-lined avenues, complete with a sporting club, racetrack, opera, and other urban "necessities." By 1917 the population of Cairo was about 800,000, and although foreigners made up only 10 percent of this figure—a rather small percentage compared with that in some other North African cities—they nevertheless controlled the city. Physically and symbolically there was a great gulf between these European colonial suburbs and the traditional quarters of Cairo.

Following World War I, however, the foreign population quickly lost its preferential status, and as Egyptians flocked to Cairo for employment in the expanded economy of the city, the foreigners became less and less of a factor. With the gradual demise of foreign influence the residential areas which began to expand after World War I became quarters for lower- and middle-class Egyptians. Many of these developments filled in the areas between the traditional city and the European-style quarters to the west, but the expansion also included areas to the north, to the south, and even across the Nile on the western shore.

Cairo's rapid population growth was due principally to increased migration from Egypt's rural areas, although the rate of natural increase was beginning to rise as well. By 1927 Cairo had reached a population of 1 million. The growth then slowed somewhat, but beginning in World War II the rural-to-urban migration to the capital began in an unprecedented fashion. In 1947 the population exceeded 2 million, representing a per annum growth rate of almost 5 percent for the decade. But the city's boundaries had increased only slightly. The population growth was being absorbed within the existing urban area, leading to high population densities. The outlying or peripheral areas of the city doubled and tripled in population as vacant and agricultural land became urban residences.

By 1960 only a third of the population lived in the old city, while about a fourth were in the modern, Western-style city and the large remainder in the new, northern suburbs being built at the expense of the rich agricultural land of the Egyptian delta. A master plan for Cairo in the mid-1950s proposed to limit the capital's population to 3.5 million; this total had already been approached by 1960.

In 1967 the Israeli invasion of the Sinai forced evacuation of the Egyptian population from the canal zone cities of Suez, Port Said, and Ismailia. Hundreds of thousands of persons had to be absorbed by the capital, which was still growing rapidly. The decade of the 1970s has seen no abatement to the rapid growth—even though Ismailia and the other Suez Canal cities have now been repopulated and are themselves growing rapidly. The annual natural increase by itself has been at a rate of 3 percent a year, and rural-to-urban migration to Cairo has continued to contribute about as many persons each year.

The story of Cairo, especially in the twentieth century, is the continued expansion into the rich agricultural land of the Nile (Fig. 8.4); the extreme population numbers have severely overloaded the urban services and caused acute housing shortages. Somehow the city has continued to function, but each year the conditions get worse.

The incredible growth of Cairo has caused a severe shortage in housing, and this situation has been met with overcrowding of the existing residences, including some unusual responses. Much of the old city or *madina* can be described as an urban slum or, at best, lower class, with its extremely substandard housing and overcrowding (Fig. 8.5). The commercial or industrial focus of the capital has long left the old city, and it has become a backwater for those individuals without the means to move to other areas of the metropolis. New migrants often occupy the *madina* dwellings, as individuals are able to move to better residential areas. Cairo itself had a high density of about 65,000 persons per square mile (25,000 persons per square kilometer) in the mid-1970s. This density is greater than that of New York City even though few apartment complexes are over four or five stories in Cairo. In the *madina* and older working-class districts densities over 260,000 per square mile (100,000 per square kilometer) can be found. By 1972 the number of persons per room for the city was about 3.1, and this continued to increase throughout the 1970s. Yet, these figures do not really indicate the nature of the overcrowding. On the eastern edge of the old city are *tomb cities*, "cities of the dead." These cemeteries are composed of tombs for former royal families and the wealthy upper classes, as well as communal burial houses of certain craft or

Figure 8.4   Growth of Cairo, 970–1966. [*Source:* Salah El-Shakhs, "National Factors in the Development of Cairo," *Town Planning Review,* 42, No. 3 (1971) 237.]

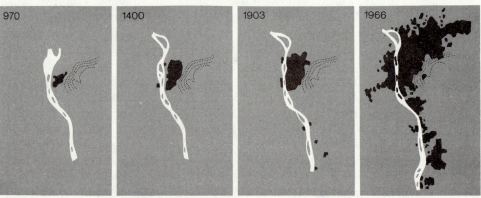

Figure 8.5 Housing in the *madina* of Cairo shows the influence of European architecture mixed with traditional features of the Middle Eastern city, such as the minarets of a mosque. The shabbiness and congestion characteristic of modern Cairo are also evident in this photo. (M. Bonine)

village migrant associations. The tombs are houses where the relatives of the deceased may come and visit, and caretakers always have stayed with some of the houses. Since World War II village migrants have swelled the population. Hundreds of thousands of people now live in this area, generally unserved by any municipal utilities.

Another way in which many lower-class and destitute Egyptians survive in Cairo is by living on rooftops. The city is a mass of apartment buildings, and an entire urban culture has developed in the poorer sections as the roof dwellers build shacks or huts on the buildings and even keep considerable numbers of animals. As long as the structures are not built of some permanent material, such as brick, they are not illegal and require no building permit. An estimated half a million persons are living on the rooftops of Cairo.

Other areas besides the *madina* have substandard housing and are overcrowded as well. The older industrial zones centered around the railroad and port districts on the east bank of the Nile actually have some of the worst living conditions in the city. The majority of the lower and lower middle classes, however, live in the northern sections of the metropolis, the area which has been expanding into rich agricultural land of the delta since World War I.

There are sections of Cairo for the upper classes and elites. The previous, Western-style city of the Europeans still houses some foreigners, although the Egyptian elite now predominate in these areas. Wealthy residences are also on the islands of Rawdah and the Gezirah and the adjacent west side of the Nile. The most expensive property is part of the east bank of the Nile where the Cairo Hilton, embassies, and exclusive apartment complexes are located. Other good neighborhoods can be found in the older community of Heliopolis to the northeast and near the pyramids to the southwest.

Premodern Cairo was a city in which the rich and poor were mixed together, although there were pockets of better or worse neighborhoods; but what has occurred in Cairo within the last hundred years has been a process of differentiation and economic segregation. As in the West, economic status and income have become the principles which influence the city's land use and the types of residential areas (Fig. 8.6). The wealthy elite have become much more segregated from the working class masses and the destitute. But the majority of the population certainly remains at the lower end of the economic scale in this impoverished metropolis.

Tehran: The Parvenu Capital

Two hundred years ago Tehran was a small village. Today it is the capital of Iran and the second largest city in the Middle East. Located just north of the ancient city of Ray, the city was established in the late 1780s as the capital of the new Qajar dynasty of Persia (the old name for Iran). A mud wall about 5 mi. (8 km.) in circumference was built to protect the nascent capital, and by 1800 Tehran already contained an estimated population of 50,000.

The selection of Tehran as the Qajar capital of Persia may seem perplexing in view of the fact that a number of well-established Iranian cities, such as Isfahan, Shiraz, Tabriz, and Mashhad, had been capitals of earlier dynasties and one of these cities might have been more logical as the capital in the eighteenth century. Tehran, however, was on a major east-west trade route as well as being at a major crossing of the Elburz Mountains to the north. Also important was the fact that the Qajars were Turkish nomads and the location of Tehran was reasonably close to their grazing and hunting grounds on the Gorgan Steppe to the northeast. And by founding Tehran they continued the ancient tradition of a dynasty establishing its own new capital.

In any case, as the capital of Persia the city soon manifested the magnetic properties created by administrative centralization and economic control. Although population estimates vary, by the end of the nineteenth-century Tehran certainly had over 100,000 inhabitants (some estimate as high as 200,000). Although there had been a few attempts at modernization in the last half of the nineteenth century and the city was greatly enlarged with a new city wall, it was well into the twentieth century before major changes began.

The Pahlavi dynasty (1925–1979) began under Reza Shah, and it was the economic and modernization programs of this monarch and his son (Mohammed Reza Shah) that were responsible for the great growth of Tehran. Reza Shah widened many of the streets of Tehran, and a grid network of broad avenues was established, although many of these followed an existing rectangular system. Streets followed a grid of water channels which came from underground *qanats* tapping the foothills of the Elburz

Major Representative Cities   295

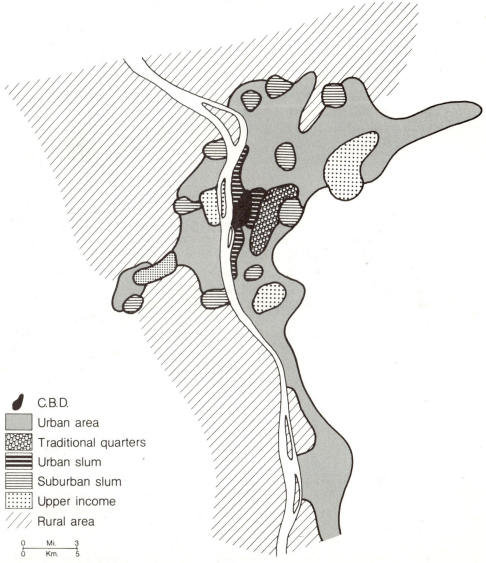

Figure 8.6 Residential Areas of Cairo. (*Sources:* Salah El-Shakhs, "National Factors in The Development of Cairo," Town Planning Review, 42:no. 3 (1971), 243, reprinted with permission, and Janet L. Abu-Lughod, *Cairo: 1001 Years of 'The City Victorious,'* copyright © 1971 by Princeton University Press.)

Mountains). The street construction occurred principally in the 1930s, and all of Iran's major cities were subjected to rudimentary planning, with broad avenues being a primary concern. Much construction of public buildings and housing occurred in the capital at this time, and numerous brickworks and other building industries were established in southern Tehran to provide the materials. Tehran also began to be linked more solidly with the rest of the country as better roads were established and railroads built. These ties resulted in the beginning of the dominance of the capital and the emergence of a primate city.

The Iranian capital had about 300,000 inhabitants by 1930, but with the impetus of Reza Shah's modernization programs the city grew to half a million by the end of that decade. Tehran began to mushroom after World War II, as increasing oil revenues promoted more projects and development; the population was almost 1 million by 1950, 1.5 million (the first census) by 1956, and 2.7 million (the second census) by 1966. By 1980 this primate city had a population of nearly 6 million and truly dominated the country demographically and economically. No other Iranian city has even a sixth of Tehran's population.

Tehran's total population makes up over a quarter of Iran's official urban population, and one out of every seven Iranians lives in Tehran. The great growth of Tehran is partly because Iran under the Pahlavis was a very centralized state, with most decision making in the capital. Although the myriad ministries had offices in the provinces as well as in the capital, the officials in Tehran made all the important decisions, even ones concerned basically with local affairs.

Tehran's growth also is related to its great industrial development. Although not located necessarily advantageously for transport, water, raw materials, or consumers, factors of agglomeration and the importance of being the locus of the central government have created an inertia for economic development which has fueled the expansion of the capital. The economic dominance of Tehran can be appreciated by knowing that approximately 30 percent of Iran's labor force in industry and services, one-third of all productive investments, and 60 percent of value-added for industry are found in the Tehran region. Although the Pahlavi government tried to prohibit new industry from being established in Tehran by offering tax incentives and other measures to locate in the provinces, the attraction and advantages for locating in the capital continued to bring industry into the region.

The population of Tehran has swelled in the last few decades because migrants have come into the metropolis for employment. Most of the unskilled migrants from villages and towns become part of the underemployed economy of the capital, most being in the large tertiary sector. Some migrants to Tehran are only temporary or semipermanent. Villagers often come to work in Tehran during the slack seasons of agriculture; others work several years before returning permanently to their settlement. Many migrants of a village, provincial town, or even region specialize in a particular occupation, and it is this job they follow in Tehran.

Also, the fact that relatives or friends are already employed in Tehran helps a migrant to obtain a particular job in the capital. A common pattern in the crafts or retail establishments is for a young boy (after finishing primary school) to travel to Tehran to be an apprentice or helper for a relative. A boy may work 5 or 10 years until he then opens up a shop himself, either in Tehran or back home in his town or village. Those individuals who remain in Tehran often still return for a wife and get married in their settlement of origin, taking their new wife back to the capital.

In nineteenth-century Tehran the elite had summer residences in Shemiran, about 6.2 mi. (10 km.) north of the city, where the higher slopes are much cooler in the hot summer. The twentieth-century areal expansion of middle- and upper-class neighborhoods has been mainly northward, so that Tehran now has reached Shemiran (Fig. 8.7). With the construction of better avenues and the use of automobiles the elite's homes are now permanently in the north. In fact, there is basically a social gradient in the capital comparable to the topography, from the most wealthy in the extreme north to the masses of poor in south Tehran. Water flows in the same direction, and so the open channels *(jubs)* on the sides of the avenues wash much garbage down to the south. The modern, Westernized city of Tehran is north of the old city, creating a bipolar character to this large metropolis. The main bazaar, located in south Tehran, is one of the few areas in which the inhabitants of the north might venture into the south. At least before the revolution of 1978–1979, a large segment of the working population of south Tehran was employed in the northern areas of the city, which daily reinforced their awareness of the two worlds.

South Tehran does not represent mass poverty, however. Even though there are

Figure 8.7 Growth of Tehran, 1868–1971. [*Source:* Adapted from Martin Seger, "Strukturelemente der Stadt Teheran und das Modell der Modernen Orientalishen Stadt," *Erdkunde,* 29, No. 1 (1975), 23.]

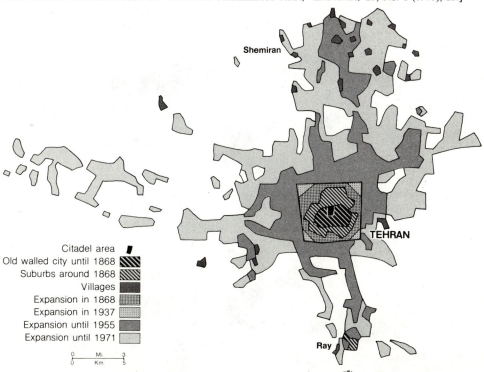

housing shortages and overcrowding, the inhabitants generally are not in as bad a situation as those in many of the poorer sections of such major Middle Eastern metropolises as Cairo, Baghdad, or Istanbul. Also, this huge city has expanded rapidly without extensive shantytowns being formed, and without the dire results found in Cairo. In 1972, for instance, it was estimated that only 4000 squatter families were in the capital. Most inhabitants have managed to find rather permanent shelter, although this often is at a cost. Many working men spend over half their income for housing, and the price of houses has led to extensive sharing by relatives of residences (and the expense), and even the renting of rooms to nonrelatives.

Most of the new housing construction in Tehran has been for large apartment complexes (Fig. 8.8), and many of these were for wealthier groups. Some housing projects have been for one single profession, such as employees of a specific ministry, teachers, or doctors, although there was a reaction against this practice and later projects had a greater mixture of socioeconomic and income groups. New towns also have been built in suburban areas in an attempt to take population pressure off the main areas of the capital.

The great expansion of the Iranian economy in the 1970s due to the increases in oil revenue (before the Islamic Republic) had especially affected housing in the capital. In fact, the cost of housing had been one of the primary ingredients of rampant inflation. Land prices and speculation have added to the cost of housing. In the mid-1970s urban land prices rose so swiftly that prices could be quoted only daily. Land

Figure 8.8 Modern apartment buildings in Tehran are typical of the efforts by many Middle Eastern governments to rehouse urban dwellers living in congested and decaying sections of the old central cities. (M. Bonine)

in south Tehran was selling for about $500 per square yard ($600 per square meter), while to the north in Shemiran, land was over $3340 per square yard ($4000 per square meter). Lots for an average-sized house in the north of Tehran were selling for several hundred thousand dollars, and houses were going for millions. Needless to say, only the wealthy could buy such land, but this upper strata has increased considerably as more and more Iranians reaped the fruits of the oil wealth. But, of course, the vast majority were left to struggle in the face of rising prices, and the widening gulf between them and the wealthy in a capital became more and more unmanageable.

Since the establishment of the Islamic Republic in 1979 Tehran has continued to have difficulties. Although there is truly a new political regime, the economic problems of the country are especially being felt in the capital. There had been an enormous influx of villagers into the city by 1982, partly due to free water and electricity provided in south Tehran by the new regime. The once elegant, Western-style shops on Ferdowsi Avenue were beginning to look like the drab shops of Eastern Europe. Peddlers and hawkers proliferated on the major avenues. Although the prices of apartments and houses dropped, traffic congestion remained as bad as ever and rapid inflation continued, coupled with acute shortages of many foods and consumer products. The fate of Tehran, and Iran, depends upon the stability of the government and the ability of the Islamic Republic of Iran to reestablish the economic foundations of the country.

Baghdad: Primate City on the Tigris

On the shores of the Tigris River is located one of the most renowned cities of the Middle East, the city of the legendary adventures of *The Thousand and One Nights.* Baghdad was founded in A.D. 762 as a planned city by the Moslem caliph al-Mansur as the capital of the newly established Abbassid dynasty. The city took four years to build and used over 100,000 laborers and craftsmen conscripted from throughout the empire. The city was round with double brick walls, a deep moat, and wide avenues radiating from the center. Yet even before the round city was completed there were surrounding suburbs with residences, markets, mosques, and other features of urban life.

Although the glory of Baghdad was in its first several centuries, it remained the capital of the Abbassids until it was partially destroyed by the Mongols in the thirteenth century. Baghdad remained a major city of Iraq and was a provincial capital for the Ottoman Empire. The city was continually plagued by floods from the Tigris, which limited the areal expansion. Until the mid-nineteenth century Baghdad consisted primarily of an east-bank city known as Rusafah and a smaller city on the west bank called Carkh. Also, several kilometers to the north of the latter was Kazimiyah, a Shiite Moslem settlement where two of the 12 Imams of this sect are buried and which was thus a major locus for pilgrimages. The population of mid-nineteenth-century Baghdad was about 60,000, but by the beginning of this century this had doubled.

In the twentieth century Baghdad began to grow into a major metropolis. Much of the physical expansion of the city has been due to the establishment of effective flood control measures. In the 1920s a major dike or bund was built under the direction of the British on the eastern side of the Tigris, and the city expanded longitudinally along this side of the river. New residential areas were constructed based upon the Western grid street patterns. One area, south of the *madina* of Rusafah, was at first inhabited mainly by the British and other Westerners, although soon wealthy native Christians and Jews began to move out of the old city to these new residences. Wealthy Sunnite Moslems moved to new residences north of the old city where the king had built a compound and where many high government officials also had moved.

The population of Baghdad was about half a million in 1947, and this doubled to 1 million by 1957. A major stimulus for the growth of Iraq's capital occurred in the 1950s: revenues from the rapidly developing petroleum industry. Many industries were begun in the city and numerous urban projects implemented. In 1956 the Wadi Tharthar flood diversion project was completed, a large diversion barrage on the Tigris River at Sammara, 68 mi. (110 km.) to the north. This provided complete flood protection for Baghdad. The Eastern Bund built in the 1920s became obsolete, so urban sprawl spread beyond it to the east.

With the oil funds came paved streets, sewage systems, and street lights, not only for the capital but in Iraq's other major cities as well. A master plan of Baghdad was begun in 1956. However, without any specific details or controls for implementing the plan, little was done, and one of the main effects was a wave of land speculation that raised the cost of land and housing. Another master plan was prepared in 1958 which had Baghdad's development focused on four major commercial-industrial zones, each surrounded by residential communities. Although some low-cost housing was eventually built on the western side of the Tigris, the 1958 revolution generally thwarted the implementation of the new master plan.

The confiscation and nationalization of the royal family's land and private estates in 1958 allowed large tracts of land around Baghdad to be developed for residences and industry (Fig. 8.9). Many residential areas became based on modern occupations or classes, replacing the kinship- or religious- based quarters which traditionally had formed the city. One scheme, professional housing cooperatives, created individual, integrated neighborhoods or "cities," named after the type of profession: Doctors' City, Engineers' City, and so forth. The homogeneity of these neighborhoods is much greater than any found in the West, although the uniformity does become diluted over time due to the selling and renting of residential units by the original owners.

Baghdad's growth has resulted partly from the great influx of rural migrants. Many have come to find employment, although large numbers also have left the countryside principally because of extremely depressed conditions. Before the 1958 revolution an oppressive land tenure system had enabled tribal sheiks to register land in their own name, and peasants were left without land. Especially in the south, in combination with floods and droughts, Iraqi peasants left the land in tens of thousands and flocked to the capital in an attempt to survive. Even after 1958 the exodus continued because the promises of land reform became enmeshed in a bureaucratic labyrinth.

The majority of the rural migrants to Baghdad settled in shantytowns, in houses made of mud, tin cans, or reeds. Called *sarifahs,* by the mid-1950s these dwellings accounted for almost half the total number of housing units in Baghdad. With the completion of the Wadi Tharthar flood diversion project in 1956, the shantytowns spread out

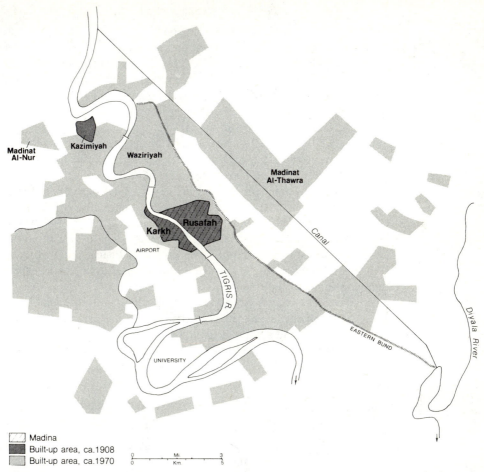

Figure 8.9 Growth of Baghdad, 1908–1970. [*Sources:* John Gulick, "Baghdad: Portrait of a City in Physical and Cultural Change," *Journal of the American Institute of Planners,* 33, No. 4 (1967), 247; and William C. Fox, "Baghdad, A City in Transition," *The East Lakes Geographer,* 5 (1969), 6.] Reprinted with permission.

eastward beyond the formerly protective bund. Usually there were no potable water, electricity, or sanitation facilities in these settlements. Health conditions were quite bad and various diseases common.

After the 1958 revolution the shantytown problem was at least officially recognized by the government and some education and health services were provided. In 1963, however, due to a change in the government and the communist sympathies of the squatters, most of the shantytowns were torn down. More than 65,000 *sarifahs* were eradicated, and a new city was established on the east bank of the Tigris for the squatters, called Madinat Al-Thawra ("revolution city"). Another project, Madinat Al-Nur ("city of light"), was built later on the west bank. It is questionable whether the government-built housing at Al-Thawra was any improvement over the *sarifahs*. Composed of row upon row of small, overcrowded concrete and brick homes, the designs did not provide air and sunlight, which at least had been available in their old structures. Also, services such as piped water, sewers, or paved streets were not provided (for example, one outside water faucet served many houses). In the second project on the west bank the government was somewhat wiser and the inhabitants were provided with materials and advice, but were allowed to build their houses more or less as they wanted as long as the structures met certain standards.

In the 1970s and 1980s urban sprawl has become a major problem, and despite attempts by the municipality to limit growth to within 9.3 mi (15 km.) of the city center, these limits have already been exceeded. Part of the reason for the continued expansion is that a large percentage of the land in the city is still owned by the government or is religious *waqf*. The latter property is leased for a period of 30 years to an individual, but the user has no control over what kind of improvements or alterations, if any, can be made. The government-owned land, also, often is only leased to individuals and so there are few incentives to improve the property. Instead of locating on the *waqf* or government land within the city, settlers choose the outlying areas, which offer greater economic incentives and opportunities.

The rapid growth of Baghdad since World War II has enabled the metropolis to become one of the largest cities in the Middle East and the primate city of Iraq. In 1980 the capital had a population of 4.5 million, which constituted over one-fourth of the entire population of the country. Although some Iraqi cities have been expanding even faster recently (Basra is approaching a population of 1 million), the primacy of Baghdad on the Tigris will continue to dominate this developing country.

Kuwait City: The Oil Urbanization

At the beginning of the twentieth century Kuwait City was a small fishing town of 35,000 at the head of the Persian Gulf. Today, the modern metropolis has a population of over 1 million. This growth represents one of the most spectacular examples of the effects of vast oil revenues—a city modernizing overnight.

Kuwait's population had only doubled by World War II, but with oil exports commencing after the war the city grew quickly. By the first census of 1957 the nation's population was over 200,000, and this reached 1.3 million by 1980, representing an incredible 9.1 percent per annum increase. The vast majority of the inhabitants of this small nation live in the conurbation of Kuwait City, with only a few smaller cities to the south around the main oil operations and industrial facilities.

Kuwait has grown because of the great numbers of foreigners who have flocked for employment to the rich country. In fact, by the early 1960s the alien population became larger than the native Kuwaitis, a dominance they have maintained until today. The foreigners live and work in the urban areas because most services, construction, hotels, restaurants and light industry are located here. Arabs constitute about 80 percent of the foreign population, about half of these being Palestinians and Jordanians; while the 20 percent non-Arabs are mainly Iranians, Indians, and Pakistanis. Aliens constitute over 70 percent of the economically active persons, including as much as 90 percent of the workers in manufacturing and 95 percent in construction.

The physical expansion of Kuwait City has been largely directed by a master plan drawn up by a British city planning firm in 1952 (Fig. 8.10). A series of four concentric ring roads were built around the *madina* (old Kuwait City), including a green belt around the old wall. Roads radiated out from the *madina,* crossing the ring roads at right angles. Within the zones created by these crossing roads, the government built major residential superblocks. Each block included services such as mosques, schools, and shops for local necessities. These blocks were reserved only for Kuwaitis, and the aliens had to settle in the nearby suburbs and in outlying areas. The *madina* was partly leveled and was developed as a new CBD for the whole metropolis. Industrial zones were planned along the coast to the west of the city. In the 1960s two more ring roads were added, despite advice from consultants that development should be concentrated and contained within the older fourth ring road.

The implementation of the 1952 master plan included acquisition of land within the *madina* by the government. The land owners were offered inflated prices, not only to induce the Kuwaitis to move to the new superblocks, but also to provide capital for investment in the private sector. The scheme provided large blocks of government land which were used to transform the *madina* to a new business center. Land prices rose over 30-fold, and housing costs increased over 15 times as a result of the program and the inflation fueled by the oil revenues. Within the superblocks the government sold plots by lottery below market values to Kuwaiti citizens who had lost property through the government purchasing or expropriation in the *madina,* as well as to government employees and to Kuwaitis of low or no income. Interest-free loans also were provided to the Kuwaitis to help finance the construction of houses.

Although many of the traditional houses in the *madina* were destroyed, about 4000 remained in the early 1970s. These are largely rented to foreign immigrants by the Kuwaiti owners at rather extreme rates. Hence, many aliens occupy a single house

Figure 8.10 Kuwait City Development Plan, 1952. (*Source:* Adapted from Colin Buchanan and Partners, *Kuwait: Studies for National Physical Plan and Master Plan for Urban Areas,* London: Colin Buchanan and Partners, 1970.)

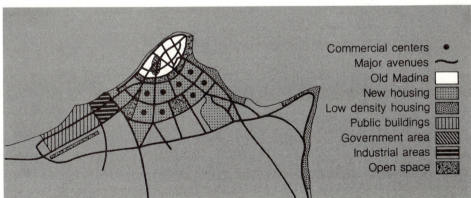

to split the rent. Most of the remaining housing in the *madina,* however, still occupies prime land for redevelopment and continues to be purchased and demolished by the government.

Despite the oil revenues and the housing programs the extreme growth of Kuwait City has created housing shortages. To the embarrassment of the government shantytowns have developed around the city (Fig. 8.11). It is not, however, the foreign workers who mainly occupy such dwellings, but Bedouin Arabs. These settled nomadic Bedouin come not only from Kuwait but also from the surrounding desert areas of Saudi Arabia and Iraq (but being Bedouin Arabs they are classified as Kuwaitis by the government). The shantytowns are built illegally on government or private land and hence are squatter settlements. But since space is not a problem in the desert, the shanty dwellings are built considerable distances from one another, in effect replicating the spatial arrangements of Bedouin tents. Hence, the shantytowns are much less dense than the rest of the urban areas, a pattern rarely found among squatter settlements elsewhere in the developing world.

The city that has developed since World War II is a modern metropolis which has little resemblance to any traditional Middle Eastern *madina.* It is a city which has

Figure 8.11 Kuwait City with Surrounding Squatter Settlements, 1970. [*Sources:* Adapted from Fred Scholz, Sesshaftwerdung von Beduinen in Kuwait," *Erdkunde,* 29 (1975), 229; and Colin Buchanan and Partners, *Kuwait: Studies for National Physical Plan and Master Plan for Urban Areas,* London: Colin Buchanan and Partners, 1970.] Reprinted with permission.

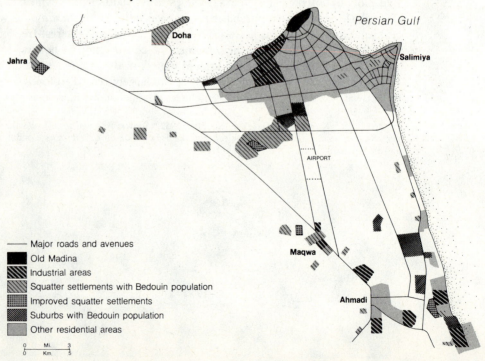

been designed for the automobile and in which that vehicle dominates. Extremely wide avenues and numerous roundabouts attempt to accommodate the great number of cars, which reached several hundred thousand by the early 1980s. The new residences tend to be outward-looking and detached, instead of the compact, inward traditional house centered around a courtyard. Elaborately landscaped parks and grounds are dispersed about the neighborhoods, quite a feat in this extremely arid desert environment.

Yet it is the rapidity of urban development which is so remarkable about Kuwait City. Even though there are problems such as housing shortages, traffic jams (despite the size of the avenues), inadequate parking, and an alien majority, the transformation nevertheless is most spectacular. The contrast with Cairo is striking. Kuwait is an affluent society, and the problem has been how to preserve an Arab/Middle Eastern society in the face of such drastic change. In the haste to modernize on the Western model the indigenous culture and urban heritage have been ignored.

Istanbul: Migrant Cosmopolis on the Bosporus

Europe and Asia, the West and the East, meet at the Sea of Marmara and two narrow straits, the Dardanelles and Bosporus, which also connect the Mediterranean Sea with the Black Sea and Russia. Where the Bosporus enters the Sea of Marmara, an inlet to the West, the Golden Horn, creates a promontory (Fig. 8.12). This inlet was a magnificent natural harbor for premodern shipping. On this strategic peninsula arose Constantinople, the capital of the Byzantine Empire, which continued as Istanbul, the capital of the Ottoman Empire.

Founded by Greeks in the first millennium B.C., the city of Byzantium became an important metropolis even before Constantine renamed the city in A.D. 330. He named it New Rome, but the city became known as Constantinople. When Rome fell in A.D. 476, Constantinople became the sole capital of the Roman Empire; by the sixth century, the golden age of Justinian, this capital and the Byzantine civilization flourished. The western part of the city had been protected by a large wall built by Constantine, but due to the growth of the city, Theodosius in the fifth century built another wall about 0.6 mi (1 km.) to the west. Although there was some later urban development in Galata across the Golden Horn (by Venetians and Genoese), until the twentieth century the population of Istanbul essentially remained on the promontory within the city wall of Theodosius.

Although Anatolia was not conquered during the initial Moslem expansion, Arab armies did reach the walls of Constantinople several times. In fact the Byzantine Empire lasted for many more centuries; there even was a second golden age in the ninth and tenth centuries, and the population of the capital reached about 400,000. However, the empire and the city then began a decline. The capital was even pillaged and sacked in the twelfth century during some of the crusades (by Christians!). The Byzantine Empire shrank as the number of Turks increased and the Ottomans gained ascendancy. By the fifteenth century the Byzantine Empire was reduced essentially to Constantinople itself. The city population, unable to recover from the effects of the crusades and the plague in the fourteenth century, had been reduced to less

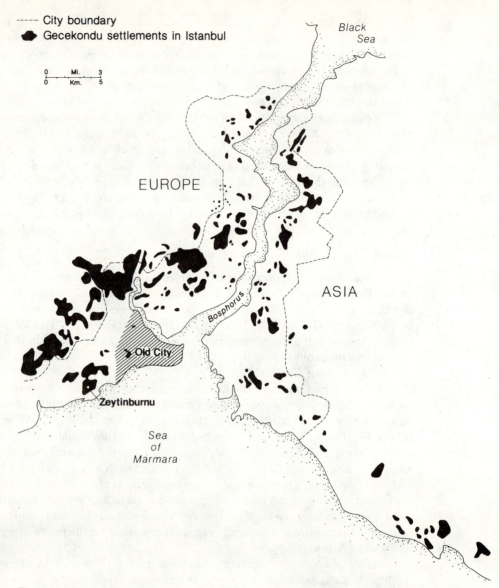

Figure 8.12 Istanbul: *Gecekondu* Settlements, ca. 1970. (*Source:* Adapted from Kemal H. Kapat, *The Gecekondu: Rural Migration and Urbanization,* London: Cambridge University Press, 1976, p. 67.)

than 100,000. In 1453 the atrophied city was taken by Fatih Sultan Mehmet II (Mohammed the Conqueror).

The Ottomans called their new capital Istanbul (perhaps from the ancient Greek *eis tēn polin,* meaning "to the city"). The conquest resulted in sudden, drastic changes in the demography of the city. Most of the Greek and other ethnic (and religious) groups either had fled or were captured and taken to Ottoman camps outside the city walls. One of the principal tasks of Mehmet, then, was to repopulate the city, with the goal of recapturing the glory of the city of earlier centuries. Some prisoners were allowed to resettle, and fugitives were encouraged to return. Christians and Jews were given certain privileges and rights in the city.

Yet the Ottoman Sultan wanted an Islamic, Turkish capital. Great numbers of Moslems from various parts of the empire, especially Anatolia, were forced to resettle in Istanbul. Mosques, religious schools, and other Moslem institutions also had to be established. The easiest way was to convert Christian religious buildings, and so many such changes took place—exemplified by the conversion of the magnificent basilica of St. Sophia into the Great Mosque of Istanbul. Much property in the capital was turned into religious endowments, *waqf* (Turkish: *vakif*), to support the Islamic institutions. The marketplaces were changed into the more typically Moslem city bazaars *(bedestan)*. The fundamental principle was to transform the Ottoman capital into an Islamic city which fulfilled the needs of its Moslem inhabitants—to turn Istanbul into a sacred city of Islam.

The Ottoman capital grew quickly. By the early sixteenth century, the population had reached 250,000; by the middle of that century, 500,000; by the end of the same century, 700,000–800,000 (including suburbs). The size of the Byzantine capital in its prime had been exceeded. Yet much of the population growth took place within the city walls, filling in and creating greater densities in the 6.64 sq. mi. (17.2 sq. km.) within those walls. The majority of the population was now Moslem, although substantial minorities still constituted parts of Istanbul. The city was organized into several hundred wards or neighborhoods. Each quarter was an organic community, settled around a mosque, church, or synagogue; groups of immigrants usually settled together in one neighborhood. By the late sixteenth century over 200 Moslem and 50 to 75 non-Moslem quarters were within the walls.

The influx of migrants into Istanbul was a pattern that had been prevalent even for the Byzantine city, and is a pattern that continues to the present day. The migration in the sixteenth century, unlike the forced resettlements of the previous century, was mainly for economic reasons. Many merchants and craftsmen immigrated from the major cities of the Ottoman Empire, especially from such centers as Konya, Bursa, Aleppo, Damascus, and Cairo. But peasants (and their families) also came to the capital, especially from the poorer agricultural regions, such as central and eastern Anatolia, and Albania. Many fled agricultural areas to escape onerous taxes and levies. They performed most of the less desirable jobs, as porters, bath attendants, peddlers, laborers, etc. Many of these peasants built houses for themselves in the outlying areas of Istanbul. In fact, shantytowns developed, a phenomenon that was to become a major feature of the cityscape in the second half of the twentieth century.

Istanbul declined with the decline of the Ottoman Empire during the eighteenth and nineteenth centuries. A census in 1885 recorded a population of 873,565 in Istanbul and its suburbs. However, following World War I, the city had to endure the end of the Ottoman Empire, extensive population transfers, and the establishment of Ankara as the capital of the new Republic of Turkey. In 1927 a population of 694,292 was recorded for the metropolitan region of Istanbul.

Modern Istanbul has few scars from its loss as a capital. Its economic importance has given it a new impetus for growth. With a heavy concentration of industry and trade, the metropolitan area represents a preponderant percentage of Turkish employees in industry and for value-added manufacturing. Istanbul contains over half of several categories of Turkey's industry, including metals, garments, printing, and leather processing.

Istanbul had reached a population of 1 million by 1950; economic development led the metropolitan area to grow by another half million by 1960. But the total has increased dramatically in the last two decades. The official city limits of Istanbul contain about 4 million inhabitants; the functional metropolitan region, a total of 4.5 to 5 million. The old city within the walls of Theodosius contains only about 500,000. The metropolitan region has expanded south along the Sea of Marmara; north across the Golden Horn and up the Bosporus; and across on the Asian side, both up the Bosporus and south along the Sea of Marmara. Although two bridges have crossed the Golden Horn for a considerable time (the first was built in the nineteenth century), only ferry service connected Europe and Asia until a bridge was completed across the Bosporus in the mid-1970s. This bridge has already paid for itself, and its success has led to plans for a second bridge. Commercial property and land values have increased considerably on the Asian side near the bridge. With easier access to the industrialized western side, residents can now live on the Asian side and work on the European side.

The recent spectacular population growth of Istanbul has resulted principally from migration. In 1965, for instance, half of the population had been born outside of the province. Since World War II these newcomers have been mainly Turkish peasants. The migrants have transformed the urban environment of Istanbul (and other Turkish cities) by the establishment of extensive shantytowns *(gecekondus)*. These "urban villagers" have imparted many of the values and ideals of the Anatolian countryside to the city, in effect "ruralizing" much of Istanbul.

Gecekondu houses usually are built overnight (*gecekondu* literally means "built in the night"), so that inhabitants can benefit from the governmental provision of prohibiting destruction of inhabited homes without due process. The initial one-room *gecekondu* often is constructed of makeshift materials. Especially over the last several decades many dealers of *gecekondu* building materials have emerged—there are even *gecekondu* builders who can be contacted to build the house (in one night!).

In 1974 there were approximately 700,000 *gecekondu* dwellings in the entire country, with an estimated 3.4 to 4.5 million inhabitants (9 to 12 percent of the total population). Yet these shanty dwellings constitute over half of the housing units in Istanbul; the total population in these shantytowns forms an even greater percentage of the inhabitants of the metropolitan area. The establishment of *gecekondus* has been responsible for much of the expansion of the city, spreading on both sides of the Bosporus and the Sea of Marmara.

Israeli New Towns: Central Places and Garden Cities

Except for several of the Persian Gulf sheikdoms, Israel is the most urbanized country in the Middle East. The 1980 population of 3.8 million was 85 percent urban. Before the advent of Zionist ideals in the late nineteenth century, most Palestinian Jews also were urbanites, living principally in the towns of Jerusalem, Safed, and Tiberias. Yet in the last quarter of that century a series of small-holder agricultural settlements, *moshavot,* began to be established. And throughout the first half of the twentieth century Zionism promoted agricultural colonization in Palestine, advocating a rural, socialist-pioneering spirit as the basis for a new Jewish society. Numerous *kibbutzim* (collective farms) and *moshavim* (cooperative farms) were established with these principles. Cities were ignored; there was even a hostility toward the urban environment.

One major Jewish urban settlement was established in 1909, before Zionist ideology turned more and more to favor only agricultural settlements. Founded as a Jewish quarter or suburb of the Arab coastal town of Jaffa, the city of Ahuzat Bait later was called Tel Aviv ("hill of spring"). Financial support came from the Jewish National Fund and a number of international Jewish organizations, and Tel Aviv was the only urban settlement to receive substantial Zionist funds until after the establishment of the state of Israel.

Despite the official Zionist neglect of the cities, the urban areas in Palestine continued to grow throughout the British mandate period (from World War I to 1948). A great number of immigrants came, especially from Germany beginning in the 1930s. Coming from cities, these Jews had no desire to settle in remote agricultural settlements. But urban growth evolved in a haphazard manner. There was no direction or planning for cities, because cities still did not have a place in Zionist ideology.

The metropolitan area of Tel Aviv especially began to expand and, secondarily, the large cities of Haifa and Jerusalem. A number of cities also evolved from *moshavot* during the mandate period. Unlike the ideological members of *kibbutzim* or *moshavim,* with their antipathy for urban life, the members of the *moshavot* did not attempt to preserve the agricultural characteristics of their settlements, since some in fact were semiurban settlements from the beginning. A number of *moshavot* were near large cities, as in the vicinity of Tel Aviv, and these settlements were soon incorporated into the expanding metropolitan areas. Other *moshavot* evolved into some of the major middle-size cities of the new state of Israel.

When Israel was established in 1948, the population was overwhelmingly urban (73 percent) in spite of the earlier Zionist ideology and efforts in agricultural colonization. Three-fourths of the urban population lived in the three cities of Tel Aviv, Haifa, and Jerusalem. Six small cities, with populations ranging from 10,000 to 22,000, were situated near or on the Mediterranean coast; but in the interior, besides Jerusalem, there were only three small towns, with 2,000 to 5,000 inhabitants each.

One of the first problems tackled by the new state was this uneven population distribution, as well as the vast number of immigrants who had flooded the nation after its establishment and needed housing. Planning goals included settling sparsely populated regions, settling frontier regions for defense and resource development, and limiting the growth of the large cities and the great number of settlements on the coast. It was realized that existing cities would continue to grow, but that the ideological *kibbutzim* and *moshavim* still could not be developed into larger urban centers.

The Israeli solution for these goals was to establish an entire system of new towns, including complete hierarchies of settlements. Central place theory was specifically used as the model (see Chapter 1), and a five-tiered hierarchy was proposed (Table 8.1). Some A- and E-level settlements already existed in some numbers; a few B centers were present; but C and D centers were found only on the coast between Tel Aviv and Haifa. Hence the new towns were to be primarily for the C and D levels. In the central place functional hierarchy the rural B centers were to be the economic, social, and cultural centers for 4 to 6 villages, *kibbutzim,* or *moshavim.* The C rural-urban centers were designed to serve about 30 villages, while the D medium-size towns were to serve as regional centers.

Approximately 30 new towns (also called development towns) were founded, most of them in the 1950s. There is no agreement on the exact number founded, due to differences in definitions of a new town. Although central place theory was the theoretical locational model for all the various regional systems, only in the Lakhish region in south-central Israel were the principles actually applied rather rigorously (Fig. 8.13). Qiryat Gat is the Lakhish regional D center, serving six subregional systems, each having four to six villages (A centers). Rural B centers were to serve each of these smaller systems, although as of 1975 only two of the rural B centers had been built. The C centers are missing entirely from the Lakhish hierarchy.

The new towns of Israel were established as "garden cities," based upon the planning principles for new towns which had originated in England at the end of the nineteenth century. Such cities also fit better into the older Zionist rural ideology, which still had a legacy, even if it was not that relevant for most Israelis. A factor also for this adoption was that most of the Israeli planners came from Europe, where the garden city concept had been a viable idea.

The Israeli town planners had an advantage over their European counterparts, for in most cases there was unlimited land for the development of their new towns. Most land in Israel was public land (including some "relinquished Arab property under trusteeship"). The earliest new towns were designed around a series of nearly self-sufficient neighborhoods. Each neighborhood had its own shopping center, schools, banks, post office, and clinic. Housing densities were low; one- or two-family homes each had 1000 to 2000 sq. yd. (832 to 1670 sq. m.) of ground. The neighborhoods were endowed with open spaces, to be planted with trees and shrubs, and to be separated from one another by green strips.

TABLE 8.1 PROPOSED MODEL OF ISRAELI CENTRAL PLACES

Level	Planned Population
A Center: village, kibbutz, or *moshav*	500
B Center: rural center	2,000
C Center: rural-urban center	6,000 to 12,000
D Center: medium-size town	40,000 to 60,000
E Center: large city	100,000 or more

Source: Adapted from Erika Spiegel, *New Towns in Israel,* New York: Praeger, 1967, p. 19.

Major Representative Cities   311

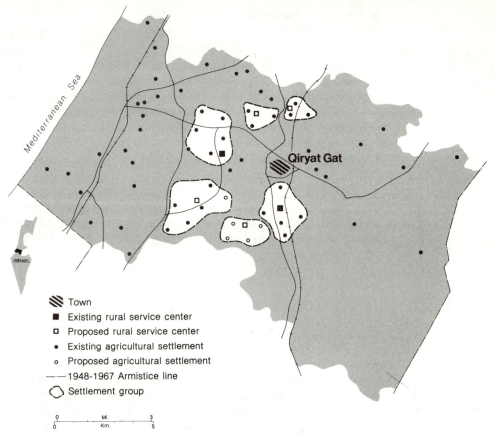

Figure 8.13   The Lakhish Regional Plan, Israel, 1964. (*Source:* Jacob Dash and Elisha Efrat, *The Israel Physical Master Plan,* Jerusalem: Planning Department, Ministry of the Interior, 1964.)

The Israeli garden cities did not function as planned. Unlike in humid Europe, water was too scarce in Israel for stretches of green, trees, shrubs, and gardens. The generous open spaces and broad avenues may have provided needed fresh air in England, but heat, glare, dust, and barren land were the result in this desert environment. The semiautonomous neighborhoods also were a failure. The population of the neighborhoods was too small to support the shops and services located there; the inhabitants preferred shopping in a central downtown area. Even by 1955 the various problems began to be realized, and newly constructed towns or additions to the older ones were built with different designs. Open space was decreased, the density of housing increased. Row houses and blocks of two- and three-story apartment buildings were constructed. The original densities of 4 to 12 dwellings per acre were increased to 60 or more dwellings per acre by the early 1960s.

The new towns provided housing and employment for some of the hundreds of thousands of immigrants who converged on Israel in the first decades of its existence.

The immigrants in these towns were largely Oriental Jews from other countries of the Middle East and North Africa. But also present was a small, core group of native Israelis, called *vatikim*. They were the local elite, holding such positions as administrators, teachers, and doctors, and they were to serve as model citizens to help integrate the immigrants into Israeli society. Only a few European Jews came to the new towns; they preferred to live in the larger cities, where the culture is more European. They also did not like the "newcomer" status attached to everyone by the *vatikim*.

The social structure in the new towns developed into a three-level hierarchy: the *vatikim* elite, the European Jews, and the Oriental Jews. The latter are the vast majority in these towns, but they are stereotyped as "primitive," or "black," and generally are excluded from the European or *vatikim* social circles. Being the least educated, they hold the lowest-paying jobs (except that Arabs also provide much of the unskilled labor in some areas). Although the new-town planners had hoped to create an ethnic melting pot, social integration of the various Jewish ethnic groups has not occurred, and the three-tiered social hierarchy has emerged to prevent the development of an egalitarian community.

The new towns have been successful, however, in the goal of shifting the population from the coasts and the larger cities. A group of middle-size towns have been created in the interior, and the primacy of Tel Aviv has been somewhat countered. Whereas Tel Aviv contained 43.1 percent of the urban population in 1948, by 1972 the metropolis had only 13.3 percent (although with outlying suburbs it was a change from about 53 to 30 percent). In 1972 Jerusalem was second with 11.2 percent (including annexed East Jerusalem), while Haifa had 8 percent. In contrast, the new towns, which contained only 1.9 percent of the urban population in 1948, had increased to 21.7 percent by 1972. Other urban settlements increased from 12.1 to 26.4 percent in the same period. Although the new towns have grown considerably, they have been only moderately successful in attracting industry, which still tends to locate in the larger cities, especially in the port cities of Tel Aviv and Haifa.

The new towns have failed as central places in most instances. These cities are not used as retail or service centers by the surrounding hinterland population; they have failed to be integrated into the regional economies. The *kibbutzim* and *moshavim* are incorporated into their own national organizations in Tel Aviv, which supply their daily needs in the village stores and arrange for the marketing of their agricultural products. Goods not found in their own settlement are purchased in Tel Aviv, Haifa, or Jerusalem instead of in a nearby middle-level town. The neglect of the new towns results partly from the small size of Israel, its well-developed road network, and the cheap public transportation system, all of which bring the cities within easy reach of the rural areas. There also is still a great antipathy by the agriculturalists for the new towns, because of Zionist ideology, the Oriental character of the new-town populations, and the practical realization that they indeed have no need for these towns. In fact, the new towns sometimes provide temporary labor for the agricultural settlements, the opposite of a normal city-hinterland relationship.

Not all the new towns are failures as service centers. Afula, for instance, is emerging as a regional center in the northern part of the country, serving as a competitor to Haifa for about 20 surrounding settlements. But the most successful new town is Beersheba, established in the Negev desert in southern Israel.

Beersheba: Primate Town of the Negev Beersheba (Beer Sheva) has been a site for a settlement since ancient times. It was the Turkish administrative center for the Negev region, resulting in a grid-pattern town being constructed during World War I. In 1922 the town had a population of only 2356, mostly Moslems. With the establishment of Israel, the settlement was selected as the focus for development of the Negev.

Beersheba was one of the few new towns developed around an existing core settlement. The garden city concept was applied; neighborhoods were built detached from one another, with no physical and social ties between them. The neighborhoods, designated only by letters of the alphabet (Fig. 8.14), filled up with immigrants who came to Israel in the 1950s and early 1960s. About half of the population are Oriental Jews, two-thirds of them second-generation.

The city suffered from its dispersed structure. Excessive expenditures were necessary for the infrastructural services, inhabitants had to walk great distances in oppres-

Figure 8.14 Beersheba According to the Master Plan of 1967. [*Source:* Adapted from Y. Gradus, "Beer-Sheva, Capital of the Negev Desert—Function and Internal Structure," *GeoJournal,* 2, No. 6 (1978), 526.] Reprinted with permission.

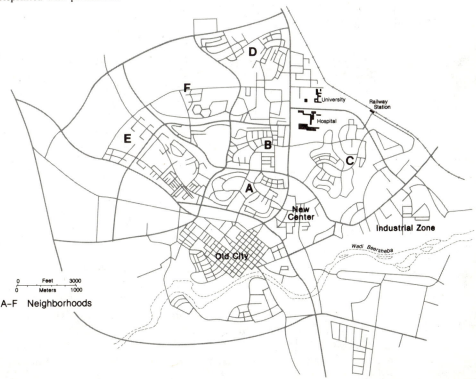

sive heat in search of goods and services, the vacant areas remained barren and increased the sense of desolation, and transportation systems did not connect the separated neighborhoods. The focus on the neighborhoods resulted in the absence of citywide functions and centers of attraction. The old Turkish city to the south of the neighborhoods became the CBD by default.

A new master plan for Beersheba, conceived in the late 1960s, focused on consolidating the city, creating a single socioeconomic unit. An integrated road network was built to connect and unify all the neighborhoods. Residences were constructed in the spaces between the neighborhoods. The city's center was transferred to a more central location. However, the old CBD was not surplanted in its commercial importance, and the new area has become mostly a cultural and administrative core. Industries mainly had been located on the eastern side of the city, resulting in obnoxious odors frequently blowing across the city. Under the new plan many of the industries are being relocated to an industrial zone about 7.5 mi. (12 km.) south of the city.

As the capital of the Southern District, Beersheba has developed a strong interrelationship with its region. It has a well-developed tertiary sector, which includes major governmental offices, medical facilities, military headquarters, and educational institutions. The city provides most of the goods and services for the inhabitants of the Negev, a hinterland containing over 100,000 inhabitants. This includes about 70,000 people in smaller new towns and 40,000 Bedouins, mostly in the last stages of sedentarization. A few thousand inhabitants are in *kibbutzim* and *moshavim,* but their dealings continue to be mostly with their national organizations in Tel Aviv.

The Negev had a population of about 200,000 in the late 1970s, half of these in Beersheba, and the population of the city is projected to double by the end of the century. Beersheba is undoubtedly the most successful new town in Israel, and the fourth largest city in the country. As the capital of the Negev, it is a new town which has become the primate city of its region.

Urban Problems and Prospects

The rapid growth of the cities of the Middle East has resulted in numerous problems. Many of the difficulties are similar to those in much of the developing world's cities: housing shortages, inadequate services, underemployment, overconcentration in primate cities, and so forth. Yet it is necessary to view many of these issues in the context of the Middle East, for several problems and complications especially manifest themselves in this cultural region.

Oil revenues have been both a benefit and a bane for the cities of Middle Eastern countries. The vast funds, especially since 1973, have enabled the inauguration of new industrial projects, the construction of gigantic housing schemes and of new towns, and often the implementation of sweeping changes in city structure. But the rapid expansion of the economies of the nations of Libya, Iraq, Saudi Arabia, Kuwait, the United Arab Emirates, and Iran (until 1978) have brought about so much development that the cities have had difficulty in coping with the situation. The boom in industrial and housing construction brings more workers into the city, and these must be housed and provided with services. The tertiary sector expands, creating the need for more shops, houses, transport systems, sewers, and so forth. Despite the great influx of capital into these cities the magnitude of development has placed a great strain on the infrastructure of the municipalities.

The cities on the Arab side of the Persian Gulf have seen some of the greatest changes under the impact of oil revenues. As previously discussed, Kuwait was completely replanned, with wide avenues and modern housing developments and the old *madina* mostly leveled to make way for the new CBD. The old houses, which were more sensibly constructed than the new ones—for example, they withstood the intense heat much better—were contemptuously razed, the huge avenues and roundabouts represent the triumph of the automobile in this metropolis. Similar developments have occurred in Abu Dhabi, Dubai, and the cities of eastern Saudi Arabia.

The surge of growth results in one characteristic which has become a major problem for some cities of these oil-producing nations. The need for manpower has been so great that thousands of foreign migrant workers have had to fill the gap. The influx of foreigners into Kuwait City soon made the native Kuwaitis a minority, a pattern which is even more pronounced in the major cities of the United Arab Emirates. Over a million foreigners are also in the cities or industrial projects of Saudi Arabia, a fact so disturbing to that government that it will not admit their presence in such large numbers. Although the foreign migrants are supposed to be only temporary, the example of Kuwait has shown that the migrants stay, even though they may not be official citizens of the country.

In fact, one of the results of the influx of foreigners into these cities is that a second-class status has been placed upon them, with many of the benefits and services of the state not open to them. A potential political crisis could occur in these municipalities. In the meantime, the native population has the easy and lucrative jobs, as in the government bureaucracy. Aliens hold most of the onerous, but necessary, labor and service occupations.

Indigenous rural migrants also have contributed to the manpower, and to the problems, of Middle Eastern cities. Being unskilled and usually illiterate, they become part of the underemployed sector of the urban economy (although this is less of a problem in the oil-rich nations with their great labor needs). Rural migrants also have problems adjusting to the urban environment and its different pace, life-styles, and values. They usually continue extensive ties to their rural areas and only gradually become assimilated into the city.

In the Middle East rural migrants include settling nomads. Attracted by the labor possibilities in the city or perhaps forced to abandon their pastoral pursuits due to loss of their flocks or government interference, the nomads have even less usable skills for the city and greater problems of assimilation. Disliking crowded conditions and the strange urban life-style, they remain on the outskirts of the metropolises. They often live in the shantytowns, or they may continue to live in their black tents (even next to a government-built house, which may be used for storage). Pastoral activities sometimes are continued by some members of the family, perhaps back in the traditional grazing grounds.

The great influx of migrants into the cities has led to formation of many shantytowns or squatter settlements. The *bidonvilles* and *gourbivilles* of North African cities, *gecekondu* of Istanbul and Ankara, and *sarifahs* of Baghdad represent this phenomenon. These settlements have enabled hundreds of thousands of migrants to provide needed labor and services for the many expanding metropolises. More importantly, perhaps, is the role of the shantytown in integrating these largely rural migrants into the life of the city. They act as a buffer and provide for a gradual transition to the status of "urbanites." It is in such areas that one can speak of the "ruralization" of the city, because many of the village (or nomadic) habits and life-styles are transferred to the shantytowns and affect the rest of the city as well. Migrants from one village or at least one region often constitute the majority of one particular shantytown, because extensive networks exist between the shantytown and the area of origin. Not only do new migrants have a place to go when reaching the city, but many relatives and friends provide aid and comfort in the new surroundings. In some instances, employment has even been arranged before the migrant reaches the city.

Although shantytowns provide a valuable function for the cities of the Middle East, they do present some sanitation and health problems, and they do not fit the tidy image of aesthetically pleasing urban environments wanted by municipalities and city planners. But as shown by the eradication of many of Baghdad's shantytowns, what replaces the shanty dwellings may be rather undesirable for the inhabitants' interests or life-styles. With their incomes at the lower end of the economic scale, even low-cost housing schemes in many cities are too expensive for the squatters.

A solution, perhaps, is for Middle Eastern governments to recognize the viability of the shantytowns, even when the inhabitants are illegal squatters (which is usually the case). With the provision of sanitation and health services, electricity, and other urban amenities the shantytowns can become a reasonable place to live. This solution is not such a drain on the municipality and its budget, which in any case can provide no viable alternatives. Cairo presents a classic case of a city without shantytowns, but with no other options either. Tomb cities, rooftop shacks, and massive overcrowding in dilapidated buildings are the consequence.

The rapidity of urban development in the Middle East has placed a great strain on the municipal services of the cities. Water, sewerage, and electrical lines must be extended as new suburbs are built. Besides the cost, these systems often get overextended for the physical plants operating them, and so electrical blackouts and loss of water pressure are common occurrences. Roads must be made available to new neighborhoods. And, unless it is an upper-class area which relies on personal automobiles, the public transport system also must be extended to the residences. New buses and taxis are added to take care of the increasing population, but more vehicles aggravate the already crowded circulation network and add to the pollution of the city.

Cairo epitomizes the crisis of municipal services. Many older residences do not have the basic necessities of piped water or electricity. The public transport system is vastly overloaded; in the mid-1970s there were only about 1300 buses, 140 trolley buses, and 230 trams for carrying 3.5 million passengers a day. But with the heavy use, lack of parts, and inadequate mechanics, in actuality, fewer than a thousand vehicles have been operational at one time. With no net increase in usable vehicles and the number of passengers increasing at about 15 percent a year, the situation continues to worsen. Also, since there is little use of bicycles or motorcycles in this metropolis, the public vehicles, taxis, private cars, donkey carts, pushcarts, and other modes of transport clog the streets and cause frequent traffic jams.

Blackouts have become common in Cairo the last several years, for there are simply too many users for the existing system. In parts of the city, blackouts sometimes have lasted for several days, especially rendering many of the middle and upper classes rather uncomfortable because they have become more dependent on electricity. Elevators will not work during blackouts, and for those inhabitants living on the upper floors of newer apartment complexes a difficult climb in totally dark corridors lessens the appeal for living in this great Arab metropolis.

Tehran also has begun to feel the strain of population numbers. As in Cairo, electrical blackouts and inadequate water pressure have become a problem. Blackouts usually have been only for a few hours at a time, purposely spread at intervals throughout parts of the city. Electrical shortages and inadequate water pressure also have affected Iran's provincial cities, which have expanded at rapid rates as well.

In terms of traffic Tehran upstages the Egyptian metropolis. There are no donkey carts or pushcarts (in the streets), but there are numerous buses (twice as many as in Cairo) and more cars. At least until 1978, about 100,000 automobiles were added to the capital every year, and Tehran had the reputation among international businessmen of having among the worst traffic in the world, a reputation well deserved.

Air pollution has become a major problem in most large cities of the Middle East. In Kuwait City before the early 1960s, there were several hundred days a year in which visibility was 6 to 9 mi. (10 to 15 km.) or more. By 1970 such visibility was uncommon, and the problem has continued to worsen. In Tehran air pollution has become a critical problem, not only due to industrial plants in the region but also to automobiles. The pollution has been increasing about 10 percent annually, and Tehran already is considered one of the most polluted cities in the world. Smog has cut visibility drastically; on most days north Tehran cannot be seen from the south, and the beautiful sight of Mount Damavand, the highest peak in Iran, is a rare occurrence indeed.

These myriad problems in the cities of the Middle East are not simply the result of increasing numbers. Part of the predicament is due to inadequate city planning, a most unenviable task in these metropolises. The municipal governments generally lack the funds, manpower, or authority to implement any rational plan of urban growth and development. Local autonomy is especially usurped by national ministries and agencies in the capitals, and so conflicting authority and interests are the norm. Rivalries between various governmental agencies for approving projects, providing funds, supervising expenditures, and implementing projects impede any proper urban planning. And even in the provincial cities the centralization of decision making in the capital city by individuals whose main interests are often couched in terms of national goals leave little room for effective local city planning.

The traditional city or *madina* has become a problem for the twentieth-century metropolis. The compactness, native housing, and traditional life-styles of the *madina* are viewed by many as anachronisms and obstructions to modernization. The narrow streets are not accessible to automobiles, there are no modern sewer systems, modern appliances do not fit easily into the traditional structures, and so forth. In fact, like the shantytowns, the *madina* is perceived by city planners and governments as a blight on the city which must be eradicated. Such extreme solutions have been followed, for example, in Kuwait City, where the Western-style CBD has replaced most of the indigenous housing and commercial area.

Madinas are "modernized" in most instances by plowing wide avenues through them to allow the circulation of wheeled vehicles. This began in Cairo with the French occupation at the end of the eighteenth century (for military reasons) and continued in the nineteenth century. It was started during World War I in Baghdad by German advisers, who stressed the need of wide avenues for moving artillery. In the 1930s Iranian cities were riddled by avenues under Reza Shah's crash modernization programs, and the bulldozing has continued under the guise of city planning (Fig. 8.15).

The major problem of most *madinas,* however, is socioeconomic. As cities have expanded there has been an exodus by the inhabitants of the old city into the new, modern suburbs. Those left are the destitute and aged, while rural migrants have replaced many of the original residents. Foreigners largely occupy the remaining houses of the *madina* of Kuwait (paying exorbitant rents), while substantial numbers of rural migrants live in the old cities of Baghdad, Tunis, and Cairo. Overcrowding and poverty accompany the changing character of the *madina.* The *madina* of Tunis provides an excellent example in which the viability of the old city has been recognized. The *madina* is seen as an integral part of the whole metropolis and performs valuable, unique functions. The key, then, is to realize the role and the actual vitality of the *madina.*

Wars and conflicts in the Middle East have affected many of its cities. Not only did the establishment of Israel begin a rapid urbanization of that country, but the displaced refugees who were not in camps flocked to Amman, Damascus, and other cities. As previously mentioned, the Palestinians constitute the largest group of foreigners in Kuwait City. The 1967 war caused the great influx of Egyptians into Cairo, and it is also at this time that Israel took over all of Jerusalem and began a detailed master plan for the old city and its immediate environs. The plan aims to preserve the traditional character of the *madina* with rigid controls on types of building and land use, attempting to keep the present balance of residences, religious land, open spaces, and commercial land (Fig. 8.16). Numerous public buildings and residences have been renovated, especially in the Jewish quarter.

One of the more recent tragedies in the Middle East is the civil war in Lebanon, resulting in the destruction of large parts of Beirut. The troubles have caused the metropolis, once proclaimed the most beautiful and international city of the Middle East, to lose its role as the headquarters for international companies and agencies and as a middleman between the West and the Arab oil-producing states. Many corporations moved to Tehran (until 1978), Manamah (Bahrain), Athens, and other cities. In 1977 about 15 percent of the city's industry had been totally destroyed, and this sector was operating at only one-third capacity. The downtown area had been largely destroyed and the seafront hotels left as lifeless shells. There is much discussion about the recon-

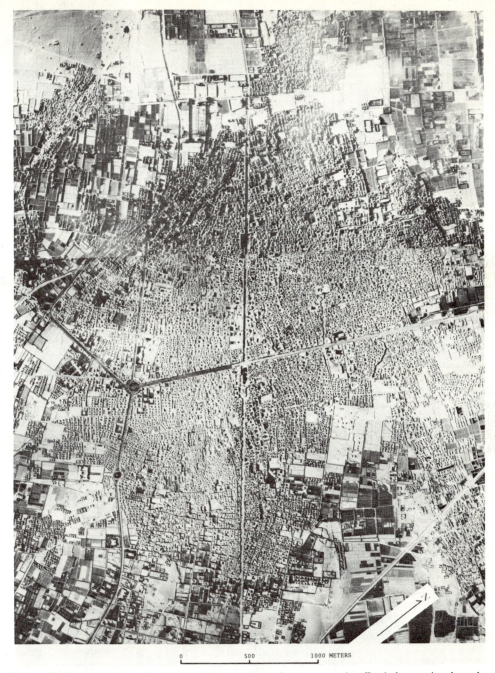

Figure 8.15 Aerial view of Yazd, Iran, 1964, showing major avenues and traffic circles running through the old city. These modern intrusions into the traditional Middle Eastern city are seen by some as necessary improvements to accommodate traffic, but seen by others as destroyers of the beauty and charm of the traditional city. (*Source:* National Cartographic Center, Plan Organization of Iran.)

Figure 8.16 Land Use in the Madina of Jerusalem. (*Source:* Adapted from Arieh Sharon, *Planning Jerusalem: The Master Plan for the Old City of Jerusalem and Its Environs,* New York: McGraw-Hill, 1973, p. 116.)

struction of Beirut; but symbolic of the struggle itself, numerous factions have very different ideas on what should be done and how it should be carried out.

The continued growth and concentration of population in the major metropolises has led to concerted efforts to decentralize these trends. Iran and Iraq have attempted to promote industrialization outside of their capital regions, with some success. Self-contained satellite cities have been built or planned to take the pressure off the major cities. Israel has been able to redistribute its population, partly due to its scheme of new towns. At least five new cities are planned around Cairo, each having a capacity between 500,000 and 1.5 million inhabitants. New water resources have been discovered recently, and these cities are being planned for the deserts, east and west of the capital. Even more satellite cities are planned for the future, and by the end of the century a projected 25 million Egyptians will be housed in the new cities in the desert.

There are no easy solutions to the problems facing the cities of the Middle East. In the final analysis, the priorities of these nations will determine whether the problems of their cities can be solved. Until these countries commit resources to bettering their urban environment, major problems will continue to plague the cities of the Middle East and North Africa.

RECOMMENDED READINGS

Abu-Lughod, Janet. *Cairo: 1001 Years of 'the City Victorious.'* Princeton, NJ: Princeton University Press, 1971.
    This elaborately illustrated book is a thorough and scholarly account of the urban history of Cairo, stressing the evolution of spatial patterns and the factors affecting the growth. The author, a sociologist, also analyzes the cultural ecology and structure of Cairo based upon the censuses of 1947 and 1960.

Abu-Lughod, Janet. "Problems and Policy Implications of Middle Eastern Urbanization." In United Nations, Economic and Social Office in Beirut, *Studies on Development Problems in Selected Countries of the Middle East, 1972.* New York: United Nations, 1973, pp. 42–62.
    A penetrating analysis of the problems of Middle Eastern cities, this article suggests several possible approaches to help alleviate these problems.

Bonine, Michael E. "From Uruk to Casablanca: Perspectives on the Urban Experience of the Middle East." *Journal of Urban History,* 3, No. 2 (1977), 141–180.
    Taking a brief glance at urbanism in the Middle East in its historical setting, this article emphasizes a review of the relevant literature. Included is a discussion of the Islamic city model.

Bonine, Michael E. "The Urbanization of the Persian Gulf Nations." In Alvin J. Cottrell, ed., *The Persian Gulf States: A General Survey.* Baltimore, MD: Johns Hopkins University Press, 1980, pp. 225–278.
    This article examines the contemporary patterns of rapid urbanization and city development in the countries of the Persian Gulf region, including Iran, Iraq, Saudi Arabia, Kuwait, the United Arab Emirates, and Oman.

Cohen, Erik. *The City in the Zionist Ideology.* Jerusalem: The Hebrew University of Jerusalem, Institute of Urban and Regional Studies, Jerusalem Urban Studies, No. 1, 1970.
    This monograph examines the disregard for the city in Zionist ideology, stressing the implications for urban planning and the establishment of the Israeli new towns.

El-Shakhs, Salah. "National Factors in the Development of Cairo." *Town Planning Review,* 42, No. 3 (1971), 235–249.
    The author, with previous experience as an urban planner in Cairo, assesses the growth of this metropolis and its problems. He also examines proposals for urban planning and future development of Cairo.

French, Geoffrey and Allan G. Hill. *Kuwait: Urban and Medical Ecology.* Berlin: Springer-Verlag, 1971.

This work includes an examination of the evolution of Kuwait City and an analysis of urban patterns through the mid-1960s.

Grunebaum, Gustave E. von. "The Structure of the Muslim Town." In Gustave E. von Grunebaum, *Islam: Essays in the Nature and Growth of a Cultural Tradition.* London: Routledge and Kegan Paul, 1955, pp. 141–158.

One of the classic essays on the Islamic city, this article discusses the characteristics of this stereotyped model.

Gulick, John. "Baghdad: Portrait of a City in Physical and Cultural Change." *Journal of the American Institute of Planners,* 33, No. 4 (1967), 246–255.

This article examines the historical evolution of Baghdad in the twentieth century and focuses on many of the urban patterns and problems of the mid-1960s.

Inalcik, H. "Istanbul." In B. Lewis et al., eds. *Encyclopaedia of Islam.* New York: Humanities Press. New Edition. Vol. 4, pp. 224–248.

A detailed, in-depth treatment of Istanbul under the Ottomans, stressing the urban structure, demography, and physical evolution of the city.

Obudho, R. A. and Salah, El-Shakhs, eds., *Development of Urban Systems in Africa.* New York: Praeger, 1979.

Four of the chapters concern urbanization in Morocco, Algeria, Libya, and Egypt and contain some of the most current information on urban development in North Africa.

Sharon, Arieh. *Planning Jerusalem: The Master Plan for the Old City of Jerusalem and its Environs.* New York: McGraw-Hill, 1973.

With colored maps and many photographs, this book illustrates the urban history and the master plan of the *madina* of Jerusalem, formulated after the Israeli occupation of the entire city in 1967.

Speigel, Erika. *New Towns in Israel: Urban and Regional Planning and Development.* New York: Praeger, 1967.

This book is an excellent account of the history, planning, and development of Israel's new towns.

United Nations, Department of Economic and Social Affairs, *Urban Land Policies and Land-Use Control Measures.* Vol. 5. Middle East. New York: United Nations, 1973.

This publication examines land use in Middle Eastern cities, including systems of land ownership, factors affecting urban land supply and demand, land control measures, and the role of urban planning in coordinating land use policy and development.

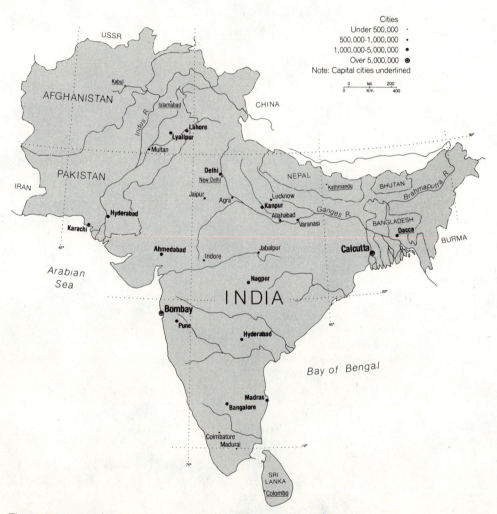

Figure 9.1 Major Cities of South Asia. (*Source:* Data derived from United Nations, Department of Economic and Social Affairs, *Global Review of Human Settlements, Statistical Annex,* published by Pergamon Press, New York, 1976.)

Chapter 9

Cities of South Asia

Ashok K. Dutt

South Asia in the World Urban System

South Asia is characterized as a whole by a low level of urbanization, 22 percent. Indeed, this is one of the least urbanized regions of the world, if examined from just the perspective of percentage of population living in urban centers. The most urbanized country in South Asia is Pakistan, at 30 percent; next is Sri Lanka at 27 percent, then India at 23 percent. The other three countries in the region are far less urbanized, however: Bangladesh is 8 percent urban, Nepal 6 percent, and tiny Bhutan less than 4 percent. Part of the explanation for this statistically low standing for South Asia is due, as with East Asia, to the huge total population of the region and the vast rural population, which produces a statistical bias even though a great many people in the region do in fact live in urban centers. In India, for example, an urban population figure of 23 percent means that about 158 million people live in cities, out of a total population of 690 million. Likewise, in Pakistan, nearly 25 million people live in cities in that country of almost 83 million. In other words, urban centers and urban life play vital roles in South Asia, even though the nations are predominantly agrarian.

The relative importance of cities in South Asia can be seen even more readily from the number of cities (Fig. 9.1). In 1980, India alone had 19 cities with a population of half a million or more, and at least 10 cities over 1 million. Pakistan had 5 cities over half a million, 4 of those of at least 1 million. Sri Lanka's relatively high standing in the region for urban population is due to the existence of a number of small to medium-size cities under half a million. Colombo, the capital, is the only city over half a million. Three of the world's largest cities, predicted to emerge as superconurbations by the year 2000, are in South Asia—the Indian cities of Calcutta, Bombay, and Delhi. These three cities already had populations of 9.5, 8.7, and 5.7 million, respectively, by 1980.

As with other regions of the developing world, rural-to-urban migration is the principal cause of this rapid growth of cities in South Asia, growth that has accelerated enormously since the independence of these countries following World War II. However, unlike regions such as Southeast Asia, no city of the subcontinent can really be called primate even in its respective country. In India, for example, Calcutta, Bombay, and Delhi jointly form a triangular primacy for North India, whereas in South India a subsidiary triangular primacy is caused by Hyderabad, Madras, and Bangalore. Likewise, Pakistan has a dual primacy produced by Karachi and Lahore, as does Bangladesh with both Dacca and Chittagong.

South Asia's cities can also be characterized as consisting of two or three types. Initially the traditional cities, such as Delhi, long antedated the arrival of Western colonialism. Indeed, this region was one of the earliest centers of city building in human history, dating back to around 3000 B.C. Large numbers of traditional cities survived into modern times, to have grafted onto them (and often be overwhelmed by) new Western colonial cities, such as New Delhi. The two most important cities of the region, Calcutta and Bombay, were entirely the creation of British colonialism. In the postindependence period, the various traditional and colonial cities have evolved further into commercial/industrial cities to serve the expanding economies and national development plans of the governments of the region. In spite of that expansion and development, however, many if not most of the cities of South Asia stand out as exhibiting among the worst urban conditions and problems to be found anywhere in the world. In this regard, Calcutta is commonly singled out as the sort of epitome of all that is bad about uncontrolled urban growth in modern times and all that can go wrong in administering a large urban center. Much is written about the cities of South Asia that is filled with bleakness and despair, as if to suggest that the urban problems of this region are beyond hope.

Evolution of Cities in South Asia

Though the realm, or the Indian subcontinent as it is often termed, was influenced by various cultures and subcultures, five distinctive civilizations made significant inroads: the civilization of the Indus Valley (3000–1500 B.C.), the Aryan Hindus (since 1500 B.C.), the Dravidians (since about 200 B.C.), the Moslems (since the eighth century), and the West Europeans (since the fifteenth century). These civilizations also affected the urban forms and patterns of South Asia, with the impact of Hindu, Dravidian, Moslem, and West European civilizations much greater than that of the Indus Valley civilization.

The Indus Valley Era

The capital cities of the Indus Valley civilization, Mohenjodaro and Harappa, were established as planned systems as early as 3000 B.C. They flourished for about 1500 years. Although approximately 400 mi. (about 650 km.) apart, the cities were situated on related rivers—Mohenjodaro on the Indus proper and Harappa on the Ravi, a tributary of the Indus. Both cities had rectangular road systems. Large elevated areas, called citadels, at the margins of both cities were assemblages for public use. The ruins of Mohenjodaro, first excavated in 1921 from sediments deposited by centuries of Indus flooding, revealed a carefully constructed citadel with an open-air great bath (39 by 29 feet and 8 feet deep—11.9 by 8.8 by 2.4 m.). At the corner of the bath lay a *hammam* or hot-air bath. The city included a large number of well-built, spacious houses of burnt brick, streets crossing at right angles to form blocks 400 by 200 feet (111 by 122 m.), an efficient drainage and sewage system with connections to it from inside the households, individualized baths and toilets inside each home, and street garbage collection. Though full excavations are still far from complete, a schematic plan consisted of five main thoroughfares: two running north-south and the other three east-west. At the time, no other city outside the Indus civilization possessed such an elaborate system of drainage, sanitation, and civic facilities as Mohenjodaro, signifying a generally high standard of living and civilization. This high-level urban civilization came to an end around 1500 B.C. when the newly immigrated Aryans, less civilized but more adept in warfare than the Indus people, overpowered the civilization and turned the northern part of the South Asian realm into a mixture of pastoralism and sedentary agriculture. The realm entered a dark age lasting approximately a thousand years.

The Aryan Hindu Impact

Eventually the needs of trade, commerce, administration, and fortification gave rise to the establishment of sizable urban centers, particularly in the middle Ganges plains. Originating from a modest fifth century B.C. fort at the confluence of the Ganges and the Son, Pathaliputra developed into the capital of a notable Indian empire, the Maurya. Its location coincides with that of modern Patna. Pathaliputra possessed the urban forms of a capital city of the Aryans. Unlike Mohenjodaro, this oblong city was surrounded by massive timber walls, 9.2 mi. (14.8 km.) long and 1.75 mi. (2.8 km.) wide, to protect it from adjacent kingdoms. The walls had 64 gates and 570 towers and were surrounded by a 60-ft.- deep (18 m.), 600-ft.- wide (180 m.) moat for additional defense. The moat was filled with water from the Son and was the main recipient of the city's sewage. The city was organized to conform with the functional requirements of the capital of a Hindu kingdom. The function-based, four-caste system of the Hindus found a place in the spatial pattern of the city. The elaborate king's palace, adorned with silver images of birds and situated in the midst of exquisite gardens and tanks for boating, occupied the center of the city.

The quarters of all four castes surrounded the palace. Near the center and a little toward the east were the temple and residences of high-ranking Brahmins (members of the priest caste) and ministers of the royal cabinet. Farther toward the east were the *Kshatryas;* members of the warrior caste, rich merchants, and expert artisans. To the south were government superintendents, prostitutes, musicians, and some other members of the *Vaisya,* the commercial and agricultural caste caste. To the west were the *Sudras* (manual-laborer members of the caste), including untouchables, along with ordinary artisans and low-grade Vaisyas. Finally, to the north were artisans, Brahmins, and temples maintained for the titular deity of the city. This functional distribution of population in Pathaliputra was accompanied by a well-organized city government, a hierarchical street system, and an elaborate drainage system. With the eclipse of the Maurya empire in the second century B.C., the city of Pathaliputra lost its importance and was eventually buried under the sediments of the Ganges and the Son. Only small parts of the city have recently been excavated. Other Hindu capitals that developed in both North and South India changed and modified the many urban forms used in Pathaliputra.

Dravidian Temple Cities

In South India, where Hindu kingdoms had relative control of the area for most of the historical period in contrast with the North, the Hindu forms of city development evolved uninterruptedly, minimizing Moslem influences. The rulers of South India constructed temples and tanks as nuclei of habitation. Around the temples grew commercial bazaars and settlements of Brahmin priests and scholars. The ruler often built a palace near the temple, turning the temple-city into the capital of his kingdom; Madurai and Kancheepuram are examples. Protective walls eventually surrounded the cities. The temple walls and gates were decorated with ornate figures depicting stories from Hindu epics. The loftiness and the grandeur of the temples imparted to the subjects a sense of protection by the Almighty. Thus, the kingdom was endowed with celestial favor, the king wielded power derived from Him, and a god-king concept was woven into the city design. Such city forms were also exported to Southeast Asia; Angkor (A.D. 802–1432) in Kampuchea is a typical example. There the concept underwent further elaboration.

Mentioned by Ptolemy, Madurai, the second capital of the South Indian Hindu kingdom of the Pandyas, dates back to about the beginning of the Christian era. The geographical advantage of the city was its situation by the side of the river Vaigai, providing natural defense. Moreover, a prescription made in Hindu religious literature that an urban site should rise gradually from northeast toward southwest was provided by the local topography of the Madurai area. Such a situation allows air and the sun's light to enter into inner apartments of the houses and the temple. In this part of the Indian subcontinent the prevailing winds are from the northeast in winter and from the southwest in summer.

However, a much greater part of the evolution of Madurai's cultural landscape dates back to 1551, when it was turned into the capital of a Hindu Nayak dynasty. A double wall, almost a square, was erected around the city to protect against Moslem invasions. Well-planned roads formed a series of three concentric squares (inner, middle, and outer) surrounding the temple. The Nayaks remodeled the main temple and added buildings to the temple complex dedicated to different gods and goddesses. The Hall of a Thousand Pillars, in which groups of pillars were carved out of single huge stones, is a masterpiece of South Indian sculpture. The palace of the Nayaks was located adjacent to and within the walls, southeast from the temple. Though Madurai city is now over five times the size of the old walled city, with imprints from a brief Moslem period and a longer British dominance, its religious importance is so great to the Hindus that it is called the Varanasi of the South; Varanasi, located in North India, is the foremost pilgrim center.

The Moslem Imprint: Shahjahanabad (Delhi)

The first permanent Moslem occupation that significantly influenced the realm began in the eleventh century A.D., and resulted in adding many Middle Eastern and Central Asian Islamic qualities to the urban landscape of South Asia. Shahjahanabad is a particularly good example of Moslem impact. The Mogul emperor Shah Jahan, who planned the Taj Mahal in Agra, moved his capital from Agra to Delhi and started the construction of a new city, Shahjahanabad, on the right bank of the Jumna. The city was built near the sites of several extinct capital cities and took nearly ten years to complete (1638–1648). Its architecture was a fusion of Islamic and Hindu influences. Though the royal palaces and mosques with their arches, vaults, and domes adhered to Moslem styles, the Hindu styles employing pillars, lintels, and pyramidal towers were found in congruous combination. The Moslem rulers were most concerned with the magnificience of their royal residences and courts, massiveness of their fortresses, and typical Islamic loftiness in the design of their mosques. These features are represented most vividly in Shahjahanabad. Surrounded by brick walls without a moat, the city was incompletely fortified. Moreover, many settlements, including the extensive remains of the earlier city, were sprawled out in four different suburbs, all outside the walls (Fig. 9.2).

Planned as a parallelogram with massive red sandstone walls and ditches on all sides except by the river, the fortress (Red Fort) had an almost foolproof defense. The fortress was situated at the eastern end of the walled city. Inside the fortress were a magnificent court, the king's private palace, gardens, and a music pavilion, all built of either red sandstone or white marble in the exquisite designs of Mogul architecture.

The two main thoroughfares, which connected the city with the fortress and the outside world, had shops of merchants along them. One, Chandni Chowk ("silver market"), ran straight westward from the Red Fort toward the Lahore Gate of the city. One hundred and twenty feet wide with a canal in its median, the Chandni Chowk was one of the great bazaars of the Orient. The other thoroughfare, Khas Road, ran straight south toward Delhi Gate. A shopping area of lesser importance, Khas Road was built a little to the east of the Great Jama Mosque, largest and most famous of all the Moslem mosques in South Asia.

Shahjahanabad ceased to be the capital of India, more precisely North India, when British rule started in the eighteenth century, but it continued to be a functional city. Today, the former Shahjahanabad area is known as old Delhi, a part of the Delhi metropolis. Most of the city walls are gone, though all the basic structures of the Red Fort and Jama Mosque remain intact. Chandni Chowk continues to be a traditional, busy bazaar.

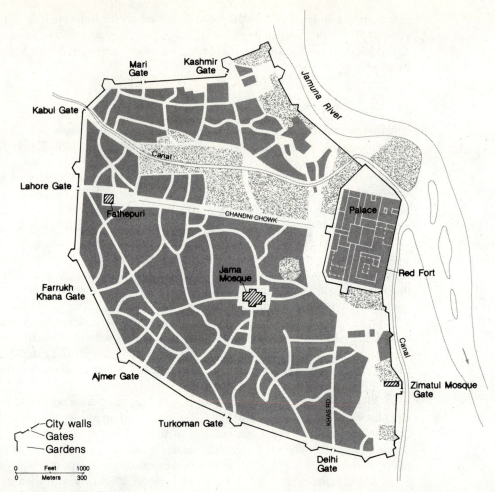

Figure 9.2 Shajahanabad City Layout. (*Source:* S. N. Sen, *Eighteen Fifty-Seven,* Calcutta: Government of India Press, 1958.)

The Colonial Period

Ever since Vasco da Gama discovered the oceanic route via the Cape of Good Hope in 1498, the Western colonial powers of Britain, France, Portugal, and Holland were greatly interested in developing a firm trade connection with South Asia. Though initially all four powers obtained some kind of footing in India, the sagacious diplomacy and "divide-and-rule" policy of the British succeeded in ousting the other Europeans from most Indian soil. Eventually, the English established three significant centers of operation: Bombay, Madras, and Calcutta. Originally in Portuguese hands, Bombay was obtained by the British Crown as a dowry when Charles II of England married Catherine of Portugal, and in 1664 Captain Cook took charge of Bombay on behalf of Britain. Due to its swampy and unattractive terrain conditions, Bombay was later transferred to the British East India Company for a nominal rent of £10 a year.

In 1639, the East India Company was granted a small territory from the local rulers of Tamil Nadu, where it later erected a fortified factory known as Fort St. George or Madras.

The most significant possession of the East India Company, however, became the site of Calcutta on the Hooghly, a distributary of the Ganges. The East India Company bought three villages, Govindapur, Sutanuti, and Kalikatta, from the Moslem rulers in 1690. The latter name would be modified for the city it was to become: Calcutta.

After successfully subjugating directly or indirectly all of South Asia, the British turned the city of Calcutta into the capital of British India in 1772. The British, or any European power for that matter, needed a firm footing on a seaport for the convenience of trading and receiving military reinforcements from the mother country whenever necessary. Calcutta, Bombay, and Madras were the seaports. Hence, these three cities were designated as the headquarters for the three different Presidencies that the British divided South Asia into for administrative purposes. Consequently, the cities are referred to as the Presidency towns.

Presidency Towns

The *Presidency towns* all developed Western-style CBDs, with banks, insurance offices, cinema halls, hotels, and large-scale retail establishments at the city center. Adjacent to this commercial core was another centrally located area containing the court houses, government offices, railway headquarters, customs buildings, and general post office. Together they formed the main focus of the empire's rule, both commercially and administratively. Like their Western counterparts, the central business areas had little residential population. This directly contrasts with the indigeneous South Asian cities, whose cores were central bazaars or *chowks,* combining high-density commercial and residential uses.

When Bombay, Madras, and Calcutta initially were established their nuclei were forts. Outside these forts were the cities. Inside the cities two different standards of living were set for two different residents, the Europeans and the "natives." The Europeans lived in their part of the city, which included broad streets, spacious houses, and, later on, sewage systems, piped water, and electric connections. This part of the city was well kept. The part of the city where the "natives" lived, with its ill-planned street patterns and unsanitary housing, was an amalgam of rich and poor. The rich were composed of the absentee rural landowners, money lenders, businessmen, and the newly English-educated elites. There was also a growing middle class of clerks. The poor comprised servants, manual laborers, street cleaners, and porters. The rich needed the service of the poor, and therefore the houses of the native rich in many instances stood by the houses of their poorer servicing people.

As local industries grew in the nineteenth century, a new working class developed. In Calcutta, the industrial workers worked mainly for jute mills and local engineering factories; in Bombay, the expanding cotton and textile-related industries; in Madras, tanning and cotton textiles.

As these trades grew, the Presidency towns turned from water to rail and roads for inland transportation. Train services were started in South Asia in 1853 when a 21-mi. (34 km.) link was established between Bombay and Thana. Delhi and Calcutta were connected by railway in 1867. The Bombay-Delhi rail line was completed in 1872. Madras Central Station, terminal of lines from Calcutta, Bombay, Bangalore, and Mangalore, opened in 1873. The Presidency towns also developed huge hinterlands that catered to the needs of the colonial economy. The hinterlands supplied the raw materials to the three seaports for exports to the United Kingdom; in return, the British sent consumer-type manufactured goods through the same ports. As a result, the Presidency towns became the main focus of colonial exploitation.

Accompanying the new technology, such as railways, were new forms of architecture, particularly the expanding use of the Western Gothic and Victorian styles. The public buildings of the Presidency towns, such as railroad terminals, post offices, the governor's house, high courts, and the central and provincial secretariats were built in these designs. One of the best examples of the use of these architectural styles in combination with some Indian forms is the Victoria Memorial Building (1906–1921) in Calcutta (Fig. 9.3). The building was done in white marble with European designs, and the architects originally intended it to surpass the Taj Mahal in massive grandeur.

Figure 9.3 The Victoria Memorial of Calcutta, erected during the early twentieth century to immortalize the late queen victoria of england. Occupying several hundred acres at the southern end of the Maidan, the site is a favorite for recreation by Calcuttans. (A. Dutt)

All three Presidency towns were seaports, of course. Bombay, which occupied a group of islands slightly separated from the west coast of India, was the only Presidency town that provided a naturally well sheltered harbor. The seven islands that formed Bombay were largely filled with swamps, but as the trading importance of the city grew and its population rose from 1600 in 1715 to 70,000 in 1744, then to 236,000 in 1836, and finally to 644,000 in 1872, large areas of the city land were filled, connected by causeways, and eventually interconnected and drained to form the one large present-day island of Bombay, south of Mahim Creek.

Bombay was called the "Gateway to India." During colonial times it was the major port of entrance from the West (Fig. 9.4). Bombay demonstrated the greatest pace of development during the second half of the nineteenth century, after railways connected the city with its extensive hinterland in northwestern India. Bombay became the leading cotton textile manufacturing center of India, profiting from the American Civil War when it exported huge amounts of raw cotton to the mills in England, temporarily supplanting the American supply. Bombay's location near the fertile cotton-producing black soils of western India was an added benefit. The opening of the Suez Canal in 1869 added to Bombay's trade advantage.

Calcutta has been characterized by Rhoads Murphey as a city in a swamp. Such

Figure 9.4   Bombay's "Gateway to India," by the side of the Arabian Sea, combines Western and Indian architectural designs. The inscription at the top reads: "Erected to commemorate the landing in India of their Imperial Majesties King George V and Queen Mary on the second day of December, 1911." (A. Dutt)

a statement not only is historically true but legitimately describes Calcutta even today. Located in the delta of the Ganges River, the site of Calcutta City (municipality) is a levee sloping eastward from the river bank. The levee has a maximum elevation of about 32 ft. (9.6 m.), though most parts of the city are less than 22 ft. (6.6 m.) above sea level (Fig. 9.5). The difficulties of the site are further aggravated by the monsoon, which brings most of the city's annual rainfall of 64 inches (1600 mm.) between June and September, when the river is also at a high level. During this time the water table rises to within about a foot of the surface, causing extensive waterlogging. Nonetheless, the population of the city grew from 12,000 in 1715 to 117,000 in 1752, then to 160,000 in 1801. Finally, when the population had reached almost 3 million after the Second World War, the city expanded by reclaiming the swamps toward the east and the south.

Situated on its eastern bank, Calcutta was given initial protection in the eighteenth century from the attacks of the Moslem rulers and Marathas from the west by the river Hooghly. Moreover, the city, situated 60 mi. (97 km.) upstream from the Bay of Bengal, was reached by full-sized, oceangoing ships of the nineteenth century. The docks were equipped to repair, paint, and service the vessels from Europe and also to manufacture smaller vessels. The unique and most significant aspect of the location of Calcutta was its command over a huge, densely populated hinterland with a very rich agricultural and mineral-based economy. This hinterland was connected to Calcutta not only by an extensive river transport system, but later by efficient railroad and road systems as well. The hinterland of neither Bombay nor Madras had an extensive and perennial river system to link it to the port city, and thus these cities were unable to take advantage of a firm sea trade base at the time (seventeenth through nineteenth centuries), when water transport was the only effective and convenient means of long-distance trade.

Madras was bought by the British East India Company in 1639 from the local representatives of the dying Hindu empire of Vijaynagar. A fort built the following year had by 1658 become the main administrative center for British operations in India. The Madras site was chosen mainly as an alternative to a nearby northern location (Masulipatnam), where the Company's headquarters was being harassed by the regional Moslem kingdom of Golconda. Madras is characterized by a low-lying, almost dead-level landscape (only 22 ft.—6.6 m. above sea level at its highest point) intersected by two small streams, Coovam and Adayar. The streams, active only during the rains, otherwise formed salt lagoons separated from the sea by a ridge of sand. Both streams were useless for either inland transportation or a supply of fresh water to the city. Only with the construction in the nineteenth century of the Buckingham Canal, which ran several hundred miles parallel to the east coast, was inland trading directed through the Madras port. Unlike Bombay, Madras did not have a natural harbor. Artificial parallel breakwaters were erected in 1881 for safe anchorage of ships. Since it did not have a rich agriculture or mineral resource base, Madras's hinterland was inferior to that of Calcutta and Bombay. Consequently, by the late nineteenth century, Madras's seaborne imports and exports ranked only fifth in British India. Apart from Calcutta and Bombay, two other parts of British India, Karachi and Rangoon (the latter now considered to be located in Southeast Asia), had already surpassed Madras.

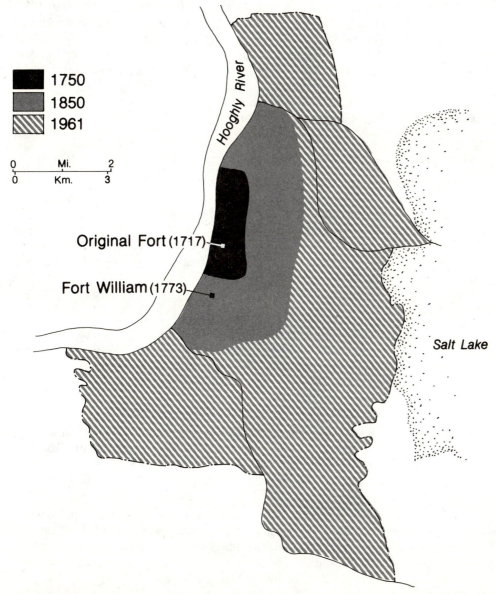

Figure 9.5 Growth of Calcutta, 1750–1961. (*Source: First Report, 1962,* Calcutta Metropolitan Planning Organization, 1963.)

Since Calcutta was more logically situated to command the major activity center of India, the Indo-Gangetic plain, Madras did not remain the capital of British India. The dual headquarters of British operations at Calcutta and Madras ceased to exist after 1772, when the latter was relegated to a secondary status. Nonetheless, Madras was the headquarters of the Madras Presidency, which had jurisdiction over most of South India. The population of Madras rose from 19,000 in 1646 to 300,000 in 1791, to 462,000 in 1822, and to 526,911 in 1921. Madras has not increased its population as rapidly as Calcutta and Bombay. Unlike Calcutta, it had adequate land free from swamps for expansion and did not witness the kind of congestion Calcutta and Bombay had to face. Madras originated with a fortified walled fort, accompanied by the "black town" of the "natives" immediately to north, with Europeans spreading out to the southwest (Fig. 9.6). Like Calcutta and Bombay, it is a city that experienced the full impact of colonial forms and then modification by traditional impacts.

Models of South Asian City Structure

The search for models to explain South Asian cities has prompted some theorists to apply mechanically the Western concentric zone theory of Burgess and to prepare all-purpose models, irrespective of their applicability. No comprehensive model explaining the growth pattern of the indigeneous city structure has yet been suggested. Two basic models depicting South Asian city forms are proposed in this chapter. Whatever model is used, it is important to note that two principal forces, colonial and traditional, have acted in designing the existing forms of the South Asian cities.

Colonial-Based-City Model

The colonial-city patterns parallel those found in other world regions, but the Indian subcontinent presents a specific and hybrid model, being neither Western nor Indian nor the same as in other world regions. The need to perform colonial functions demanded a particular form of city growth, relevant to the subcontinent, that produced the following characteristics (Fig. 9.7):

1. The need for trade and military reinforcements required a waterfront location accessible to oceangoing ships because the colonial powers operated from Europe. A minimal port facility was a prerequisite and was the starting point of the city. Thus, coastal locations became the main attractions of the colonial-city site.

2. A walled fort was constructed adjacent to the port with fortifications, white soldiers' and officers' barracks, a small church, and educational institutions. Sometimes inside the fort, factories processed agricultural raw materials to be shipped to the mother country. Thus, the fort became not only a military outpost but the nucleus of the colonial exchange.

3. An open space *(maidan)* was reserved around the fort to provide a field of fire and for other security reasons.

Models of South Asian City Structure 337

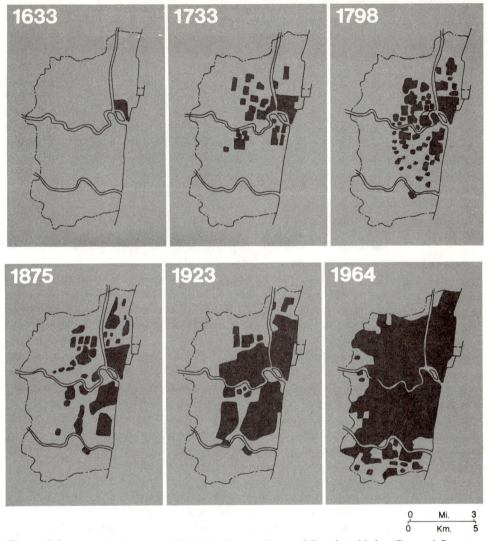

Figure 9.6 Growth of Madras, 1633–1964. (*Source: Stages of Growth in Madras City,* and *Report on Madras City Metropolitan Plan,* Directorate of Town Planning, Government of Madras, 1971.)

4. Beyond the fort and the open area, a "native town" or town for the native peoples eventually developed, characterized by overcrowding, unsanitary conditions, and unplanned settlements; it serviced the fort and the colonial administration as the CBD and further administrative activities developed near the fort and the "native town."

5. A Western-styled CBD grew adjacent to the fort and "native town", with a high concentration of mercantile-type office functions, retail trade, and low density of residential houses. The administrative quarters consisted of the

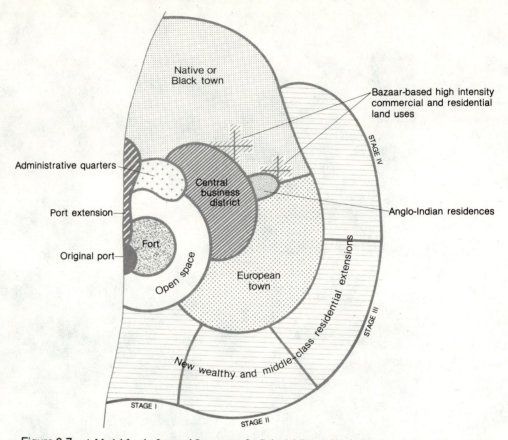

Figure 9.7 A Model for the Internal Structure of a Colonial-Based City in South Asia. (*Source:* Compiled by the author.)

governor's (or viceroy's) house, the main government offices, the high court, and the general post office. In the CBD area there also were Western-style hotels, churches, banks, and museums, as well as occasional statues of British sovereigns, viceroys, and other dignitaries at important road intersections, reminiscent of royal eternity.

6. The "European town" grew in a different area/direction from the "native town." It had spacious bungalows, elegant apartment houses, planned streets, trees on both sides of the streets, and a generally European look; clubs for afternoon and evening get-togethers and with European indoor and outdoor recreation facilities; churches of different denominations; and gardenlike graveyards.

7. Between the fort and the "European town" or at some appropriate nearby location, an extensive open space was reserved for military parades and West-

ern recreation facilities, such as race and golf courses, soccer, and cricket. The race course opened on Saturday afternoons when the whites and a few moneyed native people frequented the track to gamble after the closure of the offices at 1 P.M.

8. When a domestic water supply, electric connections, and sewage links were available or technically possible, the "European town" residents utilized them fully, whereas their use was quite restricted in the "native town."
9. At an intermediate location between black towns and white towns developed the colonies of the Anglo-Indians who were the offspring of mixed marriages (European and Indian) and were Christians; they were not accepted by the natives, nor did they belong to the "pure bred" European community.
10. Starting from the late nineteenth century, the colonial city became so large that new living space was necessary, especially for the native elites and richer people. Extensions to the city were made by reclaiming the lowland and/or developing in a semiplanned manner the existing nonurban areas. Most of these developments were done by private cooperative housing colonies and specially designated improvement trusts which received financial contributions from city revenue.

As the colonial system got deeply entrenched in the Indian subcontinent and an extensive railway network was made operational, the waterfront locations accessible to oceangoing ships were no longer a prerequisite for a colonial headquarters. Calcutta, Bombay, and Madras, classical examples of colonial-base cities and generally represented by the model, were not the only suitable locations on the subcontinent for the high levels of administration. In 1911, the capital of British India was moved to the inland city of Delhi, which was not a seaport and not accessible to oceangoing ships. Thus, a new inland colonial city was implanted by the side of a historic city, Old Delhi, and was designated New Delhi.

Three other colonial urban forms *(Cantonment, Railway Colony,* and *Hill Station),* which need separate models to explain their urban developments, were also introduced on the subcontinent. They served very specific purposes: the Cantonment was a military encampment; the Railway Colony, surrounding a railroad station, was regional headquarters of railway operation and administration; the Hill Stations, at altitudes between 3500 and 8000 feet, (1067 to 2440 m.) served as resort towns for Europeans to escape hot summers on the plains and spend time in the midst of a more exclusive European community. No separate diagrammatic models have been presented in this chapter for the above-mentioned three urban forms, but they are briefly described below. Moreover, the imprints of cantonments, railway colonies, and hill stations were much less compared with the classical colonial-city model.

Cantonment Though there were 114 specially built Cantonments in the mid-nineteenth century on the subcontinent, they housed only about 227,000 soldiers, out of which about one-third were European. Many of the cantonments were adjacent to cities, and eventually with the urban expansion they formed a part of a metropolitan complex. The layout of the cantonments was planned in rectangular design with segregation of European and native soldier's barracks, parade grounds, eating places (canteens), and recreation facilities. The class distinction was strictly maintained by separating European soldiers from the officers and designating exclusive facilities for the latter. As in the "European town," the Europeans lived in the best quarters and the British members derived maximum benefits.

Railway Colony Like the Cantonments, the Railway Colonies also were planned communities with rectangular design and separate living quarters for British and native employees. The native employees lived in houses and neighborhoods whose type depended on the employees' rank. The neighborhoods of officers also differed according to rank. Some nearby space was always reserved for a native bazaar, as in the Cantonments. Recreation facilities, such as clubs, were different for the British and natives. If the Railway Colony was situated nearby a growing urban unit, eventually it formed part of the greater urban area.

Hill Stations The Hill Stations were—and still are—resort towns, located at the lower mountain ranges of the Himalayas and at appropriate heights of the South Indian mountains. There were about 80 such stations when the British left the subcontinent. They served mainly as resorts for the British communities of Delhi, Calcutta, Bombay, Madras, and Colombo during the summer months. Some of them also were designated as temporary summer capitals of British India. Thus, a part of the capital's administrative staff moved up to the mountains in the summer for several months. In the Hill Stations, houses and hotels were built for visiting Europeans; clubs served for daily get-togethers; the mountains permitted such hobbies as walking, hiking, and birdwatching. The main thoroughfare, known as the Mall in Simla and other Himalayan stations, provided not only European living quarters, but a pedestrian street, where everyone could meet (Fig. 9.8). Wealthy Indians and those native officers/employees who also went to the Hill Stations, remained second-class citizens in a community designated exclusively for the Europeans. The bazaar staffed by the natives was located at a lower-level street, parallel to the Mall. After independence the role of the Hill Stations did not change except that they were no longer used as summer capitals, and instead of Europeans, the well-to-do natives from the urban areas visited in the same frequency as the Europeans did.

Bazaar Based City Model

The traditional *bazaar city* is widespread in South Asia and has certain features that date back to precolonial times. Ordinarily, the city grows with a trade function originating from agricultural exchange, temple location, transport node, or various administrative activities (Fig. 9.9). Usually, a crossroad is formed where commodity sales dominate. In North India such an intersection is known as *chowk,* around which develop the houses of the richer people. Most merchants live either at the upper floor or at

Figure 9.8 The mall in Simla, where no vehicular traffic is allowed, has buildings of Tudor and colonial designs on both sides reminiscent of a true colonial hill station. (A. Dutt)

the back of their shops. Often the same house is used as a warehouse. Such shop-cum-house structures generally have one story in small cities and two stories in medium and large cities, though in very large cities many reach four stories.

The bazaar or the city center consists of an amalgam of land uses, which caters to the central place functions of the city. The commercial land use, dominating the center, consists of both retail and wholesale activities, which exist either in combination with, or in partial/complete separation from, each other. As the greater portion of family income is spent for the basic necessities of life—food, clothing, and shelter—most stores are related to retail sale of foodstuffs, and clothes. Perishable goods, such as vegetables, meat, and fish, bought fresh daily by consumers because of lack of refrigeration facilities in most homes, are sold in specific areas of the bazaar, which often lack enclosed walls and instead have a common roof. In the process of bazaar evolution, functional separation of retail businesses occurs: cloth shops stay together, attracting tailors; grain shops cluster with each other near the perishable goods market; and pawn-shops are adjacent to jewelry shops. Moreover, many other retailing establishments, such as dealers in shoes, bangles, and metal goods, cluster separately. Sidewalk vendors are present almost everywhere in the bazaar.

Wholesale business establishments also form part of the bazaar landscape. Situated near a suitably accessible location, they tend to separate according to the commod-

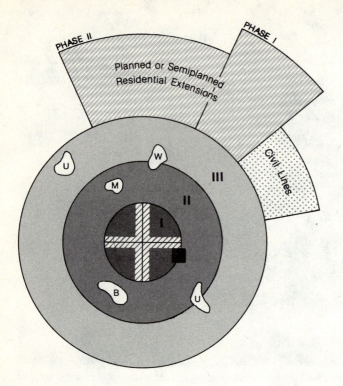

PHYSICAL SPACE

- Bazaar-based traditional city
- New extensions resulting from colonial impact
- Chowk or crossroads
- High-intensity commercial and residential land uses
- Wholesale market

SOCIOECONOMIC SPACE

- Wealthy residential and mixed commercial uses
- Mixed residential (wealthy and poor)
- Poor residential

CULTURAL SPACE

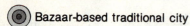
- Religious enclave (Moslem, etc.)
- Linguistic cluster (Bengali, etc.)
- Caste group (Washerman, etc.) (Untouchable, etc.)

Figure 9.9 A Model for the Internal Structure of a Bazaar-Based City in South Asia. (*Source:* Compiled by the author.)

ities they deal in, such as vegetables, grains, chillies, spices, and cloth, depending on the size of the city the bazaar serves.

Traditionally, modest overnight accommodation in the bazaar is provided by the public or nonprofit *dharmasalas* or *sarais* (inns) for a nominal fee. However, as a result of Western impact, some kind of hotel accommodation is now available in the medium-sized and large cities. Prostitutes and/or dancing girls used to be the only source of regular entertainment in the bazaars for those who wanted to visit them in the evenings. Today, movie theaters are the main recreational attractions in the evenings, though semi-Western restaurants and tea/coffee shops are used as places of recreation as well. Traditionally, the shops selling country-made liquor were never located in the bazaars, probably because liquor drinking in public places was considered ill-mannered in both Hindu and Moslem societies. As a result, such shops, where people drink indigenous *toddy* and consume snacks, are invariably located outside the center, preferably on the periphery. Only in recent years have Western-style liquor stores or bars started to be established in the center. Whereas at one time the only doctors were practitioners of indigenous medicines, now they are joined near the main streets of the bazaar by the practitioners of modern Western medicine. Barbers, who used to serve outdoors traditionally, have regular shops like those of Western countries, but many still operate on the sidewalks. Their establishments are, however, scattered all over the bazaar.

Thus, the inner core of the city develops an increased concentration of trade, commerce, and wealthy people. Beyond this inner core, in a second zone, the rich people live in conjunction with the poorer servants, but not in the same structure. The rich need the services of the poor as domestic servants, cleaners, shop assistants, and porters. The residences of the poor surround this second zone in a third area, where the demand for land is less and its price low. Whereas the contemporary Western counterpart houses much of its lower class in the city center, the bazaar city houses its lower income groups on the periphery.

As the city grows, ethnic, religious, linguistic, and caste neighborhoods are formed in specific areas. Their location varies in accordance with the time of their settlement and the availability of developable land. The untouchables always occupy the periphery of the city, although sometimes other housing develops later beyond their neighborhoods. In Hindu-dominated areas of India the Moslems always form separate neighborhoods. Often people who have migrated from other linguistic areas form specific neighborhoods of their own. For example, Bengalis migrating from Bengal to cities in the Hindi-speaking areas of the Ganges plain generally lived in neighborhoods known as *Bengali Tolas*.

Mixture of Colonial and Bazaar Models

The functional demands created by colonial and bazaar-type activities generated interaction between both. The British administrative requirements in the traditional cities resulted in the establishment of *Civil Lines*, generally on the periphery of the city. The Civil Lines were composed of a courthouse, a treasury, a jail, a hospital, police lines, a clubhouse, and residential quarters for the high administrative and judicial officials.

The streets for the Civil Lines were well planned, paved, and had trees planted on both sides. In provincial capitals, a governor's house, a secretariat, and extensive residences for different levels of government employees were also constructed. In the Native States of the subcontinent, where an indirect colonial rule was operational, a British regent with his staff resided at the state capital within a civil station, which looked like a colonial appendage attached to the bazaar city.

During the twentieth century, both before and after independence, when the local rich and the elites needed to build houses of their own, several government, semigovernment, cooperative, and private agencies planned developments outside of the traditional city. Consequently many traditional cities developed new extensions on their peripheries.

For the most part, however, the colonial cities never grew as they were conceived by the colonial masters. Traditional factors played an unavoidable role in altering the colonial forms. The traditional bazaar, inherent to the indigenous cityscape, always interacted with the colonial form. The bazaar thrived side by side with the CBD. As a result, to correctly model classical colonial cities such as Calcutta, Bombay, and Madras, it is essential to consider the impressions made on them by the traditional bazaars. All colonial cities bear imprints from bazaar forms, just as the bazaar cities received impressions resulting from colonial functional demands.

Contemporary Urban and Urbanization Characteristics

The traditional heritage, the impact of modern technology, psychological response to changing socioeconomic phenomena, regional specialization, colonial connection, and new alignments during the postindependence era have influenced contemporary urban and urbanization characteristics. First, an increasing decolonization tendency, resulted in greater agro-industrial development. This led to a reemphasis of the internal development of the countries and thereby accentuated development in such internal locations as Delhi, Lahore, Hyderabad (India), Bangalore, and Dacca. Second, the population explosion caused by a drastically reduced death rate and slowly declining birth rate created a rural labor surplus. Such conditions caused large-scale migration of unskilled labor to urban areas. This was known as the rural push. Third, after independence from British rule, the South Asian countries embarked on a large-scale expansion of college and graduate-level education. Thousands of graduates from native colleges, molded after Western systems, were either incapable of returning, or unwilling to return, to their home villages to modernize agriculture. They remained in the cities and augmented the ranks of the educated unemployed. Fourth, during the last several decades cities with a population over 100,000 persons have registered an unparalleled growth rate, until in the 1970s over 50 percent of the South Asian urban population lived in cities of this size. The increase in urban population ratio is attributable mainly to relatively greater growth rate of the larger cities compared with the medium-sized and small urban places. On the other hand, the small towns, those with fewer than 10,000 inhabitants, had stagnant or declining populations. Modern economies, based on more advanced facilities such as railroads, buses, and trucks, can be effective only if the urban centers are larger. The slow-moving bullock carts, a prevalent means of transport for

Figure 9.10 Bangalore, the cleanest of all large South Asian cities, presents a contrast in the slow-moving bullock cart on a concrete street pavement with the background of an office building built during the colonial period. Such contrasts are common in all large cities of South Asia. (A. Dutt)

the smaller towns, are becoming obsolete (Fig. 9.10). Association with traditional means of communication in the existing smaller towns restricts them from being transferred to a higher rank. However, when some towns do move up to the higher rank due to economic factors and/or natural population growth, they are replaced in the hierarchy less often now than in the past.

Fifth, cities with a population over 100,000 are generally organized now within municipal bodies. In 1687, Madras established the first South Asian Municipal Corporation with a mayor, aldermen, and burgesses. The Calcutta civic body known as the Calcutta Corporation was established in 1827. The Delhi Municipality was constituted in 1863. Most other cities were organized into municipalities starting from the nineteenth century. Sixth, the larger cities had a greater population density than did the smaller cities. Seventh, the larger cities attracted greater in-migration from both smaller urban centers and rural areas. Primarily the working-age male population comes to the cities as migrants, altering male-female ratios.

Eighth, sexual composition varies between the southern and northern cities. Northern cities have a greater proportion of males than those in the south, indicating a greater migration of single males from rural areas. In the South females generally accompany the migrating males. They move more freely because historically the Moslem impact and resultant *purdah* (seclusion of women in the home) was much greater in the North than in the South.

Two other cultural phenomena, crime and religion, present distinct regional patterns. The cities of north-central India have a greater concentration of violent crimes (murder, kidnapping, robbery, and rape). This unusual regional occurrence may be explained by the historical roots of the area, which contains a violent subculture. The religious composition of the cities of South Asia reflects the overall regional distribution of religious groups. In conformity with the religious composition of the respective countries, the cities of Pakistan and Bangladesh have a high concentration of Moslems, while those in Sri Lanka have a high concentration of Buddhists; and the Nepalese cities are predominantly Hindu. In India, even though 75 percent of the urban population is Hindu, non-Hindu religious groups are concentrated in some cities, reflecting conformity with the regional religious composition. For example, Srinagar, the capital of Kashmir, is located in the western Moslem belt of the realm and is 86 percent Moslem. In the Indian Punjab, the cities have a relatively high proportion of Sikhs. Christians are particularly concentrated on the southeastern coast. The cities of the west-central part of India have a high proportion of Jains and Buddhists. In a selected number of cities, the religious proportions do not correspond with the regional religious composition. The surburban city of Garden Reach is a typical example of such exceptions. It is situated in a Hindu-dominated region in the Calcutta Metropolitan District adjacent to the port. The seafaring Moslems, who work on the docks, were attracted to this city, while Hindus seem to avoid it.

Major Representative Cities

The main site and situation factors that have played significant roles in the making of the major cities of the subcontinent are the physical setting, the strategic location, the historical roots, the nodal and seaport locations, the industrial agglomeration, and the national and state administrative headquarters. No single factor has been instrumental in the making of a city of 1 million. Rather, a complex interplay of all or some of the above has made cities in South Asia grow.

Calcutta

From a late-seventeenth-century settlement the city of Calcutta developed a fortress at the center, a "European town" in the south, and a "native town" in the north. It grew spatially, with a CBD concentrated around the 1756 fort, which was demolished and rebuilt south of its original location. The "native town" extended considerably and many of the native rich and ever-increasing middle class filled the northern part of the city. Barbazar, an area reminiscent of the traditional bazaars, grew immediately north of the CBD. As in the past, Barabazar is still the most desirable residential area of the rich merchants (*Marwaris* and *Gujaratis*) who have migrated from the western part of India. The Marwaris and the Gujaratis are the main business community of the city. The ground floor of Barabazar is used for shopping and the upper floors for residences. Of all the places in the city, Barabazar currently has both the greatest gross and greatest floor-space density of population. Densities of over 1100 people per acre (2750 per hectare) in four-story structures have been recorded in some tracts of Barabazar. Barabazar presents the characteristics of a traditional bazaar center with commodity sales as the main business activity, high residential and commercial densities, and a large habitation of rich people. The Western-style CBD of Calcutta exists immediately south of the traditional Barabazar. The CBD is mainly an office-cum-commercial district with a low density of residential population. Extending southeastward from its eighteenth-century position, it includes a Western-style covered market facility erected in 1874 (New Market or the former Hogg Market).

As the city grew, its northern part reflected more traditional characteristics, while the southern part presented more of a European look. In between lies the CBD, including the *Chauringee,* the main activity center of the metropolis (Fig. 9.11). Since the formation of the Calcutta Improvement Trust in 1911, new areas have been reclaimed in the southern and eastern portions of the city to be inhabited mainly by wealthy Bengalis, the native inhabitants of the state.

Calcutta, a major port of India and the capital of the state of West Bengal, is India's largest metropolis. The Calcutta Metropolitan District (CMD), of which the city of Calcutta is a part, has an area of 500 sq. mi. (1300 sq. km.) and a population of 9.5 million (Fig. 9.12). The colonial characteristics of Calcutta city, however, were

Figure 9.11 Chauringee of Calcutta, which borders the eastern edge of the Maidan, is characterized by a broad street, where both buses and trolley cars operate as mass transport. An underground railway is currently under construction beneath this street. The Western-style skyscrapers have been added to the cityscape since the 1960s. (Permission of Pramob Mookerje)

348 Chapter 9, Cities of South Asia

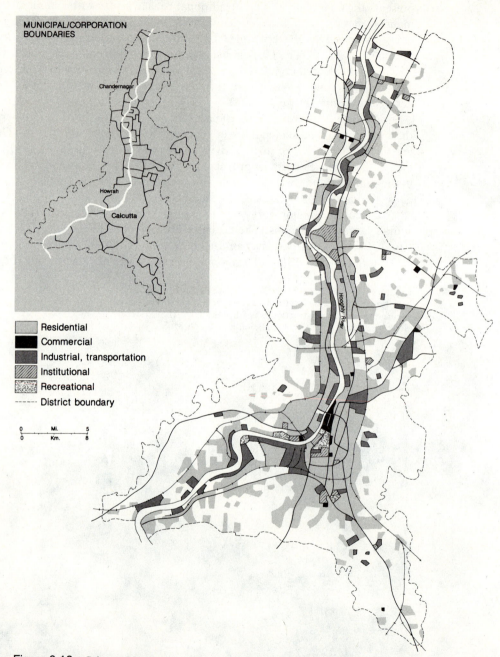

Figure 9.12 Calcutta Metropolitan District: Land Use. (*Source:* Ashok K. Dutt, S. P. Chatterji, and Margaret Geib, *India in Maps,* Dubuque, IA: Kendall Hunt Publishing, 1976.) Reprinted with permission.

restricted to its own municipal jurisdiction. The Calcutta Metropolitan District expanded along both banks of the Hooghly River in a linear and continuous pattern for about 50 mi. (80 km.) The CMD consists of about 500 local governing bodies in which the City of Calcutta is the largest, with 34 sq. mi. (88 sq. km.) and 5 million inhabitants. Away from Calcutta, the local centers of CMD typically present the traditional bazaar kind of land uses and are devoid of any imprint of a Western-style CBD.

The situation of the city was advantageous in forming an industrial nucleus. In the nineteenth century its seaport facilitated the import of wholesale machinery for the jute industry, the most significant industrial activity of the metropolis. Raw jute was produced in the nearby fields of the Ganges delta. From the mid-nineteenth century until today the jute industry has grown as a chain of mills stretching along both banks of the Hooghly River, turning the metropolis into the largest concentration of jute mills in the world.

Today the CMD is highly industrialized. It contains India's largest concentrated manufacturing capacity, accounting for 15 percent of the country's total manufactured goods. The engineering industry, the second largest in the CMD, is concentrated mainly on the right bank of the Hooghly in Howrah, Calcutta's twin city. Other important industries are paper, pharmaceuticals, and synthetic fabrics.

Being the most important commercial center of the country from colonial times, Calcutta has the largest concentration of commercial establishments, in particular, the headquarters of many native business firms, banks, and international corporations. Thirty percent of the country's bank clearances are handled in Calcutta.

In spite of recent stagnation in Calcutta's economy, the city attracts migrants from many different parts of northeastern India, the hinterland of the metropolis. After the partition of British India, a great many Hindu refugees from East Pakistan (now Bangladesh) migrated to Calcutta. In the late 1950s, 18 percent of the city's population had been born in East Pakistan. East Pakistan was also a Bengali-speaking region. As a result, the migration of East Pakistani Hindus enhanced the Bengali linguistic composition of the city. Two-thirds of the city dwellers speak Bengali, the native language of the area; one-fifth speak Hindi; and about a tenth speak Urdu. Though only a small percentage of Calcuttans can speak English, they are generally bilingual.

The lack of developable land and the employment "pull" of Calcutta cause long-distance daily commutating by both railroads and buses. Over 150,000 people commute to Calcutta daily from outside the Calcutta-Howrah twin-city complex. Though the railroads carry most long-distance commuters, buses and trolley cars service most nearby commuters. The fast-moving electric trains which move in and out of Calcutta and Howrah handle the bulk of commuters. The CBD of Calcutta, however, has no direct rail connection.

The employment pull also attracts a large number of migrants, especially from the hinterland. These migrants are largely males. Sixty-one percent of the city's population in 1971 was recorded to be male. Among the largest metropolises of the world, Calcutta is one of the most male-dominated.

Bombay

In 1672, Bombay became the capital of all British possessions on the west coast of India. The seventeenth-century British possession of the seven islands which now form this city initiated the construction of the fort. Beyond the fort grew a filthy "native town," where sanitary conditions were miserably poor. Poor drainage was the main problem. The "European town" grew around the fortress on higher ground, and protective walls were erected around it.

The main impetus to Bombay's development occurred when Britain's supply of raw cotton temporarily diminished in the early 1860s during the American Civil War and Bombay became an important supplier. This resulted in an amassing of huge capital by Bombay-based businessmen, and the city became the main cotton textile center of the realm. In 1853, the opening of railways eventually connected Bombay with a hinterland covering almost all of west India. The docks were modernized on the sheltered eastern part of the island, and Bombay served as entrepôt to the west coast of India. Bombay's physical extension occurred with its reclamation of land as the city grew from south to north.

When the fort area developed into a Western-style CBD, the British, followed by rich Indians, moved to Malabar Hill, Cumballah Hill, and Mahalaksmi on the southwest portion of the island. In the 1940s, the rich settled in another attractive area (Marine Drive), which lay along the bend of the Back Bay (Fig. 9.13). Its six-story buildings served as the mini-skyscrapers of the time. Because of an ever-increasing demand for commercial and residential land in the fort area and the lack of land on the narrow peninsula and the island city, dozens of skyscrapers have been erected since the 1950s at Nariman Point, generating a skyline resembling a miniature Manhattan. The poor, the middle class, and a few native businessmen settled mostly at the center and north of the island. Presently, the more Western colonial influence created by European settlements can be observed in the southern part of the city proper. On the other hand, the more traditional influences have remained observable in the north. In most recent times, the northern two-thirds of Greater Bombay, which lies north of Mahim Creek and the city proper, has undergone the development of planned housing suburbs and industrial parks.

Bombay, now the capital of Maharashtra, a state of India, is not only the second largest metropolis in South Asia, with a population of about 8.7 million, but also the largest port of the entire subcontinent. Though cotton textiles employ about half of the city's workers, general engineering, silk, chemicals, dyeing, and bleaching are also important employment sources.

The city attracts an enormous number of immigrants from the western part of India. Like Calcutta, it has a high proportion of males in the working-age group, which causes specific problems common to other South Asian cities as well. Two such problems are exemplified here. First, as the number of married males is far in excess of the females in Greater Bombay, a large proportion of males must live away from their wives. Second, as the number of unmarried males is much greater than that of the females, the former must search for their brides from outside the metropolis. Bombay

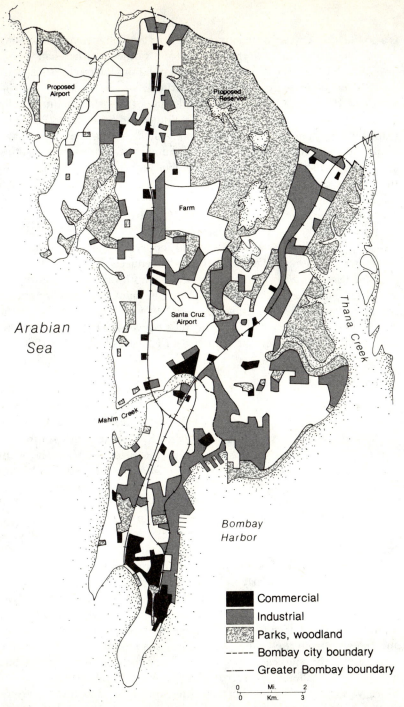

Figure 9.13 Greater Bombay: Nonresidential Land Use. (*Source:* Ashok K. Dutt, S. P. Chatterji, and Margaret Geib, *India in Maps,* Dubuque, IA: Kendall Hunt Publishing, 1976.) Reprinted with permission.

is also the most cosmopolitan among the South Asian metropolises. Bombay's diversity in religious composition surpasses that of all other South Asian cities.

Bombay further illustrates certain religious characteristics common to other South Asian cities as well. For example, the decline in the Moslem population between 1941 and 1951 resulted from the partitioning of British India into India and Pakistan in 1947, prompting a mass exodus of Hindus and Sikhs from Pakistan and Moslems from India. Indian cities such as Bombay then showed a proportionate decline in the number of Moslems and increase in the number of Hindus, whereas the cities of Pakistan showed a sharp decline in the number of Hindus and Sikhs while an increase in the number of Moslems. Other religious characteristics are typical of Bombay. First, the Zoroastrians (Parsis as they are called in Bombay) have consistently declined as a proportion of Bombay's population. They are concentrated in the city of Bombay in larger numbers than in any other place in the world. Therefore, the Parsi population has grown mainly as a result of natural increase rather than in-migration. The large in-migration of other religious communities reduced the percentile composition of Parsis, who also have a lower birth rate. Second, both Jains and Buddhists have registered significant increases in their populations. The Jains, mainly immigrating businessmen from Gujarat State, were drawn by Bombay's increasing commercial attraction. The Buddhists' increase resulted from the mass conversion of the local untouchables during the Neo-Buddhist movement launched in Maharashtra in the 1950s.

Madras

Situated by the side of the Bay of Bengal, Fort St. George was the focal point of Madras's settlement at the inception of the colonial era. The "black town" situated north of the fort walls was known as Georgetown. Georgetown's southeast corner, called Parry's Corner, forms the focal point of the present CBD. The whites' bungalows spread out toward the west and southwest from the fort and were separated by a large open space, Island Grounds, and public buildings such as hospitals. South of the "white town" was Mount Road (now Anna Salai), which eventually attracted large-scale commercial activities. In the extreme south and southwest of the city, areas were developed by government and semigovernment agencies for planned residential expansions after Independence.

The land use of Madras has a definite relationship to land value. The commercially used land, particularly in the center of the city and along Mount Road, has the greatest value. As the percentage of commercial land use increases, a significant increase occurs in the land value. Though land values in the southern portion of Madras do not decline significantly as one moves outward from the city center, in the north and the west from the center, land value falls sharply as the distance from the CBD increases. In the southeast along Mount Road the decline is gradual. Such a phenomenon reflects a differential microregional variation in distance decay of land values. Moreover, compared with Western cities, the land value gradient from the center toward the periphery is less steep, indicating lesser polarization of city land values in developing countries.

Madras, a seaport and the capital of Tamil Nadu State, has a population of 4.6 million and is a typical regional city. Three-fourths of the residents speak the language of the state, Tamil; 14 percent, Telegu; and 3 percent, Malayalam. True to its regional characteristics, 84 percent of the city's population is Hindu; 8 percent, Moslem; and 7 percent, Christian. In contrast to the North Indian cities, there is a balanced male-female ratio in Madras: 900 females for every 1000 males. This may be attributed to the South Indian women, who generally accompany their menfolk when they migrate to the city.

The existing high population density is related to the older areas of the city, particularly around the center of the city. In general, Madras's urban characteristics reflect a combination of colonial and traditional effects. The areas north of the CBD have experienced a more traditional impact, while in the south and southwest the colonial western impact is more perceptible.

Delhi

Delhi, the capital of India, combines a deep-rooted historical heritage with colonial and modern forms. Historical records confirm that 18 different capital sites in the Delhi area have been chosen in the past 3000 years; 17 actual sites have been identified (Fig. 9.14). One of the earliest capital sites, "Dilli," dates back to the first century A.D., but its location has not yet been pinpointed. Fifteen different names have been given to the various capital sites, but in spite of many efforts by the rulers to change it, the name "Delhi," derived from "Dilli" and later "Dhillika," has remained the name of the city.

The attraction for Delhi as the capital site was rooted in South Asia's physiography, locations of advanced civilization centers, and migration/invasion routes. Delhi occupies a relatively flat water-divide between the two most productive agricultural areas of the realm, the Indus and Ganges plains, where the most notable centers of civilization and power developed in the past. North of these plains and Delhi lie the insurmountable Himalayas; in the southwest lies the inhospitable Thar (Rajasthan) Desert. Following the strategic Khyber Pass and entering the vast Indus plains of Punjab, the continental migrants and invaders from the northwest frontiers of South Asia were impelled to control Delhi to insure a firm hold over the North Indian Plains. Delhi, being situated on the right bank of the Jumna, always provided an advantageous strategic location for commanding the Indus Plain to the west and the Ganges Plain to the east. The control of Delhi was so vital to the rule of North India that a popular saying arose: "He who controls Delhi, controls India." Moreover, Delhi's location by the side of the Jumna, a tributary of the Ganges, gave it access to the waterborne traffic of the Ganges system all year round.

Most of the historical sites of Delhi were located between the Delhi ridge and the Jumna, but the extensive developments that occurred after India's independence caused expansion of the city on and across the ridge. Old Delhi (the former Shahjahanabad), the only living urban relic of the past (the palaces, towers, forts, and walls of other sites are found in the form of brick and mortar complexes only) is a traditional bazaar-type Indian city with the Chandni Chowk as the main commercial center.

354   Chapter 9, Cities of South Asia

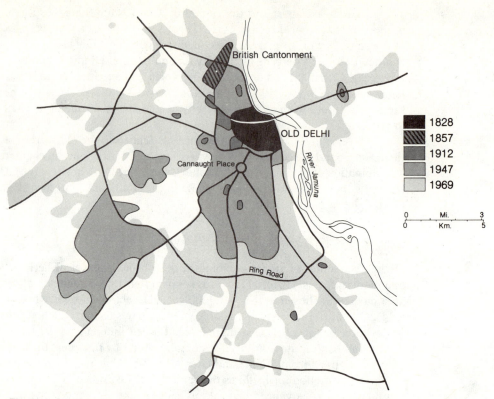

Figure 9.14 Growth of Delhi-New Delhi, 1828–1969. (*Source:* Gerald Breese, *Urban and Regional Planning for the Delhi-New Delhi Area,* Princeton, NJ: Princeton University Press, 1974.) Reprinted with permission.

New Delhi, situated south of Old Delhi, is a majestic colonial endeavor that emerged as a new city after the capital of British India was moved from Calcutta. The temporary site for the British capital from 1912–1931 was in the former cantonment and Civil Lines towards the northwest of Old Delhi, dating back to 1828. New Delhi was planned by a British architect planner, Edwin Lutyens, in a geometric form that combined hexagons, circles, triangles, rectangles, and straight lines. It became functional in 1931. Spacious roads, a magnificent viceroy's residence, a circular council chamber, imposing secretariat buildings, a Western-style shopping center (Connaught Place) with a large open space in the middle, officers' residences in huge compounds, and a gardenlike atmosphere formed the main elements of New Delhi. The new capital was separated from the congested, unsanitary, and generally poor conditions of Old Delhi by an open space. To British eyes, the congestion was so pathetic that in 1937 a Delhi Improvement Trust was formed to tackle Old Delhi's problems.

The main economic base of New Delhi is government service. After India's independence an increasing demand for housing was created by new government employees, which led to large-scale public housing developments around earlier settlements of New Delhi. The most noticeable feature of such developments was the segregation of large neighborhoods according to the rank of the government employees and foreign residents. Class rather than caste determined the new neighborhood composition. For example, diplomats and rich Indians were housed in the grand *Chanakyapuri* ("diplomat's city"), military officers in the *Dhaulakaun* complex, and lower-middle-class clerks were in the *Vinay Nagar*. Vivid imprints of a traditional city are reflected in Old Delhi, that of a colonial city in New Delhi. The modern developments are in many ways a continuation of the colonial forms.

Karachi

Karachi, the most populous city of Pakistan, is the fastest-growing metropolis in South Asia. Situated by the western edge of the Indus River delta, it is highly industrialized and has a busy port. After independence it became the federal capital of Pakistan.

In 1941 Karachi had a population of 435,000. Karachi registered a phenomenal growth rate of 161 percent during 1941–1951 and 81 percent during 1961–1972, mainly resulting from large-scale industrialization. Today the population is nearly 6 million. Before 1947, the city's industries consisted of a few servicing workshops and small handicrafts establishments located in and around the traditional bazaar-type center. By the early 1960s more than half of the city's industrial work force was employed in the newly developed, large-planned industrial estates at the periphery of the city.

The rapid industrial growth greatly accentuated the pull factor of the city. Not only Pakistanis, but Moslem refugee immigrants from India flocked to Karachi in large numbers. No other South Asian metropolis has so large a nonnative population base as Karachi. In the 1960s only 16 percent of Karachi's citizens were native born. While 18 percent were in-migrants from different parts of Pakistan, 66 percent were Indian Moslem refugee immigrants. Though the natives of the city and immigrants from India have a balanced age-sex pyramid, the in-migrants from West Pakistan, most numerous in the active age group (20 to 35), have a higher ratio of males.

Though immigration from India and in-migration from Pakistan caused greater religious homogeneity, it also turned the city heterogeneous in linguistic composition. As a result of partition, all but a few thousand Hindus left for India, and Urdu-speaking Moslem immigrants came in large numbers from the north and central parts of India. The in-migrants from Pakistan were largely Punjabi Moslems, who were bilingual (speaking Urdu and Punjabi). Thus, Karachi's population became essentially Moslem. Linguistically, Sindhi, the native language, had a minority status because of the much greater influx of Urdu speakers from Punjab and India. Moreover, since the 1947 partition, Urdu became Pakistan's national language, providing an additional impetus for becoming the majority language of Karachi's citizens. Since prepartition times, however, there was a preexistent base of Gujarati speakers, both Moslems and Hindus, further augmented by the Gujarati Moslem refugees from India. Gujaratis, in keeping with their traditional business acumen, are the well-to-do merchants and mill owners of Karachi. Thus, apart from English, a lingua franca of the elites, three languages are prevalent in the city: Urdu, Sindhi, and Gujarati. Karachi-based newspapers are published in all four languages.

The center of Karachi represents a true bazaar model: high population density, high intensity of commercial and small-scale industrial activity, and relatively higher concentration of rich people (Fig. 9.15). Toward the east from the center of the city were the planned cantonment quarters that originated during the British occupation dating back to 1839. The British Civil Lines developed farther to the north after Karachi became the capital of the new Province of Sind. During much of colonial times, Karachi remained confined to a land use pattern that placed the docks in the southwest, the bazaar in the center, and the Civil Lines and military establishments in the east and toward the north. After independence, new suburban residential developments occurred surrounding the eastern two-thirds of the colonial city, while planned industrial estates were built mainly toward the northern and western fringes. Thus the trends of colonial landscape expansion continued, with the native rich settling toward the east adjacent to the former Civil Lines and cantonment. One study points out that the southeastern section of the city has attained the highest socioeconomic status.

Dacca

Dacca, the capital and premier city of Bangladesh, is centrally located in the country on the left bank of the Burhiganga River, a tributary of the Meghna-Ganges system. The southern parts of Dacca occupy the gently rolling higher grounds of the river terrace.

Like Delhi, Dacca is an old city and is known to have existed since the seventh century A.D. Dacca was governed by the Hindu Sena kings of Vikrampur (situated near Dacca) from about the ninth century A.D. The Dacca of that time was known as Bengalla, a small marketing town with its center near the present Bangla Bazar. Thereafter, Dacca came under Moslem rule (1203–1764). Dacca intermittently served as the capital of the eastern provinces of the Mogul Empire (1608–1764) and attained great commercial importance. It is estimated that toward the end of the seventeenth century, the city had over 1 million inhabitants and stretched for 12 mi. (19 km.) in length and 8 mi. (13 km.) in breadth. The European traders, largely Portuguese, Dutch, English, and French, started coming to Dacca after 1616. In 1706, however, the capital of the eastern provinces was shifted from Dacca back to Rajmahal and Dacca began to decline.

This gradual decline continued well into the colonial period. The rise of Calcutta as the major city of the region, and of British India for that matter, further hindered the growth of Dacca. Not until 1905 did Dacca receive some impetus, when Bengal was temporarily partitioned and became the capital of the newly established Province of East Bengal (1905–1911). Although this status of Dacca was short-lived, it resulted in certain important developments in the city. The population increased slowly, however, from about 104,000 in 1901, to 239,000 in 1941.

Dacca received a fresh impetus for growth in 1947, when British India was partitioned and Pakistan was created. A large-scale immigration of Moslems from India became the major factor in its rapid population increase. In 1961, Dacca had a population of 550,000, a 132 percent increase since 1941. The establishment of jute and other manufacturing industries in Dacca and its vicinity since the partition has also contrib-

Major Representative Cities 357

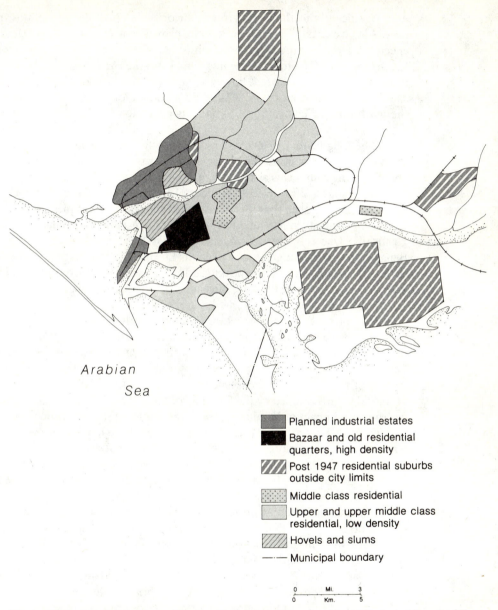

Figure 9.15 Karachi: Land Use. [*Sources:* Z. A. Khan, "Demographic and Ecological Trends of Karachi," "Population Growth of Karachi," and "Some Aspects of Industrial Land Use in Karachi," in *Pakistan Geographical Review,* 26, No. 1 (1971), 35–44; 24, No. 2 (1969), 111–129; 23, No. 2 (1968), 92–102.]

uted significantly to the city's growth. Prior to 1947, Dacca had almost no industrial base. As the capital of what was then the province of East Pakistan, Dacca also experienced the growth of multifarious administrative-commercial activities, which provided the necessary pull factors for the migrants from the rural areas and smaller towns. The most rapid growth of Dacca, however, has been since the establishment of Bangladesh as an independent country in 1971. With a population of some 3 million, Dacca is now the tenth-ranking city in South Asia; it is also one of the fastest-growing cities in the region.

The long history of Dacca has left its obvious imprints on the cityscape as well as on its internal structure. The legacies of successive Hindu, Moslem, and British rules are present in such forms as temples, mosques, churches, monuments, public buildings, and place names. With over 90 percent of the city's population Moslem, mosques are so numerous in Dacca that it is often called the City of Mosques. Hindus are the most important minority group (about 8 percent); the rest are Christians and Buddhists. Linguistically, Dacca is very homogeneous, as over 95 percent of the population speak Bengali, the native language of the land. During the Pakistani period (1947–1971), a substantial number of Urdu-speaking Moslems who came from either North India or West Pakistan were in the city; but since the creation of Bangladesh, the majority of them have departed.

The present internal structure of Dacca is closely tied to evolution of its urban form. Dacca can be divided into two sections by an old railway line passing through the city. The areas to the south and southwest of this line are considered to be old Dacca. The old town is characterized by a narrow and sinuous road pattern, a high density of population and houses, congestion, and unsanitary conditions. The nucleus of the old town, bounded by the Dulai *Khal* (canal) and the Burhiganga River, exemplifies the deep impact of Hindu culture in the names of its various localities (Goalnagar, Kamarnagar, Kumartoli, Patuatoli, and Sakhari Bazar), which are associated with different Hindu professional castes (*Goal*—milkmen; *Kamar*—blacksmiths; *Kumar*—potterymen; *Patua*—people connected with jute processing; and *Sakhari*—conch-shell cutters). The later development of the western part of the town under the Moguls took place with the construction of palaces; mosques; housing for ministers, noblemen, army commanders, traders, and professionals; and military establishments. This expansion is characterized by such districts (or *mohallas*) as Islampur and Mughaltoli. The Lalbagh Fort was built in 1676, after the old fort (present central jail) was renovated. The river became the lifeline of the city, and the *ghats* or landing places acquired new names: Sanderghat, Sawarighat, Chandnighat, and Badamtalighat. All these names of *mohallas* and *ghats* have either Persian or Arabic associations. It was during more than 100 years of Mogul rule that a more active Moslem culture was superimposed over its Hindu indigenous base in the city. The conspicuous products of Moslem construction and urban expansion led to a diversity in the Dacca landscape.

The areas to the north of the old town are generally called new Dacca. Although parts of new Dacca were settled during the Mogul period, most of its development occurred during the present century. The partition of Bengal in 1905, when Dacca became the capital of a short-lived Province of East Bengal, led to the laying out of a Civil Lines-like administrative town centering around the Ramna area. Wide roads and winding avenues enclosed administrative structures and residential housing in pleasant bungalows with large enclosed yards for high officials. These were interspersed with grass-covered open spaces, parks, and a race course. In subsequent years, the University of Dacca and other educational institutions were set up in this area. The Ramna area is still the administrative-educational focus of Dacca, maintaining its characteristics of a colonial Civil Lines. The areas to the southeast of Ramna also developed during the British period, mainly as residential districts for the upper- and middle-class native population.

The present land use pattern of the city reflects not only the evolutionary pattern of the past but also the efforts of the Dacca Improvement Trust (Fig. 9.16). The part of the business area lying in the old city shows the traditional bazaar-type characteristics, while the portion in the new city is closer to the colonial type. Other important business zones of the city manifest mixed characteristics. The major part of the city land use, however, is given to residential uses. The residential areas, in both the old and new areas of the city, have customarily assumed a neighborhood character with distinctive population differentiated by density, social class, house types, and internal road layouts.

Figure 9.16   Dacca: Land Use. [*Source:* A. U. Khan, "Land Value Pattern in Dacca City," *Oriental Geographer*, 19–20, No. 1–2 (1975–1976), 9–19.]

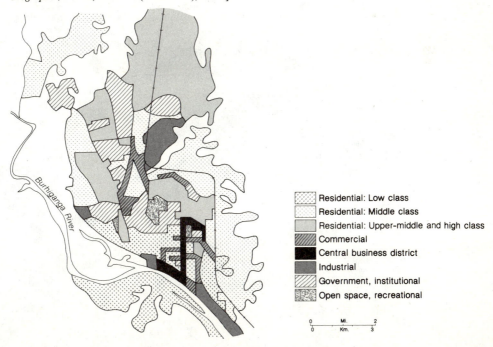

Urban Problems and Solutions

Several important urban problems, inherent in the urbanization process of the developing countries, are also prevalent in South Asian cities, among them the post-World War II urban population explosion, housing shortage, insufficient development of utilities (water supply, drainage, sewerage, and electric supply), increasing water and air pollution, and financial incapability.

The push out of the rural economy coupled with accentuated natural growth of the urban areas has augmented the city population, particularly in the large cities. This has happened without a reciprocal increase in the manufacturing sector, resulting in large-scale unemployment. Moreover, most rural migrants, being unskilled, are incapable of employment in modern industries. They are forced to swell the ranks of low-paid porters, rickshaw pullers, domestic servants, and other manual laborers (Fig. 9.17). Even a large number of educated youth find it difficult to obtain suitable employment. The following extract from a short story reflects the desperate level of Calcutta's unemployment situation:

> I have no important connections to help me, and so I have been making job inquiries at various offices and factories on my own. I even made a futile effort in bribing an agent, or you may call him a gentleman cheat, to get me a job; this I did by pawning my mother's

Figure 9.17 A street scene in central Calcutta, which was part of the native town section during colonial times. The street is characterized by ground floor shops, sidewalk peddlers selling snacks, soft drinks for sale (to the left), and (to the right) hand-pulled rickshaws, still a source of urban transport in South Asian cities. (A. Dutt)

valuables. Now I am supporting myself by tutoring pupils privately. But at the moment I am desperate. . . . There is no hope of my getting a government position because I am over the age limit, although I applied five years ago when I was eligible. I am unable to get even a coolie's job, let alone that of a bookkeeper or office peon. Can you tell me how I can get a job?[1]

Housing shortages emanating from large-scale in-migration and a relatively lower rate of new house building plague all the cities of South Asia. The demand for housing leads people to live in smaller units and in unsanitary environments. As many as 67 percent of the households in Calcutta and 83 percent in Greater Bombay have only one room, in Delhi and Madras over 60 percent. Moreover, the average number of persons per room in the households also is increasing. In Bombay there was an increase from 4.5 persons per room in one-room households in 1911 to 5.0 in 1961; 1.8 persons per room in three-room households in 1911 to 2.1 in 1961.

A large number of people who cannot afford to rent a house often turn into pavement dwellers. In 1973, there were 50,000 in Calcutta alone. Though their numbers vary from season to season they essentially are concentrated in the central areas of the city.

Slums or *bustees* have developed in almost all the major cities of South Asia (Fig. 9.18). Though the name *bustees* is used in Calcutta, it is *jhunggi* in Delhi; in Bombay it is *chawl*. The *bustees* have been defined by the government of India's Slum Areas (improvement and clearance) Act of 1954 as predominantly a residential area, where dwellings by reason of dilapidation, overcrowding, faulty arrangement, and lack of ventilation, light, or sanitary facilities—or any combination of these factors—are detrimental to safety, health, and morals. Moreover, the slums mainly consist of temporary or semipermanent huts with minimal sanitary and water supply facilities and are usually located in unhealthy waterlogged areas. In Madras, though the slums consist of 6 percent of the area, they accommodate one-third of the city population. In the city of Calcutta alone one-fifth of the city population lives in the *bustees*. Out of 30,000 huts in Calcutta *bustees,* 50 percent have no access to sewerage facilities. The unsanitary condition of such slums made Calcutta an endemic center of cholera up until the 1960s. Kipling once described Calcutta as the "cholera capital of the world."

The increasing population causes increased densities. The city of Calcutta has an average residential density of almost 300 persons per acre (750 per hectare), whereas Delhi has 200 (500). The greater number of people necessitates increased per capita water supply, school space, recreation grounds, and transportation facility developments, all of which are inadequately provided for by the cities. Bombay, for example, has only one-fourth (0.10 hectare) of an acre open space per 1000 population, though 4 acres (1.6 hectares) is the suggested standard by the Master Plan of Greater Bombay.

The CBD of Calcutta is frequented by both fast-moving vehicles and slow man-

---

[1] Prafulla Ratan Gangopadhay, "Sankat," in *Jugantar* (Calcutta), *Saradiya Sankhya,* p. 253, 1970. Translation from Bengali in Ashok K. Dutt and Ramesh C. Dhussa, "The Contrasting Image and Landscape of Calcutta through Literature," *Proceedings of the Association of American Geographers,* 8 (1976), 104.

Figure 9.18   A Thatch-Roof *Kuchcha* Slum in Bangalore City (*kuchcha* referring to any structure built of temporary materials). (A. Dutt)

pulled or animal-driven vehicles. The mixture of vehicles causes uncontrollable chaos on the streets. Free movement of animals, particularly "sacred cows" in the medium-size and small cities, adds to the traffic problems. Though almost four-fifths of the vehicles entering the CBD of Calcutta are automated, 43 percent are private automobiles and 27 percent taxis, but only 9 percent of the fast-moving ones are buses and trolley cars (trams), the mass transport carriers. These buses and trolley cars transport about 1.5 million passengers in and out of the CBD. The Howrah Bridge, the only connection between Calcutta and Howrah, is traversed by more vehicles and pedestrian commuters than any other location in Calcutta. Between 1946 and 1964, the bridge recorded a 445 percent increase in vehicular traffic, though the number of slow-moving vehicles remained stationary at 14,000. A second bridge connecting Howrah and Calcutta was under construction in 1980, but for several decades the 1941-built cantilever Howrah Bridge has been a well-known traffic bottleneck.

The increasing number of automobiles causes extensive air pollution. In Bombay, where vehicular density has been estimated to be about 800 per sq. mi. (308 per sq. km.), 15 tons of carbon monoxide are thrown into the air daily. In Madras, automobile pollution is greatest in the areas where vehicular traffic is slowest. Coal-burning industrial furnaces and domestic ovens, commonly used for cooking, are responsible for about 250 tons of particulate matter and 75 tons of sulfur thrown into the air daily in Calcutta.

South Asia's urban problems are enormous. The facilities cannot keep pace with the ever-increasing population. Because South Asian nations are poor, their limited financial resources constrict the developmental programs; even some of the rudimentary urban facilities cannot be provided.

Planning

Modern town planning began in South Asia in 1864 when Sanitary Commissions were appointed for the three Presidencies of Madras, Bengal, and Bombay. Water supply and layout of sewage systems were rudimentary elements of planning introduced. These were followed by the electric lighting of streets, the establishment of numerous parks and playgrounds, and, in some instances, the creation of mass transport facilities such as trolley cars (trams) in Calcutta, Delhi, and Karachi and suburban electric railway communications for Bombay, Madras, and Calcutta. After the establishment of the Improvement Trust in Bombay in 1898, large unsettled areas of the city were drained, reclaimed, developed, and then provided with the infrastructure of roads, sewage systems, and water lines to house the increasing number of people. The newly expanded areas were less congested, had wide streets, were provided with parks and playgrounds, and had a more substantial look than most of the older areas lived in by the poorer native peoples.

Patrick Geddes, a noted biologist who is better known as a sociologist and city planner, spent several years planning cities on the subcontinent starting in 1941. Though best known for his novel outlook in planning Indore, Lucknow, and Lahore, Geddes helped in making plans for many cities, including Baroda, Colombo, Dacca, Madras, Madurai, and Patiala. He did not care for the architect's drawing-board masterpieces, but exposed a "folk" aspect in city planning. To him, knowing what the people wanted, maintaining the historical heritage of Indian cities, and creating a garden-city atmosphere were most important. Though Geddes's ideas helped to introduce a certain human element, city planning during the colonial period in general evaded the pressing problems of congestion, lack of facilities, and unsanitary conditions of the central parts of the bazaar city.

With the formation of national governments after independence, the attitude toward city planning changed. For the first time, the old, dilapidated areas of the city were given attention. The slums became one of the main areas of improvement. Overall, systematic approaches for planning the metropolis were favored. As a result, the metropolitan planning organization that was formed for Delhi in 1956 came out with a master plan in 1961; and the organization formed in Greater Bombay in 1954 finalized a development plan in 1964. Slum clearance projects were operative in Karachi and Dacca from 1970. These two cities also were engaged in metropolitan planning.

The Delhi master plan, incorporating all of the continuous built-up areas of Delhi, visualized two complete ring roads and a national highway along the river Jumna, in addition to several major roads. High density areas were envisioned for old and adjacent parts of New Delhi and low density areas outward from the center. For the first time, plans were evolved to gradually thin out the density of Old Delhi and increase the density in New Delhi. The Connaught Place CBD shopping center was earmarked for expansion; a green belt, 1 mi. (1.6 km.) wide, surrounding the metropolis was proposed; and several towns within 50 mi. (80 km.) of Delhi were designated as secondary urban centers to promote parallel developments, reducing the pressure on Delhi.

The regional plan for the Bombay Metropolitan Region envisions the establishment of a New Bombay, a planned satellite new town on the mainland of the Indian peninsula and separated from Greater Bombay by Thana Creek, an extension of the Arabian Sea. New Bombay, planned to be a twin city with Greater Bombay, has extensive areas for industrial development along with a port and has wide green belts around its landward sides. New Bombay is expected to divert growth away from Greater Bombay and will act as parallel growth center, relieving pressure on Greater Bombay's mounting problems of employment, housing, utilities, and transportation.

The Calcutta metropolitan plan calls for three parallel development centers or "countermagnets:" Siliguir, about 200 mi. (320 km.) north; Asansol, about 100 mi. (160 km.) east; and Haldia, 40 mi. (64 km.) to the south. These centers are supposed to reduce pressure on Calcutta by industrialization and diverting potential migrants from Calcutta. Conforming with the basic linear pattern of the Calcutta conurbation, a strong linear traffic pattern with ring roads around Calcutta and a 10-mi. (16 km.) north-south underground railway have been proposed. The underground railway is expected to be completed in the early 1980s. The present mono-centered metropolis around Calcutta has been deemphasized in favor of creating another center at the northern extremity around Kalyani and Bansberia. One of the most remarkable features of Calcutta planning is the pragmatic approach toward slum improvement. The slums or the *bustees* are in the process of being cleaned up by a special legislative provision given to the Calcutta Development Authority. Through this provision, the slums are provided with underground sewerage, individual sanitary toilets in households, tap water connections inside the homes, paved lanes and streets, and electrification of homes and streets. All these improvements have been introduced by the government from tax resources. By the same special legislation, the landlords of the *bustees* are forbidden to increase rent or evict tenants unnecessarily. Thus, the public money spent for *bustee* improvement is not used for the profit of *bustee* landlords, but for the improvement of the hut dweller's sanitary conditions, without making any basic change in the structure of the buildings.

Though efforts have been made to integrate the planning activities in the metropolis, several organizations engaged in planning and improvement activities have been created without proper jurisdictional definitions. The Calcutta Metropolitan Planning Organization, the Calcutta Metropolitan Development Authority, the Improvement Trusts of Calcutta and Howrah, and the Calcutta Metropolitan Water Supply Board operate in the same area limits of the Calcutta Metropolitan District without appropriate cooperation and integration.

All areas of Dacca to the north, northwest, and east of Ramna that developed since 1947, reflect the modern town-planning endeavors of the Dacca Improvement

Trust, which, after being established in 1957, produced a master plan for the city. Planned residential districts have developed for the middle and upper-middle classes in Azimpur, Dhanmandi, and Muhammadpur and for the upper class in Gulshan. A planned commercial district in Motijhil and an industrial estate in Tejgaon have also been established. In order to improve the intracity transportation situation, the old railway line that passed through densely settled areas has been removed, and a new line and railway station have been constructed along the northeastern edge of the city.

New Towns

New towns have been built as separate entities to serve as industrial, transport, university, or capital cities. Western planning imprints are evident in all the new towns because they have been planned by either Western or native planners trained in Western systems. Broad streets separated by neighborhoods, a gardenlike atmosphere, clean housing with adequate utilities, and separation of nuisance-causing land uses such as heavy industry and transport terminals from residences are generally common to all contemporary new-town planning. The best-known new towns of South Asia are Islamabad, planned by Doxiadis, and Chandigarh, planned by Le Corbusier.

Islamabad Islamabad, capital of Pakistan and situated at the foothills of the Himalayas at an elevation of 1800 feet (540 m.), has an undulating site of exquisite natural beauty. City building started in 1961, and people started to settle there in 1963. The city plan combines an extensive Islamabad Park toward the northeast, adjacent to which administrative and university centers have been established (Fig. 9.19). Linear blocks or belts of built-up land uses separated from each other by broad boulevards, and a central open space have been designed in such a way that each one of the uses could be extended southwestward toward Rawalpindi, because it is to that direction Islamabad is most likely to grow. Only small-scale industries such as bakeries, printing, service, and others necessary to meet the daily needs of the citizens have been allowed in the inner city. As these industries do not have any nuisance value and are considered incongruous uses, they have been located by the side of the residential strips. However, a space has been reserved for the larger and nuisance-causing industries on the south-central periphery of the city. The administrative center, the seat of the central government, has been located in the north so that it can be extended along the foothills in the future. The residential area comprises small townships or neighborhoods linked by a central commercial district and several trading units. Thus, such daily requirements as shopping, schooling, and recreation can be found in the neighborhoods themselves. Pedestrian and vehicular traffic have been separated.

The CBD and special institutions have been designed in such a way that the residents can go to their place of work either by walking or by taking mass transport. The CBD (along Khyaban Igbal) has been designed to contain multistoried buildings. The Islamabad capital site has an area of 350 sq. mi. (907 sq. km.), half of which consists of Islamabad Park.

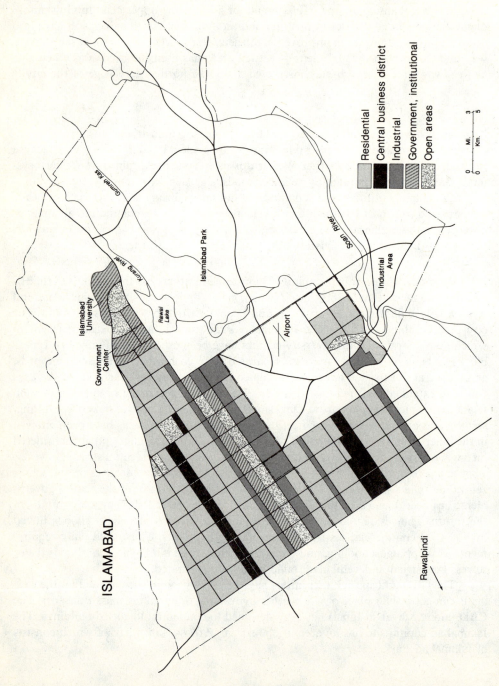

Figure 9.19 Plan of Islamabad. (*Source:* Master Plan for the Metropolitan Area of Islamabad and Rawalpindi, Capital Development Authority.)

Chandigarh Like Islamabad, Chandigarh is also located in the gently sloping terrain of the Himalayan foothills. Originally it was chosen for the capital site of East Punjab; now it functions as the joint capital of two states of India: Punjab and Haryana. The city, planned in the 1950s and mainly constructed in the late 1950s and early 1960s, is projected to accommodate a population of 500,000. It has a seven-level hierarchic road system, a government complex to the northeast, and a central commercial district out of which radiates linear commercial developments. Though the road system mostly follows the rectangular grid, the continuous open space along the median between the main roads provides an uninterrupted vista of openness. The residential area is divided into neighborhoods with primary schools, shops, and recreational facilities. A green belt surrounding the city also has been established to check unplanned developments.

Prospects

Both Chandigarh and Islamabad have been built at enormous cost. Other new towns are also too expensive. It is unlikely that construction of new towns can really solve the stupendous urban problems of South Asia. New towns will serve only the particular functions for which they are built. The future health of South Asian cities depends on comprehensive and continuous planning. Several cities already have established a basic infrastructure for such planning. The success of city planning will depend on how the planners and politicians weigh the city problems, how they make financial investments for the improvement of the city, how they integrate city planning with each country's development, and how ingenious the plans are formulated to solve the unique problems of South Asian cities.

RECOMMENDED READINGS

Breese, Gerald. *Urban and Regional Planning for the Delhi-New Delhi Area.* Princeton, NJ: Princeton University Press, 1974.
 Traces the historical background of modern Delhi in a social framework and analyzes planning activities since the turn of the century.

Brush, John E. "The Growth of the Presidency Town." In *Urban India: Society, Space and Image,* edited by Richard G. Fox. Durham, NC: Duke University Program in Comparative Studies on Southern Asia, 1970, pp. 91–113.
 The special growth patterns of Calcutta, Bombay, and Madras are evaluated.

Chandrasekhara, C. S. "India." In *Encyclopedia of Urban Planning,* edited by Arnold Whittich. New York: McGraw-Hill, 1974, pp. 514–46.
 Urban and regional planning in India are assessed in a broad historical perspective.

Dutt, Ashok K. "Delineation of the Hinterland for Calcutta Port." *The Professional Geographer,* 23 No. 1 (1971), 22–27.
 Calcutta's various levels of influence areas—catchment areas for daily perishable goods markets, the metropolitan sphere, and the economic hinterland—are delineated and their characteristics analyzed.

Evenson, Norman. *Chandigarh.* Berkeley and Los Angeles: University of California Press, 1966.
 A comprehensive anatomy of planning in Chandigarh.

Khan, Zafar Ahmad. "Population Growth of Karachi: The Example of a Large City in Developing Countries." *Pakistan Geographical Review,* 24, No. 2 (1969), 111–129.

This is the most elaborate description of Karachi's spatial growth and demographic composition, particularly after 1947.

King, Anthony D. *Colonial Urban Development Culture, Social Power and Environment.* London: Routledge and Kegan Paul, 1976.

A comprehensive sociological analysis of colonial urban forms of New Delhi, the hill station of Simla, and cantonment towns.

Mitra, Asok. *Calcutta, India's City.* Calcutta: New Age Publishers, 1963.

One of the classic socioeconomic evaluations of Calcutta.

Munsi, Sunil K. *Calcutta Metropolitan Explosion—Its Nature and Roots.* New Delhi: People's Publishing House, 1975.

Existing patterns and problems of Calcutta are portrayed historically.

Murphey, Rhoads. "The City in the Swamp: Aspects of the Site and Early Growth of Calcutta." *The Geographical Journal,* 30 (1964), 241–256.

Noble, Allen G. and Ashok K. Dutt, eds., *Indian Urbanization and Planning: Vehicles of Modernization.* New Delhi: Tata McGraw-Hill, 1977).

Contains over 20 recently written articles, including John E. Brush's "Growth and Spatial Structure of Indian Cities," Wilford A. Bladen and P. P. Karan's "Environmental Pollution and Its Perception in the Calcutta Hooghly-Side Area," Sulabha Brahme's "The Role of Bombay in the Economic Development of Maharashtra," and A. Ramesh and Allen G. Noble's "Pattern and Process in South Indian Cities."

Sundaram, V. K. *Urban and Regional Planning in India.* New Delhi: Vikas, 1979.

An exposition and critical analysis of urban and regional planning practices in India since 1947.

Turner, Roy, ed. *India's Urban Future.* Berkeley and Los Angeles: University of California Press, 1962.

A collection of articles from a group of internationally reputed scholars from different disciplines on India's urban patterns and prospects; of particular interest is the contribution made by John E. Brush, "The Morphology of Indian Cities."

Wheeler, Mortimer. *Early India and Pakistan.* New York: Praeger, 1959.

A classic reference to Indus Valley civilization cities: Mohenjodaro and Harappa.

Yadav, C. S. *Land Use in Big Cities: A Study of Delhi.* Delhi: Inter-India Publications, 1979.

An intracity spatial analysis of Delhi using quantitative techniques to test the applicability of concentric zone and sector theories.

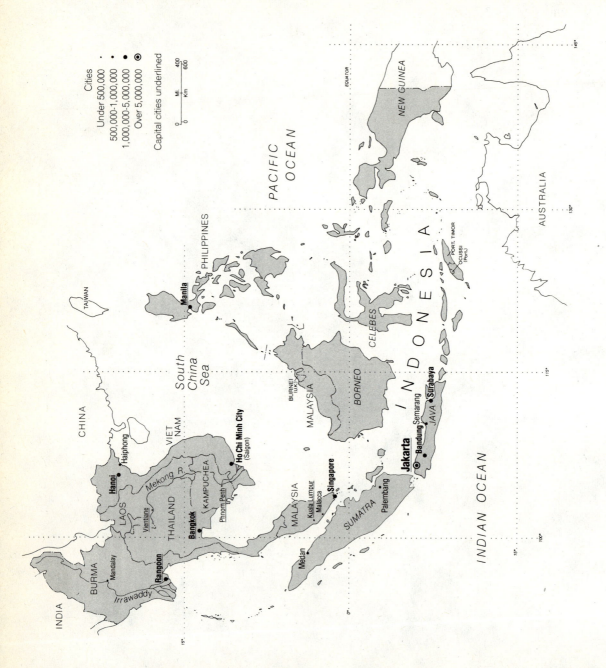

Figure 10.1 Major Cities of Southeast Asia. (*Source:* Data derived from United Nations, Department of Economic and Social Affairs, *Global Review of Human Settlements, Statistical Annex,* published by Pergamon Press, New York, 1976.)

Chapter 10

Cities of Southeast Asia

Thomas R. Leinbach
Richard Ulack

Southeast Asia in the World Urban System

Southeast Asia is one of the least urbanized regions of the world. With barely 24 percent of the population, or about 90 million of the region's some 370 million inhabitants, estimated living in cities in 1980, Southeast Asia ranks just slightly above Subsaharan Africa and South Asia. Indeed, only one independent nation in Southeast Asia is more than 50 percent urban, Singapore. With 93 percent of its population urban, Singapore is far above the average for the region; but it must be kept in mind that Singapore is a tiny city-state of a mere 2.5 million with virtually no rural hinterland, and hence a statistical exception that does not change the basically rural character of Southeast Asia as a whole. The only other political unit in the region that is more than 50 percent urban, Brunei at 63 percent, is also a statistical oddity, a ministate of barely 1.3 million, whose sole income is derived from petroleum. The rest of the countries in the region are overwhelmingly agrarian based, and hence the percentage of urban population ranges from highs of 39 and 33 percent for the Philippines and Malaysia, respectively (two of the relatively more industrialized and advanced nations in Southeast Asia), to lows of 13 and 19 percent for Laos and Vietnam, respectively. Kampuchea (Cambodia) probably has the lowest percentage of urban population, as a result of ruthless antiurban policies of the past few years, but no reliable data exist for that country today.

As with Subsaharan Africa and South Asia, although Southeast Asia remains relatively nonurban today, the growth rate of urban places is much higher than the natural population growth rate. Thus, the cities, and particularly the primate cities, are exploding. In 1950 only two cities in the whole region had a population over 1 million. By 1980 there were 11, and two of these (Jakarta and Manila) were each over 5 million, followed by five in the range of 2 to 5 million, and four in the 1- to 2-million category (Figs. 10.1). The primate city syndrome is well developed in this region, largely as a result of the colonial legacy, which created or strongly influenced the development of the primate capital cities that still dominate the region, including Manila, Jakarta, Singapore, Hanoi and Ho Chi Minh City (Saigon), Bangkok, and Rangoon. Indonesia is the only country in the entire region that has more than one major city. That country has a good half dozen major cities with a population close to or more than 1 million, but most of them again were the creation of Dutch colonialism, particularly Jakarta, which at over 7 million is three times the size of the next largest city, Surabaja.

As a result, Southeast Asia is also plagued by the urban woes found in cities throughout the Third World. A few of the more obvious problems are the large numbers of unskilled workers from rural areas who find integration into the urban way of life difficult; lack of housing and the consequent emergence of sprawling squatter and slum areas; inadequate urban services such as fresh water, electricity, public transportation, schooling, and health care; plus the ever-present unemployment and underemployment. In this regard, one of the striking aspects of Southeast Asia's urban character is the contrast between prosperous, highly Westernized, modern Singapore and the other major urban centers of the region.

Evolution of Cities in Southeast Asia

If one were to select a key phrase which might be helpful in understanding the urban characteristics of Southeast Asia today, that phrase would be "impact of external influences." The first true urban places began to emerge about the first century A.D. Initially, a few places became important centers due principally to contact with Indian sailors, merchants, and priests. Since then Southeast Asia has adapted to many cultural influences which have affected urbanism. In addition to the Indians, the Chinese, Arabs, Europeans, and, more recently, the Americans and Japanese have shaped the material form and cultural milieu of the cities.

Whereas external influences play an important role in understanding contemporary urban Southeast Asia, one must also realize that the indigenous population had its own belief systems, settlement forms, and, in short, its own cultures. It was with these cultures that the external forms were blended. Thus another key concept in understanding urban Southeast Asia is adaptation.

In thinking about these ideas of foreign impact and adaptation, the "situation" of the region relative to the rest of Asia and the world should be noted. Southeast Asia is located between the two great culture realms of China and India. The region has more coastline perhaps than any other major world region, and much of this coast is highly accessible to sea traffic. This factor led to the emergence of many settlements on or near coastal sites. Several of these became major cities in the region and have acted as centers of trade, gathering the rich agricultural and natural resources (for example, tin, rubber, spices, lumber, sugar, copra) from their hinterlands.

As is the case with other former colonial areas, the evolution of cities in Southeast Asia can be discussed in three periods. The first, which lasted until the early sixteenth century, is the period wherein Indian, Chinese, and, later, Arabic influences predominated. It was the period during which most of Southeast Asia's indigenous Indianized kingdoms existed. Each of these kingdoms had at its center a very large and ornate capital city in which a "god-king" resided. Some of the greatest of these cities have since disappeared and remain only as legacies of a glorious past. The second period began in 1509 with the arrival of the first Europeans into the area, the Portuguese. Shortly thereafter other Europeans arrived, and soon new settlements, or more often rapid expansion of existing settlements, emerged. A few such centers have since become the primate cities of the region. They are today the largest cities, the centers of commerce, education, and industry. The urban systems that exist in Southeast Asia today greatly reflect the impact of these Europeans, and more recently of the Americans and the Japanese.

Urban Southeast Asia in Precolonial Times

It is difficult to date many of the major events of precolonial Southeast Asia; much of the information available is based upon archaeological evidence and this often from only a few sites. It is generally agreed that sedentary agriculture, the earliest villages, and metal use emerged sometime during the thousand years before the Christian era began. These events first took place probably in northern Vietnam (Tonkin), and from here indigenous and early Chinese cultural practices (such as ancestor worship) diffused south to ultimately affect the rest of Southeast Asia. Thus, 2000 years ago much of the region was still characterized by small villages largely independent of one another (although in some areas local chiefdoms had emerged).

A century before the Christian era began, Indian seamen, merchants, and Brahmans (Hindu priests) entered the region, and it was through such individuals that selected Indian cultural characteristics began to appear in Southeast Asia. The characteristics most important for our purposes included Indian concepts of royalty (the god-king), of politics, and of religion. These characteristics brought about the various indigenous kingdoms that were to emerge in Southeast Asia, and with them the first true cities. During this period the more astute indigenous leaders rose to prominence by blending the advice of priests with the concepts of an Indian belief system. These central figures possessed authority which was wide ranging. By the first century A.D. true kingdoms with central cities or capitals had emerged.

Until the European period began, the urban history of Southeast Asia may be viewed through two types of cities: the inland sacred city and the coastal market city. Although both types were the base of the god-king and each performed a sacred as well as a trade function, the two differed significantly in other ways. The inland sacred city was most often the more populous and drew much of its wealth from a large rural hinterland which provided both labor and food. As a consequence it normally had a large area under its control. Furthermore, the Indian religious impact was more in evidence in the sacred city. For example, monumental stone or brick temple complexes were usually located at the city center.

Coastal market cities, located on coasts or river banks with limited hinterlands, were generally smaller and more compact and dependent upon maritime trade for their wealth. They usually did not control extensive territories. Yet another difference was that the functional and population characteristics, and therefore the morphology, of the market city was more complex than those of the sacred city. Maritime trade brought many different peoples and goods to the ports, which resulted in the establishment of clearly differentiated residential and commercial areas.

The inland sacred cities were built to function indefinitely, but the length of time they functioned was based largely on the power of the kingdom's central figure. Thus, when a ruler's authority declined the sacred city also declined and eventually disappeared. Ironically, the less permanently constructed coastal cities, because of their largely maritime, economic functions, often grew in size and importance over time.

The coastal market cities were probably the first to emerge in Southeast Asia. Examples of such cities include the trade-based capital city of the earliest important kingdom of the region, Funan. The city, called Vyadhapura ("city of hunters"), was located near the apex of the Mekong delta and was a significant port for Indian and Chinese traders. According to early Chinese accounts, Vyadhapura emerged about the first century A.D.; for five centuries, until the decline of Funan, it was a leading city of the region.

Funan was ultimately replaced by one of Southeast Asia's best-known kingdoms, that of the Khmer dynasty. At its peak this Indianized kingdom claimed a territory that included present-day Kampuchea and parts of Laos, Thailand, and Vietnam. At its center was the inland city of Angkor. The city was established in the ninth century and underwent many changes before its abandonment in the fifteenth century in the face of Thai aggression. It was perhaps the largest and most glorious of the region's early cities. During the twelfth century, the city reputedly supported a population of several hundred thousand, truly remarkable for that time. The city was carefully planned and resembled other inland sacred cities in terms of its emphasis on Hindu and Buddhist cosmology. Thus, a large brick or stone temple complex or monument was at the city center, and other religious buildings as well as the buildings of royalty, the aristocracy, and administration could be found nearby. These were usually surrounded by a walled or moated area. During the twelfth century Angkor's greatest temples (Angkor Wat and the Bayon) were constructed. These edifices stand today to remind us of a glorious past.

Few places in Southeast Asia could compete with Angkor in terms of size or splendor. Its monumental architecture was rivaled only by Borobudur, the ornate eighth-century Buddhist temple complex built during the time of the Sailendra dynasty of central Java. Another important inland sacred city was Pagan, located in Upper Burma on the Irrawaddy River. Pagan, the capital city of the Burmese kingdom from the eleventh to the thirteenth centuries (though founded in the ninth century), was an important center of Buddhist learning and architecture, as well as a powerful capital during its zenith. In addition, other lowland areas, including the Chao Phraya basin of Thailand and portions of Java, contained important inland, agrarian-based sacred cities.

In addition to Vyadhapura, other notable but more recent examples of pre-

European coastal market cities were Palembang and Malacca. Palembang, located on the southeastern tip of Sumatra, became the port capital of the maritime-trade-based Srivijayan kingdom which emerged in the seventh century and declined by the fourteenth century. The city's strategic location near the Straits of Malacca and Sunda, rather than its elaborate and functional architecture, help explain its longevity. Indeed, today the city is an important port and market city in Indonesia. Malacca, established about 1400, is one of the more recent coastal market cities of the region. It is located on the Malay Peninsula and faces the Strait of Malacca. For some time it controlled the maritime trade that passed through the Strait. Prior to European intervention the city never held a permanent population of more than a few thousand. Nevertheless, the Malacca sultanate (by the tenth century Islam had become firmly established in parts of insular Southeast Asia) was quite powerful and from its small but defensible site ruled over much of the Malay Peninsula and nearby Sumatra.

Essentially, then, two types of cities prevailed before the sixteenth century. These were found at strategic coastal trading locations and at inland sites which formed the foci of the extensive lowland "state." When the Europeans arrived few major cities were located in inland regions; most of the kingdoms had vanished or declined in power and many of their cities had been abandoned. Conversely, maritime trade was thriving and so were the coastal market cities to which, of course, the Europeans were attracted. Only in the Philippines, which primarily because of its peripheral location lacked an urban tradition, were there no cities. It was left to the Spaniards to establish the first true cities in that archipelago.

Urban Southeast Asia in Colonial Times

The impact of Europe can be dated to 1511 when the Portuguese captured the port of Malacca. A fort was constructed and served as a control point for shipping into and out of the region. The Portuguese were soon followed by the Spanish (1521), the British (1579), the Dutch (1595), and the French (mid-1600s). These Europeans, and later the Americans (1898) and Japanese (1930s), came for a variety of purposes, the most important of which was economic gain. During the first centuries after the initial penetration the Europeans were primarily interested in gaining control of the shipping routes and trade in the region. They were less concerned about other pursuits such as political imperialism or religious proselytism. Consequently, the European impact on individual cities and more specifically upon the regional urban system was only minimal and designed to aid in the control of the local trade. The Europeans captured and subsequently established garrisons in a few indigenous coastal cities such as Malacca and Ambon, the chief port of the Spice Islands in eastern Indonesia. In other coastal cities they made contact and formed treaties with local rulers. Although some impact upon city growth and territorial control was exerted as a result, these effects were minimal until the nineteenth century. Two important exceptions must be mentioned. Beginning in 1565, the Spanish established territorial control over most of the Philippines. In order to consolidate their political and economic dominance many settlements were established. Some of these grew to become important cities. This early urban system in the Philippines also served to facilitate the conversion of the population to Catholicism. The cities that ultimately emerged, such as Manila and Cebu, acted as centers from which the new religion diffused. The other exception was found in Dutch Java. During the seventeenth century the Dutch East India Company established a few permanent settlements, one of which, Batavia (now Jakarta), was to become the largest city of the region. The Europeans thus had an urban impact upon these two areas almost from the beginning of their contact with the region.

By the nineteenth century European interest in Southeast Asia had increased. Europe's industrial revolution brought about an increased demand for primary agricultural products and natural resources such as lumber, tin, and oil. Furthermore, the relative distance between Europe and Southeast Asia was beginning to shrink as improvements were made in transportation. In the nineteenth century the advent of the opening of the Suez Canal was the major reason for the increased interest in the region. All of these factors led to the political control of almost all of Southeast Asia by the late nineteenth century. In order to properly administer these newly acquired territories, old settlements rapidly expanded and newer cities emerged. Only Thailand remained independent from European control. But this nation, too, was to feel the effects of Europe, and later of America and Japan.

The effect of the colonial powers upon cities was most evident in what were to become known as the primate cities of the region. These largest cities completely overshadowed the rest of the cities in their respective urban hierarchies. They were the major commercial, administrative, financial, cultural, and educational centers within the individual countries. Included were Bangkok, Manila, Batavia, Saigon, Singapore, and Rangoon (Figs. 10.2 and 10.3). Indeed, these cities today remain as primate centers within Southeast Asia, although the overriding importance of a few of these cities has perhaps declined slightly in recent times (Fig. 10.4). Other elements of the urban hierarchy should not be ignored, and actually many other smaller cities emerged in nineteenth century Southeast Asia because of the European impact. The mining towns of Malaya, the upland resort centers or hill stations found throughout the region, and the small regional administrative centers are but a few of the examples that could be cited. All of these, however, were overshadowed by the truly great cities of the region.

These great cities at the end of the colonial era had several characteristics in common. First, all were located on or near the sea and on a river. The Europeans needed access so that their ships could export primary products from the region and import secondary products from Europe. The colonizers unknowingly encouraged the decline of inland cities, which actually began prior to European contact. Maritime trade and the establishment of foreign communities meant that the importance of these more remote cities was lessened. In a sense, Southeast Asia was turned "inside out"; that is, development was encouraged on the coast and suppressed in interior locations. Second, the city populations, especially in the twentieth century, grew very rapidly as a result of high rates of immigration. Many migrants from rural areas and immigrants from foreign nations (especially China and India) came to the cities in search of jobs or business opportunities. Beginning in the early twentieth century lower death rates brought about by improved hygiene also produced higher rates of natural population growth,

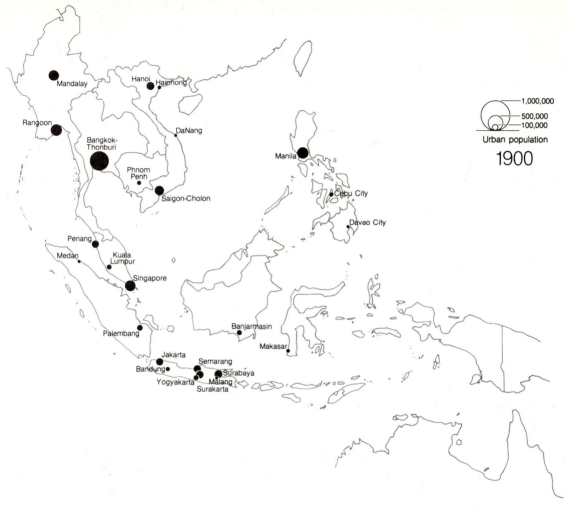

Figure 10.2 Major Cities of Southeast Asia, 1900. (*Source:* Compiled by the authors.)

especially in the urban areas. Third, these largest cities, as well as most of the other cities of the region, witnessed an expansion of their foreign populations so that in some cases they outnumbered the indigenous population. Especially significant for the cities in the region have been the large number of Chinese who worked, and lived, in the city's commercial areas. A further characteristic of the foreign populations is that they have traditionally lived in segregated residential areas. Chinatowns, such as Glodok in Jakarta, and other ethnic concentrations exist today. Fourth, all of these great cities (except Bangkok) were originally laid out in a grid pattern. And fifth, all were characterized by multiple functions although the most important were clearly the economic and related port functions.

378 Chapter 10, Cities of Southeast Asia

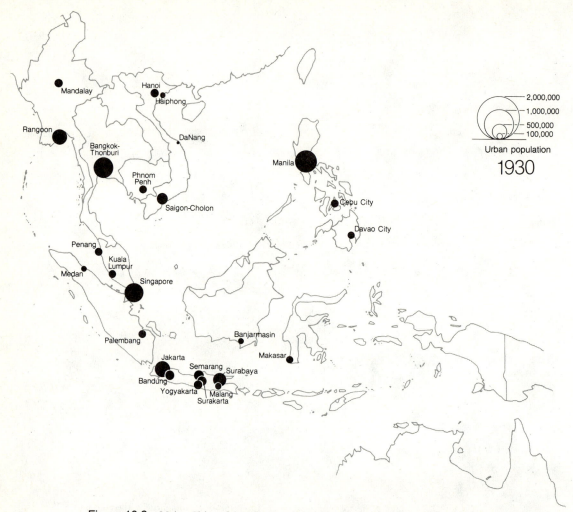

Figure 10.3 Major Cities of Southeast Asia, 1930. (*Source:* Compiled by the authors.)

As we have already noted, the first two great cities to be settled by Europeans in Southeast Asia were Manila and Batavia. Spanish conquistadores, under Miguel Lopez de Legazpi, entered Manila Bay in 1571, and it was decided that the capital of the Philippines would rise on its shore. Specifically, the settlement was built on the Pasig River where there already existed the two sultanates of Maynilad (from which the city takes its name) and Tondo. These Moslem villages were destroyed by the conquistadores, and soon after the Spaniards began construction of their city, which included the famous walled area known as Intramuros (Fig. 10.5). The city prospered and grew rapidly as the center of the Manila galleon trade with Mexico and the focus of Catholicism in the Far East. For almost four centuries the Spanish and the Ameri-

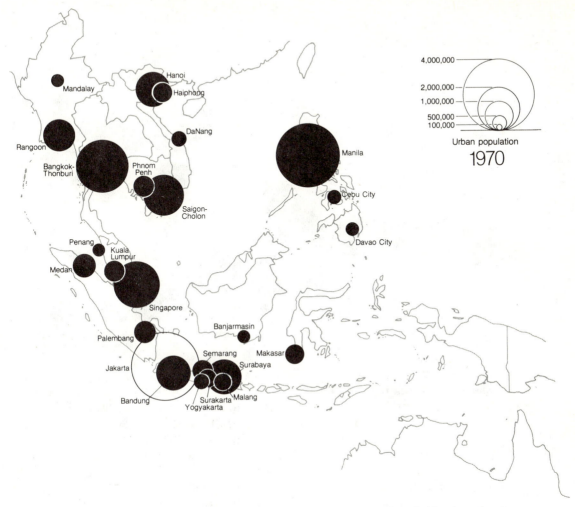

Figure 10.4 Major Cities of Southeast Asia, 1970. (*Source:* Compiled by the authors.)

cans used Manila as their administrative and economic center. Manila was, and still is, an excellent example of the primate city. The next largest metropolitan area in the Philippines, Cebu City, was only one-eighth the size of metropolitan Manila by the time of national independence in 1946.

Early Dutch settlement in Jayakarta (renamed Batavia in 1619) was established more peacefully than in Manila. Agreement was reached between the Dutch East India Company (the trading company which was to rule in Indonesia for nearly two centuries) and the indigenous ruler that allowed the Dutch to construct buildings at the mouth of the Tji Liwung, a small river upon whose banks the city stands today. The first Dutch building, a combination warehouse and residence, was built in 1611, and

Figure 10.5 Spanish-built Fort Santiago, a part of Intramuros, overlooks Manila's Pasig River. (T. Leinbach and R. Ulack)

many others soon followed. In 1619 Jan Pieterszoon Coen laid out a plan for the city, and soon Batavia replaced nearby Bantam as the preeminent city of Java. Much of early Batavia was modeled after the cities of Holland; canals were dug and the narrow, multistoried Dutch residences were also copied. It was soon discovered that the style of architecture found in Europe was not functional in places like Java, and eventually the style was altered to better fit conditions in a tropical environment. The city grew rapidly. By the time of Indonesian independence in 1948 it was already the largest city in Southeast Asia, with a population of nearly 2 million.

Singapore is truly a colonial city; at the time the British selected its site, the only human settlement nearby was a tiny fishing village. The city was founded and planned by Sir Stamford Raffles in 1819 (Fig. 10.6). The site on Singapore Island was selected in part because of its strategic location at the tip of the Malay Peninsula astride the important Strait of Malacca sea route. This locational decision of Raffles showed great foresight, since Singapore is today the largest port in Southeast Asia. In the early planning of the city, care was taken to provide separate residential areas for the diverse ethnic groups which made up the city. Indeed, this segregation is still evident today, though to a lesser degree. Singapore is an excellent example of a plural society where economic functions and cultural characteristics are attributed to different groups living in separate areas. Chinese immigration quickly overwhelmed the numbers in other ethnic groups, and today Singapore is an independent nation with a majority of its population of Chinese origin. Other nonindigenous groups important in the settlement of Sin-

Figure 10.6 Government Building Reflecting British Colonial Influence in Singapore. (T. Leinbach and R. Ulack)

gapore include Indians, Pakistanis, Ceylonese, Arabs, Bugis (from Celebes), and, of course, Europeans. In the original city plan the Europeans were accorded the best site near the city's business center, but as the city grew, population pressure forced the Europeans to the more peripheral suburbs, where they built impressive residences. This process has been repeated in the other colonial cities of the region.

Saigon, with Manila and Batavia, had on its site an indigenous settlement which included a citadel and fortress surrounded by a Vietnamese village. In fact, the French helped the Annamese build the fortress, only to destroy it when they captured the city in 1859. Thus, the history of modern Saigon, like that of Singapore, begins with the French planning and building of the city. It is true, however, that adjacent Cholon, the Chinese market center across the Saigon River from Saigon proper, has existed since the 1770s and is today a part of metropolitan Saigon. The city soon became the capital of all French Indochina (present-day Vietnam, Kampuchea, and Laos), and thus it too grew rapidly due in part to its administrative function. Furthermore, Saigon is located in the Mekong delta region, one of the world's great rice granaries, and has performed an important function as an agricultural collection, processing, and distribution center. Since Indochina's "independence" in the 1950s, the Vietnam War, and the subsequent Communist takeover there have been many alterations in the city. Today, Saigon is called Ho Chi Minh City, one of the more obvious reminders of recent change.

Rangoon, one of the last great colonial cities, both resembles and differs from the other cities. One author calls Rangoon a "grafted" city in that it, more than the others, was an important indigenous center before being captured by Europeans. The ancient Shwe Dagon pagoda, the focal point of Burmese Buddhist life, existed there for quite some time. In addition, King Alaungpaya conquered Lower Burma in 1755 and made Rangoon (which means "the end of strife") the principal port and capital city. The British took the city first in 1824 and recaptured it again in 1852, at which time it became the administrative center of Lower Burma. Soon it was the capital of the entire colony. Later, much of the city was constructed from British plans and built upon the indigenous base. Once again, European emphasis on the development of a capital on the coast led to the evolution of another primate city. Early in the colonial period the interior city of Mandalay was Burma's largest, but by the time of Burmese independence in 1948 Rangoon was more than four times as large. Rangoon also experienced the influx of foreign groups that was typical of the colonial cities. Here the Indians, by the 1930s, accounted for more than one-half of the city's population.

Bangkok, another great city of colonial times, was never colonized by Europeans. Nevertheless Western influence was exerted by the British, and to a lesser extent by the French, which had an enormous economic impact upon the city. More recently, of course, the Americans and Japanese, as is true in most Southeast Asian cities, have had an economic or military impact. The city is relatively new in that it was not settled until 1782, at which time Rama I began construction on an easily defensible but swampy site on the east bank of Thailand's major river, the Chao Phraya. For several years prior to this the capital had been located across the river in Thonburi, today a part of the Bangkok metropolitan area. Construction included a walled palace complex, one half of which included the Grand Palace. During the long reign of Rama V (King Chulalongkorn) from 1868 to 1910 Bangkok realized its greatest public works achievements. The king was an early supporter of the automobile; thus roads were built in the city. Canal building, which gained for Bangkok the nickname "Venice of the East," was continued. Port facilities, a telegraph service, and a railway were among the other public works developed. By the twentieth century, the city was as modern as any in Southeast Asia. As the focus of trade and the center of a rich agricultural hinterland, the population grew rapidly and soon Bangkok had become the epitome of the primate city.

Major Representative Cities

With the independence of Malaya in 1957, virtually all of Southeast Asia had gained its freedom. Only a few enclaves remained as remnants of colonial times. The economies of the nations, and their cities, still depend in many ways upon former colonial nations or neocolonial influences, such as that of Japan. But certainly expressions of nationalism and independence have brought about change in the cities. Ornate architectural embellishments, name changes, and the emigration, sometimes forced, of foreign populations are but a few of the more obvious changes. Political forms new to the region, such as socialism, certainly have affected urbanization. Furthermore, although the six great cities are still preeminent in their respective nations, other cities have begun to usurp at least a little of their influence. Thus, while Rangoon, Manila, and Bangkok still completely overshadow their closest national rivals, Kuala Lumpur in Malaysia, Medan, Bandung, and Surabaya in Indonesia, and Hanoi in Vietnam are a few examples of cities which have gained considerable importance. In short, some changes have occurred in the urban hierarchy of Southeast Asia. These changes have affected the cities and nations in different ways depending upon the political and economic climate in each of the nations.

A few generalizations can still be made about most of the larger cities of postcolonial Southeast Asia. First, virtually all of them have experienced rapid population growth. Second, foreign elements, especially the Chinese, still play a dominant role in the commercial activities of most cities even though their percentages have declined in the postcolonial era. More recently the Japanese influence has mushroomed and is a significant feature in the economic life of the cities. Japanese tourists, consumer goods, and investments are abundant within the cities of the region. Third, through the process of "urban concentration" many of the larger coastal cities still exert a dominant influence. Although some new seaside towns have grown to importance, the "lead effect" captured as a result of earliest settlement is dominant. These towns act as service centers and collection-distribution points for inland hinterlands. They also perform important economic functions related to external trade and shipping. The cities depend heavily upon the export of primary goods from their hinterlands and the import of processed goods from the developed nations. And fourth, the types and locations of land use in the larger cities of the region are similar, although cities in the socialist countries appear to be undergoing some dramatic changes. As we have already seen, the location of the land uses can be explained in part by the way the cities were planned during colonial times. More recently, however, factors that include rapid population growth, city expansion, and the increasing importance of local manufacturing activities also aid in explaining the location of the activities in the cities.

The last generalization about the modern city in Southeast Asia is well summarized in a model put forward by the geographer T. G. McGee (Fig. 10.7). His land-use diagram illustrates the locations of old (the port zone) and new (the industrial estate) economic activities as well as residential and commercial zones which existed during colonial times or which have arisen in more recent years. An example of a new land use is the peripheral new suburbs, which include the low income squatter areas so prevalent in Southeast Asian cities today. The squatter phenomenon is viewed by some as a problem, and it, too, will be addressed in the following section. The alien commercial zone, located in the CBD, generally has the highest population density. It is usually in this area where the Chinese reside. Often entire Chinese families will live in "shophouses" or residences attached to the small businesses they operate.

With these generalizations in mind, we can use a few selected cities in the region to illustrate some of these characteristics in more detail. The discussion which follows is not intended to encompass all of the region's major cities but rather selects a variety of different-sized cities in order to illustrate patterns and characteristics in urban Southeast Asia.

The Largest Cities: Jakarta and Manila

These two largest cities of the region resemble each other as well as other primate cities. They have both, for example, grown rapidly in terms of population. Between 1950 and

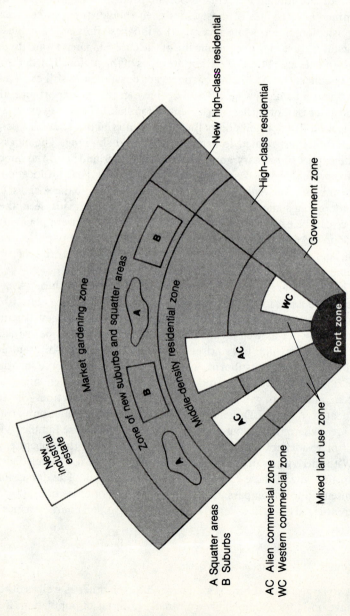

Figure 10.7 A Generalized Model of Major Land Use Areas in the Large Southeast Asian City. (*Source:* T. G. McGee, *The Southeast Asian City,* Praeger, 1967, p. 128.) Reprinted with permission of author.

1970 the population of each city nearly tripled while national populations less than doubled. In 1980 the population of the entire metropolitan area of each city stood at over 7 and 5 million respectively. In Manila, this has meant that the actual urbanized area of the city has spilled outside of the original city boundary and now includes a part of contiguous Rizal Province (Fig. 10.8). The new cities that have emerged nearby, or the older settlements that have merged with Manila, are all within the metropolitan area. Such places include Pasay City, Caloocan City, and Quezon City. Often the populations of these cities are reported separately, and thus the population given for Manila (the political city) is smaller than it is in reality. Also in the metropolitan area is the suburban town of Makati, which contains some of Manila's most expensive housing subdivisions as well as modern shopping centers and luxury hotels. If we compare the map of Manila with McGee's model it is evident that the two are similar (Figs. 10.7 and 10.8). Manila's port zone (adjacent to the old Spanish walled area and Fort Santiago) and commercial zone, as well as much of its government area (including Malacanang Palace, the presidential residence), are all located at its core on Manila Bay. From this core the other zones radiate outward until the market gardening zone is reached. Beyond that, rural lowland rice fields prevail, for Manila is located near the Philippines major rice-producing area.

In recent years Jakarta has also diffused outward very rapidly, especially along the major road axes to the south, east, and west (Fig. 10.9). One minor difference between Manila and Jakarta is that in the twentieth century the latter has had two cores, a primary and a secondary one. The primary core is that area of the city called "Kota," and the secondary core is located at Tandjungpriok, the port zone established in the late nineteenth century, some 6 mi. (10 km.) east of the primary core.

As suggested in the introduction to this section, manufacturing has become more important in the largest cities, but it is also true that industrial development has not progressed as rapidly as had been hoped. Because of this and heavy population increases, the cities still have only a small proportion (about one-fifth) of their labor force in manufacturing jobs, a characteristic different from that in most cities of the developed world. Most of the labor force is still found in the ubiquitous tertiary, or service, sector. Furthermore, a disproportionate share of manufacturing takes place in these largest cities. In Manila, for example, are located two-fifths of the industrial establishments in the Philippines. A few new industrial estates with heavy industry (especially in Singapore and Malaysia) have emerged, but most of the industries of the cities are small scale. Examples are food processing, textile manufacturing, and other small industries well known to specific cities. In Manila, for example, internationally renowned cigars are made and rope and cordage are manufactured from the locally cultivated abaca plant.

A City-State: Singapore

Singapore is an anomaly in Southeast Asia today in that it is both an independent nation and a city. In short, it is a city-state (Figs. 10.10 and 10.11). Until independence in 1965 it had been a British colony except for the period 1963–1965 when it was part

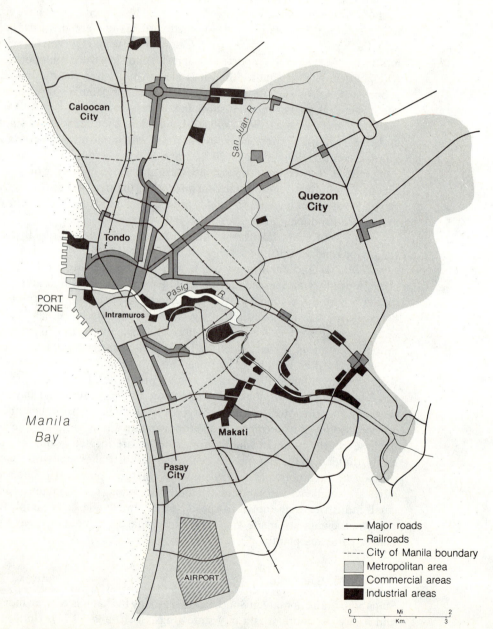

Figure 10.8 Manila Metropolitan Area. (*Source:* Compiled by the authors.)

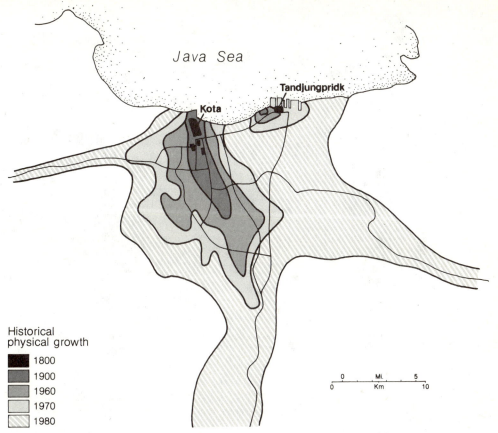

Figure 10.9 Historical Growth of Jakarta. (*Source:* Compiled by the authors.)

of independent Malaysia. The nation is unique in the region in other ways as well. Its culture and commerce strongly reflect the fact that 75 percent of its population is ethnic Chinese. A further 15 percent of the population is Malay, while 7 percent is South Asian (especially Indian). None of these groups are homogeneous; many different languages and dialects are spoken within each of the major immigrant groups. For example, among Chinese speakers dialects include Hakka, Hokkien, and Tiechiu. Actually, Singapore has four official languages, which reflects the city's diversity. They are English, Mandarin Chinese, Malay, and Tamil (a Dravidian language of southern India).

Another major difference is that in the context of Southeast Asia, an underdeveloped region, Singapore is economically well developed. Since its independence, and in large part because of the dynamic leadership of Premier Lee Kuan Yew, Singapore has been the region's leading port (and fourth largest in the world) and industrial center. The current statistics of the city demonstrate that Singapore is a developed economy. Per capita gross national product, for example, is by far the highest in the region, and is about one-third that of the United States. Demographic indicators, which coin-

Figure 10.10 An aerial view of Singapore shows the great harbor that has long been one of the city's prime assets, as well as the high-rise buildings which have rapidly become a distinctive characteristic of modern Singapore. (T. Leinbach and R. Ulack)

cide with the level of economic development, for Singapore reveal a pattern common to many Western nations with a longer industrial history. The infant mortality rate is among the lowest in the world (12 per thousand), and the rate of natural population increase (1.1 percent annually) is also quite low.

Singapore was planned by the British. Today, it reflects that heritage in many ways—for example, the architecture and cultural pluralism—but in other ways it has been altered. In recent years, perhaps the two most noticeable changes have occurred in the land-use pattern. These have resulted from the city's industrial growth and its public housing program. The rapid industrialization has depended upon the processing of raw materials, especially oil from the Middle East and rubber from neighboring Malaysia. Indeed, Singapore is the major oil-refining center in the region, and petroleum, together with rubber, accounts for nearly one-third of the value of all trade. Other heavy industries, such as plants producing transportation equipment and shipbuilding, also exist along with many light industries. Much of this is located in the Jurong Industrial Town. Singapore's public housing program is certainly the best in the region and probably the best in Asia; as a result, a number of new towns, such as Queenstown, have arisen, which contain high-rise, low-cost projects.

In the postwar years Singapore, as well as most of the largest cities of Southeast Asia, has attracted increasing numbers of tourists from Europe, North America, and, most recently, Japan. This has also affected land use with the construction of new ho-

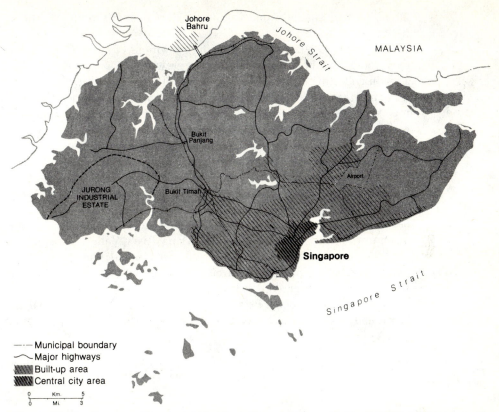

Figure 10.11 Singapore. [*Source:* Adapted from *Singapore,* Focus, 21, No. 8 (1971), 3.] Reprinted with permission.

tels, shopping areas, and additional transportation facilities. Today, Hilton Hotels and Holiday Inns are found throughout the region, supplementing (but not replacing) the lavish old colonial hotels such as Singapore's famous Raffles Hotel. Singapore is one of the major magnets for tourists and businessmen in the region. It is also a city noted for its cleanliness, which is unique among the cities of the region (and, indeed, of most world cities). Rules and regulations are strictly enforced to keep Singapore's city and port among the least polluted of the world.

A Modern Inland Capital: Kuala Lumpur

Kuala Lumpur became Malaysia's largest city after its independence in 1957, and except for the two years that Singapore was joined with Malaya to form a federation, the city has been the major city and capital of the nation. Kuala Lumpur (which means "muddy confluence," because it is located at the confluence of two rivers, the Klang and the Gombok) is at the center of Malaysia's tin and rubber belt. It is located about

25 mi. (40 km.) inland from its outport, Port Klang (formerly Port Swettenham), on the Strait of Malacca.

The city is relatively new, having grown out of a tiny Chinese tin-mining settlement established in 1857. The settlement grew rapidly and by the 1870s was flourishing as a tin-collecting center despite its malarial jungle location in hilly country. In 1880 it became the capital of the state of Selangor and from that point grew rapidly. A railroad was built linking the city with the coast, and in 1895, due primarily to its central location on the peninsula, Kuala Lumpur became the capital of the Federated Malay States (Fig. 10.12). In population size Georgetown to the north (and Singapore, of course) remained a larger city than Kuala Lumpur until about 1950, from which time the city's population grew especially rapidly. By 1950 Kuala Lumpur's population had reached about 200,000, and in 1980 the city had a population of over 580,000.

Unlike Singapore and Georgetown, which cannot expand their areas significantly because they are located on small islands, Kuala Lumpur has begun to merge with other towns and cities located in the Klang River Valley. Thus, it is estimated that by 1990 a conurbation will have emerged with a population of some 2 million. In addition to Kuala Lumpur, the conurbation will include the industrial center of Petaling Jaya, a new town begun in 1953 and apparently patterned after the new towns of postwar Great Britain. Today, Petaling Jaya is one of the most industrialized cities in Malaysia and has been successful housing some of the spillover population from Kuala

Figure 10.12 The main railway station in Kuala Lumpur, capital city of Malaysia, is one of the most distinctive in the world because of its strongly Islamic architectural style. (T. Leinbach and R. Ulack)

Lumpur. The cities of Klang and Port Klang, as well as a number of other new towns, will also become a part of the conurbation emerging in the valley.

Examples of Regional Centers

The largest cities of the region have been emphasized because of their enormous size and importance as the centers of industry, finance, education, commerce, and innovation. But there are a far larger number of smaller regional centers with specialized functions, which have become important in postcolonial Southeast Asia. Such cities include regional trade and transportation centers; cities dependent upon the gathering and processing of natural resources of agricultural products, including tin, coal, petroleum, lumber, rubber, coffee, and rice; resort cities located on the coast or in cool, interior upland areas; and a few cities, still small, which are centers of recent industrialization.

One example of a city that is both an important regional trade and transportation center and a city associated with a natural resource is Palembang in Indonesia. It is an old city, as we have already seen, having been the capital of the ancient Srivijayan empire and for some time following that an important sultanate. Since 1950 the population of this southern Sumatran port has nearly tripled, so that by 1980 its population was over 850,000. One of the major reasons for this growth is that Palembang is today a center of the Indonesian oil industry. Large oil refineries are located in the suburbs to the east of the city, and petroleum products are an important export item. In addition, the city is an important export point for the lumber, rubber, coffee, tea, and spices produced in its hinterland.

Georgetown (also called Penang) is Malaysia's second largest city, with a population exceeding 300,000. Although the city has not grown rapidly since 1947, when the population was 189,000, it has become an important tourist center for Malaysia. The city was founded on Penang Island in 1786 by the British East India Company and soon surpassed Malacca as the most important port on the Strait of Malacca. Indeed, it is still Malaysia's leading port, and is noted for its tin smelting. Historic and graceful Georgetown, and the nearby beauty of the hills and beaches of Penang Island, are tourist attractions. For these reasons tourism has become one of the more significant industries for the area, and new hotels have been added to those that have existed since colonial times.

A third type of city, one that has emerged since independence, is the small, industrializing center. An example of such a center is Iligan, on the north coast of Mindanao Island in the Philippines. Because of a tremendous hydroelectric potential nearby and because of its location in the largely underdeveloped southern Philippines, Iligan was selected as a site for large-scale industrialization. In the 1950s several industries were established, and in 1960 construction began on what was to become a fully integrated steel mill. Today, about a dozen major industries are located in the city limits and help to support a population approaching 100,000. Although the industrialization of cities like Iligan has barely made a dent in the relative importance of cities like Manila (and though Iligan's progress has not been all it was hoped to be), it is a type of city that will become more important over time.

Contemporary Major Urban Problems

In viewing the major urban problems of the Southeast Asian cities it may be useful at the outset to draw a distinction between those problems which are more distant and those which demand immediate attention. An example of the former is the development of strategies to transform these cities so that they reflect a predominantly indigenous character. In other words, an attempt must be made to preserve the local cultural characteristics while at the same time allowing for modernization. Another related problem is the more effective integration of the cities and their hinterlands into a national urban system which will allow a more efficient functioning than hinterlands based upon earlier colonial objectives. More immediate problems include rapid urban growth and the quality of housing, services, and facilities, which derive in part from the tremendous population change.

Urban Growth

In the decades from 1950 to 1980 the overall population in the region grew at a rate of about 2.8 percent per year while the urban population expanded at 5 percent per year. If this pattern is translated into future growth, the populations of these nations and cities will double in 10 to 15 years. Although the definition of "urban" varies from country to country, the implications of the data are clear. It must be mentioned too that these data disguise the variation in growth rates of cities within and between the individual nations. Although exceptions exist, Vietnam, for example, growth rates in the larger cities generally exceed those of the medium-sized and small cities. However, even among the larger cities (those over 500,000 population), considerable variation in growth rates exists. In the decade from 1960 to 1970, for example, Rangoon grew at a rate of 3.1 percent per year while Hanoi and Medan grew at rates of 8.1 percent and 7.9 percent, respectively.

The importance of the primate cities in the urban life of their respective countries can be measured in part by the percentage of the urban population they hold. Jakarta accounts for over 20 percent of Indonesia's urban population, while Manila holds over 30 percent of the urban population of the Philippines. Further appreciation of the dominance of these largest cities can be gained by holding up their material possessions and consumption statistics. It has been noted that Bangkok, for example, possesses almost 80 percent of the telephones, half of the motor vehicles and consumes over 80 percent of the electricity in Thailand. Similarly Kuala Lumpur, while not as sharp an example of primacy as Bangkok, Manila, or Jakarta, contains the bulk of the banking and manufacturing establishments in Malaysia.

The above discussion has focused on recent growth. Predicting urban growth is difficult at best. However, some recent analyses by the United States are worth noting to obtain still another dimension of the urban problems which face Southeast Asia. These data for the Philippines reveal a compound growth rate of 3.9 percent per year for the decade from 1990 to 2000. The figure for Malaysia is 3.5 percent, while for Indonesia it is 3.9 percent. It must be noted that these forecasts are conservative and could be considerably higher. Given the estimates, the magnitude of the growth problem is vividly portrayed.

Causes of Urban Growth

What is the cause of the rapid growth in the cities of Southeast Asia? In some countries, notably on the mainland, warfare and insurgent activities have affected urban growth. Recent policies in Vietnam and Kampuchea (which are discussed later in this section) have had a reversing effect on growth and urban population buildup. In addition, the expansion or relocation of urban boundaries as well as the alteration of census definitions have influenced the urban growth data. However, far and away the most important sources of growth have been and will be natural increase and rural-to-urban migration. While estimates of the contribution of natural increase to the overall urban growth vary, it is clear that with high crude birth rates in most of the Southeast Asian nations and low and falling crude death rates, that contribution is significant. United Nations data reveal that even for the most rural countries, 50 percent of the forecasted urban growth will come from the natural growth of urban populations. Research by individual scholars also points to the conclusion that natural increase is the primary factor in urban growth. This argument is strengthened if the higher fertility rates of the rural areas are exported to the cities in the migration process. Nonetheless it is generally recognized that rural-to-urban migration accounts for a significant portion of urban growth. Such migration will dominate urban growth especially in countries where only a small percentage of the population is located in urban areas. An estimated 25 to 50 percent of the residents of major primate cities were born outside the metropolis to which they migrated.

Migration to Urban Areas

On the basis of available evidence, migrants (who tend to range in age from 15 to 30 years and are mostly male) move to the largest cities largely for employment reasons. Thus it appears that rural out-migration is fueled by rather significant income differentials between the rural and urban areas. Other reasons such as the lack of work or land at the origin and the desire to seek out educational opportunities at the destination are apparently also strong influences in the migration process. Often the most important reason that a migrant selects a specific destination stems from the social relationships which link him to a job or opportunity some distance away. Simply, some people migrate to live alongside friends or relatives. The presence of these friends or family in the destination reduces the anxiety involved in a move and provides a temporary cushion for the migrant; thus the problem of searching for work and housing are made easier because someone who is familiar with the migrant's new environment is present to guide him. For some, knowledge of the conditions and opportunities existing at the destination has been transmitted from friends and relatives.

Although poor information may prevent more conservative rural people from moving, too often moves are made in ignorance of the risks involved. Migrants are confronted abruptly with the new environment and high cost of city life as well as the extreme competition for employment opportunities, which fall far behind the population buildup. Available evidence suggests that initially migrants have higher educational levels than the average at the place of origin but usually lower than that at the destination. Too often the migrant is unskilled and from an agricultural background. Some migrants will eventually be able to find employment as craftsmen, clerks, or skilled laborers, although at an unexpected expense of time and money. More realistically, and particularly in cities such as Bangkok, Manila, and Jakarta, people will turn to the traditional urban sector for employment and become part of the informal working sector. Here people are employed (or more appropriately underemployed) in the service area of the economy as hawkers (the term frequently used for people selling food items, cigarettes, simple tools and toys, etc.) and in other "occupations" such as shining shoes, washing and "guarding" automobiles, and prostitution (Fig. 10.13). Unfortunately many individuals end up as scavengers. Collecting used cigarette butts for "reprocessing" is a common trade for the street dwellers of the largest cities in the region. The capacity of the city's service sector to absorb more and more laborers and to split, share, or fractionalize employment opportunities has come to be known as *urban involution*. Two or three drivers, for example, may share the operation of a motorized vehicle or pedicab to haul passengers. Street hawkers pass the same merchandise from hand to hand, each perhaps, if lucky, taking a small profit before it reaches the consumer. Simple machine shops or garages employ relatives in small-scale operations that yield only a small return to the owner. Unfortunately these menial jobs will remain as the major support for many individuals in the region for a considerable time into the future.

Migrants in Jakarta

The discussion above has illuminated some of the aspects and spillover effects of the major problem of rural-to-urban migration. In order to appreciate fully the situation of a new migrant it is necessary to focus on a specific urban example that will point up in more detail the environment which confronts him or her as well as some of the mechanisms used to adapt to a strange and new situation. Although Jakarta, the major city of Indonesia, exhibits problems which result from a very large population (about 7 million in 1980), its circumstances are not drastically different from those of most of the other largest cities in the region.

Between 1961 and 1971 Jakarta grew at an annual rate of 4.4 percent. On the other hand, urban employment increased at a rate of only 2.8 percent and was due largely to opportunities in the service and transport sectors. Generally, urbanization in Indonesia has not been supported by the growth of manufacturing but rather by growth in the service sector. During this period 2 million people migrated to Jakarta, the majority from West Java and other parts of that island.

A recent study provides useful data surrounding these recent migrants. Most of the individuals, for example, had not moved prior to their recent migration and had migrated directly to Jakarta rather than moving to other destinations first. Apparently, transport costs are not a strong deterrent to migration, for the fare is often less than three days' wages. Although many migrants go to Jakarta expecting to remain only a short time, many change their minds and decide to make the move permanent. Most of these people manage to find some semblance of employment during the first week or so. In order to find jobs personal contacts are often crucial. For example, pedicabs or *becaks* are owned by wealthier individuals and rented to drivers who must then earn

Figure 10.13 A Hawker Selling Food Items in Jakarta. Innumerable hawkers, selling a great variety of goods and services, can be seen in virtually all the major cities of Southeast Asia, not to mention cities in other LDCs. The presence of hawkers is commonly an indication of urban unemployment and underemployment. (T. Leinbach and R. Ulack)

enough fares in a day to cover the rent on the vehicle as well as extract a small profit to purchase food and perhaps send a small amount back to their home villages. Often the driver will sleep in his *becak* to avoid the rent on a shared room. In order to qualify as a driver an individual must be recommended to the owner. Those people with few contacts therefore turn to the lowest order of employment: scavenging or prostitution. The bulk of the migrants to Jakarta earn pitifully small wages, which permit them few luxury items and almost certainly do not allow them to take advantage of electricity, water, or sewerage systems. Housing is generally a crude shelter among other squatters (Fig. 10.14). Often a migrant must repay debts from his or her wages, and this barely allows one to purchase a daily plate of rice sprinkled with a vegetable broth (or, if lucky, some vegetables or bean curd) as well as some *kreteks* (clove-scented cigarettes). Despite this meager existence most migrants feel they are materially better off in the city than in the rural areas from which they migrated. The evidence from Jakarta indicates that personal connections are an important means of choosing the destination and acquiring employment.

For some migrants the adaptation process is made easier through an institution known as a *pondok.* The *pondok* is technically a rooming house, but many of these function as much more. Essentially these lodging places serve as bases from which many small businesses are organized and operated. A group of circular migrants (those who have a family and view their rural village as a permanent home) who are often from the same village live under a common roof. Someone from the home area who

Figure 10.14   Squatter housing along Jakarta's canals reveals some of the terrible squalor and unhygienic conditions typical of squatter settlements in Southeast Asia's larger cities. (T. Leinbach and R. Ulack)

has a permanent residence permit for Jakarta will act as a supervisor and provide the lodgers with shelter, food, credit, trade equipment, and security. The supervisor will sell raw materials which he or she has purchased from a contact in a local market to the operators at a profit. Many of these operations tend to specialize as vendors of individually cooked food items.

During 1970 in an attempt to curtail further growth, the governor ruled that Jakarta was a "closed city." Essentially migrants were not permitted to enter unless they had guaranteed accommodation, regular employment, and a residence permit. The function of the *pondok* supervisor during this period of closure was to protect the migrants under his or her charge and absorb fines from the city if necessary. The *pondok* also functions to assist an individual during illness and if selling activities fail to generate sufficient income to pay back any debts.

Here in the *pondok,* as elsewhere in Jakarta, living conditions for those with marginal incomes are extremely poor. After long hours on the streets workers must return to quarters that are often cramped and unsewered and that lack water. Nevertheless, dwellers are willing to endure these hardships in the hope of saving some money so that they may return to their village able to afford new purchases. Incomes vary considerably, but a good hawker might earn Rp. 20,000 (U.S. $32) per month, which is more than the earnings of a domestic servant. A substantial portion of this income can be returned to the village, since the immediate expenses for food and lodging are small. Funds returned to the village most frequently are used for food, housing improvements, and celebrations.

Other Problems in the Indonesian Capital

The proclamation by the governor of Jakarta to close the city in 1970 was based upon the rapidly deteriorating quality of life for over a decade. Jakarta lacks a reliable supply of electricity and potable water, a waste disposal system, and adequate public schools and health facilities. In the early 1970s it was estimated that 40,000 new households were added to the city yet only 3000 new permanent housing units were approved annually. Temporary or squatter housing does not require a permit, and this variety of housing accounts for 80 percent of the total. Only 8 percent of the total housing units use both electricity and municipal water. Without taking into account the cost of land, a 500-sq. ft. (46 sq. m.) house was estimated to cost Rp. 750,000 (U.S. $1200), which places such construction well out of the range of the average worker.

The city has no sewer system except for the canals, and these often serve as catchments for refuse. The water sold by the city is not fit for drinking, and although well water is used by some it also is polluted, since the water table is near ground level. This contamination produces a constant battle against waterborne diseases such as cholera and, more commonly, dysentery. Amoebic dysentery is a strength-sapping affliction that affects a large number of people in the city. It can only be cured by strong dosages of antibiotics and in extreme cases results in death. Such medicines are not available to the broad segment of the population. Elimination of dysentery can only be accomplished by improving the water supply and sanitation.

Industry and Infrastructure

The cities of Southeast Asia, indeed all over the developing world, have an important role to play in orchestrating economic interrelationships which ultimately will yield a higher quality of life for the people within the urban as well as rural areas. Although industry is not the only element in the economic base, it is an important route to increased output, enlarged employment, and rising wages. Unemployment and underemployment remain critical problems in Jakarta, Bangkok, and all other large cities because the increase of industrial production is much too slow to meet the labor demands of the rapid population influx. Of the 30 percent of Jakarta's population considered economically active, the majority of persons are inefficiently utilized in the quasi-tertiary sector. A good example is the unincorporated transportation sector, which had over 170,000 pedicabs operated by 340,000 drivers.

The failure of governments to encourage more foreign investment can be explained by a number of factors. First, too often agreements tend to drag out and become mired in bureaucratic red tape. Although strong efforts have been made (especially in Jakarta) to control corruption, it remains a difficult problem to obliterate. Side payments are needed to reduce the long periods required for action and decisions. Instability of governments (Thailand is noteworthy as an illustration), the game of musical chairs with administrators, and overburdened, underpaid decision makers, as well as simple fear of asset expropriation are additional reasons accounting for the reluctance of foreigners to invest. In Jakarta still another problem is the high cost and lack of land and utility services. The acquisition of land is also made more difficult because of numerous agencies which have overlapping authorization to regulate such growth. On the other hand, Indonesian labor is generally very good: quick to learn, skilled when trained, and generally conscientious. Another major obstacle is the higher status accorded those in Indonesia who pursue careers in government, teaching, or the armed forces. In other words there is some cultural bias against business enterprise.

In general, urban infrastructure in Jakarta and many other large Southeast Asian cities is badly deficient. Waste disposal, water, power, buildings, telecommunications, and transportation need to be improved. The problems are made more serious because essentially they are all interrelated. The water system, for example, is affected by waste, flood control, and the power system.

A particularly conspicuous and immediate problem in Jakarta is the canal system. Originally built by the Dutch to receive wash water and to provide some flood control, the canals simply are not able to function as outlets for the garbage and excrement of seven million people. As a result of sedimentation and improper drainage the canals no longer provide flood control, so that many roads and houses become flooded during the frequent heavy tropical rains.

A plan to improve Jakarta's water supply by channeling fresh water from a river 31 mi. (50 km.) west of the city seemed viable but ultimately collapsed because of the huge costs. In addition to the external pipe required, major repairs to the existing delivery system are necessary. This problem is not faced, for example, by either the smaller

Singapore or Kuala Lumpur-Petaling Jaya urban areas, for here adequate, nonpolluted tap water is available.

Although improvements to the telephone system in Jakarta apparently have been attempted, the results leave much to be desired. Installations are slow and costly, so that people with small incomes cannot afford a hookup. Faulty connections and the difficulty of reaching many numbers successfully are commonplace, so one ultimately accepts that telephoning will be a time consuming venture. Indeed, intercity telephone communications are far superior in many instances to intracity linkages. It is more likely that one can obtain a good connection from Jakarta to Medan than across town. Unfortunately intercity calls are expensive. For example, a station-to-station call between Medan and Jakarta will cost over Rp. 4000 (U.S. $6.50) for three minutes. Communication problems in Indonesia are also reflected by the inability to communicate ideas and disseminate information to the mass of people. At the end of 1975, an estimated 50 million of the country's 132 million inhabitants had no access to mass media information. The number of telephones was estimated to be only 250,000 at the same date.

Partially as a result of the faulty and inadequate communications system the need for face-to-face meetings increases and adds to the traffic, congestion, and noise problems in many cities. The street system in and around Jakarta has been improved but not as fast as the growth in vehicles. Since the mid-1960s over one-eighth of the total budget of the city has been spent on roads. Still, maintenance has fallen behind reasonable expectations. Too frequently side streets are jammed with buses, pedicabs, horsecarts, bicycles, and vendors on foot carrying goods balanced on a long pole suspended over the shoulder so that smooth flow is prohibited. Bus transport is reasonably cheap, Rp. 30 (U.S. 5¢), but a large number of vehicles are outdated and break down frequently, further interrupting the traffic pattern. Many more buses are needed to handle the large and growing demand. As a result of the inadequate supply of buses, other, more costly forms of urban transport have appeared to add to the congestion.

While Jakarta's problems have been exacerbated by some political turmoil and particularly by the huge population burden, other cities exhibit many of the same ills. The vast, sprawling communities of squatters, each of whom inhabits only a tiny spot of vacant land, are perhaps more easily visible in Jakarta, but they also exist in the large area of Tondo in Manila and the areas of Klong Toey and Dindang in Bangkok. Kuala Lumpur does not exhibit the extreme primacy of these other cities. Yet squatter communities are now a major problem here too. Roughly one-fifth of Kuala Lumpur's population consists of squatters. An added problem is the ethnic segregation: Chinese poor and Tamil poor live in separate communities. The racial composition of the city (which heretofore had been predominantly Chinese) is changing markedly, since the Malaysian government has a specific policy to reserve urban job opportunities for underprivileged Malays or *bumiputras* ("sons of the soil"). There is concern that this added influx of Malay population will heighten tensions and create racial conflict such as that during the late 1960s. Although low-income housing is available for U.S. $13 per month, most squatter families cannot bear this cost.

Solutions to Urban Problems

Progress in Singapore

In 1960 Singapore's Chinatown was described as a mass of dingy, three-level shophouses which had been partitioned and repartitioned in an effort to accommodate more and more tiny, dark, unsanitary cubicles intended to hold entire families and their possessions. A contemporary view of Singapore must be radically rewritten, since the bulk of these squalid inner-city houses have been torn down and replaced with low-cost public housing (Fig. 10.15). The record of housing improvement in the city state is one of the outstanding examples of progress and modernization in the Third World. By 1980 more than one-third of the city's population lived in public housing, and it is estimated that by 1992 that share will be 70 percent. This success has been derived from a combination of factors, but foremost are an effective planning framework, capable leadership, and the investment derived from economic prosperity. The latter condition has resulted from a deliberate policy to diversify and broaden the entrepôt economy through an imaginative industrialization program. The bulk of the new industry has been located in new estates, the largest of which is Jurong, a former swamp on the western side of the island. Compensating for the lack of raw materials by the advantage of the locational situation and labor force, the government has struck a balance between capital-intensive and labor-intensive production.

Figure 10.15   A public housing project in Singapore shows the ultramodern architecture typical of Singapore's massive public housing program, generally regarded as the best in Southeast Asia and one of the best in the world. Eventually, most of Singapore's population is destined to live in this type of housing as the city-state continues its industrialization and urban-renewal programs. (T. Leinbach and R. Ulack)

Singapore has also provided the lead solution in an attempt to combat the growing number of vehicles within the city. Increases in road taxes, and more efficient usage and policies in the public transport area, have produced change. Most important, however, has been the policy of restricted entry to the CBD at peak hours. Vehicles such as taxis and private passenger cars must pay a fee if a journey terminates inside a cordon line during the peak hours. Taxis simply increase the fare to the customer if the destination is a downtown location. Cities such as Bangkok, Manila, and Jakarta, with large-scale problems of this nature are closely watching the Lion City's strategy.

Squatter Relocation

The housing shortage in other cities has already been noted, and especially the larger problem of squatter settlements, which by a recent estimate may include 25 percent of the population in the primate cities of Southeast Asia. Some researchers have noted that these settlements should not be viewed entirely in a negative sense. Instead they suggest that they form at least potentially stable economic and social units that function as integrative and adjusting mechanisms in the process of national and personal modernization. Nevertheless, city administrations are faced with enormous problems from these settlements, especially in the form of disease and health conditions.

In the late 1950s squatters on the edge of Manila were caught in severe flash floods resulting in a considerable loss of life. As a result, the government provided funds to purchase Sapang Palay, a site of 1850 acres (750 hectares) 23 mi. (37 km.) north of the city, which was designated as a resettlement area for the flood-afflicted squatters. By 1963 a total of 3950 acres (1600 hectares) had been set up in the areas surrounding Manila for the purpose of resettling squatters. These early concerns and actions resulted in the formation of a Squatter Resettlement Agency, whose function has been to effect an orderly and properly planned program of squatter resettlement. Although a concrete plan was devised which called for the construction of simple frame houses, the provision of water, power, markets, schools, and health facilities on the Sapang Palay site, the squatters were physically removed by court order from the Tondo and other areas before any of the preparation could be accomplished. Since that emergency, however, the Sapang Palay project has better fulfilled its purpose and represents one of the first real attempts to deal with the squatter problem. Yet here, as in many other squatter relocation projects, a major problem exists: residents are too far removed from their work places. Ultimately the solution may be to integrate squatters within existing settlements and not relocate them.

Expanding Employment

The Malaysian approach to the improvement of urban poverty is to expand productive urban-based employment at a rate which will absorb both the rural-to-urban and natural components of growth. The development of labor-intensive enterprises to increase the employment absorption ability of industry and construction, combined with tariff protection and fiscal incentives, is being stressed. Small-scale businesses and hawking operations are assisted with credit, management advice, and extension services. Such provisions are aimed at training and upgrading the skills of rural people while drawing them into the urban economy more effectively. In the short term, 100,000 housing units are being built for urban households earning less than M$200 (U.S. $90) per month. New sites and services projects for industrial, commercial, and residential purposes are also being carried out where in the latter case future residents will actually participate in the house construction. High-density public bus transport and high-occupancy private car usage is stressed within the Kuala Lumpur Urban Transport Project. The intent is that a substantial portion of the benefits of this investment will be directed to low income groups.

Solution Attempts in Indonesia

In the Second Five-Year Plan (Repelita II), the government of Indonesia, in response to housing and infrastructure deficiencies, proposed a program to construct low-cost housing; to support a site and services effort which would provide land and infrastructure to low income people, upon which they could build their own housing; and finally to undertake a large-scale *kampung* (village) improvement program to provide immediate relief to poor people in current housing. It was admitted that, with limited financial resources and a huge need, the building and sites and services programs could only alleviate the problems after several years' time had elapsed. Therefore, emphasis was to be placed on the Kampung Improvement Program (KIP). KIP, partially supported by World Bank funds, aims at improving footpaths, secondary roads, drainage ditches, schools, and health clinics. Water taps which supply 32 quarts (30 liters) of water per day per person, 12-person communal sanitary units for human waste, and facilities to collect and dispose of solid wastes were planned for an area of roughly 4,940 acres (2,000 hectares) and to affect nearly 900,000 low income residents. Through 1979, KIP has made improvements in many areas of Jakarta, although per capita expenditures (U.S. $64) are somewhat higher than estimated because areas prone to severe flooding cost more to improve. All of this, however, must be kept in proper perspective because of the extreme magnitude of the problem. Bluntly, a very long road is ahead.

It goes without saying that a major constraint in both urban and rural development in Indonesia has been communication. With a low literacy rate and low per capita income it has been difficult to disperse information on a wide variety of development issues. In 1975 the government announced its decision to procure and establish a domestic communications satellite system. That system is now in operation and has already improved the interurban telephone system. Plans are wide ranging and include a system to improve education via television as well as a nationwide service which will teach basic health, hygiene, and family planning. The expectations are ambitious and require elaborate preparations for support personnel and programs.

Resettlement Programs

Ultimately in the search for solutions to urban problems the question must be addressed: can migration be controlled? Even without additional movements the cities of Southeast Asia have a huge task ahead. But if further movements could be minimized, that task might become manageable.

For over 20 years the Malaysian government has operated a national resettlement program. The Federal Land Development Authority (FELDA) schemes are aimed at providing land and improved incomes to landless, poor rural people (mostly Malays) in areas of high-population pressure. The program provides a small farm and house along with an allotment of rubber or oil palm acreage. Proceeds from these crops are used to reduce the debts so that ultimately the land is owned by the settler. Through 1979 approximately 52,000 families had been resettled and, in the period from 1971 to 1975, around 412,000 acres were developed by FELDA. Although the development of vacant frontier lands is an objective in this program, the government also hopes to reduce the unplanned migration of rural Malays to the towns on the west coast.

In the same vein, the Indonesians are attempting to develop the Outer Islands and simultaneously alleviate some of the severest population pressure on the island of Java. In the early years of the twentieth century the Dutch began a policy to establish colonies of Javanese on the other islands in order to relieve population strains and to develop a larger labor supply for Sumatran plantations. The program has been plagued by problems of various kinds, including improper site preparation and selection of individuals. Only 54,000 families were moved in the first four years of the current five-year plan. Since 1905, fewer than 1 million people have left Java in official transmigration programs. Recently, however, the program has been receiving more emphasis and with proper planning could result in the relocation of substantial numbers of families. Whether the goal of 500,000 families (2.5 million people) set for the next five years will be realized remains to be seen.

There are continuing attempts to improve rural areas on Java through labor-intensive projects such as road and canal building, which pay local workers Rp. 350 (U.S. 50¢) per day. The cash incentive schemes aim at providing work while establishing the bases for longer-term social and economic benefits. It is doubtful, however, whether this type of program is an effective substitute for land ownership nor will it or the transmigration efforts really have the impact to reduce the flow of migrants and thus alleviate the already heavy population burden on cities.

Growth Diversion Strategies

Some scientists feel that rural-to-urban migration is caused less by the factors of population pressure and lack of work in the rural areas than by the isolation and desire to enjoy new amenities. As we have already pointed out, other researchers feel strongly that the primary motive is the search for employment. Essentially we must conclude that marginal improvements in rural incomes are unlikely to have a strong influence on migration to cities in the near future. With the possible exception of a few areas where large agricultural potential is accessible to rural populations, the migration to urban areas will be difficult to slow down.

There may be, however, the opportunity to divert this growth from larger to smaller or new urban settlements. Recognizing the strong concentration of economic activity in the largest cities of the region and the lack of alternative urban employment opportunities, some governments are working toward a growth center strategy which would decentralize industry, reduce regional disparities, and develop frontier source regions.

Although Malaysia does not have the severe urban focus problem that Bangkok, Manila, and Jakarta do, the issue is still of concern. Industrial estates have been established in the vicinity of all of the medium-sized cities on the Peninsula, so that Kuala Lumpur's proportion of total manufacturing has been substantially reduced. Over the next 20 years, the government is actually encouraging labor outflows from some of the poorest states to the industrial pockets on the west coast in order to improve their incomes with respect to the national average. The development of urban centers will also play a key role in improving the economic prosperity of the poorest states in Malaysia. Existing towns which have favorable prospects for the creation of agglomeration economies will receive mutually supportive industries and services. At the same time the development strategy will stress the buildup of existing towns and the creation of new towns in the major frontier areas of resource concentration. The overall objective is to create a more integrated urban system, especially on the east coast of Peninsular Malaysia, and to spread out urban development more evenly. Of course, the hope is to assist an increasing number of Malaysians to move into higher income urban occupations.

Although the Malaysian efforts to achieve income growth and regional equilibrium through the growth pole approach are the most noteworthy to date, other nations have similar plans in various stages of implementation. In Thailand there are plans for product diversification, income generation, and the decentralization of industries and employment based on urban centers to be established in outlying regions. The promotion of regional centers here is seen as an explicit strategy to check migration into the Bangkok Metropolitan Area. The Regional Capital Development Program in the Philippines is expected to produce similar results. For example, Iligan City, mentioned previously, is part of the strategy. Indonesia also has a scheme based upon a hierarchical system of growth centers focused largely on resource exploitation projects.

Although serious attempts have been made to incorporate a growth pole approach in the overall development strategy of these nations, the problem of implementing the plans against the constraints of fiscal capacity and organizing management remain as huge obstacles. The successful efforts, however, would move a long way toward reducing current and future urban problems.

City Problems and Solutions in the Socialist Nations

Vietnam The policies and problems within the cities of the socialist nations of Southeast Asia are more difficult to interpret because of the recent rapid changes and/or the lack of reliable data. But clearly many of the cities have problems of critical magnitude. Ho Chi Minh City (formerly Saigon), for example, has changed dramatically since the war. The Western-style establishments and customs have been replaced with a more spartan milieu. The Vietnamese administration claimed recently that while food was in short supply, five pounds of rice were guaranteed per month to each individual at controlled prices. The elimination of prostitution and the reuniting of "street children" with their parents have also been accomplished, according to reliable sources.

In an effort to rehabilitate the city, the government in 1976 encouraged the refugee population to return to the countryside and shifted many urban workers from the central area of the city to the fringe. A canal network was constructed to preserve a green belt around the town. The canals which supply fresh irrigation water are assisting in the city's transition to self-sufficiency in rice, vegetables, and meat. New economic and population dispersion zones have also been created that have spread the city's population but not reduced it. The zoning plan is intended to alleviate unemployment and to group trained industrial workers near their places of employment away from the center of the city.

It is widely acknowledged that the ethnic Chinese minorities account for a major proportion of the commerce of the Southeast Asian cities. Their role is large in the cities of Thailand, Malaysia, the Philippines, and Indonesia. The economic successes and skills of these groups continue to fuel the fires of resentment and animosity. In some nations deliberate policies have been devised to limit their economic participation. The most blatant reaction has come from Vietnam. Reliable sources report that the Hanoi government is determined to expel all of the ethnic Chinese and is stripping them of their wealth before doing so. The regime regards the Chinese as disloyal, "unproductive city dwellers" who stand in the way of rural development plans. Information from Ho Ch Minh City indicates that up to 1.2 million Chinese still reside in Vietnam following the emigration of 300,000 in 1978. To encourage them to leave, the government is resorting to harassment, curfews, intimidation, and detention. The immigration tariff of ten taels of gold or U.S. $3000 supposedly provides the largest current export revenue and replaces the previous leader, coal.

Kampuchea No city in the region has experienced more turbulence and upheaval than Phnom Penh. In early 1979 the city still reflected the effects of the policies of the Khmer Rouge victory in April 1975, when essentially the entire population was forced into the countryside in an attempt to restore the agricultural base of the country. By April the city's population was no more than 2000 and consisted mainly of soldiers and workers and their families. The current Vietnamese-supported Kampuchean National United Front has put two businesses, a soft-drink plant and a textile mill, back into operation. Supposedly the soft-drink operation can turn out Pepsi and similar beverages for two to three years on the stocks of concentrate available, but the mill has been working at levels well below capacity. Although current conditions are grim, the government has organized a ring of temporary settlements for former residents desiring to enter Phnom Penh. These camps are apparently functioning as screening centers in an attempt to rebuild some semblance of an administration. Upon establishing skills and proof of former residency, people are being assigned jobs in the capital. The most serious problem facing the new regime is that of averting a food crisis, yet as recently as June 1979 there was little evidence of a planting in preparation for the monsoon rains. Most observers agree that until the Phnom Penh government gains international recognition, Kampuchea will remain largely a Vietnamese burden and the suffering will go on.

RECOMMENDED READING

Aiken, S. Robert and Colin H. Leigh, "Malaysia's Emerging Conurbation." *Annals,* Association of American Geographers, 65 (1975), 546–563.
    Excellent description and analysis of the recent and future growth of Kuala Lumpur and nearby centers.

Coedes, George. *Angkor: An Introduction.* Hong Kong: Oxford University Press, 1963.
    Recent translation that is a thorough and well-illustrated treatment of Cambodia's ancient capital.

Fryer, D. W. "Cities of Southeast Asia and Their Problems." *Focus,* 22, No. 7 (1972), 1–8.
    A succinct discussion of the origins, morphology, functions of the major cities in Southeast Asia.

Fryer, D. W. "The 'Million City' in Southeast Asia." *Geographical Review,* 43 (1953), 474–494.
    An important earlier study which examines the differences and similarities of Southeast Asia's five largest cities.

Ginsburg, Norton S. "Planning for the Southeast Asian City." *Focus,* 22, No. 9 (1972), 1–8.
    A thoughtful, broad-ranging essay on planning and the forces and trends which affect cities in Southeast Asia.

Hardjono, J. M. *Transmigration in Indonesia.* Kuala Lumpur: Oxford University Press, 1977.
    A thorough treatment of the history, problems, and successes of the Indonesian transmigration efforts.

Jellinek, Lea. "The Pondok of Jakarta." *Bulletin of Indonesian Economic Studies,* 13 (1977), 67–71.
    Extended discussion of the nature and importance of the *pondok* in the context of circular migration.

Juppenlatz, Morris. *Cities in Transformation: The Urban Squatter Problem of the Developing World.* St. Lucia: University of Queensland Press, 1970.
    Treatment of the squatter problem with a case study from the Philippines.

Lanquian, Aprodicio A. *Slums Are For People: The Barrio Magsaysay Pilot Project in Philippine Urban Community Development.* Honolulu: East-West Center Press, 1969.
    Based upon data gathered in one of Manila's slums, this book concludes that there are a number of positive characteristics about such communities.

Lubis, Mochtar. *Twilight in Djakarta.* New York: Vanguard Press, 1963.
    Poignant interpretation of city dwellers' day-to-day activities and survival techniques.

McGee, T. G. *The Southeast Asian City: A Social Geography of the Primate Cities of Southeast Asia.* New York: Praeger, 1967.
    The classic work on the subject by one of the leading experts on the region.

McGee, T. G. and Y. M. Yeung. *Hawkers in Southeast Asian Cities: Planning for the Bazaar Economy.* Ottawa: International Development Research Centre, 1977.
    A comparative study of street vendors in Kuala Lumpur, Malacca, Manila, Baguio, Jakarta, and Bandung.

Temple, Gordon. "Migration to Jakarta." *Bulletin of Indonesian Studies,* 11 (1975), 76–81.
    Results of the interviews from a sample of recent migrants to the Indonesian capital.

Ulack, Richard. "The Role of Urban Squatter Settlements." *Annals,* Association of American Geographers, 68 (1978), 535–550.

A case study of the characteristics of squatter settlements in Cagayan de Oro City, the Philippines.

Yeung, Y. M. and C. P. Lo, eds. *Changing South-East Asian Cities: Readings on Urbanization.* Singapore: Oxford University Press, 1976.
A topically arranged reader including articles by some of the experts (mostly geographers) on the region.

Yeung, Y. M. "Southeast Asian Cities: Patterns of Growth and Transformation." In *Urbanization and Counterurbanization. Urban Affairs Annual Reviews,* Vol. 11, *Reviews,* edited by B. J. L. Berry. Beverly Hills, CA: Sage, 1976, 285–309.
An excellent essay on urbanization, urban problems and issues, and future prospects.

Figure 11.1 Major Cities of East Asia. (*Source:* Data derived from United Nations, Department of Economic and Social Affairs, *Global Review of Human Settlements, Statistical Annex*, published by Pergamon Press, New York, 1976.)

Chapter 11

Cities of East Asia

Jack F. Williams

East Asia in the World Urban System

As a region, East Asia ranks toward the bottom of the scale in percentage of urban population. About 33 percent of its people lived in urban places in 1980 compared with about 41 percent for the world as a whole. Only South Asia, Southeast Asia, and Subsaharan Africa ranked lower. This relatively low standing is due to the statistical bias that China's vast rural population produces. Japan is about 79 percent urbanized, on a par with much of Western Europe and North America, while Taiwan's urban population is now above 70 percent, that of South Korea 53 percent, and North Korea's slightly less at around 47 percent. At the bottom is China, with perhaps 20 percent urban population at best (the data for China are the least reliable).

The high figures for urban population (exclusive of China) are the result of fairly recent urbanization. Even Japan did not pass the 50 percent figure until the 1950s. The remaining countries of the region have seen explosive growth in urban centers (with the exception of China and North Korea) within the last quarter century also. Certainly prior to the twentieth century, the rate of urban growth in these countries was far closer to the rate of total population growth than is true today.

More significant than mere percentages of total population are the numbers and sizes of cities in the region. From this perspective, East Asia is among the most important world urban regions. Three of the 10 largest cities in the world are here (Tokyo, Shanghai, and Peking) (Fig. 11.1). Of the 94 cities in the world with a population over 2 million, 19 are in East Asia, 13 in China. One of the world's two existing superconurbations is in East Asia (Tokyo; the other is New York), and of the 17 other superconurbations predicted to emerge by the year 2000, three will be in East Asia (Shanghai, Peking, and Seoul). China has as many "million" cities as the United States (about

27). Another way of looking at the situation is to note that the total urban population of China today is nearly twice the total population of Japan, yet China is still overwhelmingly a rural nation. Finally, because of the vast population in East Asia as a whole (nearly 1.1 billion), the nearly 360 million people living in cities account for the largest share (19 percent) of the world's urban population, ahead even of Western Europe (15 percent).

Beyond these statistics, however, is the fact that two radically different urban systems exist today in East Asia. One is the socialist urban system that has developed in China (and to a lesser extent in North Korea) since 1949 on the dual base of the traditional Chinese city and the colonial treaty port. The other system is that found in Japan, South Korea, Taiwan, and Hong Kong, a system with considerable variations among those four states but which has much in common with the Western industrial cities and the cities of the developing nonsocialist LDCs. These two urban systems are the products of very different political/economic orders—one reclusive, suspicious of the outside world, determinedly self-reliant; the other open to the outside world, interdependent with other economic and political systems. The cities of this latter system contain some of the truly great world cities, best typified by Tokyo and Hong Kong, but also include lesser cities such as Seoul and Taipei. The importance of these cities extends beyond the national territory in which the cities are located; the hinterland of these cities is the world, or at least large parts of the world. By contrast, the cities of China were turned inward once again after 1949, closing the circle begun by the forced opening of China in the nineteenth century. China has huge cities today, but even the greatest of them, Shanghai (the greatest legacy of the Western impact on China) is no longer truly a world city as it once was. Indeed, at least one observer has quipped that China's major cities are trying to behave as villages, referring to the peculiar efforts at decentralization that are one aspect of socialist urban planning in China discussed later in this chapter. To be sure, since the death of Mao, China's stance vis-à-vis the outside world has changed substantially, and China is no longer as reclusive and determinedly self-reliant as it pretended to be just a few years ago. However, the permanence of these policy switches is uncertain.

Introduction

> As regards the size of this city, you must know that it has a compass of 24 miles, for each side of it hath a length of 6 miles. . . . And it is all walled round with walls of earth which have a thickness of full ten paces at bottom and a height of more than 10 paces. . . . The streets are so straight and wide that you can see right along them from end to end and from one gate to the other. And up and down the city there are beautiful palaces, and many great and fine hostelries, and fine houses in great numbers . . . thus the whole city is arranged in squares just like a chess-board, and disposed in a manner so perfect and masterly that it is impossible to give a description that should do it justice.[1]

[1] Sir Henry Yule, *The Book of Ser Marco Polo, the Venetian, Concerning the Kingdoms and Marvels of the East,* II (New York: Charles Scribner's Sons, 1929), pp. 374–375.

So wrote Marco Polo of Peking (or Cambaluc, as he called it) in the thirteenth century, marveling at the splendors of China's capital city at a time when Europe was still centuries away from creating cities of comparable size and magnificence.

Contrast Marco Polo's enraptured account with that of a modern-day traveler to the urban landscape of socialist China:

> It is not easy to foresee how future centuries will judge the Maoist rule, but one thing is certain: despite all it has done, the name of the regime will also be linked with the outrage it inflicted on a cultural legacy of all mankind: the destruction of the city of Peking. . . .[2]

Other visitors to the People's Republic of China might quarrel with Simon Ley's jaundiced impression of present-day Peking (Beijing), although he is hardly alone in his criticism of what has been done to Chinese cities in the name of modern urban planning. Regardless, this seven-century leap between two widely divergent views is employed merely to illustrate that Chinese cities have long held a fascination to Westerners, because of the unique character of the classic Chinese city, some aspects of which have survived into the contemporary period. Moreover, some might argue that the present Chinese model of urban development may be the model of the future.

Cities and urbanism in East Asia (China, Japan, Korea, Taiwan, and Hong Kong) began with the classic Chinese city and its spread to other parts of the region. Indeed, China was one of the original world centers of the city. Unlike the other early centers, China's traditional old cities, with few exceptions, have been continuously occupied ever since they were founded. In fact, China has the distinction of containing probably the greatest number of continuously occupied cities dating to the pre-Christian era of any country in the world.

At the same time, although much of the urban character of China, and to a lesser degree of the rest of East Asia, was established centuries before Westerners came to the area in any significant numbers, many of the major cities of the region today were the creation in entirety or in large part of the colonial and postcolonial industrial periods of the nineteenth and twentieth centuries. In fact, essentially three major types of cities and periods of city development can be discerned in East Asia. The first was the traditional or preindustrial city, dating from antiquity to the arrival of Westerners in the sixteenth century, but really continuing on in diminishing importance even into the twentieth century. The second was the colonial city, starting in the sixteenth century and ending abruptly, with one or two exceptions, with the end of World War II, but having the greatest impact in the late nineteenth and early twentieth centuries. The third type has been the postcolonial and industrial city of the era since 1945, the period that has witnessed the greatest growth in cities and the most rapid increase in the rate of urbanization.

---

[2]Simon Leys, *Chinese Shadows* (New York: Penguin Books, 1978), p. 53.

Evolution of Cities in East Asia

The Traditional or Preindustrial City

The highest form of the earliest-known cities in East Asia was the ceremonial center of the capital cities of Shang China, beginning with Ao (sixteenth century B.C.) near present-day Chengchou (Zhengzhou) followed by the great city Shang (fourteenth century B.C.) near present-day Anyang, and some others. These centers consisted of a centrally situated ceremonial and administrative enclave, but the peasantry who produced the agricultural surplus to support the cities lived in villages dispersed through the surrounding countryside.

This ceremonial and administrative function, which was stamped on the earliest cities in China, was to persist as a major function until the arrival of Westerners many centuries later. In this regard then, the traditional Chinese city was not unlike the preindustrial city of other early civilizations. The uniqueness of the Chinese city, however, came from the way most cities were established and the morphology that the cities took on. Cities were established through the succeeding centuries largely by the government, as the Chinese state expanded outward from the culture hearth in North China. The Chinese civilization was based on intensive lowland agriculture, irrigated where possible. This meant that centers of government administration had to be located in the areas where the bulk of the population was located, in the valleys and plains where rich agricultural soils could be found. As the Chinese state grew in size and population, the numbers and sizes of cities naturally increased. Indeed, the spread of these administrative centers can be traced down through the centuries. At the highest level was the national capital, which remained in North China throughout most of China's history, except for a few periods when it was located in the central part of the country, principally the Yangtze Valley. At the next level were the provincial capitals, and below them hundreds of *hsien* (county) capitals.

The establishment of these cities and towns was the result of military expansion by the government for the purpose of protecting trade routes and consolidating control over newly acquired agricultural land. China's historic cities thus were located in the great fertile plains and river valleys of North, East, and South China, primarily the Yellow, Yangtze, and Hsi (Xi) rivers and their tributaries. Many of the largest and most important cities of China today date back many centuries to their original founding in these areas during the expansion of the Chinese state. These include such historic centers as Chungking (Chongqing) in the Szechuan (Sichuan) Basin, which was founded in the pre-Christian era and served as a capital city of an early state in that region. There was also Canton (Kuangchou, or Guangzhou, as the Chinese call it) near the mouth of the Hsi (Xi) River in South China, founded in the third century B.C., when the Chinese state first penetrated the tropics, and which served as China's principal southern port until the establishment of Hong Kong in the nineteenth century. Another example would be Nanking (Nanjing, which means "southern capital"), founded in the fifth century B.C. and located at a strategic point on the lower Yangtze River. Nanking (Nanjing) served as national capital for various periods over the centuries, most recently as the capital of Nationalist or Republican China (Taiwan) until 1949.

Peking Of all the historic, traditional cities, however, none is more famous than Peking (Beijing), the present national capital. Peking was originally a garrison town called Chi when it was founded during the Chou dynasty (a town may have existed here as early as 2000 B.C. according to some accounts). Even then, the city's strategic site on the border zone between the North China plain and the mountainous southern fringes of the Mongolian plateau was already evident. Peking was the capital of the Chin dynasty in the twelfth century A.D. The city then was destroyed by the invading Mongols, but rebuilt in 1260 by Kublai Khan (and called Ta-tu, "great capital") as his winter capital. It was this Peking that Marco Polo saw. The city was destroyed yet again with the fall of the Mongols and the establishment of the Ming dynasty in 1368. Nanking (Nanjing) served as national capital briefly after that, but in 1421 the capital was moved back to the rebuilt city, now named Peking (meaning "northern capital") for the first time, where it has remained with few interruptions until today. It is this city that can still be partially seen within the walls of the former Forbidden City, which the government today calls the Palace Museum (Figs. 11.2 and 11.3). Tremendous urban expansion in modern times, especially since 1949, including the tearing down of all the city walls except the one surrounding the old Forbidden City, has drastically altered the appearance and character of Peking.

A distinctive feature of the classic Chinese city was the wall surrounding the city. Initially, the wall served as a means of defense. But over time the wall also took on

Figure 11.2 Tienanmen (Gate of Heavenly Peace) Square in Peking, a vast open area created in front of the Palace Museum (the former Forbidden City) after the 1949 Revolution to serve the political needs of the new government of China. This square, larger than Red Square in Moscow, is still the focal point of celebrations and rallies and of China's capital city. (J. Williams)

the function of dividing line between what was urban and what was rural. Urban centers all had walls, from the smallest *hsien* capital up to the national capital. Indeed, purely agricultural villages could normally be distinguished from urban centers by the lack of walls around the villages. The walls varied in size, shape, and method of construction. The most imposing and permanent were the walls around capital cities at the provincial and national level.

The wall was only one part of the structure of the traditional city, however. In its idealized form, the traditional Chinese city reflected the ancient Chinese conception of the universe and the role of the emperor as intermediary between heaven and earth. This idealized conception was most apparent in the national capitals, but many elements of this conception could be seen in lesser cities at lower administrative levels.

Changan The Tang capital of Changan (present-day Sian or Xi'an) was one of the best early expressions of the classic Chinese capital city. Founded over 3000 years ago, Changan was the capital of a number of dynasties and states in the region of the Wei River Valley. But the city reached its true flowering during the brilliant period of the Tang dynasty (A.D. 618–906). The city, as typified by Changan, was regarded as a microcosm (Fig. 11.4). The arrangement of its parts was the visible expression of cosmological beliefs, which were those of an agricultural people. Thus, the city was divided in a grid pattern into four main quadrants representing the four quadrants of the heavens translated into the four directions or four seasons. Each side of the square enclosed by the city wall could be identified with the daily position of the sun or with each of the four seasons. The royal palace represented the polar star; as the polar star dominates the universe, so the palace at the center dominated the city (and in a broader context, the nation as a whole). The main north-south street through the city represented the celestial meridian. The palace at the center separated the markets from the centers of religious observance. The city wall and gates were oriented to the cardinal directions. South was the most favorable direction, toward the world of man; hence the palace (or lesser administrative headquarters in lower-order cities) always faced south. Some cities did not even have north gates. In short, the city was a cosmo-magical symbol, representing in highly formalized morphology the interrelationships of man and nature.

In reality, deviations from the ideal were common, particularly in cities at lower levels, such as *hsien* capitals. Many factors caused these less-than-perfect morphologies. Topography, for example, sometimes made it physically impossible to have a perfectly square or even rectangular wall. Population growth over time commonly produced a spillover effect of urbanization outside the original city wall, and eventually the need to build another to enclose the "suburbs." Over centuries, this process sometimes produced cities with walls within walls, or with walls of highly irregular shape.

Regrettably, the demands of modern urban development in China have necessitated, in the eyes of planners at least, the tearing down of most city walls, removing a colorful legacy of the past. The sites of the old walls commonly become the routes of new, broad boulevards. One of the few cities whose original wall has been retained almost in entirety is Sian (Xi'an). Because of the historic role of this city, the wall has been repaired and kept largely intact in its great rectangle surrounding the city.

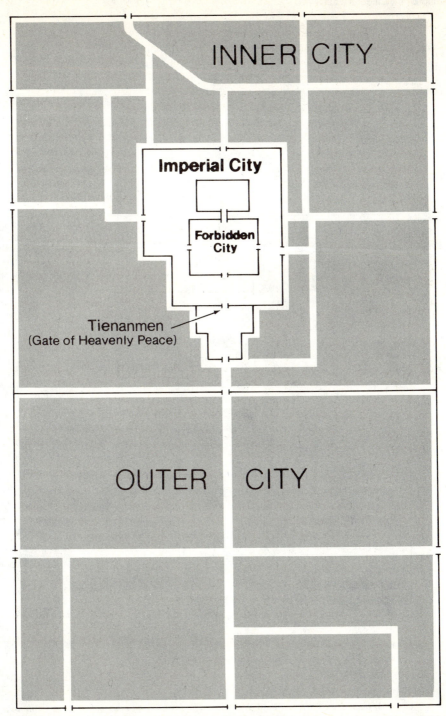

Figure 11.3 Old Peking. (*Source:* Sketched by J. Williams from an old map of nineteenth-century Peking.)

416 Chapter 11, Cities of East Asia

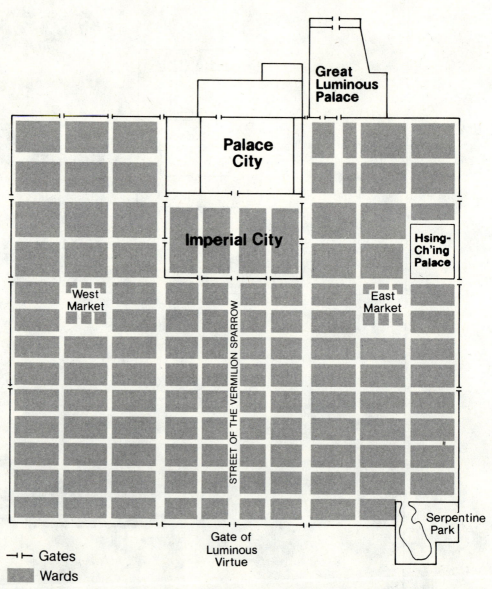

Figure 11.4 Ancient Changan—the City as Cosmo-Magical Symbol in China. (*Source: K'ao-ku*, No. 11, 1963, plate 2, as shown in Paul Wheatley, *The Pivot of the Four Quarters, A Preliminary Enquiry into the Origins and Character of the Ancient Chinese City,* Chicago: Aldine, 1971, p. 412.)

The Chinese City as Model: Japan and Korea Changan was the national capital of China at a time when Japan was a newly emerging civilization and was adopting many features of China, including city planning. As a result, the Japanese capital cities of the period were modeled after Changan. Indeed, the city as a distinct form first appeared in Japan at this time, beginning with the completion of Keijokyo (now called Nara) in 710. Although Nara today is a rather small and insignificant prefectural capital, it once represented the grandeur of the Nara period (710–784), a grandeur still evident today in the form of magnificent shrines and temples, if not in the original plan. Keiankyo (modern-day Kyoto) was to survive as the best example of early Japanese city planning. Serving as national capital from 794 to 1868, when the capital was shifted formally to Edo (now Tokyo), Kyoto still exhibits the original rectangular form, grid patterns, and other features copied from Changan, although modern urban/industrial growth has greatly increased the size of the city and covered or confused much of the original form. Nonetheless, the Chinese city morphology, with its rigid symmetry and formalized symbolism was still essentially alien to the Japanese culture and its basically asymmetrical tendency. Even the rugged character of the Japanese landscape, with the shortage of level land needed to fully realize the Chinese concept of the city, militated against the Chinese city as a long-range model for city planning in Japan. Hence, although Kyoto and Nara are of great historic interest, their influence on the morphology of the Japanese city as it developed in later centuries was relatively minor.

Korea also experienced the importation of Chinese city planning concepts. The Chinese city model was most evident in the national capital of Seoul (literally "capital"), which became the premier city of Korea in 1394. The city has never really lost its dominance since. Early maps of Seoul reveal the imprint of Chinese city forms, with the wall, street patterns, and placement of palaces and other city functions. The form was not completely achieved, however, in part because of the rugged landscape around Seoul, which was located initially in a confining basin just north of the lower Han River. Succeeding centuries of development and rebuilding, especially in the twentieth century with the Japanese occupation (1910–1945) and the Korean War (1950–1953), obliterated most of the original form and architecture of the historic city. A modern commercial/industrial city, one of the largest in the world, has arisen on the ashes of the old city. Occasional relics of the past still stand though, through restoration efforts such as some of the palaces and a few of the main gates.

Colonial Cities

Important as the traditional cities were, the present urban patterns and character of many of the major cities of East Asia are the result in large part of the colonial history of the region.

The First Footholds: The Portuguese and Dutch The Portuguese and Dutch were the first to arrive in East Asia. Their impact on urban development, while not major compared with that of later colonial powers, was not insignificant. The Portuguese were the more important of the two. Seeking trade and the opportunity to spread Christianity, the Portuguese made some penetration of southern Japan via the port of

Nagasaki in the latter 1500s, but their influence was short-lived there. They actually had a greater, but indirect influence on Japanese city development by introducing firearms and military technology into Japan. This led to the development of stronger private armies among the *daimyo* or feudal rulers of Japan, and that in turn led to the building of large central castles in the center of each daimyo's domain. These castles, which were modeled after fortresses in the West, were commonly located on strategic high points, surrounded by the *daimyo*'s retainers and a commercial town. These centers eventually served as the nuclei for many of the cities of modern Japan.

The Portuguese also tried to penetrate China. Reaching Canton in 1517 they attempted to establish themselves there for trade, but were frustrated in their efforts by the Chinese and forced to accept the small peninsula of Macao, near the mouth of the Pearl River south of Canton. The peninsula was walled off by Chinese authorities, and rent was paid for the territory until the Portuguese declared it independent from China in 1849. With only 10 sq. mi. (26 sq. km.) of land, Macao remained the principal Portuguese toehold in East Asia, especially after the eclipse of their operations in southern Japan in the seventeenth century. Macao was most important as a trading center and haven for refugees. The establishment of Hong Kong in the nineteenth century on the opposite side of the Pearl River estuary signaled the beginning of Macao's decline, from which it has never recovered. Although Portugal retains control of Macao (since 1974 as a "Chinese territory under Portuguese administration"), the tiny colony, with under 300,000 inhabitants (with only 7,000 Europeans), is a rather shabby remnant of Portugal's colonial empire. The colony survives economically largely on tourism and gambling, drawing eager customers by the thousands from Hong Kong across the bay, where gambling is illegal.

The Dutch impact in East Asia was much less important. Primarily concerned with Southeast Asia and the Dutch East Indies, Dutch penetration of East Asia was limited largely to a brief period of control of the island of Formosa (now called Taiwan) from 1624 to 1662. During that time they began to develop modern agriculture and established the original site of the city of Tainan, the original capital and oldest city on the island.

Treaty Ports of China   It was the other Western colonial powers, arriving in the eighteenth and nineteenth centuries, that had the greatest impact on the growth of cities and urbanization in China. Most important were the British and Americans, but the French, Germans, Belgians, and others were also involved, as were the Japanese, who joined the action toward the close of the nineteenth century.

It all began officially with the Treaty of Nanking (Nanjing) in 1842, under the terms of which the British were ceded the island of Hong Kong and allowed to reside and trade in five ports—Canton (Guangzhou), Amoy, Fuchou (Fuzhou), Ningpo, and Shanghai. Further refinements of this treaty in succeeding years gave to the other foreign powers the same rights as the British. A second set of wars and treaties, 1856–1860, led to the opening of further ports to Western trade and settlement. By 1911, approximately 90 cities of China, along the entire coast, up the Yangtze valley, in North China and Manchuria, were opened as treaty ports or open ports, with a third of a million foreign residents (Fig. 11.5).

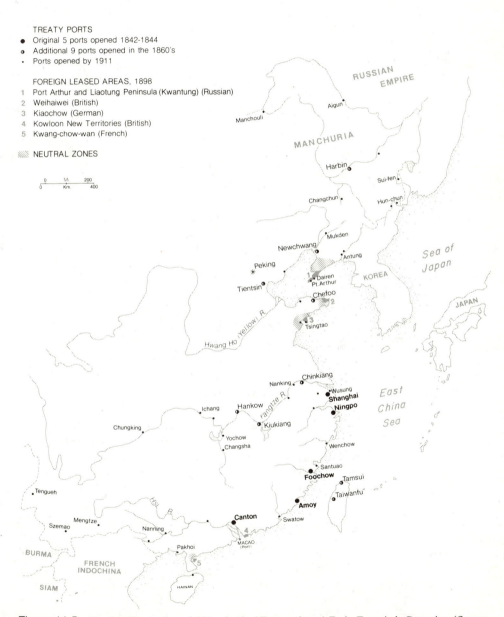

Figure 11.5 Foreign Penetration of China in the Nineteenth and Early Twentieth Centuries. (*Source:* J. Fairbank, et al., *East Asia, Tradition and Transformation,* Boston: Houghton Mifflin, 1973, p. 577.)

The treaty ports represented an aggressive and dynamic new order introduced into the traditional fabric of Chinese society, a new order based on organized competition. The Westerners established themselves in the ports primarily to make money. But the treaty ports represented much more. Foreign residents in these ports were under the legal jurisdiction of their respective consuls; that is, they had the right of extraterritoriality. Western legal procedures covered the merchants and missionaries, their goods and property, and in practice even their Chinese servants and assistants. By degree, taxation, police forces, and other features of municipal government were developed in the treaty ports under Western control. China's sovereignty was thus largely supplanted in these cities in the concession areas, which were the areas of land in each treaty port leased in perpetuity by the foreigners for modest rents from the Chinese government. The treaty ports thus became Western-secured havens in the increasingly unstable Chinese nation.

Shanghai Of all the treaty ports, Shanghai quickly became the most important and eventually rose to become China's premier city, a position it retains to this day. Shanghai is a classic example of both the treaty port system and of the role that situation can play in the growth of a city. Shanghai, which literally means "on the sea," had existed as a small settlement as early as the Warring States period (403–221 B.C.). By the eighteenth century, the city was a medium-sized county seat with a population of about 200,000, built in traditional city style with a wall. Deposition of silt by the Yangtze River over the centuries, however, had made Shanghai no longer a port directly fronting the sea. The town was now located about 15 mi. (24 km.) up the Whangpoo (Huangpu) River, a minor tributary of the Yangtze. Western control of Shanghai began with the British concession in 1846, followed by expansion of these areas over the years to cover most of the city. In 1863 the British and American areas were joined to form the Shanghai International Settlement, which, by the heyday of the 1920s, contained some 60,000 foreigners, the largest concentration in China. The Shanghai Municipal Council dealt with all the problems of the large city—roads, jetties, drainage, sanitation, police, recreation, etc. Shanghai remained Chinese territory, but was free from Chinese taxation and under foreign consular control. Hence, Shanghai, and the other treaty ports as well, served as magnets for wealthy Chinese entrepreneurs and for millions of impoverished Chinese peasants seeking a haven. The wealthy Chinese invested in manufacturing and other aspects of the commercial economy; the peasants provided cheap labor. Shanghai was unique in all this, however, in that it grew in the short period of a hundred years out of the traditional agrarian economy of China, before China had a modern railway network or a single national market and before other Chinese commercial cities of metropolitan size had appeared, to become China's most important city. By the end of its first century under Western control, just before World War II, Shanghai handled half of China's foreign trade and had half the country's mechanized factories. The city's population of 4 million made it one of the five or six largest cities in the world and was over twice the size of its nearest rivals, Peking and Tientsin (Tianjin) (Fig. 11.6).

This phenomenal rise to greatness was the result in part of situation. The city's location near the mouth of the Yangtze delta was a natural one for a great seaport

Evolution of Cities in East Asia 421

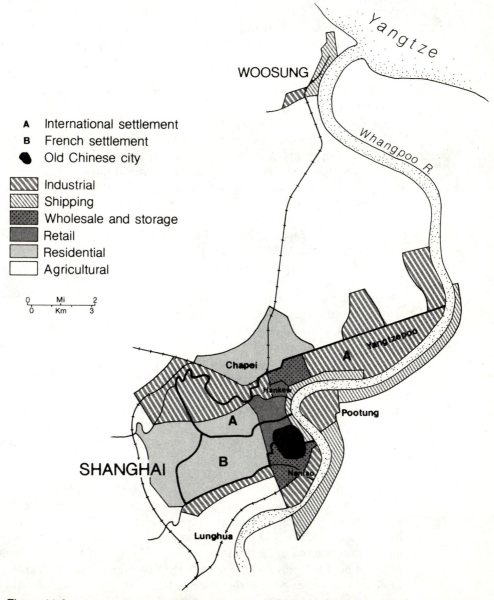

Figure 11.6 Shanghai, Land Use During the Colonial Era. (*Source:* Rhoads Murphey, *Shanghai, Key to Modern China,* Cambridge, MA: Harvard University Press, 1953, p. 26.)

city of the modern commercial age. The Westerners simply profited from a natural locational advantage for handling the trade of the largest and most populous river basin in China. In addition, the city became the major financial center for the Chinese government as well as for the economic life of Shanghai itself and its commercial hinterland. During the twentieth century, manufacturing developed in the city, aided by the accumulation of foreign and Chinese capital from trade, and enhanced by the protection and advantages of the treaty port system. Manufacturing was able to compete successfully with other manufacturing centers emerging in China, despite the absence of local supplies of raw materials, because of the ease and cheapness of water transport. And the rich agricultural hinterland immediately surrounding Shanghai provided ample foodstuffs to maintain the city's population.

This was all achieved, too, in spite of a relatively poor site. The city is located in the Yangtze Delta, an area of deep silt deposits, high water table and poor natural drainage, difficult water supply, poor foundations for modern buildings of any great height, and a harbor on a narrow river that required considerable dredging to maintain its utility for oceangoing ships. Shanghai illustrates well that a superb situation can usually outweigh a poor site, which can be improved through modern technology. Indeed, it has been said that a great city would probably have arisen here eventually anyway. Western colonialism, via the treaty port system, simply hurried the process along.

There was a colonial impact on other Chinese cities, too, of course. Particularly significant was the Japanese impact. In Manchuria, which the Japanese eventually took over outright in the 1930s, many of the major cities were modernized and developed along the Western lines that the Japanese had adopted in the development of their own cities after 1868 (see below). The Japanese also introduced the beginnings of the industrial base that was to make Manchuria the most important industrial region in China, an importance it retains today. The industry was concentrated in a string of major cities connected by the railway network that the Japanese built, particularly Harbin (Ha'erbin), Changchun, and Mukden (Shenyang). As with Shanghai, in these cities of Manchuria there arose a new Western-type commercial/industrial city alongside the traditional Chinese city, which eventually was engulfed and left as a remnant of the past. Not until after 1949, really, was this duality of China's former treaty ports largely eliminated through urban renewal and development under socialism.

Taiwan and Korea: The Japanese Impact The Japanese also greatly influenced the urban landscape of their two other colonies in East Asia. During their rule of Taiwan (1895–1945) and Korea (1910–1945), the Japanese introduced essentially the same Western-style urban planning practices that they brought to Manchuria's cities. Taipei was made the colonial capital of Taiwan and transformed from a rather sleepy, backward Chinese provincial capital of no real consequence into a relatively modernized city of about 250,000. The city wall was razed, roads and other infrastructure, such as water and sanitation facilities improved, and many of the public buildings still in use today built to house colonial government functions. The most prominent of these buildings, the former governor's palace, with its tall red brick tower, still stands in the heart of Taipei as the main headquarters of the Nationalist Chinese government-in-exile, and the square in front of the building is used for mass rallies and celebrations in much the same fashion as Tienanmen (Tiananmen) Square in front of the Palace Museum in Peking. Seoul likewise was transformed much as Taipei, to serve the needs of the Japanese colonial rule in the Korean peninsula.

Hong Kong Hong Kong differed from the treaty ports in that there was no pretense of Chinese sovereignty here. Founded by the British at the same time Shanghai was opened up in the 1840s, Hong Kong became second only to Shanghai as the most important entrepôt center on the China coast during the century following its founding.

The reasons for the importance of Hong Kong are not difficult to find. Site and situation played major roles again. The colony consists of some 400 sq. mi. (1040 sq. km.) of mountainous, rocky land on the east side of the Pearl River estuary, some 70 mi. (113 km.) downstream from Canton (Fig. 11.7). The original acquisition by the British consisted of just Hong Kong Island, about 36 sq. mi. (93 sq. km.). The Kowloon Peninsula (another 4 sq. mi. or 10 sq. km.) across the harbor was obtained in a separate

Figure 11.7 Hong Kong. (*Source: Hong Kong's New Towns, Sha Tin,* Hong Kong: Public Works Department, 1972.)

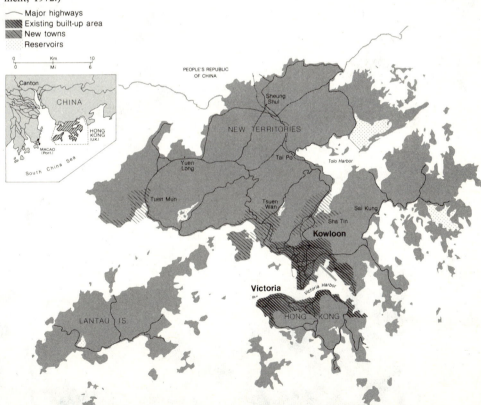

treaty in 1858. In theory these two parts belong to Britain in perpetuity. In 1898 the New Territories, some 360 sq. mi. (932 sq. km.) of islands and land on the large peninsula north of Kowloon, were leased from the Chinese for 99 years. Strictly speaking, there is no city named Hong Kong (which means "fragrant harbor," rather a misnomer today because of pollution). The two main urban centers in the colony thus are the cities of Victoria on the north shore of Hong Kong Island and Kowloon ("nine dragons," from the nine hills surrounding the city) on the mainland across from Victoria. About 4 million out of Hong Kong's 5 million residents live in these two cities. The site factor that so strongly favored Hong Kong's growth was the superb harbor, one of the world's great natural harbors. Protected by Hong Kong Island to the south, the deep waters of the bay between the two cities made this an ideal location for a major port. Indeed, the advantages of the harbor outweighed the disadvantages of the site, including limited level land for urban expansion, an inadequate water supply, and insufficient land nearby to feed the colony (Fig. 11.8).

As for situation, the colony's location at the mouth of southern China's major drainage basin, the Hsi (Xi) River, gave Hong Kong the same advantage that Shanghai had. When the north-south railway from Peking was pushed through to Canton (Guangzhou) in the 1920s, Hong Kong also had improved land connections with the rest of China, strengthening the entrepôt function of the colony. Thus, for about a century, Shanghai and Hong Kong completely dominated the foreign trade of China.

Figure 11.8 Hong Kong, as viewed from the peak on Hong Kong Island. The city of Victoria, the main commercial/banking center of the colony, skirts the north shore of the island, facing the larger city of Kowloon across the harbor that has always been one of Hong Kong's greatest natural assets. (J. Williams)

Japan: The Asian Exception

Japan is referred to as the Asian exception because it did not go through a true colonial experience. Indeed, Japan was itself a colonial power. Hence, the urban history of Japan involved an evolution directly from the premodern or traditional city to the modern commercial/industrial city.

It has already been observed that the city originated in Japan around the eighth century with the classic capitals of Nara and Kyoto. Other cities followed, principally the centers of feudal clans. Most of these were transitory; a few survived into the modern era, such as Kamakura, now an important satellite city of the Tokyo complex. Also noted was the emergence of the fortified castle towns that flourished on trade and piracy. The most famous of these was Sakai, just south of present-day Osaka. Because of its excellent harbor and its strategic location vis-à-vis the trade routes to China and Southeast Asia, Sakai became the major port of Japan from the fourteenth to seventeenth centuries. Almost none of these early cities retained its original function or importance, however. Sakai is now simply a major suburb of the Osaka metropolitan complex. Kyoto was one of the few cities of this era to survive down to the modern period; by the middle of the sixteenth century it had a population of over half a million, larger than that of any European city of the day.

Osaka Gradual political unification during the Tokugawa period (1603–1868) led to the establishment of a permanent network of cities. The castle town served as the chief catalyst for urban growth. One of the most important of these new castle towns to emerge at this time was Osaka. In 1583 a grand castle was built here, which served as the nucleus for the city to come. Various policies stimulated the growth of Osaka and other cities, including the prohibitions on foreign trade after the mid-1630s which signaled the decline of centers such as Sakai, the destruction of minor feudal castles, and prohibitions on the building of more than one castle to a province. These policies had the effect of consolidating settlements and encouraging civilians to migrate to the more important castle communities, a trend that was to be repeated in the twentieth century in a somewhat different form.

The new castle towns, such as Osaka, were ideally located. Because of their economic and administrative functions, they generally were located on level land near important landscape features such as river crossings or harbors. These locations gave the castle towns a natural advantage for future urban growth in their respective regions. Thus, Osaka emerged as the principal business, financial, and manufacturing center in Tokugawa Japan, a role it still retains, in competition with Tokyo, even today. The cities of this period were tied together by an impressive network of highways that stimulated trade and city growth. The most famous of these early roads was the Tokaido Highway, running from Osaka eastward through Nagoya (which emerged as another major commercial and textile manufacturing center) to the most important city of this period and after, Edo (Tokyo).

Tokyo Among the major cities of Asia, Tokyo was a relative latecomer. It was founded in the fifteenth century, when a minor feudal lord built a rudimentary castle on a bluff near the sea, about where the Imperial Palace stands today. The site was a good one, however, for a major city: a natural port with hills that could easily be fortified, and plenty of room on the Kanto plain behind for expansion (Fig. 11.9). But Tokyo really got its start a century later when Ieyasu, the Tokugawa ruler at that time, decided to make Edo his capital. Much of Tokyo still bears the imprint of the grand design that Ieyasu and his descendants laid out for Tokyo. The Imperial enclosure, a vast area of palaces, parks, and moats in the very heart of Tokyo, was planned by them. Much of the land on which central Tokyo stands today was reclaimed from the bay, a method of urban expansion that was to typify Japanese city building from then on, reflecting the shortage of level land and the need for good port facilities. By the early seventeenth century, Edo already had a population of 150,000 surrounding the most magnificent castle in Japan. By the eighteenth century, the population was well over 1 million, making Edo the largest city in the world, a distinction Tokyo retains today.

Edo's growth, then, was based initially on the role as political center of Japan, tied to the other cities by an expanding network of roads. An early dichotomy was established between Osaka, as the business center, and Tokyo, as the cultural and political center, that lingers on even today in the form of regional dialects and attitudes. With the restoration of Emperor Meiji in 1868, Japan's modern era began. For many reasons, it was decided that the emperor's court would leave Kyoto and move to Edo, which was renamed Tokyo ("eastern capital") to signify its additional role now as national political capital of Japan. This transfer of political functions, plus the great industrialization and modernization program that was undertaken from the 1870s on, gave Tokyo a further boost that started it on its astounding growth during the last century.

Major Representative Cities of East Asia Today

Since the latter 1940s, as was noted in the introduction to this chapter, the end of colonialism in East Asia brought independence and new paths of national development along two distinctly different lines: the socialist and nonsocialist approaches. This basic dichotomy between the cities of China and North Korea on the one hand, and the cities of Japan, South Korea, Taiwan, and Hong Kong on the other, is the most fundamental classification of cities one could make for the region today.

One can also classify the major cities of the region on the basis of functions and size. From this perspective, the largest city in each of the states of East Asia can serve as a major example of a certain type of city.

Superconurbations: Tokyo and the Tokaido Megalopolis

Japan illustrates especially well the phenomenon of superconurbations. A distinctive feature of Japan's urban pattern is the concentration of its major cities into a relatively small portion of an already small country, and in particular into one superconurbation linking the three largest urban nodes of Tokyo-Nagoya-Osaka, known as the Tokaido Megalopolis (after the historic highway).

Most of the major cities in Japan are found in the core region, a narrow band

Major Representative Cities of East Asia Today 427

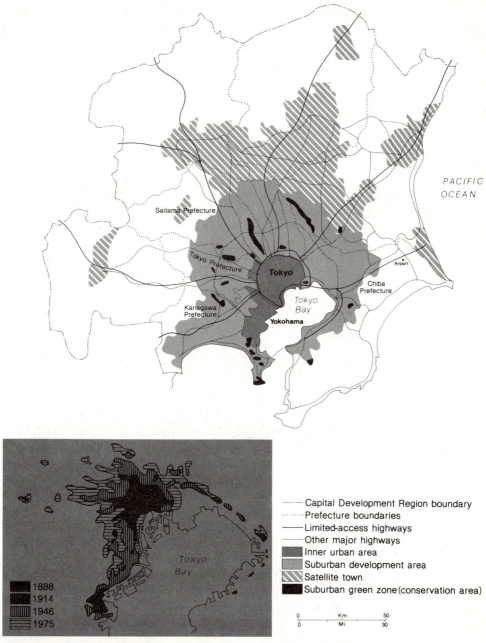

Figure 11.9 Tokyo Capital Development Region. (*Source: Planning of Tokyo, 1980,* Tokyo Metropolitan Government, 1980.)

stretching from the urban node of Fukuoka-Kitakyushu-Shimonoseki at the western end of the great Inland Sea, which separates the major islands of Japan and serves as the internal waterway linking the industrial nodes of the core, eastward as far as the giant urban agglomeration of the Tokyo region. In between, along the coastal fringes of the islands, are strings of industrial cities that grew to importance largely in the last century, such as Hiroshima and Okayama (Fig. 11.10). During the 1960s, Japan's lead-

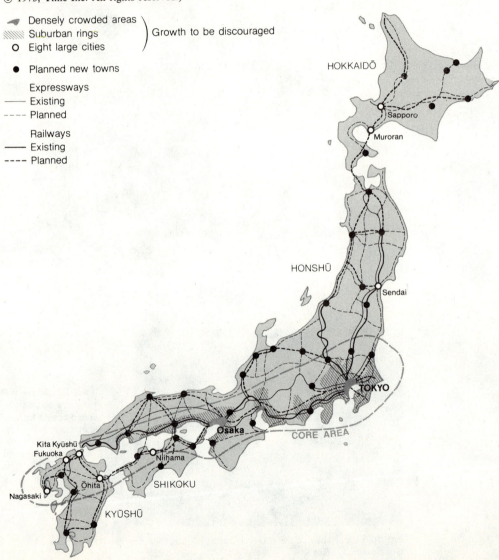

Figure 11.10 Japan's Core Area and Industrial Cities, Present and Projected. (*Source:* Louis Kraar, "Japan Sets Out to Remodel Itself," *Fortune,* March, 1973, 100. *Fortune* Art Department/Vahé Karishjian, © 1973, Time Inc. All rights reserved.)

ers encouraged the relocation of rural people to smaller and newer cities in this belt and oversaw the construction of huge industrial complexes known as *kombinats*. As a result, not only did the big cities grow, but numerous secondary and tertiary industrial cities thrived as well. Between 1950 and 1970 the percentage of Japanese living in cities with a population of 50,000 or more rose from 33 to 64 percent, while the proportion of the population living in cities of 100,000 or more increased from 25 to 52 percent. By 1970, some 70 percent of the Japanese lived in urban areas. Hence, Japan became a predominantly urbanized nation only within the last 30 years.

Beyond these figures, however, is the more startling fact that over one-third of the Japanese are concentrated in a 30-mi. (48-km.) radius of the three biggest metropolises of Tokyo, Osaka, and Nagoya, which together cover only slightly more than one percent of Japan's land area. The Greater Tokyo Metropolitan Region, which includes Metropolitan Tokyo with its port city of Yokohama (built in the late 1800s to service the Tokyo region and still one of Japan's most important ports) and the three neighboring prefectures of Chiba, Kanagawa, and Saitama contains about 25 million inhabitants (about 22 percent of the national total) and has a population density of around 8,000 per square mile (20,800 per square kilometer). Osaka is the center of the second most important node. It includes the main port of Kobe (also built in the late 1800s to service that region) and the historic city of Kyoto to the northeast, which is now merging with the Osaka conurbation. This region holds another 15 million people. Third in size is the Nagoya node with about 6 million people. In other words, over 40 million people lived in the Tokaido Megalopolis by the late 1970s and a major share of the 70 million remaining Japanese lived in other cities in the core region. Few other countries in the world exhibit such an extraordinary degree of concentrated urbanization. The reasons for this concentration are too complex to explore in detail here, but are the result of such factors as the shortage of level land, the need to import almost all raw materials and to export finished goods to pay for them, and the desire to locate industry along the coast to reduce transportation costs and to take advantage of economies of scale in order to make Japanese goods more competitive abroad.

Not only is Tokyo itself part of this superconurbation, but it is also a primate city in many respects. Tokyo is the center of the business, banking, financial, and publishing world in Japan, the center of all mass communications media, and the headquarters for all political parties. It is as if Washington, D.C., New York, Chicago, Philadelphia, Pittsburgh, Boston, and Detroit were all rolled into one, as a Japanese observer put it once. Hence, for people eager to be in the mainstream of modern Japan, living in or near Tokyo is essential. In other words, Tokyo's importance in the minds of most Japanese is far greater than that of any American city in the minds of Americans. A closer parallel would be the roles of Paris or Moscow in their respective countries.

A distinctive feature of many of Japan's major cities, particularly Tokyo, is the radial morphology they exhibit today. This is not surprising, because the castle served as the original nucleus of the town and remained the center of the city until modern times. Hence, the towns grew outward from the central point and commonly along the road network centered on the castle. A strong parallel can be seen here between this pattern and that of such cities as Moscow, with its dominating Kremlin. Modern transportation development, in the form of expressways and railways, has continued this radial pattern, and suburbanization has tended to follow the transportation networks.

Colonial Cities: The Anachronism of Hong Kong   Only two colonial cities are left in East Asia—Hong Kong and Macao. Hong Kong is far the more important of the two, and remains today one of the last remnants of the British Empire and one of the few colonial enclaves left in the whole world. At the same time, Hong Kong is a mini-industrial state and financial center of considerable importance.

Hong Kong's locational advantage became even more important after 1949 when Shanghai became part of socialist China and its functions as a major financial center for the China coast and East Asia ceased, along with much of its trading function with the outside world. During the Korean War (1950–1953), however, things looked bleak for Hong Kong. The UN blockade effectively shut off most of the colony's entrepôt trade. In addition, the colony was flooded with refugees from the mainland. The population soared from half a million in 1946 to over 2 million by 1950. For a while, it looked as if the colony would either be taken over by the new Chinese government or else wither and die anyway. That did not happen, obviously. Instead, there was a dramatic reorientation of the colony's directions, away from just the trading of other people's goods to the manufacturing and exporting of goods by the colony itself. The British rulers and Chinese entrepreneurs got together and decided to diversify the economic base, beginning in the early 1950s with a massive industrialization program, based on production of light industrial goods, most importantly textiles. Foreign and domestic investors, at the start wily Chinese capitalists who fled Shanghai, but eventually including British, Americans, overseas Chinese, and Japanese, were encouraged to put their money into the colony. The lures were cheap labor and a laissez-faire economic system that provided minimum government interference in the operations of the economy. Site limitations were overcome by massive landfill projects to provide new land for factories, the infrastructure of the colony was drastically improved, and tax incentives initiated to provide as attractive an investment climate as possible. There still are site problems, however, particularly the shortage of water (over half the local supply is still piped in from China's Kwangtung (Guangdong) province), and the meager local production of food (about 95 percent of demand must be imported, over half from China).

The strategy worked, but in part because the Chinese government allowed it to work. One of the paradoxes of Hong Kong is that the government of China has continued to permit this arch symbol of unrepentant Western capitalism and colonialism to exist and thrive on what is rightly Chinese territory. The Chinese have done this because Hong Kong makes money for them too (several billion dollars a year in foreign exchange). The Chinese government is heavily involved in the industry, banking, and commerce of the colony, along with all the foreign and domestic capitalists. One of the striking sights of Hong Kong is to stand in Statute Square on Queens Road Central in Victoria and see there lined up side by side the Bank of China (originally built by the Nationalist government but taken over by the new communist government in 1949) and the Hong Kong and Shanghai Banking Corporation, the local financial strongholds of China and Great Britain, respectively. Looming over these banks a few blocks away is the 52-story Connaught Center, a striking steel and glass tower that houses, among other things, the headquarters of Jardine Matheson and Company, the colony's premier *hong,* or trading firm, that helped put Hong Kong on the map in the nineteenth century. This firm is now a powerful conglomerate with its hands in all types of activities in many countries of Asia.

Hong Kong's trade with China now is largely a one-way street, with the importation of foodstuffs and raw materials for the colony's industry from China, and the export of manufactured goods throughout the world, but principally to Japan and the United States. Totally dependent on the vagaries of world trade and the export of consumer goods that threaten to glut the big markets of the developed world, competing as they do with similar goods from South Korea, Taiwan, and elsewhere, Hong Kong's economic future is fraught with as much uncertainty as its political future. Theoretically, the Chinese have the legal right to demand return of the New Territories in 1997. To do so would seriously jeopardize the continued functioning of Hong Kong as it exists today. Militarily, the Chinese could take the colony in a day. It is widely felt they will not do this, at least not until 1997, because Hong Kong is too profitable for them the way it is, even though their tolerance of it is a glaring contradiction of socialist and nationalist principles. Hong Kong is clearly living on borrowed time. It stands as a rich, artificial, glitteringly modern patch of Western capitalism, colonialism, and materialism on the doorstep of austere, socialist China. While it lasts, however, Hong Kong will stand as one of the world's most fascinating, and in certain respects most beautiful, cities.

Primate Cities: Seoul   The primate city is a phenomenon confined essentially to nonsocialist East Asia. Japan, South Korea, and Taiwan all suffer to some extent from this problem, but it is most pronounced in the case of South Korea and its capital city of Seoul. With a population of nearly 9.5 million, Seoul contains almost one-quarter of the population of South Korea (Fig. 11.11). The next largest city is the southern industrial port of Pusan, with somewhat under 3 million, a sizable and important city in its own right, but completely overshadowed in functional importance by Seoul.

The rise of Seoul, within the span of about two decades, to one of the largest cities in the world is surprising, if only from a locational viewpoint. The city's site, midway along the west coast plain of the Korean peninsula, where most of the people are located, was originally a logical place for the national capital under a unified Korea. However, since the division of the peninsula in the late 1940s, and the bitter stalemate between North and South Korea since 1953, Seoul's location just 20 mi. (32 km.) from the demilitarized zone makes the city a highly vulnerable national capital. Yet, the population grew from a few hundred thousand at the time of the Korean War to its present bloated size. Most of this growth was the result of rural-to-urban migration from the overcrowded countryside. Fewer than half the people living in Seoul were born there. Hence, Seoul represents one of the most intense and compressed examples of urbanization anywhere in the world.

Figure 11.11 Seoul, South Korea's capital and primate city, largely a creation of the post-Korean War reconstruction, fills the constricting basin of the Han River in which the city is centered, with newer urban growth spilling over the hills into adjacent valleys. (J. Williams)

These migrants, coming as families and as single people, especially young women, sought the employment opportunities available in Seoul, which has been the center of South Korea's phenomenal industrial transformation since the late 1950s. Yet manufacturing alone has not accounted for the city's growth. Seoul is also the national capital with the attendant administrative and civil service employment, the preeminent education and research center, the locus of culture and entertainment, the banking and financial capital, and the focus of tourism. With a per capita income more than twice the national average, Seoul resembles Tokyo in the late 1950s in many respects. There is a combination of modern Westernization mixed with considerable congestion and shabbiness, reflecting the housing shortage that still plagues the city and the confining terrain of the basin in which the city is located. Seoul is not a beautiful city. Rather, it gives the impression of a society too busy building and growing, always with the threat of military catastrophe hanging over it, to worry overly about aesthetics and where the development path may be taking the city and nation.

Regional Centers: Taipei Another distinctive type of city is the regional center. Although these centers are found throughout East Asia, a particularly good example is the city of Taipei. Since 1950 the "temporary" capital of the Nationalist Chinese government-in-exile, Taipei has experienced phenomenal growth beyond what it probably would have undergone if it had remained solely a provincial capital of an island province of China.

When the Nationalist government retreated to the island in 1950, the provincial capital was shifted to near the town of Taichung in the center of Taiwan's west coast plain. That political change did not alter Taipei's position as the real regional center for the island, however. In fact, Taipei came to assume certain primate city functions, even though its population of now over 2 million is only twice that of the next largest city, the industrial port of Kaohsiung in the south. Being the national capital, Taipei has strengthened its hold on education, culture, entertainment, banking and finance, manufacturing, and tourism, initiated during the Japanese era. As with Seoul, much of the city's eightfold increase in population in the span of two decades was the result of in-migration from the densely populated countryside, responding to the frenetic industrialization program of the government.

In some respects, Taipei looks like Seoul, on a smaller scale, with modern buildings and broad, tree-lined boulevards and a relatively high standard of living mixed with a certain degree of shabbiness, although on the whole Taipei is a more attractive city and its urban problems seem less severe than those of Seoul (Fig. 11.12). As with Seoul, there is a certain austerity to the political atmosphere, reflecting the changing international political fortunes of the Nationalist government as well as the unbending policy of preparing the island and its people for the eventual downfall of the mainland regime. Political posters and slogans adorn the walls of public buildings or span major

Figure 11.12 A water buffalo grazes contentedly in a field across the street from one of Taipei's newest high-rise office buildings on Tunhua North Road, the heart of one of the most fashionable commercial/residential districts of New Taipei. This scene could be duplicated in many of Asia's rapidly growing cities, where the rural/urban boundary is often sharply defined. (J. Williams)

streets in Taipei, and the military is highly visible. All this, combined with the frantic pace of construction and growth, gives Taipei a slight air of unreality.

Socialist Cities: Shanghai Since 1949 the Chinese have been creating their own peculiar variant of the socialist city, which is also found in the Soviet Union and Eastern Europe (see Chapter 4). Of all the Chinese cities one might use as an example of the Chinese socialist city, Shanghai, the largest and most Westernized city in 1949, offered the biggest challenge to the urban planners of China. Shanghai still is China's largest and most Westernized city, and still has the highest standard of living in China. But even the casual visitor can see that the Western aura is now relatively superficial, primarily in the legacy of Western-style buildings dating from before 1949, and that a socialist transformation has indeed taken place.

The principles of socialist urban planning in the Chinese model are discussed in detail later in this chapter. Suffice it to note here some of the basic changes that have taken place in Shanghai since 1949. First of all, Shanghai has not diminished in total importance within the sphere of China, although its relative importance has declined as the result of the growth of many other cities, particularly those in the interior. The government's general policy since the 1950s, although somewhat inconsistently followed, has been to promote more balanced regional development, so that the extreme imbalance in urbanization and modern industrial/commercial development inherited in 1949 could be righted. Thus, virtually every city has seen the development of a manufacturing sector in its economy and growth in population. For example, Lanchou (Lanzhou) in Kansu (Gansu) province in the northwest has become a major industrial city and transportation node of nearly 2 million as the main jumping-off point for the trans-Sinkiang (Xinjiang) railway and all of northwest China's frontier region. As another example, Kunming, in the southwest province of Yunnan, has become a city of over 1.2 million and serves as the industrial node for that formerly underdeveloped part of China.

Shanghai itself is now part of Shanghai Municipality, one of three municipalities in China enjoying provincial status (the others are Peking and Tientsin [Tianjin]), comprising 10 urban districts and 10 rural counties with a combined total population of approximately 11 million. The population of Shanghai City, in the 10 urban districts, is actually just over 5 million. All major cities have substantial rural hinterlands administered by the cities. The people in these rural districts are counted as part of each city's gross population. Hence, Shanghai shows up as one of the five or so largest cities in the world, when in fact it is actually smaller in terms of true urban population than some 15 to 20 other cities of the world. This urban/rural population mix can make working with Chinese urban data hazardous unless one is aware of the peculiar administrative setup.

Size aside, the locational advantage of Shanghai has continued to serve the city well. Shanghai has remained as China's most important commercial and industrial city, the largest port in volume of foreign and domestic freight handled. In terms of meeting the criteria of a true "producing" city (see below), Shanghai comes the closest of just about any Chinese city today. Indeed, it is the attraction of Shanghai, with its broad-based economy and relatively high standard of living, that has served as a magnet, just as in colonial days, for Chinese migrants. Only the most energetic efforts of the government at controlling rural-to-urban migration have succeeded in holding down the growth of the city. Shanghai's recent record of the 1970s has been one of capital-intensive development and high rates of labor force participation. Particularly rapid growth has been experienced in electronics, shipbuilding, heavy machinery, computers, and electric generators, all made possible by Shanghai's position as one of the three largest iron-steel centers in the nation and its relatively sophisticated and well-trained labor force. Some of the flavor of the old international settlement is also returning to the city as a result of the influx of foreign businesses and tourists in the post-Mao period.

Major Urban Problems: The Experience of Nonsocialist East Asia

As with big cities around the world, the industrial cities of nonsocialist East Asia are experiencing the same profound problems of overcrowding, pollution, traffic congestion, crime, shortages of housing and other urban services, etc. These problems are certainly not unique to East Asia. The region's dubious distinction in regard to these problems, however, is that they have escalated to appalling dimensions in some of the biggest cities of the region. The cause of the problems is too many people occupying too little land and competing for too few services. The result is a somewhat paradoxical situation of seeming affluence in the midst of great urban problems. Residents of the cities of Japan, South Korea, Taiwan, and Hong Kong have standards of living among the highest in the world, certainly the highest in Asia (adding Singapore to the list). They dress smartly, and many own and drive their own cars or at least motorcycles, which have long since replaced the bicycle as the main means of private urban transportation. These urban dwellers eat well and increasingly eat more Western-style foods, especially in Japan. The ubiquitous golden arch of McDonald's hamburger chain and other American fast-food merchants are increasingly evident, catering to the modernized tastes of especially the younger generation in these countries. Retail stores of a thousand and one types, ranging from small family operations to the gaudy emporiums of mass merchandising, best typified by department stores such as Mitsukoshi's on the Ginza in Tokyo, provide every conceivable consumer good for the affluent residents of these cities. At night, the big cities glitter with eye-popping displays of neon, nowhere more dazzling than in Tokyo, advertising the goods and services to be had there. In short, superficially the big cities seem to provide a rich and tempting life for their residents.

Closer observation reveals the severity of the problems, however. The cities of Japan epitomize the major ills that afflict the region primarily because of that country's longer experience with industrialization. Unfortunately, it sometimes seems as if South Korea, Taiwan, and Hong Kong are madly rushing down the Japanese road to development in their excessive pursuit of the GNP at the expense of the social and urban environment, with the result that their biggest cities are experiencing many of the same problems as Japan.

Much of the urban chaos in Japan results from the fact that Japan's leaders put off investment in social overhead such as housing, sewage, and refuse treatment for many years, and only belatedly began to think about correcting these deficiencies. Hence, zoning and city planning tend to be compromises, with different land-use functions, such as residential, retail, and industrial, all mixed together in seemingly random patterns (Fig. 11.13).

The housing shortage in Tokyo is particularly acute. Even the casual visitor can see this, sitting in a taxi as it whisks one from airport to downtown along one of the elevated expressways, themselves reflections of the shortage of land for transportation and the necessity to stack roadways one above another off the ground. Even the space directly under expressways is often used for homes or other building sites. The residential pattern that meets the eye is one of primarily single-story, small wood-frame or concrete structures, densely packed together, with little or no open space. There is no discernible alignment of the houses, as in the United States, no lawns or gardens, precious few trees or other greenery, and a lack of color (most structures are a drab brown or gray). In short, the view is not a pretty one. One could quote statistics to demonstrate various aspects of this intense urban crowding, such as the fact that a tiny two-room apartment with a kitchen and dining area of 84 to 96 sq. yd. (67 to 77 sq. m.) in central Tokyo costs the equivalent of about U.S. $238,000 (Tokyo is annually rated as one of the most expensive cities in the world to live in). As land prices go up in Tokyo, the

Figure 11.13 A perspective view from the Tokyo Tower reveals the incredible congestion and overcrowding typical of Japan's, and the world's, largest city. Detached private homes increasingly are giving way to low-rise apartment buildings and commercial structures in more Western style, interspersed with elevated expressways to handle the ever-growing hordes of motor vehicles. Staggering land costs spell the eventual doom of private homes for the mass of Japanese in the central cities. (J. Williams)

detached single-family home, however inadequate, is falling to the wrecking ball, to be replaced by high rise structures. Tokyo is following in the footsteps of New York and most other large cities. Indeed, the high rise syndrome is spreading throughout nonsocialist East Asia and producing an increasing homogenization of the physical appearance of the cities. Aside from the obvious problems of high rise structures, such as increased demands on local transportation, sewage, and other services, a problem peculiar to Japan has appeared. Since most Japanese residences lack central heating, the winter sun is highly appreciated. High rises are beginning to block that winter sun for many, adding yet one more aggravation to an already trying existence for the majority of citizens in Tokyo.

The most dramatic upward movement is in the form of the few true skyscrapers that have appeared, especially in the newer commercial/entertainment district of Shinjuku, where several commercial buildings dramatically tower 50 stories or more over the still generally low skyline of Tokyo, or the spectacular new office/retail complex of "Sunshine City" in Ikebukuro. These structures offer a portent of things to come, even though these super high-rises have not yet had their supposedly earthquake-proof foundations really tested. The Japanese have also made extraordinary use of underground space in Tokyo and the other big cities, with enormous underground shopping centers, connected with the subway systems, that provide all the services and shopping opportunities one could want.

Movement outward from the central city is the only other alternative to going upward or downward. Skyrocketing land values, suburbanization, and rapid population increases have been experienced around the big cities, especially Tokyo. New communities have sprung up, bedroom towns in the American fashion, where young couples can obtain better housing for less money, with cleaner air and less noise, even though it often means commuting to work as much as two hours each way on a train that is sometimes crowded to 300 percent of capacity.

Like Americans, the Japanese have flocked to the private automobile as an illusory means of finding private space and independence from the herd. By the mid-1970s, Japan had 480 registered vehicles per square mile (165 per square kilometer), eight times the concentration of motor vehicles in the United States. and the highest density in the world. And this all took place within a period of about 15 years, starting in the early 1960s. No other country has experienced such a rapid adoption of the automobile society. The consequences for Japan's urban environment have been disastrous, even while the national economy rose to new heights of prosperity because of mushrooming auto production and its spinoffs on other segments of the economy. Although Tokyo has roughly the same ratio of vehicles to population as New York City, only about 12.5 percent of Tokyo's land is used for streets, compared with 30 percent for New York. In addition, most streets in Tokyo, reflecting their construction in days of simpler life-styles, lack sidewalks and are narrow and twisting. Add to this lethal situation the generally poor driving skills and attitudes of most drivers, plus lack of parking facilities, and the result is high rates of traffic accidents, deaths and injuries.

Autos have also been a major contributor to the severe air pollution problem in

Tokyo and other cities. Air pollution monitoring stations have been built in strategic places around the city, with electronic signs that constantly inform the public of pollutants in the air at any given moment. Traffic police at particularly bad intersections have oxygen supplies nearby for periodic relief. Air pollution is worst, nonetheless, near the major heavy-industry belt in Kanagawa Prefecture, or around Yokohama.

Another problem in Tokyo and elsewhere is subsidence of the land, resulting from overuse of ground water because of heavy industrialization and overpopulation. This problem also occurs commonly in the coastal areas where landfill techniques have been used to create new land for urban/industrial expansion. Much of the reclaimed land is built from compressed garbage.

Water pollution is another obvious and serious problem of rapid urban growth. The Sumida River, flowing through Tokyo, once was called "a stinking open sewer" even by the government. Tokyo Bay was worse off, because of the vast quantities of pollutants dumped into the bay by many of the more than 83,000 factories in the area, not to mention untreated human sewage. Water pollution in other parts of the country, particularly associated with industrial centers, has been grimly documented in the tragic stories of heavy metals and chemicals, such as mercury at Minimata in the southwest and polycholorinated byphenyls (PCBs), that have entered the food chain and resulted in deaths and deformities for many Japanese.

These problems may seem almost repetitious or exaggerated by the time the reader gets to this chapter and has read the depressing litany of urban problems around the world. If anything, however, the urban problems of East Asia have been understated here. A sobering lesson is to be learned from Japan's urban experience. In their frantic haste to modernize Japan and in their imitation of Western ways, the Japanese turned Tokyo, and most of the rest of Japan's major cities, into ugly "shantytowns," as some observers have called them. The cities look unplanned to a degree that makes even America's worst cities seem good. This hodgepodge character to the urban landscape occurred, too, in spite of the physical insecurity of the cities and their frequent destruction from natural or man-made calamities, and hence the opportunity to redesign the cities in more rational manners. Most notable of these catastrophes, and lost opportunities, were the great 1923 earthquake that leveled Tokyo and the bombing of World War II. To be sure, reconstruction after the war, aided by new building techniques and architectural styles, partially modernized the face of Japan's big cities. One can find handsome modern buildings and occasional pockets of urban beauty, even in the heart of Tokyo. But by and large, Japan's cities still convey a congestion, lack of planning, and neglect of the urban environment that is depressing, even while one can delight as a tourist or short-term visitor in the many pleasures to be experienced in cities such as Tokyo and Osaka.

Solutions to Urban Problems

The Nonsocialist Way

The nonsocialist cities of East Asia have seen the beginnings of efforts to soften, if not eliminate, the major problems afflicting them. The battle is just starting, however, and some might question whether it is too little, too late, to have any lasting and significant impact.

In Japan, for example, the government did attempt through the late 1950s and 1960s to enact pollution control laws of one sort or another, usually as the result of heavy pressure from victims of pollution. Finally, in 1971 the Environment Agency (EA) was established, modeled after the Environmental Protection Agency in the United States. Inroads on pollution problems have been made since then, but the record still leaves much to be desired. Auto emissions standards, controls on factory effluents, and other curbs have been issued. Their combined effect, however, has been mainly to moderate further pollution rather than to eliminate it. The EA remains part of a conservative, big-business-oriented government that associates antipollution activities with the opposition. Nonetheless, it does appear that the Japanese government and public are swinging around to a greater recognition of the need to improve air and water quality in the cities, and by 1980 there was noticeable improvement in Tokyo's environmental problems. Some reports even optimistically predict that the problems will be eliminated by 1990, but that is probably an unrealistic projection.

One tack the government has been taking to "solve" both pollution and the extreme congestion of the core region, especially the Tokaido Megalopolis, is to further decentralize the urban pattern of Japan. This concept was best expressed in the Tanaka Plan announced in 1971 for building many new cities with a population of about 250,000 outside the core region of Japan (Fig. 11.10). Each city would serve as the focus for new industrialization and growth, with the intent that these cities would draw industry and people away from the core region. These cities would be connected by vast new expansions of the rail system and expressways that already dominate the core region. Although never formally approved by the National Diet, this plan has begun to be implemented, even though it represents a continuation of the policy of high economic growth rates of the past and huge consumption of resources and would allow, in the eyes of critics, the spreading of pollution into yet-untouched regions of the country. This development path is running head-on into the criticism of those who would like to see a change in the attitude that rapid industrial expansion is Japan's only means of survival in the modern world. The outcome of this clash has yet to be fully felt.

Elsewhere in East Asia, the record on solving urban problems is hardly any better, and in some cases is worse than in Japan. In Hong Kong, the lack of green space and recreation facilities, the terrible traffic congestion, and the high incidence of crime, drug use, and other social problems resulting from excessive population density and the socioeconomic colonial structure are frequent topics in the news. Hong Kong's problems are somewhat unique, of course, because of the refugee problem and the political uncertainty of the future. The colony must be given credit for having one of the better urban resettlement programs in the region. Huge apartment blocks in new integrated settlement estates have arisen over the past three decades and now house half the colony's population (Fig. 11.7). Yet so many still live in squalor, in decrepit shacks clinging precariously to the steep hillsides, in old and cramped boats in the harbors, or in decaying buildings left over from the prewar period. While the housing problem has been attacked, with some success, one major problem that results from the fierce materialistic competition in Hong Kong, deeply ingrained corruption, persists. This problem is probably unsolvable within the existing social/political system.

In South Korea, the biggest urban problems are those of Seoul. As with Hong Kong, squatters form a sizable share of the population and present one of the biggest headaches to the government. An estimated 130,000 squatter huts sprawl along the major streams and hillsides, housing about one-fifth of Seoul's population, even though the government has been building resettlement estates as rapidly as it can, under the much-vaunted *Saemaul* (new village) movement. The seeming intractability of Seoul's problems, plus the military vulnerability of the city, led the government to announce in the mid-1970s that it planned to build a new capital city further south. That action, plus efforts to build up industry elsewhere in the country, such as the Masan Export Processing Zone in the south near Pusan, might signal at the least a leveling off in the growth of Seoul.

In Taiwan, particularly Taipei, the problems are much the same, and the attempts at solution also similar. A subway is being talked about (one already exists in Seoul, and one is under construction in Hong Kong). Squatter resettlement and urban renewal have been underway many years now in Taipei, and it is true that here one finds the lowest incidence of abject urban poverty in East Asia, outside of Japan. There is still a housing shortage, however, resulting in part from the city's primate city character and the shortage of land. Traffic congestion seems almost unsolvable, with the continuing rush to own automobiles, or at least motorcycles, even with high taxes and very expensive gasoline. A problem that Taipei shares with Hong Kong and Seoul is the lack of cultural and entertainment facilities. Aside from movie houses, which are normally jam-packed with people watching mostly old grade-B films from Hollywood and regional film producers, the big cities of this region, with the exception of Japan, are cultural deserts, relatively speaking. Taipei has seen some notable advances in recent years, the most spectacular being the gigantic new cultural center built right in the heart of Taipei in classic monument style as a memorial to Chiang Kai-shek.

The Socialist Way

As part of the process of building a new socialist society, the Chinese have followed a quite different path of urban development from the nonsocialist states of East Asia. This path has been characterized by a peculiar blend of pragmatism and idealism, reflecting the needs of the Chinese to solve the enormous urban problems that face the country, but at the same time to fit that solution into the framework of the socialist transformation of the nation. On a smaller scale, the socialist state of North Korea has been doing much the same thing since the end of the Korean War in 1953 and the rebuilding of its war-shattered cities, particularly the capital of Pyongyang, which has been transformed into a modern, albeit austere socialist city of nearly 2 million, differing little in character from the major cities of China.

The Chinese view the city not as a separate entity, but as an integral part of a region. This is reflected in several ways. One is the distinction the Chinese make between what they call "consuming cities" and "producing cities." The latter are those with a comprehensive or diversified industrial base, able not only to meet the needs of the city for industrial products, but also to export industrial products to the region of which the city is a part, and to the nation as a whole, or even overseas. Consuming cities are obviously the opposite of this. Almost all the cities of pre-1949 China are classified by the Chinese today as having been consuming cities. The goal is to transform all of these into producing cities. Political rhetoric aside, this is an obvious recognition by the Chinese that every city should have a solid economic base.

This producing-city concept also has the implication of ensuring that all able-bodied workers are employed, and that there should be no unemployment in the cities, as commonly occurred before 1949. By extension, any person in a city who is not employed there does not belong in that city and is subject to deportation to the countryside.

The motive here is controlling city size. This has been a consistent theme of China's national development since 1950. In large part, it is the familiar problem of controlling rural-to-urban migration, or as the Chinese call it, "blind infiltration" of the cities. Uncontrolled migration not only runs counter to Marxist-Maoist principles, but also creates innumerable urban problems. Since the early 1950s, there have been periodic campaigns to control "unproductive elements" in the cities by "mobilizing" (deporting) them out of the cities. Hence, urban residents are required to have certificates of employment or some other document from an urban agency for the administration of population registers, approving their residence in the cities.

These measures have been only partially successful. Shanghai, for example, experienced fluctuating population growth through the 1950s and 1960s, in a two-way flow of legal and illegal migrants moving to the city and mobilized people moving out of the city. It appears the population of Shanghai City itself is now stabilized at about where it was in the early 1950s. As another example, a city official in Sian (Xi'an) gave the natural rate of population growth for that city in 1977 as 0.7 percent, but because of illegal in-migration from the countryside the actual rate of population growth was "much higher." Given the degree of control over the lives of urban residents by the government, it is a wonder how any illegal migrants can long remain undetected in the cities, but apparently substantial numbers do, often with the aid of friends and relatives. Nonetheless, although not totally successful, these efforts to stabilize the population of the biggest cities have clearly helped to keep them from experiencing the explosive, uncontrolled growth that nonsocialist East Asia has experienced.

There are other ways of controlling city size. One way is to emphasize the building of smaller cities. Those with a population of 100,000 to 250,000 are regarded as the optimum size, in terms of a balanced economic base and a livable urban environment that can be controlled. Many of these small cities have been built or are under construction now, often in proximity to the large cities. Many are preexisting towns being revitalized and expanded. Those in the vicinity of major cities commonly serve as centers of specific industries, as satellite cities, to aid in decentralizing the large central city and to alleviate environmental degradation in the central city. In the case of Shanghai, for example, the old port of Wusung (Wusong), on the Yangtze, is one of the iron/steel centers for the Shanghai region. Chinshan (Jinshan) and Kaochiao (Gaoqiao) are centers for Shanghai's petrochemical manufacturing.

A major characteristic of China's cities today, one already alluded to, is the large area of rural/suburban territory under the jurisdiction of the cities. The basic function of these rural areas is to provide the food supply for the central city. These rural areas are commonly many times the size of the city itself, the area being dependent on the population of the city, its location, and the food-producing potential of the hinterland. In the case of Peking, for example, the built-up area of the city itself is under 154 sq. mi. (400 sq. km.), while the administrative boundaries of the Peking district encompass some 2625 sq. mi. (6800 sq. km.) (Fig. 11.14). Each city will have contracts with its rural communes to guarantee food deliveries to the city. In return, the city provides much of the industrial manufactures for the rural area, and even helps out with labor needs at critical times of the year, such as harvesting, when urban workers are commonly mobilized and go out to the rural communes to help for a few days or weeks.

A political and social objective of all this is to reduce, if not eliminate, what the Chinese call the "contradictions" between city and countryside, between urban and rural dwellers. These contradictions are in standards of living and in attitudes toward work and social classes. The government is trying to do away with the rigid classes and elitism that characterized presocialist China. Recent policy switches, however, suggest that the Chinese are swinging back more toward pragmatism and away from idealism for at least the coming few years, in their efforts to lift the country's economy to new levels. Thus, an urban-based, highly educated elite (many of whom are likely to receive their training abroad) may appear on the rise in the near future, along with a reduction in the mixing of rural and urban residents.

Within the cities themselves, the socialist urban planning principles of the Chinese are reflected in many ways. At the broadest level, planning is carried out within the context of the "Four Services," namely, to serve proletarian politics, central leadership, industrial/agricultural production, and the laboring masses. Within these rather vague political slogans, urban planning has more specific objectives and policies.

Urban Land Use   A vital policy is in urban land use and particularly the location of industry. In the West, especially in the United States, urban land use is determined by the interplay of private and public interests, with distance and access to transportation routes playing major roles. All of these forces are modified in varying degrees by zoning restrictions and land use codes. None of this exists in China, where the city government has virtually absolute power over allocation of land use. This makes city planning vastly easier.

Land in the cities is classified into two major types: industrial land and "land for the people's livelihood." The latter includes green space, streets and roads, public and commercial buildings, and residential structures. The relative proportions of these land uses will naturally vary between cities. In Sian (Xi'an), for example, industrial land occupies 20 percent of the city's built-up area, and land for the people's livelihood the remaining 80 percent.

Within this land-use system, then, city planning is carried out. One of the objectives is to locate industry in the best place, in order to provide balance to the city and to protect the environment. As much as possible, heavy industries and polluting industries are located on the periphery of the city (or in satellite cities). Nonpolluting indus-

Solutions to Urban Problems   443

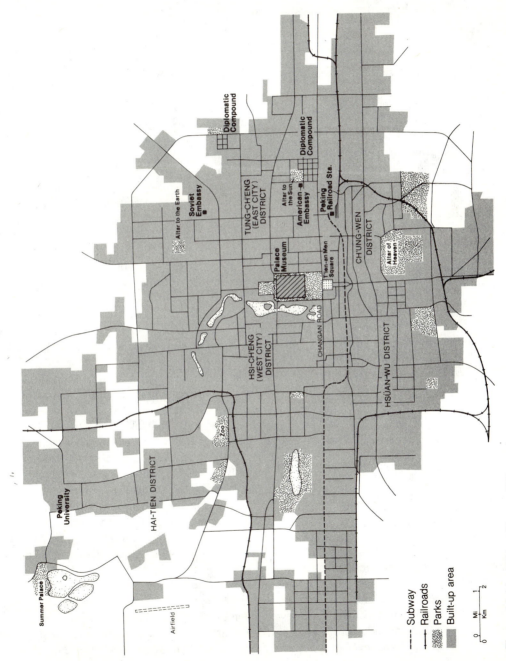

Figure 11.14 Peking. (*Source:* CIA map.)

try, on the other hand, is distributed throughout the city, such as handicrafts and light industry of various kinds. In Peking, for example, heavy industry is being located on the leeward side of prevailing winds and in the lower reaches of the drainage system, which are the east and southeast suburbs.

Administration and Socialization Another aspect of city planning is in the neighborhood unit concept. The goal is for self-contained neighborhoods, with residents living in large apartment blocks in close proximity to factories and their sources of employment. These neighborhoods will have supporting services such as shopping, schools, entertainment, and medical care nearby. Minimizing travel time to work not only saves the energy and time of the residents, but also reduces the strain on the overtaxed urban transportation systems. The policy also helps to foster the building of integrated neighborhoods along socialist lines.

The administrative organization of the cities contributes to the neighborhood unit concept also. Large cities, such as Nanking (Nanjing), are divided first into districts, then into communes. Small and medium cities, such as Kueilin (Guilin), are divided directly into communes. These administrative units were run, from the Cultural Revolution period on, by "revolutionary committees" (RCs), composed, in theory at least, of old, middle-aged, and young citizens drawn from the leading cadres and "representatives of the masses." The size of the committees varied, but they could be quite large. Decision-making power, however, was in the hands of the Standing Committee, which was strictly controlled by the Party. Under the city RC, there was a planning bureau, responsible for overall planning of the city. There also were city-level bureaus for other urban functions, such as architecture, engineering, public utilities, housing, gardens and forestry, and environmental protection. Each district and commune had its RC and subunits of the city-level bureaus.

At the lowest level in this nested hierarchy, each urban commune was organized into Street Residents Revolutionary Committees, a form of mass organization, for the purpose of improving the urban environment at the local level, enhancing productive work, and (implicitly) for strengthening political control by the party and government. Residents could organize various activities, such as units to sell goods on behalf of overburdened state stores, and establish small restaurants, nurseries, middle-school student services, sewing clubs, and so on. All these establishments were collectively owned. Income from such services was locally used by the resident committees to improve facilities and pay salaries. Residents also collectively saw that the streets and facilities in their jurisdiction were well kept and planted and maintained trees and gardens. The purpose of these activities was to involve everyone in the running of the affairs that affect their daily lives and immediate environment. It was compulsory group participation, using social pressure to coerce mass participation.

In the late 1970s, the RCs were abolished, with the de-Maoification of China that began then, and some reorganization of the urban administrative hierarchy begun. In spite of these changes, however, much of which are simply changes in name only, the basic principles of decentralization of urban administration and of involving citizens at the local level in the running of their daily lives remain important characteristics of city life in China today. Moreover, there is tolerance, even encouragement, now of what might be called "petty capitalism," in which individuals are being allowed to open up small business enterprises of their own. This compromise with socialist principles is a pragmatic effort to reduce the unemployment problem that has grown alarmingly in China's cities since 1976. Thus, hawking, small family-run restaurants or other types of shops, and similar small-scale enterprises, run strictly on a profit-making basis, are increasingly common in the cities of China.

Role of the City Center This effort to decentralize the cities into relatively self-contained units is reflected further in the function of the city center, used primarily for administration and political activities. Most cities of any size have a central square for political rallies, celebrations, parades, etc. Political indoctrination of the citizens is particularly evident here, with statues and portraits of the fathers of Marxism-Leninism and Mao visible everywhere. Slogans in bright characters are painted or hung here and there. The city center still retains a commercial function, but it is not nearly as important as in the CBD of a typical nonsocialist city of Asia or the West. In Peking, for example, the main commercial street is two blocks east of the Palace Museum and Tienanmen Square and contains department stores and other retail/service establishments, but it hardly compares with the Ginza in Tokyo or Nathan Road in Kowloon.

Housing One of the biggest urban problems the Chinese have had to wrestle with is the massive housing shortage (Fig. 11.15). In spite of nearly three decades of work at solving the problem, it persists because of the sheer size of the problem. Housing programs in the cities consist of two aspects: the building of new apartment blocks, usually near factories and other sources of employment in keeping with the neighborhood unit drive; and the refurbishing of old housing. No new detached single-family dwellings are being built in the cities, although one can still see them in rural communes (and even there, the apartment block is increasingly common). The apartment blocks used to be no more than three or four stories, without elevators, but taller structures are going up, with elevators, as building standards improve. However, the typical apartment is austere by most Western standards. Usually it will consist of two small multipurpose rooms, with communal kitchen and bath. Rent and utilities, however, are cheap. In 1977, rent was about 5 yuan per month (about U.S. $2.50), utilities about the same total, out of a typical income (for a family of two full-time workers, the norm) of 100 to 120 Yuan (U.S. $50 to 60). Unfortunately many people, the majority in most cities in fact, still live in old housing dating from pre-1949, normally refurbished at least to some degree. However, the relativity of Western and Chinese concepts is evident in the fact that the Chinese officially classify only 10 percent of Shanghai as "slums," whereas Westerners would be more likely to raise that percentage substantially.

Since all buildings are owned by the city, there are two ways of allocating housing. One is to turn over apartment blocks to factories and other large urban units. These units have their own housing bureaus that then decide who moves into which apartments. Allocation is usually on the basis of seniority, age of applicants, and number

Figure 11.15 Canton (Guangzhou), one of China's oldest cities, dating back some twenty centuries, exhibits the sprawl, congestion, shabbiness, and inadequate housing that most of China's urban residents still must put up with. Housing demand persistently exceeds the ability of the government to construct new apartment blocks. (J. Williams)

of persons in the household. Other new buildings are allocated to the housing management bureau of each district of the city. Residents then apply to the bureau for new housing.

Urban Services Other urban necessities are also inexpensive, although not necessarily in abundant supply. Most shopping by residents is done at the neighborhood level for everyday necessities, with perhaps trips to the district commercial center or the city center at less frequent intervals, such as a combined shopping/social trip on the weekend with the whole family.

Food and consumer goods are relatively plentiful and inexpensive. Some items are still rationed, however, such as cooking oil and cotton cloth. Ration coupons are a fact of everyday life, as is queuing to buy almost anything. Some goods much in demand, such as bicycles, require long waiting periods and are quite expensive. Other items are clearly luxuries that the average resident cannot yet afford, such as television sets and refrigerators, although one can see these displayed in stores.

Urban Transportation Another major unique feature of Chinese cities is the relative absence of the automobile. Indeed, the Chinese have firmly indicated that they never intend to allow private ownership of automobiles, although apparently no law actually prohibits such ownership. The limited supply, high cost, and social criticism hinder people from buying cars. Hence, all the other urban features associated with the automobile society elsewhere are largely lacking in China.

This is not to suggest there are no urban transportation problems. They are simply of a somewhat different character. These problems center around the huge numbers of bicycles that must coexist with still sizable and growing fleets of trucks, buses, and other motorized vehicles, as well as animal- and human-drawn carts (although these are usually banned from the central districts of major cities). The problem is compounded by poor driving skills and attitudes of people, attitudes attacked at major intersections by traffic control police who sit in booths with loudspeakers and do not hesitate to use the power of highly public criticism to chastise and reform errant drivers and pedestrians. City authorities also attempt to alleviate transportation problems by widening and improving roads, expanding bus services, and in the case of Peking by building China's first subway system.

Green Space The urban environment is also being improved quite noticeably by the development of green space, which refers to all parks, recreation sites, ponds, and gardens. Every city has a tree-planting program. Nurseries on the outskirts of the city provide millions of trees, which are planted along all the major thoroughfares, as well as side streets. (Fig. 11.16). This is one of the most striking and appealing features of Chinese cities today. The close-spaced trees improve the microclimate, provide pleasant shade in the summer, and hold down noise and dust levels. This is particularly important in the hot summer, when the streets become extensions of cramped residences that lack air conditioning. Although the buildings are often shabby, the residential neighborhoods often have a certain charm, because of the greenery, that one looks for in vain most of the time in Japanese cities.

Controlling Pollution Improvement of the urban environment is also carried on through efforts at controlling pollution. Each city has a program for dealing with the "three wastes" (water, gases, and solids). As much as possible, the wastes are processed and recycled to be used for other purposes. Sewage, for instance, is handled with both the old "honey buckets" system (manual collection each morning of raw sewage) and more modern sewage pipeline systems. Both remove the sewage from the city to where it is treated and then used as fertilizer in suburban communes. Industrial waste water is used for electricity generation. Methane is produced from waste solids. Waste material from coal is used to make bricks for building construction. And so on. Although this system makes sound ecological sense, the Chinese admit they are a long way from eliminating pollution from their cities. Shanghai, for example, has serious air pollution, as do other cities to varying degrees.

Chinese Urban Planning: Portent of the Future? Authorities in China are quick to point out that they are a long way from achieving all of their principles of urban planning and readily admit past mistakes. But they contend that their cities (and their society in a larger context) offer a healthier and more enlightened environment in which to live than that offered in the nonsocialist countries, even though Chinese cities do

Figure 11.16 A pleasant, tree-lined street in one of Shanghai's residential/commercial districts. Sycamores and other trees have been planted along major thoroughfares in virtually all of China's cities as one means of improving the urban environment, dressing up the otherwise generally shabby-clean urban landscape, and improving the microclimate of the urban areas. Bicycles predominate as the principal private form of transportation in China's cities. (J. Williams)

not have the luxurious comforts and distractions enjoyed by the middle and upper classes outside of China. Indeed, the relative austerity of China's cities today is what most strikes the outsider's eye at first glance. Until the late 1970s there were no advertising (that is now changing, to the dismay of some, as the government attempts to promote consumerism to boost economic growth), no garish neon displays, little or no night life, and a general lack of the urban sophistication (pretentiousness?) so evident in cities such as Tokyo or Hong Kong. People go to bed early and get up early, and at night the cities are unusually dark and lacking in public lighting, reflecting the conservative use of resources. Some might argue that the Chinese are developing a model of urban development and urbanism that the rest of the world may one day have to adopt whether or not it wants to, as resources dwindle and it becomes prohibitively costly to maintain the extravagant use of resources so typical of nonsocialist cities in the developed world. Whether or not this will come to pass is debatable, but no one can argue that the Chinese are not moving along a distinctly different path of modern urban development that is well worth watching.

RECOMMENDED READINGS

Bonavia, David, and the editors of Time-Life Books. *Peking*. Amsterdam: Time-Life Books, 1978.

  A lavishly illustrated, highly readable, and popular account of Peking's past and present, as one volume in the excellent Great Cities Series.

Chang, Sen-dou. "The Historical Trend of Chinese Urbanization." *Annals of the Association of American Geographers,* 53 (June 1963), 109–143.
  A thorough study of the spread of the Chinese walled city from earliest times, and the regional patterns produced. Well illustrated with maps.

Chang, Sen-dou. "Some Observations on the Morphology of Chinese Walled Cities." *Annals of the Association of American Geographers,* 60 (March 1970), 63–91.
  The best comprehensive study of the character of the Chinese walled city over time and over space within China. Well illustrated.

Elegant, Robert and the editors of Time-Life Books. *Hong Kong.* Amsterdam: Time-Life Books, 1977.
  A lavishly illustrated, highly readable, and popular account of Hong Kong's past and present, as one volume in the Great Cities Series.

Elvin, Mark and G. William Skinner. *The Chinese City Between Two Worlds.* Stanford: Stanford University Press, 1974.
  One of three volumes resulting from conferences on the Chinese city held in 1968–1969. The other two: *The City in Communist China* (John W. Lewis, ed.), 1971; and *The City in Late Imperial China* (G. W. Skinner, ed.), 1977. All three are scholarly compendiums of the current state of knowledge about Chinese cities, past and present.

Huddle, Norie, Michael Reich, and Nahum Stiskin. *Island of Dreams: Environmental Crisis in Japan.* New York: Autumn Press, 1975.
  The best summary of the environmental impact of Japan's modern industrial development on the land and people of Japan, with good discussion of the grim problems of Tokyo and other cities. A highly readable and chilling story.

Kornhauser, David. *Urban Japan: Its Foundation and Growth.* New York: Longman, 1976.
  One volume in the World's Landscapes series. A fine overview of the geographic and historical aspects of Japan's urban experience from earliest times to the present. Best for the historical coverage of pre-World War II eras.

Leys, Simon. *Chinese Shadows.* New York: Penguin Books, 1978.
  A controversial but highly readable impression of the People's Republic of China by a respected Old China Hand, who gives a currently unpopular view of the "New China."

Ma, Laurence J. C. *Cities and City Planning in the People's Republic of China: An Annotated Bibliography.* Washington, DC: U.S. Department of Housing and Urban Development, USER Bibliography Series, September 1980.
  An extremely useful compendium of 194 publications about cities, past and present, in China. The title is thus somewhat misleading.

Maraini, Fosco and the editors of Time-Life Books. *Tokyo.* Amsterdam: Time-Life Books, 1976.
  A lavishly illustrated, highly readable, and popular account of Tokyo's past and present, as one volume in the Great Cities Series.

Murphey, Rhoads. *The Fading of the Maoist Vision: City and Country in China's Development.* New York: Methuen, 1980.
  An examination of the urban and rural balance in China's development since the treaty port days and the initial revolution of 1911, but with emphasis on the role of cities and urbanization in Maoist China and what has been happening since the death of Mao.

Murphey, Rhoads. *Shanghai, Key to Modern China.* Cambridge, MA: Harvard University Press, 1953.

The definitive study of Shanghai's first century, up until the takeover by the new Chinese government in 1949. A very readable account of one of the world's most interesting cities.

Wheatley, Paul. *The Pivot of the Four Quarters: A Preliminary Enquiry into the Origins and Character of the Ancient Chinese City.* Chicago: Aldine, 1971.

A massive and extremely scholarly tome on the early Chinese city and its comparison with early cities in other regions. A classic and exhaustive study, but not for the casual browser.

Yule, Sir Henry. *The Book of Ser Marco Polo, the Venetian Concerning the Kingdoms and Marvels of the East.* 3rd ed. New York: Charles Scribner's Sons, 1929.

The classic translation and annotated study of the classic work by Marco Polo. Lavishly illustrated and painstakingly researched. Fascinating reading, particularly for cities in China at that time.

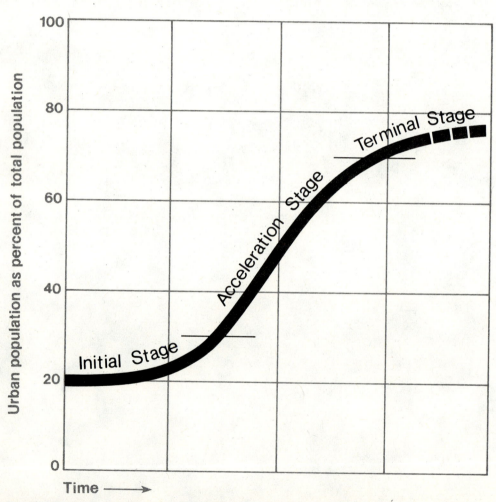

Figure 12.1 Urbanization Curve. (*Source:* Ray Northam, *Urban Geography,* New York: John Wiley, p. 66. Copyright © 1979. Reprinted by permission of John Wiley and Sons, Inc.)

Chapter 12

Cities of the Future

Stanley D. Brunn

Thus far we have observed the historical processes and contemporary patterns of urbanization and major urban problems in 10 major world regions. By treating both the salient features of urbanization processes and the distinctive characteristics of major cities in each region, we have emphasized the geographic arrangement and internal structure of the world's major urban agglomerations. Neglected has been a discussion of the settlement processes and patterns of the future, the major urban regions in the year 2000, and the forms and functions of cities in the future, all topics addressed in this concluding chapter. The overlap from concepts introduced, materials discussed, and cities examined in earlier chapters is anticipated, as some authors have included materials on urban settlement futures and the futures of selected cities. What is sought in this chapter, as in Chapter 1, is a global coverage of world urbanization; the major difference is focus on the future.

Examining future urbanization and cities of the future calls for assessing the impact that future economies, social structures, and governance as well as transportation, communication, and machine technology will exert on human interaction, human activities, and settlement patterns. Advances in energy, transportation, and communication technology have affected settlement forms and patterns historically, as previous chapters have demonstrated. It is likely that similar advances, coupled with economic, political, and social changes, will operate to create some new urban geographies of the future. Eight major themes are discussed below: (1) an overview of global urban population in 2000, (2) urban growth and primacy, (3) major agglomerations in 2000, (4) the structural components of a shrinking world, (5) the emergence of city systems, (6) characteristics of the global village and world cities, (7) urban morphology and functions, and (8) urban problems and priorities.

A major source for many of the tables and graphs is the *Global Review of Human*

Settlements prepared by the UN in conjunction with the Habitat Conference in Vancouver in 1976. This is the same data set used in the introductory chapter and for the prefacing statement to the individual regional chapters. Data in this volume provide the projections for total population and urban population for individual countries in 1980, 1990, and 2000 as well as the size of many major urban agglomerations in the same years. The above volume provides the single most valuable data set available for describing and analyzing future urbanization at the global and comparative regional scales.

Global Urban Settlement in 2000

The dramatic increases in urban population this century, and particularly in the LDCs in the last several decades, are portrayed in the estimated urban population among the major regions in 2000 and the percentage of the total population living in urban areas. Within the 1980–2000 period alone the total global urban population is expected to increase by 1.3 billion, of which more than 1 billion will be in LDCs (Table 12.1). The urban population in the MDCs will increase 30 percent, while the urban population in the LDCs will skyrocket by more than 110 percent. In spite of the high absolute and relative urban increases in the LDCs, still slightly more than one-third of the total population in LDCs will be living in cities by 2000. Approximately three-quarters of the population in the MDCs will be living in cities by 2000, a slight increase over two decades earlier.

Dividing global urban population numbers in 2000 into two broad categories, viz., MDCs and LDCs, belies significant variations within regions included in each

TABLE 12.1 WORLD URBAN POPULATION, BY REGION, 1980 (EST.) AND 2000 (EST.)

World Region	1980 (est.) Urban Population (Millions)	(%)	2000 (est.) Urban Population (Millions)	(%)
North America	196	79	256	86
Western Europe	268	74	321	83
Oceania	17	73	26	78
Latin America	237	64	464	75
Eastern Europe/Soviet Union	243	62	344	74
North Africa/Middle East	112	48	243	50
East Asia	358	33	591	43
Southeast Asia	90	24	207	34
South Asia	199	22	441	31
Subsaharan Africa	80	22	210	37
World	1800	41	3103	50
More Developed Countries	850	72	1107	77
Less Developed Countries	950	30	1996	35

Source: Derived from Table 1 in *Global Review of Human Settlements, Statistical Annex,* United Nations: Department of Economic and Social Affairs, published by Pergamon Press, New York, 1976, pp. 22–49.

group. Among developing world regions, the absolute increases in urban population are especially great in North Africa/Middle East, Southeast and South Asia, and Subsaharan Africa. In each of these four regions more than twice as many urban residents are estimated in 2000 than were expected in 1980. The increases will be substantial in Latin America as well as East Asia, although not the magnitude of other developing regions. By the year 2000, more urban residents will be in Latin America, East Asia, and South Asia than in North America, Western Europe, and the Soviet Union/Eastern Europe. Among MDC regions, North America and Western Europe are expected to add about 60 million urban residents each from 1980 to 2000. The Soviet Union/Eastern Europe will add about 100 million; this same region is the least urbanized of any developed world region.

The increasing percentages of populations classified as urban is illustrated further by the number of countries in which half or more of the population lives in cities. In Chapter 1, 21 MDCs and 26 LDCs with a population of least 1 million were estimated to have 50 percent or more of their population living in cities in 1980. By 2000 there are expected to be 71 such countries, 28 MDCs and 43 LDCs (Table 12.2). The major changes in a listing of countries having a majority of their population living in cities between the years 1980 and 2000 is the addition of more LDCs to Subsaharan Africa, the Middle East/North Africa, and Latin America. South Asia in 2000, as in 1980, will have no country with at least half the population living in cities; rural majorities will exist in India, Pakistan, and Bangladesh as well as in Ethiopia, Zaire, Nigeria, Ivory Coast, Thailand, Indonesia, and Burma. These "rural" countries will probably not become defined as urbanized until the early decades of the twenty-first century. In regards to the developed world, all countries with a population of 1 million or more in Western Europe and the Soviet Union/Eastern Europe will become urbanized by the year 2000 except Portugal. Additions to the list of urbanized countries by 2000 are those that two decades earlier had large rural populations, such as Norway, Ireland, Yugoslavia, Albania, and Hungary.

Not only will more people be living in cities in the developing world than in the developed world, but more cities will be of varying sizes (Table 12.3). In 1980 roughly half the world total of 2,201 cities of more than 100,000 were in LDCs. By the year 2000 almost two-thirds will be in these same countries. At the turn of the century more cities in each of the six city-size classes presented in Table 12.3 will be in the developing than in the developed world. For example, the number of million cities in the LDCs will increase from 116 in the year 1980 to 264 by the year 2000; a comparable increase in the MDCs will be from 110 to 150 between the years 1980 and 2000. The number of supercities, those with 5 million plus, will increase dramatically in the LDCs, from 15 to 43 in only 20 years. The MDCs will have only 16 by the year 2000, only 5 more than in 1980. The increased number of cities in the population range from 100,000 to 200,000 and from 200,000 to 500,000 will be just as sharp in the LDCs as the number in the higher size categories. The increased number of cities in the developing world in the year 2000, the larger total urban population in LDCs, and the rapid rates of urban population increase demonstrate one salient fact about the global urban population at 2000: the ever-increasing dominance the LDCs will achieve in total urban population numbers and urban settlements.

TABLE 12.2 THE WORLD'S MOST URBANIZED NATIONS, 2000 (EST.)
(At least 1 million population, 50% or more urban)

Region and Nation	Urban Population (%)	Region and Nation	Urban Population (%)
Western Europe		**Latin America (cont.)**	
Sweden	92	Panama	68
West Germany	91	Jamaica	65
Denmark	90	Nicaragua	63
France	87	Dominican Republic	63
Netherlands	87	Ecuador	58
United Kingdom	85	Costa Rica	54
Belgium	82	Bolivia	53
Spain	82	El Salvador	53
Italy	79	Paraguay	50
Greece	73	**Subsaharan Africa**	
Finland	73	Mauritius	64
Switzerland	72	Republic of South Africa	63
Ireland	70	Zambia	60
Austria	65	Central African Republic	60
Norway	61	Congo	58
Eastern Europe/Soviet Union		Ghana	52
East Germany	83	**North Africa/Middle East**	
Bulgaria	77	Kuwait	96
USSR	76	Israel	91
Czechoslovakia	73	Lebanon	80
Poland	73	Iraq	78
Romania	63	Jordan	73
Hungary	63	Tunisia	66
Yugoslavia	57	Egypt	64
Albania	56	Turkey	63
North America		Iran	61
Canada	88	Syria	60
United States	86	Morocco	56
Oceania		**South Asia**	
Australia	92	(none)	
New Zealand	91	**Southeast Asia**	
Latin America		Singapore	97
Chile	92	Philippines	51
Venezuela	92	**East Asia**	
Uruguay	90	Hong Kong	98
Argentina	89	Japan	87
Colombia	78	Taiwan	80
Mexico	78	Mongolia	72
Brazil	76	South Korea	69
Cuba	75	North Korea	63
Peru	72		

Source: Derived from Table 1 in *Global Review of Human Settlements, Statistical Annex,* United Nations: Department of Economic and Social Affairs, published by Pergamon Press, New York, 1976, pp. 22–49.

TABLE 12.3 CITIES OF THE WORLD
100,000 or More Population,
1980 and 2000 (est.)

	1980 (est.)	2000 (est.)
World Total		
Over 5 million	26	59
2–5 million	71	134
1–2 million	129	221
500,000–1 million	249	395
200,000–500,000	727	1057
100,000–200,000	999	1458
Total	2201	3324
More Developed Countries		
Over 5 million	11	16
2–5 million	31	51
1–2 million	68	83
500,000–1 million	118	152
200,000–500,000	351	403
100,000–200,000	482	559
Total	1061	1264
Less Developed Countries		
Over 5 million	15	43
2–5 million	40	83
1–2 million	61	138
500,000–1 million	131	243
200,000–500,000	376	655
100,000–200,000	517	899
Total	1140	2061

Source: Derived from Table 5 in *Global Review of Human Settlements, Statistical Annex,* United Nations: Department of Economic and Social Affairs, published by Pergamon Press, New York, 1976, pp. 60–61.

Urban Growth and Urban Primacy

Two major features of urban settlements that provide evidence of internal demographic, economic, and policy changes within a country or region are the directions of urban growth, especially for the largest cities, and what is taking place vis-à-vis the primate city and second largest city.

Stages and Rates of Growth

The position of a country with respect to urban growth is measured by the urbanization curve (see Fig. 12.1 at the beginning of the chapter). This S-shaped curve, or logistic curve, plots the percentage of the population living in cities at a given point in time.

In tracing a country's urban population over time, three stages have been identified. In the first stage the population lives mainly in rural areas and is engaged in primary-sector occupations. The growth of industries and mass rural-to-urban migration lead to the second or accelerating stage. During this time the rate of urban growth is most rapid. Eventually the rate of urban increase begins to decline, as indicated most markedly toward the upper end of the curve, and the population disperses into sparsely populated areas (not counted as urban) and becomes engaged in nonindustrial occupations or (especially in the case of retirees) receives aid from various government welfare programs. Small settlements and dispersed settlements, including the various new-town planning schemes, also characterize the terminal stage.

The utility of the urbanization curve is that we can observe through past or future time the evolution of urban development for individual countries and major regions. As we have seen from earlier chapters, for most of recorded history, the world's population and economy has been tied to an agrarian life; this characterized Europe and North America until the beginnings of the Industrial Revolution in the eighteenth and nineteenth centuries. Cities of 100,000 or more in Europe contained less than 20 percent of the total population in 1600 and only slightly more by 1800. Kingsley Davis has estimated that by 1900 less than 5 percent of the world's population lived in cities.

The sharp upswing in total global urban population has occurred in the past several decades, particularly in the developing countries. In 1950 approximately 29 percent of the world's population lived in cities; by the year 2000 nearly half of all humankind will be urban dwellers. Measured in absolute numbers this represents an increase from 715 million urban residents in 1950 to 3.1 billion by 2000, a fourfold increase at the same time the world's total population is expected to double. The urban growth rate in 2000 will still be high (2.6 percent) but somewhat lower than in 1960 (3.4 percent) and 1980 (2.8 percent). A gradual lowering of the global urban growth rate parallels the existing and anticipated lowering of the world population growth rate, a trend begun in the mid-1970s and earlier in many LDCs.

Urbanization curves exhibit a variety of S shapes, some shallow, some steep, and others with some combination. The varying slopes indicate when the percentage of the urban population began increasing and the rate of that growth over time (Fig. 12.2). The United Kingdom, the Netherlands, Belgium, Sweden, and West Germany have experienced urban growth for nearly two centuries; their curves show a very slow beginning, gradual rise, and recent leveling off of the population residing in cities to between 75 and 85 percent. The percentage living in urban areas between 1950 and 2000 in many industrial European countries is expected to remain high and increase slightly; the annual increase, which was slightly above 1 percent in 1950, is expected to be less than that by 2000 as the urban population approaches a *zero growth* state. Canada, Japan, Australia, the United States, and the USSR, all experiencing industrial and urban growth later than Europe, will have urbanization curves by 2000 that assume the present appearance of many Eastern and Western European countries.

The directions in urban growth existing within an individual country also apply to individual cities and agglomerations. Decennial growth rates from the years 1970 to 2000 for most large agglomerations in Western Europe, Eastern Europe, the USSR, North America, and Japan will be less than 1.5 percent during the last decade of the

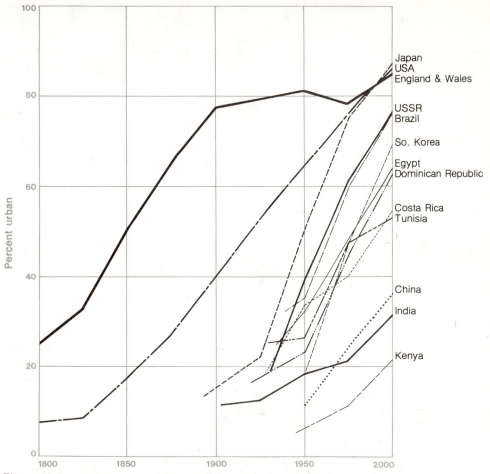

Figure 12.2 Urban Growth Curves for Selected Countries. (*Sources:* Adapted in part from "The Urbanization of The Human Population" by Kingsley Davis. Copyright © 1965 by Scientific American, Inc. All rights reserved. Data also derived from United Nations, Department of Economic and Social Affairs, *Global Review of Human Settlements, Statistical Annex,* published by Pergamon Press, New York, 1976.)

century. In some cases the rates will be approaching a 1 percent increase (the Tokyo-Yokohama, Paris, Milan, Budapest, Chicago, and New York City agglomerations) or less than 1 percent (Rhine-Ruhr area, London, and Birmingham). The largest agglomerations in these MDCs will increase absolutely but at a decreasing rate each successive decade (Fig. 12.3). During the 1990s several major agglomerations will add fewer than 1 million residents: Chicago, Toronto, Sydney, Melbourne, London, Madrid, Leningrad, and the Rhine-Ruhr area. Athens, Vienna, Warsaw, and Philadelphia are among those expected to add 500,000 or fewer.

In sharp contrast to the gradual absolute population increases and near-zero growth rates for major agglomerations in MDCs are the overall high rates of absolute and relative increase for LDCs (Fig. 12.4). Decennial increases for Kinshasa, Nairobi,

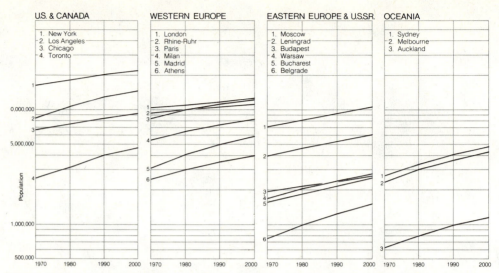

Figure 12.3 Urban Growth Curves for Selected Agglomerations in MDCs, 1970–2000. (*Source:* Data derived from United Nations, Department of Economic and Social Affairs, *Global Review of Human Settlements, Statistical Annex,* published by Pergamon Press, New York, 1976.)

Karachi, Tehran, Hanoi, and Lima were estimated to be above 8 percent from 1970 to 1980. Rates above 5 percent between 1970 and 1980 were projected for two dozen large agglomerations. During the 1990s rates above 5 percent are predicted for Bangkok, Hanoi, Dacca, Karachi, and most agglomerations in Africa, save those in the Republic of South Africa. The growth rates for most major agglomerations in the LDCs will have declined several percentage points from 1970 to 2000. This fact, while not an indication that urban problems are necessarily being solved, illustrates that the peak of urban growth will have occurred sometime during the 1980s. Slower rates will be attributed to reduced rural-to-urban migration, successful family planning programs, increased abortions, voluntary sterilization, and the increased attraction of secondary and tertiary cities within a country. A number of agglomerations will have added 8 million or more residents in the 1970–2000 period; these include Lagos, Kinshasa, Baghdad, Manila, Bangkok, and Shanghai. Mexico City, São Paulo, Rio de Janeiro, Calcutta, Bombay, Karachi, Jakarta, and Seoul will each have added 12 million by the year 2000 from their 1970 bases. Cairo and Tehran will each add 10 million by the year 2000 from their 1970 population. The critical and obvious question is how these large cities, already plagued by populations which they cannot support, are going to absorb so many millions of residents. It is worth noting that annual growth rates of 5 percent between the years 1990 and 2000, albeit lower than the previous decade, can still be responsible for several million residents being added to very large agglomerations during a 10-year span. Cities growing 5 percent annually will double their population in 15 years. The *doubling rate* for cities growing 3 percent annually is 25 years.

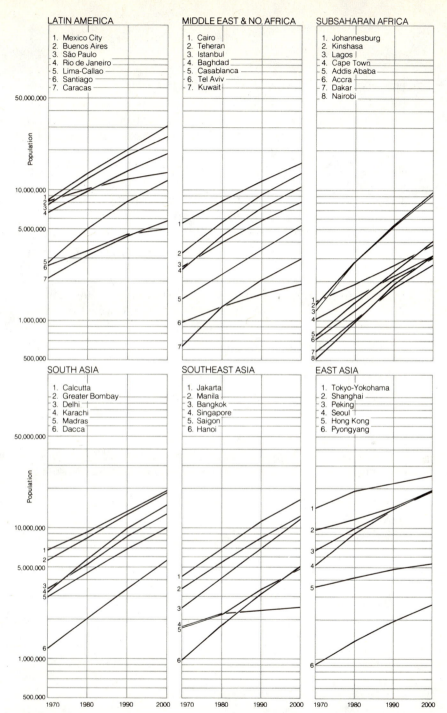

Figure 12.4 Urban Growth Curves for Selected Agglomerations in LDCs, 1970–2000. (*Source:* Data derived from United Nations, Department of Economic and Social Affairs, *Global Review of Human Settlements, Statistical Annex,* published by Pergamon Press, New York, 1976.)

Primacy Ratio

The *primacy ratio,* defined as the ratio of the first to the second largest city in a country, reflects the degree of population dominance of the largest urban center. Primacy ratios that increase over time demonstrate that the primate city is becoming more important in population, and probably in key social, economic, and political functions within a country. Higher ratios of rural-to-urban migration to the primate city than to the second largest city, as well as initially higher fertility rates in primate cities, are reasons for primacy ratios increasing over time in developing countries. When primacy ratios decrease over time, the population differences narrow between the two largest places. The smaller ratio may be explained by government programs successfully decentralizing government offices, businesses, and industries to the second largest city and by individual migrants being attracted to cities other than the primate city.

Part of the difficulty in discerning the directions of primacy ratios over the past and for the future is the lack of sound historical or predictive data for cities in both the developed and developing countries. Fortunately the aforementioned *Global Review of Human Settlements* contains data for cities in selected developing and developed countries for the 1950–2000 period.

From data available for the first and second largest cities in selected countries, five generalizations can be made regarding primacy rates from 1950 to 2000 (Table 12.4). First, the ratios tend to increase in most LDCs. In some countries, for example, Colombia, Egypt, Indonesia, and Pakistan, the primate city agglomeration increases at a lower rate than in South Korea, Nigeria, and Iran. The higher ratios in 2000 than in 1950 indicate that the dominance of Bogotá, Cairo, Jakarta, Karachi, Seoul, Lagos, and Tehran vis-à-vis the second largest cities continues to increase. The second largest cities of Medellín, Alexandria, Surabaja, Lahore, Pusan, Ibadan, and Isfahan, respectively, are attracting not only fewer rural migrants but also probably fewer key economic, social, and political functions.

Second, in populous LDCs that have a number of large urban agglomerations, the primacy ratio declines. This decline is evident, for example, in Mexico, India, and China. While Mexico City, Calcutta, and Shanghai had or are estimated to have the largest populations in their respective countries each decade from 1950 to 2000, the second largest cities of Guadalajara, Bombay, and Peking are increasing at a more rapid rate. By 2000 the Calcutta and Bombay agglomerations are both estimated to have nearly 19 million residents each, as are Shanghai and Peking. Within these three countries a number of additional urban centers also are attracting rural migrants, businesses, and industries. Monterrey, Vera Cruz, Tampico, and Puebla in Mexico are examples, as are Delhi, Madras, and Hyderabad in India and Tientsin (Tianjin), Shenyang, Wuhan, Lanchou (Lanzhou), and Canton (Guangzhou) in China. By the year 2000 India and China are expected to have 8 and 22 agglomerations, respectively, with a population between 2 and 5 million.

Third, the primacy ratios in most MDCs from 1950 to 2000 will decline or remain fairly static. Primate cities in France, the U.K., the U.S., and the USSR will experience slower rates of increase than the second largest cities. In each country the primate city

TABLE 12.4 PRIMACY RATIOS FOR SELECTED COUNTRIES, 1950–2000

	1950	1960	1970	1980	1990	2000
Less Developed Countries						
China	2.41	1.66	1.43	1.17	1.04	1.00
Colombia	2.00	2.31	2.33	2.45	2.52	2.54
Egypt	2.56	2.47	2.79	2.87	2.91	2.93
India	1.53	1.35	1.19	1.10	1.05	1.03
Indonesia	2.30	2.81	2.97	3.16	3.31	3.36
Iran	5.66	6.11	6.59	6.93	7.14	7.20
Mexico	7.16	6.04	5.76	5.39	5.18	5.12
Nigeria	1.49	1.33	1.96	2.74	3.35	3.58
Pakistan	1.24	1.46	1.72	1.90	2.02	2.06
South Korea	1.97	2.09	2.91	3.31	3.57	3.67
More Developed Countries						
Australia	1.21	1.15	1.13	1.11	1.09	1.09
Belgium	1.62	1.59	1.55	1.59	1.59	1.59
Canada	1.17	1.16	1.08	1.05	1.03	1.03
France	7.48	8.15	7.50	6.93	6.63	6.52
Italy	1.32	1.41	1.54	1.61	1.66	1.68
Japan	1.75	1.85	1.95	2.03	2.07	2.08
Netherlands	1.15	1.10	0.02	1.07	1.11	1.12
Poland	1.67	1.65	1.61	1.60	1.59	1.59
Soviet Union	1.85	1.82	1.79	1.77	1.76	1.76
Spain	1.42	1.45	1.80	2.01	2.15	2.59
Sweden	2.10	2.02	2.04	2.03	2.02	2.02
United Kingdom	4.08	4.03	3.79	3.67	3.61	3.59
United States	2.50	2.17	1.94	1.68	1.54	1.50
Yugoslavia	1.20	1.35	1.37	1.42	1.46	1.47

Source: Derived from Table 6 in *Global Review of Urban Settlements, Statistical Annex,* United Nations: Department of Economic and Social Affairs, published by Pergamon Press, 1976, pp. 77–87.

agglomeration will continue to have a much larger total population than the second largest center. The Paris, London, New York, and Moscow agglomerations will continue to overshadow the populations of Lille, Manchester, Los Angeles-Long Beach, and Leningrad.

Fourth, stable primacy ratios and those with very slight increases or decreases are characteristic of countries where there are two large dominating urban agglomerations or where the natural increase is nearly zero. In Canada, Australia, and the Netherlands, the two largest agglomerations are becoming more similar in size. In Sweden, Poland, and Belgium the population increase is approaching zero.

A fifth and final generalization regarding primacy ratios is their increase in selected countries. Increases are found particularly in countries where there has been and remains a single dominating primate city: Tokyo-Yokohama in Japan, Madrid in Spain, Rome in Italy, and Belgrade in Yugoslavia. In each of these four countries the rate of growth is much greater than in the second largest agglomeration of Osaka-Kobe,

Barcelona, Naples, and Zagreb. In summary, the primate city ratios for both developed and developing countries illustrate trends during the 1950–2000 half-century indicative of continued and increasing and decreasing primacy as well as stability.

Rank-Size Relationships

Changes in the population size and ranking of a country's largest cities over time can be illustrated by the *rank-size curves*. The curves are based on the population and rank of each successively smaller agglomeration. A steep rank-size curve depicts primacy, that is, where the primate city may have three, four, or five times the population of the second largest city. A flat or shallow rank-size curve demonstrates that the largest-ranked cities have a similar population.

Rank-size curves can be constructed for a number of years to show whether primacy has increased or whether secondary, tertiary, or successively large cities have increased at uniform rates. If primacy has increased over time, the curves would become steeper. If the primate city has grown less than the other large cities within a country, the curve would be flatter. If, on the other hand, the curves for different years are widely spaced, the growth of all ranked cities has increased over time. Closely spaced curves indicate little absolute growth from decade to decade and probably little change in the rankings of the largest agglomerations.

Curves for a number of selected MDCs and LDCs for 1950, 1975, and 2000 are shown in Fig. 12.5. For the three MDCs, the curves for the U.K. and U.S. are basically flat, especially for the former, where there is little variation in the slope for the three years. In the U.K., London will remain the primate city until 2000, and the rankings for Birmingham, Manchester, Leeds-Bradford, Glasgow, and Liverpool will remain essentially the same for 2000 as they were for 1950 and 1975. The rank-size curves for the six largest U.S. urban agglomerations for the three years are fairly evenly spaced and almost parallel, indicating that the increases among the ranked cities are uniform. While the curves have similar slopes, the largest cities undergo some change in rank each year. New York-Northeast New Jersey was the largest agglomeration in 1950 and 1975 and will remain so in 2000, but the Los Angeles-Long Beach agglomeration was second in 1975 and will be second in 2000; it replaced Chicago-Northwest Indiana, which was second in 1950, third in 1975, and will be third in 2000. Shifts in rankings also occurred or will occur among Philadelphia, Detroit, San Francisco, and Boston. Boston, the sixth largest agglomeration in 1950, dropped out of the top six in 1975 and will remain out in 2000. The curves for the six largest Japanese agglomerations for 1975 and 2000 are similar to those for the U.S. except that the curves are slightly steeper, an indication of the degree of primacy held by the Tokyo-Yokohama area.

The rank-size curves for Indonesia, China, and Brazil reveal some striking similarities; all these curves are more widely spaced than those for the U.K., the U.S., and Japan. Indonesia's curves illustrate rapid population increases (wide spaces between curves) from 1950 to 1975 and from 1975 to 2000 for each of the six largest cities. Jakarta, Surabaja, and Bandung remain the three largest each year; Medan, Palembang, and Semarang shift ranks. The slightly steeper curve for 2000 than for 1950 reveals that the primacy is increasing particularly for Jakarta. China's flat curves, which are ap-

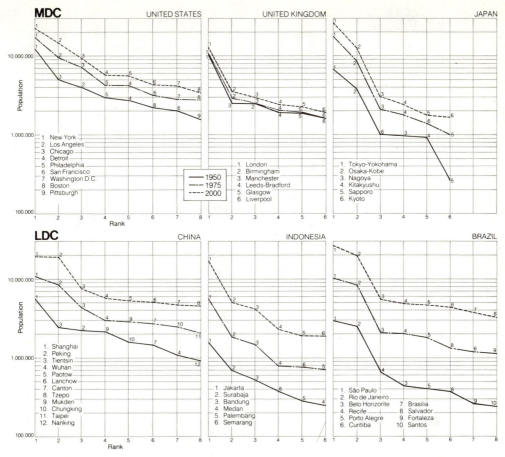

Figure 12.5 Rank-Size Distribution of Settlements for Selected Countries, 1950, 1975, and 2000. (*Source:* Data derived from United Nations, Department of Economic and Social Affairs, *Global Review of Human Settlements, Statistical Annex,* published by Pergamon Press, New York, 1976.)

proaching those for the U.S. and U.K., reflect the success of government programs to decentralize the concentration of economic activities away from the largest agglomerations, especially Shanghai and Peking, and into smaller large regional centers. Other large cities in China have been growing at the expense of Shanghai and Peking. The two largest cities are estimated to have a similar population by the year 2000. Shanghai remains the largest agglomeration in each year. Peking (third largest in 1950), Tientsin, (Tianjin), Wuhan, Mukden (Shenyang), Taotou (Baotou), Chungking (Chongqing), Canton (Guangzhou), and Langchou (Lanzhou) are among the other five largest cities in one year or more. Brazil's curves for 1950, 1975, and 2000 are more akin to China's than to Indonesia's. The flattening appears after São Paulo and Rio de Janeiro, the two largest agglomerations. Belo Horizonte, Recife, Pôrto Alegre, Curitaba, Fortaleza, Salvador, and Brasilia (in 2000 only) are also among the seven largest agglomerations for 1950, 1975, and 2000. The planned growth of regional capitals in Brazil resembles the growth pattern evident in China. Steeper curves for both China and Brazil in 1950 and 2000 indicate the higher growth rates for third, fourth, fifth, and sixth largest cities than for the two largest agglomerations in each country.

Major Agglomerations

The largest and greatest number of agglomerations in 1975 were in East and South Asia and North America (see Chapter 1). Sixty-eight of the 181 "million" cities were in Asia, with another third in Europe and North America. The U.S. and China had 27 and 26 agglomerations above 1 million, respectively. The USSR, India, and Brazil had from 9 to 12 agglomerations of that size.

The distribution of the largest agglomerations in 1980, that is, those above 5 million, was similar to that of those over 1 million. Most were in Asia, North America, and Europe (Table 12.5). Their combined population approached 246 million, a figure slightly more than the total U.S. population in 1980. The U.S. was the fourth largest

TABLE 12.5 LARGEST URBAN AGGLOMERATIONS: 1980

Rank	Country	Urban Agglomeration	Population (in thousands)
1.	Japan	Tokyo-Yokohama	19,705
2.	United States	New York City-Northeast New Jersey	17,909
3.	Mexico	Mexico City	13,878
4.	Brazil	São Paulo	12,494
5.	China	Shanghai	12,002
6.	United Kingdom	London	10,962
7.	United States	Los Angeles-Long Beach	10,658
8.	Argentina	Buenos Aires	10,375
9.	China	Peking	10,216
10.	Brazil	Rio de Janeiro	10,016
11.	West Germany	Rhine-Ruhr	9,949
12.	France	Paris	9,908
13.	Japan	Osaka-Kobe	9,731
14.	India	Calcutta	9,583
15.	Korea	Seoul	9,443
16.	India	Bombay	8,722
17.	Egypt	Cairo	8,391
18.	U.S.S.R	Moscow	8,160
19.	United States	Chicago-Northwestern Indiana	7,484
20.	Indonesia	Jakarta	7,191
21.	Italy	Milan	6,513
22.	Pakistan	Karachi	5,971
23.	Iran	Tehran	5,804
24.	India	Delhi	5,704
25.	Philippines	Manila	5,593

Source: Derived from *Global Review of Human Settlements, Statistical Index,* New York: Pergamon Press, 1976, pp. 77–87. Data prepared by the Statistical Office of the Department of Economic and Social Affairs of the United Nations.

nation. The five largest agglomerations in 1980, each with a population of 12 million or more, had a combined population of nearly 75 million, a figure equivalent to the total population of Nigeria (tenth largest nation) or all the urban population in Africa save that in Egypt and South Africa. Substantial future growth is anticipated for those agglomerations of 5 million or more. In 1950 six agglomerations over 5 million contained a total population of 47 million, less than 1 percent of the world's total urban population. By 2000 an estimated 59 5-million-plus agglomerations will have a combined population of 646 million, a figure that represents 21 percent of the total urban population and 10 percent of the total population of the world.

As discussed above, the most rapid rates of growth of large cities are in the LDCs. Many capital cities, which are also primate cities, were experiencing annual increases in the mid-1970s above 6 and 8 percent, figures that mean the population will double in less than 15 years. Many of the world's fastest growing large cities were not ranked among the largest agglomerations in 1975. By 1980 Addis Ababa, Accra, Tunis, Khartoum, Guatemala City, Brasilia, Lucknow, Tangshan, Kuwait City, and Haiphong were "million" cities. Kingston-St. Andrew, Colombo, Phnom Penh, and Fuchou (Fuzhou) will approach that level by the year 2000. Agglomerations expected to reach 5 million by 1980 were Delhi, Jakarta, Tehran, Karachi, and Manila. Alexandria, Casablanca, Guadalajara, Belo Horizonte, Dacca, Wuhan, Bangalore, Surabaja, Pusan, and Ho Chi Minh City will pass that threshold before the end of the century.

A ranking of the largest agglomerations for 2000 is expected to be similar to that for 1975 except that a larger number will be in the LDCs (Table 12.6). In 1975, 11 of the top 21 were in Latin America, Africa, and Asia (excluding Japan) (Fig. 12.6). By 2000, 25 of the 35 largest agglomerations will be in the developing world. São Paulo, Peking, Calcutta, Seoul, and Jakarta will replace several large North American and European cities that have long been considered major world population centers. New cities added will be Bogotá, Lagos, Kinshasa, and Lahore; each will have more people by the year 2000 than Toronto, Philadelphia, Detroit, Sydney, Leningrad, Madrid, and Rome. By 2000 more people will be in Addis Ababa than in San Francisco-Oakland, more in Caracas than in Montreal, and more in Ho Chi Minh City than in Melbourne. The absolute growth of some of these agglomerations in Africa, Latin America, and Asia during the 1950–2000 period will be nothing short of astronomical. Seoul and Baghdad will have grown 18 times their 1950 populations, and Lagos will have grown 31 times. Kinshasa will have grown from 160,000 (a small urban center in 1950) to over 9 million, an increase of over 5000 percent. The largest agglomerations in the MDCs, including Tokyo, New York City, London, and Moscow, will have increased by twice (or less) their 1950 populations. During the 1950–2000 period, Mexico City is expected to have added an average of 574,000 people per year (the approximate 1980 population of metropolitan Omaha and Winnipeg), while São Paulo will have added 470,000 each year (the size of Edinburgh). From 1950 to 2000 the urban population in the MDCs will have increased 1.4 times and nearly 7 times in the LDCs. It is estimated that by the turn of the century more people will be in the Mexico City agglomeration than in Canada or Australia and New Zealand combined. Only 10 countries by

TABLE 12.6 LARGEST URBAN AGGLOMERATIONS

Rank	Country	Urban Agglomeration	Population 2000 (in millions)	Population 1950 (in millions)	Percent Change, 1950–2000
1.	Mexico	Mexico City	31.6	2.87	1001
2.	Japan	Tokyo-Yokohama	26.1	6.74	287
3.	Brazil	São Paulo	26.0	2.45	959
4.	United States	New York City-Northeast New Jersey	22.2	12.34	80
5.	India	Calcutta	19.7	4.45	342
6.	Brazil	Rio de Janeiro	19.4	2.89	571
7.	China	Shanghai	19.2	5.78	232
8.	China	Peking	19.1	2.16	784
9.	India	Greater Bombay	19.1	2.90	559
10.	Korea	Seoul	18.7	1.02	1733
11.	Indonesia	Jakarta	17.0	1.57	782
12.	Egypt	Cairo-Giza-Imbada	16.4	2.38	589
13.	Pakistan	Karachi	15.9	1.03	144
14.	United States	Los Angeles-Long Beach	14.8	4.05	265
15.	Argentina	Buenos Aires	13.9	4.50	490
16.	Iran	Tehran	13.8	1.04	1227
17.	India	Delhi	13.2	1.39	850
18.	United Kingdom	London	12.7	10.25	24
19.	Philippines	Manila	12.7	1.53	730
20.	Japan	Osaka-Kobe	12.5	3.83	226
21.	France	Paris	12.3	5.44	126
22.	Peru	Lima-Callao	12.1	.61	1883
23.	West Germany	Rhine-Ruhr	11.2	6.82	64

Source: Derived from *Global Review of Human Settlements, Statistical Index,* New York: Pergamon Press, 1976, pp. 77–87. Data prepared by the Statistical Office of the Department of Economic and Social Affairs of the United Nations.

the year 2000 are expected to have more people than the combined population (126 million) of the five largest agglomerations.

Human Geography of Shrinking Urban Worlds

A useful concept within which to examine the more tightly integrated urban centers and networks emerging at national and global scales is *time-space convergence*. As the concept has been developed by geographers, it refers to the rate at which places are moving closer together, measured by travel time and communication time. That is, while absolute distances remain the same, improvement in transportation and communication make it possible to overcome the friction of distance. The fact that railroads and automobiles permit easier contact between two cities than do horses or stage coaches and that airlines and telephones further reduce the travel and communication time between two nodes demonstrates the geographic consequences of a shrinking world. The concept of time-space convergence can be applied to preindustrial, industrial, and postindustrial societies and urban nodes within them. Ultimate time-space con-

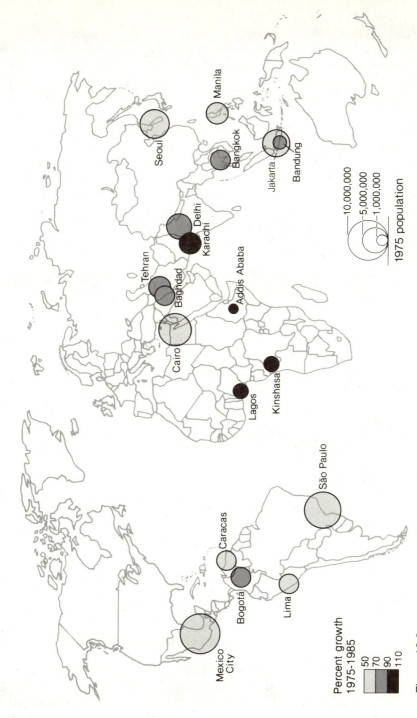

Figure 12.6 Fastest-Growing Cities of the World, 1975–1985. (*Source:* United Nations, *Development Forum*, December 1975.)

vergence in a globally integrated and interdependent urban world would reveal all places could be reached within the same amount of time, regardless of the absolute distances separating them.

Whether or not the consequences of time-space convergence are fully realized at the national or international level will depend on the introduction, adoption, and diffusion of such technologies by a society. Faster railroads, automobiles, and aircraft, as they are developed, may be easier to adopt and integrate within the MDCs than in many LDCs. Likewise, the ability to purchase, adopt, and diffuse communications technologies (radio, television, satellite) is not likely to be shared equally by wealthy and poor countries. In the case of LDCs, only the largest cities may be converging in transportation and communication time, both to one another and to selected major cities in the developed world. Cities in LDCs are often more similar to their counterparts in the MDCs than to towns and villages in their own hinterlands. Rural areas that are isolated may remain so because of the high costs needed to integrate them into the shrinking urban worlds. That is, the advances in transportation and telecommunications that shrink the worlds of humankind are likely to result in some spaces and places shrinking more than others. In a futuristic context, it is most likely that the small and large places in the wealthy MDCs and the largest cities in the LDCs will be the first to experience the benefits (or ill effects) of improved transportation and communications technologies. Some countries, cities, and individuals may choose not to adopt the above technologies; if so, they will not become an integral part of the shrinking worlds where the times needed to visit or contact distant spaces are constantly reduced.

Time-space convergence can be measured in terms of both travel time and costs. The realization that individuals traveling between major cities, such as Paris, New York City, or Tokyo, can travel faster via the Concorde than the 747 or DC-7, shows the ease in reaching cities once considered distant. The DC-7, the fastest commercial plane in 1950, flew about 350 miles (560 km.) per hour; the 747 jumbo jet in the 1980s flew about 640 miles (1030 km.) per hour. The Concorde, which still probably will be the fastest commercial aircraft in the year 2000 (until a liquid-hydrogen plane is operative), flies at maximum speeds over 1300 miles (2090 km.) per hour. With each advance, major world cities that were 24 hours distant in travel time in 1950 will be less than 6 or 8 hours apart by the year 2000. The examples of time bands from Paris would be similar to those from New York City, Moscow, Rio de Janeiro, Sydney, and other large cities (Fig. 12.7). *Cost-space convergence* has occurred along with faster modes of transportation and communication. That is, it is less expensive to travel 500 to 1000 mi. (800 to 1600 km.) by airline in the 1980s than in the 1950s; the same applies to placing intranational and international phone calls in the 1980s compared with three decades earlier. The costs of long-distance telephone calls from New York City to San Francisco (roughly 2500 mi. or 4020 km.) dropped from $21 to less than $1 (weekdays for the first minute), and the time to establish connections from 14 minutes to less than 30 seconds with direct long-distance dialing, from 1920 to 1970. Complete cost-space convergence would mean the costs of phoning any location would be the same regardless of distance; that is, phoning New York City from Chicago would be the same as

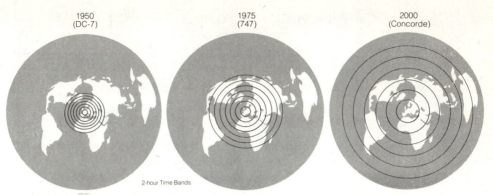

Figure 12.7 Shrinking World: Air Travel Times from Paris, 1950, 1975, 2000. (*Source:* Compiled by the author.)

phoning Tokyo, London, Rome, or Nairobi. Uniform rates regardless of distance are easier to attain for postage than for telephone.

The significance of time-space convergence in a futuristic context is how it will affect human decision making and interaction in an urbanized world. By 2000 almost half of humankind will be living in cities and more than that percentage will experience first or second hand the effects of *space-adjusting technologies*. Possibly, though not necessarily, the instant or nearly instant communication among those in industries, governments, and universities, as well in as households in the MDCs and LDCs, will promote a greater global awareness and resolution of pressing international problems. Rapid transportation as well will facilitate the ease and extent of mobility, not only for individuals but also for those transnational corporations seeking new industrial sites and markets in the MDCs but even more so in the LDCs, where labor, assembly, and energy costs may be lower and where the population is expanding.

Complete time-space convergence exists when the world becomes a single point. When all places or points, regardless of size or distance between any other points, can be reached within the same amount of time, distance ceases to become a barrier. Differences between locations are relative only in the amount of time needed to establish contact. The demise of distance as a barrier to interaction can be illustrated by international offices headquartered in Cairo, an international city. Phone contacts, made possible by satellites, can be made just as easily with affiliates and subsidiaries in Nairobi, Lagos, Cape Town, and Algiers as with those in Paris, Buenos Aires, San Francisco, or Singapore. Supersonic flights in the future would place Melbourne, Bombay, Moscow, and New York City almost as close as Dakar, Kinshasa, and Dar es Salaam. The "urban worlds" of business, government, industry, and the university are likely to assume global proportions. The emerging interdependent urban worlds just described may also reduce human barriers to interaction. Increased interregional and international ties, particularly among institutions and individuals in urban areas and urbanized environments, may also reduce psychological and political barriers that may have stemmed from linguistic, cultural, religious, and ideological differences. While differences between and among societies and economies will continue, their emergence into increasingly urbanized and shrinking worlds, at a global scale, will mark a significant feature of the future.

Emergence of City Systems and Systems of Cities

The large, medium-sized, and small urban agglomerations increasing the most rapidly in population and expanding in area are adjacent to the existing largest nodes along major transportation arteries. Coastlines where major ports handle substantial national and international commerce and which are sites for tourist/recreation activities and retirement settlements are additional areas experiencing rapid urban growth and expansion. Faster and improved transportation, which facilitates and increases population mobility and regional and interregional transfers of commodities, as well as advances in telecommunication, have fostered the emergence of *city systems.* Large and small urban centers become economically integrated into systems that transcend numerous political divisions and subdivisions at regional and national levels.

At both national and regional levels, individual city systems focused on single major nodes, may eventually become a part of more tightly integrated nationwide urban systems. *Systems of cities* or megalopolises form by places in between existing individual systems "growing together." The "filling in" process occurs most frequently along major transportation and communication networks linking major nodes. A useful analogy to envisage this spatial and temporal process is comparing the growth of an urban system to the "growth" of beads on a string. At an initial period few beads (urban nodes) are widely spaced, except for those near the largest beads (major nodes). As the urban population expands, the existing beads grow and a few new ones appear on the string (major transport artery). Eventually the smaller and medium-sized beads as well as the largest ones expand so that few open spaces remain. At this stage an urban corridor or system links people, companies, and offices throughout the entire system.

Examples of "systems of systems" are evident in a number of countries. The U.S. Commission on Population Growth and the American Future identified 25 *urban regions* expected by the year 2000 (Fig. 12.8). Some of the coalescing and converging urban strips have been given humorous labels: Bowash (Boston to Washington), Chipitts (Chicago to Pittsburgh), and San San (San Francisco to San Diego). Others rapidly emerging are along the Texas-Louisiana-Mississippi-Alabama-West Florida Gulf Coast and the Florida peninsula. Smaller megalopolises are emerging along the east face of the Rockies, where Denver-Boulder-Pueblo are the major nodes; in Texas, where Dallas-Fort Worth-Austin-San Antonio form the largest clusters; in Oklahoma, from Tulsa to Oklahoma City; and in the Piedmont, from southwest Virginia to northern Georgia. Outside the U.S. the "Canadian Main Street" (identified by Maurice Yeates) stretches from Quebec to Windsor. Similar urban systems also exist in the U.K., Japan, Australia, and South Africa (Fig. 12.9).

Figure 12.8 Urban Regions in the United States in the Year 2000. (*Source:* Report on the Commission on Population Growth, *Population and the American Future*, Washington, DC, 1973, p. 33.)

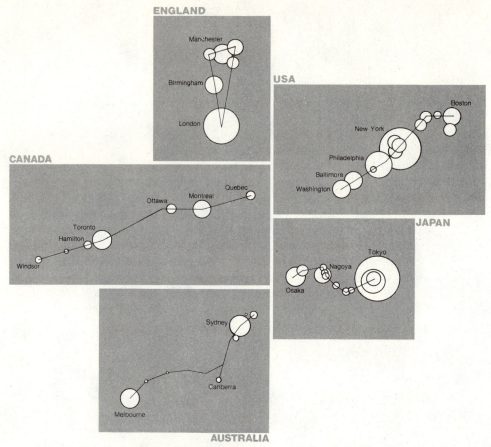

Figure 12.9 Patterns of Urban Systems in MDCs. (*Source:* Adapted in part from Maurice Yeates, *Main Street, Windsor to Quebec City,* Toronto: Macmillan, 1975, p. 35.)

The filling-in process described above that leads to the formation of regional and national urban systems is not a phenomenon restricted to the developed world. The rapid increase in the number, population, and expansion of urban agglomerations in certain LDCs will result in large and medium-sized cities in close proximity forming the foci of a large urban network. The nodal growth of primate cities and major regional centers will gradually assume a linear form with the spaces in between being filled up by currently existing smaller nodes or new nodes being developed at major transportation junctions, new administrative centers, or new industrial sites. The beginnings of such systems are apparent in several countries, in southeast Brazil, for example, where the major nodes are Rio de Janeiro-Belo Horizonte-São Paulo; in Mexico, where Mexico City-Puebla-Vera Cruz form the major nodes; and in Egypt, where Alexandria and Cairo are the two major cities (Fig. 12.10). Elsewhere urban growth is around one or two major nodes, as in Lagos and Ibadan, Nigeria; in Valparaiso and Santiago, Chile;

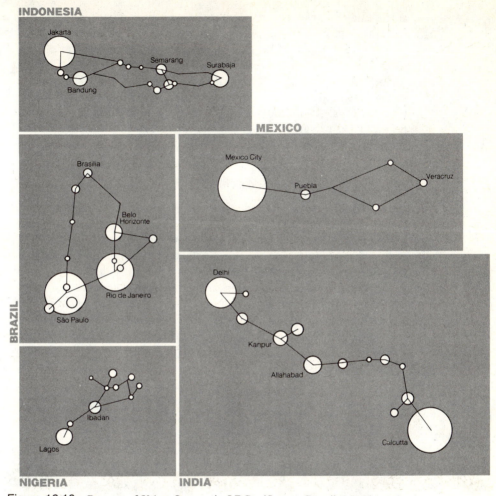

Figure 12.10 Patterns of Urban Systems in LDCs. (*Source:* Compiled by the author.)

and in Jakarta and Surabaja on Java. Future sprawling agglomerations will also appear in southern and eastern China and in northern, western, and eastern India. Possibly the largest cities that form the urban systems in the LDCs will become more integrated into the systems of the MDCs than the lower levels of the settlement hierarchy in their own country. The *urban global core* and *rural periphery* form a more likely scenario than one completely integrated urban system.

National urban growth and expansion accounts for both a clustering of the population around selected centers (primate cities and other high-ranking cities) and a dispersion of the population into less dense areas in between. Density surfaces are likely to contain a series of peaks and troughs representing nodes of concentration in central-city locations and broad plateaus of less dense population interspersed with occasional ridges (major transport corridors) in the suburbs and outlying "rural" or nonmetropolitan areas. Improved transport systems and modes of communication, plus the desire of some members of the population to reside in less crowded areas, will also contribute to the dispersion. The Greek planner Constantine Doxiadis predicted that national urban systems, of the type just described, will eventually become integrated into an *ecumenopolis,* the ultimate form of human settlement (Fig. 12.11). By 2060, such an ecumenopolis, (containing most of the world's population) will be highly integrated into a global urban network. The consequences of time-space convergence described previously will contribute to places being located in closer relative space to each other.

The Global Village and World Cities

Small and large urban centers, those in preindustrial, industrial, and postindustrial societies and those in highly accessible and previously remote locations will become part of the *global village.* As time and space converge, the scale, perception, and dimensions of human problems change. The satisfaction of human needs is attained via a system of spatial organization that is progressively more urbanized, more complex, and more reflective of global interdependency. In this regard Doxiadis has also projected a multi-centered transportation and communication network for the twenty-first century where the major world capitals and cities are linked (Fig. 12.12). The major difference the "wired global village" at 2000 and beyond has with previous national and continental urban systems is in the scale of the linkages and the number of nodes forming the network.

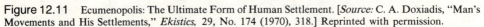

Figure 12.11 Ecumenopolis: The Ultimate Form of Human Settlement. [*Source:* C. A. Doxiadis, "Man's Movements and His Settlements," *Ekistics,* 29, No. 174 (1970), 318.] Reprinted with permission.

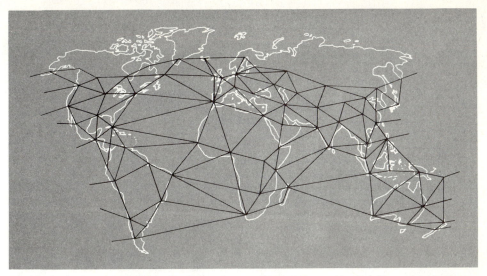

Figure 12.12 Multicentered International Transportation and Communications Network in the Twenty-First Century. [*Source:* C. A. Doxiadis, "Man's Movements and His Settlements," *Ekistics,* 29, No. 174 (1970), 321.] Reprinted with permission.

Within the global village some cities will attain a global character. These *world cities* are significant nodes for international decision making. Major governmental and nongovernmental organizations and agencies together with transnational corporations have head offices in these cities. These cities already are or are destined to become the important centers for political, economic, and cultural activities; such cities are not necessarily the largest within a country, but are those with an international atmosphere and profile. Peter Hall in *The World Cities* identified a number of characteristics that can be applied to these cities (Table 12.7). Rio de Janeiro, Lagos, Hong Kong, and Cairo would qualify as world cities in the LDCs as would Tokyo, New York City, London, Paris, Sydney, and Moscow in the MDCs. The greater role the LDCs are exercising in global economies and politics will lead to a number of major cities within the LDCs assuming as great a part in global decision making as traditional European "world capitals." The realities of the shrinking world and the significance of new world cities are observed when international meetings are convened and attended by delegates from 150 or more countries. UN conferences on food (Rome), environment (Stockholm), population (Belgrade), the law of the sea (Caracas), women (Mexico City), and desertification (Nairobi) in essence are "miniworld" settings where within one room or building participants can listen to the pressing problems as expressed by friends, acquaintances, and possibly even adversaries. That views expressed and resolutions adopted can reach other regional and world capitals and thousands of medium-sized and small centers at the same time further illustrates the realities of the shrinking world and major urban centers within it.

TABLE 12.7 CHARACTERISTICS OF WORLD CITIES

Major centers of political power
Seats of national and international governmental and nongovernmental agencies
Major headquarters of transnational corporations
Headquarters of major professional organizations and trade unions
Major centers of industrial activity
Major railroad, highway, port, and airline centers
Headquarters of major banks and insurance companies
Major medical and legal centers
Headquarters of national courts of justice
Major universities and research institutes
Major libraries, museums and churches
Major theaters, opera halls, restaurants, etc.
Headquarters of information dissemination—publishers, advertisers, radio, television, and satellite data
Large populations and an international labor force
Increasing share of employees in services as opposed to industry
Centers of very specialized goods and services
International markets
Sites of global conferences: governments, industries, and volunteer organizations

Source: Adapted in part from Peter Hall, *The World Cities,* New York: McGraw-Hill, 1966, pp. 7–9.

Urban Forms and Functions

Numerical growth in the number of future urban settlements, their areal expansion and filling in of the open spaces between large cities, and the extension of transportation and communication networks are likely to attain several forms. Likewise, changes in the economy of individual MDCs and LDCs, especially as reflected in the labor force and income generated, will bring about some new and different functional orientations of cities in the future.

Urban Forms

Broad, clustered strips, corridors, and megalopolises will be a major form evident on an international scale. Transport corridors and amenity environments (rivers, coastlines, and scenic attractions) will become major foci for future urban growth and expansion. Railroads, highways, rivers, and coastlines together will serve as the impetus for horizontal urban settlement. Much of the horizontal growth that has occurred previously in suburbs, especially in North America, Western Europe, Japan, and Oceania, has been due to inexpensive and abundant fossil fuels, the popularity of the automobile, and the freedom to select areas of lower density near larger cities. The extent to which energy in similar amounts is available in the future will help determine the face of extensive horizontal urban developments.

Doxiadis and others who have advanced notions regarding the future ecumenopolis and future megalopolises and conurbations have identified major national and international highways as the "major rivers" of the twenty-first century. Primate cities, secondary and tertiary centers, and in many cases regional centers will form systems where people, raw materials, finished products, and services are exchanged among the multitude of places accessible to the major transport arteries. Within the developing world completed and projected highways along the Amazon, on the east face of the Andes, in East and West Africa (Nairobi-Lagos-Dakar), between Cairo and Cape Town, and from Turkey to Singapore are major land routes both where existing urban centers will grow and where some entirely new rapidly growing centers will develop at critical junctions. With national urban systems emerging in more countries, the economic and social integration of old and new settlements are expected to be more closely integrated into new major agglomerations, which will create some new problems and may call for new ways to resolve them.

Another question related to urban forms is the physical appearance cities may assume in the future. Probably most cities will bear a strong resemblance to the present. Clustered buildings in downtown centers, high residential densities at city centers, and broad commercial strips intermixed with commercial nodes of varying size will be found. The slower-growing older cities in Europe and North America will probably see a continuation of the forms acquired in the first six decades of the twentieth century. Higher energy costs may lead to somewhat higher densities in the peripheries of the largest cities. These densities may be associated with high rise apartments, clusters of townhouses or condominiums, or new towns immediately beyond but close to large cities. It is tempting to assume that within the LDCs the salient appearance of future cities will be "more of the same." However, this in part is probably a premature description, since rapid growth is still occurring and the economic and social fabric of many countries is being profoundly altered by new and rapid urban growth. The "sorting out" of distinct social groups, income classes, and land uses is far from attaining the degree of permanence apparent in the MDCs. The more-of-the-same scenario may not hold in the LDCs where national urban planning programs are successful in stemming the tide of rural-to-urban migration to the primate city and if efforts to decentralize industries, government offices, and businesses away from the compacted downtowns of many old cities are successful.

Some entirely new architectural forms for cities are also likely. Even though they may be expensive, they may be vehicles to revitalize the human spirit within a country and demonstrate a break with previous tradition, for example, colonialism. Newly designed capital cities in the LDCs include Brasilia, Islamabad, and Gabernoes (Botswana). Unique architectural layouts have been planned for some new towns in the U.S.; Jonathan, Minnesota, and Paolo Soleri's Arcology (near Phoenix) are two examples. Underground architecture or terratecture has been used for high-technology industries and warehouses in the Kansas City area, the UNESCO building in Paris, defense facilities in Colorado, and libraries, shopping malls, and transportation (subways and people movers) in various locations. Skyscrapers and subdivisions in Japan, the Netherlands, and the U.S. (Florida) have been extended into bays, lagoons, and former marshes. Domed enclosures are currently limited to botanical gardens, shopping centers, and large entertainment complexes (the Houston Astrodome, Toronto's Eaton Place, and the New Orleans Superdome). It may be only a matter of time before an entire city is enclosed in a climate-controlled dome; such an enterprise will probably not become a reality until the post-petroleum age.

Urban Functions

An equally pertinent question concerning future urban form is what functions cities will perform and how individuals will interact with them. The preindustrial cities much in evidence in the LDCs today and the industrial cities found primarily in the MDCs will be joined by a third group of cities: postindustrial cities that are foci for economic activities of a nonindustrial nature; These cities specialize in performing a variety of services, including research-and-development technology, tourism and recreation, publishing and telecommunications, and a variety of government functions.

The economic functions of cities are closely associated with changes in the composition of the labor force. As we have seen in previous chapters dealing with the LDCs, the preindustrial city is associated with rural economies; these economies have the largest percentage of their labor force engaged in the *primary sector.* The economic activities associated with that sector are agriculture, fishing, forestry, mining, and hunting and gathering. Preindustrial cities have been historically, and still are where they survive, commercial islands in a sea of a rural-oriented population. The rise of the industrial revolution in Europe initially and its diffusion to Europeanized areas elsewhere in the world triggered the emergence of cities with an industrial base. Cities grew in number and population and over larger areas with increasing demand for industrial goods. The *industrial or secondary sector* of the labor force increased the demand for a variety of larger and smaller industries within urban nodes. Retail, transportation, government, personal, and professional services also began to increase with larger percentages of the population living in cities. The *tertiary or services sector* grew at the expense of primary and secondary sectors, declining in their proportions of the total labor force. The labor force composition or "mix" that identifies the economic orientation at a particular period within a country also can be associated with specific stages in humankind's urban development (Fig. 12.13).

The association between urbanization and industrialization has been characteristic of Europe, North America, the USSR, Japan, Australia, and New Zealand. That is, cities grew as industries grew, and industries grew as did cities. In many parts of Africa, Asia, and Latin America, as previous chapters have demonstrated, many cities that recently have been increasingly urban (especially since 1955) have not experienced a corresponding increase in the industrial or secondary sector of the labor force. Rather than their secondary sector undergoing large increases in the work force, the services sector often shows the most rapid increase. That services sector would include not only small retailers, government servants, teachers, professionals, and bankers, but also a sizable number of part-time and underemployed adults. The *informal working sector,* as it is sometimes called, includes those members willing to perform odd jobs (watch parked cars and run personal errands) and those working only part-time as gardeners, peddlers, and construction workers. This relationship between urban growth and the composition of the labor force is important in attempting to project the economic futures for cities in both the MDCs and the LDCs.

It is reasonably safe to assume that in many of the MDCs the cities will increase the percentage of their labor force in the services sector—tertiary and *quaternary.* Some

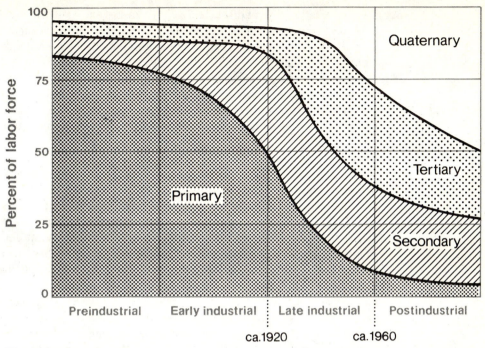

Figure 12.13 Labor Force Composition at Various Stages in Human History. (*Source:* from Ronald Abler, Donald Janelle, Allen Philbrick, and John Sommer, *Human Geography in a Shrinking World.* © 1975 by Wadsworth Publishing Company, Inc. Reprinted by permission of Wadsworth Publishing Company.)

geographers have identified a fourth sector of the economy, the quaternary sector, which includes the most specialized and highly trained members of the labor force. These individuals are associated with knowledge and information industries, including teaching, medicine, journalism, law, advertising, banking, computer systems, and research and development. The quaternary sector is separated from the barbers and beauticians, small shop owners, and truck drivers that make up of the tertiary sector. Postindustrial cities tend to have the largest percentage of their labor force in service-oriented occupations. These members perform services for each other and for those in the industrial and primary sectors. A major feature of postindustrial economies is the gathering, processing, analyzing, and disseminating of information rather than the manufacturing of industrial goods (secondary sector). Information in increasing amounts is in demand by individuals, firms, libraries, and governments.

Inasmuch as postindustrial cities and cities in postindustrial societies will have a different labor force composition than industrial and preindustrial periods, the cities themselves may assume some different form and structure. Preindustrial and industrial cities were and will remain basically compact; that is, places of activity are usually within a relatively short distance of one's residence. Places of work, shop, worship, and play can be reached easily by walking, driving a personal automobile, or taking public transportation a short distance. Even businesses and industries tend to agglomerate or at most locate not too far in travel time from the sources of their raw materials, their subsidiaries, their markets, and the many services they need (banking, law, government, and advertisers). Cities with a highly compact form and clusters of businesses, industries, and residences basically represent the preauto era; those with a bit more horizontal form, that is, urban sprawl, are likely to have felt the impact of the automobile. Industrial parks, commercial strips, regional shopping centers, and residential subdivisions, all of which define suburbanization, are reflected in an urban form that contrasts sharply with cities not experiencing the impact of massive mechanized transportation.

If we assume that more rapid transportation and communication are two attributes of postindustrial cities in the affluent developed world, what forms might such cities assume? Some answers to this question have been raised above, viz., the emergence of agglomerations or supercities or large clusters of individual nodes merging together. It stands to reason that a more dispersed and horizontal development will be a major distinguishing feature of future cities, especially those in the developed world. The availability and cost of energy may define the degree of that sprawl. The spread character will be related to an intricate highway system for private automobiles and mass transit but also to individuals who will be able to be employed at home or in small, nearby employment nodes rather than at gigantic office complexes. If much of the employment in the future includes those working in information and information-based industries, many highly skilled or semiskilled tasks could be done at a home, that is, connected with other places via telephone, television, and computer. A wired home (an "electronic cottage"), office, or industry that permits easy, cheap, and rapid interaction with other places short and long distances away will eliminate much of the need for personal travel for medical checkups, conferences, and voting and will also facilitate merchandise orders and letter writing. Wired cities composed of wired homes and offices that make all spaces equally accessible are likely to result in more dispersed populations.

The developments described above are unlikely to appear on even a small scale in the LDCs within the next 50 years. Cities, especially primate cities, are still experiencing the transportation, communication, and marketing impacts of cities in the MDCs. The introduction and widespread diffusion of satellite-television-computer technologies have yet to achieve a major impact on urban forms and functions. A question that needs asking is to what extent will postindustrial economies and rapid transportation and instant communication be reflected in the urban morphology of LDCs. Since many cities in the LDCs are likely to skip the industrial stage in their development (an absence of abundant and available industrial raw materials and inexpensive energy sources that fostered the industrial revolutions), will they assume a horizontal form analogous to the postindustrial urban development anticipated for many of the MDCs? Whether future growth is more dispersed and horizontal rather than clustered and vertical will depend on such factors as government policies, energy supplies and costs, existing infrastructures, and the successes of sound urban planning. The rate of the transition from a preindustrial to postindustrial economic orientation and the spatial dimensions of that transition will reveal whether the morphology will assume a character similar to urban processes and planning occurring in MDCs. The evolution of societies and cities where the industrial component is skipped, or not of major economic and political importance, represents a major distinguishing feature of many LDCs that will doubtless have an imprint on their large cities' form and function.

Future Urban Problems

Problems individual cities and urban regions will face in the next several decades have been identified and discussed in previous chapters. The economic, social, political, and environmental problems that cities and their residents experience and will experience are numerous. While global urban problems and those of individual countries and cities may not necessarily be similar, some underlying continuities and characteristics can be identified. Below we will examine four salient urban problems for each broad regional grouping. Those discussed for the LDCs are: (1) satisfying and providing basic human needs, (2) efforts to decentralize urban activities, (3) efforts to stem the tide of rural-to-urban migration, and (4) the wrenching adjustments preindustrial cities and residents will experience. Four major problems cities in the MDC grouping will face are: (1) improving the physical quality of life, (2) adjusting to slow and zero population growth, (3) adapting to energy crises, and (4) planning appealing alternative settlements. While it is convenient to discuss these four problems in the MDCs and LDCs, many of the problems are not mutually exclusive. There are cities and countries within the LDCs that are and will be severely affected by higher energy costs, just as there are cities within the MDCs where urban primacy is a major economic and political concern.

The Developing World

Basic human needs are those needs essential to all members of a population, regardless of age, culture, nationality, or political ideology. These needs are identified as potable water, health services, schools to improve literacy, model farms and marketing systems, and rudimentary transportation and communication systems. Both providing for these needs and implementing successful delivery systems are considered vital. A major goal of many developing countries and international lending institutions is to provide these needs at even a minimal level. A problem many LDCs face is funding and planning for such basic needs in the face of rapid population growth, increasing indebtedness, and conflicting development priorities. It is indeed possible that with the increasingly limited financial resources available in many LDCs distinct spatial priorities will have to be identified. The result of such development policies may mean that a few cities or regions will be "salvaged" or "saved," while many more towns and villages will experience little relief. Deciding what cities will be assisted raises a series of ethical questions similar to those lifeboat or sorting-out strategies mentioned when discussing what LDCs will be fed with the limited resources available.

The second problem identified above is how to decentralize urban activities within a country. High primacy rates, and rates which increase over time, suggest that programs and plans need to be implemented to "break down" the urban system and extend the benefits of urbanization to other major urban centers. The primate city that becomes more important economically, socially, and politically within a country also may become increasingly isolated from the rest of the country. The urban "island" has and develops an existence more akin to that of cities outside the country or region than to that of other centers inside the country. Alternative solutions need to be developed that will promote decentralization rather than agglomeration. China, Tanzania, and Israel have been particularly vigorous in trying to eliminate rural-urban dichotomies.

Stemming the tide of rural-to-urban migration is closely linked with the efforts to decentralize urban economies. With the high rates of migration, especially to primate cities, governments face difficulties in attempting to provide basic human needs for urban residents and to secure employment, permanent or semipermanent. High unemployment and underemployment will remain serious problems until successful alternative growth regions or centers are established and perceived as realistic employment nodes, or until the rural-to-urban growth rate begins to slack. As various authors have mentioned, efforts to stem the tide of that migration have not been very successful to date, in large part because the freedom to migrate had no restrictions. Even "forced" or monitored migration movements have not been successful in resolving the increasingly higher densities in cities. A long-term, more realistic solution may be to await the declines in the rural-to-urban migration, declines likely to be explained more by the successes of extensive family-planning programs than of planned secondary and tertiary growth centers.

A final problem facing many traditionally oriented LDCs is their transition into the worlds of rapid change going on around them. The transportation and telecommunications advances discussed above seem likely to question and possibly alter the basic economic, social, and political fabric of many preindustrial cities and their residents. Two basic questions that will need to be addressed are: (1) how will those anticipated changes occur, and (2) what will be their impact? Whether those changes will be gradual or rapid, be accepted or rejected, and be forced or voluntary is essential to understanding the future of preindustrial cities not only in the developing world but in the global urban community. Transitions from pre- to postindustrial cities that are humane, planning oriented, and gradual may ease adjustments into the ever-shrinking world.

The Developed World

Whereas a major concern of governments, scholars, and planners interested in the LDCs are the basic human needs, the major concern in the MDCs is to improve the physical quality of life, since basic human needs are provided at a minimal level for almost everyone in the MDCs. To many governments and planners this means providing a clean, safe, healthy environment. Air, water, and noise pollution are chief concerns, as are providing for equity in policy, employment, education, and justice. All are critical issues in societies entering the postindustrial phase of their economies. As in other problems facing the LDCs, dealing with these issues will call for increased planning and citizen participation. Interest in and concern for the quality of life stand in sharp contrast to the emphasis on the quantity of the production of goods, and is a trademark of industrial economies and societies.

The demographic present and future of the MDCs would seem to facilitate planning for an improved quality of life because the growth rate will level off and possibly even decline. Social, economic, and environmental planning would be expected to be easier with a constant population. Eastern and Western European countries are already at or approaching *zero population growth* (ZPG); the U.S. and Canada will probably be at the same stage in three or four decades. The number of legal and illegal immigrants from LDCs added to the populations of selected rich countries will prolong the arrival of ZPG. The addition of these refugees may pose serious economic, social, and political problems in specific coastal cities and in cities with a cosmopolitan and international profile. The political, social, and economic adjustments to slow and no growth will be among the most critical problems facing many MDCs. That transition, gradual rather than rapid, is unlikely to be smooth, because these countries have epitomized the essence of growth. Economic growth, another trademark of the industrial world, occurred at the same time there was a constantly growing population for the many industrial items produced. Adjusting to a society that is older and slowly growing (or declining) seems likely to affect the amount of risk individuals and governments will take, the types of goods produced, entry into the job market, and the tenor of policies (possibly more conservative). While serious problems face cities and regions experiencing slow or no growth, there are also benefits, among which are the ease in providing health, leisure, and education services for a constant population and the ability to make the physical environment more livable.

The higher energy costs and shortened supplies, especially of petroleum, are directly affecting the fabric of current urban settlement. These costs affect not only the way cities are designed (horizontal or vertical) but the way individual residents transport themselves, re-create, and consume products. Automobile-dependent societies like Japan and North America are most affected by higher fuel prices. Less affected are the more clustered European cities. The importance of energy in the daily life of all populations is being recognized as one of the critical issues facing settlement form and function, regardless of location, culture, or political ideology. Two major questions are what energy mix is likely to be characteristic of individual cities and urban regions in the future (nuclear, solar, wind, geothermal, etc.) and whether that transition to the post-petroleum world will occur without a great deal of physical, economic, and emotional trauma. At issue with respect to energy is the way future cities and their residents will exist, whether at a survival level or with some degree of comfort.

Energy costs are also related to the fourth and final problem facing the MDCs: the degree of success enjoyed in planning for alternative forms and types of settlements. Whether they occur in downtowns, suburbs, or exurban areas, new and different types of settlements have energy costs built in for construction, for the transportation, or for the delivery of basic human needs and luxuries. As a number of previous chapters in the first half of the book have shown, new-town planning and settlement schemes have met with varying successes. Governmental and private corporations have entered

486 Chapter 12, Cities of the Future

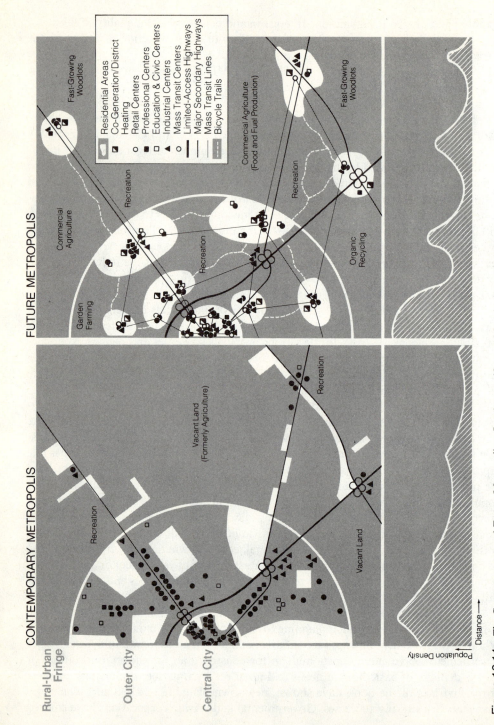

Figure 12.14 The Contemporary and Future Metropolitan Landscape. (*Source:* Model by D. J. Zeigler in H. E. Koenig and L. M. Sommers, eds., *Energy and the Adaptation of Human Settlements: A Prototype Process in Genesee County, Michigan*, East Lansing, MI: Michigan State University, Center for Environmental Quality, 1980.)

the picture to revitalize downtowns, to build townhouses and condominiums, and to finance new towns and settlements, all in an attempt to create or recreate living spaces that are more livable, that is, places that are esthetically pleasing and convenient places to work, shop, re-create, or retire (Fig. 12.14). While only a small portion of any nation's urban residents live in what might be termed new towns, new cities, or alternative forms of settlement, the question is whether efforts to provide such will occur at a larger scale in the future. Answers seem to await market, energy, and social costs in the future.

RECOMMENDED READINGS

Abler, Ron et al. *Human Geography in a Shrinking World.* North Scituate, MA: Duxbury Press, 1975.

The 21 chapters, by 14 authors, introduce geographers to economic, social, urban, environmental, and technological futures. Good conceptual statements, literature reviews, and futuristic methodologies are included, as are some futuristic maps and graphics.

Bell, Daniel. *The Coming of Post-Industrial Society,* New York: Basic Books, 1973.

One of the early critics of postindustrial economies and societies addresses the roots in industrial society evident in the present period of transition. The analysis and commentary are useful in comprehending social and political changes in Europe, North America, the USSR, and Japan.

Berry, Brian J. L. "The Geography of the United States in the Year 2000." *Transactions of the Institute of British Geographers,* 51 (1961), 21–53.

A descriptive and cartographic presentation of the demographic and urban geographies of the U.S. within the next two decades. Good examination of geographic concepts within an evolving national urban system.

Brunn, Stanley D. and James O. Wheeler, eds. *The American Metropolitan System: Present and Future.* New York: John Wiley, 1980.

Thirteen chapters address a series of economic, social, and political problems of U.S. urban systems. Specific chapters investigate the impacts of slow growth, inner-city revitalization, mortgage-lending practices, geopolitical fragmentation, corporate control, communication technology, and regional and metropolitan impacts of energy supplies and demands.

Hall, Peter and Dennis Hay. *Growth Centers in the European Urban System,* Berkeley and Los Angeles: University of California Press, 1980.

A descriptive and analytical treatment of evolving urban systems regions in Northern, Central, and Southern Europe. Detailed examinations of population and economic shifts on a regional and country-by-country basis. Numerous maps and tables accompany the text.

Phillips, Phillip D. and Stanley D. Brunn. "Slow Growth: A New Epoch of American Metropolitan Evolution." *Geographical Review,* 68 (1978), 274–292.

An analysis of recent economic, demographic, and geographic changes suggests the U.S. is entering a new stage in its metropolitan evolution. Sun Belt and Frost Belt contrasts are described. Numerous maps depict changes at national and regional scales.

Toffler, Alvin. *The Third Wave.* New York: William Morrow, 1980.

The author of *Future Shock* describes the characteristics of postindustrial economies and societies. Good insights into urban and industrial futures of MDCs and LDCs and prospective human, technological, and political problems.

Appendix 1

Major Cities of the World (Estimated and Projected Population of Cities of 500,000 or More as of 1970)

	Population (in thousands)		
Regions and Cities	1950	1980	2000
North America			
Canada			
Montreal	1,360	3,409	4,833
Toronto	1,158	3,236	4,681
Vancouver	545	1,280	1,791
*Ottawa	283	727	1,034
Winnipeg	345	611	81
United States			
New York-Northeastern New Jersey	12,340	17,909	22,212
Los Angeles-Long Beach	4,046	10,658	14,795
Chicago-Northwestern Indiana	4,945	7,484	9,347
Philadelphia-New Jersey	2,938	4,489	5,616
Detroit	2,769	4,500	5,695
San Francisco-Oakland	2,031	3,423	4,362
Boston	2,238	2,829	3,412
*Washington, DC-Maryland-Virginia	1,298	3,095	4,211
Cleveland	1,393	2,204	2,773
St. Louis	1,408	2,087	2,593
Pittsburgh	1,540	1,970	2,379
Minneapolis-St. Paul	995	2,045	2,704
Houston	710	2,239	3,209
Baltimore	1,168	1,754	2,183
Dallas	546	1,805	2,609
Milwaukee	886	1,434	1,829

*National Capital

	Population (in thousands)		
Regions and Cities	1950	1980	2000
Seattle-Everett	627	1,559	2,134
Miami	466	1,677	2,462
San Diego	440	1,666	2,468
Atlanta	513	1,546	2,192
Cincinnati-Ohio-Kentucky	817	1,233	1,532
Kansas City, Missouri-Kansas	703	1,281	1,651
Buffalo	900	1,158	1,395
Denver	505	1,332	1,840
San Jose	182	1,792	3,168
New Orleans	664	1,085	1,363
Phoenix	221	1,340	2,156
Portland, Oregon-Washington	516	962	1,237
Indianapolis	505	961	1,240
Providence-Pawtucket-Warwick-Rhode Island	585	880	1,086
Columbus, Ohio	441	955	1,263
San Antonio	454	917	1,196
Louisville, Kentucky-Indiana	476	853	1,088
Dayton	350	854	1,155
Fort Worth	319	864	1,191
Norfolk-Portsmouth, Virginia	388	861	1,202
Memphis, Tennessee-Mississippi	409	776	999
Sacramento	216	894	1,336
Fort Lauderdale	83	1,165	2,186
Rochester, New York	411	677	845
San Bernardino	139	920	1,493
Oklahoma City	0	1,513	3,652
Birmingham	447	601	709
Akron	369	605	740
Jacksonville	246	668	900
Springfield, Massachusetts-Connecticut	359	567	690
St. Petersburg	118	770	1,224
Puerto Rico			
San Juan	468	1,037	1,445

Western Europe

	1950	1980	2000
Austria			
*Vienna	1,787	1,950	2,411
Belgium			
*Brussels	968	1,136	1,316
Antwerp	599	714	829
Denmark			
*Copenhagen	1212	1,421	1,528
Finland			
*Helsinki	365	719	877

*National Capital

	Population (in thousands)		
Regions and Cities	1950	1980	2000
France			
*Paris	5,441	9,908	12,293
Lyon	572	1,430	1,884
Marseilles	660	1,191	1,475
Lille	727	991	1,163
Bordeaux	308	720	936
West Germany			
Rhine-Ruhr	6,818	9,949	11,288
Hamburg	1,787	2,263	2,495
Munich	959	1,970	2,380
Frankfurt	942	1,912	2,304
Stuttgart	983	1,824	2,160
Mannheim	581	935	1,078
Nuremberg	547	922	1,072
Hanover	565	904	1,041
Bremen	497	895	1,054
Wiesbaden	391	710	837
Berlin	2,146	2,038	2,128
Greece			
*Athens	1,347	3,034	3,982
Thessaloniki	292	651	851
Ireland			
*Dublin	632	980	1,428
Italy			
Milan	3,641	6,513	8,267
Naples	2,754	4,036	4,932
*Rome	1,701	3,520	4,586
Turin	884	2,020	2,677
Genoa	909	1,707	1,443
Florence	649	1,036	1,283
Palermo	523	770	938
Bologna	347	639	813
Catania	381	566	691
Netherlands			
*Amsterdam	855	1,098	1,297
Rotterdam	741	1,178	1,449
The Hague	614	749	874
Norway			
*Oslo	492	704	914
Portugal			
*Lisbon	790	1,426	2,212
Porto	285	1,019	1,624

*National Capital

	Population (in thousands)		
Regions and Cities	1950	1980	2000
Spain			
*Madrid	1,618	4,065	5,893
Barcelona	1,280	2,018	2,676
Valencia	509	741	967
Seville	377	646	871
Sweden			
*Stockholm	740	1,258	1,497
Goteborg	352	619	741
Switzerland			
Zurich	474	816	1,037
United Kingdom			
*London	10,247	10,962	12,693
Birmingham	2,497	2,988	3,534
Manchester	2,509	2,599	2,990
Leeds-Bradford	1,907	2,064	2,395
Glasgow	1,876	1,957	2,255
Liverpool	1,600	1,647	1,892
Newcastle-upon-Tyne	1,126	1,178	1,357
Sheffield	762	825	957
Bristol	596	746	890
Nottingham	600	731	867
Coventry	519	757	929
Cardiff-Rhondda	590	645	750
Edinburgh	586	638	741
Middlesborough/Hatt	479	629	757
Belfast	436	632	774
Leicester	425	565	682
Stoke-on-Trent	488	542	631

Soviet Union/Eastern Europe

Eastern Europe

Bulgaria			
*Sofia	568	1,180	1,498
Czechoslovakia			
*Prague	1,000	1,145	1,385
East Germany			
*Berlin	1,189	1,126	1,275
Leipzig	618	611	698
Dresden	494	536	623
Hungary			
*Budapest	1,630	2,150	2,660
Poland			
Katowice	1,689	3,288	4,360

*National Capital

	Population (in thousands)		
Regions and Cities	1950	1980	2000
*Warsaw	1,014	2,056	2,746
Lodz	725	1,014	1,259
Krakow	363	777	1,045
Gdańsk	365	899	1,242
Poznań	355	631	819
Wrocław	309	644	862
Romania			
*Bucharest	1,111	1,850	2,561
Yugoslavia			
*Belgrade	397	990	1,508
Zagreb	331	695	1,023
Soviet Union			
*Moscow	4,841	8,160	10,623
Leningrad	2,623	4,614	6,052
Kiev	743	2,168	3,131
Tashkent	613	1,857	2,702
Baku	708	1,559	2,134
Kharkov	710	1,495	2,029
Gorki	718	1,403	1,877
Novosibirsk	645	1,441	1,978
Kuibyshev	595	1,289	1,759
Sverdlovsk	569	1,273	1,748
Minsk	291	1,376	2,178
Odessa	477	1,122	1,554
Tbilisi	530	1,076	1,449
Donetsk	541	1,053	1,408
Chelyabinsk	517	1,060	1,431
Kazan	491	1,071	1,463
Dnepropetrovsk	485	1,066	1,457
Perm	454	1,068	1,480
Omsk	402	1,063	1,505
Volgograd	415	1,047	1,470
Rostov-on-Don	448	972	1,327
Ufa	378	1,002	1,420
Yerevan	315	1,055	1,564
Saratov	424	937	1,283
Alma Ata	286	1,020	1,530
Riga	437	887	1,195
Voronezh	298	878	1,269
Zaporozhe	301	872	1,256
Krasnoyarsk	280	878	1,284
Krivoy Rog	275	747	1,063
Lvov	297	694	961
Karaganda	221	710	1,044
Yaroslavl	306	627	846
Novokuznetsk	280	616	842

*National Capital

	Population (in thousands)		
Regions and Cities	1950	1980	2000
Oceania			
Australia			
Sydney	1,628	3,324	4,695
Melbourne	1,350	3,000	4,303
Adelaide	422	1,028	1,499
Brisbane	441	1,021	1,473
Perth	302	807	1,192
New Zealand			
Auckland	335	802	1,154
Latin America			
Argentina			
*Buenos Aires	4,500	10,375	13,978
Rosario	570	927	1,169
Córdoba	426	992	1,338
La Plata	325	595	767
Bolivia			
*La Paz	321	790	1,649
Brazil			
São Paulo	2,450	12,494	26,045
Rio de Janeiro	2,890	10,016	19,383
Recife	650	2,380	4,654
Belo Horizonte	370	2,593	5,732
Pôrto Alegre	430	2,275	4,766
Salvador	395	1,595	3,174
Curitiba	140	1,768	4,353
Fortaleza	260	1,431	3,007
Belém	235	886	1,733
Santos	240	774	1,469
*Brasilia	0	1,261	3,742
Chile			
*Santiago	1,256	3,472	5,119
Colombia			
*Bogotá	655	4,415	9,527
Medellín	328	1,804	3,743
Cali	241	1,599	3,428
Barranquilla	276	955	1,808
Cuba			
*Havana	1,106	2,631	4,451
Dominican Republic			
*Santo Domingo	182	1,230	3,251
Ecuador			
Guayaquil	253	1,296	3,109
*Quito	206	808	1,841

*National Capital

	Population (in thousands)		
Regions and Cities	1950	1980	2000
Guatemala			
*Guatemala City	294	1,036	2,422
Jamaica			
*Kingston-St. Andrew	260	684	1,037
Mexico			
*Mexico City	2,872	13,878	31,616
Guadalajara	401	2,573	6,176
Monterrey	354	2,026	4,751
Peru			
*Lima-Callao	614	5,157	12,130
Uruguay			
*Montevideo	800	1,702	2,223
Venezuela			
*Caracas	677	3,244	5,963
Maracaibo	231	867	1,521
Subsaharan Africa			
Ethiopia			
*Addis Ababa	225	1,431	4,170
Ghana			
*Accra	250	1,241	3,165
Kenya			
*Nairobi	135	1,021	3,371
Nigeria			
*Lagos	288	2,899	9,437
Ibadan	428	1,059	2,635
Senegal			
*Dakar	155	1,048	2,590
South Africa			
Johannesburg	900	1,949	3,933
*Cape Town	618	1,545	3,201
East Rand	546	1,227	2,487
Durban	485	1,175	2,413
Pretoria	275	823	1,758
Sudan			
*Khartoum	216	1,059	3,013
Zaire			
*Kinshasa	164	2,957	9,112
Middle East/North Africa			
Algeria			
*Algiers	515	1,410	2,861

*National Capital

	Population (in thousands)		
Regions and Cities	1950	1980	2000
Egypt			
*Cairo	2,377	8,391	16,398
Alexandria	927	2,927	5,599
Iran			
*Tehran	1,041	5,804	13,785
Esfahān	184	838	1,913
Iraq			
*Baghdad	579	4,565	10,907
Israel			
Tel Aviv	416	1,305	1,935
Kuwait			
*Kuwait City	85	1,310	3,047
Lebanon			
*Beirut	190	1,632	3,775
Morocco			
Casablanca	633	2,316	5,248
Syria			
*Damascus	325	1,339	3,231
Aleppo	388	886	1,898
Tunisia			
*Tunis	482	1,090	2,073
Turkey			
Istanbul	950	4,022	8,284
*Ankara	288	2,275	5,262
Izmir	228	1,122	2,371
South Asia			
Bangladesh			
*Dacca	396	2,069	5,936
India			
Calcutta	4,446	9,583	19,663
Bombay	2,901	8,722	19,065
*Delhi	1,390	5,704	13,220
Madras	1,397	4,658	10,375
Hyderabad	1,122	2,425	4,972
Ahmedabad	859	2,530	5,502
Bangalore	764	2,462	5,448
Kanpur	691	1,815	3,863
Poona	592	1,609	3,446
Nagpur	474	1,346	2,908
Lucknow	488	1,128	2,344
Coimbatore	265	1,159	2,717

*National Capital

	Population (in thousands)		
Regions and Cities	1950	1980	2000
Madurai	358	1,012	2,183
Agra	368	888	1,858
Jaipur	285	945	2,103
Varanasi	348	852	1,789
Indore	306	789	1,673
Jabalpur	251	788	1,733
Allahabad	327	700	1,431
Pakistan			
Karachi	1,028	5,971	15,862
Lahore	826	3,144	7,706
Lyallpur	169	2,045	6,159
Hyderabad	233	1,345	3,512
Multan	182	1,189	3,166
Sri Lanka			
*Colombo	388	738	1,269

Southeast Asia

Burma			
*Rangoon	686	3,124	7,372
Cambodia (Kampuchea)			
*Phnom Penh	269	701	1,392
Indonesia			
*Jakarta	1,565	7,191	16,933
Surabaja	679	2,273	5,038
Bandung	511	1,836	4,126
Semarang	371	893	1,858
Medan	245	989	2,270
Palembang	277	859	1,876
Philippines			
Manila	1,532	5,593	12,683
Singapore			
*Singapore	484	2,260	3,029
Thailand			
*Bangkok-Thonburi	964	4,258	11,030
Vietnam			
*Hanoi	225	1,851	5,109
Haiphong	140	1,099	2,974
*Ho Chi Minh City (Saigon)	970	2,419	5,066

East Asia

China			
Shanghai	5,781	12,002	19,155
*Peking (Beijing)	2,163	10,216	19,064

*National Capital

	Population (in thousands)		
Regions and Cities	1950	1980	2000
Tientsin (Tianjin)	2,392	4,741	7,488
Mukden (Shenyang)	2,229	3,025	4,433
Wuhan	1,088	3,364	5,766
Canton (Guangzhou)	1,456	2,974	4,705
Chungking (Chongqing)	1,573	2,746	4,210
Nanking (Nanjing)	917	2,146	3,477
Harbin (Ha'erbin)	960	1,988	3,144
Lüta (Luda)	488	2,417	4,514
Sian (Xi'an)	561	2,223	3,977
Langchou (Lanzhou)	273	2,445	5,107
Taiyuan	572	1,766	3,012
Tsingtao (Qingdao)	802	1,511	2,343
Chengtu (Chengdu)	722	1,482	2,334
Changchun	784	1,367	2,085
Kunming	600	1,325	2,113
Tsinan (Jinan)	581	1,338	2,149
Fushun	530	1,343	2,197
Anshan	425	1,387	2,380
Chengchou (Zhengzhou)	502	1,316	2,166
Hangchou (Hangzhou)	644	1,081	1,632
Tangshan	630	1,072	1,622
Taotou (Baotou)	0	2,033	5,252
Tzepo (Zepo)	0	1,816	4,562
Changsha	618	892	1,300
Shihkiachwang (Shijiazhuang)	273	1,106	1,961
Tsitsihar (Qiqihaer)	222	1,103	2,033
Kalgan (Zhangjiakou)	170	1,178	2,314
Suchou (Suzhou)	391	876	1,387
Kirin (Jilin)	365	879	1,410
Hsü Chou (Xuzhou)	251	952	1,665
Fuchou (Fuzhou)	515	731	1,059
Nanchang	339	825	1,324
Kueiyang (Guiyang)	179	978	1,830
Wusih (Wusi)	561	669	936
Hofei (Hefei)	131	1,012	2,020
Huainan (Huainan)	242	783	1,325
Chinchou (Jinzhou)	260	766	1,272
Penki (Benqi)	427	655	960
Loyang	138	892	1,719
Nanning	159	796	1,461
Huhehot (Huhehete)	0	918	1,947
Sining (Xining)	0	846	1,762
Urumchi (Urumuchi)	0	847	1,765
Hong Kong	1,561	4,340	5,515

*National Capital

	Population (in thousands)		
Regions and Cities	1950	1980	2000
Japan			
*Tokyo-Yokohama	6,737	19,705	26,128
Osaka-Kobe	3,828	9,731	12,553
Nagoya	956	2,346	3,006
Kitakyushu	935	1,946	2,416
Kyoto	1,001	1,455	1,687
Sapporo	254	1,211	1,758
Hiroshima	266	632	803
North Korea			
*Pyongyang	430	1,406	2,717
Hamhung-Huangan	145	882	1,916
South Korea			
*Seoul	1,021	9,443	18,711
Pusan	518	2,857	5,104
Taegu	338	1,579	2,726
Inchon	272	857	1,373
Taiwan			
Taipei	609	2,377	4,245
Kaohsiung	261	1,127	2,023

Source: Derived from Table 6 in *Global Review of Human Settlements, Statistical Annex,* United Nations: Department of Economic and Social Affairs, 1976, pp. 77–87.

*National Capital

Index

Abidjan, 252, 262, 266, 267
Abu Dhabi, 289, 315
Accra, 244, 248, 271, 461, 467
Addis Ababa, 247, 250, 252, 267, 271, 272, 461, 467
Adelaide, 163, 166, 169, 173, 190, *191*, 195
Administrative organization of cities, 37–38
Albania, 5, 123, 149, 455, 456
Alexandria, 288, 289, 462, 467, 474
Algeria, 12, 32, 91, 282, 289
Algiers, 244, 289, 471
Amsterdam, 105, 107, 108
Ankara, 307, 316
Apia, 169, 173, 196
Archangel, 128, 142
Argentina, 5, 12, 14, 199, 200, 203, 204, 206, 207, 234–237, 456, 466, 468
Athens, 86, 105, 318, 459, 460
Atlanta, 44, 53, 55, 70, 77
Auckland, 163, 165, 169, 170, 172, 189–192, 193, 460
Australia, 12, 162–187, 193–197, 456, 458, 463, *474*
Austria, 12, 107, 149, 152, 456

Baghdad, 28, 282, 288, 298, 299–302, *301*, 316, 318, 460, 461, 467
Baku, 135, 143
Baltimore, 44, 49, 77
Bandung, 382, 464, 465
Bangalore, 326, 332, 344, *345*, 362, 467
Bangkok, 14, 372, 376, 382, 392, 394, 398, 399, 404, 460, 461
Bangladesh, 325, 326, 344, 346, 349, 356–360, 363, 364–365, 455
Barcelona, 107, 464
Basic functions of cities, 24–25
Basic human needs in cities, 31–32, 483
Beersheba, 313–314, *313*
Beirut, 318
Belfast, 28
Belgium, 5, 12, 88, 92, 107, 111, 456, 458, 463
Belgrade, 151–152, 159, 460, 463
Belo Horizonte, 465, 467, 474
Berlin, 90, 105
Birmingham, U.K., 92, 97, 107, 173, 459, 464, 465
Bogota, 14, 204, 213, 215, 216, 234, 235, 236, 239, 462, 467

Bolivia, 204, 456
Bombay, 14, 325, 330, 331, 332, 333, *333*, 334, 335, 339, 340, 344, 350–352, *351*, 361, 362, 363, 364, 460, 461, 462, 466, 468, 471
Boston, 6, 45, 48, 49, 51, 66, 77, 79, 429, 464, 465, 472
Brasilia, 9, 180, 206, 231–234, *232*, *234*, 465, 467, 479
Brazil, 7, 9, 12, 14, 32, 199, 206, 207, 218, 226–234, 263, 456, 459, 464, 465, 466, 468, 474, *475*
Brisbane, 163, 169, 173, 187, 190
Brussels, 86, *98*
Bucharest, 153–154, *154*, 460
Budapest, 124, 151, 155, *157*, 159, 160, 459, 460
Buenos Aires, 14, 199, 203, 204, 206, 207, 223, 227, 234–237, *235*, 239, 461, 466, 468, 471
Bulgaria, 12, 123, 149, 152–153, 456
Burma, 334, 372, 376, 381–382, 455

Cairo, 14, 271, 282, 283, 288, 290–294, *292*, *293*, *295*, 298, 305, 307, 316–317, 318, 320, 460, 461, 462, 466, 468, 471, 474, 477, 479
Calcutta, 14, 325, 326, 330, 331, 332, *332*, 333, 334, 335, *335*, 339, 340, 344, 345, 346–349, *347*, *348*, 350, 354, 356, 360, *360*, 361, 362, 363, 364, 460, 461, 462, 466, 467, 468
Canada, 12, 42–83, 92, 164, 456, 458, 463, *474*, 485
Canberra, 167, 172–173, 180–182, *181*, 187, 188, 189, 195
Canton, 412, 418, 423, 424, *446*, 462, 465
Cape Town, 248, *249*, 272, 461, 471, 479
Capitalism and cities, 19
Caracas, 239, 461, 477
Casablanca, 289, 461, 467
Center-periphery concept, 8
Central African Republic, 243, 252, 273, 456
Central place theory, 22–23
Chandigarh, 367
Chelyabinsk, 129, 140
Chicago, 26, 44, 48, 49, 52, *62*, 64, 67, 68, 69, 70, 77, 182, 206, 208, 234, 429, 459, 460, 464, 465, 466, 470, 472
Chile, 12, 200, 202, 203, 204, 205, 206, 456, 474
China, 4, 8, 14, 16, 19, 30, 43, 409, 410–411, 412–416, 418–424, *419*, 430–435, 440–448, 459, 462, 463, 464, 465, 466, 468, 475, 484
Chungking, 412, 465

500

Cincinnati, 45, 48
Circular and cumulative causation, 23–24
Cities
  location and growth of, 22–25
  theories on internal spatial structure of, 25–30
  types of, 22–23
City
  concept of, 6
  optimum size of, 4
City system, 7, 472
Cleveland, 50, 52, 55, 77, 208
Colombia, 12, 14, 28, 204, 206, 207, 219, 456, 462, 463
Colombo, 325, 340, 363, 467
Colonial city, 8
Concentric zone theory, 26
Congo, 243, 252, 456
Conurbation, 6
Copenhagen, 85, 88, 105, 106
Cost-space convergence, 470–472
Cuba, 12, 238, 456
Czechoslovakia, 12, 123, 149, 151, 155–158, 159

Dacca, 326, 344, 356–360, *359,* 363, 364–365, 460, 461, 467
Dakar, 244, 250, 262, 266, 267–270, *268, 269,* 271, 272, 461, 471, 479
Damascus, 288, 307, 318
Dar es Salaam, 250, *251,* 252, 471
Delhi, 14, 325, 326, 329, *330,* 339, 340, 344, 345, 353–355, *354,* 361, 363, 364, 461, 462, 466, 467, 468
Denmark, 5, 12, 88, 106, 456
Denver, 213, 372
Detroit, 44, 49, 50, 52, *61,* 77, 135, 208, 429, 464, 465, 467
Djibouti, 243, 250, 271
Dominican Republic, 203, 204, 456–459
Donetsk, 129
Doubling rate, 460
Dual city, 8
Dual primacy, 7
Durban, 250, 272
Düsseldorf, 89, *96,* 109

East Asia, 10, 11, 12, 19, 20, 325, *408,* 409–450, 454–456, 461, 466, 480
  British colonial impact, 418–422, 423–424
  Chinese city as model, 417
  colonial cities, 417–424, 430–431
  evolution of cities, 412–426
  Japanese colonial impact, 422–423
  major representative cities, 426–435
  Marco Polo and Chinese cities, 410–411
  Portuguese and Dutch colonial impact, 417–418
  preindustrial city, 411, 412–417, 425–426
  primate cities, 431–432
  regional centers, 432–434
  socialist cities, 434–435
  socialist urban system, 440–448
  solutions to urban problems in nonsocialist countries, 438–440
  solutions to urban problems in socialist countries, 440–448
  superconurbations, 426–430
  Tokaido megalopolis, 426–430, 439
  treaty ports, 418–422
  urban problems in nonsocialist countries, 435–438
  in world urban system, 409–410
Eastern Europe, 10, 11, 12, 86, 91, *122,* 123–124, 149–160, *150,* 458, 480, 485. *See also* Soviet Union/Eastern Europe
  German influences in city development, 150–151
  historical development of cities, 149–151
  major representative cities, 151–159
  socialist cities, 158–159
  Turkish influences in city development, 151
  urban problems, 159–160
East Germany, 12, 123, 149, 151, 158, 159, 456
Economic base concept, 24–25
Ecumenopolis, 7, 476
Egypt, 12, 14, 16, 271, 282, 283, 288, 289, 290, 290–294, 298, 307, 316–317, 318, 456, 459, 462, 463, 466, 467, 468, 474
Environmental degradation in cities, 36
Essen, 89, 92, 105, 109
Ethiopia, 247, 250, 252, 267, 271, 272, 455
Excessive size of cities, 30

Fiji, 163, 164, 165, 169, 170, 192–193
Finland, 12, 118, 456
France, 5, 12, *38,* 85, 86, 87, 88, 91, 101–105, 107, 111, 112, 115, 119, 174, 456, 462, 463, 466

Gabon, 243, 249
Georgetown, 390, 391
Ghana, 5, 243, 244, 247, 248, 272, 273, 456
Gheorghe Gheorghiu-Dej, 159
Glasgow, 464, 465
Global village, 476
Gorki, 130, 134–135
Greece, 5, 12, 456
Guadalajara, 462, 467
Guatemala City, 207, 467
Guayaquil, 204

The Hague, 108
Haifa, 309, 312
Hamburg, *19,* 92, 95, 105, 107
Hanoi, 372, 382, 392, 460, 461
Harbin, 422
Havana, 204, 238
Hiroshima, 428
Ho Chi Minh City, 372, 376, 378, 381, 404–405, 461, 467
Homogenization of cities, 43
Hong Kong, 12, *33,* 223, 410, 411, 412, 418,

Hong Kong *(Continued)*
    423–424, *423, 424,* 430–431, 435, 439–440, 445, 448, 456, 461, 477
Houston, 44, 70–73, *71,* 479
Hungary, 149, 151, 152, 155, 158, 455, 456
Hyderabad, 326, 344, 462

Ibadan, 247, 249, *263,* 366, 462, 474
India, 14, 32, 254, 283, 290, 325, 326, 327–336, 346–355, 363–365, 455, 459, 462, 463, 466, 468, *475*
Indonesia, 91, 164, 371, 372, 374, 375, 376, 377, 378, 379–380, 381, 382, 383–385, 391, 392, 394–397, 398–399, 402, 403, 404, 405, 455, 462, 463, 464, 465, 466, 468, *475*
Industrial city, 19
Industrialization and growth of cities, 21–22
Informal working sector of economy, 480
Inverse concentric zone theory, 27–28
Iran, 14, 282, 287, 289, 294–299, 314, 317, 318, 320, 456, 462, 463, 466, 468
Iraq, 12, 28, 282, 288, 289, 298, 299–302, 304, 314, 316, 318, 320, 456
Ireland, 5, 455, 456
Irkutsk, 141
Isfahan, 288, 294, 462
Islamabad, 180, 365, *366,* 479
Ismailia, 291, 292
Israel, 5, 12, 281, 290, 308–314, *311,* 456, 484
Istanbul, 151, 282, 288, 298, 305–308, *306,* 316, 461
Italy, 107, 115, 456, 463, 466
Ivory Coast, 252, 262, 266, 267, 273, 455

Jakarta, 371, 372, 376, 377, 379–380, 381, 383–385, *387,* 392, 394–397, *395, 396,* 398–399, 402, 404, 460, 461, 462, 464, 465, 466, 467, 468, 475
Japan, 12, 20, 36, 70, 173, 382, 383, 409, 410, 411, 417, 418, 425–426, 426–430, *428,* 431, 435–438, 439, 445, 448, 456, 458, 459, 463, 464, 465, 466, 468, *474,* 479, 485
Jerusalem, 287, 288, 309, 312, *320*
Johannesburg, 252, 257–260, *257, 259,* 461
Jordan, 290, 318, 456

Kampala, 250, 252
Kampuchea, 328, 371, 374, 381, 393, 405
Kano, 244, 247, 265, 273
Kaohsiung, 433
Karachi, 326, 334, 355–356, *357,* 363, 460, 461, 462, 466, 467, 468
Kazan, 135, 140
Kenya, 244, 248, 250, 252–256, 262, 267, 271, 272
Kharkov, 130, 134, 138
Khartoum, 249, 250, 273, 467
Kiev, 123, 125, 130, 134, 135, 138, 147
Kinshasa, 243, 244, 245, 247, 252, 260–262, *260,* 265, 267, 271, 273, 459, 460, 461, 467, 471

Kitakyushu, 428, 465
Kobe, 429, 463, 465, 466
Krakow, 151, 158–159
Kuala Lumpur, 382, 389–391, *390,* 392, 399, 402, 404
Kunming, 434
Kuwait, 12, 281, 282, 289, 302–305, 314, 315, 317, 318, 456
Kuwait City, 282, 289, 302–305, *303, 304,* 317, 318, 461, 467
Kuybyshev, 130, 135, 140, 141
Kyoto, 20, 417, 425, 465

Lack of social responsibility in cities, 34
Lagos, 243, 244, 261, 262–267, *264, 266,* 271, 272, 273, 460, 461, 462, 467, 471, 474, 477, 479
Lahore, 326, 344, 363, 462, 467
Lanchou, 434, 462, 465
Laos, 371, 381
Latin America, 3, 4, 10, 11, 12, 20, 70, 165, *198,* 198–240, *201, 205, 217,* 454–456, 461, 480
    Amerind cities, 16, 200–202
    architectural change, 211
    central business district, 213–215
    core area slums and homelessness, 218–219
    European urbanization, 202–206
    evolution of cities, 200–213
    expansion of central business district, 207–208
    expansion of urban services and suburbanization, 210–211
    favelas, 32, 218, 229–230
    filter-down housing and squatter settlements, 211–213
    industrialization and cities, 208–210
    internal structure of cities, 213–219
    major representative cities, 219–237
    mercantilism, 203–204
    pre-Columbian urbanization, 200–202
    spine and elite residential sector, 215–216
    traditional city, 200, 206–207
    transformation of city structure, 207–213
    urban primacy, 200, 223, 227, 236
    urban problems and solutions, 237–239
    in world urban system, 199–200
    zone of *in situ* accretion in cities, 217–218
    zone of maturity in cities, 216–217
    zone of peripheral squatter settlements in cities, 218
Lebanon, 12, 282, 318, 456
Leeds-Bradford, 88, 464, 465
Leningrad, 123, 124, 128, 129, 130, 134, 135, 137, *139, 140,* 142, 147, 154, 459, 460, 463, 467
Less Developed Countries (LDCs), 4–5
Liberia, 249, 272
Libya, 289, 314
Lima, 14, 204, 205, 208, 213, 235, 236, 460, 461
Lisbon, 105
Liverpool, 88, 464, 465

London, 16, 85, 86, 90, 92, 93, *93*, 95, 97, 98–101, *100, 101*, 102, 103, 111, 115, 118, 137, 223, 237, 459, 460, 463, 464, 465, 466, 467, 468, 471, 477
Los Angeles, 14, 36, 44, 49, 53, 55, 64, 67–70, *68*, 71, 73, 177, 208, 213, 460, 463, 464, 465, 466, 468
Luanda, 248, 250, 271

Macao, 418, 430
Madras, 326, 330, 331, 332, 334, 335, *337*, 339, 340, 344, 345, 352–353, 361, 362, 363, 461, 462
Madrid, 105, 106, 459, 460, 463, 467
Madurai, 328, 363
Magnitogorsk, 139–140
Malacca, 375, 391
Malaysia, 371, 375, 382, 387, 389–391, 392, 399, 401–402, 403, 404, 405
Mali, 252, 267
Manchester, 88, 463, 464, 465
Manila, 14, 371, 372, 376, 378–379, *380*, 381, 382, 383–385, *386*, 391, 392, 394, 399, 401, 404, 460, 461, 466, 467
Maracaibo, 206
Market centers, 22–23
Marseilles, 86, 267
Mecca, 288
Medan, 382, 392, 399, 464, 465
Megalopolis, 4, 6
Melbourne, 163, 168, 169, 170, 173, 182–185, *183, 184*, 195, 459, 460, 471
Mercantilism, 18–19
Metropolis, 6
Metropolitan area, 6
Mexico, 5, 12, 16, 199, 202, 204, 207, 219–226, 456, 462, 463, 466, 468, 474, *475*
Mexico City, 14, 36, 199, 200, 204, 206, 207, 208, *209*, 210, *212*, 213, 219–223, *220, 221*, 234, 236, 237, 239, 460, 461, 462, 466, 467, 468, 474, 477
Miami, 35, 44, 55, 78
Middle East/North Africa, 20, 28, *280*, 281–322, 454–456, 461, 480
   evolution of cities, 282–290
   gecekondu, 32, 308, 316
   Islamic city model, 284–287
   Israeli new towns, 308–314
   madina, 292–293, 300, 303, 304, 315, 317–318
   major representative cities, 290–314
   Middle Eastern city, 281, 282, 287
   processes of urbanization, 287–290
   sarifahs, 300–301, 302, 316
   tomb cities, 292–293
   urban primacy, 289
   urban problems and prospects, 314–321
   in world urban system, 281–282
Milan, 105, 107, 459, 460, 466
Millionaire (million) city, 6

Minneapolis-St. Paul, 57–58, *57*
Mombasa, 247, 248, 250, 252
Monrovia, 249, 272
Montevideo, 200, 206, 207
Montreal, 45, 50, 52, 58
More Developed Countries (MDCs), 3–4
Morocco, 32, 388, 389, 456
Moscow, 123, 124, 125, 126–127, *127*, 128, 129, 130, 134, 135–137, *136, 137, 138*, 140, 145, 147, 160, 429, 460, 463, 466, 467, 470, 471, 477
Mukden, 422, 462, 465
Multiple nuclei theory, 27
Munich, 89, 95, 107
Murmansk, 142

Nagasaki, 418
Nagoya, 426–430, 465
Nairobi, 244, 250, 252–256, *253, 256*, 262, 267, 271, 272, 459, 461, 471, 477, 479
Nanking, 412, 413, 418, 444, 465
Naples, 107, 464
Netherlands, 12, 85, 88, 91, 108–109, 111, 115, 456, 458, 463, 479
Newcastle-upon-Tyne, *95*, 111–112
New Orleans, 45, 48, 72, 479
New towns concept, 8–9
New York City, 6, 44, 45, 48, 49, 55, *61*, 64–67, *65*, 68, 69, 73, 77, 79, 83, 102, 137, 173, 213, 222, 223, 292, 409, 429, 437, 459, 460, 463, 464, 465, 466, 467, 468, 470, 471, 477
New Zealand, 5, 12, 162–173, 189–192, 193–197, 456
Nigeria, 243, 244, 247, 248, 249, 252, 261, 262–267, 271, 272, 273, 455, 462, 463, 467, 474, *475*
Nonbasic functions of cities, 24–25
North America, 3, 10, 11, 12, 20, 28, *42*, 43–83, *46, 47, 52*, 86, 97, 123, 207–208, 210, 211, 213, 215, 216, 218, 222, 236, 237, 258, 409, 454–456, 458, 460, 466, 480, 485
   Bowash megalopolis, 51–52
   business and wholesaling activities in cities, 59–60
   commercial activities in cities, 58
   counterurbanization, 54–55
   deconcentration of continental urban growth, 52–53
   differential growth within urban systems, 81–83
   fragmentation of metropolitan regions, 76–81
   ghettos, 62
   Great Lakes megalopolis, 52
   internal structure of cities, 56–64
   major representative cities, 64–76
   manufacturing activities in cities, 56–58
   megalopolitan development, 51–52
   redlining, 62
   retail structure of cities, 58
   residential patterns, 60–64

504 Index

North America *(Continued)*
  segregation in cities, 62, 64
  suburbanization, 53–54
  urban problems and solutions, 76–83
  urban system development, 44–55
  in world urban system, 43–44
North Korea, 409, 410, 411, 417, 422–423, 431, 440, 456
Norway, 88, 113, 115, 455, 456
Novosibirsk, 141
Nowa Hutta, 158–159

Oceania, 10, 11, 12, 20, 70, 86, *162,* 163–197, 454–456, 460, 480
  the archipelagos, 165
  changing the urban system, 193–195
  colonial seeds of primate dominance, 170–171
  corridor cities, 195
  internal metropolitan changes, 195–196
  major representative cities, 172–193
  nature and evolution of urban system, 164–165
  problems of island cities, 196
  technology and urbanization intensity, 171–172
  territorial framework for urban evolution, 165–168
  urban primacy, 164, 167, 168–170, 173–174, 193–195
  urban problems and solutions, 193–196
  in world urban system, 163–164
Odessa, 124, 128–129, 130
Osaka, 425, 426–430, 438, 463, 465, 466
Oslo, 86, 95, 113

Pakistan, 16, 254, 290, 325, 326, 334, 344, 346, 352, 355–356, 363, 365–366, 455, 462, 463, 466, 468
Palembang, 375, 391, 464, 465
Papua-New Guinea, 163, 164, 166, 169, 172, 173, 187–189
Paris, 85, 90, 92, 93, *94,* 95, 101–105, *102, 103, 105,* 112, 174, 206, 222, 223, 234, 237, 291, 429, 459, 460, 463, 466, 470, 471, 477, 479
Peking, 14, 409, 410–411, *413,* 413–414, *415,* 423, 424, 434, 442, *443,* 445, 461, 462, 465, 466, 467, 468
Perth, 164, 166, 169, 170, 185–187, *186,* 190, 195
Peru, 12, 14, 16, 32, 204, 205, 208, 456
Philadelphia, 44, 45, 49, 55, 66, 77, 429, 459, 464, 465, 467
Philippines, 14, 371, 372, 376, 378–379, 381, 382, 383–385, 391, 392, 394, 399, 401, 404, 405, 456, 466
Phnom Penh, 405, 467
Pittsburgh, 50, 52, 55, 173, 429, 464, 472
Poland, 12, 123, 149, 151, 154–155, 456, 463
Port Moresby, 163, 164, 166, 169, 172, 187–189, *188,* 193, 196
Postindustrial city, 7
Prague, 151, 155–158, *158,* 159, 160
Preindustrial city, 7, 16–21

Primacy ratio, 462–464
Primary sector of economy, 480
Primate city, 7
Pusan, 431, 440, 462, 467
Pyongyang, 440, 461

Quaternary sector of economy, 480–481
Quebec City, 45, 52, 472

Racial and social issues in cities, 35
Randstadt, 85, 107, 108–109, *108,* 119
Rangoon, 334, 372, 376, 381–382
Rank-size curve, 464–466
Rank-size rule, 8
Rhine-Ruhr cities, 85, 88, 107, 109–111, *110,* 114, 459, 460, 466
Riga, 143–144, 146
Rio de Janeiro, 2, 14, 199, 200, 204, 205, 207, 218, 226–231, *227, 230,* 233, 236, 239, 460, 461, 465, 466, 468, 470, 474, 477
Romania, 149, 151, 153–154, 159, 160, 456
Rome, 16, 19, 86, 87, 89, 105, 107, 222, 305, 463, 467, 471, 477
Rotterdam, 92, 105, 108

Salisbury, 250, 252
Samarkand, 125, 142
San Francisco, 48, 49, 68, 72, 79, 80–81, *80,* 164, 177, 464, 465, 467, 470, 471, 472
Santiago, 203, 205, 239, 461, 474
São Paulo, 7, 14, 36, 199, 206, 207, 222, 223, 227, *228,* 233, 237, 239, 460, 461, 465, 466, 467, 468, 474
Saudi Arabia, 288, 289, 304, 314, 315
Secondary (industrial) sector of economy, 480
Sector theory, 26–27
Senegal, 5, 243, 244, 250, 262, 266, 267–270, 271
Seoul, 14, 36, 409, 410, 417, 423, 431–432, *432,* 433, 440, 460, 461, 462, 466, 467, 468
Shanghai, 14, *31,* 409, 410, 418, 420–422, *421,* 424, 430, 434–435, 441, 445, 447, *448,* 460, 461, 462, 465, 466, 468
Shortage of urban services, 31–32
Sian, 20, 414, *416,* 441, 442
Singapore, 12, 164, 371, 372, 376, 380–381, *381,* 385–389, *388, 389,* 390, 399, *400,* 400–401, 435, 456, 461, 471, 479
Site, 22
Situation, 22
Slums, 32
Socialist city, 8, 30
Sofia, 152–153, *153*
South Africa, 12, 35, 243, 248, 249, 250, 252, 257–260, *257,* 271, 272, 456, 460, 467
South Asia, 10, 11, 12, 243, *324,* 325–368, *338, 342,* 371, 409, 454–456, 461, 466, 480
  Aryan Hindu impact on cities, 327–328
  Bazaar-based city model, 340–343
  bustees, 32, 361
  cantonments, 339–340

Civil Lines, 343–344
colonial-based city model, 336–339
colonial period and cities, 330–336
contemporary urban and urbanization
    characteristics, 344–346
Dravidian temple cities, 328–329
evolution of cities, 326–336
hill stations, 340
Indus valley era and cities, 326–327
major representative cities, 346–359
mixture of colonial and bazaar models, 343–344
models of city structure, 336–346
new towns, 365–367
Presidency towns, 331–336
railway colonies, 340
urban planning, 363–365
urban problems and solutions, 360–367
in world urban system, 325–326
Southeast Asia, 10, 11, 12, 35, 70, 328, *370,*
    371–408, 377, 378, 379, 384, 409, 454–456,
    461, 480
coastal trade city in precolonial times, 373–375
evolution of cities, 372–382
expanding employment in cities, 401–402
growth diversion strategies, 403–404
industry and infrastructure in cities, 398–399
inland sacred city in precolonial times, 373–375
major representative cities, 382–392
migration to urban areas, 393–394, 394–397
model of land use in cities, 383–384
regional centers, 391
resettlement programs, 402–403
solutions to urban problems, 400–405
squatter relocation, 401
urban development in colonial times, 375–382
urban development in precolonial times,
    373–375
urban growth and its causes, 392–393
urban involution, 394
urban primacy, 376, 392
urban problems, 392–399
urban problems and solutions in socialist
    nations, 404–405
in world urban system, 371–372
South Korea, 12, 14, 36, 290, 409, 410, 411, 417,
    422–423, 431–432, 433, 435, 440, 456, 459,
    462, 463, 466, 468
Soviet Union, 3, 8, 9, 10, 11, 12, 30, *122,*
    123–124, 124–149, *131, 132, 133,* 456, 458,
    459, 462, 463, 466
agricultural triangle (urban core), 124–125
cities of commercial and early industrial period,
    1700–1917, 128–129
cities of Soviet period, 1917 to Second World
    War, 129–135
early urbanization, 125–127
entertainment in cities, 146
historical development of cities, 124–135
housing in cities, 144–145
Kremlin, 125, 126

major representative cities of the Soviet period,
    135–144
recreation in cities, 147
shopping in cities, 145–146
socialist city, 148–149
socialist urban planning, 148
solutions to urban problems, 147–149
urban problems, 144–147
urban transportation, 145
Soviet Union/Eastern Europe, *122,* 123–161, 199,
    454–456, 458, 460, 480
in world urban system, 123–124
Space-adjusting technologies, 471
Spain, 12, 87, 106, 115, 223, 283, 456, 463
Specialized-function cities, 22–23
Squatter settlements, 32
Sri Lanka, 325, 346, 363
Standard Consolidated Statistical Area (SCSA), 6
Standard Metropolitan Statistical Area (SMSA), 6
Stockholm, 86, 93, 95, 105, 106, 115, 118, 119,
    119, 477
Subsaharan Africa, 10, 11, 12, 20, *242,* 243–279,
    245, 246, 272, 281, 371, 409, 454–456, 461,
    480
apartheid, 35, 258, 260
earliest centers of urbanization, 244–247
evolution of cities, 244–252
major representative cities, 252–270
medieval trade centers of Eastern Africa,
    247–248
prepartition European influence, 248–250
rural-to-urban migration, 273–274
site and situation of cities, 271–273
solutions to urban problems, 275–278
urbanization in postpartition era, 250–252
urban primacy, 254, 262, 265, 270, 274–277
urban problems, 271–275
in world urban system, 243–244
Sudan, 247, 249, 250, 252, 273, 288, 289
Supercity, 6
Superconurbation, 4, 6, 12–14
Supermetropolitan region, 6
Surabaja, 372, 382, 462, 464, 465, 467, 475
Suva, 163, 169, 170, 192–193, 196
Sweden, 5, 12, 85, 88, 92, 106, 115, 118, 456, 458,
    463
Switzerland, 12, 92, 115, 456
Sydney, 163, 164, 166, 167, 168, 169, 170, 172,
    173–180, *174, 175, 176, 178, 179,* 181, 183,
    185, 187, 190, 192, 195, 459, 460, 467, 470,
    477
Syria, 288, 307, 318, 456
Systems of cities, 472–476

Taipei, 410, 422–423, 432–434, *433,* 440, 465
Taiwan, 12, 36, 409, 410, 411, 422–423, 432–434,
    435, 440, 456
Tallin, 143–144
Tanzania, 250, 252, 273, 484
Tashkent, 135, 142–143

Tbilisi, 135, 143
Tehran, 14, 282, 288, 294–299, *297, 298,* 317, 318, 460, 461, 462, 466, 467, 468
Tel Aviv, 309, 312, 461
Tertiary (service) sector of economy, 480
Thailand, 14, 372, 376, 382, 392, 394, 398, 399, 404, 405, 455
Tientsin, 420, 434, 462, 465
Tijuana, 224–226, *224,* 239
Time-space convergence, 468–472
Tokyo, 20, 137, 409, 410, 417, 425–426, 426–430, *427,* 432, 436–438, *436,* 439, 445, 448, 459, 461, 463, 464, 465, 466, 467, 468, 471, 477
Toronto, 44, 52, 58, *59,* 73–76, *74,* 78, 459, 460, 467, 479
Traffic congestion, 32
Transport cities, 22–23
Tunis, 86, 244, 288, 289, 318, 467
Tunisia, 12, 282, 288, 289, 318, 456, 459
Turkey, 32, 151, 152, 153, 155, 282, 288, 289, 298, 305–308, 316, 456, 479

Uganda, 250, 252, 253
Unemployment and underemployment in cities, 34–35
United Arab Emirates, 289, 314, 315
United Kingdom, 9, 12, 21, 28, 48, 85, 86, 87, 88, 89, 91, 98–101, 114, *117,* 167, 176, 263, 291, 332, 431, 456, 458, 459, 462, 463, 464, 465, 466, 468, *474*
United States, 5, 6, 9, 12, 14, 21, 28, 30, 35, 36, 37, 42–83, 92, 144, 164, 168, 225, 409, 436, 439, 442, 456, 458, 459, 462, 463, 464, 465, 466, 468, *473, 474,* 479, 485
Urban agglomeration, 4
Urban expansion and loss of agricultural land, 36–37
Urban forms of the future, 478–479
Urban functions of the future, 480–483
Urban global core and rural periphery, 475
Urbanism, 3–9
Urbanization
   curve, 452, 457–461
   definition, 3, 5
   and economic development, 4
   history of, 16–22
   relationship with political and economic power, 4
Urbanized, concept of, 3, 5
Urban pattern in 1900, 3
Urban pattern in 1980, 3, 9–16
Urban pattern in 2000, 454–466
Urban primacy, 7
Urban problems, 30–38, 483–486
Urban regions, 472
Uruguay, 12, 200, 206, 207, 456

Vallingby, 115, *116,* 118
Vancouver, B.C., 44, 50, 53

Venezuela, 5, 12, 200, 206, 456
Vera Cruz, 204, 462, 474
Vienna, 107, 154, 159, 459
Vietnam, 371, 372, 376, 381, 382, 392, 393, 404–405
Volgograd, 130, 135, 138, 139–140, 141

Warsaw, 124, 154–155, *156,* 159, 160, 459, 460
Washington, D.C., 6, 48, 52, 77, 180, 182, 429, 465, 472
Wellington, 164, 165, 169
Western Europe, 10, 11, 12, 30, 34, 84–121, *84, 91,* 123, 409, 410, 454–456, 458, 460, 480, 485
   conurbations, 107–111
   future urban trends, 119–120
   ghettos, 95
   historical evolution of cities, 86–90
   industrial revolution and urban development, 87–90
   major representative cities, 98–114
   medium-sized cities, 111
   nature of cities, 92–98
   new towns, 115–118
   profile of cities, 92–93
   regional planning, 118
   residential patterns, 94
   small towns, 112–114
   solutions to urban problems, 115–118
   urban core, 90
   urban land use, 95
   urban population densities, 93
   urban problems, 114–115
   urban regions, 90–92
   urban transportation, 95
   in world urban system, 85–86
Westernization versus modernization in cities, 35–36
West Germany, 12, 35, 85, 86, 87, 88, 89, 91, 106, 109–111, 114, 115, 456, 458, 466
West Samoa, 164, 165, 169, 173, 190
Windsor, 52, 472
World city, 477–478

Yazd, *285, 286, 319*
Yugoslavia, 123, 149, 151–152, 159, 160, 455, 456, 463

Zaire, 92, 243, 244, 247, 250, 251, 252, 260–262, 265, 267, 271, 455
Zero growth, 458
Zero population growth (ZPG), 485
Zimbabwe, 247, 250, 252